HANDBOOK OF
Child and
Adolescent
Psychiatry

VOLUME THREE

HANDBOOK OF
Child and Adolescent Psychiatry

Joseph D. Noshpitz / Editor-in-Chief

VOLUME THREE

Adolescence: Development and Syndromes

LOIS T. FLAHERTY AND RICHARD M. SARLES

EDITORS

John Wiley & Sons, Inc.
New York • Chichester • Weinheim • Brisbane • Singapore • Toronto

This text is printed on acid-free paper.

Copyright © 1997 by John Wiley & Sons, Inc.

All rights reserved. Published simultaneously in Canada.

Reproduction or translation of any part of this work beyond
that permitted by Section 107 or 108 of the 1976 United
States Copyright Act without the permission of the
copyright owner is unlawful. Requests for permission or
further information should be addressed to the Permissions
Department, John Wiley & Sons, Inc.

This publication is designed to provide accurate and
authoritative information in regard to the subject matter
covered. It is sold with the understanding that the publisher
is not engaged in rendering professional services. If legal,
accounting, medical, psychological, or any other expert
assistance is required, the services of a competent
professional person should be sought.
ISBN 0-471-55079-5 (vol. 1)
ISBN 0-471-55075-2 (vol. 2)
ISBN 0-471-55076-0 (vol. 3)
ISBN 0-471-55078-7 (vol. 4)
ISBN 0-471-17640-0 (set)

10 9 8 7 6 5 4 3 2 1

DEDICATION

This set of volumes grows out of an attitude that reflects the field itself. To put it succinctly, the basic theme of child and adolescent psychiatry is hope. Albeit formally a medical discipline, child and adolescent psychiatry is a field of growth, of unfolding, of progressive advance; like childhood itself, it is a realm of building toward a future and finding ways to better the outcome for the young. But within the field, an even greater theme inspires an even more dominant regard. For, beyond treating children, child and adolescent psychiatry is ultimately about rearing children. This is literally the first time in human history that we are on the verge of knowing *how* to rear a child. While people have reared children since we were arboreal, they did it by instinct, or by cultural practice, or in keeping with grandma's injunctions, or by reenacting the memories, conscious and unconscious, of their own childhood experiences. They did what they did for many reasons, but never because they really knew what their actions portended, what caused what, what was a precondition for what, or what meant what.

At this moment in history, however, things are different. The efforts of researchers, neuroscientists, child developmental specialists—in short, of the host of those who seek to understand, treat, and educate children and to work with parents—are beginning to converge and to produce a body of knowledge that tells us what children are, what they need, what hurts them, and what helps them. Hard science has begun to study the fetus, rating scales and in-depth therapeutic techniques have emerged for the mother with the infant in her arms, increasing precision is being achieved in assessing temperament, in measuring mother/infant fit, and in detecting the forerunners of person-

ality organization. Adolescence and the intricacies of pubertal transformation are being explored as never before. Indeed, a quiet revolution is coming into being: the gradual dissemination of knowledge about child rearing that, within a few generations, could well alter the quality of the human beings who fall under its aegis.

If children—all children—could be reared in a fashion that gave them a healthier organization of conscience, that preserved the buds of cognitive growth and helped these to flower (instead of pinching them off as so many current practices do), that could recognize from the outset any special needs a child might have in respect to impulse control or emotional stability—and could step in from the earliest moments in development with the appropriate tactics and strategies, anodynes and remedies, techniques of healing and practices of enabling to allow the youngster to better manage his or her inner life and interpersonal transactions—consider what fruit this would bear.

Today this is far more than a dream, far more than a wistful yearning for a better day to come. The beginnings are already accomplished, much of the initial work has been done, the directions of future research are becoming ever more evident. As the heretofore cryptic equations of development are beginning to be found and some of their solutions to be discerned, the once-mystical runes are being read—and are here inscribed in page after page of research report and clinical observation.

Some of the initial changes are already well under way. As with all science, first a process of demystification must occur. Bit by bit, we have had to unlearn a host of formulaic mythologies about children and about parenting that have been part of Western civilization for centuries.

We have indeed begun to do so. We have been able to admit to the realities of child abuse, first to the violence directed toward children and then to their sexual exploitation. And we have had to admit to children's sexuality. Simply to allow those things to appear in print, to become part of common parlance, has taken immense cultural energy, the overcoming of tremendous defensiveness; after all, such things had been known but not spoken of for generations. Right now the sanctity, the hallowed quality of family life, is the focus of enormous cultural upheaval. There is much to suggest that the nuclear family set in the bosom of a body of extended kin relationships that had for so long served as the basic site for human child rearing is no longer the most likely context within which future generations of our children will grow. The quest is on for new social arrangements, and it is within this milieu that the impact of scientific knowledge, the huge and ever-increasing array of

insights into the nature of childhood, the chemistry of human relationships, the psychodynamics of parent-child interplay—in short, within the area of development that this work so carefully details—that we find the wellsprings of hope. As nursery schools, kindergartens, grade schools, and high schools become more sophisticated, as the psychiatric diagnostic manuals become more specific and more differentiated, as doctors become better trained and better prepared to address human issues with dynamic understanding, as what children need in order to grow well becomes ever more part of everyday cultural practice, the realization of this hope will slowly and quietly steal across the face of our civilization, and we will produce children who will be emotionally sounder, cognitively stronger, and mentally healthier than their parents. These volumes are dedicated to advancing this goal.

Joseph D. Noshpitz, M.D.
Editor-in-Chief

PREFACE

Some 16 years ago the first two volumes of the *Basic Handbook of Child Psychiatry* were published, to be followed shortly by volumes III and IV, and then, in 1985, by the fifth volume. More than a decade has passed since that volume was released, during which time the field of child psychiatry has advanced at a remarkable pace. Indeed, it has even changed its name to be more inclusive of the teenage years. New advances in neuroscience, in genetics, in psychoanalytic theory, in psychopharmacology, in animal studies—new findings in a host of areas have poured out during these years. It is therefore necessary to revise the handbook, to reorganize it, to update many of the clinical accounts, and to bring it to the level where the active practitioner can use its encyclopedic format to explore the enormous variety of clinical possibilities he or she may encounter.

The focus of this work is on development. It is no exaggeration to look on child development as the basic science of child and adolescent psychiatry. Development is so vital a concern that in this revision, we have abandoned the classical way of presenting the material. Rather than following tradition, wherein development, diagnosis and assessment, syndromes, treatment, and so on are discussed for a variety of related topics, in these volumes the bulk of the material is presented developmentally. Thus, volumes I, II, and III focus on development and syndromes of infancy and preschool, of grade school, and of adolescence, respectively. Within each of these larger sections, the material on development comes first, followed by chapters on syndromes, conceptualized as disturbances of development. While syndromes are described in depth, they are discussed only within the framework of the developmental level under study. Volume IV, entitled *Varieties of Development,* explores a host of ecological niches within which children are reared.

Volumes V and VI will contain sections on consultation/liaison, emergencies in child and adolescent psychiatry, the prehistory of child and adolescent psychiatry, current cultural issues that impinge on young people, forensic issues involving children and youth, and professional challenges facing the child and adolescent psychiatrist. Volume VI will include a most unusually rich banquet of studies on the assessment and evaluation of children, adolescents, and their families, plus reports on the basic science issues of the field and the current status of the various treatment techniques.

The intention of the work is to be as comprehensive and as readable as possible. In an encyclopedic work of this sort, concerns always arise as to how much space to allot to each topic and to which topics should be covered. To deal with such questions, a number of readers reviewed each submission. One editor had primary responsibility for each section; often a coeditor also reviewed submissions. Then the editor of another section reviewed the submissions, exchanging his or her chapters with the first colleague so that someone outside the section read each chapter. In addition, one editor reviewed all submissions with an eye to contradictions or excessive overlap. Finally, the editor-in-chief reviewed and commented on a large proportion of the materials submitted. In short, while the submission process was not juried, a number of readers reviewed each chapter. Each author was confronted with their cumulative critiques and asked to make appropriate changes. Most did so cheerfully, although not always with alacrity.

The writing and review process lasted from about 1990 to 1996. For much of this time, a host of authors was busy writing, revising, and polishing their work. The editors worked unstintingly, suffering all the ups and downs that accompany large projects: many meetings, huge expenses, moments of despair, episodes of elation, professional growth on the part of practically all the participants (a couple of authors who never came through with their material may be presumed to have shrunk), profound disappointments and thrilling break-throughs, lost causes that were snatched from the jaws of defeat and borne aloft to victory, and, ultimately, the final feeling that we did it!

I speak for all the editors when I say that it was our purpose and it is our earnest wish that these volumes make for better understanding of young people, greater access to knowledge about children and adolescents, a richer sense of what this field of human endeavor entails, and a better outcome for the growth, development, mental health, and happiness of all the young in our land and of those who would help them.

Joseph D. Noshpitz, M.D.
Editor-in-Chief

CONTENTS

SECTION I / Normal Adolescent Development

Contents

SECTION II / Syndromes of Adolescence

SECTION III / Special Aspects of Psychiatric Treatment of Adolescents

---

CONTRIBUTORS

MARCELINO AMAYA, M.D.
Director, Children's Psychiatric Institute, John Umstead Hospital, Butner, North Carolina; Clinical Professor of Psychiatry, University of North Carolina, Chapel Hill, North Carolina; Emeritus Professor, Department of Psychiatry, Duke University, Durham, North Carolina.

BRUNO J. ANTHONY, PH.D.
Associate Professor of Psychiatry, University of Maryland School of Medicine, Baltimore, Maryland.

CLAUDIA K. BERENSON, M.D.
Associate Professor of Psychiatry and Pediatrics, Medical Director, Partial Hospital of Children's Psychiatric Hospital, Interim Director of Training, Division of Child and Adolescent Psychiatry, Health Sciences Center, University of New Mexico, Albuquerque, New Mexico.

IRVING H. BERKOVITZ, M.D., PH.D.
Clinical Professor of Psychiatry, University of California School of Medicine; Private Practice, Los Angeles, California.

CAROLE M. BOOTH, M.D.
Psychiatric Chief of Children's Services, North Baltimore Center; Clinical Instructor, Department of Family Medicine, University of Maryland School of Medicine, Baltimore, Maryland.

W. V. BURLINGAME, PH.D.
Assistant Director of Adolescent Services, Children's Psychiatric Institute, John Umstead Hospital, Butner, North Carolina; Clinical Professor of Psychology, University of North Carolina, Chapel Hill, North Carolina.

DENNIS P. CANTWELL, M.D.
Joseph Campbell Professor of Child Psychiatry, Neuropsychiatric Institute, Department of Psychiatry and Behavioral Sciences, University of California, Los Angeles, California.

AUDREY J. CLARKIN, PH.D.
Clinical Assistant Professor of Psychology in Psychiatry, Cornell University Medical College, New York, New York; Director of Psychology, Scarsdale School District, Scarsdale, New York

LEONARD J. COMESS, M.D., PH.D.
Training and Supervising Analyst, Southern California Psychoanalytic Institute, Private Practice, Beverly Hills, California.

NEIL COMESS-DANIELS, B.A.
Rabbi, Temple Beth Shir Shalom, Santa Monica, California.

TOBY COMESS-DANIELS, B.A.
Certified Hypnotherapist, Los Angeles, California.

KEITH FLAHERTY, B.S.
Medical Student, Johns Hopkins University School of Medicine, Baltimore, Maryland.

LOIS T. FLAHERTY, M.D.
Clinical Associate Professor of Psychiatry, Department of Psychiatry, University of Pennsylvania School of Medicine, Philadelphia, Pennsylvania; Adjunct Associate Professor of Psychiatry, University of Maryland School of Medicine, Baltimore, Maryland.

BARONESS GHISLAINE D. GODENNE, M.D.
Director Emerita, Counseling and Psychiatric Services, Johns Hopkins University, Professor of Psychiatry, Pediatrics and Mental Hygiene, Johns Hopkins University School of Medicine and Public Health, Clinical Professor of Psychiatry, University of Maryland School of Medicine, Baltimore, Maryland.

MOHAMMAD HAERIAN, M.D., M.P.H.
Senior Psychiatrist, Sheppard Pratt Hospital, Clinical Associate Professor of Psychiatry, Associate Director, Child Psychiatry Residency Program, University of Maryland School of Medicine, Baltimore, Maryland.

Contents

ROBERT L. HENDREN, D.O.
Professor of Psychiatry and Pediatrics, Director, Division of Child and Adolescent Psychiatry, University of Medicine and Dentistry of New Jersey, Robert Wood Johnson Medical School, Piscataway, New Jersey.

DOUGLAS HOLLAN, PH.D.
Associate Professor of Anthropology, University of California, Los Angeles, California; Research Clinical Associate, Southern California Psychoanalytic Institute, Beverly Hills, California.

HARVEY A. HOROWITZ, M.D.
Senior Attending Psychiatrist, Institute of Pennsylvania Hospital, Clinical Associate Professor of Psychiatry, University of Pennsylvania School of Medicine, Philadelphia, Pennsylvania.

SUSHMA JANI, M.D.
Clinical Assistant Professor of Child and Adolescent Psychiatry, University of Maryland Medical System, Baltimore, Maryland.

ALEXANDER KALOGERAKIS, M.D.
Clinical Instructor in Psychiatry, New York Hospital-Cornell Medical Center; Psychoanalyst, New York Psychoanalytic Institute; Private Practice, New York, New York.

DEBRA M. KATZ, M.D.
Medical Director, Child and Adolescent Division of the Mental Health Mental Retardation Authority of Harris County, Houston, Texas.

STEVEN E. KATZ, M.D.
Professor of Psychiatry, New York University Medical Center, New York, New York; Clinical Professor of Psychiatry, University of Vermont College of Medicine, Burlington, Vermont; Executive Vice President and Chief Medical Officer, Community Care Systems, Wellesley, Massachusetts; Executive Vice President and Medical Director, Jackson Brook Institute, South Portland, Maine.

CHARLES R. KEITH, M.D.
Associate Professor, Division of Child and Adolescent Psychiatry, Department of Psychiatry, Duke University Medical Center, Durham, North Carolina.

JOHN G. LOONEY, M.D., M.B.A.
Professor of Psychiatry, Duke University, Durham, North Carolina.

RICHARD C. MAROHN, M.D.
Richard C. Marohn, M.D. passed away in November of 1995. At the time of his passing he was a Professor of Clinical Psychiatry, Northwestern University Medical School and a Member of the Faculty, Institute for Psychoanalysis, Chicago, Illinois.

JOHN E. MEEKS, M.D.
Clinical Professor of Psychiatry, Georgetown University School of Medicine, Washington, D.C.; Medical Director, The Developmental School Foundation, Rockville, Maryland.

ROBINSON J. MUNOZ-MILLAN, M.D.
Assistant Professor, Department of Psychiatry, University of Maryland School of Medicine, Center for Infant Study, Baltimore, Maryland.

GLEN T. PEARSON, JR., M.D.
Director, Child and Adolescent Services, Dallas County Mental Health, Clinical Professor of Psychiatry, University of Texas Southwestern Medical School, Dallas, Texas.

SHERIDAN PHILLIPS, PH.D.
Associate Professor of Psychiatry and Pediatrics, University of Maryland School of Medicine, Baltimore, Maryland.

LYNN E. PONTON, M.D.
Professor of Child and Adolescent Psychiatry, University of California, San Francisco, California.

RICHARD A. RATNER, M.D.
Clinical Professor of Psychiatry and Behavioral Sciences, George Washington University School of Medicine, Adjunct Professor of Law (Psychiatry), Georgetown University Law Center, Consultant, Forensic Programs Division, Commission on Mental Health Services, Washington, D.C.; Secretary-Treasurer, American Board of Adolescent Psychiatry, Bethesda, Maryland.

REBECCA RENDLEMAN, M.D.
Assistant Professor of Psychiatry, Cornell University Medical College, Payne Whitney Clinic, New York Hospital/Cornell Medical Center, New York, New York.

SUSAN KAUSCH RICHTER, M.D.
Clinical Instructor, Departments of Neurology and Psychiatry, Albany Medical College, Albany, New York; Staff Psychiatrist, Outpatient and Consult Liaison, Ellis Hospital, Schenectady, New York.

DIANA S. ROSENSTEIN, PH.D.
Research Scientist and Consulting Psychologist, Institute of Pennsylvania Hospital, Private Practice, Philadelphia, Pennsylvania.

RICHARD M. SARLES, M.D.
Professor and Director, Division of Child and Adolescent Psychiatry, University of Maryland School of Medicine, Baltimore, Maryland.

THEODORE SHAPIRO, M.D.
Professor of Psychiatry, Professor of Psychiatry in Pediatrics, Cornell University Medical College; Director, Child and Adolescent Psychiatry, Payne Whitney Clinic, New York Hospital/Cornell Medical Center, New York, New York.

Contributors

JOYANNA L. SILBERG, PH.D.
Senior Psychologist, Coordinator, Dissociative Disorder Services for Children and Adolescents, Sheppard Pratt Health System, Towson, Maryland.

BERTRAM SLAFF, M.D.
Associate Clinical Professor of Psychiatry, Mount Sinai School of Medicine, City University of New York, New York, New York.

DESANKA STIPIC, M.D., FRCP [C]
Medical Director, Adult Partial Hospital Program, St. John's Hospital, Detroit, Michigan; Private Practice, St. Claire Shores, Michigan.

BARRI KATZ STRYER, M.D.
Clinical Instructor of Psychiatry, Department of Psychiatry and Behavioral Sciences, Neuropsychiatric Institute, University of California; Private Practice, Los Angeles, California.

MAX SUGAR, M.D.
Clinical Professor of Psychiatry, Louisiana State University School of Medicine, Clinical Professor of Psychiatry, Tulane University School of Medicine, New Orleans, Louisiana.

FEREIDOON TAGHIZADEH, M.D.
Senior Psychiatrist, Service Chief, Adolescent Inpatient Service, Sheppard Pratt Health System, Clinical Assistant Professor, Department of Psychiatry, University of Maryland, Baltimore, Maryland.

JOHN T. WALKUP, M.D.
Associate Professor, Division of Child and Adolescent Psychiatry, Johns Hopkins Medical Institutions, Baltimore, Maryland.

MARK D. WEIST, PH.D.
Assistant Professor, Department of Psychiatry, University of Maryland, Baltimore, Maryland.

1 / Introduction

Lois T. Flaherty

Adolescence is a time of paradox. The early years of this developmental period are marked by callousness and egocentricity, but by late adolescence relationships and mental life are infused by sensitivity and altruism. Societal attitudes toward adolescents are often inconsistent and contradictory; there is tension between the wish that adolescents would remain children and follow unquestioningly the precepts of their elders, and the hope that they will not repeat the mistakes of past generations and become saviors who lead society into a better future. They are simultaneously blamed for ills such as crime and teen pregnancy and adulated as sports stars and sex symbols.

Anna Freud summarized this paradox succinctly:

I take it that it is normal for an adolescent to behave for a considerable period of time in an inconsistent and unpredictable manner: to fight his impulses and to accept them; to ward them off successfully and to be overrun by them; to love his parents and to hate them; to revolt against them and to be dependent on them; to be deeply ashamed to acknowledge his mother before others and, unexpectedly, to desire heart-to-heart talks with her; to thrive on imitation of and identification with others while searching unceasingly for his own identity; to be more idealistic, artistic, generous, and unselfish than he will ever be again, but also the opposite—self-centered, egoistic, calculating. Such fluctuations between extreme opposites would be deemed highly abnormal at any other time of life. (1958/1969, pp. 164–165)

Compared to childhood and adulthood, adolescence has been less well defined. Indeed, it became a focus of study relatively late in history. From a scientific point of view, it can be argued that this developmental stage has been the least well researched of the developmental stages. Consequently, our understanding of normal adolescent development as well as of psychopathology during this period is still developing, albeit rapidly.

Historical Perspective

Both as individuals and members of groups, adolescents have played leading roles in history. Alexander the Great commanded the Greek troops in Macedonia at the age of 16 and became king at the age of 20. Joan of Arc became a military leader at the age of 19. By the end of his adolescence, Mozart had written some of his major musical works. In a high school essay written when he was 16, Albert Einstein had posed the question: "What would happen if a man tries to catch a light ray?" Ten years later came the answer, the theory of relativity.

In groups, adolescents have had a defining role in many watershed political and social movements, many of which originated as youth movements. In the Middle Ages, they went off to fight in the Crusades, including the ill-fated Children's Crusade of 1212. In the 20th century, they made up the Young Communists, Zionist youth groups, Mao's Red Guard, and the Hitler Jugend. They were leaders in the protests in the United States against the Vietnam War in the 1960s and the uprising in Tiananmen Square in Beijing, China, in 1989. As Rakoff (1996) has pointed out, all of these movements "shared in a mythology that youth was a transforming agent of history."

In our present-day world, adolescents play an important role in industrialized societies as consumers of goods and services. They are the targets of vast industries that vie for their spending on clothes and entertainment. They also serve as role models in cultures in which there is an idealization of youth, strength, and sexuality; many of our admired athletes, models, film stars, and beauty queens are adolescents. The other side of the coin is the publicity focused on adolescent drug dealers, murderers, thieves, vandals, and rapists.

1

Destructiveness

On a more negative note, many criminal careers have begun during the teenage years. Although the vast majority of adolescents do not become criminals, a great many do engage in some form of delinquent behavior on occasion, if delinquent behavior is defined as that which is illegal. Most of this behavior is relatively harmless, but serious criminal activity, sometimes involving gratuitous violence, does occur, and group antisocial activity including gang rapes, armed robberies, and murders are an unfortunate feature of this age.

Adolescents, as is discussed in Chapter 2, have always been considered somewhat troublesome. Indeed, it was their troubles that first brought them to the attention of behavioral scientists, as the first studies of this developmental period focused on delinquent or otherwise deviant youth. Even viewed through the distortions of psychopathology, it was possible to discern that adolescence was a period of dramatic changes and of paradoxes and inconsistencies.

A flowering of creativity, furthering of moral development, deepening capacity for relationships, and an expanding and more complex sense of self are all some of the possibilities of this period. However, these progressions are not guaranteed and are dependent to a large degree on the presence of favorable conditions in the adolescent's social and intellectual environment. In addition, the adolescent brings into this developmental period all of his or her preceding life experience, which has already shaped the development of the individual to a great extent.

Crises of Adolescence

Adolescents are confronted with the necessity of adapting to new bodies, new emotions, and new intellectual capacities. Commensurate with their new abilities, more is expected of them by others. These conditions inevitably create a crisis (or, more accurately, multiple crises), to which adolescents must adapt and respond. As is ex-plained in Chapter 3, most youngsters are able to respond to these rapidly changing internal and external realities without developing psychiatric symptoms or impaired functioning. The fact that, by and large, adolescents and their families weather successfully the teenage years does not mean that this period is devoid of stress or inner turmoil. Because adolescence brings with it new capacities and new opportunities, there is the possibility of reworking and resolving earlier problems during this developmental phase. Therein lies the appeal of therapeutic approaches with this age group.

Onset of Psychiatric Illness

Many of the major psychiatric disorders have their onset during the adolescent or young adult period. Whether for reasons of biological vulnerability or increased environmental stress, or, more likely, some interaction of both, the onset of puberty and the late adolescent period are times of particular risk. The data from the landmark National Institute of Mental Health Epidemiological Catchment Area Study revealed a much earlier age of onset than had formerly been believed for nearly all of the psychiatric disorders studied (Burke, Burke, Regier, & Rae 1990). This important new knowledge lends an even greater urgency to the study of adolescent psychiatry.

A word is in order about the organization of this volume. When the *Handbook of Child and Adolescent Psychiatry* was conceptualized, it was agreed that each of the syndromes would be treated in the volume covering the developmental period during which they have their peak occurrence. Thus, the primary treatment of attention deficit hyperactivity disorder (ADHD) is in Volume 2, *The Grade-School Child*, because this is the age at which the syndrome most commonly comes to the attention of clinicians. Although this volume contains some material on ADHD, its definitive treatment is provided elsewhere. By organizing the *Handbook* in this fashion, the editors have hoped to avoid unnecessary repetition.

REFERENCES

Burke, K. C., Burke, J. D., Regier, D. S., & Rae, D. S. (1990). Age at onset of selected mental health disorders in five community populations. *Archives of General Psychiatry, 47,* 511–518.

Freud, A. (1969). Adolescence. In *The Writings of Anna Freud* (Vol. 5, pp. 136–166). New York: International Universities Press. (Originally published 1958.)

Rakoff, V. (1996). Adolescence and youth movements. *Newsletter of the American Society for Adolescent Psychiatry,* (Winter), 1–3.

2 / A Historical Overview of Adolescence and Adolescent Psychiatry

Bertram Slaff

In Act III, Scene 3 of Shakespeare's *The Winter's Tale,* an old shepherd speaks: "I would there were no age between ten and three and twenty, or that youth would sleep out the rest, for there is nothing in the between but getting wenches with child, wronging the ancientry, stealing, fighting—"

Historical Background

Although Shakespeare recognized that the period of life we now know as adolescence had unique characteristics, the conceptualization of adolescence as a distinct stage of development did not exist in his time. In fact, neither childhood nor adolescence was acknowledged throughout most of recorded history. Philippe Aries (1962), in his *Centuries of Childhood,* examined the life cycle from the Middle Ages to the present and concluded that during the Middle Ages, the concept of childhood as we know it today simply did not exist. A stage of infancy, lasting until about age 7, was generally acknowledged. Thereafter, what we would consider children were simply assimilated into the adult world. The art, literature, and social documents of these times show children and adults dressed similarly, sharing in similar pursuits, and undifferentiated with regard to status or psychological development. The concept of childhood as a separate stage of life began to emerge slowly during the 17th and 18th centuries.

The concept of adolescence is of even more recent origin. Keniston (1971) considers that, while puberty as a biological state had been recognized, adolescence, as we think of it today, was discovered only during the 19th and 20th centuries, and the extension of adolescence as a stage of psychological growth is far from complete even

today. He observes that three changes occurred during the last century:

First, adolescence as a stage of life has been socially recognized and acknowledged. Second, society has begun to sanction and support adolescence, increasingly buttressing it with educational, familial, institutional, and economic resources. Third, these new resources, coupled with other changes in society, have opened up to an even larger proportion of the thirteen to eighteen-year-old age group the possibility of continuing psychological growth during the adolescent years. A further protection from adult responsibilities has been granted, educational institutions have been created to fill this moratorium, and a positive image of a postchildhood, preadult stage of life, adolescence, is now almost universally held. (P. 165)

This discovery of adolescence is closely related to other social, economic, and historical changes. Increasing industrialization has freed postpubertal youngsters from the requirements of farm and factory labor. The rising standards of economic productivity make the adolescent, especially the uneducated adolescent, a burden on the labor market. Growing affluence enables families and society as a whole to support economically unproductive adolescents in school.

Alternative Responses to Adolescence

Stone and Church (1957) state:

In primitive societies, there is no equivalent for our concept of adolescence. In some primitive societies, the transition from childhood to adulthood is so smooth that it goes unrecognized. More frequently, we find that the young person on the threshold of maturity goes through a ceremonial adolescence. Such ceremonial observances are called *puberty* rites, since they are usu-

5

ally timed to the onset of sexual maturity. . . . At the conclusion of the puberty rite, the young person is granted full adult status and assumes it without any sense of strain or conflict. . . . The essential fact that emerges from comparing our own culture with others is that the psychological events of adolescence in our society are not a necessary counterpart of the physical changes of puberty, but a cultural invention—not a deliberate one, of course, but a product of an increased delay in the assumption of adult responsibilities. (Pp. 271–272)

G. Stanley Hall's two-volume work on adolescence was published in 1904. It is widely regarded as the first scholarly work to focus on adolescent development. Weiner (1970) states that Hall, heavily influenced by Charles Darwin's theory of biological evolution, had formulated an essentially evolutionary theory of psychological development based on a "law of recapitulation." Individuals were thought to develop through predetermined stages from primitiveness to civilized behavior in a manner that re-creates the development of the human race (p. 8).

Noshpitz (1979) has noted that the early history of child and adolescent psychiatry in the United States was focused on the area of delinquency. Gardner (1972) has described the seminal development connected with the long and singularly productive life of William Healy (1869–1963). A group of philanthropically minded individuals in Chicago had proposed a 5-year study of Illinois delinquents that would, according to Jane Addams, one of the sponsors, "get at the root of the exact causes that make children go wrong" (K. Jones, 1987). On the recommendations of Adolf Meyer and William James, a 40-year-old neurologist, William Healy, was asked to head the research project at the Juvenile Psychopathic Institute, later to be known as the Institute for Juvenile Research. In 1909 he was charged to work with the Juvenile Court of Chicago, providing the court with a detailed scientific record on each subject; he also was to collect data about the medical, psychological, and social background of frequent offenders in an effort to determine the causes of juvenile delinquency. In 1915 *The Individual Delinquent* was published. In this work Healy introduced a psychodynamic perspective, demonstrating the role of disturbing social and developmental events in bringing about delin-

quent behavior. Each youth's actions had a meaningful history, and only through studying this background could one hope to understand and to help. Healy included psychoanalysis in his 1915 list of "working methods" and made use of a psychologist and a social worker in a collaborative effort to study the emotional problems of children, introducing Southard's term "clinic team" to describe this activity.

Organizations to Serve Youths

Disappointed at the lack of adequate facilities for the treatment of delinquents in Chicago, Healy and Dr. Augusta Bronner, a psychologist, his principal collaborator, moved to Boston and opened the clinic known as the Judge Baker Foundation (later the Judge Baker Guidance Center), after receiving assurances of improved opportunities for the treatment of delinquents there. He continued to be active in the Boston area until his death at the age of 94.

In 1909 Clifford Beers founded the National Committee for Mental Hygiene. Its slogan was "the prevention of insanity and delinquency," and it emphasized preventive work with children. In 1918 the Commonwealth Fund was established with the goal of furthering medical knowledge; its interests came to include delinquency. The National Committee for Mental Hygiene and the Commonwealth Fund proposed, in 1922, that 8 test clinics be established in various cities with 5-year support to be given by the fund; afterward, these clinics were to be supported locally.

These 8 "child guidance" clinics were established successfully and gained community support; many additional clinics were founded subsequently. They provided psychiatrists who worked with children and adolescents with an institutional base for their activities. Diagnosis took up most of their energies, but they also did some pioneer treatment. The "team approach" prevailed. Generally, the psychiatrist treated the child, the social worker took a history and worked with the parents, and the psychologist did testing. The clinics discovered that, in addition to their basic tasks, they had to function as child advocates, work with com-

6

munity groups, and liaison with other agencies that dealt with children.

Disruptive Behavior

Thus, in the early years of child and adolescent psychiatry, delinquency was the prime object of study; in the 1920s, attention began to be paid to children whose behavior was disruptive at home or a school but who had not come to the attention of the law.

In 1923 Karl Menninger (Lowrey, 1948, p. 190) wrote to 26 psychiatrists, stating "In spite of the rapidly increasing prestige of neuropsychiatry and the behavioristic or psychological attitude toward conduct disorder, there exists no centralizing organization of the representatives of the neuropsychiatric or medical view of crime." This led ultimately to the formation of the American Orthopsychiatric Association (AOA, or "Ortho"). The 1926 program included the statement

The American Orthopsychiatric Association has as its purpose the centralizing of the techniques, objectives, and aspirations of psychiatrists, psychologists and social workers, whose primary interests lie in the problems of human behavior, particularly conduct disorders of the antisocial types, providing a common meeting ground for students of these problems, and fostering scientific research in this field. (Lowrey, 1948, p. 198)

Psychoanalytic and Psychological Contributions

During the 20th century the influence of Sigmund Freud and his followers has been outstanding in the development of child and adolescent psychiatry. Ernest Jones (1922/1948) presented an evolutionary view of adolescent development that was seen as a reexperiencing of the first years of life. He propounded "the general law . . . that adolescence recapitulates infancy, and that the precise way in which a given person will pass through the necessary stages of development in adolescence is to a very great extent determined by the form of his infantile development" (p. 399).

With the publication of *The Ego and the Mechanisms of Defense* (1946), Anna Freud is acknowledged as having been instrumental in ushering in the era of "ego psychology." In her paper on adolescence, she described this phase as a period of normative upheaval and turmoil:

I take it that it is normal for an adolescent to behave for a considerable length of time in an inconsistent and unpredictable manner; to fight his impulses and to accept them; to ward them off successfully and to be overrun by them; to love his parents and to hate them; to revolt against them and to be dependent on them; to be deeply ashamed to acknowedge his mother before others and, unexpectedly, to desire heart-to-heart talks with her; to thrive on imitation of and identification with others while searching unceasingly for his own identity; to be more idealistic, artistic, generous, and unselfish than he will ever be again, but also the opposite—self-centered, egoistic, calculating. Such fluctuations between extreme opposites would be deemed highly abnormal at any other time of life. At this time they may signify no more than that an adult structure of personality takes a long time to emerge, that the ego of the individual in question does not cease to experiment and is in no hurry to close down on possibilities. (1958, pp. 275–276)

Erikson (1950) has been another powerful influence in enriching the field of developmental psychology with its emphasis on crucial stages in personality development as "normative crises"—critical points that determine the outcome of subsequent developmental stages. His concepts of identity formation and the experiences of adolescence in promoting the sense of personal identity have been widely accepted, as has his formulation of a basic conflict area of this period as "identity vs. identity diffusion."

Alternative Views on Adolescent Turmoil

A challenge has arisen to Anna Freud's view of adolescence as a period of disturbance. According to Offer (1969):

Studies of normal populations that exhibit little behavioral disequilibrium might eventually lead to the concept that adolescence as a period of growth can be undergone without serious disruptions between the generations or between the adolescent and his former identity. The transition to adulthood may be accomplished gradually, but accomplished all the same. Our findings emphatically suggest that a state of inner turmoil need not be the password of adolescence. (P. 192)

Masterson, too, has questioned the ubiquity of adolescent turmoil. It is his view that turmoil is not normative; when the adolescent appears to be disturbed, he or she is indeed disturbed and treatment is indicated (1968).

In 1926 Piaget published *The Language and Thought of the Child,* which was republished in 1957. In this and many succeeding works, he was able to show the development of cognitive structures in an orderly and predictable developmental sequence. He described the sensorimotor stage until about 18 months, the preoperational stage until 5 to 6 years, the stage of concrete operations from about 6 to 11, and finally, the potential for abstract thought, the highest level of intellectual development, beginning at about 11.

Recent Developments

ADOLESCENT PSYCHIATRIC WARDS

In 1937 an adolescent psychiatric ward was opened at Bellevue Hospital in New York City under the direction of Frank Curran (1939). Although in recent years there has been a proliferation of specialized inpatient services for adolescents, for many years this was a unique program. It served as a focus of research and training as well as service delivery. The establishment of such a program grew out of the recognition that adolescents needed specially designed services apart from those developed for adults.

SUPEREGO LACUNAE

The 1940s saw an interesting development in the realm of delinquency. An early concept emerged that was to make child psychiatry especially cognizant of the power of family factors in

the genesis of emotional disorders. Articles appeared describing the unconscious fostering by parents of child acting-out behavior, formulations later to be couched in Johnson's term of parental "superego lacunae" (1949).

RESIDENTIAL TREATMENT CENTERS

In 1946 Fritz Redl organized a research-oriented residential treatment center, which accepted a number of "hyperaggressive" boys. This was in the tradition of the work August Aichhorn had done in Vienna in 1918, which had led to the publication of *Wayward Youth* (1925). From this research, "Children Who Hate" and "Controls from Within" were published by Redl and David Wineman. They were included in *The Aggressive Child* (1957).

GROUP FOR THE ADVANCEMENT OF PSYCHIATRY

In 1946 the Group for the Advancement of Psychiatry (GAP) was formed, with William Menninger as a guiding figure. Its membership of approximately 186 psychiatrists was organized in the form of a number of working committees, including a Committee on Adolescence. This committee has published a number of influential works, beginning with its report, *Normal Adolescence,* in 1968.

EVOLUTION OF CHILD PSYCHIATRY INTO AN ACADEMIC DISCIPLINE

Early child psychiatry evolved in the freestanding community service units, the child guidance clinics. Now many were growing as subunits of departments of general psychiatry. Before the decade was over, however, in many an academic setting, battle lines would be drawn between the parent department of psychiatry and the younger child psychiatry division. By 1979 child psychiatry had become, in large measure, an academic discipline.

ADOLESCENT PSYCHIATRIC HOSPITAL SERVICES

The growth of psychiatric units attached to general hospitals went on apace. In many institutions, as I have reported (1980), adolescent patients were housed on the adult units and treated by general psychiatry residents under the supervision of adolescent preceptors. Gradually, a trend toward adolescent inpatient units developed.

MULTIPLE DETERMINANTS IN THE AREA OF ADOLESCENT PSYCHIATRY

Thus, the development of psychiatric services for adolescents as well as the advancement of knowledge of adolescent development and psychopathology took place both within and outside of child psychiatry and general psychiatry. In some cases, leaders in the field came from backgrounds in pediatrics; in other cases, from a perspective of general psychiatry. Adolescents were seen in the child guidance clinics as well as in facilities for adults. Much of the impetus for research and services came from the areas of juvenile justice, social services, and education. Increasingly, adolescents were seen as needing specialized treatment facilities and expertise, apart from that necessary to treat either adults or children. It was inevitable that issues of training, credentialing, and professional qualifications would arise.

AMERICAN ASSOCIATION OF PSYCHIATRIC CLINICS FOR CHILDREN

In 1948, 54 child guidance clinics came together and created the American Association of Psychiatric Clinics for Children (AAPCC) under Frederick Allen's leadership. This was to be the first standard-setting body for child and adolescent psychiatric services and for the training of child and adolescent psychiatrists. These clinics manifested the multidisciplinary "team approach" and were not necessarily under medical supervision.

AMERICAN ACADEMY OF CHILD PSYCHIATRY

In 1953 the American Academy of Child Psychiatry (AACP) was formed, with George Gardner as its president. The organization was made up of the recognized leaders in the field who proclaimed the goal of setting and maintaining the highest standards. Membership was to be by invitation; only individuals who had made "outstandingly significant" contributions would be asked to join. In 1967 the AACP radically transformed itself, abandoning its invitation-only position and opening itself to become the professional organization

of the rank and file of trained child-adolescent psychiatrists (Slaff, 1989). In 1987 it changed its name to the American Academy of Child and Adolescent Psychiatry. As of June 30, 1996, it had 6,053 members.

DEVELOPMENTS IN BIOLOGIC PSYCHIATRY

In the same year of the founding of the AACP, 1953, it became known that chlorpromazine affected the symptoms of psychosis. This discovery had tremendous import for the field of psychiatry as well as for the care of mentally ill patients of all ages. It led to a refocusing of psychiatry on the biological roots of mental illness, a trend that we are in the midst of today.

AMERICAN SOCIETY FOR ADOLESCENT PSYCHIATRY

In 1958 the Society for Adolescent Psychiatry was formed in New York City under the leadership of James Masterson. General psychiatrists who were interested in and active in treating adolescents as well as child psychiatrists (as they were then known) were welcomed into membership. Subsequently, local societies were formed in Philadelphia, Chicago, and Southern California. In 1967 these four groups confederated to form the American Society for Adolescent Psychiatry (ASAP), with William A. Schonfeld as president. The founders of ASAP saw their role as stimulating interest in this age group and providing a common meeting ground for child psychiatrists with an interest in adolescence, adolescent psychiatrists, and adult psychiatrists, many of whom were active in treating adolescents. There was great concern about what was seen as a severe shortage of adolescent psychiatrists, with a goal of promoting education and training in this field (Slaff, 1970). In contrast to the AACP, which initially sought to limit membership, ASAP began as a relatively open professional organization, a confederation of local groups, motivated by a desire to meet the manpower emergency in adolescent psychiatry. In July 1996 it had 763 members.

SPECIALTY CERTIFICATION

The American Board of Psychiatry and Neurology (ABPN) set up a Committee on Certification in Child Psychiatry in 1959; in 1987 this was renamed the Committee on Certification in Child and Adolescent Psychiatry. Training requirements were defined and examinations were established for psychiatrists who had been previously certified in psychiatry. The ABPN examination includes a focus on adolescents; candidates are examined on their ability to interview an adolescent patient and, based on the interview, demonstrate knowledge of differential diagnosis and treatment planning.

AMERICAN BOARD OF ADOLESCENT PSYCHIATRY

Many of the members of ASAP are credentialed as child and adolescent psychiatrists. Nevertheless, a significant number have come from adult psychiatry, drawn by their interest in adolescence. Many of these have had specialized training in working with adolescents but lack experience with younger children. ASAP took the position that this group should have the opportunity to be credentialed specifically in adolescent psychiatry, and developed its own certifying examination, which was given for the first time in 1992 by the American Board of Adolescent Psychiatry. A requirement for admission to this examination is previous certification in psychiatry by the ABPN or the Royal College of Physicians of Canada.

Undertreatment of Adolescent Psychopathology

Although there are widespread concerns about specialty training today, with questions being raised about whether there are too many specialists, including psychiatrists, there can be no doubt that adolescents with psychiatric disorders always have been and still are significantly undertreated. An additional problem is the apparent increased prevalence and severity of adolescent psychopathology. Are adolescents getting worse now in terms of mental health and problem behaviors, or are we better able to diagnose mental illness and detect problems? While some would point out that increased awareness has contributed to what seems to be an epidemic of mental illness among adolescents, objective signs indicate that much is not well with today's youth. Epidemiological data

(Fleming, 1996) reveal that the suicide rate is increasing for young people. Access to firearms figures prominently in this picture. Although young white males are at greater risk for suicide, suicide rates increased most rapidly for young African American males. Homicide rates are also increasing.

Changing Social Demographics in the United States

Elliot and Feldman (1990) have remarked on the changing social demographics in the United States; these changes have important implications for adolescent psychiatry. By the year 2000, 31% of adolescents will belong to a racial or ethnic minority: 12% Hispanic, 16% African American, and 3% of Asian or Pacific Island descent. Yet a most striking observation is the degree to which research on normal development has been restricted to middle-class whites. Far too little information is available about African Americans and Hispanics, and even less is known about other minority groups. These authors give several examples of changes in social attitudes toward and expectations for adolescents: a high school education has become a minimal expectation; work for this age group is typically part-time, low-paying, service-oriented activity; the proliferation of entertainment and leisure activities also has altered the adolescent experience; marked changes in women's roles mean that young people now see a much wider array of options for females; access to illicit drugs has become a common feature of growing up, as has the danger of being physically victimized. They conclude:

Growing up has always carried risks, but the nature of those risks is changing. Adolescents are less likely than in the past to suffer debilitating or fatal childhood diseases. Increasingly the sources of immediate distress and long-term problems are becoming instead socially mediated conditions such as poverty and marital disruption. It is crucial to learn how changes like these affect ability of the young to navigate this crucial stage of development. (Pp. 8–9)

In summary, adolescent psychiatry, which had its beginnings in the early part of the 20th century, is a new and still-growing field. Adolescence itself is changing, as is our knowledge of normal adolescent development and psychopathology. While there is much that has been learned, much remains unknown. Services, research, and training have developed slowly, and adolescents' mental health needs remain largely unmet. Many of the significant health and mortality problems of adolescents are linked to mental illness or various kinds of psychological dysfunction. Meeting the mental health needs of today's adolescents has become increasingly challenging, as is evident in many of the chapters that follow.

REFERENCES

Aichhorn, A. (1925). *Wayward youth.* New York: Viking.

Aries, P. (1962). *Centuries of childhood.* New York: W. W. Norton.

Curran, F. (1939). Organization of a ward for adolescents in Bellevue Psychiatric Hospital. *American Journal of Psychiatry, 95,* 1365–1388.

Elliot, G. R., & Feldman, S. S. (1990). Capturing the adolescent experience. In S. S. Feldman & G. R. Elliot (Eds.), *At the threshold—the developing adolescent* (pp. 6–9). Cambridge, MA: Harvard University Press.

Erikson, E. H. (1950). *Childhood and society.* New York: W. W. Norton.

Feinstein, S. C., & Slaff, B. (1971). Another society! Why? *Newsletter, American Society of Adolescent Psychiatry* (April 1971), 12.

Fleming, M. (1996). *Healthy youth 2000. A mid-decade review.* Chicago: Department of Adolescent Health, American Medical Association.

Freud, A. (1946). *The ego and the mechanisms of defense.* New York: International Universities Press.

Freud, A. (1958). Adolescence. *Psychoanalytic Study of the Child, 13,* 255–278.

Gardner, G. (1972). William Healy, 1869–1963. *Journal of the American Academy of Child Psychiatry, 11,* 1–29.

Group for the Advancement of Psychiatry. Committee on Adolescence (1968). *Normal adolescence.* New York: Author.

Hall, G. S. (1904). *Adolescence.* New York: Appleton.

Healy, W. (1915). *The individual delinquent.* Boston: Little, Brown.

Johnson, A. M. (1949). Sanctions for superego lacunae of adolescents. In K. R. Eissler (Ed.), *Searchlights on delinquency* (pp. 225–245). New York: International Universities Press.

Jones, E. (1922). Some problems of adolescence. Reprinted in E. Jones (Ed.) (1949). *Papers on psychoanalysis* (p. 399). Baltimore: Williams & Wilkins.

Jones, E. (1948). Some problems of adolescence. *Papers on Psychoanalysis.* London: Bailliere, Tindall & Cox.

Jones, K. (1987). "Straightening the twig": The professionalization of American child psychiatry. New Brunswick, NJ: Rutgers University, Department of History. Typescript.

Keniston, K. (1971). Youth as a stage of life. *Adolescent Psychiatry, 1,* 161–175.

Lowrey, L. (1948). The birth of orthopsychiatry. In L. Lowrey (Ed.), *Orthopsychiatry, 1923–1948, retrospect and prospect* (pp. 190–208). Menasha, WI: George Banta Publishing.

Masterson, J. F. (1968). The psychiatric significance of adolescent turmoil. *American Journal of Psychiatry, 124,* 1549–1554.

Noshpitz, J. D. (1979). *History of childhood and child psychiatry in the 20th century.* Unpublished manuscript.

Offer, D. (1969). *The psychological world of the teenager.* New York: Basic Books.

Piaget, J. (1957). *The language and thought of the child.* Glencoe, IL: Free Press.

Redl, F., & Wineman, D. (1957). *The aggressive child.* Glencoe, IL: Free Press.

Slaff, B. (1970). The manpower emergency in adolescent psychiatry. *Psychiatric Opinion, 7,* 25–28.

Slaff, B. (1980). The history of hospital adolescent psychiatry. In D. R. Heacock (Ed.), *A psychodynamic approach to adolescent psychiatry—The Mount Sinai Experience* (pp. 3–12). New York: Marcel Dekker.

Slaff, B. (1989). History of child and adolescent psychiatry ideas and organizations in the United States: A twentieth century review. *Adolescent Psychiatry, 16,* 31–52.

Stone, L. J., & Church, J. (1957). *Childhood and adolescence—a psychology of the growing person.* New York: Random House.

Weiner, I. B. (1970). *Psychological disturbance in adolescence.* New York: John Wiley & Sons.

SECTION I
Normal Adolescent Development

3 / Overview of Normal Adolescent Development

Susan Kausch Richter

INTRODUCTION

An understanding of normal development is paramount to prevention, diagnosis, and treatment of adolescent disorders that may have links to abnormal development. Only by first defining "normal" can we begin to recognize that which is abnormal. This chapter provides a brief overview of normal adolescent psychological development. The concepts of adolescence, normality, and adolescent emotional turmoil are examined, followed by a discussion of the stages of adolescent development. Within this framework, continuities and discontinuities in human development as related to adolescence and its place in the life course are described.

Before turning to normal adolescent development, what is meant by "adolescence" and "normal" should first be clarified. Adolescence is a transitional stage in human development during which the individual undergoes marked physiological, psychological, and social change in the process of growing from a child into an adult. The precise onset, duration, and termination of adolescence varies with cultural context and individual rate of maturation. Puberty is often the developmental marker used to designate the onset of adolescence (Brooks-Gunn & Petersen, 1984; Greene & Boxer, 1986). However, there is a wide variation in both onset and duration of normal puberty. For girls, puberty usually occurs between the ages of 8 and 18; for boys, between the ages of 9 and 19. Girls experience the onset of puberty approximately 18 months prior to boys. Because our society uses the system of age-grading, which emphasizes chronological age in conferring certain rights, responsibilities, and privileges to the individual, it is useful to consider other, socially defined markers of entry into adolescence, such as starting junior high school (Hamburg, 1974). Although different researchers use different definitions, it is convenient to consider adolescence in our culture as roughly encompassing the second decade of life (Petersen, 1988) or ages 12 to 19 (Offer & Boxer, 1990). The end of adolescence is defined by social factors such as marriage, entry into the workforce, and financial independence and is therefore more ambiguous. Depending on the personal choices made within available options, adolescence may end for some in the teens with early termination of schooling and entrance into the workforce. Due to the prolonged education necessary to enter certain careers, adolescence may not end for others until the late 20s. Therefore, length of adolescence is both biologically and socially determined.

NORMALITY

Whether a particular behavior or path of development is deemed normal or abnormal depends largely on the particular definition of normality being employed. According to Offer and Sabshin (1974), normality can be organized into four main perspectives, each having different implications for both data interpretations and patient diagnosis and treatment. Normality can be defined as *utopia*, the perspective of many psychoanalysts. From this standpoint, normality is equivalent with optimal functioning or self-actualization, which few individuals achieve. Normality also can be viewed as *health*, or absence of disease, and implies reasonable rather than optimal functioning. This is the traditional medical-psychiatric position, and normality is considered to be a ubiquitous phenomenon. The third perspective, normality as the *statistical average*, is the usual approach taken by the behavioral scientist in the analysis of data. The fourth and most complex model defines normality as a *transactional system*, with normal behavior being the end result of interacting systems which change over time. The unique individual and his or her environment are both considered to be in a continual state of flux, and both are seen as participating in the production of healthy as well as maladaptive behavioral patterns.

ADOLESCENT EMOTIONAL TURMOIL

An example of the importance of defining which perspective of normality is being taken is seen in studies of adolescent emotional turmoil. The seemingly contradictory psychoanalytic viewpoint asserts that adolescent turmoil is not only normal but necessary to the continuing development of the adolescent. However, the gradual nature of the transitions associated with adolescence allow for growth without the experience of undue turmoil as was once believed. By studying normal (modal) adolescent development using multiple, diverse groups of adolescents from all over the world, Offer and associates have found that most adolescents (80%) do not experience emotional turmoil. For this significant majority of teenagers, the passage into adulthood can be described as smooth (Offer, 1969; Offer & Offer, 1975; Offer, Ostrov, & Howard, 1981; Petersen & Leffert, 1995), rather than full of "storm and stress" (Freud, 1958; Hall, 1904). Other investigators have demonstrated similar findings (Douvan & Adelson, 1966; Rutter, Graham, Chadwick, & Yule, 1976). Nevertheless, although the average adolescent may not experience normative turmoil, it is important not to ignore the impact our rapidly changing society may have on normal adolescent development. The lengthening of adolescence, disjunction between the attainment of social and biological maturity, abundance of different options available for adult roles, erosion of family and social support networks, along with greater access to life-threatening activities may combine to make modern adolescence more difficult than in the past (Hamburg & Takanishi, 1989).

Social Forces as Shapers of Adolescence

Changing social forces will necessarily alter the experience of being adolescent, as adolescence is essentially a time of changing biologically and psychologically from a child to an adult within a social context. Most social scientists believe that the place of adolescents within society, behaviors deemed characteristic of adolescents, and the length of adolescence itself are largely culturally determined. When drastic changes occur in societal construction, so, too, must individuals change in terms of psychological adaptation. For example, the changes brought about by the industrial revolution radically altered our human social experience and are associated with adolescence being recognized as a discrete stage in human development (Esman, 1990; Lewis & Volkmar, 1990). The examples of consumerism, cultural definitions of female beauty, substance use, and parental divorce will serve to illustrate the interaction between cultural values and adolescent behavior. The experience of growing up in a country at war or being the victim of natural and economic disaster is an unfortunately common experience in many parts of the world. How these experiences impinge on adolescent development is a complex topic; the reader is referred to Jensen and Shaw (1993) and to Shannon, Lonigen, Finch, and Taylor (1994).

Adolescent subcultures and the behavioral features defining them are often expressions of adult values in larger society. Peer groups, in turn, tend to reinforce rather than contradict parental and dominant cultural values (Brown, 1990; Dornbusch, 1989). For example, adolescent consumerism in Western culture could be viewed as the outcome of growing up within the economic system of capitalism and its attendant market forces, where one major role of the adult is that of consumer. In other words, the shop-till-you-drop mentality and the idea that "he who dies with the most toys wins" didn't originate with adolescents. Training to become an adolescent consumer of sneakers, magazines, records, and makeup begins with childhood television exposure. This process continues with multimedia marketing strategies specifically designed for adolescent appeal, the classic example being the marketing of rock music idols, which translates into huge record company sales, as the main consumers of popular music are adolescents (Esman, 1990).

The changing face of the cultural dictates of female beauty is another powerful example of adolescent susceptibility to adult values. As tall and slender describes the current preferred female body type, the majority of normal-weight adult females view themselves as overweight (Brooks-Gunn & Reiter, 1990). Young adolescents, in their desire to conform, may attempt to emulate this narrow definition of beauty, resulting in preoccupation with weight, dieting, and a negative body image (Caspar & Offer, 1990).

Lest adolescent drug use be mistakenly belied as a form of rebellion, it should be recalled that rates of adolescent alcohol use cross-culturally tend to parallel the rates of their respective adult counterparts (Kandel, 1984). Use of marijuana and other psychoactive drugs by adolescents appears also to be related to rates of use by adults. However, experimental use and abuse need to be distinguished for clinical purposes and to determine overall social cost (Zinberg, 1984). Although adolescent use of alcohol and illicit drugs has declined from its peak in the 1980s, it is still very common. In 1993, about one-third of adolescents reported drug use within the past year and about one-quarter admitted to binge-drinking (5 or more drinks) within the preceding 2 weeks (Johnston, O'Malley, & Bachman, 1994). A survey of college students, originally done in 1980 and repeated at the same school in 1992, found declines in use of all drugs, with marijuana going from 72 to 52%; cocaine, from 38 to 14%; hallucinogens, from 30 to 21%; amphetamines, from 26 to 10%; and sedatives, from 17 to 7%; Although frequency of alcohol use had declined, the prevalence of binge-drinking and its negative consequences on functioning rose, with more students reporting blackouts, missed classes, arrests, and loss of friends related to their drinking (Schuckit, Klein, Twitchell, & Springer, 1994).

Parental divorce and remarriage is so prevalent that growing up in a single-parent or blended family is now a nearly normative alternative experience to living with ones' original parents throughout childhood and adolescence (Hill, 1993). Divorce appears to be related to negative shaping of the adolescent experience and is correlated with increased risk for school failure, substance use, and delinquency (Furstenburg, 1990). Teasing out protective and risk factors for developing divorce-related problems is required, however, as divorce is not a uniform hazard and is not an event unto itself (Hetherington, 1989).

For example, interparental conflict before and after divorce appears to be a main risk factor for the development of disturbance in children and adolescents. However, adolescents from divorced families experience less intergenerational conflict and more autonomy than those from intact families. Additionally, a good relationship between the adolescent and at least one parent may act as a buffer against the stress of parental breakup. In summary, how the adolescent experience is shaped by a cultural phenomenon such as a high parental divorce rate is, like other social forces, dependent on the interaction between the individual and what makes up his or her environment (Hill, 1993).

Stages of Adolescent Development

Previously adolescence had been thought of as a single stage of development, which was a useful concept in that adolescence was of relatively short duration. Over the last 80 years adolescence in Western cultures has progressively lengthened (Kett, 1977), with puberty occurring earlier and entrance into adult roles later. Recent researchers in development have thus begun to subdivide adolescence into early, middle, and late stages, as life events will impact differently on the adolescent depending on his or her developmental level. The divisions of secondary education into junior high, high school, and college also roughly correspond to the stages of adolescence. Each stage can be given a somewhat arbitrary age range during which important developmental tasks need to be accomplished. These primary developmental tasks do overlap stages, and many researchers now consider that while the most rapid growth in a particular area may occur during a specific stage, many issues in development require continuous integration of new events and experiences and may be considered to be issues for the lifespan. Human development in any stage of the life course, including adolescence, thus can be conceptualized as involving progressive, continual change within a given context rather than involving transformations from one stage to the next (Petersen, 1988; Stern, 1985).

IDENTITY DEVELOPMENT

A review of the theoretical and empirical work in the area of identity formation as summarized by Hill (1993) will serve to illustrate how the view of a fundamental developmental task has evolved. While identity development was thought to be primarily a task for adolescence, empirical research has shown that identity only begins to become a salient issue during adolescence, peaks during young adulthood, and is subject to refinements throughout the rest of the lifespan.

Erikson (1959) first put forth a theory of identity formation, which he believed was the central developmental issue for the adolescent. He postulated that the adolescent ego identity proceeds from a state of diffusion to the achievement of a solid sense of who he or she is by the time young adulthood is reached. During this time, the adolescent tries on various social roles and possible selves. This experimentation with possibilities requires a time of psychological moratorium such that one's truest identity may be discovered and consolidated. A major underlying conflict is maintaining a sense of personal continuity over time while the physical changes associated with puberty and changes in societal demands are also occurring (Harter, 1990; James, 1982).

Marcia's work (1980) built on that of Erikson by establishing a model for identity development where 4 possible identity statuses could result from the interaction of the dimensions of exploration of possible identities and the degree of commitment to a personal identity. A state of identity *diffusion* results when exploration and commitment are low, while *moratorium* occurs when commitment is low but options for possible identities are kept open by active exploration. Identity *foreclosure* ensues when one firmly commits to a personal identity before allowing for exploration. Identity *achievement*, the most mature form of identity resolution, is characterized by a clear personal identity preceded by a period of careful, active exploration.

Empirical research has tested, expanded, and refined these theoretical assumptions. For example, Berzonsky's model (1992) of identity development incorporates information processing into Marcia's identity statuses. Those who are *information oriented* educate themselves as to available alternatives before making decisions, characteristic of those in moratorium or achievement. *Avoidant-oriented* individuals stay in diffusion by neglect and forestallment of decision making. Adolescents who are *normative oriented* foreclose on further individual identity development by adopting the preset standards of parents and community.

Longitudinal studies also have shown that identity is not a unitary concept but involves various domains, such as vocation, religious and political beliefs, and gender-related roles. Late adolescents may be at different points across these domains—for example, achieved in vocation and diffused in religion. Furthermore, few youths studied had reached achievement status in even one domain by the end of adolescence (Archer 1989; Kroger, 1988). Therefore, it appears that most adolescents, while beginning to find their own voice across these domains, still remain in diffusion or passive conformity characteristic of identity foreclosure. Additionally, trying on different selves per Erikson is difficult in a practical sense, as high school society does not readily allow sudden shifts in peer group memberships. For example, for a "druggie" to associate with a new crowd requires time and experience, during which others' perceptions of him or her based on old behaviors shift (Brown, 1990). In Western culture, then, active exploration and consolidation of identity across various domains seems to be a more salient issue in the development of young adults; additional refinements take place in later stages of the life course.

EARLY ADOLESCENCE

During early adolescence (ages 12 to 14), the rapid physical changes associated with puberty occur and the adolescent has to accept the changes in his or her body (Offer & Boxer, 1990) and incorporate the changes into the self-image. While the sequence of pubertal changes is relatively constant, the age of onset and rate of progression are not. Pubertal change can have varying psychological effects, depending on pubertal timing and status in relation to peers and the particular meaning the adolescent attaches to the changes. Research has shown both positive and negative consequences of both sexes when pubertal development is off time in relation to peers. Early maturation in boys has been found to be associated with greater self-confidence and less dependency

(Mussen & Jones, 1957). Early-maturing boys also were considered to be more attractive to peers and adults; they perceived themselves as more attractive and reported a more positive body image and higher self-esteem (Blyth et al., 1981; Jones, 1965; Tobin-Richards, Boxer, & Petersen, 1983). Late maturation in boys has been associated with both personal and social maladjustments, such as a more negative body image and decreased sense of attractiveness (Mussen & Jones, 1957; Tobin-Richards, et al., 1983). However, Petersen and Crockett (1985) found improved psychological adjustment for both later-developing boys and girls. The effects of pubertal timing appear to be more complex in girls, with those who are developmentally on time in comparison with peers reporting a better body image and feeling more attractive than those who are either early or late (Tobin-Richards et al., 1983). Late-maturing boys and early-maturing girls are thought to be at risk for poor adjustment. Not only are they off time relative to their same-sex peers, but they are even more discrepant from those of the opposite sex, when the fact is considered that females, on average, mature 18 months earlier than males (Brooks-Gunn, Petersen, & Eichorn, 1985). The cultural importance placed on strength and athletic ability in boys and thinness and breast development in girls may influence in part some of these differences (Petersen, 1988; Tobin-Richards et al., 1983).

The physical changes associated with puberty may coincide with entry into junior high school, which is associated with increased academic demands and the social expectation that adolescents have entered the teen culture (Hamburg, 1974). Significant others may begin to react differently to adolescents in response to these changes, bringing about a subsequent shift in the socially shared definitions of the self (Tobin-Richards et al., 1983). Peer interactions also are beginning to shift as adolescents begin to spend more time with each other and less with adults. This shift is made apparent to family members with the oft-heard statement, "Aw, Mom, I want to go, everybody else is!" Time spent with friends is the best part of the daily life of an adolescent; similarly, adults also report feeling best with friends (Csikszentmihalyi & Larson, 1984). There are, however, large cross-cultural differences in the amount of time adolescents spend with friends (Savin-Williams &

Berndt, 1990). Throughout adolescence the peer group gradually shifts from same-sex groups and dyads to opposite-sex groups and finally dyads (Csikszentmihalyi & Larson, 1984). Young adolescents seem to travel in packs, with one parent heard to state dryly that it was his turn to take his daughter and the other "teenlings" to the mall. And who has not observed, while chaperoning a junior high school dance, the herds of boys and girls conducting separate meetings in the bathrooms over their respective romantic involvements? The intimacy of these initial tentative dyads does increase throughout adolescence, paving the way for close relationships in young adulthood. Cliques and close same-sex friendships are characteristic of this period but by no means exclusive to early adolescence. Both boys and girls are beginning to show a strong interest in the opposite sex, and about half report infrequent petting (Crockett, Losoff, & Petersen, 1984). Sexual expression during this phase usually involves fantasy and masturbation. Transient homosexual contact is not rare. The few studies reporting on sexual intercourse in early adolescence show it to be a relatively uncommon event (Crockett et al., 1984; Katchadourian, 1990).

Changes in cognition and moral development also are beginning to occur, as early adolescents begin to develop a capacity for abstract thought. As they begin to be able to take into account another's viewpoint, they may display the adolescent form of egocentric thinking, manifesting itself in self-consciousness (Elkind, 1967; Keating, 1990). These biological, social, and psychological changes may interact to make early adolescence a particularly challenging and stressful time in life, although most youths display healthy development through this period (Blyth, Simmons, & Carlton-Ford, 1983; Hamburg, 1974; Petersen & Ebata, 1987).

MIDDLE ADOLESCENCE

Midadolescents (ages 15 to 16) move increasingly toward independence, as they separate and individuate themselves from the family. This does not imply detachment but rather a redefinition of family relationships, as the ties of adolescents to those outside the family continue to widen and intensify. Much of the bickering with parents over everyday issues, common in middle adolescence, decreases by late adolescence (Montemayor, 1983; Steinberg, 1990). In general, adolescents report positive feelings toward their families (Offer et al., 1981). As adolescents continue to experiment with a variety of relationships, heterosexual relationships gain increasing importance. There is a gradual advancement in sexual behaviors with progression through adolescence. The age of first sexual intercourse, usually unplanned and unprotected, is decreasing, with a current average age of 16 (Brooks-Gunn & Paikoff, 1997).

During this stage adolescents typically enter high school, but the transition is felt to be smoother, as adolescents have had the previous experience of junior high (Hamburg, 1974). As adolescents progress through high school, the importance of crowd membership (a larger, more reputation-based group than a clique) begins to fall, coinciding with a fall in relative vulnerability to peer pressure. It also becomes more likely that adolescents may belong to several crowds at once—"jock," "brain," "druggie," and "in" crowd. Serious delinquent behavior as a group norm remains within a small number of these crowds, with aggressive children finding each other and staying together before and during adolescence (Brown, 1990). Cognitive abilities and the practical use of abstract thought continue to increase, although the timing and extent of the development of formal operational thought is variable (Dulit, 1972; Keating, 1980, 1990). In addition, use of formal thought process depends on content and context (Mussen, Conger, Kagan, & Huston, 1990).

Moral development also may undergo important progressions during adolescence, although like other developmental domains, timing and final level of development vary with the individual. Conventional morality is the dominant mode of moral thinking in adolescents. Conventional moral thinking involves the consideration of both the individual and society in moral decisions. Adolescents at this level mainly concern themselves with being "good people." Some individuals do advance to postconventional morality, involving a sense of social contract between the individual and society and universal ethical principles (Kohlberg, 1976). Gilligan (1982) considers the moral development of women to be oriented more toward care in relationships than the justice and rights model of Kohlberg. Others, however, have not demonstrated any significant sex differences in moral development (Walker, 1989).

LATE ADOLESCENCE

Late adolescence (ages 17 to 19 and beyond) is the time of addressing identity issues, especially involving vocational choice and sexual identity (Erikson, 1968; Offer & Boxer, 1990). As discussed earlier, however, much identity formation and consolidation probably occurs during young adulthood. Adolescents gradually develop a sense of personal continuity over time and an integrated, coherent theory of the self, as more advanced cognitive abilities allow them to resolve diverse self-attributes that sometimes are more apparent in one social role than another. For example, adolescents can comfortably characterize themselves as "rowdy" with friends, "thoughtful" with teachers, and "flirtatious" with romantic partners. The extent of social networks continues to expand, and romantic relationships become increasingly important, with most adolescents experiencing dating before ending high school (Harter, 1990; Savin-Williams & Berndt, 1990). For those who continue their education, this stage corresponds to finishing high school and entrance into college. In terms of adult roles in the past, older adolescent males typically oriented themselves toward work and careers, while female adolescents focused on marriage and raising children. As different options for female adolescents are becoming more available, there is an increased need to integrate work and family. This ability to choose from a wider range of adult roles may make identity consolidation more difficult (Flaherty, 1982; Marcia, 1980). Throughout late adolescence, intimate relationships continue to evolve, and optimally, the ability to sustain a lasting, mutually satisfying relationship will eventually emerge. As adult roles and responsibilities are gradually assumed, adolescence ends, merging with the beginnings of young adulthood.

Continuities and Discontinuities in Adolescent Development

Whether aspects of the developing individual are continuous or discontinuous over phases of the life course is controversial and continues to be an interesting challenge to modern psychiatry. Here the continuity/discontinuity dilemma is first viewed in a historical sense before the implications for adolescence and its place in the life course are discussed.

As summarized by Rutter (1989), the belief that the first few years of life were most critical to psychological development and that following this period, personality remained consistent dominated the field until challenged by longitudinal studies. For example, the idea that maternal deprivation in infancy invariably caused permanent, irreversible damage was challenged by longitudinal studies showing that the outcome of early deprivation was diverse and dependent on subsequent life experiences (Rutter, 1989). It was then argued that certain developmental domains may, in fact, have little continuity over time and that, in looking for continuities, continuing social influences and contexts may have been largely overlooked (Brim & Kagan, 1980; Bronfenbrenner, 1979). For example, the driving forces behind the increasing rates of both suicide and pregnancy among adolescents are not likely to be clarified by examination of connections from early childhood to adolescence. These problems are more likely to be connected to current societal norms and cohort effects (Offer & Schonert-Reichl, 1992). Research now demonstrates development to be a complicated mix of both continuity and discontinuity (Rutter, 1993). Psychiatric treatment issues, however, continue to aid in driving this controversy. For example, if personality patterns are believed to be set early in life and thereafter remain constant, then the amount of change from maladaptive patterns hoped for in treatment is limited and would be thought to require long-term intervention to achieve. Alternatively, if development is generally considered to be more discontinuous and subject to the influence of current context, then perhaps a great deal of change could occur with proper interventions and environmental changes.

Certain aspects of the individual may be more continuous, such as temperament and self-image, while others may be more discontinuous across developmental stages (Offer & Sabshin, 1984). Furthermore, patterns of normal development are multiple (Block, 1971; Offer & Offer, 1975; Rutter, 1993). This viewpoint is also more consistent with understanding development as a transactional system, with normal behavior being the end result of interacting systems that change over time (Offer & Sabshin, 1984).

Because of the transitional nature of the progression from childhood to adolescence and adolescence to adulthood (Petersen, 1988), it is important to consider the existence of homotypic and heterotypic continuities as well as discontinuities. Heterotypic continuities occur when behavioral expression changes but the underlying process driving the behavior remains the same (Kagan, 1971; Rutter, 1989); homotypic continuity implies constancy in behavioral expression over time. Heterotypic continuities that have withstood the test of longitudinal replication, for example, are the associations between social isolation, peer rejection, odd behavior, and attention deficits in childhood with schizophrenic psychosis in adults (Neuchterlein, 1986; Rutter, 1984). Conduct disorder in childhood also has been shown to have continuity with a broad range of adult disorders, with gender playing a mediating role in modifying expression of the underlying disturbance. While conduct disorder in boys tends to lead to the more homotypically continuous antisocial personality disorder in men, conduct-disordered girls tend to have an increased risk for depression in addition to other disorders as adults. This is more consistent with a pattern of heterotypic continuity (Robins, 1986). Studies of personality development, temperament, and cognition will serve as further illustrative examples of developmental continuity and change during adolescence.

Kagan and Moss (1962) found personality structures that tended to remain stable over time were those that were in accordance with sex roles deemed appropriate by society. Those traits that were not congruent with sex roles were suggested to be heterotypically continuous, such as passivity in young males being expressed in adulthood as noncompetitiveness, a more socially acceptable trait.

Block's (1971) longitudinal study assessing personality development from early adolescence to adulthood demonstrated considerable personality continuity over time, especially between junior and senior high. However, on an individual level, there was marked variability in that certain subjects underwent character stabilization early, while others did change considerably over the years (Brim & Kagan, 1980).

The longitudinal study of shy persons showed that this behavioral style is continuous across the life course, and has different consequences for males and females. Shy boys were more likely to enter into marriage, parenthood, and stable careers later than their peers, while shy girls tended to more frequently enter into the conventional female pattern of marriage, childbearing and homemaking than their more outgoing counterparts.

This study highlights the possibilities for how continuities may develop. *Cumulative continuity* refers to behavior sustaining itself as a result of the consequences of that behavior. For example, ill-tempered adolescents who drop out of school place themselves in a situation of limited opportunity, providing circumstances against which to continue to strike out, perpetuating a cycle of frustration—explosive striking out—opportunity limitation. Alternatively, adolescents who have learned that explosive striking out is a way to get what they want or have come to expect a hostile response may behave in such a way as to elicit hostility from others. This is an example of *interactional continuity,* which arises as a result of reciprocal social interaction (Caspi, Elder, & Bem, 1988).

Offer and Offer (1975) found three general patterns of psychosocial development—continuous, surgent, and tumultous—in their study of white, middle-class male adolescents, demonstrating the presence of both continuities and discontinuities in normal development. Similar findings were reported by Golumbek and Marton (1992), who examined personality functioning in adolescents with yearly assessments from ages 10 to 19. Personality functioning was defined as preferred ways of relating and coping both in quiet times and under duress. They found the teens fell into three general patterns of personality functioning: consistently clear, fluctuating, and consistently disturbed. The personality patterns of the clear and disturbed groups support the notion that personality functioning, while undergoing maturation during adolescence, is fairly stable at the core. The fluctuating group also could represent an underlying continuous process of stable instability. However, Nesselroade and Baltes (1974) reported current culture to be more important than change in age when assessing adolescent personality development, and emphasized the importance of taking context into account. Other studies have reiterated these themes of both stability and change in personality development (Haan, Millsap, & Hartka, 1986; Stein, Newcomb, & Bentler, 1986; Stokes, Mumford, & Owens, 1989) across adolescence and beyond.

Clausen's investigation (1991) of the relationship between adolescent competence and the subsequent life course alludes to possible effects of stability and change. Those considered to be highly competent in adolescence by measures of self-confidence, intellectual investment, and dependability were found to exhibit greater personality continuity over the life course.

Studies of the type A behavior pattern suggest both heterotypic and homotypic continuities from childhood to adolescence, depending in part on the method of assessment used (Keltikangas-Jarvinen, 1990; Steinberg, 1986). Cairns, Cairns, Neckerman, Ferguson, and Gariepy (1989) examined aggressive behavior from childhood to early adolescence in normal children. Individual differences demonstrated continuity over time, but themes of aggression for the group shifted with maturation and gender. Boys continued to use physical aggression in male-male conflicts but much less so in male-female confrontations, while girls showed a decrease in overall physical aggression but developed an increase in the use of social aggression and ostracism. In their review, Parke and Slaby (1983) discuss the need to consider the effects of social norms, roles, and context in modifying the expression of aggressive behavior through development, while Olweus (1979) attests to the individual stability of aggressive behavior in boys.

In his review of continuities and discontinuities in the specific factor of temperament, McDevitt (1986) notes stability in early childhood, with global measures of ill-temperedness in particular having significant ties to adolescence and young adulthood. Korn (1984) demonstrated a strong association between teenage and young adult temperament in a follow-up of the New York Longitudinal Study (Thomas, Chess, & Birch, 1968). However, the correlation between early childhood and young adult temperament was low, indicating, perhaps, the stabilization of temperament with age or the effect of time lapse between two assessments.

Work in the area of cognition also demonstrates the possibility of continuity within change. While tests of intelligence before the age of 2 have poor predictive ability for later scores, tests in middle childhood are predictive of performance in adolescence. In turn, prediction of test scores as an adult is most reliable at adolescence. However, it is important to be conservative in test interpretation, as individual variation with age is not uncommon. While intelligence as measured by standard testing tends to remain stable with age, cognitive ability does not. Throughout adolescence gains continue to be made in practical use of abstract thought, social cognition, information processing, and perceptual ability (Conger, 1991; Keating, 1980).

CONCLUSION

Normal development can occur across multiple pathways. The complex effects of unique genetic inheritance interacting with shared and unshared aspects of the environment in producing the continuities and discontinuities in individual development are only beginning to be understood. The effects of nature and nurture are no longer viewed in a mutually exclusive manner. Similarly, the effects of past and present experience on behavior should not be polarized as either/or (Rutter, 1993). Adolescence is a transitional period in human development, and future research needs to be directed toward understanding the complex links between adolescence and other stages in the life course. Only by understanding normal development can we begin to understand and provide appropriate interventions for those on an abnormal developmental trajectory.

REFERENCES

Archer, S. (1989). The status of identity: Reflections on the need for intervention. *Journal of Adolescence, 12*, 345–359.

Berzonsky, M. (1992). A process perspective on identity and stress management. In G. R. Adams, T. P. Gullotta, & R. Montemayor (Eds.), *Adolescent identity formation* (pp. 193–215). Newbury Park, CA: Sage.

Block, J. (1971). *Lives through time*. Berkeley, CA: Bancroft Books.

Blyth, D. A., Simmons, R. G., Bulcroft, R., Felt, D., VanCleave, E. F., & Bush, D. M. (1981). The effects of physical development on self-image and satisfaction with body image for early adolescent males. In R. G. Simmons (Ed.), *Research in community and mental health*, Vol. 2 (pp. 43–73). Greenwich, CT: JAI Press.

Blyth, D. A., Simmons, R. G., & Carlton-Ford, S. (1983). The adjustment of early adolescents to school transitions. *Journal of Early Adolescence, 3*, 105–120.

Brim, O. G., & Kagan, J. (1980). *Constancy and change in human development*. Cambridge, MA: Harvard University Press.

Bronfenbrenner, U. (1979). *The ecology of human development: Experiments by nature and design*. Cambridge, MA: Harvard University Press.

Brooks-Gunn, J. & Paikoff, R. (1997). Sexuality and developmental transitions during adolescence. In J. Schulenberg, J. L. Maggs, & K. Hurrelman, (Eds.), *Health risks and developmental transitions during adolescence* (pp. 190–219). New York: Cambridge University Press.

Brooks-Gunn, J., & Petersen, A. C. (1984). Problems in studying and defining pubertal events. *Journal of Youth and Adolescence, 13*, 181–196.

Brooks-Gunn, J., Petersen, A. C., & Eichorn, D. (1985). The study of maturational timing effects in adolescence [Special issue]. *Journal of Youth and Adolescence, 14*, (3, 4).

Brooks-Gunn, J., & Reiter, E. (1990). The role of pubertal processes. *Journal of Youth and Adolescence, 13*, 16–53.

Brown, B. (1990). Peer groups and peer cultures. In S. S. Feldman & G. R. Elliot (Eds.), *At the threshold: The developing adolescent* (pp. 171–196). Cambridge, MA: Harvard University Press.

Cairns, R. B., Cairns, B. D., Neckerman, H. J., Ferguson, L. L., & Gariepy, J-L. (1989). Growth and aggression: 1. Childhood to early adolescence. *Developmental Psychology, 25*, 320–330.

Caspar, R. C., & Offer, D. (1990). Weight and dieting concerns in normal adolescents: Fashion or symptom? *Pediatrics, 86*, 384–390.

Caspi, A., Elder, G., & Bem, D. (1988). Moving away from the world: Life-course patterns of shy children. *Developmental Psychology, 24*, 824–831.

Clausen, J. S. (1991). Adolescent competence and the shaping of the life course. *American Journal of Sociology, 96*, 805–842.

Conger, J. J. (1991). *Adolescence and youth: Psychological development in a changing world* (4th ed.). New York: Harper-Collins.

Crockett, L., Losoff, M., & Petersen, A. C. (1984). Perceptions of the peer group in early adolescence. *Journal of Early Adolescence, 4*, 155–181.

Csikszentmihalyi, M., & Larson, R. (1984). *Being adolescent: Conflict and growth in the teenage years*. New York: Basic Books.

Dornbusch, S. (1989). The sociology of adolescence. *Annual Review of Sociology, 15*, 233–259.

Douvan, E., & Adelson, J. (1966). *The adolescent experience*. New York: John Wiley & Sons.

Dulit, E. (1972). Adolescent thinking à la Piaget: The

formal stage. *Journal of Youth and Adolescence, 1,* 281–301.

Elkind, D. (1967). Egocentrism in adolescence. *Child Development, 38,* 1025–1034.

Erikson, E. (1959). Identity and the life cycle. *Psychological Issues, 1,* 18–164.

Erikson, E. H. (1968). *Identity: Youth and crisis.* New York: W. W. Norton.

Esman, A. (1990). *Adolescence and culture.* New York: Columbia University Press.

Flaherty, L. T. (1982). To love and/or to work: The ideological dilemma of young women. In S. C. Feinstein, J. G. Looney, A. Z. Schartzberg, & A. D. Sorosky (Eds.), *Adolescent psychiatry* (Vol. 10, pp. 41–51). Chicago: University of Chicago Press.

Freud, A. (1958). Adolescence. *Psychoanalytic Study of the Child, 13,* 255–278.

Furstenburg, F. F., Jr. (1990). Divorce and the American family. *Annual Review of Sociology, 16,* 379–403.

Gilligan, C. (1977). In a different voice: Women's conceptions of self and morality. *Harvard Educational Review, 47,* 481–517.

Gilligan, C. (1982). *In a different voice: Psychological theory and women's development.* Cambridge, MA: Harvard University Press.

Golombek, H., & Marton, P. (1992). Adolescents over time: A longitudinal study of personality development. In S. C. Feinstein, A. H. Esman, H. A. Horowitz, J. G. Looney, G. H. Orvin, J. L. Schimel, A. Z. Schwartzberg, A. D. Sorosky, & M. Sugar (Eds.), *Adolescent Psychiatry* (Vol. 18, pp. 213–284). Chicago: University of Chicago Press.

Greene, A. L., & Boxer, A. M. (1986). Daughters and sons as young adults: Restructuring the ties that bind. In N. Datan, A. L. Greene, & H. Reese (Eds.), *Lifespan developmental psychology: Intergenerational relations* (pp. 125–129). Hillsdale, NJ: Lawrence Erlbaum.

Haan, N., Millsap, R., & Hartka, E. (1986). As time goes by: Change and stability in personality over fifty years. *Psychology and Aging, 1,* 220–232.

Hall, G. S. (1904). *Adolescence: Its psychology and its relations to physiology, anthropology, sociology, sex, crime, religion, and education.* New York: Appleton.

Hamburg, D., & Takanishi, R. (1989). Preparing for life: The critical transition of adolescence. *American Psychologist, 44,* 825–827.

Harter, S. (1990). Self and identity development. In S. S. Feldman & G. R. Elliot (Eds.), *At the threshold: The developing adolescent* (pp. 352–387). Cambridge, MA: Harvard University Press.

Hetherington, E. M. (1989). Coping with family transitions: Winners, losers, and survivors. *Child Development, 60,* 1–14.

Hill, P. (1993). Recent advances in selected aspects of adolescent development. *Journal of Child Psychiatry and Psychology, 34,* 69–99.

James, W. (1982). *Psychology: The briefer course.* New York: Holt, Rinehart, & Winston.

Jensen, P., & Shaw, J. (1993). Children as victims of war: Current knowledge and future research needs. *Journal of the American Academy of Child and Adolescent Psychiatry, 32,* 697–708.

Johnson, L. D., Bachman, J. G., & O'Malley, P. M. (1988). *Drug use, drinking, and smoking: National survey results from high school, college, and young adult populations* [Press release]. Washington, DC: National Institute on Drug Abuse.

Johnson, L. D., O'Malley, P. M., & Bachman, J. G. (1994). National survey results on drug use from Monitoring the Future Study, 1975–1993. Washington, D.C.: U.S. Department of Health and Human Services.

Jones, M. C. (1965). Psychological correlates of somatic development. *Child Development, 36,* 899–911.

Kagan, J. (1971). *Change and continuity in infancy.* New York: John Wiley & Sons.

Kagan, J., & Moss, H. A. (1962). *Birth to maturity.* New York: John Wiley & Sons.

Kandel, D. (1984). Substance abuse by adolescents in Israel and France: A cross-cultural perspective. *Public Health Reports, 99,* 277–283.

Katchadourian, H. (1990). Sexuality. In S. S. Feldman & G. R. Elliot (Eds.), *At the threshold: The developing adolescent* (pp. 330–351). Cambridge, MA: Harvard University Press.

Keating, D. P. (1980). Thinking processes in adolescence. In J. Adelson (Ed.), *Handbook of adolescent psychology* (pp. 211–246). New York: John Wiley & Sons.

Keating, D. P. (1990). Adolescent thinking. In S. S. Feldman & G. R. Elliot (Eds.), *At the threshold: The developing adolescent* (pp. 211–246). Cambridge, MA: Harvard University Press.

Keltikangas-Jarvinen, L. (1990). Continuity of type A behavior during childhood, preadolescence, and adolescence. *Journal of Youth and Adolescence, 19,* 221–231.

Kett, J. F. (1977). *Rites of passage: Adolescence in America, 1790 to the present.* New York: Basic Books.

Kohlberg, L. (1976). Moral stages and moralization: The cognitive-developmental approach. In T. Lickona (Ed.), *Moral development and behavior* (pp. 31–53). New York: Holt, Rinehart, & Winston.

Korn, S. J. (1984). Continuities and discontinuities in difficult/easy temperament: Infancy to young adulthood. *Merrill-Palmer Quarterly, 30,* 189–199.

Kroger, J. (1988). A longitudinal study of ego status interview domains. *Journal of Adolescence, 11,* 49–64.

Marcia, J. E. (1980). Identity in adolescence. In J. Adelson (Ed.), *Handbook of adolescent psychology* (pp. 159–177). New York: John Wiley & Sons.

McDevitt, S. (1986). Continuity and discontinuity of temperament in infancy and early childhood: A psychometric perspective. In R. Plomin & J. Dunn (Eds.), *The study of temperament: Changes, continuities, and challenges* (pp. 27–38). Hillsdale, NJ: Lawrence Erlbaum.

Montemayor, R. (1983). Parents and adolescents in conflict: All families some of the time and some families most of the time. *Journal of Early Adolescence, 3,* 83–103.

Moss, H. A., & Susman, E. J. (1980). Longitudinal study

of personality development. In O. G. Brim & J. Kagan (Eds.), *Constancy and change in human development* (pp. 530–595). Cambridge, MA: Harvard University Press.

Mussen, P. H., Conger, J. J., Kagan, J., & Huston, A. C. (1990). *Child development and personality* (7th ed.). New York: Harper & Row.

Mussen, P. H., & Jones, M. C. (1957). Self-conceptions, motivations, and interpersonal attitudes of late and early maturing boys. *Child Development, 28*, 243–256.

Nesselroade, J. R., & Baltes, P. B. (1974). Adolescent personality development and historical change: 1970–1972. *Monographs of the Society for Research in Child Development, 39* (1, Serial No. 154).

Nuechterlein, K. (1986). Childhood precursors of adult schizophrenia. *Journal of Child Psychology and Psychiatry, 27*, 133–144.

Offer, D. (1969). *The psychological world of the teenager: A study of normal adolescent boys.* New York: Basic Books.

Offer, D., & Boxer, A. M. (1990). Normal adolescent development: Empirical research findings. In M. Lewis (Ed.), *Child and adolescent psychiatry* (pp. 266–278). Baltimore: Williams & Wilkins.

Offer, D., & Offer, J. B. (1975). *From teenage to young manhood: A psychological study.* New York: Basic Books.

Offer, D., Ostrov, E., & Howard, K. I. (1981). *The adolescent: A psychological self-portrait.* New York: Basic Books.

Offer, D., & Sabshin, M. (1974). *Normality: Theoretical and clinical concepts of mental health* (2nd ed.). New York: Basic Books.

Offer, D., & Sabshin, M. (1984). *Normality and the life cycle.* New York: Basic Books.

Offer, D., & Schonert-Reichl, K. (1992). Debunking the myths of adolescence: Findings from recent research. *Journal of the Academy of Child and Adolescent Psychiatry, 31*, 1003–1014.

Olweus, D. (1979). Stability of aggressive reaction patterns in males: A review. *Psychological Bulletin, 86*, 852–875.

Parke, R. D., & Slaby, R. G. (1983). The development of aggression. In P. H. Mussen (Series ed.) & E. M. Heatherington (Vol. ed.), *Handbook of child and adolescent psychology* (4th ed., pp. 547–641). New York: John Wiley & Sons.

Petersen, A. C. (1988). Adolescent development. *Annual Review of Psychology, 39*, 583–607.

Petersen, A. C., & Crockett, L. J. (1985). Pubertal timing and grade effects on adjustment. *Journal of Youth and Adolescence, 14*, 191–206.

Petersen, A. C., & Ebata, A. T. (1987). Developmental transitions and adolescent problem behavior: Implications for prevention and intervention. In K. Hurrelman, F. X. Kaufman, & F. Losel (Eds.), *Social intervention: Potential and constraints* (pp. 167–184). New York: Walter de Gruyter.

Petersen, A. C., & Leffert, N. (1995). What is special about adolescence? In M. Rutter, (Ed.), *Psychological disturbances in young people: Challenges for pre-*

vention (pp. 3–36). New York: Cambridge University Press.

Robins, L. (1986). The consequences of conduct disorder in girls. In D. Oleus, J. Block, & M. Radke-Yarrow (Eds.), *Development of antisocial and prosocial behavior: Research, theories and issues* (pp. 385–408). New York: Academic Press.

Rutter, M. (1984). Psychopathology and development. I: Childhood antecedents of adult psychiatric disorder. *Australian and New Zealand Journal of Psychiatry, 18*, 314–327.

Rutter, M., Graham, P., Chadwick, O., & Yule, W. (1976). Adolescent turmoil: Fact or fiction? *Journal of Child Psychology and Psychiatry, 17*, 35–56.

Rutter, M., & Rutter, M. (1993). *Developing minds: Challenge and continuity across the life span.* New York: Harper Collins.

Savin-Williams, R. C., & Berndt, T. (1990). Friendship and peer relations. In S. S. Feldman & G. R. Elliot, (Eds.), *At the threshold: The developing adolescent* (pp. 277–307). Cambridge, MA: Harvard University Press.

Schuckit, M. A., Klein, J. L., Twitchell, G. R., & Springer, L. M. (1994). Increases in alcohol-related problems for men on a college campus between 1980 and 1992. *Journal of Studies of Alcohol, 55*, 739–742.

Shannon, M., Lonigan, C., Finch, A., & Taylor, C. (1994). Children exposed to disaster: I. Epidemiology of post-traumatic symptoms and symptom profiles. *Journal of the American Academy of Child and Adolescent Psychiatry, 33*, 80–93.

Stein, J. A., Newcomb, M. D., & Bentler, P. M. (1986). Stability and change in personality: A longitudinal study from early adolescence to young adulthood. *Journal of Research in Personality, 20*, 276–291.

Steinberg, L. (1986). Stability (and instability) of type A behavior from childhood to young adulthood. *Developmental Psychology, 22*, 393–402.

Steinberg, L. (1990). Autonomy, conflict, and harmony in the family relationship. In S. S. Feldman & G. R. Elliot (Eds.), *At the threshold: The developing adolescent* (pp. 255–276). Cambridge, MA: Harvard University Press.

Stern, D. N. (1985). *The interpersonal world of the infant.* New York: Basic Books.

Stokes, G. S., Mumford, M. D., & Owens, W. A. (1989). Life history prototypes in the study of human individuality. *Journal of Personality, 57*, 510–545.

Thomas, A., Chess, S., & Birch, H. G. (1968). *Temperament and behavior disorders in children.* New York: New York University Press.

Tobin-Richards, M., Boxer, A. M., & Petersen, A. C. (1983). The psychological significance of pubertal change: Sex differences in perception of self during early adolescence. In J. Brooks-Gunn & A. C. Petersen (Eds.), *Girls at puberty: Biological and psychosocial perspectives* (pp. 127–154). New York: Plenum Press.

Walker, L. J. (1989). A longitudinal study of moral orientation. *Child Development, 60*, 157–166.

Zinberg, N. (1984). *Drug, set and setting.* New Haven, CT: Yale University Press.

4 / Protective Factors in Childhood and Adolescence

Mark D. Weist

A central and prominent theme in child psychiatric research has been the evaluation of factors that influence children's developmental trajectories. Early on, a major focus of this research was on assessment of variables that increase children's risk for the development of psychopathology. For example, genetic risk studies such as the seminal work by Mednick and Schulsinger (1968) documented increased levels of psychopathology in children of schizophrenic mothers. Reports on the Isle of Wight studies conducted by Rutter and his colleagues (Rutter, Quinton, & Yule, 1977) initially focused on identification of rearing conditions (marital distress, overcrowding, parent criminality) that increased the risk of psychiatric disturbance in children. More recently, investigators have turned to the identification of protective or "resilience" factors, which in contrast to risk factors, serve to reduce the probability of illness or maladaptation in children and adolescents.

The search for protective factors implies some negative circumstance that youths must contend with during a phase (or phases) of their development. Most of the initial studies attempting to identify these protective factors were conducted with children of mentally ill parents (Bleuler, 1978). These studies have been followed by others evaluating coping among youths who experience ongoing familial discord (Wallerstein & Kelly, 1980) or contend with chronic physical illness (Cerreto & Travis, 1984), studies on children growing up in war (Rosenblatt, 1983), and studies that have assessed variables promoting resilience in disadvantaged urban youth (Clark, 1983). In this chapter I review variables that have served to promote adaptive functioning in children of mentally disordered parents and in underprivileged youths. Key conceptual issues are then highlighted. The chapter concludes with a case example that illustrates attention to protective factors in therapy efforts with adolescents.

Protective Factors in Youth with Mentally Ill Parents

Most studies of adjustment variables contributing to adaptive functioning in children of mentally disordered parents have targeted latency-age and, to some extent, early adolescent youths. However, these studies illuminate variables that also may be of importance to older adolescents. Musick, Stott, Spencer, Goldman, and Cohler (1987) evaluated factors that influenced responsiveness to an intervention for 25 latency-age children of chronically mentally ill mothers. The authors concluded that the most significant factor in the children's ability to make use of the intervention program was the "enabling quality" of their relationships with their mothers. Mothers of children who did well in the program were characterized as being "likable," having friends, being emotionally responsive, and being receptive and encouraging of outside assistance to the family.

Fisher, Kokes, Cole, Perkins, and Wynne (1987) conducted a developmental study of 145 families in which one adult member (most commonly the mother) was hospitalized for psychiatric disturbance. Parents and youths (including early adolescents) were studied over several weeks on a variety of measures including family interaction, parent marital relations, and child behavioral functioning and school competence. As expected, youths were found to function better on measures of behavioral and school adjustment when their parent's disorder was brief or intermittent versus prolonged or chronic and when their parents were diagnosed with affective disorders versus thought disorders. Notably, youths displaying the highest levels of school competence were more likely to display balanced and warm interaction with their parents on the family observation measure than were less-competent youth.

Other studies point to the important influence of extrafamilial social support on the development of latency-age children with at least one mentally disturbed parent. Kauffman, Grunebaum, Cohler, and Gamer (1979) found competence in these children to be associated with their having families in which the mother had adequate social supports and with the children's having regular contact with nonfamilial adults. Werner and Smith (1982) found that the more caregivers present in the child's home, the more likely positive developmental outcomes would be obtained in children and early adolescents of parents with psychiatric disturbance.

In addition to family and other social support variables, personal characteristics of children of mentally disordered parents may serve to protect them from maladaptation. In an extensive study of these intrapersonal variables among children of parents with psychiatric disorders, Murphy and Moriarty (1976) found that resilient children were more humorous and confident, and more frequently exhibited advanced problem-solving and coping abilities than less-competent children. Other individual factors such as positive temperament, intelligence, social responsiveness, and the capacity to function autonomously have been associated with adaptive functioning in children of mentally ill parents (Anthony, 1987; Cohler, 1987; Cowen & Work, 1988).

As mentioned, few studies have assessed variables that affect the adjustment of adolescents living with a parent with a mental disorder. The literature is particularly limited for older adolescents. However, this brief review does highlight familial, social, and intrapersonal factors that may be important influences on the adjustment of these youth and that warrant further study.

Protective Factors in Disadvantaged Urban Youths

The relatively severe levels of life stress that inner-city youths must contend with has been documented by a number of studies. Too many of these youths are exposed to abuse and neglect (Garbarino, 1976); live in single-parent families, with poorly educated, overwhelmed, and depressed mothers (Rutter & Quinton, 1977; West & Farrington, 1977); and face frequent violence and crime in their neighborhood (Spencer, 1993). In turn, these factors serve to increase the likelihood that these youths will feel alienated and hopeless (Paster, 1985), develop severe behavior problems (Farrington, 1987), and become involved in drug dealing and/or use (Rhodes & Jason, 1988). Further, there is a very high rate of academic failure among inner-city youths, which some authors have suggested is equal to or greater than 50% of students (Rhodes & Jason, 1990).

However, in spite the severe and chronic stressors associated with life in our inner cities, some urban youths manage to display social and academic competence, while remaining free from emotional/behavioral disorder or involvement in delinquent or criminal activity. Selected studies have attempted to document variables that characterize these successful, or resilient, inner-city youths. For example, Garmezy and colleagues (Garmezy, 1987; Masten et al., 1988) conducted a longitudinal study assessing variables that moderate the influence of life stress in around 200 elementary-age and preadolescent children from Minneapolis. In these youths, positive family qualities such as family stability and organization (frequency of moves, upkeep of the home) and family cohesion (presence of rules, adequacy of communication, level of manifest affection) served to promote competent functioning under stress. In a study of 144 urban ninth-grade students, Luthar (1991) found that social skills and internal locus of control served to protect youths from the effects of life stress. She also reported the counterintuitive finding that students who had relatively higher grade point averages were more prone to develop depression and anxiety under high stress.

Family variables have been found to have a critical influence on the adjustment of inner-city youths. For example, Rhodes and Jason (1990) evaluated family influences on substance use in 124 urban (84% minority) high school students. Youths who reported positive sibling and parental relationships and high levels of support and encouragement from family members were less likely to evidence substance abuse problems than youths from more conflicted and less supportive families. Felner, Abu, Primavera, and Cauce

28

(1985) examined the impact of school and family support on academic achievement and self-concept in inner-city ninth graders. Perceived support from teachers was found to predict overall self-concept and academic self-concept. Family support was also positively related to academic self-concept and inversely related to absences from school. Rumberger, Ghatak, Poulos, Ritter, and Dornbusch (1990) evaluated family influences on dropping out from school in 1,300 urban high school students from San Francisco. Compared to enrolled students, dropouts reported that their parents played a more passive role in their lives, they were less involved in ongoing decision making, were more permissive, and paid less attention to the students' education.

Clark (1983) examined family qualities associated with academic achievement among impoverished African American youth. In contrast to parents of low achievers, parents of high achievers were characterized as: (1) frequently initiating contact with teachers, (2) playing a major role in the child's schooling, (3) establishing and enforcing clear rules and role boundaries, (4) engaging in deliberate academic training, (5) providing frequent nurturance and support, and, at times, (6) deferring to the child's knowledge on academic matters.

Weist and coworkers (1995) assessed a range of variables that may contribute to resilient functioning in a sample of 164 ninth graders from a high school in an economically deprived area of Baltimore. Our goal was to further assess variables holding promise in the literature as moderators of psychological and academic outcomes for disadvantaged youth. In particular, we assessed variables of locus of control, family environment, social support, and coping style, variables various studies have suggested are important in influencing developmental outcomes for urban youths.

For boys, the reported level of family cohesion (closeness, supportiveness) was found to protect against the development of depression and discipline problems (suspensions) as stress levels increased. For girls, a different pattern of findings emerged. Unlike the boys, adaptive coping was found to promote competent functioning under stress. That is, generating problem-focused solutions (efforts to modify or change a problem or one's reaction to it) to school problems was found to protect against depression and behavior prob-

lems and also to protect against declines in self-concept. Overall social support from adults, from nonfamily members as well as from family, served to protect the girls' grades and positive teacher impressions from declines under stress. Reported family cohesion also protected the girls from increases in negative impressions by teachers as stress levels increased.

Summary of Protective Factors

The previous review provides highlights of studies that identified factors which may serve to protect children and adolescents from deleterious impacts of growing up with a mentally disturbed parent or within the context of poverty. These resilience factors can be grouped into three main categories: intrapersonal aspects of the youths, family qualities, and external support systems (Werner, 1989).

Intrapersonal aspects of youths that have been associated with resilience include positive temperament, intelligence, and internal locus of control. The capacity to function autonomously, use problem-solving abilities, and use constructive, problem-focused approaches also are related to effective coping with stress. Social skills such as interpersonal warmth, expressiveness, responsiveness, and sense of humor also have been found in adolescents who are successful despite difficult environments.

Important personal qualities in parents include being friendly, emotionally responsive, actively involved in the child's education, and accepting of outside assistance. Key family characteristics include stability and adequacy of living conditions and family closeness and flexibility in solving problems. Also crucial are adequate social support and assistance in child rearing for parents.

In addition to family support, external social support, such as that provided by teachers, other nonfamilial adults, or from organizations such as churches, sports teams, or employers may play a very important role in protecting children and adolescents from maladaptive development. Such extrafamilial support may be particularly critical for youths from conflicted, neglectful, or abusive families (Rutter, 1979).

Key Conceptual Issues

A number of leading investigators working in the fields of child and adolescent development and developmental psychopathology have provided important reviews of critical issues relating to the identification of risk and resilience factors for youths. Articles by Garmezy and Masten (1986), Pellegrini (1990), Rutter (1987), and Werner (1989) delineate critical findings and provide a conceptual grounding in this rather large and complex literature. The following summary highlights key conceptual issues.

SPECIFICITY VS. GENERALITY OF PROTECTIVE FACTORS

It appears that some protective factors act in limited and highly specific ways, while other factors seem to have a more generalized impact. For example, in our research (Weist et al., 1995), certain variables (problem-focused coping) served as a protective factor for girls but not for boys, and almost all of the hypothesized protective variables protected only certain outcomes. In contrast, family variables were found to have protective influences for boys and for girls, and across a number of emotional/behavioral outcomes (depression, discipline problems). Findings supporting the importance of family environment are congruent with findings from a number of other studies (Clark, 1983; Felner et al., 1985; Garmezy, 1987) and indicate that family stability, cohesion, and supportiveness may be centrally important and generalized protective factors.

Other variables, such as nonfamilial social support and locus of control, have been found to promote competent functioning in youths in a number of studies, but not to the extent of familial variables. At the low end of the continuum are a number of factors that have received only limited support as serving protective functions for youths, such as child coping style and involvement in meaningful activities (Maton, 1990).

We are not yet at the point where we can confidently define whether specific protective factors other than family variables have limited, moderate, or generalized protective functions. Family factors clearly have received the most support for serving generalized protective functions; however,

these variables also have received the most attention in research studies. Therefore, it is difficult to determine if, for example, internal locus of control serves limited protective functions, or alternatively, is actually a powerful generalized protective factor that requires further investigation. More studies on promising protective factors such as nonfamilial social support, locus of control, and coping style are needed, followed by meta-analysis to begin to document their strength and generality. The ultimate aim of such research would be to identify protective factors that operate for specific children in specific risk contexts (factors operating for inner-city preadolescent boys) and factors that operate generally for youths across risk contexts. Such an empirically validated template of resilience factors for youths could then serve as the basis for comprehensive intervention programs; for example, programs could aim at bolstering school and family support and promoting mastery experiences (to enhance internal locus of control) for inner-city middle-school children identified as being at risk for dropping out (Weist, Ollendick, & Finney, 1991).

DEFINING RESILIENCE

Another concern is attempting to define just what comprises resilient functioning in children and adolescents. Standards vary; however, most definitions focus on external behavior, such as academic performance or behavior problems. Following these criteria, resilience for youths under adversity has been defined by maintaining good grades and staying out of trouble; indices of emotional functioning are not used. Luthar (1991) found that academic performers in her sample (defined as "resilient") were more prone to depression and anxiety under high stress than youths who were not performing as well academically. This labeling of depressed and anxious children (regardless of their exemplary school performance and behavior) as resilient must be questioned.

In any given sample of youths contending with adversity, there may be very few who are truly resilient, or functioning adaptively across psychological, social, and societal domains of functioning. For example, in our study with inner-city ninth graders, we attempted to analyze psychosocial qualities in adolescents who met minimal cutoffs in terms of being below the median for depression, anxiety, behavior problems, discipline problems, and absences and above the median for grade point average. Only 6 out of our 164 adolescents (3.6%) met these cutoffs, and inspection of individual scores revealed that all of them had scores that were very close to the median for at least two variables (Weist et al., 1995).

These findings indicate that the definition of resilience in youths will necessarily be a somewhat subjective and arguable process in the absence of a clear marker variable that definitively identifies youths as successful performers in the situation or context of interest. Such precise identification of resilient youths can be approximated for children contending with chronic illness—for example, using glycosylated hemoglobin scores with youths with diabetes to assess overall management of the illness (Weist, Finney, Barnard, Davis, & Ollendick, 1993). But even with such children, it could be argued that a child may manage his or her illness well but still not be resilient (as in the case of a child with diabetes well under control but who presents emotional or behavioral disturbance).

ENVIRONMENTAL INFLUENCES

Bloom (1964) presents the concept of "powerful environments," which are characterized as

relatively uniform in preventing individuals from securing the necessary nutriments, learning experiences or stimulation necessary for growth, . . . that all (or almost all) individuals are affected in similar ways and to similar extents. In such powerful environments, only relatively few individuals are able to resist the effects of environmental pressure. (p. 212)

Clearly, the deprived and crime-ridden neighborhoods that many inner-city youths grow up in would be considered powerfully harmful environments, and relatively few of these youngsters overcome these environmental obstacles to go on to lead successful lives.

While study of the individuals who overcome the odds of disadvantage to become successful is critically important, interventions based on removing children from these environments need to be considered. Kaufman and Rosenbaum (1992) studied adolescents participating in a residential program that enabled impoverished African American families to move from segregated housing projects to other city residences or to middle-income, primarily Caucasian suburban neighborhoods in Chicago. Followed over a 4-year period, compared to city movers, youths moving to the suburbs were less likely to drop out from high school (20% vs. 5%) and were more likely to attend college (21% vs. 54%) or, if not in college, to be employed (41% vs. 75%). The authors concluded that problems that urban African American youths encounter in educational and occupational attainment may arise from deficiencies in their environments, not in themselves.

These findings are congruent with observations by Spencer (1993), who has conducted extensive developmental studies of inner-city boys. She writes: "While impoverished boys growing up in high risk environments have the same societally mandated needs for adult instrumentality as high-resource youth, they both lack opportunities and role models for learning legal, valued, developmentally appropriate, and competence-promoting work roles" (p. 9).

Pragmatically, often it is not possible to explicitly remove a child from a disadvantaged and deleterious home environment. But at times, this opportunity does arise. Practicing clinicians likely have cases in mind where an acting-out child was removed from a home due to abuse and/or neglect and then "blossomed" in a nurturant foster home or other placement. Alternatively, an older adolescent can be assisted in problem solving to identify methods (such as attending college) or familial or other living resources that are away from the inner city in safe and positive communities. Often simple techniques have significant therapeutic impacts, such as helping adolescents to realize that opportunities to escape their home environments do exist and helping them to believe that some day they will actually move into the light at the end of the tunnel.

Knowledge of resilience factors can be used in therapy with adolescents to focus attention on variables shown empirically to contribute to adaptive outcomes in youths under similar stressful circumstances. Throughout the evaluation process, the clinician considers the role personal and environmental factors are playing on each youth's adjustment. Particular attention is paid to factors that have been identified to be associated with successful functioning by youths in the context of interest (e.g., poor, inner-city neighborhoods).

The following case example illustrates how to consider variables of family environment and support, extrafamilial social support, and locus of control in developing interventions for inner-city youths under stress.

CASE EXAMPLE

Tamika: Tamika was a 17-year-old African American female referred for evaluation of suicidal ideation. She had no history of previous counseling. Diagnostic evaluation suggested adjustment disorder with depressed mood, with symptoms of sleep disturbance, irritability, anhedonia, hopelessness, and inability to focus on schoolwork. These symptoms coincided with mother's relapse into substance abuse (crack cocaine, marijuana, and alcohol) and consequent familial neglect around 3 months ago. Tamika did not have active suicidal intent or plans and was willing to contract for no attempts at self-harm. Her history was notable for being raped at age 12 by a 17-year-old male from the neighborhood and behavior problems in school, including fighting, cutting classes, and talking back to teachers that contributed to failure of the ninth grade. Tamika was now in the 11th grade and trying to do well in school but was feeling stressed and overwhelmed. She harbored considerable anger and resentment toward her mother for her drug problem, family neglect, and lack of support.

Psychotherapy was aimed at addressing Tamika's emotional distress and depression related to the rape and to historical and recent family stress. Interventions included encouraging emotional expression, providing information on the impacts of sexual trauma, training cognitive restructuring skills, and developing coping skills to use at home. In addition, considerable effort was made toward improving her family and social support systems. Along these lines, the therapist encouraged a rapprochement with her father, who had a college degree and worked as a computer operator. He had provided financial support but otherwise played an inconsistent role in Tamika's life since she was around age 9. Tamika expressed her feelings to him regarding his minimal involvement; he apologized to her, admitting that he had put his second marriage before her, and they began to renew a positive and supportive relationship. In addition to his developing supportiveness, father's role as a positive role model for Tamika was made more salient to her.

The therapist also strongly supported Tamika's burgeoning efforts at becoming involved in extracurricular activities in school. She was beginning to work for the high school newspaper but had doubts about her abilities to really contribute. The therapist reviewed some of her writings, saw her writing ability, and praised her efforts. In addition, he encouraged her to show him poetry she had written, and Tamika complied, surprised that anyone would be interested. Eventually, they made plans for Tamika to solicit writings from her classmates in the next academic year, which the therapist would review with her for possible publication in the newsletter or other informal media.

In therapy Tamika was encouraged to make or solidify other adaptive social connections. These included: talking to each of her teachers, to express renewed motivation to do well and to request compensatory or remedial assignments; phoning a mentor (older African American businessman) who had taken an interest in her in middle school but had since lost contact; and discussing ways for her relationships with successful students in her high school to develop into real friendships.

In addition to assisting Tamika increase positive social supports, some discussion was held on ways to interact with friends who continued to get in severe trouble. Support was given for Tamika's approach of being sociable to them at school but avoiding involvement with them outside of school by citing school or home responsibilities. Time was spent discussing the negative peer pressure that often occurs when a formerly troublemaking adolescent decides to go in a more positive direction (criticism and teasing sometimes occurs related to jealousy). In the context of these talks, the therapist introduced the notion of life trajectories, pointing out that Tamika's former close friends had trajectories that would predict future failure and suffering; she was altering her trajectory away from that of her friends to one of success and accomplishment. These discussions served to help Tamika focus on her own strengths and to realize that she could control the way her life develops. They were followed by asking her to relate in detail her fantasy for her life at age 25. She imagined being in medical school, with a nice car and home in the suburbs. She was encouraged to visualize this on a daily basis to engender conscious and unconscious goal striving.

Over time, Tamika's depression began to lift, her school performance progressively improved, and she began to really believe in the new narrative that she had formed for her life. In her previous scenario, she was a worthless, unintelligent, tramp of a drug-abusing mother. After seven sessions, she was beginning to see herself as a talented, intelligent, giving person who was on her way to success. She clearly made a dramatic shift in self-perception, behavior, and future outlook. This shift occurred in the context of improvement in family and social support and increased focus on personal strengths and control that occurred over the course of a relatively brief therapy experience. Attention to resilience factors provided a framework for therapy efforts with Tamika, which, in her case, appeared to be essential elements of her positive response to treatment. Tamika was last seen around 14 months following the termination of this therapy. At this follow-up, she was a senior in high school, doing reasonably well, and planning for entrance into community college. She reported only brief episodes of mild depression (without suicidal ideation) and conveyed overall satisfaction with her life.

Conclusion

Leading investigators have underscored the importance of research on the identification of factors that serve to protect children and adolescents from harmful life circumstances. Garmezy and Masten (1986) call the search for factors associated with resilient functioning the "necessary base" for the development of "truly preventive" interventions. Segal and Yahraes (1978) write: "The study of so-called invulnerability may be among the most important research projects underway in child development today. If we can discover what the factors are that make the difference between prevailing over and succumbing to

adversity, we can hope to learn how to impart these capacities to the children who need them" (p. 288). Similarly, in discussing stress resilient urban youth, Rhodes and Jason (1990) state: "By studying how these resilient children and their experiences differ from those with similar high-risk status who have problems, we may be able to identify important prevention factors" (p. 396). The importance of supportive adults, both within and outside the family, is a consistent finding in the high-risk studies of two otherwise very different groups, children of mentally ill parents and inner-city youth.

A number of efforts to further identify resilience factors that operate for youth are now under way. Findings from these studies should bolster our understanding of the nature and generality of factors that protect the development of children and adolescents who grow up in the context of conflict, deprivation, or abuse. Following the example of Kaufman and Rosenbaum (1992), these efforts should be augmented by further exploration of methods to alter negative environments and/or to remove children from them.

REFERENCES

Anthony, E. J. (1987). Risk, vulnerability, and resilience: An overview. In E. J. Anthony & B. J. Cohler (Eds.), *The invulnerable child* (pp. 3–48). New York: Guilford Press.

Bleuler, M. (1978). *The schizophrenic disorders: Long term patient and family studies.* New Haven, CT: Yale University Press.

Bloom, B. S. (1964). *Stability and change in human characteristics.* New York: John Wiley & Sons.

Cerretto, M. C., & Travis, L. B. (1984). Implications of psychological and family factors in the treatment of diabetes. *Pediatric Clinics of North America, 31,* 665–673.

Clark, R. M. (1983). *Family life and school achievement: Why poor black children succeed or fail.* Chicago: University of Chicago Press.

Cohler, B. J. (1987). Adversity, resilience, and the study of lives. In E. J. Anthony & B. J. Cohler (Eds.), *The invulnerable child* (pp. 363–424). New York: Guilford Press.

Cowen, E. L., & Work, W. C. (1988). Resilient children, psychological wellness, and primary prevention. *American Journal of Community Psychology, 16,* 591–607.

Farrington, D. P. (1987). Epidemiology. In H. Quay (Ed.), *Handbook of juvenile delinquency.* New York: John Wiley & Sons.

Felner, R., Abu, M., Primavera, J., & Cauce, A. (1985). Adaptation and vulnerability in high risk adolescents: An examination of environmental mediators. *American Journal of Community Psychology, 13,* 365–380.

Fisher, L., Kokes, R. F., Cole, R. E., Perkins, P. M., & Wynne, L. C. (1987). Competent children at risk: A study of well functioning offspring of disturbed parents. In E. J. Anthony & B. J. Cohler (Eds.), *The invulnerable child* (pp. 3–48). New York: Guilford Press.

Garbarino, J. (1976). A preliminary study of some ecological correlates of child abuse: The impact of socioeconomic stress on mothers. *Child Development, 47,* 178–185.

Garmezy, N. (1987). Stress, competence, and development: Continuities in the study of schizophrenic adults, children vulnerable to psychopathology, and the search for stress-resistant children. *American Journal of Orthopsychiatry, 57,* 159–174.

Garmezy, N., & Masten, A. S. (1986). Stress, competence and resilience: Common frontiers for therapist and psychopathologist. *Behavior Therapy, 17,* 500–521.

Kauffman, C., Grunebaum, H., Cohler, B., & Gamer, E. (1979). Superkids: Competent children of psychotic mothers. *American Journal of Psychiatry, 136,* 1398–1402.

Kaufman, J., & Rosenbaum, J. E. (1992). The education and employment of low-income black youth in white suburbs. *Educational Evaluation and Policy Analysis, 14*, 229–240.

Luthar, S. S. (1991). Vulnerability and resilience: A study of high-risk adolescents. *Child Development, 62*, 600–616.

Masten, A. S., Garmezy, N., Tellegen, A., Pellegrini, D. S., Larkin, K., & Larsen, A. (1988). Competence and stress in school children: The moderating effects of individual and family characteristics. *Journal of Child Psychology and Psychiatry, 6*, 745–764.

Maton, K. I. (1990). Meaningful involvement in instrumental activity and well-being: Studies of older adolescents and at risk urban teen-agers. *American Journal of Community Psychology, 18*, 297–320.

Mednick, S. A., & Schulsinger, F. (1968). Some premorbid characteristics related to breakdown in children with schizophrenic mothers. In D. Rosenthal & S. Kety (Eds.), *The transmission of schizophrenia* (pp. 267–291). Oxford: Pergamon Press.

Murphy, L. B., & Moriarty, A. (1976). *Vulnerability, coping and growth: From infancy to adolescence.* New Haven, CT: Yale University Press.

Musick, J. S., Stott, F. M., Spencer, K. K., Goldman, J., & Cohler, B. J. (1987). Maternal factors related to vulnerability and resiliency in young children at risk. In E. J. Anthony & B. J. Cohler (Eds.), *The invulnerable child* (pp. 229–252). New York: Guilford Press.

Paster, V. S. (1985). Adapting psychotherapy for the depressed, unacculturated, acting-out, black male adolescent. *Psychotherapy, 22*, 408–417.

Pellegrini, D. S. (1990). Psychosocial risk and protective factors in childhood. *Journal of Developmental and Behavioral Pediatrics, 11*, 201–209.

Rhodes, J. E., & Jason, L. A. (1988). *Preventing substance abuse among children and adolescents.* New York: Pergamon Press.

Rhodes, J. E., & Jason, L. A. (1990). A social stress model of substance abuse. *Journal of Consulting and Clinical Psychology, 58*, 395–401.

Rosenblatt, R. (1983). *Children of war.* Garden City, NY: Anchor Press.

Rumberger, R. W., Ghatak, R., Poulos, G., Ritter, P. L., & Dornbusch, S. M. (1990). Family influences on dropout behavior in one California high school. *Sociology of Education, 63*, 283–299.

Rutter, M. (1979). Protective factors in children's response to stress and disadvantage. In M. W. Kent & J. E. Rolf (Eds.), *Primary prevention of psychopathology: Vol. 3. Social competence in children* (pp. 49–74). Hanover, NH: University Press of New England.

Rutter, M. (1987). Psychosocial resilience and protective mechanisms. *American Journal of Orthopsychiatry, 57*, 316–331.

Rutter, M., & Quinton, D. (1977). Psychiatric disorder: Ecological factors and concepts of causation. In H. McGurk (Ed.), *Ecological factors in human development.* Amsterdam: North Holland.

Segal, J., & Yahraes, H. (1978). *A child's journey: Forces that shape the lives of our young.* New York: McGraw-Hill.

Spencer, M. B. (1993). Personality and social adjustment of children in poverty, or character development in a combative context. *Child, Youth and Family Services Quarterly, 16*, 8–9.

Wallerstein, J. S., & Kelly, J. B. (1980). *Surviving the breakup: How children and parents cope with divorce.* New York: Basic Books.

Weist, M. D., Finney, J. W., Barnard, M. U., Davis, C. D., & Ollendick, T. H. (1993). Empirical selection of psychosocial treatment targets for children and adolescents with diabetes. *Journal of Pediatric Psychology, 18*, 11–28.

Weist, M. D., Freedman, A. H., Paskewitz, D. A., Jackson, C. Y., Flaherty, L. T., & Proescher, E. J. (1995). Urban youth under stress: Empirical identification of risk and resilience factors. *Journal of Youth and Adolescence, 24*, 705–721.

Weist, M. D., Ollendick, T. H., & Finney, J. W. (1991). Toward the empirical validation of treatment targets in children. *Clinical Psychology Review, 11*, 515–538.

Werner, E. E. (1989). High-risk children in young adulthood: A longitudinal study from birth to 32 years. *American Journal of Orthopsychiatry, 59*, 72–81.

Werner, E. E., & Smith, R. S. (1982). *Vulnerable, but not invincible: A longitudinal study of resilient children and youth.* New York: McGraw-Hill.

West, D. J., & Farrington, D. P. (1977). *The delinquent way of life.* London: Heinemann Educational Books.

5 / Brain Development in Adolescence

Keith T. Flaherty

Introduction

The human brain undergoes marked transformation throughout childhood and adolescence, reaching a structurally stable form in adulthood. Clinical research in psychiatry and psychology has provided qualitative descriptions of the ontogeny of sensory perception and cognitive abilities. (See chapter 9 for further discussion.) Recently, the disciplines of cell biology and neurobiology have begun to elucidate the structural mechanisms behind these systems. The changes that occur anatomically and at the molecular level have been well characterized in animal models, and have been correlated with cognitive development in nonhuman species. In humans, observational studies using noninvasive experimental techniques such as magnetic resonance imaging (MRI), positron emission tomography (PET), and electroencephalography (EEG) have provided correlative evidence about the relationship between structural and cognitive changes that occur in human brains during adolescence. MRI is useful in identifying regions of neocortex that undergo changes in size during development. In evaluating age-dependent changes in human cortex, it has been hypothesized that cell death and the elimination of synapses result in cortical thinning, while synaptogenesis and increased myelination are thought to correlate with cortical thickening. PET detects metabolic activity in neurons by localizing the uptake of radioactively labeled glucose. EEG studies measure the electrical excitement of neuronal populations based on changes in the ionic composition of the extracellular environment. Together, these technologies are able to assess metabolic and electrical activity among large populations of neurons in the brain.

The ability to dissect the molecular constituents of complex neuronal circuits has become possible with genetic cloning, cell culture, and monoclonal antibody methodology. These techniques have given rise to the modern discipline of developmental neurobiology. In recent years it has become possible to characterize many of the key cellular events that occur throughout the development of the central nervous system in vertebrates. These experimental systems have been of greatest value in describing the events surrounding embryological and neonatal development. However, the principles of postpubertal brain development are just now being addressed.

Principles of Brain Development

In humans, cell division among neurons commences in the fetal period and continues until about 1½ years of age. Following the attainment of a maximum complement of neurons, a process of selective attrition begins and continues throughout childhood and adolescence, finally leveling off around age 20. In conjunction with this gradual decrease in the number of neurons, growth of axons and modification of synapses occurs, processes that persist throughout life and are responsible for the human brain's remarkable degree of plasticity. Brain development following infancy consists of changes in cell morphology, alteration of synaptic connections and strength, and selective elimination of neurons through cell death. The death of some cells is a normal process in brain maturation, unrelated to pathology, and is actually a prerequisite for normal physiologic development. After neurons undergo terminal differentiation in the embryo, they sprout axons and dendrites that grow in the direction of target neurons. Neuronal processes grow in response to neurotrophic factors that are secreted by the target neurons and taken up by the growing neuronal processes. They also respond to components of the extracellular matrix that direct the migration axons and dendrites. Both the neurotrophic factors and the extracellular matrix provide cues to the cell processes regarding the direction in which they are to grow. Neurons that do not take in enough neurotrophic factor or do not respond to the cues of these extracellular molecules undergo a programmed cell death, or apoptosis. Since the supply of trophic factors is limited, neurons growing in the same microenvironment in the brain literally must compete with each other for trophic factors in order to survive. While the majority of neuronal cell death occurs in the perinatal period, this process continues throughout development. The process of neuronal death that occurs throughout childhood and adolescence is accompanied by changes in synaptic density, local brain activity, and neuronal plasticity. The process of cell loss during brain development can be conceptualized as a kind of pruning that allows for more reliable and stereotypical functioning of the remaining cells. In other words, although the number of possible synaptic pathways decreases, the routes that persist are well traveled. If one thinks of neuronal pathways as transportation routes for brain communication, the situation is analogous to the elimination of scenic, more convoluted byways and secondary roads in favor of major highways that are more efficient and faster to use. At different stages of development, different parts of the brain are undergoing these processes at different rates.

Synaptogenesis, or synapse formation, is the critical process in the formation of a functional neuronal network. There are two hypotheses regarding synaptogenesis. One hypothesis holds that this process is characterized by events that occur prior to the arrival of a growing axon at the site of its target. The leading edge of the axon, known as the growth cone, contains all of the signal transduction machinery necessary to respond to soluble and matrix-bound extracellular signals. Additionally, the growth cone releases neurotransmitters into the extracellular environment prior to reaching its target cell. This release can trigger a depolarizing response in a target neuron. It is thought that, following the depolarization, the postsynaptic neuron secretes a soluble factor which, when taken up by the presynaptic cell, results in the formation of a synapse. Another hypothesis suggests that contact between the growth cone and its target induces this transformation. In other words, the interaction between cell surface proteins might provide the cue that a migrating

growth cone has reached its intended target. Currently there is evidence to support both models.

The principle of neuronal plasticity is central to the understanding of brain maturation during the adolescent period. Plasticity, or remodeling of neuronal connections, is most evident early in development when most areas of the brain are establishing connections for the first time. However, the human brain maintains the ability to modify synapses and sprout new axons throughout life. Studies done by a number of researchers on adolescent rat neocortex have shown that neurons in developing areas of cortex form new synapses, synthesize synaptic enzymes, increase neurotransmitter production, and demonstrate increased levels of activity (Epstein, 1979). Elimination of synapses occurs concomitantly. Therefore, the maturation of neocortex consists of both activity-dependent synaptogenesis and synapse elimination.

Experiments performed on the rat hippocampus have found that simultaneous depolarization in the pre- and postsynaptic cells are sufficient to strengthen a preexisting synapse in a way that persists upon removal of that stimulation (Nicoll, Kauer, & Malenka, 1988). In a 3-cell system, with 2 presynaptic cells and 1 postsynaptic, the presynaptic cell that demonstrates synchronous electrical activity with the postsynaptic will have its synapse strengthened while the asynchronous synapse will be weakened. This effect has been termed long-term potentiation (LTP), a model that accounts for the modulation of synaptic efficiency at any time during development. Long-term potentiation is integral to the understanding of neuronal plasticity in the developing human brain. It provides a mechanism for understanding how neuronal activity determines brain architecture, and how these structures can be modified.

Anatomical Changes in Adolescence

In the human brain, although the functional development of certain cortical regions is complete before the onset of puberty, the process of maturation in other areas of the brain, such as frontal cortex, continues through the second decade of life. The exact mechanisms of brain development in these higher cortical centers are not well understood, but it is reasonable to suppose that they are similar to those involved in the development of the visual cortex and other more fully understood systems. This model of brain development has emerged out of research on visual cortex in animal models (Hubel, 1988). The visual cortext reaches an adult level of maturation in humans· by the age of 10 or 11. It is characterized by an early proliferation of axonal projections to the visual cortex. At this stage there is a high level of synaptic density. As certain synapses are strengthened, others are selected against in an activity-dependent manner. As development proceeds, the target cells receive fewer inputs. The result is a decrease in one aspect of neuronal plasticity, as inputs to the visual cortex are not altered after this developmental window has passed. This process is required to establish and maintain a precise visual field for each cell in the visual cortex receiving input from the retina. In other words, the representation of the visual fields in the cortex becomes more refined as certain synapses are selectively eliminated. A kind of fine-tuning of the neuronal circuitry occurs, with surviving neurons and connections becoming specialized to process visual input in a way that allows the brain to perform specialized functions with a greater degree of precision than would be possible with a larger number of less well differentiated interconnections.

The extension of these principles to the development of higher cortical functions in humans is still tenuous because the neurobiological basis of cortical function is still so incompletely understood, but an analogous mechanism is hypothesized to apply to the maturation of higher cortical centers. In contrast to the visual cortex, most regions involved in higher cortical functions do not reach an adult level of maturity until the end of puberty. Thus considered, the pruning of synaptic inputs in the cerebral association cortex would result in more refined neuronal circuits, which are required to perform complex tasks. In fact, noninvasive recordings of neuronal activity in humans have shown changes in electrical and metabolic activity in the human cortex that are presumed to be associated with a similar process of cellular remodeling as that described for the visual cortex.

Frontal Lobe Changes in Adolescence

It is in the association cortex that the most striking changes have been observed during the adolescent period. Using MRI, Jernigan and Tallal (1990) observed that cortical volume in these areas decreased throughout late childhood and adolescence. In a subsequent study they localized this reduction to the superior aspects of the frontal and parietal lobes (Jernigan, Trauner, Hesselink, & Tallal, 1991). Huttenlocher (1979) reported a concomitant reduction in synaptic density in these areas during this period. If the massive reduction in the number of neurons and synapses is related to functional maturation, then a similar reduction in the electrical activity in regions of the brain that undergo the greatest alteration should be seen. Feinberg and others have used electroencephalography and positron emission tomography to analyze the adolescent brain (Feinberg, Thode, Chugani, & March, 1990). Measurements of electrical and metabolic activity in the frontal cortex of child and adolescent brains indicate a peak in neuronal activity at age 5 followed by a decline that continues throughout adolescence. Adult levels of activity are reached around age 20. A parallel pattern has been observed in the level of synaptic density in frontal cortex from childhood to adulthood, with progressive reduction in the number of neurons and synapses, apparently related to functional maturation. Thus, the development of frontal cortex is characterized by a decrease in both synaptic density and neuronal activity. By the end of adolescence these parameters reach a level that is maintained throughout adulthood. These observations suggest that adolescent brain development is characterized by a partial loss of plasticity in frontal cortex. The fact that these processes of cortical thinning and synaptic reduction are going on simultaneously suggests that the late stages of maturation involve fine-tuning of neuronal circuits. Assuming that once a synapse cannot be regenerated once it has been eliminated, the removal of synapses represents a certain alteration in the ability of the brain to undergo further modification later in life. Or, on the cytoarchitectural level, neuronal plasticity decreases as synapses are pruned during development. How do we reconcile this fact with the fact that neuronal plasticity persists throughout life? Plasticity is made possible by the fact that the efficiency of preexisting synapses can always be modified. It is the reduction in cell number and synaptic density that limits the ability of the cortex to undergo further changes in adulthood.

Theoretically, any abnormalities in this stage of brain development could result in impaired brain functioning. One possible explanation for the fact that many psychopathological syndromes thought to be related to brain disorders are more common during adolescence is that the thinning out of synaptic connections during this developmental period may allow pathological brain functioning to emerge. The existence of a larger number of neurons and synapses prior to puberty may have had a protective effect that disappears with the thinning out of neuronal structures. This hypothesis provides an explanation for how brain development during adolescence, and its associated changes in functioning, could be influenced by environmental factors ranging from physical health and nutrition, to social influences, since the manner in which the thinning out process occurs is highly dependent on the environment of neurons and the interactions between them. It could also explain how developmental deviations acquired early in life could reemerge as psychopathology in adolescence, a commonly observed clinical phenomenon.

Hormonal Influences

As other chapters have explicated, the onset of puberty is associated with a dramatic elevation in the serum levels of testosterone in males and estrogen in females. These hormones mediate the maturation of reproductive organs and secondary sexual characteristics. They are also important in the development of the central nervous system. This effect is most evident in the perinatal period and adolescence, when the levels of sex steroids are highest. Estrogen and testosterone in the neonate seem to be responsible for the sexually dimorphic development of several brain structures. However, the specific role of sex steroids in the

organization of neuronal systems is not well understood. Furthermore, the effects of estrogen and testosterone on the adolescent brain are considerably more subtle than the changes these hormones produce during neonatal development. Much of our understanding of the role of endogenous steroids on the adolescent brain is derived from research on the effect of gonadal hormones on individual neurons in vitro.

Estrogen and testosterone are potent modulators of neuronal activity and plasticity. In the male brain, testosterone is converted intracellularly to estradiol, the same hormone derived from estrogen in females. Although testosterone has been shown to have direct effects on behavior, its role in molecular and cellular changes in the adolescent brain has not been worked out. The action of estradiol in the male and female brain is widespread during fetal, neonatal, and adolescent development. These functions have been best described in vitro, with explanted neurons. It has been demonstrated that estradiol binds to a cytoplasmic steroid receptor that can then bind to DNA and alter gene transcription. Estradiol also has been shown to elicit calcium mediated action potentials, decrease monoamine oxidase activity, and reduce uptake of norepinephrine and serotonin by some neurons (Kopera, 1980). These various effects imply that the hormone affects many of the functions that control neuronal activity. Additionally, estradiol causes axonal sprouting in some experimental systems. This activity has particular relevance to the question of adolescent brain development. It has been shown, in vivo, that estradiol promotes synaptogenesis during the prepubertal period (Gorski, 1985). Considered with the in vitro data, this result indicates that estradiol may be a catalyst of neuronal alterations in the adolescent brain when the levels of circulating hormone are peaking. The search for estradiol's site of action has revealed that the estradiol receptor is present at high levels in the hypothalamus and limbic system, with lower levels found throughout the central nervous system. Estrogen receptors are expressed at high levels in frontal, auditory, and visual cortex in developing rat brains (Katawa, 1995). How the hormone affects neuronal structure and function in these regions is unknown, but several studies have suggested that estradiol acts as a neurotrophic factor. In this capacity the presence of steroid either promotes axonal migration or prevents cell death. Therefore, in the adolescent brain, estradiol may act to save a population of neurons from programmed cell death. If this is the case, estradiol may mediate the fine-tuning of neuronal function that results from selective cell and synapse survival.

Clinical Implications of Brain Changes in Adolescence

The current understanding of the adolescent brain sheds some light on the possible connection between abnormal development and mental disorders that emerge at this age. It seems likely that developmental abnormalities during adolescence may play a role in psychiatric disorders that are known to begin during this period. The greatest attention has been focused on schizophrenia and bipolar disorder because of the rise in incidence of these disorders during adolescence compared to childhood and their prevalence among young adults. Some investigators have proposed that the alterations that bring on these disorders are subtle and widespread, reflecting an overall failure to follow the normal developmental pathway. One possible explanation is that brain abnormalities may be present all along but masked by the overabundance of synaptic connections that prevails prior to the thinning-out process that occurs during adolescence. The thinning of synaptic connections may allow for pathological brain functioning to emerge (Weinberger, 1996). Early in development, the presence of aberrant projections to the frontal lobe might be masked by the presence of other appropriate inputs. Theoretically, elimination of appropriate synaptic inputs could result in the maintenance of abnormal connections. The reduction in synaptic density and neuron number that has been found to occur during this time might preclude modification of these synapses, resulting in a chronic condition of cognitive or affective disturbance. The finding of preexisting deficits in cognitive functioning, including attentional and learning difficulties in individuals who later become schizophrenic, lends support to this hypothesis. One competing model proposes that in individuals who develop schizophrenia, pro-

grammed synaptic elimination in early adolescence is delayed or decreased, allowing inappropriate inputs to persist. These types of cellular events are presumed to result in macroscopic changes that can be appreciated with neuroimaging.

Jernigan and others (1991) applied the same techniques used to quantitate the morphological changes during adolescence to address possible abnormalities in the schizophrenic brain. They observed that regions in the basal ganglia were abnormally large in schizophrenics. This finding, in combination with previous evidence of reduced volume in the limbic system, suggests that the aberrant survival of certain projections or elimination of others may result in psychopathology. However, Jernigan's study was unable to replicate the finding of limbic system alteration found in other schizophrenic patients. And while some investigators also have identified enlargement of the basal ganglia (Swayze, Andreason, Alliger, Yuh, & Ehrhardt, 1992), others have not. In his review of neuroimaging in adolescent psychiatric disorders, Peterson (1995) evaluates the studies using structural and functional brain imaging in schizophrenics. He concludes that the preponderance of evidence supports metabolic and structural abnormalities in the frontal and temporal lobes of schizophrenics. Recent findings of altered neurotransmitter receptor expression in the hippocampus of schizophrenic brains (Benes, Khan, Vincent, & Wickramasinghe, 1996) combined with the structural and metabolic defects described in this same region suggest that various lines of investigation are closing in on common ground in the pathology of this complex disease. The investigation of structural abnormalities in bipolar disorder is still in its infancy. However, several recent magnetic resonance imaging studies have found increased signal intensity in the subcortical white matter of some adolescent patients with bipolar disorder. These results imply that neuroimaging will continue to provide insights into the basis of these two psychiatric illnesses that evolve during adolescence.

Saugstad (1989) has combined epidemiologic data with the evidence of neuronal death and synaptic elimination to construct a model that attempts to explain the etiology of schizophrenia and bipolar disorder. He recognizes that adolescent brain development is characterized by extensive synaptic elimination (estimating the reduction at 40% of all brain synapses). Supposedly, any alteration in the extent of elimination, either too little or too much, might result in psychopathology. Specifically, he advances the hypothesis that bipolar disorder is associated with the persistence of synapses that would normally be removed. This result would be achieved in people whose maturation period is shortened. He proposes that the early onset of puberty would cause such a reduction in the duration of brain development. In the case of schizophrenia, Saugstad suggests that the disorder is caused by excessive synaptic elimination, resulting in the loss of appropriate projections. He correlates this endpoint with the late onset of puberty. Over the past century, the average age at which puberty begins has decreased by 4 years in developed countries. Saugstad's model predicts that this trend would be accompanied by an increase in the prevalence of bipolar disorder and a decrease in the prevalence of schizophrenia. Epidemiologic data for these disorders support this prediction. Therefore, Saugstad argues against the hypothesis that there is a specific lesion associated with the onset of schizophrenia and bipolar disorder. He asserts that the pathology involved in these syndromes is more subtle than other investigators have implied. The identification of local enlargement and atrophy in many cortical regions of schizophrenic brains highlights the fact that the defects are widespread. Further research is needed to confirm that schizophrenia and bipolar disorder result from developmental abnormalities in systems that relay neuronal projections to and from the entire neocortex. Saugstad's model provides one set of hypotheses that could guide the direction of future investigations.

Galdos, van Os, and Murray (1993) have provided more epidemiological data to support the concept that the onset of schizophrenia is dependent on events that transpire after the onset of puberty. Comparing the prevalence of schizophrenia in adolescent males and females, they found that the male-to-female ratio of patients increases with age. This trend reflects the fact that girls begin puberty 2 years earlier than boys, on average, corresponding with a delayed onset of disease in boys. These results and those of Saugstad's study solidify the hypothesis that alterations in brain structure and function that occur during puberty are associated with the emergence of psychopathology.

Current Technology and Future Directions for Research

There is much still to be understood regarding adolescent brain development. The current theories rely on the data produced by imaging and electrical recording of neuron populations. The limitation in these systems is the inability to monitor the activity of individual neurons. Electroencephalography is able to detect electrical activity only of large populations of cells. The electrical excitation of small subpopulations of neurons is indistinguishable from background noise. Similarly, PET scans detect concurrent metabolic activity among millions of cells, while the important events of cellular maturation and plasticity most probably occur at the synaptic level. The modifications of activity at a developing synapse are far too subtle to be detected with this technology. Forming firmer associations between developmental brain abnormalities and psychopathology will require more thorough understanding of the molecular determinants of neuronal development and function. Our understanding of schizophrenia and bipolar disorder on the molecular and cellular level awaits the development of methods for detecting pathology at the level of individual neurons in these diseases. Investigation of brain activity at this level is possible only within the disciplines of cellular and molecular biology.

Recombinant DNA technology has provided the tools necessary to begin to dissect neuronal function at the molecular level. It has become possible to characterize cell adhesion molecules, membrane receptors, and signal transduction systems that are unique to certain cells. The ongoing effort to identify molecules involved in cell migration, recognition, and differentiation provides hope that, some day, we will be able to recognize each subpopulation of neurons based solely on their surface antigens or other markers. The presence of a given constellation of proteins will correlate with the developmental and functional identity of these neurons. The development of monoclonal antibodies directed against these epitopes will provide investigators with the means to map the projections made by individual neurons and monitor the fate of these axons. Using animal models and postmortem human brains, it should be possible to chronicle the modifications of specific neurons throughout development. Histologic experiments should be able to detect axon sprouting, synaptogenesis, and synaptic elimination in cells that are labeled with antibodies against their specific antigens. The sequencing of the entire human genome will contribute greatly to this effort by making it possible to characterize all of the molecules that identify a given neuron. In short, the technology necessary to address the questions raised about adolescent brain development is rapidly becoming available.

Conclusion

Brain development during the first decade of life is characterized by the proliferation of neurons in the neonate followed by a progressive thinning out of neurons during the next decade. The second decade consists of synaptic pruning and a subsequent fine-tuning of higher cortical function. These processes reflect the refining of neuronal plasticity with increasing age. Confirmation of this model is limited to qualitative data from imaging studies and in vitro experiments with explanted neurons. Research efforts in the past 20 years have approached this system from two directions. Molecular and cell biologists have sought to characterize the molecular players in neuronal development and plasticity that are important throughout development. Meanwhile, neuroanatomists have tried to describe large-scale morphological changes during this period. Neither of these systems is able to integrate all of the diverse molecular, cellular, and structural aspects of brain development. In combination, these approaches have produced data that attempt to describe some global principles of brain development. Further investigation will require more sensitive imaging technology and specific markers for neuron populations. Greater understanding of the mechanisms that underlie neuronal plasticity will shed more light on the changes that occur in the adolescent brain. The effect of subtle cellular modifications on cognitive processing and other higher cortical functions has yet to be fully elaborated.

REFERENCES

Benes, F., Khan, Y., Vincent, S., & Wickramasinghe, R. (1996). Differences in the subregional and cellular distribution of GABAa receptor binding in the hippocampal formation of schizophrenic brain. *Synapse*, 22, 338–349.

Botteron, K., Figiel, G., Wetzel, M., Hudziak, J., & VanEerdewegh, M. (1992). MRI abnormalities in adolescent bipolar affective disorder. *Journal of the American Academy of Child and Adolescent Psychiatry*, 31, 258–261.

Epstein, H. (1979). Correlated brain and intelligence development in humans. In M. Hahn, C. Jensen, & B. Dedek (Eds.), *Development and evolution of brain size* (pp. 111–131). New York: Academic Press.

Feinberg, I., Thode Jr., H. C., Chugani, H. T., & March, J. D. (1990). Gamma distribution model describes maturational curves for delta wave amplitude, cortical metabolic rate and synaptic density. *Journal of Theoretical Biology*, 142, 149–161.

Galdos, P., van Os, J., & Murray, R. (1993). Puberty and the onset of psychosis. *Schizophrenia Research*, 10, 7–14.

Gorski, R. A. (1985). Gonadal hormones as putative neurotrophic substances. In C. W. Cotman (Ed.), *Synaptic plasticity* (pp. 287–310). New York: Guilford Press.

Hubel, D. H. (1988). *Eye, brain, and vision.* New York: Scientific American Library.

Huttenlocher, P. R. (1979). Synaptic density in human frontal cortex-development changes and effects of aging. *Brain Research*, 163, 195–205.

Jernigan, T. L., & Tallal, P. (1990). Late childhood changes in brain morphology observable with MRI. *Developmental Medicine and Child Neurology*, 32, 379–385.

Jernigan, T. L., Trauner, D. A., Hesselink, J. R., & Tallal, P. A. (1991). Maturation of human cerebrum observed in vivo during adolescence. *Brain, 114*, 2037–2049.

Jernigan, T. L., Zisook, S., Heaton, R. K., Moranville, J. T., Hesselink, J. R., & Braff, D. L. (1991). Magnetic resonance imaging abnormalities in lenticular nuclei and cerebral cortex in schizophrenia. *Archives of General Psychiatry*, 48, 881–890.

Kandel, E. R., Schwartz, J. H., & Jessell, T. M. (1991). *Principles of neural science* (3rd ed.). Norwalk, CT: Appleton & Lange.

Katawa, M. (1995). Roles of steroid hormones and their receptors in structural organization in the nervous system. *Neuroscience Research, 24,* 1–46.

Kopera, H. (1980). Female hormones and brain function. In D. de Wied & P. A. van Keep (Eds.), *Hormones and the brain* (pp. 189–204). Baltimore: University Park Press.

Nicoll, R., Kauer, J. A., & Malenka, R. C. (1988). The current excitement in long-term potentiation. *Neuron, 1,* 97–103.

Peterson, B. (1995). Neuroimaging in child and adolescent neuropsychiatric disorders. *Journal of the American Academy of Child and Adolescent Psychiatry, 34,* 1560–1576.

Saugstad, L. F. (1989). Mental illness and cognition in relation to age at puberty: A hypothesis. *Clinical Genetics, 36,* 156–167.

Stevens, J. R. (1992). Abnormal reinnervation as a basis for schizophrenia: A hypothesis. *Archives of General Psychiatry, 49,* 238–243.

Swayze, II, V. W., Andreason, N. C., Alliger, R. J., Yuh, W. T. C., & Ehrhardt, J. C. (1992). Subcortical and temporal structures in affective disorder and schizophrenia: A magnetic resonance imaging study. *Biological Psychiatry, 31,* 221–240.

Weinberger, D. (1996). On the plausibility of "The neurodevelopmental hypothesis" of schizophrenia. *Neuropsychopharmacology, 14,* 1–11S.

6 / Encounter with New Body Changes

Richard M. Sarles

Introduction

In biological terms, puberty is defined as the state of transition in physical development when sexual reproduction becomes possible. As such, it is a critical stage of a complex process that involves changes in the reproductive organs as well as in many other body features. However, the term "puberty" is commonly used to refer to the entire period of development during which both primary and secondary sexual characteristics evolve into their mature state. Except during the first 2 years of life, no other period of human development involves such dramatic and striking physical changes. Both the rate and the magnitude of change during puberty distinguish it from other periods in the life cycle.

Psychologically, the profundity of these changes requires an entire reorganization of the adolescent's body image and, indeed, self-concept in the larger sense. Indeed, adolescence, especially early adolescence, may be defined as the process of accommodation to the significant psychological and social changes stimulated by the body changes of puberty. Viewed in this manner, adolescence comprises the sum of the psychosocial responses to puberty and thus epitomizes the biopsychosocial paradigm.

For both males and females, the changes that occur during this period may seem to both child and parents to be occurring at breakneck speed. Hair appears where it never grew before, breasts bud and grow, penises enlarge and spring into spontaneous erections, menstruation occurs (and the girls often ambivalently tell their mothers, sisters, and friends about the event), nocturnal emissions occur (and the boy tells no one), pimples pop out, clothes will not tuck in, graceful coordination disappears, clumsy, gawky awkwardness erupts, and strong erotic and aggressive impulses seem to leap out of nowhere. Numerous visits to the bathroom are common along with frequent recourse to mirrors in order to check privately on the new changing body. Time exploring the new body may include an examination, indeed a precise count, of axillary hair growth; examining pubic hair, with special attention to its quantity, texture, and distribution; a check on breast size and contour, noting the balance of growth between right and left breast; evaluation of the color and size of the testicles; and learning ever more about the capacity for erection and orgasm through masturbation. Voyeurism, exhibitionism, and intense narcissism and egocentrism are normal for pubertal boys and girls who spend a great deal of time looking at their own bodies and the bodies of others to validate their own normality. Secrecy from adults and sharing with peers are common.

Boys seem more concerned about their height, their musculature, the breadth of their shoulders, and the slimness of their hips. Girls are more concerned about being pretty, being attractive, having breasts that are not too big and yet not too small, and about being too tall or too heavy (Brooks-Gunn & Reiter, 1990). Secondary sexual characteristics are extremely important to the pubertal-age child because these readily observable physical features are the foci of attractiveness between the sexes.

To be normal and in step with the physical development of one's peers are crucial. For the pubertal-age child, life often feels out of control, the body is new and clumsy, body secretions give off new odors, pimples erupt, and the mind is suddenly and unpredictably flooded with erotic thoughts. Prepubertal-group games such as "spin the bottle" and "postman" give way to disco dances, often ambivalently uncomfortable for both sexes. Facts and fantasies deriving from friends; from school health and science classes; from sex information pamphlets, pop songs, and music videos; and from late night X-rated television shows or videos influence new and powerful feelings, thoughts, and desires.

The Biology of Puberty

Puberty represents the culmination of a long maturational process that began in utero. It does not occur as a result of a single biologic event but arises out of a complex and not yet fully understood interrelated series of hormonal and neuroendocrine changes. The hypothalamic-pituitary-gonadal axis, active during infancy, becomes relatively quiescent during the school-age period and is reactivated between the ages of 10 and 12. The mechanism that triggers this reactivation is thought to involve a complicated interaction of genetic, hormonal, and environmental factors. One of these factors is an increase in growth hormone releasing hormone (GHRH) as well as luteinizing hormone releasing hormone (LHRH), both of which are neuroendocrine hormones produced by cells in the hypothalamic area. GHRH is released in a pulsatile fashion, and the amount released in each pulse increases; this in turn causes the release of larger pulses of growth hormones. The increase in GHRH is thought to occur through disinhibition of a regulatory mechanism that is active during childhood. Both estrogen and testosterone increase growth hormone release, as well, and thyroid hormone plays a permissive role. These changes are in concert with other maturational brain changes that include enhancement of intellectual capacity and alterations in behavior and personality (Reichlin, 1992).

Between early childhood and puberty, the hypothalamic-pituitary-gonadal axis is relatively inactive. Accordingly, a slow growth rate is characteristic of the school-age period; this in turn contributes to a stable body image. Indeed, by the end of the late school-age period, good control of the body has been achieved, and the child is generally well coordinated and strong and smooth in performance. A thorough familiarity with one's body in space and with its boundaries and extensions is characteristic of this era. The body image is part and parcel of the sense of self and is generally clear and comfortable. Finger-to-elbow and knee-to-toe distance is firmly programmed on the cerebral cortex. Late school-age children have developed a good sense of self and their place in the family; in addition, they are aware of their ethnic and cultural traditions and have achieved a firm identity. Thus, by the end of the school-age period,

children usually demonstrate a considerable measure of self-confidence. As they approach puberty, however, they become ever more aware of internal sensations and note the visible changes in slightly older peers. In short, late school-age children become explicitly conscious of the rapidly impending changes of puberty.

The body changes of puberty involve both discrete events, such as menarche and first ejaculation, and more gradual changes, such as the growth of breasts and muscle development. The physical stages of puberty have been outlined by Tanner (1962) and are described in terms of genital development (boys only), breast development (girls only), and pubic hair development (both sexes). Although the stages of development occur in fairly characteristic succession, the relationships of the sequences vary significantly both between and within individuals. In general, estrogens are primarily responsible for breast development, and androgens are responsible for genital and pubic hair development. Figures 6.1 and 6.2 summarize the physical changes of puberty.

In the female, the most notable marker for the onset of pubertal processes is breast bud development. This occurs anywhere from 8 to 13 years of age, with a mean age of onset of 10.6 years. It is secondary to pituitary follicle stimulating hormone and ovarian estrogen production. Actually, breast bud development is preceded by the growth of downy pubic hair. By 9½ years the size of the uterus has already increased, although for the late school-age girl, this is an internal and unrecognized change in her body. Another physical change that may be unrecognized is enlargement of the labia and their gradual development into an adult configuration. It should be noted that many girls study this part of their bodies with a hand mirror in order to learn about this emotionally vital part of the self they cannot otherwise observe.

Peak velocity of growth and height occurs on the average of 1 year following the onset of breast bud development. Menarche then follows approximately 2 to 2½ years after early breast bud development. Thus, in the female, the growth spurt has already begun when first breast buds become apparent. Thereafter, the rate of growth progressively accelerates, and peak height velocity occurs at about 12 years of age. The acceleration in growth declines rapidly after this peak; the total

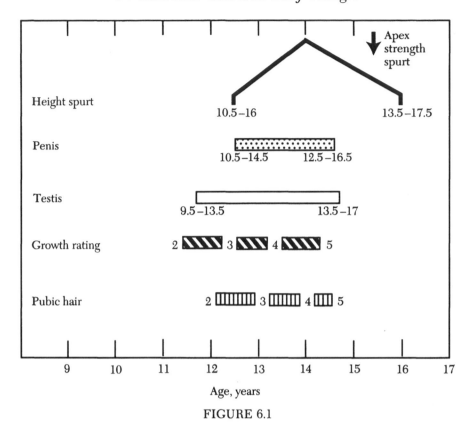

FIGURE 6.1

The developmental course of five pubertal processes for boys.

time of the female adolescent growth curve is approximately 4 years. The average increase in height during this period is between 10 to 14 inches. Epiphysial closure, marking the end of skeletal growth, occurs at 16 to 17 years of age.

Following the peak height velocity, menarche occurs within 6 months to 1 year. The first period is commonly regarded as the marker for the onset of female puberty and early adolescent development; in reality, however, it occurs late in the course of puberty.

The development of the mature menstrual cycle is a relatively long process, and ovulation does not occur on a regular monthly basis for several years after menarche.

Much of the girl's sexual development occurs within her body and is thus unseen; this fact has important consequences for her psychosocial development.

The onset of puberty is influenced by nutritional status. It is closely related to body weight as a ratio of fat to lean composition (Brooks-Gunn & Reiter, 1990). Since the turn of the century, in

industrial, developing countries menarche has occurred at progressively younger ages. Between 1900 and 1960 the average age of menarche decreased from 15 to 12.6 years; in 1990 it was 12.5 years. The decline in age is assumed to be related to the control of infectious diseases and more adequate nutrition. As nutrition and health improved, optimal growth potential was reached, and the age of menarche has accordingly remained stable.

During the preadolescent years, growth is primarily due to elongation of the limbs. Immediately prior to puberty, the distal parts of the extremities—the hands and feet—grow before the proximal parts. A rapid increase in shoe size is usually a harbinger of the impending pubertal growth spurt. This is a relatively slow process. During the pubertal growth spurt, the increase in height is primarily due to truncal growth. For the female, there is a widening and realignment of the pelvis to accommodate for the enlargement of the birth canal; this in part accounts for the pelvic "wiggle" of the mature female gait.

45

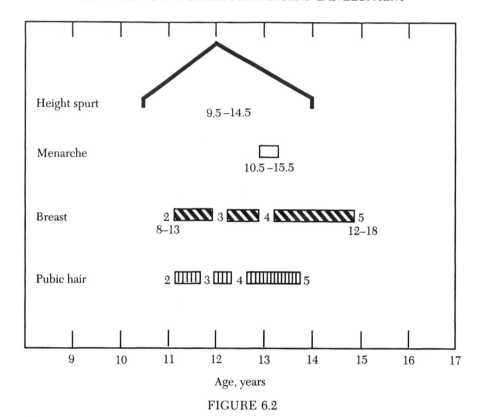

FIGURE 6.2

The developmental course of four pubertal processes for girls. From J. M. Tanner,
Growth at Adolescence (Oxford: Blackwell Scientific, 1962), p. 36. Copyright © 1962 by
Blackwell Scientific. Reprinted with permission.

The female secondary sex characteristics that emerge at puberty are stimulated mainly by estrogen production. In addition to stimulation of breast development; enlargement of the labia, the uterus, fallopian tubes; and thickening of the vaginal mucosa, estrogen leads to fat deposition around the hips and buttocks, which gives the maturing adolescent a rounder and softer appearance and the typical hourglass shape of the adult female. Estrogen secretion also develops a cyclical pattern; in concert with progesterone secretion, this accounts for the monthly menstrual cycle.

Androgens secreted by the adrenal glands bring about pubic and axillary hair growth and enlargement of the clitoris. Androgens also account for sebaceous and apocrine sweat glands in the axillary and genital areas. These glands, in turn, produce increased oiliness of the face, often leading to pimples and occasionally to acne.

Characteristically, puberty in males occurs 2 years later than in females and lasts longer. Sec-ondary to pituitary interstitial stimulating hormone production and testicular androgen (testosterone) production, enlargement of testes and penis occurs as the first outward signs of pubertal change in the male. This is usually identifiable at approximately 11 to 11½ years of age. Male growth spurt also begins about this time, and peak height growth velocity occurs at about 13 to 14 years of age. Males achieve about the same overall total growth as females (10 to 14 inches); however, since males begin puberty later, they experience a longer prepubertal growth time with resultant longer extremity growth.

Peak height growth velocity coincides with spermarche, the onset of the release of spermatozoa, commonly described as first ejaculation and generally occurring at about 14 years of age. Spermarche may occur as a result of masturbation or nocturnal emission. Information about spermarche is less easily obtained than that about menarche, because this event is more likely to be

46

kept secret. It is seen as having a "sexual" nature, in contrast to the "normal" cyclical body function of menstruation (Gaddis & Brooks-Gunn, 1985). The first ejaculation occurs at a time when only minimal secondary sexual characteristics are present in the male. It is thus an early pubertal event for males in contrast to menarche, which occurs toward the end of puberty in females.

In boys, pubic hair growth precedes that of axillary hair by about 2 years, and the appearance of facial hair generally coincides with axillary hair growth. Full facial hair does not occur until late adolescence; only 50% of 17-year-old males are shaving. In addition to full facial hair growth, another noticeable change in the adolescent male is the deepening of his voice secondary to enlargement of the larynx, a transformation that occurs at age 14 or 15. The accumulation of musculature in the pubertal male is associated with a deceleration of fat deposition and is coupled as well with a wider shoulder girth and narrow hips. These changes give males their characteristic triangular body habitus. However, the transient and very common phenomenon of gynecomastia secondary to estrogen production by the testes occurs unilaterally in 25% of boys and bilaterally in 50 to 65% of boys. When it does occur, it is often a source of confusion and embarrassment for the pubertal-age boy. Equally embarrassing is the androgen driven growth of skin glands. This leads to an increase in oiliness of the skin, pimples, and occasionally to acne.

AROUSABILITY

Masturbation—Males: Although genital stimulation and masturbatory activity begin in infancy, the drive to masturbate to orgasm characteristically begins during puberty. Erection in the male infant occurs spontaneously during the sleep cycle, and it is common for most male infants to have experienced and touched their erect penises at least by their first birthday. Erections continue through the preschool and school-age years, often spontaneously or in response to pain, fright, or other nonsexual and/or sexual stimuli. Masturbation to orgasm is possible during these years, with all the accompanying physiological responses typical of an adult orgasm except for ejaculation (Masters, Johnson, & Kolodny, 1986). However, in the prepubertal era, spontaneous erection and masturbation are less likely to be erotically focused than they are after puberty. At puberty, under the stimulation of sex hormones, the capacity for erotic thought, fantasy, and feeling evolves, and erections and masturbatory activity become closely associated with erotic-sexual content. Erotic thoughts can stimulate an erection, but a spontaneous erection also can stimulate erotic thoughts and feelings. This connection of erotic fantasy with sexual behavior plays out for the remainder of adult sexual life. In fact, direct genital stimulation in the adult does not necessarily lead to erection unless accompanied by erotic thought and/or fantasy. Awareness of the tremendous importance of cognitive and affective processes as components of sexual behavior has led clinicians in the field of human sexuality to observe that sex is really between the ears, and only the sex organs are between the legs.

The pubertal-age boy is ambivalently pleased about his capacity for erection, because, albeit rewarding, it is not under his control. Thus, he may be dismayed at the occurrence of spontaneous erections at inappropriate times. An erection gives the pubertal boy visible, palpable evidence of his enlarging phallus and an immediate sense of growth and strength. The difference in the size of the penis in the flaccid and erect states is a source of wonder, with the erect phallus symbolically demonstrating power and size. Boys often display their genitals to each other to compare sizes. A spontaneous erection, however, during a gym class shower, at the beach, in history class, or when talking with a girl is usually embarrassing, confusing, and anything but reassuring to the boy's sense of masculinity.

The occurrence of erections and the capacity for erotic thought and fantasy lead to an increasing percentage of males who masturbate during the adolescent years and to an increase in the frequency of masturbation. In the not too distant past, folklore and myths attributed many maladies to masturbation, including blindness, acne, warts, insanity, impotence, and early sterility. Religious traditions held it to be sinful. Even with such ominous associations, all studies have shown that as they get older, more and more boys masturbate, so that by early adulthood up to 85 to 90% of males are so engaged (Kinsey, Pomeroy, & Martin, 1948; Sorensen, 1972). Some clinicians assert that, in fact, 95% of adolescent males masturbate and 5% lie. Nevertheless, although masturbation is an almost universal occurrence during adolescence, for most teenagers it is still shrouded in secrecy and accompanied by some guilt. In today's world of sex education classes, abundant medical pamphlets, and open discussions of sexuality, the fact that secrecy and guilt still attach to masturbation may attest to the fact that old myths die hard. An alternative explanation for the ubiquitousness of guilt is the universal presence of masturbatory fantasies, many of which represent oedipal wishes in various degrees of disguise. No matter how much openness exists with regard to sexual expression, no society is free of some taboos, and, in Western society, the prohibition of incest is certainly one of the most prevalent and powerful interdictions.

For the majority of males, masturbation leads to the first ejaculation. A smaller number experience their first ejaculation through nocturnal emissions or intercourse. It is not unusual for adolescent boys to engage in mutual masturbation, to masturbate simultaneously together, or to do so in a group as a "circle jerk" to see who can ejaculate first and farthest. Pubertal-age boys generally experience the act of ejaculation with mixed emotions. Prior to the capacity for ejaculation, the boy may experience orgasm through masturbation, intense physical exercise, or even pain. When the capacity for ejaculation is attained, the built-up intensity and release that accompany the orgiastic discharge can often be shocking, startling, and frightening. As the seminal fluid "shoots" out, the ejaculate is visible, tangible evidence that the boy is sexual. He now has the capacity to impregnate and reproduce and to be sexually potent as a mature grown male. The residues of nocturnal emissions in bedclothes alert siblings and parents to the boy's sexuality. While masturbatory ejaculates can be kept covert, spontaneous ejaculation, or "coming in the pants," while dancing or making out is a humiliating experience. Most adolescent males are astounded to learn that the ejaculate that creates such a large stain and feels like such an incredible amount of liquid involves only about 3.5 cubic centimeters of seminal fluid, less than a full teaspoon.

Spermarche, the onset of the release of spermatozoa, as manifested by the first ejaculation, initiates a lifelong capacity for fertility. This stands in contrast to the female menarche, which introduces fertility for a period of approximately 35 years. For the male, the potential to impregnate occurs with every ejaculation, whereas throughout her reproductive years the female produces only approximately one egg per month.

Most pubertal-age boys are aware that the ejaculate carries sperm and is capable of impregnating a female. Most adolescent boys do not, however, wish or plan to impregnate a girl during intercourse, and most teenage pregnancies are not planned.

Male Fantasy Life: It is very difficult to determine at what point during puberty male and female erotic fantasies begin and equally difficult to know the content and scope of these fantasies. In one report (Coles & Stokes, 1985), 72% of teenagers ages 13 to 18 admitted to erotic fantasies; of these fantasies, 94% involved television or movie stars and 51% involved boyfriends or girlfriends. The majority of available data are, however, outdated, and contemporary concerns about obtaining such sensitive information from adolescents and parents have virtually eliminated further chances of collecting epidemiological data on sexual behavior and concerns from this age group.

The surge of erotic fantasy that suddenly and inexplicably intrudes into the adolescent boy's thoughts is often confusing and embarrassing to him. He therefore avoids sharing these thoughts and feelings with anyone lest his inner life, about which he is quite anxious, be revealed. Therefore, the meager anecdotal accounts of the erotic fantasies, sexual feelings, and the accompanying joys and fears attending these newfound thoughts and sensations have been obtained either from adult retrospective accounts or from isolated psychoanalytic reports of pubertal-age boys. The limited information available indicates that the pubertal-age boy is extraordinarily sensitive to the aroma of perfumes or facial powder on girls, to the sound of a girl's clothes rubbing or the wiggle of her hips as she walks by, to her erect nipples, or to her fleeting glances. Erotic fantasies stimulated by such encounters include thoughts of undergarments, nudity, genital size, breast firmness, and sexual exploration.

Masturbatory fantasies may include any of the day's events and usually incorporate various scenarios of seduction, petting, disrobing, genital stimulation, and intercourse. For the majority of pubertal-age boys, the masturbatory fantasies precede actual sexual experiences and are colored by thoughts, feelings, and fantasies of what their sexual experiences will be like. The early masturbatory fantasies and experiences serve a number of important functions for the pubertal adolescent. First, as noted previously, these erotic fantasies are a source of sexual arousal. Second, they allow for behavioral rehearsal, setting patterns of response for actual experiences yet to come. Third, they permit adolescents to learn about their own bodies, their own sexual responses, and the power of their own thoughts, impulses, and self-regulating capabilities. Sadomasochistic fantasies, incestuous fantasies, homosexual fantasies, and fantasies of bestiality are generally confusing and threatening to the pubertal adolescent. Such inner images probably are not uncommon, but it is rare that such fantasies are ever made known.

Masturbation—Females: The female infant, like the male, generally discovers her genitalia through normal body exploration. The female infant and child have the capacity to reach orgasm, demonstrating all of the physiological responses noted in adulthood. In contrast to visible, spontaneous penile erections, it is unclear if female children experience spontaneous clitoral engorgement. In addition, the relatively internal nature of the clitoris makes it somewhat less accessible to the girl than the penis is for the boy. Anectodal accounts of preadolescent female masturbatory activity described by Kinsey (1958) and others report that the female child tends to use rocking, bouncing, or crural rubbing in the service of masturbatory activity.

Female orgasm has been shrouded in myth. Psychoanalytic theorists proposed that clitoral orgasm was a precursor and that only vaginal orgasm was a true, mature adult response. Masters and Johnson's pioneering work (1966), however, demonstrated that all orgasms are clitoral in nature. Subsequently the Women's Liberation Movement of the 1970s spoke up for the role of self-stimulation as a mechanism for the female to learn about her own body and body responses. Only then did female masturbation become more openly discussed and acceptable. Thus, as recently as the 1970s for a multitude of reasons, female masturbation was a far more secret, far more guilt-evoking practice than male masturbation. Reports in 1958

(Kinsey), 1972 (Sorenson), and 1966 (Masters & Johnson) indicated that the percentage of adolescent females who acknowledged masturbation increased from 20% in 1958 to 40% in 1973, to over 75% in 1986.

Female Fantasy Life: Even less is known about the pubertal girl's erotic fantasies than the males. It is clear that pubertal females develop the capacity for erotic thought and fantasy, which can lead to masturbatory activity. It is also known that adult females experience periodic nocturnal clitoral engorgement and vaginal lubrication similar to males' nocturnal erections. In contrast to males, females utilize body touch and caress far more as a part of the sequence leading to masturbation than do males. Females caress their breasts, abdomen, thighs, and clitoris with or without digital insertion in the vagina and utilize devices such as vibrators, whereas males generally only stimulate the penis and occasionally the testes. In contrast to males' erotic thoughts, which are primarily sexual scenarios, female fantasy is generally more romantic in nature with gradual evolution of sexual themes.

For girls' psychosexual development, puberty has been held to be a more important stage than the oedipal phase. In particular, it allows for a consolidation of the body image that had previously been unclear because of misinformation, confusion of vaginal and clitoral sensations prior to puberty, and concrete thinking. Almost all agree that the lack of visibility of the vagina complicates female development. For prepubertal girls, the body image is mysterious and accompanied by a sense of incompleteness. One of the major psychological tasks of the pubertal period is to integrate inner genital sensations with the changes taking place in the outer body. Menarche is particularly important in female psychosexual development as it helps to resolve the ambiguities of the prepubertal period.

Freud had emphasized the centrality of the girl's preoedipal tie to her mother and the castration complex. This view has been reevaluated in the light of current knowledge and is generally understood to have been related both to unspoken and shared assumptions about women in the Victorian era and to a misunderstanding of female infantile masturbation. Masturbation in the female was anthropomorphized, as it was assumed that all libido was masculine, and theory about this was generalized to the entirety of female psychology and character. Freud did see bisexuality as universal and innate. His view (and that of his followers) was that femininity derived from a series of events beginning with the girl's discovery of the anatomical differences between the sexes, followed by her identification with her mother, and her shift in libidinal object interest from her mother to her father. Recent psychoanalytic views hold that prolonged penis envy is not the norm in female development and that menarche is an event that is often associated with joy (Fischer, 1991).

In the female, the onset of menstruation, the menarche, is a marker commonly cited by girls and their culture as the end of childhood and the entry into adolescence and adulthood. Menstruation occurs only in humans, apes, and some monkeys. Albeit a normal function of the reproductively mature human female, negative attitudes toward menstruation and toward the menstruating woman are found in many cultures. Within such context, a woman in this state is seen as unclean, a source of contamination, not to be touched or allowed into the home, and not permitted to touch food. In most cultures, until recently, menstruation was shrouded in mystery and approached with disdain by both males and females (although to be sure, some cultures have always had positive attitudes toward it, as shown in some Native American groups). In the last few years in most industrialized enlightened societies, particularly among the educated, a more modern view of the biologic process of menstruation has evolved. Linked to this changed attitude is the availability of feminine hygiene products permitting women full access to all activities during the menstrual period, including sports and swimming.

In the United States, most school-age children are exposed to classroom family life and personal hygiene courses. These curricula include classes in human growth, development, and reproduction. School-age boys and girls are taught about the normal physical developments of puberty, including the emergence of secondary sexual characteristics, ova and sperm production, and the menstrual cycle. Since it exists apart from sexual activity, the menstrual cycle usually is described in detail as part of the normal functioning of the body. However, male erection and ejaculation, which are direct components of sexual activity and associated with sexual feelings and pleasure, are still taboo subjects and usually are described only superficially. The result is that most boys learn more about females and menstruation than they learn about their own bodies.

Although reliable data are unavailable for all ethnic groups and socioeconomic classes, most middle-class girls talk with each other and older female siblings about menstruation. Girls also hear their mothers discussing their own menstrual periods with other women, so young girls usually have some knowledge and preparation for menarche. This is the single event that is usually cited as the transition point from child to woman. Unlike spermarche, menstruation is not inherently a pleasurable experience, although it is an important milestone on the road to maturity. Reactions to menarche are very much influenced by the kind of preparation received. Many girls are not attuned to the subtle physical signs preceding the menstrual period, and most are not prepared for the unesthetic experience of the blood leaving the body, blood that is often clotted, heavy, and brownish black, typical of an anovulatory cycle. Girls may be intellectually prepared for incipient menstruation, but they are not always ready emotionally for the reality of actual menstrual flow. Even in an enlightened, educated society where menstruation is viewed as a female normalcy, it requires a real leap of logic for the pubertal female to understand that, while in general bleeding means injury, menstrual bleeding means health. Among pubertal girls, it is evident that menstruation evokes a wide array of feelings. When asked about the subject, 20% of adolescent girls are positive, 20% are negative, and 20% report no feelings or feeling indefinite. The remainder experience mixed positive and negative feelings (Ruble & Brooks-Gunn, 1982). While menstruation is the marker for adulthood and reproductive capacity, it may also be experienced as an uncomfortable monthly chore of managing menstrual flow, bloating, and cramping. Dysmenorrhea is a significant cause of school or work absence during adolescence, and among adolescents, the level of knowledge about effective treatment for it is low. There is strong evidence that the attitudes toward the first menstrual period, which, as we have seen, are influenced by the quality and source of information received, continue throughout adolescence and into adulthood (Brooks-Gunn, 1987). These attitudes form an important part first of the girl's and later of the woman's self-concept. Thus, improved knowledge about menstruation is an important health need for adolescents.

Menstruation is a visible sign of the maturation of the uterus and ovaries; the development of these internal organs is otherwise invisible. While the majority of pubertal-age girls do not use tampons initially, their subsequent use permits the girl to have her first experience with something entering and leaving her vaginal space. The girl has a special opportunity and permission to touch, explore, and even look at her genitalia in order to insert the tampon properly. The pubertal-age girl thus learns of the location, size, flexibility and distensibility, ease or difficulty of insertion (pene-

tration), and sensitivity or lack of sensitivity of her genital organs.

Summary

The biological events of puberty set in motion a dynamic, evolving growth pattern of biopsychosocial interaction. Physical maturation, menstruation, ejaculation, and the capacity for reproduction are all biological in nature, but mature sexual behavior is not a biologic given. It is the interaction of the adolescent, the family, the school, peers, religion, and society with the biological aspects of puberty that is critical for the successful psychosocial maturation of the adolescent in society.

REFERENCES

Brooks-Gunn, J. (1987). Pubertal processes and girls' psychological adaptation. In R. Lerner & T. T. Foch (Eds.) *Biological-psychosocial interactions in early adolescence: A life-span perspective* (pp. 123–153). Hillsdale, NJ: Lawrence Erlbaum.

Brooks-Gunn, J., & Reiter, E. O. (1990). The role of the pubertal process. In S. S. Feldman & G. R. Elliott (Eds.), *At the threshold: The developing adolescent* (pp. 16–53). Cambridge, MA: Harvard University Press.

Coles, R., & Stokes, G. (1985). *Sex and the American teenager.* New York: Harper & Row.

Fischer, R. (1991). Pubescence: A psychoanalytic study of one girl's experience of puberty. *Psychoanalytic Inquiry, 11*, 457–479.

Gaddis, A., & Brooks-Gunn, J. (1985). The male experience of pubertal change. *Journal of Youth and Adolescence, 14*, 61–69.

Katchadourian, H. A. (1989). *Fundamentals of human sexuality* (5th ed.). New York: Holt, Rinehart, Winston.

Kinsey, A. C., & Gebbard, P. H. (1953). *Sexual behavior in the human female.* Philadelphia: W. B. Saunders.

Kinsey, A. C., Pomeroy, W. B., & Martin, C. E. (1948). *Sexual behavior in the human male,* Philadelphia: W. B. Saunders.

Masters, W. H., & Johnson, V. E. (1966). *Human sexual response.* Boston: Little Brown & Co.

Masters, W. H., Johnson, V. E., & Kolodny, R. C. (1986). *Masters and Johnson, On sex and human loving.* Boston: Little, Brown.

Reichlin, S. (1992). Neuroendocrinology. In J. V. Wilson & D. W. Foster (Eds.), *Williams textbook of endocrinology* (p. 181). Philadelphia: W. B. Saunders.

Ruble, D. N., & Brooks-Gunn, J. (1982). The experience of menarche. *Child Development, 5,* 1557–1566.

Sarrel, L. J., & Sarrel, P. M. (1979). "The Concept of Sexual Unfolding." In L. J. Sarrel & P. M. Sarrel, *Sexual unfolding.* (pp. 17–44) Boston: Little, Brown.

Sorensen, R. C. (1973). *Adolescent sexuality in contemporary America.* New York: World Publishing Co.

Tanner, J. M. (1962). *Growth at adolescence* (2nd ed.). Oxford, UK: Blackwell Scientific Publishers.

7 / The Development of Affect

Carole M. Booth

Affect is a complex construct that encompasses bodily sensations, facial expression, and cognition. Since alterations in affect are found in many psychiatric disorders, the observation of affect is considered an important aspect of the mental status examination. In current psychiatric thinking, affect is described as "the visible and audible manifestation of the patient's emotional response to external and internal events, that is thoughts, ideas, evoked memories, and reflections. It is expressed in autonomic response, posture, facial and reactive movements, grooming, and in tone of voice, vocalizations, and word selection" (Othmer and Othmer, 1994). Smiling, crying, stiffening, trembling, quickly straightening up, patting one's hair in place, and yelling are all examples of affective responses. These brief, often momentary behaviors are visible to others and convey information to them.

The terms "affect," "mood," "feeling," and "emotions" are often used interchangeably. Mood, however, is a more sustained internal feeling state than affect. It involves subjective awareness and can be described only by the person who is experiencing it. Sadness, joy, and boredom are examples of moods. While affect is an immediate response to a stimulus, mood is more durable and exists apart from stimuli. Both mood and affect can vary in intensity as well as in degree of pleasure. Thus, mild irritation and extreme rage both represent manifestations of anger. Emotions have a positive or negative valence, as well; joy is a pleasant affect, disgust is unpleasant. For humans, emotions play a critical role in self-awareness and identity, as they are linked with perception and cognition.

Affective expression begins in infancy and develops toward increasing complexity and differentiation throughout the life cycle. The earliest manifestations of affect include interest, excitement, startle responses, fear, and distress, all of which can be seen in infants. These varying emotional responses are stimulated at first by visceral and other somatic sensations, but very quickly they also become associated with social interactions. While some aspects of affective responses are probably innate, social interaction has a profound effect on shaping them. Others' reactions to the child's affective expressions shape the form they take as development proceeds. Mirroring, for example, by smiling back in response to a child's smile, encourages the child to smile even more. A caregiver's negative response or no response at all discourages further smiling.

As children develop, feeling states become increasingly linked to cognitive awareness as they learn to identify and label emotions. Young children can describe feeling happy, sad, or angry. Older children can identify greater numbers of feelings and experience each of these as different. Children also learn to bear painful emotions, such as sadness or anger, with relative equanimity and to manage them in ways that reduce their noxious impact.

The ability to label emotion and to communicate about it to others who are able to help children feel better are important components of this maturational process. As children grow older, they begin to be able to soothe and calm themselves, things they previously depended on others to do.

By the time they reach preadolescence, most children are able to experience within a brief period a range of feelings that differ from each other in intensity and quality and can even experience a mixture of feelings. A child feels sad, for example, to be leaving a well-liked teacher at the end of the school year but pleased and proud to be moving up to a higher grade. Preadolescents are capable of showing a wide range of affective expression. They recognize that others' facial expressions do not always accurately reflect feelings. They can respond accurately to cues from the context of social situations as opposed to facial expressions alone.

Various affects play a role in defensive operations; for example, disgust over his own feces in a 3-year-old child is a reaction against an earlier fascination with them. In addition to signaling to others that the child is a member of civilized society, this affective reaction reassures the child that he has distanced himself from infancy.

Replacing a strong but unacceptable feeling with its opposite helps the child to master infantile impulses, give up regressive behaviors, and conform with social expectations. Children's sensitivity to the emotional tone of social situations is an important facilitator for social interactions and contributes to their being liked by peers (Denham, McKinley, Couchoud, & Holt, 1990). Children learn to hide their own emotions when the situation demands it—for example, not crying or having a temper tantrum when losing a game. When their emotions become too intense, these capabilities disappear temporarily, as they do for adults, as well, but most preadolescent children are able to maintain an even emotional keel most of the time.

The passage from preadolescence to adolescence is accompanied by changes in affective intensity, variety, and modes of expression. Sigmund Freud (1929/1963) noted that intense and unstable affects characterized entry into puberty. He theorized that this resulted from the increase in sexual and aggressive urges that occur during puberty and the role of affects in repressing these inner drives. Anna Freud (1958) saw emotional instability during adolescence as in part a consequence of withdrawal of intense feelings from their original objects, preparatory to the reattachment of the feelings to others outside the family, ultimately to sexual partners. Early adolescence is thus a period of transition when the child's intense attachment to parents is being weakened, but there is not yet the capacity for equally sustaining relationships with others.

The child's attention becomes focused inwardly on the self as well as on others who represent for the child the kind of person he or she longs to be. Thus, intense relationships may be formed that are actually narcissistic attachments. The young adolescent falls in love, or develops crushes on idealized peers, who are often older, very physically attractive, or seem to have some other highly admired qualities. Because the relationship is not based on mutual sharing or even on real attributes of the other person, it usually falls apart quickly once the other person becomes better known or once the adolescent moves on to other interests.

The brevity of these relationships and alacrity with which they are abandoned accounts for what often appears as the adolescent's callous disregard for the feelings of others.

Empirical research has provided conflicting results on affective intensity and instability during adolescence. Offer, Ostrov, Howard, and Atkins (1990) attempted to measure the various components of affect in large nonclinical populations of adolescents, in studies of adolescent mental health using the Offer Self-Image Questionnaire. The questionnaire included an "emotional tone" subset, a group of questions designed to measure harmony, control, and fluctuation of affect. The authors found that most adolescents experienced many affects satisfactorily, enjoyed life, and were happy with themselves.

Golombeck (1986) included measures of some affects in a study that compared the personality traits of the same group of adolescents at age thirteen and age 16. Forty-seven percent of the adolescents did not demonstrate persistent or excessive anxiety or depression at either time. However, as a group, middle adolescents were more affectionate and experienced more pleasure and less anxiety and depression than early adolescents. The older group also showed more emotional involvement with others and awareness of feelings and thoughts of others. These results support the notion of early adolescence as a period of more dysphoric moods with middle adolescence being a time of relative calm and increasing maturity.

One of the methods used to study affect in nonclinical populations of adolescents is exemplified by Larson and Lampman-Petraitis (1989), who used the experience sampling method to collect data concerning the hourly mood changes experienced by children and adolescents, ages 9 through 15. They concluded that their findings "suggest that the onset of adolescence is not associated with appreciable differences in the variability of emotional states experienced during daily life." (p. 1252). However, older participants reported more dysphoric average states. Greene (1990) also used the experience sample method to measure affectivity, daily affect, affect lability, and feeling states in male and female students in fifth through ninth grades.

The students carried pagers and a booklet of

self-report forms for 1 week, rating their moods and feelings when they were paged at random intervals 7 times a day. The average daily affect derived fom the adolescents' self-reports was less extreme among older than among younger adolescents, and Greene concluded that there was a linear trend in the direction of more emotional stability with increasing age. Greene found that the underlying dimensions of adolescents' emotions was not different from that experienced by adults. While average daily mood was similar in adults and adolescents, adolescents experienced more extreme positive and negative moods and this variability seemed to be occurring in response to social situations. Greene also reviewed several studies that compared affective lability in high school students and adults; these studies showed conflicting results. Greene proposed that the inconsistencies in the findings of these studies was related to their focus on the intensity and change of individual emotions rather than on a qualitative change in the underlying dimensions of affect. This conclusion is supported by other research that indicates that the intensity of affect is increased during adolescence, but not its overall type of variability; thus, adults have as many moods as adolescents and they change just as often, but their intensity is less.

This transition toward decreased intensity is illustrated by the following case example.

Mary at age 10 was an active, competent fifth grader; as she entered puberty, she became shy and moody around adults but "loud" and "silly" with her friends. At age 12 she was critical of parents' dress and behavior and was "mortified" to be forced to eat in a restaurant with her family. At age 14 she became infatuated with a boy and became involved in a relationship that she described as intensely exciting but engendering moments of extreme despair. At age 16, Mary says she feels calmer and does not feel the urgency to be with someone all the time. She continues to date but also enjoys spending time with her family and friends.

The increased intensity of affective experience pushes the adolescent to find new ways of coping with affects. Healthy adolescents learn how to cope with their moods in a constructive fashion rather than being at the the mercy of their moods. Sports can provide an outlet for controlled expression of aggressive impulses that might otherwise lead to outbursts of anger. Seeking reassurance

from friends or trusted adults can help counter feelings of self-deprecation. Offer's classic studies (1969) of normal adolescent boys showed that although these adolescents did experience transient depressed moods, they coped with them by becoming active physically. Talking with others, confronting others, using humor, and seeking interpretations of their behavior from others were also strategies these adolescents used when faced with difficult situations.

One unquestionable change is that adolescents acquire new abilities to talk about their feelings, and girls, in particular, seem to spend endless amount of time doing so. A tendency to develop and use their own language with expressions to describe strong emotions—"awesome" or "amazing," for example—is part of the teenage culture. It is as if the everyday language of adults is too pale and emotionless to contain their feelings. For further discussion of adolescents' language, see Chapter 22.

Schave and Schave (1989), synthesizing the work of infant researchers, self psychologists, and Piaget, have described a theory of the development of affects in early adolescence that links affective and cognitive development. In their view, affective development in adolescence is a reaction to dramatic changes in cognition during early adolescence that force adolescents into a different awareness of themselves and the world around them. They describe a "quantum leap" in cognitive thinking from present to future orientation that in turn results in a softening of the adolescent's psychic structure. They state:

The intensity of cognitive and emotional disequilibrium during this phase leads to egocentrism that activates very intense affects, such as shame, humiliation and other feeling states. Early adolescents protect themselves from these intense feeling states, most particularly shame, by using primitive defense mechanisms, especially disavowal and denial. The extensive use of disavowal and the resulting disconnection from the unconscious lives of early adolescence makes this phase developmentally unique. (p. 27)

Because of the early teenager's fragile self-structure, Schave and Schave (1989) see shame as the core affect of early adolescence. Yorke et al. (1990) describe shame as a powerful and painful affect, which carries with it a strong sense of exposure. Shame always has an external referent—an awareness of an observer—as well as an internal feeling. The typical young adolescent perceives an imaginary audience always watching him or her with a critical eye. This perception can lead to explosive rage or bouts of despair. The young adolescent can have moments of great pride and elation when perceived as perfect by this same imaginary audience. If these affects become too intense, the adolescent may resort to "disavowal," a state of mind in which there is cognitive awareness of an event that produced an intense and painful affect but the affect is not experienced.

The enormous leap in cognitive ability from concrete operational thinking to formal operational thinking and the rapid physiological changes that occur during early adolescence are reminiscent of the toddler's struggles for autonomy. Increased egocentrism and concerns about shame and abandonment are common to both developmental periods. Like the toddler, the early adolescent needs external support as internal structures weaken. Kohut's (1971) concept of the parent's functioning as a stimulus barrier or, as expressed by Schave and Schave (1989), as a protective umbrella also applies to the role of the parent of the young adolescent who tests the limits of his or her new cognitive and physical abilities. Without consistent external structure and support, adolescents may become anxious and "raise the ante" by acting out until there is some response. According to Schave and Schave, "The same issues of affective attunement, mirroring, idealization and capacity to accept, tolerate, define and integrate different affect states [that apply to toddlers] apply to young teenagers as well."

Parents can provide affective soothing through attunement to the young adolescent's affective needs and by providing a protective umbrella of consistency and limits. The adolescent's use of "disavowal" or "denial" to avoid feelings of shame or anxiety makes the task of the parent to remain affectively attuned to the young adolescent difficult. Stein, Golombeck, Marton, and Korenblum (1987) note that in middle adolescence there is some resolution of the ambivalence of early adolescence, with an increase in affection and acknowledgment of closeness expressed toward the mother. This change in affective expression is compared to the rapprochement phase. As in the

rapprochement phase, the resolution of earlier ambivalent feelings allows for greater comfort in expressions of closeness.

An important quality of adolescent emotional experiences arises out of their newness and the adolescent's lack of the experience to put them in perspective. For the adolescent, experiences of such intensity, occurring for the first time, have profound effects on cognition and behavior, not only in the immediate present but often throughout life. A friend's death by suicide, for example, engenders suicidal impulses. Rage at having been insulted is a common cause for gang fights and even killings. Falling in love for the first time is such an intense and unique experience that it does not fade from memory no matter how many years pass.

While not all adolescents achieve formal operational thinking, one consequence of this level of cognition is the ability to imagine hypothetical situations. Doing so allows a greater capacity for empathy, as the adolescent can imagine how he or she would feel in a variety of situations and can figuratively walk in another's shoes. This allows for emotions to be experienced vicariously; another's joy or sorrow can be shared. Future feelings also can be recognized, as can more subtle nuances of emotion (Lane & Schwartz, 1987). The capacity for abstract thinking also allows for the association of feelings with symbols—words, music, artistic creations, ideologies—and allows these abstractions to be imbued with an intensity of feeling heretofore not possible. The passionate commitment to a political cause or to an artistic endeavor are examples of this. For further discussion of these issues, see Chapters 9 and 10.

With the transition to adulthood, further development may occur with regard to affect. Emotions themselves do not change, but the understanding of them may, depending on the individual's capacity to think analytically and his or her efforts at self-observation. The change is mainly in the direction of increased introspection and deepening self-understanding, and can continue throughout life. Brown (1993) has described the developmental task of the adult with respect to affect as to recognize fully one's own emotional states and learn to distinguish between events themselves and the thoughts, fantasies, and behaviors that are associated with the emotional responses to the events. In summary, the task for adults is to become as fully aware as possible of emotions as part of a deepening capacity for self-observation.

CLINICAL IMPLICATIONS OF INCREASED INTENSITY OF EMOTIONAL EXPERIENCES

An important clinical consequence of the development of increased and persistent negative affect during adolescence is the increase in depressive symptoms in adolescent girls. Offord et al. (1990) found that among children from age 4 to 11, the rate of emotional disorder was higher for boys than for girls (19.5% vs. 13.5%). Prepubertal depression is found either equally represented in both boys and girls or slightly increased in boys. From ages 12 to 16, there is a more than twofold increase in disturbance in adolescent girls in comparison with adolescent boys (21.8% vs. 18.8%). The increased incidence of disturbance in adolescent girls is related to their increased levels of depression. Velez, Johnson, and Cohen (1989) reported that in a sample of 456 adolescents ages 13 to 18, the depressed adolescents were more likely to be girls. An epidemiologic survey of 5596 adolescents ages 11 to 17 found a 2.5 to 1 predominance of major depressive disorder in adolescent girls compared to boys (Offord et al., 1987). Peterson, Sarigiani, and Kennedy (1991) discuss the possible causes of the increase in depression in adolescent girls. Both biological and environmental factors are considered influential. Early-developing girls who reach puberty before their peer group have more problems with body image and self-esteem when compared to on-time or later-developing girls. Early puberty timing shows long-term negative effects only for girls. Petersen et al. found that regardless of timing of puberty, girls on the whole showed significantly more depressed affect and poorer emotional tone than boys by the 12th grade. This difference appeared to emerge in the eighth grade and then to increase over subsequent years. Negative family events and changes in school had negative effects on girls and positive effects on boys. Perhaps males respond positively to the challenges of adolescence because for most males, entry into puberty results in an increased size and strength resulting in increased self-esteem. For females, a larger height and weight may not be desirable because a slim preadolescent body type is preferred by Western society. Females are also concerned about menstruation and the possibility of pregnancy. Peterson et al. (1991) also noted that close relationships with parents provide "an arena of comfort" and moderate the negative effects of early adolescent changes on emotional tone and depressive episodes.

Hormonal changes also may correlate with increased risk of developing depression. Brooks-Gunn and Warren (1989) reported a significant relationship between rising estradiol levels and self-reports of negative mood in adolescent girls.

Differences in ways of coping with dysphoric mood also may account for difference in clinical presentation of boys and girls. Adolescent girls may find the expression of depressed affect more acceptable. According to Peterson et al. (1991), there is a significant negative relationship between masculinity and depression.

Adolescent boys may use the defenses of disavowal and denial to avoid affects that they consider unacceptable. Adolescent boys also engage in increased risk-taking behavior and increased use of alcohol and drugs to manage negative affects. In a survey of high school seniors, Johnson and O'Malley (1986) found that heavy substance users were more likely to report using alcohol to cope with unpleasant affect. McKay et al. (1992) also found adolescent psychiatric patients used alcohol and drugs to manage painful affective states. When aggressive, oppositional behavior has already manifested itself in childhood, it often intensifies during early adolescence. Increasing affective instability combines with an increase in sexual and aggressive drives and larger size to create an increased potential for violent acting-out behavior, as illustrated by the following case example.

At age 10 Joe had a history of fighting in school and disobeying family rules; at age 12 he had begun to drink alcohol with his friends and was suspended from school for fighting. At age 14 he was charged with assault and selling drugs. At age 15, Joe was placed in an alternative school program where he developed in interest in carpentry through a supportive relationship with a counselor. Family therapy lead to an improved relationship with his parents. At age 18 Joe has a steady girlfriend and is in his senior year at a vocational high school. He looks back on his earlier teenage years with some relief that he was able to "turn the corner in time."

Summary

Affective development is one of many developmental lines proceeding from childhood through adolescence and into adulthood. Growing capacities to express affect and understand its manifestations in others affect how the adolescent copes with biological, social, and psychological change. Increasingly complex affective responses provide a richer mode of communication with friends and family and lead to a more mature sense of self.

Many adolescents have a positive response to the changes in affective intensity and variety that they experience. For others, inability to cope with painful affects is an important component of their psychopathology. Early adolescence is a time of affective instability brought on by the physiologic changes of puberty and a quantum leap in cognitive ability. During middle adolescence affects again become more manageable. For the older adolescent and young adult, further development within the realm of affect may take place if the individual possesses the capacity for abstract thinking and the inclination for introspection.

REFERENCES

Blos, P. (1962). *On adolescence.* New York: Free Press.

Brooks-Gunn, J., & Warren, M. (1989). Biological and social contributions to negative affect in young adolescent girls. *Child Development, 60,* 40–55.

Brown, D. (1993). Affective development, psychopathology, and adaptation, in S. L. Ablon. *Human feelings: Explorations in affect development and meaning* (pp. 5–66). Hillsdale, NJ: Analytic Press.

Cantor, M. P., & Glucksman, M. L. (1983). *Affect: psychoanalytic theory and practice.* New York: John Wiley & Sons.

Denham, S. A., McKinley, M., Couchoud, E. A., & Holt, R. (1990). Emotional and behavioral predictors of preschool peer ratings. *Child Development, 61,* 1145–1152.

Drellich, M. G. (1983). Psychoanalytic Theories of Affect. In M. P. Cantor & M. L. Glucksman (Eds.), *Affect: Psychoanalytic Theory and Practice* (pp. 11–23). New York: John Wiley & Sons.

Freud, A. (1958) Adolescence. *Psychoanalytic Study of the Child, 13,* 255–276.

Freud, S. (1963). Three essays on the theory of sexuality. In *Standard edition of the complete psychological works of Sigmund Freud,* ed. J. Strachey (Vol. 7). London: Hogarth Press. (Originally published 1905.)

Freud, S. (1963). Introductory lectures on Psychoanalysis. In *Standard Edition of the complete psychological works of Sigmund Freud,* ed. J. Strachey (Vols. 15 & 16). London: Hogarth Press. (Originally published, 1929.)

Golombeck, H., & Kutcher, S. (1990). Adolescence: Psychopathology, normality, and creativity. *Psychiatric Clinics of North America, 13,* 443–454.

Golombeck, H., Martin, P., Stein, B., Korenblum, M. (1986). A study of disturbed and non-disturbed adolescents: The Toronto Adolescent Longitudinal Study. *Canadian Journal of Psychiatry, 31,* 532–535.

Greene, A. L. (1990). Patterns of affectivity in the transition to adolescence. *Journal of Experimental Child Psychology, 50,* 340–356.

Izard, C. (1991). *The psychology of emotion.* New York: Plenum Press.

Johnson, L., & O'Malley, P. (1986). Why do the nation's students use drugs and alcohol? Self-reported reasons from nine national surveys. *Journal of Drug Issues, 16* (1), 29–66.

Kohut, H. (1971). *The analysis of the self.* New York: International Universities Press.

Kohut, H. (1977). *The restoration of the self.* New York: International Universities Press.

Kohut, H. (1987). *The Kohut seminars on self psychology and psychopathology with adolescents and young adults,* Ed. M. Elson. New York: Analytic Press.

Lane, R. D., & Schwartz, G. E. (1987). Levels of emotional awareness. *American Journal of Psychiatry, 144,* 133–143.

Larson, R., & Lampman-Petraitis, C. (1989). Daily emotional states as reported by children and adolescents. *Child Development, 60,* 1250–1260.

Marton, P., Golombeck, H. Stein, B., & Korenblum, M. (1987). Behavior disturbance and changes in personality dysfunction from early to middle adolescence. *Adolescent Psychiatry, 14,* 394–416.

McKay, J., Murphy, R., Maisto, S., & Rivinus, T. (1992). Characteristics of adolescent psychiatric patients who engage in problematic behavior while intoxicated. *Journal of the American Academy of Child and Adolescent Psychiatry, 31,* 1031–1040.

Offer, D. (1969). *The psychological world of the teenager.* New York: Basic Books.

Offer, D. (1986). Adolescent development: A normative perspective. *American Psychiatric Association Annual Review, 5,* 404–419, Washington, DC: American Psychiatric Press.

Offer, D., Ostrov, E., Howard, K., & Atkins, R. (1990). Normality and adolescence. *Psychiatric Clinics of North America, 13,* 377–388.

Offer, D., & Schonert-Reichl, K. (1992). Debunking the myths of adolescence: Findings from recent research. *Journal of the American Academy of Child and Adolescent Psychiatry, 31,* 1003–1011.

Offord D. R., Boyle M. H., Szatmari P., Rae-Grant N. I., Links P. S., Cadman D. T., Byles J. A., Crawford J. W., Munroe Blum, H., Byrne, C., Thomas H., & Woodward C. A. (1987). Ontario Child Health Study, II: Six-month prevalence of disorder and rates of service utilization. *Archives of General Psychiatry, 44,* 832–836.

Othmer, E., & Othmer, S. C. (1994). *The clinical interview using DSM-IV, Vol. 1: Fundamentals.* Washington, DC: American Psychiatric Press.

Peterson, A. C., Sarigiani, P., & Kennedy, R. (1991). Adolescent depression: Why more girls? The emergence of depressive symptoms during adolescence [Special Issue]. *Journal of Youth and Adolescence, 20,* 247–271.

Schave, D., & Schave, B. (1989). *Early adolescence and the search for self.* New York: Praeger.

Stein, B., Golombeck, H., Marton, P., & Korenblum, M. (1987). Personality functioning and change in clinical presentation from early to middle adolescence. *Adolescent Psychiatry, 14,* 378–393.

Velez, C., Johnson, J., & Cohen, P. (1989). A longitudinal analysis of selected risk factors for childhood psychopathology, *Journal of the American Academy of Child Psychiatry, 28,* 861–864.

Yorke, C., Balock, T., Cohen, P., Davids, J., Gaushon, A., McCutcheon, M., McCutcheon, R. A., McLean, D., Miller, J., & Szydlo, J. (1990). The development of the sense of shame. *Psychoanalytic Study of the Child, 45,* 327–409.

8 / The Upsurge of Erotic and Aggressive Urges at Puberty

Charles Keith

Puberty and the onset of early adolescence are among the most sudden and dramatic developmental watersheds of the human life cycle (Tobin-Richards, Boxer, & Petersen, 1983). Pubertal cognitive and bodily changes, described elsewhere in this volume, are certainly striking, but it is the new sexual and aggressive urges that provide the electrifying fuel which changes the latency-age child into a suddenly restless, searching youth. Of course, these urges are not new; there has already been a complicated developmental course since early infancy involving the control and sublimation of sexual and aggressive impulses (Blos, 1963). However, the easily observable quantitative and qualitative upsurge of these pubertal impulses put the previous psychic structure "to the test" (A. Freud, 1958). The focus of this chapter is on these surging erotic and aggressive urges. The reader must keep in mind that these impulses never appear outside of the context of personality structure that is constantly modifying, controlling, and sublimating the impulses and the resulting guilt and anxiety stirred up by their latent and/or overt expression. In a similar vein, these urges are always connected with and directed toward human and/or nonhuman objects. This upsurge of drives fundamentally springs from the biological, hormonal changes of puberty. Thus, this is a period in life when the edges of the mind-body gap come close together.

External Manifestations of the Pubertal Urges

What are some of the observable, external manifestations of these up-swelling urges? To observe these, one need but sit in a fifth- or sixth-grade classroom. One can see the unmistakable signs of increased bodily squirming, flirtatious looks at the opposite sex, increased awareness and preoccupation with how one looks resulting in preening and showing off, all of which are accompanied by excited giggles and twitters. Those youths not yet in puberty still appear like latency children, while those entering puberty obviously no longer appear childlike. Increased aggressive urges manifest themselves through poking, shoving, motor restlessness, and displays of strength, all of which are more obvious in boys. These signs of increased drive activity peak during the seventh and eighth grades (around ages 13 to 14) with some settling down and calming observable in the high school years.

All of these signs of puberty are exacerbated when class is over and the youths surge into the hallways. Boys and girls pair up, hold hands, and kiss behind locker doors while others look on with embarrassed fascination. The shoving and playful jabbing in the classroom are now accompanied in the hallway by body slams and loud shouting. Banging of bathroom doors adds exclamation points to this din of sexual and aggressive urges. Junior high and middle school teachers often take special pride in managing, teaching, and surviving in this early adolescent environment in contrast to the quieter pace in grade school and senior high school.

Internal Psychological Processes

The internal psychological processes accompanying these easily observable external manifestations of drive upsurge are, of course, more difficult to observe and often require the use of inferential data. Most clinicians agree that the erotic and aggressive urges appear to be the fundamental fuel that energizes the central developmental task of early adolescence, that is, the embarking on the final separation-individuation of the youth from the childhood dependency ties with parental caregivers. The search for new sexual objects both in fantasy and reality turn the adolescent away from the childhood, dependent sexual ties on parents. It is likely that the new cognitive and abstractive abilities appearing at puberty play a role in expanding the youth's object-seeking horizons. However, the specific interactions between these formal intellectual operations and the movement from parental dependency to the search for new objects remains unclear.

Pubertal youth may fall in love with older persons, such as a school teacher, as a way-station between the old ties with the parent and same-age sexual relationships (Goldings, 1979). Poster music stars become exciting safe "distant" sexual objects. This is most striking in girls, who often plaster every inch of bedroom walls with portraits of teenage male rock stars. Boys may turn to sexually explicit photos, particularly when masturbating. One purpose of these photos is to divert the youth's attention away from sexual urges toward immediate female family members. The upsurge in pubertal drives brings with them old incestuous temptations, which often break through into consciousness in normal adolescence. These incestuous urges are manifested as peeking at and occasionally sexually touching siblings, exhibitionistic activities with siblings, and looking through Mother's closet or underwear, which is a common exciting yet guilt-ridden activity of boys.

Masturbation

The most important genital sexual activity of early adolescence is masturbation. This subject is still shrouded in considerable mystery and guilt as our society concerns itself with feared heterosexual activity on the part of early adolescents.

During the pubertal years, male masturbation to the point of ejaculation probably occurs in over 90% of youths and is almost always accompanied by varying degrees of guilt. Masturbating in the presence of other boys occurs frequently as a means to gain reassurance about the safety and adequacy of one's sexuality and as a protection against emerging incestuous fantasies. These mutual masturbatory activities often result in lingering doubts and fears about homosexuality. Pubertal sexual jokes are common, particularly among boys. These jokes often concern the prowess and

large magnitude of the female sexual organs and thus serve at once to express and to reduce sexual anxiety. Absence of masturbation in the boy usually indicates a severe repression of sexual urges and resulting inhibition of sexual activity, which is a danger signal of potential derailment of the adolescent developmental process. The detailed description of genital masturbation in early adolescent girls comes mostly from occasional psychotherapy and psychoanalytic case studies (Clower, 1975). Most observers believe that masturbation in girls is less frequent than in boys and that sexual self-stimulation is more easily displaced onto other areas of the body (Clower, 1975; Kinsey, Pomeroy, Martin, & Gebhard, 1953).

Revision of superego beliefs and the resulting relaxation of moral standards occurring in normal early adolescence permits the gradual incorporation of these sexual urges and activities into the evolving adolescent sexual identity.

Parental Responses to the New Pubertal Urges

Common sense tells us that the normal parent allows the pubertal process to unfold while at the same time maintaining an appropriate protective "holding" environment, a phrase just as applicable to adolescence as to infancy. Definitions of the early adolescent holding environment differ across generations and social class. However, there is a general assumption that the majority of normal parents protect their adolescents from too-early stimulating heterosexual contact through rules such as no "alone" dating until age 16, curfews, and restrictions on the youths' use of the family automobile. Restrictive rules usually are stated more explicitly for girls and laid out more implicitly for boys, consistent with our historical background of granting the male permission to "prowl" while putting restraints on girls. This gender asymmetry is rapidly changing concurrent with the redefinition of sexual and gender roles (Mussen, Conger, Kagan, & Huston, 1984).

A firm position taken by normal parents concerning early adolescent sexual activity often belies the considerable internal parental turmoil. There can be constrained jealousy both in the mother and father as their daughters become more sexually attractive and their sons more sexually assertive (Beiser, 1977). These changes in early adolescence often are occurring in the context of the parents' "aging out" of the usual standards of sexual attractiveness. Normal parents often subtly tease and demean their early adolescent's sexual choices at the same time they are pleased with the adolescent's forward developmental moves. Normal fathers find their pubescent daughters sexually attractive and can have conscious sexual fantasies that are troubling and guilt-provoking. Fathers can then become overly cross and stern in reaction to this sexual stimulation. How to appreciate and show pleasure in their daughters' blossoming sexuality without undue seductiveness or reactive anger is a challenge to fathers (Josselyn, 1974; Ravenscroft, 1974). Another crucial facet of the normal early adolescent parental holding environment is to allow signs of masturbatory activity to go unnoticed and uninterrupted by the parents.

Pubertal upsurge of sexual and aggressive urges and the concomitant forward thrust in adolescent development can proceed normally only if the parents provide sufficient appreciation, acceptance, and the proper amount of control of their sons' and daughters' emerging genital sexuality.

Siblings

It must not be forgotten that siblings are important participants in this early adolescent development of sexual urges. A younger sibling often experiences a sense of loss and jealously as the older adolescent sib moves on to extrafamily sexual objects. The amount of normal sexual attachment between siblings is often underappreciated. Mild depression in a younger sibling is a common accompaniment as an older adolescent youth moves into extrafamily sexual searching.

Homosexual Urges

Normal homosexual urges also increase at puberty and take on an increasingly genital aspect. Sexual urges toward the same-sex parent are as important

in development as are the heterosexual urges toward the opposite-sex parent. The urges are displaced onto same-sex peers in puberty. Twenty to 25% of males stated they reached orgasm in peer homosexual activity during early and middle adolescence (Kinsey, Pomeroy, & Martin, 1948). Two to 3% of girls attest to orgasmic homosexual activity in early adolescence (Kinsey et al., 1953). This unfolding of the homosexual developmental line began in early childhood with exploratory sexual activity, formation of same-sex friendships, and an evolving identification with the same-sex parent (Fraiberg, 1964). Overt manifestations of homosexual impulses include mutual sexual activity such as looking at same-sex genitals and shared masturbatory activities. Nongenital same-sex activities such as hugging, kissing, and hand holding are more common with girls but are often conflictual and dystonic with boys, particularly in our current culture. Homosexual urges at puberty combining with heterosexual impulses, plus the resulting defensive configurations and life experiences, lead to most youth settling on a sexual identity somewhere along the homosexual-heterosexual continuum in late adolescence.

Conclusion

Little current systematic epidemiological or anthropological data exists concerning these important, normal developmental issues at puberty. Emerging conservative trends in our country make Kinsey-like epidemiological studies in early adolescence increasingly difficult to carry out. The conclusions described herein arise primarily from older epidemiological studies from the 1950s and 1960s, pooling of clinical case material, self-revelatory artistic and literary contributions, and commonsense observations of parents, teachers, and professionals who work with early adolescents. Current data continue to suggest that the pubertal, biological upsurge of erotic heterosexual and homosexual urges fuel the final separation-individuation from the caregiving parents. These sensuous events enable youths to experience heightened genital sexual excitation; this in turn results in their seeking out of nonincestuous sexual relationships. This sequence sets the stage for eventual crystallization of sexual identity in late adolescence. An insufficient physiological puberty, excessive use of repressive and inhibitory defenses or a breakdown of defensive structure, and a lack of appropriate parental facilitation can either singly or in combination derail early adolescent development leading to the psychopathological syndromes of adolescence described elsewhere in these volumes.

REFERENCES

Beiser, H. (1977). Sexual factors in antagonism between mothers and daughters. *Medical Aspects of Human Sexuality 11*(4), 32–47.

Blos, Peter (1963). *On adolescence.* New York: Free Press.

Clower, V. L. (1975). Significance of masturbation in female sexual development and function. In I. Marcus & J. J. Francis (Eds.), *Masturbation from infancy to senescence* (pp. 107–143). New York: International Universities Press.

Fraiberg, S. (1964). Homosexual conflicts. In S. Lorand & H. Schneer (Eds.), *Adolescents* (pp. 78–112). New York: Harper & Row.

Freud, A. (1958). Adolescence. *Psychoanalytic Study of the Child, 14,* 255–278.

Goldings, H. J. (1979). Development from ten to thirteen years. In J. D. Noshpitz (Ed.), *Basic handbook of child psychiatry* (Vol. 1, pp. 199–205). New York: Basic Books.

Josselyn, I. (1974). Adolescence. In S. Arieti (Ed.), *American handbook of psychiatry* (2nd ed., Vol. 1, pp. 382–398). New York: Basic Books.

Kinsey, A. C., Pomeroy, W. B., & Martin, C. E. (1948). *Sexual behavior in the human male.* Philadelphia: W. B. Saunders.

Kinsey, A. C., Pomeroy, W. B., Martin, C. E., & Gebhard, P. H. (1953). *Sexual behavior in the human female.* Philadelphia: W. B. Saunders.

Mussen, P. H., Conger, J. J., Kagan, J., & Huston, A. C. (Eds.). (1984). Adolescence: Physical changes, mental growth and socialization. In *Child development and personality* (6th ed., pp. 460–508). New York: Harper & Row.

Ravenscroft, K. (1974). Normal family regression at adolescence. *American Journal of Psychiatry, 131* (1), 31–35.

Tobin-Richards, M. H., Boxer, A. M., & Petersen, A. C. (1983). The psychological significance of pubertal change—Sex differences in perceptions of self during early adolescence. In J. Brooks-Gunn and A. C. Petersen (Eds.), *Girls at puberty* (pp. 127–154). New York: Plenum Press.

9 / Cognitive Development in Adolescence

Bruno J. Anthony

A widely accepted characteristic of cognitive development is that qualitative shifts in thinking occur during three transitional phases: infancy to early childhood, early childhood to the school years, and late childhood to adolescence. The notion that adolescence represents the end point of this process has been overemphasized, resulting in unrealistic expectations of competence and ill-advised educational practices. Moreover, this notion is incompatible with the extensive variation in cognitive competence evident even in adulthood and neglects huge amounts of variation within the adolescent and adult period that can be attributed to individual, social, and cultural influences. There is increasing evidence that the development of a more sophisticated and integrated cognitive system is a much more continuous process. The acquisition of knowledge seems less the result of the development of basic principles applied to broad areas than shifts in the accessibility of specific domains of knowledge as a function of experience.

Oddly, the belief that cognitive maturity is largely achieved by adolescence has had little effect on how teenagers are treated. Significant changes in thinking and their impact on functioning are often largely ignored by parents, educators, and policy makers, resulting in overprotective, stifling, and inappropriate actions. Recent attention to the development of specific areas of cognition and the influences on this development has brought about advances in the understanding of adolescent thought and behavior.

This chapter covers the major approaches to understanding cognitive development during adolescence and then, in the context of these different theories, reviews the changes in thinking occurring during this period. A section follows examining significant factors affecting knowledge acquisition and the development of cognitive structures. The final section covers implications of the changes in thinking for adaptive adolescent functioning in the areas of critical thinking, decision making, and social cognition.

Theoretical Approaches

Understanding of the changes occurring in thinking during adolescence has moved away from an approach stressing a universal sequence of stages toward a more differentiated view. Influences of process-oriented and contextualist theories have focused attention on the unevenness of cognitive performance, stressing domain-specific development resulting in part from particular experience.

STAGE/STRUCTURAL THEORIES

The most influential theory of cognitive development remains Piaget's (Inhelder & Piaget, 1958) *stage theory,* which posits an invariable sequence of changes in underlying logico-mathematical structures, resulting from interaction of the individual with the physical and social world. Briefly, different stages have a global or unified character derived from an organization of cognitive actions. This *structure d'ensemble* causes information to be processed and problems to be solved according to a general set of strategies across all domains. In this scheme, adolescent thinking is characterized by the end point of the developmental sequence—*formal operational logic,* based on 16 binary operations of propositional logic. Unlike previous stages in which cognitive operations remain centered on concrete and immediate objects and events, formal operational thought involves symbolic (second-degree) functions that operate on the product of concrete (first-order) functions and that manipulate abstract propositions. The "formal" nature of formal operations refers to the ability to compare propositions—abstract logical relations—rather than empirical phenomena.

Piaget (Piaget & Inhelder, 1969) characterizes "formal" problem solving as "hypothetico-deductive" as opposed to "empirico-inductive." The ability to hypothesize about explanations in a purely conceptual way, not tied to the physical reality, allows all possible solutions to a problem or all possible linkages between objects to be entertained and hypotheses formed concerning the likelihood of each linkage. Adolescents then can deduce what would occur given the various alternatives and then finally test the deduction by comparing it with what really occurs. In practice, indications of preference beginning with "all other things being equal" reflect the systematic variation of a single aspect of various situations to determine its significance.

Several questions have been raised concerning universal stage theories (Brainerd, 1993; Broughton, 1984; Sugarman, 1987). First, relatively abrupt, qualitative change in a range of cognitive processes seems less the case than more gradual, domain-specific changes. In response to these observations, Fischer and colleagues (Fischer, 1980; Fischer, Kenney, & Pipp, 1990) have built on the stage notion and propose that several factors preclude the observation of discontinuities or sudden developmental spurts in performance. In their *skill theory*, they suggest that true cognitive developmental levels will be evident only under specific environmental conditions that optimize performance. In particular, they propose that two circumstances are necessary to build a new skill: a supportive environment and the opportunity to practice the skill. Environmental support includes providing examples of the operation of the mature skill and the opportunity to use the skill. The skill approach accounts for other related problems with stage theory: the large variation in task performance across individuals and low intertask correlations.

A second problem area for stage theory has been the difficulty in identifying underlying changes in logic as the source of developmental changes in thinking. Concurrent changes in other functions may underlie performance differences across age. In Case's (1984) neo-Piagetian stage theory, growth in memory capacity and efficiency allows for transitions in cognitive function. Stage-like changes result from the integration of previously separate "control structures," plans for solving problems that involve representations of the situation, objectives, and strategies. This integration is assumed to occur in short-term or *working* memory and is constrained by the amount of space available. Over development, the amount of working memory increases either as a result of

maturation or more efficient execution of cognitive operations. Others suggest that the ability to reason effectively is related to increases in specific *knowledge and task familiarity* rather than to universal changes in logical structures (Sternberg, 1984). As a result, the content and rate of development are highly dependent on specific experiences and opportunities to learn. Truly logical thought, independent of such specific contexts, has been difficult to document in adolescents and even adults.

PROCESS THEORY

A second explanation of growth in cognitive functioning emphasizes the development of separable processes rather than general logical structures. Unlike stage theorists, these *process-oriented* approaches emphasize the independence of skill across domains. For instance, Keil (1984) proposes a biological view of "constrained faculties" in which humans are seen as developing "specialized organs" that deal with different aspects of the physical world. Process views emerged in concert with the development of computers and gradually gained in influence during the 1960s and 1970s as an approach to understanding normal human cognition.

A central construct in the information-processing approach to cognition is the notion of limited processing resources (Kahneman, 1973; Shiffrin & Schneider, 1977). Mental activities are divided into those that are completed slowly in a serial fashion and demand attention of conscious effort and those that occur quickly and automatically in parallel (Shiffrin & Dumais, 1981). Automatic processes are critical to efficient cognitive processing since the amount of attention-demanding activity that can occur is severely limited. Developmental change has been proposed to result from either an increase in the automatization of cognitive work or an increase in the extent of processing resources. Instance theory (Logan, 1988) is one variant of the automatization position. Increased efficiency is obtained through the shift from performance based on algorithms, slow, step-by-step routines, to relatively rapid, direct retrieval of appropriate responses. Repeated task performance leads to increased likelihood that such direct, automatic processes will take place. This specific-skills view assumes that adolescents and adults are more likely to have extensive task-relevant experience than younger children and therefore more ready access to rapid retrieval processes. Critics of the process approach cite a lack of specificity in the changes that occur in critical mechanisms (e.g., automatization, increased processing capacity) and their method of operation (Miller, 1989).

Neuropsychological investigations also employ a process view. This field began as a means of localizing neural injury but, as more sophisticated techniques emerged, now involves the study of brain-behavior relationships with special emphasis on deficits in cognitive functions. Developmental theories stress the interaction of multiple brain systems that mature in a hierarchical fashion (Anthony & Friedman, 1991; Goldman-Rakic, 1987; Luria, 1980). Neuropsychological investigations during adolescence have concentrated on processes associated with the frontal lobes. These processes have been termed executive functions and comprise goal-directed behaviors such as planning, organization, and impulse control. It was thought that children under 12 years showed little evidence of executive functions, performing in a manner similar to adults with frontal lobe damage (Luria, 1980; Stuss & Benson, 1984). However, studies using developmentally appropriate measures have documented a more gradual growth of skills, beginning in early childhood, with more complex and integrated sequencing and planning skills emerging in adolescence (Becker, Isaac, & Hynd, 1987; Passler, Isaac, & Hynd, 1985).

CONTEXT THEORIES

Stage and process theories stress development of internal cognitive structures that, through a process such as equilibration or automatization, come to represent external reality in a more differentiated manner. In contrast, the *contextualist* and *cognitive socialization* approaches emphasize the importance of environmental influences in determining the nature of thinking. Vygotsky (1978) pioneered the notion that cognitive development is unique to a certain cultural milieu, mediated by specific tools (technical and psychological) and demands of the environment. In particular, he stressed the internalization of speech in structuring and guiding thought. During development, the overt, "egocentric" speech that guides thought

and behavior in early childhood converts to inner speech and finally, in adolescence and adulthood, to internalized cognitive processes. The active, guiding nature of inner speech is the cornerstone of cognitive-behavioral therapy (Meichenbaum, 1977). Contextualists stress the importance of broad cultural and social differences but also particular social interactions. In adolescence, cognitive development is more dependent on such environmental influences, particularly peer and school factors, than in earlier years.

PSYCHOMETRIC THEORIES

Measurement of individual differences represents the earliest approach to adolescent cognition and continues to have the greatest practical impact, determining educational and career paths (Phillips, Anthony, & Tepper, 1992). Although based on the notion that components of intelligence grow in quantity with age, psychometric models tend not to be concerned with determining qualitative developmental changes. The standardized instruments employed have good reliability and replicability; however, they are complex, making it difficult to determine what cognitive constructs they reflect. Moreover, they are not designed to examine skills that may be critical for adaptation during the adolescent years, such as higher-order or critical thinking.

Description of Adolescent Thought

Even though aspects of logic-based stage theory have been questioned, the emphasis on adolescence as a transitional period in cognitive development remains justifiable given the systematic differences in performance across a range of mental functions. This section examines adolescent thinking in those areas most relevant to adaptive functioning. We begin with the changes in brain development.

BRAIN DEVELOPMENT

Major neuroanatomic changes in the brain (neuron and axon growth) are largely over by early infancy, and the pace of dendritic branching and synaptogenesis falls to adult levels at age 7 years (Goldman-Rakic, 1987; Huttenlocher, 1979). However, measurement of a variety of brain growth indices suggest that significant changes continue to occur into adolescence (Chugani, Phelps, & Mazziotta, 1987; Epstein, 1974; Thatcher, Walker, & Giudice, 1987) and appear linked to general cognitive advances (Epstein & Toepfer, 1978; Fisher, 1987). Changes in myelination at both cortical and subcortical levels (Yakovlev & Lecours, 1967) as well as more subtle synaptogenesis and regional pruning in specific cortical areas occur well into adulthood. Greenough (Greenough, Black, & Wallace, 1987) believes that the later neuronal changes occur rapidly and are "experience-dependent," triggered by specific environmental events, as opposed to "experience-expectant" synapse formation, which is activated early in development by events common to all species members (such as pattern perception).

REASONING

It is generally accepted that two broad areas of reasoning skills begin to develop in late childhood and early adolescence: those promoting systematic deductive reasoning (Keating, 1980; Ward & Overton, 1990) and those involved in judging hypotheses against available information. Younger children tend to derive possible outcomes of events only as generalizations from the current situation—an inductive analysis of observed, concrete relations. Beginning at around age 10 years, the ability to reason deductively develops in a well-defined manner. The current situation is seen as only one possibility of a set that can be generated a priori through hypothetical transformations of all permutations of elements of the situation. For instance, by age 13, 80 to 90% of adolescents can display the ability to reason in this combinatorial way to some extent in certain situations (Byrnes & Overton, 1988). However, evidence suggests that logical strategies are not particularly well entenched or available even in adults (Bartsch, 1993).

The second aspect of this formal reasoning process involves evaluating the set of possible real-world outcomes that would confirm or negate each hypothesis. In Piaget's view, the adolescent becomes capable of varying factors or envisaging the various models that might explain a phenomenon

and checking them through actual experimentation. However, evidence for consistent use of the hypothesis-generating/evaluation process in adolescents and even adults is sparse. Rather, there is a strong tendency to evaluate by verifying instead of falsifying; evidence is ignored if it goes against a held theory and given inordinate weight if it is supportive. There is often a strong belief that confirming a prediction means that it is true. Thus, although late adolescents can demonstrate a high level of competence in deductive analysis, it is not manifested in all contexts. Various factors have been found to promote sophisticated reasoning. In particular, material that is familiar to the individual (Griggs & Cox, 1983; Overton, Ward, Noveck, Black, & O'Brien, 1987) or meaningful (Ward & Overton, 1990) promotes accurate deductive reasoning in older adolescents.

MEMORY

Most research on memory development has dealt with the extremes of the age continuum, leaving the impression that memory skills have reached a relatively stable, asymptotic level by adolescence. This lack of emphasis is particularly surprising given that associative and organizational strategies, skills key to efficient remembering, show rapid development during adolescence. However, more recent work suggests that memory efficiency continues to improve during the period of adolescence (Ryan, 1990). The reasons for this improvement appear to result from both changes in the encoding of information in short-term memory and in the representation of knowledge in long-term store.

Short-term or working memory (Baddely, 1986) refers to a limited-capacity system where information is briefly stored and manipulated prior to decay or more permanent storage in long-term memory. The amount of information able to be retained in short-term memory increases throughout adolescence. For example, Ryan asked adolescents (ages 12 to 19) to remember a string of digits, a common test of short-term memory, and, in another task, a list of highly imagable words after completion of a brief (5 to 30 second) distraction task (counting backward by threes). Within the adolescent period, the number of digits recalled increased with age. Also, older adolescents recalled more words than younger adolescents, most clearly at the longest retention interval. Results from these and other studies suggest that the capacity of short-term memory increases substantially during the adolescent years through more efficient encoding of information, memorial strategies (rehearsal, grouping), and attention allocation. These developments are discussed in a later section.

Mature mechanisms of retrieval from long-term store seem well established quite early; however, the connectedness and complexity of knowledge structures or semantic networks develop rapidly in adolescence (Chi & Koeske, 1983). As a result, older children and adolescents can access information from memory with less mental effort. For instance, Bjorkland and Buchanan (1989) showed that, compared to fourth graders, seventh graders remembered more words from a particular category; however, the advantage was greater for words less typical of a category (such as ties or belts for clothing) than for highly typical words (pants or shirts for clothing). The dramatic improvement in performance on memory tasks during adolescence (Beuhring & Kee, 1987) also appears due to an improvement in the use of memorial strategies, particularly elaboration. Adolescents are more likely to create a relationship between to-be-remembered items in order to facilitate their storage in memory.

REGULATION

One of the most important developments in adolescence concerns the growth of regulatory mechanisms to control, monitor, and understand cognitive activity. Several concepts fall under this topic.

Plans and Strategies: Adolescents show more strategic and efficient organization of cognitive activity and manipulation of information. In contrast to younger children, they tend to impose their own structure on a task situation rather than decipher the structure that is already there. Adolescents are more likely to plan problem-solving steps with an eye to the variety of options and the consequences of a particular path. *Strategies* refer to goal-directed mental operations employed to facilitate task performance. Current research suggests that younger children do use strategies, without direct training. However, their use tends to be more restricted. That is, with age, children

become less context dependent, being able to apply strategies over a broader array of stimuli and situations (Bjorkland & Muir, 1988; Ornstein & Naus, 1985). Older children are more apt to begin tasks with a clear strategy, to acquire a strategy if they do not use one initially, and to demonstrate greater benefits of training with the strategy. Of equal importance, children begin to use more complex strategies, such as the sophisticated associative memory strategies.

Attention: The allocation of *attention* becomes more task-driven in the adolescent years. Concurrent developments in cognitive psychology, neuropsychology, and neuroanatomy point to a multi-component view of attention (Mirsky, Anthony, Duncan, Ahearn, & Kellam, 1991; Posner & Peterson, 1990). This work suggests the existence of several linked attentive functions including the ability to focus in the face of distraction, sustain that focus over time, shift focus in an adaptive fashion, and exert attention to memorial activities. These functions seem to mature at different rates; however, adolescence is marked by a greater flexibility in the deployment of these attention functions. That is, the direction and maintenance of attentive focus becomes less determined by salient features of the environment and more task oriented. For instance, the ability to allocate attention in response to the level of mastery of a task increases. Older high school and college students shift attention more quickly to new sections once they master material than younger individuals (Brown, Bransford, Ferrara, & Campione, 1983).

Metacognition: Metacognition refers to knowledge of knowing and thinking that allows us to monitor mental activity for the adequacy of its operation (Brown et al., 1983; Flavell & Wellman, 1977). This concept has received an enormous amount of attention over the last decade and is particularly relevant to adolescence since these skills are assumed to be late-occurring. Within a given situation, metacognitive knowledge involves knowing about persons, tasks, and strategies (Flavell, 1985).

Adolescents come to understand that cognitive functions differ in efficiency within a person ("I have a much harder time with math than English") and between persons (Jane understands how to read maps better than John) but also that there are universal similarities (short-term memory sometimes fails). Knowledge about what information is involved in various tasks strongly affects performance. Task knowledge grows substantially in late childhood and adolescence. For instance, teenagers know that recognizing recently learned material is easier than trying to recall it, particularly if the material is unfamiliar. Finally, knowledge about strategies involves what tactics are likely to be successful in a certain situation and how well they are working. This monitoring aspect of performance is particularly crucial, allowing for adaptive alterations to cognitive operations.

Although metacognitive skills are conceived of as general procedures, they have been studied most intensively in the area of memory, where the awareness of one's own memory processes has been shown to have a major influence on the ability to maintain, store, and recall information. Aspects of *metamemory* include monitoring what is actually stored in memory, the capacity of one's memory, and what factors inhibit or facilitate recall. Although individual aspects of metamemory appear in place by middle childhood, the impact of combinations of these memory skills is not recognized until adolescence. For instance, older adolescents are more likely to report that they used a certain strategy in a task and to recognize how efficient it was (Beuhring & Kee, 1987; Waters, 1982). Moreover, the extent of metamemory knowledge influences the use of strategies, which has implications for interventions to improve memory. The more understanding adolescents have of their memory skills, the task demands, and the usefulness of particular strategies, the more likely it is that the strategies will be used.

EFFICIENCY

Results from studies using a variety of cognitive tasks show that there is a substantial improvement in the speed of response throughout childhood and adolescence, reaching a peak in young adulthood (Kail, 1991a). However, the developmental pattern is exponential; decreases in processing time are less precipitous in adolescence (Kail, 1991b). These developmental improvements in response speed appear to result from changes in processing resources and in the time to carry out basic cognitive operations rather than changes in logical structures (Kail, 1991a). Important changes in cognitive functioning may be attributable, in part, to alterations in the speed of information processing. For instance, part of the reason why

a young adolescent may not use a certain memory strategy may be because the information is presented at too fast a rate.

CONTENT

One reason why adolescent thought might seem qualitatively different from that of younger children is that adolescents have accumulated much more organized and elaborated knowledge, sometimes termed expertise, in many more domains. Having expertise can improve cognitive functioning, by allowing one to solve problems more by memory processes—well-learned, efficient responses to particular situations—than by complex reasoning processes. Adolescents might look more like younger children if operating in a domain where they had little knowledge. How much of cognitive development can be accounted for by the acquisition of domain-specific knowledge is a hotly debated issue in developmental research (Bjorkland, 1987; Ornstein & Naus, 1985).

Factors Influencing Cognitive Development

Different theories of cognitive development vary in their emphasis on social, cultural, and individual effects on thinking. However, no approach denies that these factors in part determine the nature of information to which children are exposed, creating the specific funds of knowledge, and the use of particular cognitive skills. Such influences are particularly salient during adolescence, when change occurs in every aspect of individual and social life. Cognitive skills of late childhood are achieved by almost all individuals, except for those with major genetic or environmental perturbations; however, this is not the case for higher-level thinking skills that develop in adolescence. The development of these latter skills are more crucially dependent on noncognitive factors.

GENDER

Some 20 years ago, Maccoby and Jacklin (1974) carried out a comprehensive review of gender differences in cognitive development and reported significant superiority for males in verbal, spatial, and quantitative abilities. More recent meta-analytic work (Hyde & Linn, 1988) has shown that male-female differences have declined rapidly over time in each of these areas. Gender differences in adolescence for verbal abilities are now negligible (Feingold, 1988); however, differences in spatial and quantitative ability continue to be observed and still generate the greatest amount of research because they are often hypothesized to underlie the reduced female presence in science and mathematics.

Early work seemed to point to early adolescence as the time when gender differences emerge; pubertal influences on the brain were assumed to result in alterations in cognitive processes (Carey & Diamond, 1980; Merola & Liederman, 1985). Waber (1976, 1977) suggested that the earlier pubertal maturation in girls curtailed the process of hemispheric lateralization leading to poorer spatial skills but better verbal skills. However, recent negative findings have called into question the relation of pubertal timing and spatial ability (Newcombe & Dubas, 1992) and suggest that male-female differences occur much earlier than adolescence (Linn & Peterson, 1985). Moreover, the differences are not widespread but limited to certain aspects of spatial processing (Gilger & Ho, 1989).

Scores by children and young adolescents on national aptitude tests of quantitative skills continue to indicate a significant superiority for teenage males on the math portion of the Scholastic Aptitude Test (SAT). There is some indication that females are better at computation, while males excel in more complex and applied areas (reasoning, estimation). The SAT differences appear to reflect, in part, less preparation by females; there continues to be reduced enrollment of females in higher mathematics and science courses during high school. Hill and Lynch (1983) suggest that, during adolescence, expectations for conformity to sex-role stereotypes increases. Thus, traditionally male careers emphasize spatial and mathematic skills, leading to familial and peer pressure to succeed in these areas. Social pressure on females emphasizes interpersonal skills. In this vein, the possession of intellectual characteristics often stereotyped as masculine (striving, high standards for self, assertiveness, persistence) predict performance on various spatial tasks both concurrently

and over the adolescent period (Newcombe & Dubas, 1992; Ozer, 1987).

CULTURAL AND SOCIAL FACTORS

Aspects of adolescents' culture may influence which cognitive skills and strategies are valued and thus which are practiced. The mass media play a very important role in teenagers' lives, determining knowledge base, attitudes, and behavior. For example, the present culture, particularly television, emphasizes the presentation of information in ways that do not support reflective and reasoned thinking (Keating, 1990). Material is presented at a rapid pace, with little regard for accuracy, and at an emotional rather than a cognitive level.

Differences between cultural groups in academic performance have been documented; however, attributing differences to variations in basic cognitive skills is very difficult without specifying how such skills may be assessed independent of experience and knowledge. Moreover, cognitive skills that are essential to success in one culture may be less important in another. For instance, minority youths often reject academic achievement in others as "acting white" (Fordham & Oghu, 1986). Also, social interactions that affect self-confidence, expectations for achievement, and a sense of purpose undoubtedly influence the development of cognitive skills. Teenagers with satisfying and supportive peer relations place more value on what they learn and achieve at a higher level.

INDIVIDUAL FACTORS

Aspects of the self such as interest, motivation, and expectations likely have significant effects on the amount of effort and attention paid to activities that promote cognitive advances. The metacognitive beliefs that adolescents hold about their own thinking skills orient them toward pursuing certain goals. If they believe that their skills are a fixed trait, then they become quite discouraged in the face of failure because they view it as a result of their own inadequacies. In contrast to this "helpless" pattern, those who see their skills as malleable, able to be changed through learning experiences, tend to persevere more readily (Henderson & Dweck, 1990). Adolescents with the latter pattern are more likely to possess the intrinsic motivation to tackle new tasks and to feel more self-control and higher self-esteem. The latter characteristics are associated with higher achievement and greater interest in creative tasks. For instance, cross-cultural studies reporting higher levels of achievement in Asian than American children have shown that Asian parents put more emphasis on effort as a means to achievement than American parents, perhaps promoting more feelings of mastery in their children (Stevenson, Lee, & Stigler, 1986)

Implications of Cognitive Changes in Adolescence

Changes in thinking occurring in adolescence have implications for the understanding and promotion of adaptive functioning in three major areas: critical thinking, decision making, and social cognition.

CRITICAL THINKING

Skills in critical thinking, or systematic methods for gaining and evaluating knowledge, are based on the cognitive advances that are associated with adolescence: increases in the ability to reason logically, to maintain and integrate multiple representations of information, to develop hypotheses, to apply strategies, and to monitor outcomes. The coordination of these various skills is difficult, and research indicates that efficient critical thinking is not characteristic of a majority of adolescents or adults. Indeed, the perceived lack of analytic abilities has led to initiatives to inject problem-based learning into curriculums from elementary through graduate school.

Efforts to enhance critical thinking skills, particularly logical competence, have not been particularly successful. Keating (1990) suggests several reasons behind these failures. First, these interventions have tried to teach general analytic skills, in the hope that they could be applied to all knowledge areas. Evidence for such a transfer of skills is weak, however. Interventions to improve critical thinking and the monitoring of one's own cognitive activity are more effective when organized within the context of content-based instruction. As Mandler (1983) observes, "Typically, people think and

solve problems in the context of familiar routines and on the basis of knowledge they have accumulated in those domains" (p. 475). The injection of case-based learning into the medical school curriculum is an example of this trend.

Second, even when analytic skills are taught within the framework of specific domains of knowledge, progress is not achieved unless there is a concurrent communication of the value of such skills. Whether in formal (classroom) or other mentoring or therapeutic settings, the teacher or therapist must convey a commitment to the analytic process in order to pass it on to the adolescent and allow meaningful material to be discussed in depth.

Constraints on learning critical thinking skills also can arise from the individual's goals, motivations, and commitments. Factors that make adolescents value these activities need to be determined and applied to both formal and informal teaching. For instance, identifying the nature of an adolescent's attributions concerning success may inform instructional approaches. Training low-achieving students to attribute failure to a lack of effort has been shown to improve persistence and motivation (Schunk, 1982).

The fit between cognitive changes and classroom environment is poor in junior high school, which increases the risk for poor outcomes. Opportunities for decision making and for the exercise of higher-level cognitive skills are deemphasized at a time when the desire for such activity is increasing (Eccles et al., 1993)

Finally, passive consumption of information impedes the active attention, reflective thinking, and rational decision making, which are vital components of critical thinking. It is clear that watching commercial television represents the model for such passive consumption. Moreover, unless video presentations and computer-assisted learning are used properly, they can fall prey to the same criticism.

DECISION MAKING/RISK TAKING

Current society demands that teenagers make decisions that are critical for their well-being. Experimental examination of decision-making skills indicates a developmental trend in keeping with the advances in reasoning (Mann, Harmoni, & Power, 1989). Compared to children, young adolescents (11 to 12 years) tend to generate more solution options in a problem situation, to examine the situation from more perspectives, to anticipate the consequences better, and to evaluate the reliability of the sources of information more accurately. Older adolescents (14 to 15) do even better.

This apparently sophisticated style of decision making is at odds with the view that adolescence is a time of extreme risk taking. For example, recent surveys have found that, compared to adults, teenagers are far more likely to contract a sexually transmitted disease and to be involved in traffic accidents. Keating (1990) reviews several reasons to account for poor decision making displayed in real-world settings. One popular notion is that adolescents feel invulnerable to the threats of these high-risk behaviors, focusing only on their benefits. As a result, the evaluation process is distorted and faulty decisions are reached. Elkind (1967) links these feelings of invulnerability to a type of egocentrism developing in adolescence, associated with increases in logical capacities. In his theory, based mainly on clinical experience, teenagers view their thoughts and feelings as unique, highly differentiated from others (the Personal Fable). Elkind argues that this sense of uniqueness is so strong that teenagers feel that misfortune will not happen to them. However, recent comparisons of feelings of invulnerability between adolescents and adults found little difference; both age groups tended to overestimate risks to others and underestimate their own risk (Quadrel, Fischhoff, & Davis, 1993). However, Quadrel et al. (1993) point out that the same amount of perceived invulnerability may put adolescents at more risk because the consequences of decisions may be greater and resources to recover fewer.

Estimates of risk-taking behavior are usually gathered in benign settings (reduced peer and time pressure) with procedures that direct teenagers to consider facets of the process that are often less obvious in real-life situations. Keating (1990) suggests that the stresses in the environment lead to reduced cognitive resources and thus more of a reliance on automatic, and possible more risky, kinds of responses. Adolescents need opportunities to practice decision making under realistic situations.

Finally, adolescent decisions, although counter to the beliefs of parents or society, may reflect a decent decision-making process, involving careful assessment of options, risks, and benefits. For instance, a teenager's decision to experiment with drugs may be a carefully thought out response, influenced by factors such as knowledge of risk and the need to maintain peer relations (Helwig, 1995).

In sum, while it has been assumed that adolescents have deficient skills in decision making or underestimate risk, this does not seem to be the case. Effective interventions need to more carefully evaluate factors that lead adolescents to make a decision. As Keating (1990) warns, "If we dislike the choices adolescents make, perhaps we need to give them better opportunities from which to choose" (p. 244). These type of experiences need to occur in a variety of settings. Families, schools, and communities as well as therapeutic interventions need to provide adolescents with adequate models of decision making, discussions of the process, and opportunities for the exercise and monitoring of such skills.

SOCIAL UNDERSTANDING

The growth in abstract reasoning, attention, and cognitive flexibility during adolescence has a large impact on what has been termed social cognition, inferences, beliefs, or conceptions about the inner psychological processes or attributes of oneself and others. *Person perception,* the understanding of others, is one important aspect of social cognition. In early childhood, perceptions are based mainly on observable characteristics ("Jim is tall, smells bad, and picks his teeth with a pencil"), while in middle childhood they involve specification of stable, internal states ("He has no sense of humor and is very stupid"). The adolescent's emerging understanding of causality and logical reasoning skills results in more subtle and complex inferences about intentions and feelings of others. This is signaled by the increased use of qualifiers ("He is silly sometimes," "She is quite sad") and organizing terms, explicit or implicit explanations of when and why behaviors occur or traits are expressed ("Jim is very shy and modest around strangers, but he is talkative with friends"). The increasingly differentiated nature of adolescent thought allows for an understanding of multiple causal influences in a situation. In addition, adolescents are aware that other views of the person are possible. Adolescents flexibly and planfully select ideas from a wide range of possibilities, and carefully shape them into an organized, integrated portrait of the other. Moreover, they know that this impression in unique and therefore may be inaccurate or different from that of others.

The ability to infer or *take the perspective* of others is another aspect of social cognition that develops in concert with major cognitive changes. The shift to nonegocentric thought, differentiating one's knowledge, viewpoint, and feelings from those of others, is necessary for mature role-taking. This shift is largely completed by adolescence; however, role-taking becomes quite sophisticated with the awareness that social knowledge is reciprocal. This understanding is based in part on the ability to think in a recursive fashion ("I think that you think that I think"). A surprising amount of the ordinary, everyday social thought and communication of adolescents seems to presuppose this knowledge ("I thought you knew that Billy liked Cindy"). Selman (1980) proposed a sequence of stages of social understanding that holds that adolescence is marked by recursive thinking and the ability to observe the "mutuality" of interactions.

Empathy is an instance of perspective taking where one understands and/or experiences another's affective or emotional state. During adolescence, inferences about affect tend to occur more spontaneously, to require fewer cues, and to be more accurate. With increased recursive abilities, adolescents are more aware that emotional states may be linked to others' behavior. Also, empathy becomes more abstract and broad ranging. For instance, with more advanced categorization abilities, an adolescent may empathize with the suffering of children in different parts of the world as well as the pain of a jilted friend. Also, adolescents become more adept at monitoring their own feelings and putting forth an appropriate expression of emotion as well as recognizing that others can deliberately modify the inner nature or the outward expression of their emotions.

Whatever the orientation of the clinician, in order to deal therapeutically with adolescents, it is critical that he or she understand changes in cognitive skills during adolescence and their implications for conceptions of the self and others. However, when treating internalizing (Wilkes, Belsher, Rush, & Frank, 1994) and externalizing (Barkley, Guevremont, Anastopoulos, & Fletcher, 1992; Kendall & Morris, 1991) problems in adoles-

cents, clinicians using cognitive approaches need to take an informed developmental perspective to utilize techniques such as increasing awareness of emotional variability, detecting automatic thoughts, and identifying, evaluating, and altering thoughts and beliefs.

Cognitive advances in adolescence and the coincident growth in social understanding leads away from defining *friendship* in concrete and surface terms ("I like to play with him"), toward seeing friends as sharing similar internal dispositions, thoughts, and feelings (Shantz, 1983). Adolescents' increased awareness of their own traits leads to choosing friends more on the basis of compatibility of personality attributes. Further, growing recognition of the reciprocal nature of social interaction leads to an emphasis on trust as the critical feature of a friendship. Greater skills in directing and sustaining attentive focus also benefit the development of more consistent social interaction (Wilcox, 1993).

Increased differentiation of the *self-concept,* the understanding of one's own attributes and personality, parallels the increased awareness of characteristics of others and also appears related to cognitive developments of adolescence. Flavell (1985) feels that understanding of the self closely follows the growth of metacognitive skills, as adolescents become more able to monitor and comment on their own behaviors and thoughts and thus more aware of similarities and differences with others. Also, hypothetical thinking allows adolescents to make inferences about the stability of their psychological attributes and the likelihood that they may change toward some "ideal" self.

Developments in self-concept and perspective taking, both linked in part to cognitive advances, complement each other in producing more differentiated social understanding. Often, however, this synergy can become unbalanced (Harter, 1990). The process of defining the self, one of the major developmental tasks of the period, is a necessarily disrupting process since there is a constant reintegration of the views of others and a changing hypothetical "ideal" self. The precarious nature of the self-concept can cause some adolescents to insist on absolute autonomy, setting up a me versus them (parent, school) conflict. In addition, the intense introspection and preoccupation with the self may lead to the assumption that others are just as concerned with their behavior and appearance but that no one else can understand their unique experience. Alternatively, increasing perspective-taking skills may allow adolescents to now use interpretations of others' view of them in the construction of their self-concept. However, when overemphasized, these interpretations may result in self-definitions based on the standards and desires of others.

The support that parents and others provide for practicing critical types of thinking appears important in the development of self-identity and self-esteem. Harter (1990) believes that *democratic* parents who help teenagers to consider alternatives and think through consequences foster the development of self-identity, whereas *autocratic* parents, who prevent expression, and *permissive parents,* who allow freedom of decision but without guidance, do not. Interventions both formal and informal must understand the difficult task that adolescents face in coordinating the tasks of constructing an autonomous self and evaluating the positions, views, and desires of others. Significant adults who explain their views and opinions, sanction questioning, and empathize appropriately enable both cognitive and emotional independence in adolescents.

Summary

An understanding of developmental trends in cognition during adolescence, their variation as a result of external and internal factors, and their influence on social and emotional awareness is important for those working with teenagers in educational and therapeutic settings. As children enter adolescence, changes in thinking continue to occur reflecting increases in abstract ideation, processing efficiency, automatization of cognitive functions, and metacognitive functions. Instead of a broad, stagelike shift, these changes appear more domain-specific. Cognitive competence varies greatly within and across individuals, depending in part on the extent of experience with various knowledge bases, cultural and social factors, and personality and self-concept. Development of critical thinking skills is not obligatory but depends to a large extent on opportunities to exercise such thinking and support from others in this process. Cognitive development requires a process of scaffolding (Fischer & Silvern, 1985) in which child and adolescent skill development occurs in the context of careful monitoring of structures, interests, and goals by adults. Processes, strategies, and information implicitly or explicitly provided by adults are internalized by adolescents to varying degrees, depending on characteristics of each participant in this transactional process. Assessment of adolescent cognitive status cannot be identified independently of the type and availability of environmental support, and interventions at the individual, family, and community level must provide the atmosphere to promote higher-level and adaptive cognitive skills.

REFERENCES

Anthony, B. J., & Friedman, D. (1991). Development of processing control mechanisms. In J. R. Jennings & M. G. H. Coles (Eds.), *Handbook of cognitive psychophysiology: Central and autonomic nervous system approaches* (pp. 657–683). New York: John Wiley & Sons.

Baddely, A. (1986). *Working memory.* Oxford: Clarendon Press.

Barkley, R. A., Guevremont, D. C., Anastopoulos, A. D., & Fletcher, K. E. (1992). A comparison of three family therapy programs for treating family conflicts in adolescents with attention-deficit hyperactivity disorder. *Journal of Consulting and Clinical Psychology, 60,* 450–462.

Bartsch, K. (1993). Adolescents' theoretical thinking. In R. M. Lerner (Ed.), *Early adolescence: Perspectives on research, policy, and intervention* (pp. 143–157). New York: John Wiley & Sons.

Becker, M. G., Isaac, W., & Hynd, G. W. (1987). Neuropsychological development of nonverbal behaviors attributed to "frontal lobe" functioning. *Developmental Neuropsychology, 3,* 275–298.

Beuhring, T., & Kee, D. W. (1987). Developmental relationships among metamemory, elaborative strategy use, and associative memory. *Journal of Experimental Child Psychology, 44,* 377–400.

Bjorkland, D. F. (1987). How age changes in knowledge base contribute to the development of children's memory: An interpretive review. *Developmental Review, 7,* 93–130.

Bjorkland, D. F., & Buchanan, J. J. (1989). Development and knowledge base differences in the acquisition and extension of a memory strategy. *Journal of Experimental Child Psychology, 48,* 451–471.

Bjorkland, D. F., & Muir, J. (1988). Children's development of free recall memory: Remembering on their own. In R. Vasta (ed.), *Annals of child development* (Vol. 5, pp. 79–123). Greenwich, CT: JAI Press.

Brainerd, C. J. (1993). Cognitive development is abrupt (but not stage-like). *Monographs of the Society for Research in Child Development, 58* (9), 170–190.

Broughton, J. M. (1984). Not beyond formal operations but beyond Piaget. In M. L. Commons, F. A. Richard, & C. Armon (Eds.), *Beyond formal operations: Late adolescent and adult cognitive development* (pp. 395–411). New York: Praeger.

Brown, A. L., Bransford, J. D., Ferrara, R. A., & Campione, J. C. (1983). Learning, remembering, and understanding. In J. H. Flavell & E. M. Markman (Eds.), *Handbook of child psychology* (Vol. 3, pp. 77–166). New York: John Wiley & Sons.

Byrnes, J. P., & Overton, W. F. (1988). Reasoning about logical connections: A developmental analysis. *Journal of Experimental Child Psychology, 46,* 194–218.

Carey, S., & Diamond, R. (1980). Maturational determination of the developmental course of face encoding. In D. Caplan (Ed.), *Biological studies of mental processes* (pp. 60–73). Cambridge, MA: MIT Press.

Case, R. (1984). The process of stage transition: A neo-Piagetian view. In R. J. Sternberg (Ed.), *Mechanisms of cognitive development* (pp. 19–44). New York: W. H. Freeman.

Chi, M. T. H., & Koeske, R. D. (1983). Network representation of a child's dinosaur knowledge. *Developmental Psychology, 19,* 29–39.

Chugani, H. T., Phelps, M. E., & Mazziotta, J. C. (1987). Positron emission tomography study of human brain functional development. *Annals of Neurology, 22,* 487–497.

Eccles, J. S., Midgely, C., Wigfield, A., Buchanan, C. M., Reuman, D., Flanagan, C., & Mac Iver, D. (1993). Development during adolescence: The impact of stage-environment fit on young adolescents' experience in schools and in families. *American Psychologist, 48,* 90–101.

Elkind, D. (1967). Egocentrism in adolescence. *Child Development, 38,* 1025–1034.

Epstein, H. T. (1974). Phrenoblysis: Special brain and mind growth periods. *Developmental Psychobiology, 7,* 207–216.

Epstein, H. T., & Toepfer, C. F., Jr. (1978). A neuroscience basis for reorganizing middle grades education. *Education Leadership, 35,* 656–660.

Feingold, A. (1988). Cognitive gender differences are disappearing. *American Psychologist, 43,* 95–103.

Fischer, K. W. (1980). A theory of cognitive development: The control and construction of hierarchies of skills. *Psychological Review, 87,* 477–531.

Fischer, K. W. (1987). Relations between brain and cognitive development. *Child Development, 58,* 623–632.

Fischer, K. W., Kenny, S. L., & Pipp, S. L. (1990). How cognitive processes and environmental conditions or-

ganize discontinuities in the development of abstractions. In C. N. Alexander & E. J. Langer (Eds.), *Higher stages of human development* (pp. 162–187). New York: Oxford University Press.

Fischer, K. W., & Silvern, L. (1985). Stages and individual differences in cognitive development. *Annual Review of Psychology, 36,* 613–648.

Flavell, J. H. (1984). Discussion. In R. J. Sternberg (Ed.), *Mechanisms of cognitive development* (pp. 187–209). New York: W. H. Freeman.

Flavell, J. H. (1985). *Cognitive development* (2nd ed.). Englewood, NJ: Prentice-Hall.

Flavell, J. H., & Wellman, H. M. (1977). Metamemory. In R. V. Kail & J. W. Hagen (Eds.), *Perspectives on the development of memory and cognition.* Hillsdale, NJ: Lawrence Erlbaum.

Fordham, S., & Oghu, J. U. (1986). Black students' school success: Coping with the burden of "acting white." *Urban Review, 18,* 176–206.

Gilger, J. W., & Ho, H.-Z. (1989). Gender differences in adult spatial information processing: Their relationship to pubertal timing, adolescent activities, and sex-typing of personality. *Cognitive Development, 4,* 197–214.

Goldman-Rakic, P. S. (1987). Development of cortical circuitry and cognitive function. *Child Development, 58,* 601–622.

Greenough, W. T., Black, J. E., & Wallace, C. S. (1987). Experience and brain development. *Child Development, 58,* 539–559.

Griggs, R. A., & Cox, J. R. (1983). The effects of problem content and negation on Wason's selection task. *Quarterly Journal of Experimental Psychology, 35,* 519–533.

Harter, S. (1990). Self and identity development. In S. S. Feldman & G. R. Elliott (Eds), *At the threshold: The developing adolescent* (pp. 352–387). Cambridge, MA: Harvard University Press.

Helwig, C. C. (1995). Social context in social cognition: Psychological harm and civil liberties. In M. Killen & D. Hunt (Eds.), *Morality in everyday life: Developmental perspectives* (pp. 166–200). New York: Cambridge University Press.

Henderson, V. L., & Dweck, C. S. (1990). Motivation and achievement. In S. S. Feldman & G. R. Elliott (Eds), *At the threshold: The developing adolescent* (pp. 308–329). Cambridge, MA: Harvard University Press.

Hill, J. P. & Lynch, M. E. (1983). The intensification of gender-related role expectations during early adolescence. In J. Brooks-Gunn & A. C. Petersen (Eds.), *Girls at puberty: Biological and psychosocial perspectives* (pp. 201–228). New York: Plenum Press.

Huttenlocher, P. R. (1979). Synaptic density in human frontal cortex: Developmental changes and effects of aging. *Brain Research, 163,* 195–205.

Hyde, J. S., & Linn, M. C. (1988). Gender differences in verbal ability: A meta-analysis. *Psychological Bulletin, 104,* 53–69.

Inhelder, B., & Piaget, J. (1958). *The growth of logical thinking from childhood to adolescence.* New York: Basic Books.

Kahneman, D. (1973). *Attention and effort.* Englewood Cliffs, NJ: Prentice-Hall.

Kail, R. (1991a). Development of processing speed in childhood and adolescence. *Advances in Child Development and Behavior, 23,* 151–184.

Kail, R. (1991b). Processing time declines exponentially during childhood and adolescence. *Developmental Psychology, 27,* 259–266.

Keating, D. P. (1980). Thinking processes in adolescence. In J. Adelson (Ed.), *Handbook of adolescent psychology* (pp. 211–246). New York: John Wiley & Sons.

Keating, D. P. (1990). Adolescence thinking. In S. S. Feldman & G. R. Elliott (Eds.), *At the threshold: The developing adolescent* (pp. 54–89). Cambridge, MA: Harvard University Press.

Keil, F. C. (1984). Mechanisms in cognitive development and the structure of knowledge. In R. J. Sternberg (Ed.), *Mechanisms of cognitive development* (pp. 81–99). New York: W. H. Freeman.

Kendall, P. C., & Morris, R. J. (1991). Child therapy: Issues and recommendations. *Journal of Consulting and Clinical Psychology, 59,* 777–784.

Linn, M. C., & Hyde, J. S. (1991). Trends in cognitive and psychosocial gender differences. In R. M. Lerner and A. C. Petersen (Eds.), *Encyclopedia of adolescence* (pp. 139–150). New York: Garland Press.

Linn, M. C., & Petersen, A. C. (1985). Emergence and characterization of sex differences in spatial ability: A meta-analysis. *Child Development, 56,* 1479–1498.

Logan, G. D. (1988). Toward an instance theory of automatization. *Psychological Review, 95,* 492–527.

Luria, A. H. (1980). *Higher cortical function in man.* New York: Basic Books.

Maccoby, E. E., & Jacklin, C. N. (1974). *The psychology of sex differences.* Palo Alto, CA: Stanford University Press.

Mandler, J. M. (1983). Representation. In J. H. Flavell & E. M. Markman (Eds.), *Handbook of child psychology* (Vol. 3, pp. 420–494). New York: John Wiley & Sons.

Mann, L., Harmoni, R. V., & Power, C. N. (1989). Adolescent decision making: The development of competence. *Journal of Adolescence, 12,* 265–278.

Meichenbaum, D. (1977). *Cognitive behavior modification: An integrative approach.* New York: Plenum Press.

Merola, J. L., & Liederman, J. (1985). Developmental changes in hemispheric independence. *Child Development, 56,* 1184–1194.

Miller, P. H. (1989). *Theories of developmental psychology.* New York: W. H. Freeman.

Mirsky, A. F., Anthony, B. J., Duncan, C. C., Ahearn, M. B., & Kellam, S. G. (1991). Analysis of the elements of attention: A neuropsychological approach. *Neuropsychology Review, 2,* 109–145.

Newcombe, N., & Dubas, J. S. (1992). A longitudinal study of predictors of spatial ability in adolescent females. *Child Development, 63,* 37–46.

Ornstein, P. A., & Naus, M. J. (1985). Effects of the knowledge base on children's memory strategies. In H. W. Reese (Ed.), *Advances in child development and behavior* (Vol. 19, pp. 113–148). New York: Academic Press.

Overton, W. F., Ward, S. L., Noveck, L., Black, J., & O'Brien, D. P. (1987). Form and content in the development of deductive reasoning. *Developmental Psychology, 23,* 22–30.

Ozer, D. J. (1987). Personality, intelligence, and spatial visualization: Correlates of mental rotations test performance. *Journal of Personality and Social Psychology, 53,* 129–134.

Passler, M. A., Isaac, W., & Hynd, G. W. (1985). Neuropsychological development of behavior attributed to frontal lobe functioning in children. *Developmental Neuropsychology, 1,* 349–370.

Phillips, S. A., Anthony, B. J., & Tepper, V. T. (1992). Use of psychometrics with adolescent patients. *Adolescent Medicine State of the Art Reviews, 3,* 111–129.

Posner, M. I., & Peterson, S. E. (1990). The attention system of the human brain. *Annual Review of Neuroscience, 13,* 25–42.

Quadrel, M. J., Fischhoff, B., & Davis, W. (1993). Adolescent (in)vulnerability. *American Psychologist, 48,* 102–116.

Ryan, C. M. (1990). Age-related improvements in short-term memory efficiency during adolescence. *Developmental Neuropsychology, 6,* 193–205.

Schunk, D. H. (1982). Effects of effort attributional feedback on children's perceived self-efficacy and achievement. *Journal of Educational Psychology, 74,* 548–566.

Selman, R. L. (1980). *The growth of interpersonal understanding.* New York: Academic Press.

Shantz, C. U. (1983). Social cognition. In J. H. Flavell & E. M. Markman (Eds.), *Handbook of child psychology* (Vol. 3, pp. 495–555). New York: John Wiley & Sons.

Shiffrin, R. M., & Dumais, S. T. (1981). The development of automatism. In J. R. Anderson (Ed.), *Cognitive skills and their acquisition* (pp. 111–140). Hillsdale, NJ: Lawrence Erlbaum.

Shiffrin, R. M., & Schneider, W. (1977). Controlled and automatic human information processing. II: Perceptual learning, automatic attending, and a general theory. *Psychological Review, 84,* 127–190.

Sternberg, R. J. (1984). Mechanisms of cognitive development: A componential approach. In R. J. Sternberg (Ed.), *Mechanisms of cognitive development* (pp. 163–186). New York: W. H. Freeman.

Stevenson, H. W., Lee, S., & Stigler, J. W. (1986). Mathematics achievement in Chinese, Japanese, and American children. *Science, 231,* 693–699.

Stuss, D. T., & Benson, F. (1984). Neuropsychological studies of the frontal lobes. *Psychological Bulletin, 95,* 3–28.

Sugarman, S. (1987). *Piaget's construction of the child's reality.* New York: Cambridge University Press.

Thatcher, R. W., Walker, R. A., & Giudice, S. (1987). Human cerebral hemispheres develop at different rates and ages. *Science, 236,* 1110–1113.

Vygotsky, L. (1978). *Mind in society: The development of higher psychological processes*. Cambridge, MA: Harvard University Press.

Waber, D. P. (1976). Sex differences in cognition: A function of maturation rate? *Science, 192*, 572–574.

Waber, D. P. (1977). Sex differences in mental abilities, hemispheric lateralization, and rate of physical growth at adolescence. *Developmental Psychology, 13*, 29–38.

Ward, S. L., & Overton, W. F. (1990). Semantic familiarity, relevance, and the development of deductive reasoning. *Developmental Psychology, 26*, 488–493.

Waters, H. S. (1982). Memory development in adolescence: Relationships between metamemory strategy use, and performance. *Journal of Experimental Child Psychology, 33*, 183–195.

Wilcox, C. L. (1993). *The relationship between attention and social status*. Unpublished M.A. thesis, University of Maryland Baltimore County.

Wilkes, T. C. R., Belsher, G., Rush, A. J., & Frank, E. (1994). *Cognitive therapy for depressed adolescents*. New York: Guilford Press.

Yakovlev, P. I., & Lecours, A. R. (1967). The myelogenetic cycles of regional maturation of the brain. In A. Minkowsky (Ed.), *Regional development of the brain in early life* (pp. 3–70). Oxford: Blackwell.

10 / Creativity in Adolescence

Robinson J. Munoz-Millan

Adolescence is the period when creativity begins to crystallize in its mature form. Creativity in adolescence is of interest to the child and adolescent psychiatrist from at least three perspectives. The first is based on the hope that the clinical experience with adolescents will allow further understanding of creativity in general. The psychiatrist also needs to understand the function of creativity and art in the psychic organization, in order to interpret the psychological significance and implicit meaning of a specific patient's artistic work. Third, an understanding of the developmental processes of talent and creativity is essential when one of the psychotherapeutic goals is facilitating the career of an obviously gifted youngster. This chapter addresses these three topics.

Concepts of Creativity

Creativity is seen by some as the exclusive province of the extraordinarily gifted, while others conceive creativity as the capacity for innovative problem solving whether it is applied in daily life or in the arts and sciences. According to this latter point of view, the difference between the pragmatic creativity and that of artistic or scientific accomplishment is only a matter of degree of complexity and level of abstraction; there is no implicit qualitative difference. As a heightened capacity for problem solving, creativity implies the ability to redefine issues, to pose questions or problems in new contexts and conceptual perspectives, and to find original and innovative solutions to the questions thus posed. This process differentiates the creative person from those who simply apply to new situations solutions already designed by somebody else. A classical example of creative thinking is the discovery of penicillin by Sir Alexander Fleming. Confronted with the concrete problem of inhibited growth of bacteria in contaminated cultures, Fleming envisioned the application of the capacity to inhibit growth found in

Penicillium nonatum to the treatment of infectious diseases. The problem in the laboratory was redefined as a question about the clinical application of a well-known phenomenon. Such a conceptual leap clearly exemplifies creativity. Creativity, therefore, implies not only the solution of a problem, whether scientific, artistic, or pragmatic, but implies also the capacity to change the rules by which solutions to the problems will be found. The capacity for redefining the issues under new parameters differentiates the innovative creator from the merely competent.

There is an interesting difference between scientific and artistic creativity. Besides encompassing the manipulation of reality-oriented concepts crucial to scientific thinking, artistic creativity also involves the elaboration of personally meaningful affective material. This subjective material is processed not according to the demands of logic and causation but in relation to aesthetic demands. Such elaboration of affective material, while an essential part of artistic creativity, is not necessarily part of the creative process in mathematics and the sciences. On the contrary, in those disciplines it can be a disturbing impediment to reality-oriented thinking.

Characteristics of Adolescent Creativity

Psychiatrists who treat adolescents are confronted frequently with the artistic work (poetry, drawings, songs, etc.) of their patients. These works are often rich in meaning and emotion: at times intriguing in their aesthetic naïveté, at times impressive in their artistic accomplishment and promise. The naive work will inform us of the specific preoccupations of the specific patient, without telling much of the development of creativity in general. From the more accomplished group, we can learn also about the developmental stages of creativity.

Compared to the artistic production of the child, the adolescent's work begins to show genuine innovation and concerns itself not only with what is present and actual but with what is hypothetically possible. Adolescent creativity demonstrates also the capacity to integrate personal expression in the context of a formal structure such as aesthetic norms or the requirements of the scientific method. This new capacity is due in part to increased training in artistic and scientific techniques, the increased number and significance of life experiences, and the biologically increased intensity of affective events. An equally important factor is the increased capacity of the adolescent to sustain, in consciousness, dysphoric and anxiety-laden fantasies and affects, as a result of maturation of psychic functioning. This development of the ego capacities is responsible for the more "mature" quality of the artistic product but cannot account for the momentous increase in the adolescent's capacity to conceive innovative contextual structures and patterns of thought. How far the adolescent progresses at this level is determined by cognitive development, the further maturation of the primary process, and the increased capacity of the adolescent to integrate primary and secondary processes in the service of creativity.

Cognitive Factors in Adolescent Creativity

INTELLIGENCE AND CREATIVITY

Early in the development of psychometric techniques, researchers expected to find a direct correlation between creativity and a high IQ, equating intelligence and creativity. However, longitudinal studies have failed to support these expectations. Even a very high IQ does not correlate necessarily with creativity.

COGNITIVE STYLE AND CREATIVITY

The expectation persisted, however, that definable cognitive factors would be found to be the underpinnings of creativity, that such factors could be objectively measured with appropriate tests, and that consequently the recognition of potential creativity would be feasible. Based on these assumptions, emphasis has been placed on the study of cognitive styles or problem-solving strategies that may be predictive correlates of creativity. Guilford (1967) developed the concept of "convergent" and "divergent" styles of psychological functioning based on features such as verbal fluency, ideational fluency, redefinition, and originality. He postulated a correlation between a divergent cognitive style and creativity. However, later studies using similar measures found no differential correlation of "creativity" and these cognitive styles, but report that those "divergers" who were creative tended to choose the arts and humanities, while those who were "convergers" moved into mathematics and sciences.

FORMAL OPERATIONS AND CREATIVITY

There is, however, a high level of agreement that the emergence and consolidation of formal operational thinking, first described by Piaget (1952), is a necessary condition for creativity in adolescence. The capacity for formal operations, which becomes apparent around the age of 11 years, allows the adolescent to postulate hypothetical alternatives, to deduce patterns from observational data, and to propose new logical possibilities. Since this new reasoning process is not limited to the application of logical operations to concrete objects or events actually present (as in the earlier stage of concrete operations), entities never before seen can be imagined and pursued and novel solutions can be found to problems old and new. It is this achievement of formal operational reasoning that most closely correlates with creativity. Formal operational reasoning allows for true innovation rather than the repetitive application of familiar solutions to concrete events. The accomplishment of this developmental stage represents a further development of the secondary process, increasing its capacity to deal more effectively with reality.

Maturation of the Primary Process and Creativity

"Primary process" is a term used to describe a particular type of mental functioning thought to be the most primitive, basic, and earliest in the life of the individual. Primary process was originally described by Freud as the mode of operation of the unconscious system. The primary process has been invoked to understand creativity as well as dreams, parapraxes, and jokes. The primary process as conceived by Freud is characterized by its orientation toward immediate discharge of drives, hence operating under the pleasure principle. The primary process uses three main mechanisms: condensation, displacement, and symbolism. Because of its lack of regard for the reality principle, the "illogical" quality of its contents (it ignores logical demands for causal reasoning, the resolution of contradictions, and the respect for time and spatial relations), and its propensity for unmodulated discharge, the primary process has been considered a primitive and chaotic mode of ideation. Classical psychoanalysis sees the primary process as eventually superseded by the secondary process, the organizational mode of the system conscious, of logical thinking and reality-oriented behavior. However, primary process remains active in the dynamic unconscious system and continues to influence thoughts, feelings, and behavior, albeit in ways of which the individual is generally unaware.

From this perspective, the creative person is assumed to have an enhanced capacity to access the primary process content in a controlled and reversible fashion. Mental content thus retrieved is then processed according to the secondary process organization, which would be responsible for the formal excellence of the work of art or music, or for the logical structure of a scientific communication.

According to this point of view, the artist, through the creative process, has access to unconscious wishes and through sublimation gratifies them. The artwork represents a means to convey the wishes in such a way that both expresses the wish and simultaneously avoids censorship and repression. The artistic production is, in this sense, similar to a dream. However, it is different from a dream in that the work of art is a form of communication directed to others (the viewers). As such, it allows the observer to recognize the unconscious meaning of the work and by identification with the artist undergo similar wish fulfillment also in a sublimated way. This view of art as a sublimated discharge of drives implies a basic allegiance to the pleasure principle and a transient regression to the primary process (albeit a regression in the service of the ego).

However, more recent theorists have questioned the basic assumption that the development of the primary process arrests once the secondary process begins to dominate the conscious psychic organization. They propose that the primary process continues to develop at the same pace as the development of the secondary process.

Noy (1969) in particular proposes that the primary process does not remain an archaic, primitive organization but that it develops around functions related to the regulation, maintenance, and integration of the self, in contrast to the secondary process, which organizes around the relation of the ego to reality. This model envisions both processes as equal in their importance to development but different in terms of their function. According to this model, the primary process is not an obsolete, irrational process but one that is eminently suited for its task: the organization of the self. This organization of the self includes assimilation of new experience into the self, accommodation of the self to changing experience and growing reality demands, and integration of the self to safeguard its cohesion, unity, and continuity. These functions of maintaining a cohesive sense of the self are accomplished by dreams, fantasy, and artistic creativity. The creative act may be understood not only as sublimated discharge of drives but as a manifestation of the synthetic function of the ego.

Creating works of art, from this perspective, serves the needs of the self with regards to definition, differentiation from the object, adaptation of reality to the self and of the self to reality. Artistic productions also involve communication and sharing self-experiences with others (Noy, 1979b). These functions of art with regards to the self make artistic production such an appealing activity for those adolescents who are able to transcend the solitary pleasures of fantasy and daydreaming. While the development of the self begins prior to adolescence, it is during this developmental stage that the most active increase in complexity of the self occurs. This complexity calls for the active integration of contrasting parts of the self, to avoid its fragmentation under the forces of conflicting emotions and drives. Noy (1979a) advances the theory that the creative artists' search for the "perfect form" is part of the synthetic functions of the ego in an attempt to reconcile contrasting ideas or feelings into an integrated whole. He quotes Storr (1972) who adds that "by identifying ourselves, however fleetingly, with the creator, we can participate in the integrating process which he has carried out for himself" (p. 236).

With this model, the emphasis has moved from the concept of art as the sublimated discharge of drives to the idea of creativity as a manifestation of the synthetic functions of the ego, with particular reference to the consolidation and preservation of the integrity of the self. This approach dispenses with the concept of regression as a necessary aspect of the creative process.

Other writers have developed concepts that represent parallel views of the development of the primary process.

Rothenberg (1990) describes two modes of psychological functioning: the homospatial and janusian processes, which first manifest themselves in adolescence. The homospatial process "consists of actively conceiving two or more discrete entities occupying the same space" (p. 418). This capacity, considered by Rothenberg as crucial to creative imagination, allows the artist or scientist to envision multiple images or representations (sounds, visual images, smell, or any other sensorial experience) as occupying the same spatial location and facilitates the conception of innovative concepts and ideas. The janusian process is described as the capacity to conceive multiple opposite ideas or antitheses simultaneously. Although these ideas are illogical and contradictory, they are transiently held in consciousness during rational states of mind. Rothenberg proposes a dynamic origin for these processes, relating them to the adolescent conflicts about autonomy and social involvement.

Smolucha and Smolucha (1985) also envision development of the primary process after the secondary process is acquired. One manifestation of this development is the ability of creative persons to perceive and manipulate perceptual resemblances (isomorphisms) between different entities. An example of the use of isomorphism in art can be found in Picasso's sculpture of a bull using a bicycle seat and handlebar. These writers understand this ability—an important feature of adult creativity—to be the result of maturation of the analogical thinking seen in children engaged in symbolic play. According to them, the maturation of the primary process allows conscious control of analogical thinking and the ability to alternate between analogical thinking and secondary process in an harmonious manner.

Integration of Primary and Secondary Processes

In the creative event, the ego uses an appropriate combination of primary and secondary processes without implying a hierarchical stratification between the two. Arieti (1976) proposed the term "tertiary processes" for this synthesis of processes seen in creativity. Regardless of the model used, there is some agreement that creativity occupies an intermediate position between self (primary process) and nonself reality (secondary process). This intermediate position is elaborated in object-relations terms by Winnicott (1971). He proposes that such a transitional space, which is intermediate between self and nonself, is the field where creativity occurs. Transitional objects and related phenomena acquire increasing levels of abstraction and become the objects and processes of culture that in the civilized person can stimulate and comfort. He states:

This intermediate area of experience, unchallenged in respect of its belonging to inner or external (shared) reality, constitutes the greater part of the infant's experience, and throughout life is retained in the intense experiencing that belongs to the arts and to religion and to imaginative living and to creative scientific work. (P. 14)

HEMISPHERIC SPECIALIZATION AND CREATIVITY

In the last decade, there has been increasing interest in the correlation between the special functions and abilities of each cerebral hemisphere and the creative process. Hemispheric specialization greatly increases the functional flexibility of the brain. The right hemisphere is particularly able to detect and create gestalt and patterns. Applying these abilities, the right brain develops images that are then manipulated in the serial processes typical of the left brain. Bogen and Bogen (1988) hypothesize that in the creative process, two consecutive events occur. Initially, there is an incubation period during which partial and reversibly independent function of the hemispheres allows for separate lateralized cognition. A second phase involves active communication between the hemispheres and represents the moment of "illumination" where the creative answers are first conceived. Since interhemispheric communication occurs via the corpus callosum, that structure mediates creativity. These propositions are supported by observation of patients who have undergone commissurotomy and whose fantasies are "unimaginative utilitarian, and tied to reality; and their symbolizations concrete, discursive and rigid" (Hoppe, 1988, p. 303).

Future research will clarify further the correlation of creativity and the functions of the hemispheres, of the commissures, and perhaps of the frontal lobe with its synthesizing and integrating capabilities.

Motivational Factors

While creativity can be seen as a basic drive, present in all human beings and irreducible to further constituent elements, motivation toward creativity can be identified in several developmental events that are particularly significant in adolescence.

CREATIVITY AT THE SERVICE OF IDENTITY CONSOLIDATION

I have already discussed the significance of art in the maintenance and integration of the self. Since in adolescence issues of identity, self-definition, and self-expression are paramount, the interest of many adolescents in art becomes easily understandable.

CREATIVITY AS REPARATION

Segal (1957) conceives the basis of sublimation and creativity in the wish to restore and re-create the lost loved object both outside and within the ego. To be able to use reparation and guilt to deal with loss, the person must have achieved the "depressive position." This implies the capacity to relate to whole objects and the capacity to experience guilt for the primitive aggressive attacks on the external or internal objects.

Because the objects are seen as whole, with integrated positive and negative valences, aggression directed to them is followed by the fear of their loss. In adult life, mourning represents a reliving of the early depressive anxieties. Alongside the mourning for the recent loss of the object in the real world are reactivated memories of the loss of the early objects, the parents, experienced as lost both in the real and inner worlds.

Adolescence represents the giving up of the early objects as the adolescent works toward autonomy and independence. The mourning is for the parents as actual objects in the external world and the parents as inner representations. If the adolescent can avoid the manic defenses of omnipotence and prevent the regression to primitive defenses of the paranoid position (splitting, idealization, denial, projective identification, etc.), then the reparatory functions of creativity can be brought forth and the lost object can be re-created, this time with the immortality of the artwork.

The Talented Adolescent

Whether a talented adolescent will succeed in the field of his or her greatest gift is dependent on both intrinsic and extrinsic factors. Intrinsic to the adolescent are talent, perseverance, intellectual daring, and ability to ignore convention. Extrinsic factors include those related to the immediate family and cultural environment: stimulation, support, stability, and opportunities for training. Finally, there are factors having to do with society at large: historical times and imponderables that can be called luck.

A specially talented or creative adolescent may be referred to an adolescent psychiatrist for various reasons. If the patient presents with any of the usual pathological conditions that affect adolescents, therapy should proceed as with any other patient. There is no support for the romantic assumption that pathology stimulates creativity or that talent is dependent on internal conflict. This chapter has already reviewed the notion that creative work may relate in content to intrapsychic conflicts, mourning, and other events, and that creativity may be used by the ego for sublimatory discharge of drives, mastery of traumatic events, and preservation of the self. However, pathology represents a failure of the ego to perform its functions, and that failure does not facilitate creativity. Some adolescents can be creative in spite of their pathology but not because of it.

A talented adolescent may come to a psychiatrist because of performance anxiety, creative block, and other symptoms that prevent the pursuit of creative work or training. In such a case it is important to differentiate between neurotic symptoms and a more existential crisis regarding the meaning of the special talent in the adolescent's life.

In the first case, the symptom may express or attempt to resolve intrapsychic or interpersonal conflicts. Neurotic symptoms in the talented adolescent often relate to the intense competitiveness in some of the creative fields. The adolescent may experience guilt about success or shame about failure. Problems associated with the disparity between the demands of the ego ideal and the realities of the capacities of the ego may be resolved through neurotic symptoms. Often symptoms that interfere with the creative work of the adolescent represent transferential conflicts with teachers, mentors, or coaches. In those cases treatment aims at the removal of symptoms and the resolution of the underlying conflicts. Multiple treatment modalities may be needed, including expressive psychotherapy, psychopharmacology, behavior therapy, and family therapy.

When the therapist is confronted with an existential crisis in a talented adolescent who has already achieved success and recognition, the issues and the approach are different. The adolescent may already be at a point in his or her career that others will not reach for years. This career state may confront the adolescent with issues beyond his or her developmental capacities: management of high income, exploitation by others, overwhelming admiration or adulation. Many gifted adolescents genuinely enjoy the exercise of their talent, while others may feel that their talent forces them to a career choice that may be at odds with their identity, goals, and ideals. The adolescent may deal with these issues in the context of adolescent rebellion or may address them in a more mature, although not necessarily less painful, manner. For example, a youngster may question the

significance of his creative work in a social perspective—comparing the human relevance of a career as a pianist to that of social work. Or the adolescent may ponder the economic consequences of embarking in a career with uncertain financial rewards. When these questions are brought into the adolescent's psychotherapy, the therapist must decide how best to deal with them. There are many possible therapeutic approaches to these real-life dilemmas, ranging from review of reality issues to the analysis of unconscious motivation. The best solution for the adolescent may be a moratorium on making a decision while maintaining a maximum of open possibilities. In such cases a more traditional expressive psychodynamic psychotherapy or psychoanalysis would be of particular help to the youth. The goal of this therapy is not simply to remove symptoms or prevent their recurrence but to increase awareness of the multiple factors that influence human feelings, behavior, and preferences. Insight into those unconscious determinants and resolution of intrapsychic conflicts will allow the adolescent to make choices with increased freedom.

Conclusion

Research in the areas of ego psychology, cognitive development, and neurophysiology has offered suggestive initial findings toward an understanding of creativity. The various psychoanalytic perspectives are conceptualizations of mental activity that presume a relationship to the neurobiological functioning of the brain but were developed independently of biological studies of brain and behavior. It is fascinating that new knowledge about brain functioning has led to hypotheses that are similar to the concepts of primary and secondary thought processes and the idea that creativity results from a synthesis of these two very different kinds of thinking. However, an in-depth understanding of the creative process and its developmental stages remains elusive. It is equally difficult to measure and predict creativity from early-life indicators. Discovering innovative answers may take a redefinition of the questions about creativity under new conceptual perspectives. The subject of creativity may reveal itself only when addressed according to new and truly creative parameters. At present, psychiatry can best contribute to the emergence of creativity in adolescents by removing the motivational and intrapsychic conflicts that may interfere with its development.

REFERENCES

Arieti, S. (1976). *Creativity: The magic synthesis.* New York: Basic Books.

Bogen, J. E., & Bogen, G. M. (1988). Creativity and the corpus callosum. *Psychiatric Clinics of North America, 11,* 293–301.

Guilford, J. P. (1967). *The nature of human intelligence.* New York: McGraw-Hill.

Hoppe, K. D. (1988). Hemispheric specialization and creativity. *Psychiatric Clinics of North America, 11,* 303–315.

Noy, P. (1969). A revision of the psychoanalytic theory of the primary process. *International Journal of Psycho-Analysis, 50,* 155–178.

Noy, P. (1979a). Form creation in art: An ego-psychological approach to creativity. *Psychoanalytic Quarterly, 48,* 229–256.

Noy, P. (1979b). The psychoanalytic theory of cognitive development. *Psychoanalytic Study of the Child, 34,* 169–216.

Piaget, J. (1952). *The origin of intelligence in children.* New York: International Universities Press.

Rothenberg, R. (1990). Creativity in adolescence. *Psychiatric Clinics of North America, 13,* 415–434.

Segal, H. (1957). A psychoanalytical approach to aesthetics. In M. Klein, P. Heiman, and R. E. Money-Kyrle (Eds.), *New directions in psychoanalysis* (pp. 384–405). New York: Basic Books.

Smolucha, L. W., & Smolucha, F. C. (1985). A fifth Piagetian stage: The collaboration between analogical and logical thinking in artistic creativity. *Visual Arts Research, 11,* 90–99.

Storr, A. (1972). *The dynamics of creation.* London: Secker and Warburg.

Winnicott, D. W. (1971). *Playing and Reality.* New York: Basic Books.

11 / Changing Relationships with Parents

Sushma Jani

During early adolescence, the intensity and exclusivity of parental attachments begins to change. What appears on the surface to be a process of distancing is often accompanied by discomfort and conflict and, in extreme cases, anguish and dysfunction for both the adolescent and his or her family. Often this process of transformation of the childhood attachments, and its accompanying behavioral manifestations, is the source of much of what brings adolescents and their families to the attention of the mental health system. Current theories of attachment have led to the recognition that adolescents, as they mature, do not totally give up their ties to their parents; rather these ties undergo profound changes throughout adolescence.

In the process of establishing distance from the dependency and control of early childhood, adolescents use a variety of defenses and character traits. These defenses may take the form of displacements or substitutions and may be played out through imitation of the parental interactions with their own friends; or they may show up in the form of ego disturbances, such as acting out, negativism, exaggerated moodiness, or episodic acts of aggression. Traces of these behaviors may be first noted among toddlers but often become more pronounced in adolescence. For example, a toddler who is required to sit at the dinner table when he was previously engrossed in playing with beads may express his anger by throwing his beads or exhibit a full-blown temper tantrum, play with the food, or not eat at all. Similarly, an adolescent who is reminded to complete an expected weekly chore while leaving the house for a social event may respond with a negative remark that may or may not lead to a negative interaction with the parent. For example, the adolescent may say, "Why do you always remind me as I'm about to leave the house?" and the mother may respond, "Why don't you do what you're supposed to do so that I don't have to remind you! Why should I even have to remind you, you are grown-up, you

should know it by now! If you would act responsible, then I wouldn't have to remind you!" The adolescent's response could be "Stop fussing at me, I'm going to do it, don't tell me what to do, I KNOW WHAT TO DO!" At this point, she may begin to drag an improperly tied trash bag with trash falling out. In this example, the adolescent's behavior suggests that she is ambivalent about establishing distance from the dependency and he puts himself in a situation that invites the parent to participate in the negative interaction, so that the adolescent can feel angry and not guilty for establishing the distance. The anger thus serves as a way to sever the ties and move the adolescent toward separation and independence. Thus, distancing behaviors, devaluing authority, and altered parental relationships are the important factors of adolescent identity consolidation.

Blos (1962) described three stages of adolescence—early, middle, and late—and the linkages between family life and identity consolidation during each phase. Early adolescence generally encompasses ages 10 to 13; middle adolescence, ages 13 to 16; and late adolescence, ages 16 to 19. These chronologic and arbitrary stages acknowledge that all of the developmental period of adolescence cannot be lumped together, since, for example, a 13-year-old is much different from a 16-year-old or 19-year-old in regard to altered relationships with parents. Hauser (Hauser, Borman, & Bowlds, 1991) recently broadened Blos's work to include interpersonal relationships and conceptualized ego development into three types of ego development: preconformist, conformist, and postconformist. During the preconformist stage of ego development, high dependent interaction with parents occurs; adolescents are almost unaware of differences between themselves and others and relate to peers and adults through largely exploitative styles. Hauser also characterizes these adolescents as having simple cognitive constructions; they respond to situations and questions with few options and exhibit "either/or," "black/white" thinking. In the conformist stage, adolescents are preoccupied with being accepted by friends and complying with prevailing social rules. However, they are more aware of individual differences and complex views, although they tend not to question socially popular traditions and slogans. During the postconformist stage, adolescents exhibit an advanced stage of ego development; they stick to norms based on inner standards and express increased autonomy from their parents' views. Adolescents in this stage also show more interest in mutuality with others and in the complexity of the experience.

Preadolescent children generally are comfortable with the views, precepts, and values they have learned from parents, family, and the sociocultural milieu and do not see these views and values as things to be discarded.

In contrast, mid-to-late adolescents are faced with establishing an identity separate from that of the parents. This process involves gaining emotional independence from what adolescents may perceive as inordinate control by parents but in reality is control that is being exercised by the internalized affects and associated parental identifications that were attained during the preadolescent period (Blos, 1962). One important way in which adolescents establish their identity is by internalizing their own values, distancing themselves from parental values and setting up an authority conflict. These new values form an integral part of each adolescent's self and yet are clearly derived from the familial and larger cultural group. One of the key developmental tasks of adolescence is determining how to develop a sense of values as truly one's own and at the same time acknowledge a debt to adults. That this task is not accomplished without some degree of both internal and external conflict should not be surprising. At the same time, for normal adolescents and their families, the degree of conflict with parents that is manifest externally as well as that which is experienced internally by the adolescent is not as great as might be inferred from the magnitude of the developmental task of separation-individuation during the adolescent period.

The importance of parent-adolescent relationships as a barometer of adolescent functioning cannot be overemphasized. Comparing normal with troubled adolescents in a large, nonclinical sample, Offer, Ostrov, Howard, and Atkinson (1990a) found that the major difference between the two groups could be seen in their parent-child relationships; over 60% of normal adolescents viewed their parents as people to confide in regarding problems, whereas only 35% of disturbed adolescents did. Two explanations for this finding are possible. The development of disturbed adolescents may involve greater distancing from their parents as a consequence of the adolescents' greater degree of conflict over dependency. A second possibility is that parents' lack of emotional availability may create distance between them and their adolescents that both facilitates the development of disturbance and makes disturbed adolescents realistically perceive their parents as unlikely to be helpful. It is quite possible that both mechanisms occur and may operate separately or synergistically.

Early Adolescence

In early adolescence, children are dependent on their parents and still rely to a great extent on their parents' value system and beliefs (Blos, 1967). Early adolescents generally possess relatively limited formal operational thinking, tending to see most situations as either black or white. They tend to distance themselves from parents by being impulsive and acting in a manner that can be a distorted mirror image of parental values. For example, a 13-year-old girl with a very messy bedroom littered with piles of clothes and books on the floor may criticize her mother's housekeeping skills. The teenager may say, "When I have my own house, I'll keep it clean and not be lazy like you, lying around all day long not doing anything." At the same time, the adolescent may help organize her friends' room and closets.

Adolescents in this age group may also show a deference to authority that is designed mostly to avoid trouble or confrontations with superior power or prestige (Offer et al., 1990a). For example, a group of 13-year-olds in a mall may play around in a loud manner and draw attention to themselves. However, if the mall security officer approaches them, they generally respond to the officer's request for moderation, unlike 15- or 16-year-olds, who may argue or protest. Early adolescents have an egocentric orientation; they assume that a proper course of action is one that satisfies their needs first and, occasionally, the needs of others (Hauser, 1990). For example, a 14-year-old may demand that the parents drop him first at the skating rink to meet friends before they take his younger sister to her doctor's appointment.

Early adolescents exhibit an interpersonal style that is alternately dependent, exploitative, and manipulative, and they seem unaware of individual differences between themselves and others. They tend to be self-protective with a fear of being caught and are consciously preoccupied with their physical selves, especially regarding sexual and aggressive feelings (Hauser, 1990).

Further evidence of the early adolescent's egocentric way of thinking is the imaginary audience, which some theorists view as a resurgence of infantile narcissism, an extension of the "See how cute I am" behavior of childhood (Hauser et al., 1991). The "imaginary audience" is a phenomenon in which adolescents imagine that they are being watched very closely by everyone around them. For example, 13-year-olds would not leave the house without wearing a certain type of clothes or with a certain hairstyle; they feel very "conscious" of being watched or observed by this imaginary audience. The "odd" or eccentric styles or trends of clothing or hairstyles are also to please and draw attention from this imaginary audience. To a lesser degree, normal adolescents do not want to be caught dead with their parents at a restaurant. "What if some one sees me?! I can't go with you to the mall!" This imaginary audience is a major source of embarrassment for most teenagers, and many act out to draw attention from that audience. In essence, the imaginary audience reflects the adolescents' beliefs that their appearance, actions, and influence on their peers is the same as their own egocentric view. The imaginary audience clearly demonstrates to them that their world truly revolves around them.

Adolescents who do not advance beyond this stage may fail to establish their own identity and may remain copies of their parental models. For example, these children may not exhibit autonomy in their choice of clothing style or of music and feel safer and more secure in behaving like their parents. These adolescents tend to be isolated from their peers by being "different" or "old-fashioned" and may be picked on as "nerds." In general, these children do not seem to challenge or question parental authority and on the surface appear to have a relatively "good" and conflict-free adolescence.

Middle Adolescence

By middle adolescence, most teenagers have had enough experience with reality to begin dispensing with their imaginary audience. Their "testing" of this fictional construct allows them to replace it with a more realistic framework. This shift away from egocentrism allows the world at large to come into focus for them. Cognitively, adolescents in this middle stage of development, ages 15 to 17, have an orientation to approval, pleasing others by helping, conforming to stereotypes or commonly held values or roles, and experiencing guilt at breaking rules or conventions. At this point, as Kohlberg (1964) notes, an adolescent's moral development is still quite limited and is perceived mostly in terms of "doing one's duty" and observing the expectations of others. Middle adolescents show a healthy respect for authority figures and seem to have an emotional stake in maintaining the status quo. In their interpersonal relationships, middle adolescents begin to relate to the family by belonging and helping, as a way of meeting others' expectations. As Hauser notes, middle adolescents achieve a dawning realization of the difference between the self and others, an awareness of individual differences in motivations, actions, and interests (Hauser et al., 1991). As a result, they begin to exhibit a relatively superficial awareness of individual relationship patterns among different family members—in effect, a nascent, though incomplete, appreciation of the richness of individual patterns of interrelating to others. As adolescents become aware of individual motivation, actions, and interests in context of relationships, their own testing of this newly acquired knowledge leads to experimentation with "new styles" of relating with parents and their peers. These new styles of relating seem to manifest themselves in distancing from parents, but in fact the parent-child bond remains, albeit with different behavioral manifestations. The adolescent chooses peer-group values and interactions in preference to parental standards and associations.

Late Adolescence

By age 17, adolescents are capable of greater conceptual complexity, self-criticism, and differentiated feelings, motives, and forms of self-expression. In terms of moral development, late adolescents begin to recognize the difference between mere conventions and laws or mores rooted in matters of conscience. As a result, authority conflicts take the form of appeals to a higher authority or appeals to universal conscience. According to Hauser (Hauser et al., 1991), the late adolescent is more intensive and responsible, and shows deepened interest in interpersonal relations, as illustrated by an interest in awareness of the styles other family members exhibit in relating to each other. In addition to this heightened interest in interpersonal relations, late adolescents show respect for the autonomy of others and respect for the individuality of the person to whom they are relating. Distancing at this stage often takes the form of "quasi-legalistic" posturing, perhaps quibbling over the arbitrary elements of rules of laws.

Altered Parent-Child Relationships

Besides disengaging the self from parental egos, adolescents also face the task of reorganizing the superego. This process can be difficult, depending on the success of early ego organization and parental support for children's individuation and separation. Thus, altered relationships with parents can be seen as springing in part from children's growing cognitive abilities and their capacity to make moral judgments outside of the parents' moral milieu. The adolescents' growing ability to perceive differences among people and their increasing capacity to weigh moral dilemmas presage a

new way of relating to others and provide the mechanisms for important steps toward identity consolidation.

The parents' personal experiences with their own adolescent years have a great impact on how they view this period in their children's lives. Parents who enjoyed their adolescence are likely to view their children's impending teen years favorably. Conversely, those whose adolescence was consistently painful are likely to expect, and perhaps re-create, difficulties for their children. Parents not infrequently undergo unconscious identification with their adolescent children. For example, a father who was afraid of engaging in sex at a younger age may act overvigilant with his daughter by not trusting her with her friends. In response, the daughter may overreact and force premature sexual activity.

In a society that places so much value on youthfulness, parents may envy, consciously or unconsciously, the youthfulness of their teenage children. This parental envy may include sexually laden conflicts. At a time when women themselves are going through the normal midlife changes of menopause and men through waning sexual potency, competitive, sexually charged strivings of parents with a same-gender adolescent may be troublesome for both. In addition, parents may couple competitive strivings with sexually seductive patterns of relating to their opposite-gender adolescent or that adolescent's same-sex peers.

Adolescents have their own version of these sexual issues: their powerful new sexual urges contrast starkly with their former selves. Young children wonder about the sexuality of their parents and tend to want to see them as asexual. During adolescence teenagers come to fully understand that their parents are sexual creatures. Anna Freud interpreted the rebellion of adolescents against their parents as a function of the resurgence of infantile sexuality. She believed that the infant's libidinal attachments to the opposite-sex parent and rudimentary identification with the same-sex parent and related conflict resurface in adolescence (Freud, 1958). For example, an adolescent girl may actively participate with and support her mother in discussions of women's issues while constantly challenging and taunting her father's authority. At some point, however, the daughter may find herself distancing. For example, the girl may say "My mother put up with a lot and never questioned my father! She would not even listen to me or accept my support, but tolerated my father's behaviors. I'm so angry with her, she deserves what she got!"

Parents are confused as well. Cuddling that was once asexual may now be accompanied by conscious and unconscious sexual feelings in both the parent and the child, causing discomfort or embarrassment for both. Fearful about sexual feelings, parents may inadvertently reject their opposite-sex children. In dysfunctional families, incest may occur when a child reaches adolescence, or parents may create a double bind for the adolescent by overtly admonishing particular behaviors but at the same time communicating that they expect them, frequently because the parents themselves engaged in such behaviors as adolescents. Adelaide Johnson (1949) described this phenomenon as the "superego lacuna." For example, a chief computer security officer's son may create a virus that disables many computer systems. It is possible that during his own adolescence, the security officer had wanted to break into computer systems. Perhaps in later years he channeled his impulses in a more productive way and became a security officer. However, his son might have acted on his father's unconscious impulses, and at an unconscious level, the father may have encouraged his son's impulses. In extreme cases, parents may arouse premature development of certain inclinations by proscribing and describing in great detail behavior that the child does not even understand. More commonly, parents who have experienced difficulty in some area during their own adolescence have difficulty setting consistent and appropriate limits with their adolescent children in that area, although their guidance may be very appropriate in other matters. Regardless of what they may say about their parents' expectations, adolescents usually try to fulfill them, and they complain of experiencing problems with self-esteem when they do not.

Devaluation

Devaluation is a process by which adolescents reduce the value of previously assimilated sets of ideas, goals, objectives, and relationship patterns

(Hauser, 1990). The family may recognize the increasing independence of its adolescent member and may accept and encourage continued differentiation, supporting new opinions and insights even if they are at odds with those previously shared by all family members. On the other hand, family members may be surprised or alarmed by unexpected disagreements and challenges by the previously agreeable adolescent. The family that feels threatened by these challenges may respond by devaluing the new opinions. For example, the level-headed adolescent may criticize his mother's cooking after he has explored new tastes in his broader world, may choose not to eat with the rest of the family, or may grab a TV dinner.

Adolescent criticisms may extend to parental likes and dislikes, their views or ideas regarding social norms or values, their careers, and their political and religious beliefs. Adolescents' ability to criticize their parents is related to their enhanced perception of behavior and its underlying meanings. The nature of the criticism also reflects differing levels of cognitive development associated with different phases of adolescence. Early adolescents tend to challenge obvious and observable contrasts in the behaviors parents engage in versus what they preach. For example, in the early stage of adolescence, a child of alcoholic parents, for instance, may exhibit devaluation by being very critical of parental drinking. In middle adolescence, with enhanced cognitive ability, the adolescent may be equipped to question parents' personal likes and dislikes. The adolescent begins to recognize that he or she has acquired the parents' likes and dislikes at some point in development. The middle adolescent of traditional parents may be critical of his or her parents' clothing preferences or choice of furniture or music. The late adolescent, who is more capable of abstract thinking, begins to understand societal norms and values that other subsets of people within the same culture ascribe to but are totally different from the parents' value system. The late adolescent of a military family, for example, may begin to become critical of his or her parents' traditional patriotism.

These challenges to parental values set up the distancing that allows the children to see themselves as distinct individuals, with unique identities apart from those of their parents, and capable of deciding for themselves whether parental val-

91

ues are good or bad. Viewed in this manner, devaluation is a part of normal adolescent development. It can have a positive value, not only for an adolescent's own development but even for society as a whole. Having perceived what they deem to be the imperfections of the adult world with their newly discovered cognitive skills, adolescents are determined to do better—to supplant their parents' outdated moral precepts with state-of-the-art morality designed to work perfectly in the "New World Order" that will be ushered in when their generation assumes the mantle of authority. The realization that they may ultimately return to the old values in adulthood is little comfort to adolescents—or to their parents. They will embrace the moral "antiques" of their childhood too late to prevent the conflict that naturally must ensue during adolescence. At the same time, those same values provide a sense of security. They are the moral equivalents of baseball cards or stamp collections, providing the nostalgic warmth of a simpler time, when moral issues were black and white and not so loaded with guilt or self-interest. Adolescents also may use parental values as a security blanket, to establish uniqueness, an assurance that the adolescent or later adult really has a distinct identity.

What kinds of ideologies qualify as values? Traditionally, strongly held religious or political beliefs have been the most obvious examples. Unfortunately, many studies have shown that neither political nor religious views are meaningful to adolescents (Hess & Torney, 1967; Jennings & Niemi, 1968). That has led to conflicting conclusions: that these values are acquired before adolescence or, conversely, that they are acquired later. There is yet a third possibility: that current values are more global or metaphysical than the traditional religious or political beliefs. Current societal values are less simplistic or reductionistic in nature. Today's values are not simply the good vs. evil that the child perceived during the concrete stage of cognitive development.

Significant family interaction may constrain (restrict, limit) or enable (facilitate, enhance) communication in the following, and other, areas. As a result of an adolescent's provocative comments, parents may withdraw or give uncharacteristically authoritarian or harsh responses. In one case, the parents stopped offering suggestions and did not even ask about their adolescent's progress in com-

pleting job applications due to his repeated rejection of their advice. Distraction creates withdrawal, another form of constraining interaction. Family members may interfere with the expressed perceptions, thoughts, or feelings of one another by making tangential points, by changing the subject entirely, or by making self-contradictory responses. For example, a father may insert seemingly irrelevant or vaguely formed ideas whenever the adolescent offers a new perception or thought. A mother may interfere with her son's self-awareness or poise so that his train of thought or concentration is unsettled or, at the extreme, undermined.

On the other hand, enabling interactions are explaining, problem solving, expressing curiosity, focusing, accepting, and empathizing. For example, a son's thoughtful explanation of a new perspective may elicit helpful paraphrasing (focusing) and continued curiosity from his parents.

Distancing

The term "adolescent turmoil" becomes more understandable if one recognizes that the emotional conflict that accompanies devaluation and the rejection of parental morality combined with the loss of security of those values is occurring simultaneously with biologically based increases in sexual drives.

According to Mahler (1967), distancing is a normal phenomenon; it actually begins early in life and intensifies in adolescence. An infant learns to walk by venturing out into the unknown, exposing him- or herself to injury; only by taking a few staggering steps and falling down can he or she master walking. In some cases, parents may not be ready for their baby to take this first step toward self-sufficiency. But ultimately, infants discover this new skill allows them to leave the warmth and safety they found in their parents' laps and also gives them the freedom to return to that safety and security at will.

Because of their limited cognitive skills, the preconformist adolescent has a great deal of difficulty establishing distance from parental values and responds with impulsive actions. The child of alcoholic parents, though devaluing parental drinking, may respond impulsively by taking drugs. In middle adolescence, the conformist teen may reject parental styles and adopt an eclectic, bohemian, or "punk" style in attitude or clothing. And in later adolescence, the moral, conscientious "army brat" may embrace pacifism. Not surprisingly, the adolescent's struggle for his or her own identity may cause a variety of reactions in the parents. Some families, often inadvertently, obstruct the adolescent's attempts to establish relationships that allow an appropriate degree of autonomy.

In addition, other parents may feel envious of their child's sexual freedom or experimentation, and may be driven by their own fantasies of what their children are doing. Mothers worry about what happened to their little boys, while fathers may react jealously to a maturing daughter's boyfriends, projecting and displacing their own incestuous fantasies. Alternately, parents may revel in their children's exploits, too easily abandoning the parental role and implicitly encouraging dangerous or immoral behavior. Many of these extremes—harsh rules, overprotection, or implicit encouragement—may result in such behavior.

The pace of distancing often reflects the adolescent's development pattern. Offer describes three types of adolescent growth: continuous, sergeant, and tumultuous (Offer, 1969; Offer & Offer, 1975; Offer et al., 1990b). Each type of growth is likely to manifest distancing in a different way. Adolescents in the continuous-growth group progress steadily through adolescence, showing self-assurance in their transition to adulthood. Their family history and childhood were relatively stable, and parents were able to encourage their children's independence. As a result, this group exhibits relatively little disruption in the distancing process.

Those adolescents in the sergeant-growth group were likely to have experienced a series of developmental spurts, resulting in significant emotional conflict as they distance themselves from their parents. Despite the need to devote more energy toward mastering developmental tasks, their long-term adjustment is usually just as adaptive and successful as that of the first group.

The third group, those experiencing tumultuous growth, generally demonstrates significant turmoil and psychopathology. Generally these adolescents come from a less stable background than the other two groups; many of these adolescents experience greater psychological pain and may require psychotherapy.

In general, studies indicate that families are able to make the process of distancing easier by promoting new patterns of individual authority and encouraging different types of relationships or connections with outsiders. Other strategies that work effectively for parents include allowing their adolescents to make decisions of increasing importance and giving them responsibility for an ever-widening array of moral choices.

Authority Conflict

The related concepts of devaluation and distancing create a parental paradigm resulting in conflict in which the child must distance him- or herself in order to individuate.

For most adolescents, the way they resolve conflict in the home reflects how they will resolve issues in adulthood. Adolescents both adapt and exercise the skills they learned in the family setting, applying them to the demands of society at large. The world presents its own challenges, of course, alternately demanding the skills of both follower and leader from adolescents—which causes authority confusion. The children will resolve this confusion only by developing their own value system—which, of course, begins at home. Adolescents need to know how far they can go on their own, but they also need to be able to return to the security and safety of the parental relationship. Their ambivalence toward authority in the midst of growing individuality, their confusing and contradictory actions, is their way of attempting to determine how well they can deal with their own impulses and frustrations.

For parents, the conflict of values is a double-edged sword: If they attempt to force their children to maintain their values, they face constant conflict. But if they allow their children to abandon their values too quickly, they show their own lack of moral commitment and cut their children adrift in a sea of moral uncertainty.

For that reason, parents must maintain their most important precepts even in the face of the guerrilla warfare waged by their teenagers. In fact, parents who only give lip service to their moral values create a tumultuous situation for their adolescent children. How can these children develop the perfect moral solution, when they have an uncertain footing? By all indications, parental values are the building blocks adolescents will use to fashion their own new, improved system of morality and values.

It is not uncommon for parents who were themselves rebellious as teenagers to have a rude awakening when their adolescent offspring begin to mature. The adolescent "antiauthority" stance takes on an entirely different aspect when an angry teenager is confronting the once-rebellious parent as the quintessential authority figure, forcing the parents to rethink their own views on authority and to be appropriately decisive. Suddenly parents must replay their own adolescence, searching for solutions.

Individuals who fail to resolve, during adolescence, the issues of having a separate identity while still being connected to parents may continue to display devaluation and distancing into adulthood, manifested by such behaviors as continuing defiance of authority figures, disparagement of parents, and devaluation of past connections. In some people, the struggle to distance themselves from parental values goes on for decades and is displaced onto cultural institutions or value systems: the aging hippie or the rebel without a cause, for instance.

THE END OF FOND IDEALS; OR IS IT?

In an extensive systematic empirical study, Offer and his associates found that normal adolescents did not perceive any major problems between themselves and their parents. No evidence was presented for major intergenerational conflict in his sample involving 30,000 teenagers in 10 countries, over three decades. In 1960 study, American teenagers described their parents in somewhat more positive terms than did these teenagers surveyed in the 1970s and 1980s (Offer, Ostrov, Howard, & Atkinson, 1988). The parents were described as patient, reasonable adults who knew what they were doing.

In the 1980s, teenagers were more inclined to say that, although their parents may have been satisfied with them, they were not necessarily satisfied with their parents. The family of the 1980s

seemed to be somewhat more distant; there seemed to be less cohesion and more taking of sides among family members. And the family was seen as less democratic than the families of the 1960s.

In addition, 1960s' adolescents had a more positive psychologic self (believing that it is normal for young people to enjoy life and to be happy with themselves most of the time) than did the adolescents from the 1970s and 1980s. In terms of scale means, all three social-self scales showed that teenagers had a more positive psychologic self in the early 1960s than their counterparts did in the 1970s. It is of particular note that the 1960s' subjects had the highest standard score on the moral scale among all the groups studied; this may indicate that the adolescents of the 1960s had more stable and well-structured ethical standards than did their successors.

Any discussion of values must make note of the sociocultural framework. American values have undergone a series of shifts over the last 40 years, making it relatively more difficult for adolescents to develop individual values. One interpretation of the Offer studies might be that this shift in values necessarily led to the narcissistic styles of 1980s' teenagers. As their parents of the 1950s and 1960s were undergoing a series of shifts, they themselves did not have a firm footing.

Ironically, the formative experiences of adolescents of the 1960s led to positive self-esteem. Even as the hippies of the 1960s, they described their parents in a positive light. But their behaviors went to extremes in distancing, devaluation, and authority conflicts, fighting for a unified cause or moral value. Conversely, the narcissistic children of the 1980s gave their parents a much lower approval rating, reflecting their own poor self-image. Behaviors, in addition, underscore the lack of self-esteem, hollowly imitating the 1960s in everything from fashions and musical styles to politics and art.

There is hope, however, in the observation that such occurrences are cyclical. All is not lost—enough of the pre-1960s' values remain in our cultural heritage. Whether as an old-fashioned revival or as a recycled version of that "old-time religion," we can expect to see values come back into fashion. A new generation of parents will raise their children with a firm hand and a clear sense of values, so that their children, in turn, can liberate themselves anew and become the "flower children" of the next century.

Parents can help or hinder the process. By bringing their own jealousies or unresolved conflicts into the fray, they often place roadblocks to their child's development. And if they fail to press home their values, they provide no basis their offspring can use to fashion their own system of morality.

REFERENCES

Blos, P. (1962). On adolescence. A psychoanalytic interpretation. In P. Blos (Ed.), *Phases of adolescence* (p. 52). New York: Free Press.

Blos, P. (1967). The second individuation process of adolescence. *Psychoanalytic Study of the Child, 22,* 162–186.

Freud, A. (1958). Adolescence. *Psychoanalytic Study of the Child, 16,* 225–2728.

Hauser, S. T. (1990). Adolescence: Psychopathology, normality & creativity. *Psychiatric Clinics of North America, 13* (3), 495.

Hauser, S. T., Borman, E., & Bowlds, M. (1991). Understanding coping within adolescence: Ego development and coping strategies. In A. L. Greene, E. M. Cummings, & K. Karraker (Eds.), *Life-span developmental psychology: Perspectives on stress and coping.* Hillsdale, NJ: Lawrence Erlbaum.

Hess, R. D., & Torney, J. (1967). *The development of political attitudes in children.* New York: Aldine.

Jennings, M. K., & Niemi, R. G. (1968). The transmission of political values from parent to child. *American Political Science Review, 62,* 169–184.

Johnson, A. M. (1949). Sanctions for superego lacunae of adolescents. In K. R. Eissler (Ed.), *Delinquency* (pp. 225–245). New York: International Universities Press.

Kohlberg, L. (1964). Development of moral character and moral ideology. In M. C. Hoffman & L. W. Hoffman (Eds.), *Review of child development research* (Vol. 1, pp. 383–432). New York: Russell Sage Foundation.

Mahler, M. (1967). On human symbiosis and the vicissitudes of individuation. *Journal of the American Psychoanalytic Association, 15,* 740–763.

Offer, D. (1969). *The psychological world of the teenager: A study of normal adolescent boys.* New York: Basic Books.

Offer, D., & Offer, J. B. (1975). *From teenage to young manhood: A psychological study.* New York: Basic Books.

Offer, D., Ostrov, E., Howard, K., & Atkinson, R. (1990a). Adolescence: Psychopathology, normality and creativity. *Psychiatric Clinics of North America, 13* (3), 377–388.

Offer, D., Ostrov, E., Howard, K., & Atkinson, R. (1990b). Normality and adolescence. *Psychiatric Clinics of North America, 13* (3), 317–388.

Offer, D., Ostrov, E., Howard, K. I., & Atkinson, R. (1988). *The teenage world: Adolescents self-image in ten countries.* New York: Plenum Press.

12 / Attachment in Adolescence

Diana S. Rosenstein and Harvey A. Horowitz

> The family experience of those who grow up to become relatively stable and self-reliant is characterized not only by unfailing parental support when called upon but also by a steady but timely encouragement toward increasing autonomy, and by the frank communication by parents of working models—of themselves, of [the] child, and of others—that are not only tolerably valid but are open to be questioned and revised.
> —BOWLBY, 1973, pp. 322–323

Although attachment theory has been central to the understanding of the social development of infants and young children for the past 30 years, the vicissitudes of attachment in the adolescent years did not receive comparable attention until relatively recently (Kobak & Sceery, 1988; Weiss, 1982). In fact, it was commonly thought that adolescence was a period of weakening attachment to the family, with increased separation from parents and growing autonomy. It is true that direct and immediate parental influence is less apparent during adolescence than in earlier stages of childhood, but adolescence is a time when relationships with parents come again to the fore and are heightened in intensity compared to preadolescence. The emergence of emotionally charged issues such as separation, identity formation, and autonomy, while confronting the adolescent with difficult developmental tasks, present opportunities for further differentiation and integration of the individual within the context of relationships.

Attachment theory is a developmental theory, and it is grounded in a perspective that views development as a goal-directed process of change, during which new competencies and adaptive patterns emerge from the reorganization of previous patterns, structures, and competencies. According to Werner (1957), this process "proceeds from an initial stage of globality and lack of differentiation to increasing states of articulation, differentiation and hierarchical integration" (p. 126). This developmental perspective is defined by four basic assumptions:

1. The dialectical and paradoxical: Development is a dynamic process that embodies both structure and process, organization and activity, differentiation and integration, continuity and discontinuity, stability and change.
2. The relational and contextual: Development proceeds within a relational matrix; it is interactive and contextual. In human development, the individual is seen as emerging or differentiating from within a matrix of relationships and remaining interdependent within relational contexts throughout the life span.
3. The constructivist and metaphoric: Development is a co-construction of meaning and knowledge through a coordination of actions, affective communication, language, awareness, and shared experience. All human categories, including "reality" and "objectivity," are metaphoric, constructed from experience, constrained by biology, and finding stability in the consensual domain of human meaning systems.
4. The cybernetic and recursive: Development is a living process with systemic and holistic properties embodying complex circular causality, self-reference and self-generation (autopoiesis), and part-whole relation and coherence.

By understanding these aspects of attachment theory, it is possible to comprehend the paradox of the increasingly autonomous adolescent who is firmly embedded in and profoundly influenced by attachment to parents.

Review of Attachment Theory

BOWLBY: THE ATTACHMENT BEHAVIORAL SYSTEM AND INTERNAL WORKING MODELS

Bowlby (1958, 1969/1982, 1973, 1980) devised attachment theory as a combination of features of ethology, control systems theory, cognitive science, and psychoanalytic theories. Following the British Object Relations school, Bowlby postulated the primacy of social affectional ties between a child and his or her caregiver, independent of the secondary reinforcement of caregiving practices.

Using ethological explanations, the child's tie to the mother subserved a biological and adaptive function in an evolutionary context. The goal of enhanced survival of the child is mediated by the proximity of the child to the caregiver to accomplish the caregiver's protective and nurturing abilities, which fulfills a complementary evolutionary function. From these basic premises, Bowlby attempted to explain childhood psychopathological disorders, reactions to separation from parents, and mourning as examples of behaviors designed to increase proximity to the caregiver, thereby enhancing survival. As the child developed, the easily observed behavioral aspects of attachment were enhanced and supplanted by the emotional and cognitive aspects that subserved the same adaptive function of increasing access to the caregiver and hence survival.

Drawing on control systems theory, Bowlby posited an attachment behavioral system that could be activated when access to the caregiver was threatened. This system coexisted in reciprocal interplay with the exploratory system, which accomplished exploration of the environment and the development of autonomy and competence. Only when the child was confident in his or her access to the caregiver did the child feel confident to engage in exploration. Ainsworth (Ainsworth, Blehar, Waters, & Wall, 1978) called this the secure base phenomenon, and reformulated the goal of attachment behavior as both proximity to the caregiver and emotional security in the availability of the caregiver. Thus, three criteria define a relationship as fulfilling the function of attachment: (1) the need for ready access to the attachment figure—"accessibility"; (2) the desire for the proximity to the attachment figure in times of stress— "proximity seeking under conditions of threat"; and (3) diminished anxiety in the company of the attachment figure and increased anxiety when the attachment figure is unavailable—"secure base and felt security" (Weiss, 1982).

During the first year of life, the infant's attachment behaviors become organized around maintaining access to a specific, preferred figure, the primary caregiver (typically the mother). The goal of attachment is achieved when the infant is sufficiently near the attachment figure and attachment behaviors such as crying or clinging are not expressed. The infant is then free to explore the environment, and through this exploration, cognitive development, mastery, and self-reliance are fostered. A mother's (or other primary caregiver's) ability to create a secure base works jointly with her ability to foster appropriate levels of autonomy in her infant. As cognitive ability develops, the toddler becomes less dependent on immediate sensory experiences and is able to use cognition to ascertain maternal availability, cope with separations, and explore the environment. What Bowlby (1969/1982) termed the "goal-corrected partnership" emerges. The toddler is now able to engage in communication with the mother about her availability and can negotiate shared plans about the maintenance of security in her absence (e.g., "Mommy will be in the kitchen. You play here and get me if you need me.") Quality of attachment in the preschool years should, therefore, include aspects of child reciprocity, perspective-taking, management of relationships, and empathy (Crittenden, 1992, p. 211).

Also accompanying the toddler's increasing cognitive and linguistic sophistication is Bowlby's notion of an "internal working model." In this model the history of the child's relationship to caregivers, particularly information about the caregiver's availability and quality of responsiveness, and complementary aspects of the child's self are cognitively represented. Such a model would guide expectations and attitudes about current and future relationships and organize an individual's behavior in all emotionally significant relationships. Although they are updated by ongoing experience, working models become resistant to change beyond early childhood because they develop preverbally, are affectively laden, and tend to be reinforced by ongoing experience. Attachment, therefore, is one means of conceptualizing and describing a basic intrapsychic organization that is a "tolerably accurate reflection" (Bowlby, 1973) of actual relationship experiences. This view of internal working models as affectively charged representations of self and important others is very close to psychoanalytic formulations of self and object representations.

Bowlby's models were based on actual experience. He saw that the competence of the caregiver directly affects the quality of caregiver-child relations. Children whose caregivers are sensitive, attuned, and accepting expect to continue to be treated in this way. In contrast, inconsistency or insensitivity in parental responsiveness encourages children to develop defenses (in Bowlby's terminology, "defensive biases") that allow the children to cope with the painful affects they experience and simultaneously to maintain access to the caregiver. Bowlby postulated that such defensively biased models were even more enduring than models based on security and confidence in the caregiver. Thus, defensively biased models formed the initial stages of defensive structures, which would ultimately lead to distortions in personality and psychopathology.

ATTACHMENT THROUGHOUT THE LIFE SPAN

Despite the focus in developmental psychology on the nature and function of attachment in infants and toddlers, Bowlby viewed attachment as developing throughout the life span. Indeed, one of his most important contributions was to point out that an increased need and desire for closeness in times of stress is normal rather than a sign of maladaptive dependency. However, how these attachment functions are played out beyond early childhood was less well studied. While Bowlby strongly affirmed the existence of attachment, especially the secure base phenomenon, in adolescence and adulthood, he did not consider that it changed in quality. He explained the fact that older children and adolescents tolerated longer and more distant separations from attachment figures on the basis of their advancing cognitive and ego development, which in turn permitted greater internalization of self-regulatory abilities previously supplied by the attachment figure and allowed for substitution of symbolic methods of proximity seeking (e.g., phone calls, letters, photographs) for the physical closeness required by the young child. Changes in the hierarchy of attachment figures also occur beginning in adolescence (Bowlby, 1969/1982; 1988). Romantic partners replace parents as primary attachment figures, and attachment is directed toward groups and institutions. Adolescents who have had inadequate attachments to their parents may form relationships with other, more responsive adults, to replace these deficient relationships. Although the adolescent may be able to tolerate, or more correctly seeks and welcomes, increased physical and psychological distance from early attachment figures, he or she is able to do so only with the knowledge that a secure base awaits a call. In Bowlby's words, "All of us,

from the cradle to the grave, are happiest when life is organized as a series of excursions, long or short, from the secure base provided by our attachment figure(s)" (1988, p. 62).

Weiss (1982) echoes much of Bowlby's theorizing regarding the role of attachment in adolescence and beyond. The three basic criteria for identifying a relationship as an attachment relationship—accessibility, proximity seeking, and a secure base—can be found in "relationships of central emotional importance" (p. 174) throughout the life span. Several important distinctions exist between childhood and adult attachments, however. The first concerns the asymmetry inherent in childhood attachment relationships, with the attachment figure viewed not only as a safe haven but as a source of other forms of caregiving. Another aspect of this asymmetry is that the attachment figure may be imbued with powers beyond the range of the child, such as greater competence, wisdom, or strength. In adolescence, one of the central transformations revolves around the deidealization of the attachment figure (Blos, 1967) and hence the more objective recognition of that figure's abilities. With the parent-adolescent relationship put on a more equal footing, attachment figures come to be used to foster the adolescent's own capacity to master challenges, as allies. Weiss (1982) describes parents of adolescents as "attachment figures in reserve" (p. 176).

Increased adolescent autonomy is implied in this now more equal relationship with parents, making the adolescent less susceptible to anxiety-triggered activation of the attachment system. Whereas in infancy and early childhood, lack of physical access to the attachment figure when desired is highly affectively arousing or even disorganizing, adolescents can utilize more symbolic access to attachment figures and do not experience major disruptions when access is denied. In contrast to younger children, adolescents seek out longer intervals away from parental supervision or direct contact with parents. Weiss (1982) views the process of relinquishment of the parents as attachment figures not as a gradual one but as one in which the ongoing relationship is punctuated by more frequent and longer separations with briefer resurgences of attachment seeking. An attachment/autonomy dialectic proceeds; during these separations, adolescents test out their own competence, seek out new attachment figures, and increasingly come to rely on their own ability to function autonomously. The new attachment figures are usually peers for younger adolescents and romantic partners for older adolescents. Attachment is not forsaken, since parents are "in reserve," and new attachment relationships take on the same properties as the original ones with parents.

INDIVIDUAL DIFFERENCES IN ATTACHMENT

Mary Ainsworth, an American developmental psychologist and colleague of Bowlby's, set out to provide "a normative account of the development of attachment during the first year of life . . . and . . . an examination of individual differences in the qualitative nature of the attachment" (Ainsworth, 1989, p. 709). From home observations of mother-infant pairs and a laboratory paradigm called the Strange Situation (Ainsworth & Wittig, 1969), in which the separation and reunion behavior of infants with their mothers is observed, three patterns of attachment were identified, one secure and two insecure (avoidant and ambivalent) (Ainsworth, et al., 1978). Although her goal was only to identify patterns in infancy, the same basic patterns have been utilized to recognize behavioral patterns in older children, adolescents, and adults that are the developmentally reorganized and transformed enactments of working models. Subsequent research has described a fourth, insecure (disorganized) pattern (Main & Solomon, 1986, 1990). The same four patterns of attachment have been found in infants, toddlers (Crittenden, 1992), school-age children (Main, Kaplan, & Cassidy, 1985), adolescents (Kobak & Sceery, 1988; Rosenstein & Horowitz, 1993), and adults (Main & Goldwyn, 1985–1991). Each attachment pattern corresponds to a working model that guides behavior on the part of the child as well as the mother. The insecure models involve defensive biases leading to characteristic defensive behaviors. The attachment types and their behavioral and defensive correlates are described next.

Secure/Autonomous Attachment: Most infants (65–75%) in American middle-class samples are secure. Secure infants acknowledge maternal absence on separation, either through protest or diminishment in the quality of play, but greet the mother with pleasure on reunion. If distressed, the infant is calmed by the mother's return or ministrations, such as holding or reassurance. These infants have a working model of their mother as "sensitively responsive" to their needs, which refers to the caregiver's capacity to understand the needs of the infant accurately and respond to those needs. Securely attached infants expect that their mothers will see their distress and also will respond to their signals about how to end that distress.

Secure toddlers and school-age children are not distressed by brief separations from parents and affectionately and confidently initiate conversation or contact with their parents on reunion. Their conversations are distinguished by fluidity and a sense of ease. When asked to fantasize about separations from parents, their descriptions show an openness to the topic, an ease with both positive and negative aspects of the situation, an ability to become absorbed in other activities during the separation, and the anticipation of a happy reunion.

Secure (autonomous) adolescents and adults value attachment relationships and regard attachment-related experiences as pleasurable. They are relatively independent and objective regarding any particular experience or relationship. Their view of parents is coherent and consistent. Typically, in discussing their relationships with their parents, they are fluent and relaxed. They seem at ease with the topic of relationships with parents and therefore able to reflect objectively on experiences with them.

Avoidant/Dismissing Attachment: A second group of infants (20 to 25% of middle-class samples) is characterized as having insecure-avoidant attachments. These infants rarely show overt distress over separation. On reunion they are indifferent to their mother's return and literally avoid interaction with her, usually turning their attention to toys, exploration of the room, or the company of the stranger. As with the other types of attachment, this avoidant behavior develops in the context of a particular kind of mother-infant relationship. These infants have been emotionally and physically rejected, particularly in times of distress (Ainsworth et. al., 1978). The avoidant infant has created an adaptative strategy to deal with rejection and to regulate his or her affective response to this rejection. The mother's rejection of the infant's attachment behavior leads to anger and anxiety within the infant. Avoidance is a compromise between alienating the attachment figure with angry demands for attention and maintaining an intolerably angry, rejected position in the absence of a comforting attachment figure. Avoidance serves to cut off the affective arousal before it is experienced as distress. This allows the infant to regulate affect, thereby maintaining some organization during times of distress, and to maintain some comforting physical proximity to the attachment figure.

Avoidant toddlers and children show the same pattern of indifference to relationships and heightened interest in the environment. Avoidant (dismissing) adolescents and adults either dismiss the importance of relationships or dismiss the extent of the impact of the relationship on the self. They idealize their parents or portray negative experiences with their parents as normal. Frequently they lack memories of childhood; if negative memories are present, they regard themselves as unaffected by them. Often they highly value achievement, self-reliance, personal strength, or cunning. Sometimes they cite these qualities as rationalizations for the lack of effect of negative experiences on the self. The dismissing organization functions defensively to exclude from awareness any information that may evoke attachment behaviors and hence make a person vulnerable to being rebuffed, resulting in painful affects of anger and sadness. To make a bad situation worse, if these feelings are revealed, the parents are not able to respond to them in a way that alleviates the adolescent's distress, nor does the adolescent have sufficient self-regulatory capacity to acknowledge and tolerate negative affect. The result is that negative affects can be neither displayed nor tolerated in order to achieve mastery over threatening or frustrating situations. Hence, denial, falsification of affective expression, and displacement of aggression are used as the primary defenses of dismissing individuals.

Ambivalent/Preoccupied Attachment: The third attachment classification, the insecure-ambivalent attachment, is the rarest organization in infancy (less than 10% of Ainsworth's middle-class sample). It is characterized by cyclical efforts to gain security from the attachment figure and avoidance of that figure. These infants are distressed by novel environments and cling to their mothers. On separation they are excessively distressed and uncontrolled. On reunion these infants alternate bids

for physical contact with their mothers with angry rebuffs of their mothers. They fail to be soothed by their mothers' attentions and therefore cannot use their mothers as a secure base. These infants have experienced inconsistent sensitivity from their mothers (Ainsworth et al., 1978), leading them to become uncertain of the mother's availability. In order to elicit and maintain the mother's attention, the infant intensifies attachment behaviors and vigilance regarding her whereabouts, leading to a pattern of exaggerated emotionality and angry rebuff of maternal soothing and anxiety.

Ambivalent toddlers and preschoolers show inappropriate or exaggerated emotional expressions and chronic low-level dependency on adults, and are socially incompetent with peers. Ambivalent (preoccupied) adolescents and adults appear highly conflicted and in an ongoing cycle of fruitless reflection on relationships with parents and disavowal of interest in maintaining these relationships. Identity diffusion is common. The "actively preoccupied" adolescent shows extreme anger toward parents and blames them for his or her problems, together with placating attitudes toward the parents. "Passively preoccupied" adolescents oscillate between positive and negative characterizations of parents, or give descriptions of their parents that are so vague that they are nearly incomprehensible. Preoccupied individuals' bids for attachment are partially or inconsistently met, and the behavior of parents of such adolescents is such that it prevents disengagement from the relationship. Patterns of hysteric, obsessional, and borderline defenses are therefore common in these adolescents.

Disorganized/Unresolved Attachment: Infants in the fourth category, whose attachment has been characterized as "disorganized," do not possess a coherent and functional strategy for regulating their distress on separation and therefore engage in behaviors that seem inexplicable or contradictory in intent or function (Main & Solomon, 1990). Behaviors seen in these infants include "approaching with the head averted, stilling or freezing of movement with a dazed expression, walking backwards toward the mother, calm, contented play suddenly succeeded by distressed angry behavior" (Main & Solomon, 1990, p. 122). In low-risk (middle-class) samples, infant disorganization has been found to be associated with the mother's unresolved mourning for her own attachment figure (Ainsworth & Eichberg, 1991). According to Main and Hesse (1990), the mother's lack of resolution of mourning leads to frightened and frightening behavior by the mother with her own infant. The infant is placed in the intolerable position of having the source of his or her distress and haven from that distress embodied in the same person— the attachment figure. In high-risk samples (impoverished individuals; individuals with abusive, neglectful, or psychopathological attachment figures), infant disorganization is also strongly related to maternal lack of resolution of trauma, typically parental history of childhood abuse or neglect (Carlson, Cicchetti, Barnett, & Braunwald, 1989).

Disorganized (unresolved) attachment in adolescents and adults results from unresolved responses to trauma in childhood (typically physical or sexual abuse) or from unresolved mourning of an attachment figure lost when the individual was young. In both cases, unresolved individuals cannot move beyond the events in question to form an abstract understanding of their effect. They continue to experience disorganization and disorientation, as manifest in irrational thought processes surrounding the traumatic or loss event, unfounded fear, unfounded guilt, and continuing disbelief that the traumatic events occurred. While this category frequently is viewed as a separate attachment organization, it can occur in adolescents or adults who had developed any of the other types of attachment organizations prior to the trauma or loss. In such persons, both the superimposed unresolved attachment and the preexisting attachment type should be discernible. Preliminary studies have shown that unresolved attachment is associated with dissociative experiences in adults (Main, van IJzendoorn, & Hesse, 1993).

Attachment and the Tasks of Adolescence

SEPARATION-INDIVIDUATION AND IDENTITY FORMATION

Until recently, the dominant view of an adolescent's relationship with parents emphasized the adolescent's developmentally appropriate need to create emotional and physical distance from the family of origin. Distancing was viewed as a necessary component of the separation-individuation task for the adolescent, in the service of enhanced individuation. These processes have been held to result ultimately in the adolescent's self-reliant adaptation, with internalized affective and cognitive controls, and a replacement of relationships with parents with peer and romantic relationships. The end result of the separation-individuation process is a cohesive identity and sense of self, allowing for independent functioning. This view has long-standing roots in the psychoanalytic literature (A. Freud, 1958), with the most recent and influential voice articulated by Blos (1967). According to Blos, individuation results from the adolescent's relinquishment of dependence on infantile parental introjects. Separation, defined as a distinct sense of self as a separate person from the parents, then occurs. The adolescent thereby becomes capable of taking over functions that were previously performed by parental ego supports and parental introjects. Blos describes this process as the "second separation-individuation," likening it to the separation-individuation process that occurs in toddlerhood (Mahler, Pine, & Bergman, 1975), through which a sense of self, as distinct from mother, is first established. The rekindled need for separation-individuation in adolescence is prompted by puberty and the urge toward sexual object choice outside of the family this entails. Hence failures in the separation-individuation process can lead to difficulty in accepting sexuality and in the development of intimacy.

With the growing attempt to understand the role of attachment beyond its origins in infancy and toddlerhood, the prevailing view of adolescence as a progressive movement away from emotional reliance on parents and family and toward complete self-reliance has come into question. According to attachment theory, the attachment system is active throughout the life span, although reorganized in its behavioral expression to meet the needs of the individual at every point in development (Sroufe & Waters, 1977). The first separation-individuation process in toddlerhood does not dissolve the child's attachment relationship when a sense of self is established. Rather, attachment is reorganized in the context of developmental transformations. Attachment behaviors in toddlerhood continue to be organized around maintenance of security, although incorporating the toddler's capacity for understanding the goals and intentions of the attachment figure in order to negotiate the attachment figure's availability. Similarly, attachment is maintained in adolescence, albeit with transformed behavioral expressions and transformations in the contexts in which it occurs. That is, adolescents maintain attachment relationships with parents, although attachment behaviors may be emitted less frequently, with less intensity and urgency, and increasingly come under the control of higher-order cognitive processes such as abstraction, formal reasoning, and metacognitive monitoring.

Just as attachment functions early in life to provide security to the vulnerable child, so it functions in adolescence to provide security under instances of heightened vulnerability, fear, and stress. Just as in the preschool years, more and more self-regulatory functions are assumed by the child, secure in the knowledge of parental availability if needed, so in adolescence, more and more self-regulatory functions typical of adulthood are assumed by the adolescent, in the context of parental availability if needed. Rice (1990) cites the contingent necessity of parents and contingent awareness of attachment longings as one of the reasons that links between attachment and adolescent adjustment have been so variable:

[the link] waxes and wanes during one's development. It may be that a stronger association between attachment and adjustment occurs prior to important developmental transitions (e.g., admission to college, graduation from college). Once the transition is made, the adolescent may rely on other sources to help him or her adjust (e.g., peer groups, counselors). Since multiple attachment figures are possible, the adolescent may at certain times and in certain situations utilize attachment relationships with someone other than parents. (Pp. 534–535)

Parents continue to serve as a "secure base" for their adolescent children. They serve both as proximal sources of aid in times of need or distress and as distal sources of potential aid. The assurance of their availability frees the adolescent to utilize his or her capacities to explore the environment. Hence, as the attachment behavioral system is deactivated, the exploratory behavioral system can come in to play.

Beyond the secure base functions provided by parents of adolescents, parental encouragement of appropriate levels of autonomy also is associated with adolescent attachment security. For parents to encourage autonomy and at the same time provide support, they must intuitively understand the needs of their adolescent children. This empathic sensitivity is analogous to that needed for infants and toddlers. Just as maternal sensitivity to her infant predicts security of the infant's attachment, so, too, does parental sensitivity to the adolescent's developmental needs predict attachment security. Not only are attachment behaviors in adolescence redefined in light of the organizational perspective, but so are reciprocal parental behaviors. Sensitive parents of infants and toddlers maintain close contact and provide room for exploration. Sensitive parents of adolescents maintain themselves as available for emotional contact while actively promoting and supporting the adolescent's appropriate efforts at self-reliance, self-governance, individual identity, and autonomy. Ryan and Lynch (1989) underscore this view:

We suggest that individuation during adolescence and into young adulthood is facilitated not by detachment . . . but rather by attachment where the latter is appropriately conceptualized . . . [as] those relationships that are optimal and appropriate to a person's developmental level, thereby enabling the person to function with a degree of coherence and integrity that would not otherwise be possible. In adolescence and young adulthood, gratifying relationships with parents would involve emotional closeness and a sense of support within a context of encouragement for one's efforts at individuation and autonomy. . . . Indeed, individuation is not something that happens *from* parents but rather *with* them. (Pp. 340–341)

ATTACHMENT AND PEER GROUP RELATIONS

Early adolescence is a time during which the peer group takes on prominence and in which susceptibility to peer influence is at its height. Traditional accounts have interpreted the peer group as supplanting parental influence and providing support for adolescent independence and individuation in the service of the first steps toward separation from parents. The peer group further functions as a normative reference group in which adolescents come to evaluate their own behavior, increase social skills, and consolidate their identity. Blos (1967) views these extrafamilial influences as essential in the consolidation of identity, a process that cannot take place solely within the confines of the family. Steinberg and Silverberg (1986) take an essentially consistent view, that normative development consists in "a trading of dependency on parents for dependency on peers rather than straightforward and uni-dimensional growth in autonomy" (p. 848). Autonomy is then reserved for a later stage in adolescent development, when the support of the peer group is no longer vital.

Ryan and Lynch (1989) have questioned this belief in the relative functions of parents and peers in the lives of early adolescents. They cite data that show that those adolescents who are most reliant on peer support are doing so in a compensatory manner to make up for feelings of rejection and detachment from parents. Therefore, those adolescents who trade emotional support on parents for emotional support on peers are insecurely attached to parents. Adolescents who are secure with parents are also secure with peers. Armsden and Greenberg (1987) similarly showed the more predominant effect of parental attachment security on adolescent adjustment over and above the effect produced by peer attachment security, highlighting the causal role of parental attachment quality in producing adequate peer relationships.

But how does attachment theory account for the increasing interest in and importance of peers in adolescence? Attachment provides a model that underscores the continued importance of parents as attachment figures in adolescence, both in the ongoing influence on adolescents and in the effect of internalized representations of parents. A timetable for the relinquishment of the immediate aspects of parental influence is suggested, as peers and ultimately romantic partners supplant parents on the hierarchy of attachment figures. Hazan (1991) has most closely studied this issue and posits a developmental sequence in which four basic attachment functions—proximity seeking, separation protest, safe haven, and secure base—shift in object from preadolescence to early adulthood. In preadolescence, all four functions are directed toward parents. Proximity seeking is the first function to shift to peers in early adolescence. By late adolescence, only the secure base function is retained by parents, and this, too, will shift to a

romantic partner when a committed relationship is established.

The sequence of this developmental progression can be altered by the quality of the adolescent's relationship with parents. Varying types of insecure attachment can lead to individual differences in the desire for and adequacy of parents as attachment figures, and this in turn affects relationships with peers. Late adolescents classified in traditional attachment groups (i.e., secure, dismissing, preoccupied) had parents who remained prominent as attachment figures when compared with peers and romantic partners (Smith & George, 1993). This was especially true for the secure and preoccupied groups, the latter group being characterized by its enmeshment with parents. Dismissives were relatively more reliant on peers than were the other two groups. The unresolved adolescents did not rely on any individuals for attachment functions; their isolation from intimate contact was a striking feature of their relational lives.

Empirical Studies of Adolescent Attachment

ATTACHMENT AND SOCIAL DEVELOPMENTAL OUTCOMES

A large body of empirical work has linked the quality of adolescent relationships to their overall emotional adjustment. (See Armsden and Greenberg, 1987, and Rice, 1990, for reviews of this literature.) A much smaller number of investigators have attempted to narrow the construct of "relationships" to Bowlby's ideas of attachment relationships. In keeping with the perspective that views attachment as an organizational construct whose expressions vary both behaviorally and intrapsychically with development, adolescent attachment researchers have attempted to delineate the central functions of attachment in adolescence. Most common, and in keeping with findings of non–attachment-based studies linking relationships and emotional adjustment, are studies that explore the relative contributions of peer and parent attachment to adolescent social and emotional development, especially social competence, self-esteem, identity formation, and emotional adjustment. Investigators have hoped to show either prospectively or concurrently that adolescent adjustment is facilitated by positive attachment to parents, in which parental availability in times of stress, parental support, and warmth are most highly associated with adolescent social and emotional adjustment. Most studies show that a secure relationship to parents continues to have a positive effect on adjustment well into adolescence (Armsden & Greenberg, 1987; Papini, Roggman, & Anderson, 1991; Ryan & Lynch, 1989) and that the quality of the adolescent's relationship with parents is a more important determinant than peer relationships on the adolescent's adjustment. These studies also show that secure adolescents not only feel accepted by parents, but seek out involvement with them.

While the studies just reviewed agree on the association among attachment, social competence, and interpersonal functioning, Rice (1990), in a review of the correlative adaptations of adolescent attachment, cites several inconsistent findings, particularly with regard to identity formation (Lapsley, Rice, & FitzGerald, 1990; Quintana & Lapsley, 1987). Since identity integration was viewed by Erikson (1968) as the essential task of adolescent development, failure to find a link between attachment and identity development undercuts the premise of attachment as basic to all processes of social and emotional development. Nevertheless, some aspects of attachment have been found to be related to identity. Lapsley et al. (1990) did show that communication with parents (one aspect of attachment) was correlated with personal and social identity. Kroger and colleagues (Kroger, 1985; Kroger & Haslett, 1988) related attachment style to identity status, defined according to a developmental model, including an identity crisis leading either to foreclosure, commitment, moratorium, or diffusion. While securely attached adolescents were the most likely to be committed and those who were insecurely attached most likely to be foreclosed, no predictions could be made about the other two identity statuses. Because of the cross-sectional nature of the studies, it is possible that moratorium or diffused individuals were simply delayed in acquiring commitment or foreclosure and that knowing how they eventually resolved their identity crisis might

have allowed greater predictive power from their prior attachment status.

In a meta-analytic review, Rice (1990) concluded, however, that the association among adolescent attachment security, social/emotional adjustment and identity formation did indeed hold: "There appeared to be a consistent positive association between attachment and measures of social competence, self-esteem, identity, and emotional adjustment. Negligible correlations emerged between attachment and measures of college adjustment" (p. 534). He offers two speculations about inconsistencies in results. The first is based on differences in measurement instruments. No studies used multiple measures of attachment or identity, which would have allowed for convergent and discriminant validation of the attachment and identity measures. Using more assessment tools to measure each of these constructs may have revealed more definitively that certain aspects of identity are related to certain aspects of attachment. The second speculation involves time of assessment. Rice posits that

the association between attachment and indices of adjustment waxes and wanes during one's development. It may be that a stronger association between attachment and adjustment occurs prior to important developmental transitions (e.g., admission to college, graduation from college). Once the transition is made, the adolescent may rely on other sources to help him or her adjust (e.g., peer groups, counselors). (Pp. 534–535)

While the studies just reviewed allow for greater specificity of prediction by using constructs from attachment theory, they all allow predictions only regarding the secure/insecure dimension of attachment. None of these studies allows for a description of the emotional and interpersonal difficulties specific to each insecure attachment type. Several other studies have remedied this deficiency. Resnick (1991) reported a correspondence between security and self-esteem, and additionally demonstrated that individuals classified as preoccupied showed the lowest rating of all groups on attachment to peers. Jenkins and Fisher (1989) showed that avoidant individuals reported poor relations with both parents and viewed their mothers as unresponsive, troubled, and demanding, while ambivalent individuals reported poor relations with their mothers and positive ones with their fathers, whom they viewed as understanding and sympathetic. Based on attachment classification, Bartholomew and Horowitz (1991) made predictions about aspects of late-adolescent self-esteem (self-confidence, self-reliance, positive versus negative view of self) and aspects of relationships to others (level of involvement in relationships, emotional expressiveness in relationships, trust). Secures are positive about both self and others, allowing them to maintain close relationships without loss of autonomy, to express interpersonal warmth, and to exhibit coherence and thoughtfulness in discussing relationships. Dismissives have high self-regard and low regard for others, predisposing them to high self-confidence, independence, and self-reliance, but they lack interpersonal trust and closeness and have restricted emotional expressiveness. Others view them as hostile. By contrast, preoccupied individuals have a negative view of self and positive view of others. They are highly emotionally expressive and self-disclosing, highly dependent and caregiving, over-involved in relationships, and incoherent in their discussion of relationships. Others view them as exploitable. The fourth category, unique to this system but paralleling some aspects of the infant disorganized classification, is fearful. These individuals have negative evaluations of both self and others. They avoid closeness because of fear of rejection, distrust others, and are personally insecure. They have low levels of romantic involvement and no reliance on others yet lack self-confidence. They exhibit the most social problems, including lack of assertiveness and social inhibition.

While this study represents a significant advance in predicting the particular problems in social relations and self-concept associated with each attachment type, it does not answer questions regarding the etiology of the types or the dynamic underpinnings that perpetuate dysfunctional relationships. Such deficiencies are remedied by an exemplary study conducted by Kobak and Sceery (1988). Attachment was conceptualized as (among other functions) a theory of affect regulation, which incorporates the idea of defensive bias (Cassidy & Kobak, 1988; Kobak, 1986). An understanding of the styles of affect regulation led to predictions about representation of self and others. In a college (late-adolescent) sample, securely attached adolescents self-reported little distress

and high levels of social support from friends and family. Parents were viewed as loving and available. Kobak and Sceery (1988) conclude that loving and supportive experiences with parents directly lead to the ability to report childhood experiences with clarity, coherence, and balance in the presentation of both positive and negative evaluations. The group dismissing of attachment rated themselves as lonelier, with little support from family, but they had as little distress as the securely attached group. Memory for childhood was poor, presumably protecting these individuals from the negative affect associated with self-acknowledged parental rejection and lack of love. Peers viewed dismissives as more hostile than any attachment group and more anxious than secures. Preoccupied adolescents rated themselves as highly distressed, with poor dating skills, although with high support from parents. They saw parents as loving but role-reversing, leaving them vulnerable to incoherence and continuous efforts to gain support from parents. Others viewed them as more anxious than secure individuals. Taken together, these results suggest deficits in the regulation of negative affect in insecure individuals and differential strategies for the regulation of negative affects leading to differential deficits in self-awareness, symptomatic expression, and social competence. Secure individuals are accurate in self-awareness and socially competent with little distress. Dismissing and preoccupied individuals distort self-awareness for defensive purposes. Dismissives exclude from awareness information that would lead them to confront the anger generated by parental rejection. Preoccupied individuals cannot move beyond a cyclical state of intensive distress, promoting efforts to gain parental support that fail, thereby increasing distress, especially anxiety.

PARENT-ADOLESCENT COMMUNICATION

Less well explored than the relation of attachment to social competence is the relation of family functioning to attachment status. This line of research grows from a tradition in family theory relating patterns of family functioning to ego development (Bell & Bell, 1982; Hauser et al., 1984), identity formation and role-taking skill (Cooper, Grotevant & Condon, 1983), resistance to psychopathology (Wynne, Jones, & Al-Khayyal, 1982), and academic and social competence (Baumrind, 1991). Since each of these areas of adolescent development has been shown to be affected by the attachment status of the adolescent, it stands to reason that adolescent attachment should be directly affected by the quality of family functioning. The results of three studies, to be reviewed, show this to be the case. All three studies use an analysis of observed family interactions as their main source of data. This strategy connects two important strands in family research, what Reiss (1989) refers to as the individual's subjective or "represented" family and the interactive or "practicing" family. The represented family is the family as the developing individual understands or cognitively represents it; this is the concept that has been explored by attachment research. The term "practicing family" refers to the current organization and interactional processes of the family. This aspect of the family has been the focus of both family therapy and parenting practices research. Reiss (1989) emphasizes that both the represented and the practicing families are important regulatory contexts of adolescent development that need to be understood in conjunction with one another but most often are studied in isolation. In the studies that follow, the characteristics of the represented family, defined as the adolescent's attachment organization, and of the practicing family, described by family interaction processes, were found to be linked and to be associated with important aspects of adolescent development.

In our own research, the represented family for each adolescent was assessed by the Adult Attachment Interview. The practicing family was assessed by observing families of psychiatrically hospitalized adolescents using the Beavers Interactions Scales, drawn from the Beavers-Timberlawn Model of family functioning. Factor analysis of the subscale scores yielded two distinct factors: responsivity and behavioral control. Responsivity refers both to the degree of empathy and connectedness within the family as well as the intentional facilitation of individuation or psychological autonomy. Parental control taps the degree to which parents set clear standards for behavior and maintain those standards. Results showed an association between attachment and family responsivity (Reimer, Overton, Steidl, Rosenstein, & Horowitz, 1996). Dismissing adolescents came from families rated as less responsive

while preoccupied adolescents were equally likely to come from families rate high and low in responsivity. These results underscore the psychological detachment inherent in the families of dismissing adolescents and the confounding of factors of empathy and promotion of individuation in the families of preoccupied adolescents.

Kobak and colleagues (Kobak, Cole, Ferenz-Gillies, Fleming, & Gamble, 1993) took the perspective of the ongoing utilization and development of emotion regulation to describe parent-adolescent communication. In a problem-solving task designed to place parent and adolescent in moderate conflict (i.e., discussion of an area of disagreement in their relationship), communication patterns between parent and adolescent were found to depend on attachment classification. Adolescents with secure attachment engaged in less dysfunctional anger and less avoidance of problem solving, and maintained balanced assertiveness with their mothers. Adolescents with a dismissing attachment style employed high levels of dysfunctional anger, and the interactions were characterized by higher levels of maternal dominance. Kobak et al. (1993) interpret these findings as exemplifying the dysfunctional aspects of insecure attachment on the attainment of joint goals even into adolescence. In keeping with Bowlby's notion of the "goal-corrected partnership" in toddlerhood (1969/1982), in which mother and child reciprocally set goals and plans and carry them out in the service of increasing autonomy for the child, adolescents with secure attachments are able to balance individual and relational needs, while those with insecure attachments are not. Insecure attachment can compromise the adolescent's ability to either individuate from parents or maintain close relations with them.

Drawing on similar constructs regarding the balance of autonomy and relatedness, Allen and Hauser (1993) examined continuities between adolescent-family interactions and attachment organization 11 years later, when the adolescents had become young adults. Again using an adolescent-parent interaction revolving around resolving a disagreement, both normal and psychiatrically hospitalized adolescents and their families were observed. Results showed that coherence in the young adults' descriptions of their attachment relationships were predictable from qualities of autonomy and relatedness in their families' interactions when they were adolescents. These predictions could be obtained both from adolescents' behavior toward their parents and from parents' behavior toward their adolescents. However, the one insecure attachment indicator in young adulthood that could be predicted from parent-adolescent interaction (passivity of thought processes) could be predicted only on the basis of adolescents' behavior toward parents and not vice versa. These adolescents were inhibited in the development of autonomy by personalizing disagreements with parents or by failing to recant their positions.

CLINICAL IMPLICATIONS
OF ATTACHMENT CLASSIFICATION

From the standpoint of psychopathology, links between attachment insecurity and increased symptomatology have been shown consistently for adolescents. Insecure adolescents are more depressed, anxious, resentful, and alienated (Armsden & Greenberg, 1987; Armsden, McCauley, Greenberg, Burke, & Mitchell, 1990) and are more likely to engage in problem drinking (Hughes, Francis, & Power, 1989; Kwakman, Zuiker, Schippers, & deWuffel, 1988) or drug abuse (Allen, Hauser & Borman-Sporrell, 1996). The links between depression and preoccupied attachment (Cole-Detke and Kobak, 1996; Kobak, Sudler, & Gamble, 1991) and eating disorders and dismissing attachment (Cole-Detke & Kobak, 1996) have been demonstrated. Adam, Sheldon-Keller, and West (1996) have demonstrated that adolescents unresolved with respect to trauma or loss were at greater risk for suicide attempts. Dozier (1990) showed that insecure attachment was associated with treatment noncompliance in severely disturbed late adolescents.

Rosenstein and Horowitz (1996) have examined the relationships among attachment classification, psychopathology, and personality traits in a group of psychiatrically hospitalized adolescents. These adolescents were overwhelmingly insecure (97%) in their current state of mind with respect to attachment. The adolescent group dismissing of attachment was associated with conduct and substance abuse disorders; denial of psychiatric symptomatology; and narcissistic, antisocial, and histrionic personality traits. The group preoccupied by attachment was associated with affective

disorders; overt disclosure of symptomatic distress; and avoidant, dependent, schizotypal, and dysthymic personality traits. Sex differences in both diagnosis and attachment classification were found, with males more likely to be dismissing and conduct disordered or substance abusing and females more likely to be preoccupied. We interpreted these findings in the context of the emergence of styles of regulating distress from working models, which evolve in the course of development into styles of adaptation and defense. Ultimately these styles coalesce into personality traits and symptomatology. Therefore, in adolescence, distinctive personality traits and attachment organizations are well established. Symptomatology, personality, and attachment organization are integrally related, since they result from the same context in development.

Adolescents whose attachment organization was dismissing relied on a strategy of defensive exclusion from awareness of information that portrayed attachment relationships in a negative light. This strategy is shared by adolescents with externalizing disorders, that is, conduct and substance abuse disorders, and by those with narcissistic and antisocial personality disorders and traits. The pernicious effect of this exclusion from awareness of negatively charged information is inferred from the individual's self-defeating behavior (e.g., aggressiveness that is interpersonally alienating or runs afoul of the law, or substance abuse that compromises health and academic functioning). The widely observed affective regulatory function of substance abuse can be viewed from an attachment theoretic perspective as a means to cut off awareness of negative affects surrounding attachment, thereby maintaining an idealized view of attachment figures and dismissing personal distress. Symptomatic behavior, such as substance abuse or the aggression seen in a conduct-disordered adolescent, thus may be seen as reflecting, in a displaced manner, the anger generated in the adolescent by ongoing parental rejection or intrusion, coupled with the adolescent's failure to acknowledge his or her own anger.

By contrast, adolescents in the preoccupied group were extremely sensitive to difficulties in their attachment relationships and overwhelmed by negative perceptions of parents. Preoccupied adolescents were unduly sensitive to their own distress and characteristically exaggerated their affect in order to elicit comfort from the attachment figure, in a manner that blocked autonomy. Thus they were likely to have an affective disorder and personality traits that emphasized exaggerated emotionality and overt conflict, such as histrionic, borderline, or dependent traits.

Conclusion

A knowledge of attachment theory is important to the understanding of adolescent development. There is a significant body of knowledge related to the study of attachment; the literature converges on the view that security of attachment predicts more competent social and emotional functioning throughout childhood and adolescence. Insecure attachment forms a major risk factor in the development of impoverished or conflictual relationships, negative mood states, and psychopathology. Empirically, the relation of each type of attachment insecurity to specific symptomatic patterns in childhood has been inconsistent. Not until adolescence can the latent effect of attachment insecurity, coupled with the renewed press for the adolescent to separate from parents, specify the pattern of psychopathology and character.

REFERENCES

Adam, K. S., Sheldon-Keller, A. E., & West, M. (1996). Attachment organization and history of suicidal behavior in clinical adolescents. *Journal of Consulting and Clinical Psychology, 64*, 264–272.

Ainsworth, M. D. S. (1989). Attachments beyond infancy. *American Psychologist, 44*, 709–716.

Ainsworth, M. D. S., Blehar, M. C., Waters, E., & Wall, S. (1978). *Patterns of attachment: A psychological study of the Strange Situation.* Hillsdale, NJ: Lawrence Erlbaum.

Ainsworth, M. D. S., & Eichberg, C. G. (1991). Effects on infant-mother attachment of mother's unresolved loss of an attachment figure or other traumatic experience. In P. Marris, J. Stevenson-Hinde, & C. Parkes (Eds.), *Attachment across the life cycle.* (pp. 160–183). New York: Routledge.

Ainsworth, M. D. S., & Wittig, B. A. (1969). Attachment and the exploratory behavior of one-year olds in a strange situation. In B. M. Foss (Ed.), *Determinants of infant behavior* (Vol. 4, pp. 113–136). London: Methuen.

Allen, J. P., Hauser, S. T., & Borman-Spurrell, E. (1996). Attachment theory as a framework for understanding sequelae of severe adolescent psychopathology: An 11-year follow-up study. *Journal of Consulting and Clinical Psychology, 64*, 254–263.

Allen, J. P., & Hauser, S. T. (1996). Autonomy and relatedness in adolescent-family interactions as predictors of young adults' states of mind regarding attachment. Manuscript submitted for publication.

Armsden, G. C., & Greenberg, M. T. (1987). The Inventory of Parent and Peer Attachment: Individual differences and their relationship to psychological well-being in adolescence. *Journal of Youth and Adolescence, 16*, 427–454.

Armsden, G. C., McCauley, E., Greenberg, M. T., Burke, P. M., & Mitchell, J. R. (1990). Parent and peer attachment in early adolescent depression. *Journal of Abnormal Child Psychology, 18*, 683–697.

Bartholomew, K., & Horowitz, L. M. (1991). Attachment styles among young adults: A test of a four-category model. *Journal of Personality and Social Psychology, 61*, 226–244.

Baumrind, D. (1991). Parenting styles and adolescent development. In R. Lerner, A. C. Peterson, & J. Brooks-Gunn (Eds.), *The encyclopedia of adolescence* (pp. 746–758). New York: Garland Press.

Bell, D. C., & Bell, L. G. (1982). Family climate and the role of the female adolescent: Determinants of adolescent functioning. *Family Relations, 31*, 519–527.

Blos, P. (1967). The second individuation process of adolescence. *Psychoanalytic Study of the Child, 22*, 162–186.

Bowlby, J. (1958). The nature of the child's tie to his mother. *International Journal of Psycho-analysis, 39*, 350–373.

Bowlby, J. (1973). *Attachment and loss: Vol. 2. Separation, anxiety and anger.* New York: Basic Books.

Bowlby, J. (1980). *Attachment and loss: Vol. 3. Loss.* New York: Basic Books.

Bowlby, J. (1982). *Attachment and loss: Vol. 1. Attachment* (2nd ed.). New York: Basic Books. (Originally published 1969.)

Bowlby, J. (1988). *A secure base.* New York: Basic Books.

Carlson, V., Cicchetti, D., Barnett, D., & Braunwald, K. (1989). Disorganized/disoriented attachment relationships in maltreated infants. *Developmental Psychology, 25*, 525–531.

Cassidy, J., & Kobak, R. R. (1988). Avoidance and its relation to other defensive processes. In J. Belsky & T. Nezworski (Eds.), *Clinical implications of attachment* (pp. 300–323). Hillsdale, NJ: Lawrence Erlbaum.

Cole-Detke, H., & Kobak, R. (1996). Attachment processes in eating disorder and depression. *Journal of Consulting and Clinical Psychology, 64,* 282–290.

Cooper, C. R., Grotevant, H. D., & Condon, S. M. (1983). Individuality and connectedness in the family as a context for adolescent identity formation and role-taking skill. In H. D. Grotevant & C. R. Cooper (Eds.), *Adolescent development in the family* (pp. 43–59). San Francisco: Jossey-Bass.

Crittenden, P. M. (1992). Quality of attachment in the preschool years. *Development and Psychopathology, 4,* 209–241.

Dozier, M. (1990). Attachment organization and treatment use for adults with serious psychopathological disorders. *Development and Psychopathology, 2,* 47–60.

Erikson, E. H. (1968). *Identity, youth and crisis.* New York: W. W. Norton.

Freud, A. (1958). Adolescence. *Psychoanalytic Study of the Child, 13,* 255–278.

Hauser, S. T., Powers, S. I., Noam, G. G., Jacobson, A. M., Weiss, B., & Follansbee, D. J. (1984). Familial contexts of adolescent ego development. *Child Development, 55,* 195–213.

Hazan, C. (1991). *The process of relinquishing parents as attachment figures.* Paper presented at the biennial meeting of the Society for Research in Child Development, Seattle.

Hughes, S. O., Francis, D. J., & Power, T. G. (1989). *The impact of attachment on adolescent alcohol use.* Paper presented at the biennial meeting of the Society for Research in Child Development, Kansas City.

Jenkins, V. Y., & Fisher, D. A. (1989). *Patterns of adolescent attachment and coping.* Paper presented at the biennial meeting of the Society for Research in Child Development, Kansas City, MO.

Kenny, M. E. (1987). The extent and function of parental attachment among first year college students. *Journal of Youth and Adolescence, 16,* 17–29.

Kobak, R. R. (1986). *Attachment as a theory of affect regulation.* Unpublished manuscript.

Kobak, R. R., Cole, H. E., Ferenz-Gillies, R., Fleming, W. S., & Gamble, W. (1993). Attachment and emotion regulation during mother-teen problem solving: A control theory analysis. *Child Development, 64,* 23–245.

Kobak, R. R., & Sceery, A. (1988). Attachment in adolescence: Working models, affect regulation and representation of self and others. *Child Development, 59,* 135–146.

Kobak, R. R., Sudler, N., & Gamble, W. (1991). Attachment and depressive symptoms during adolescence: A developmental pathways analysis. *Development and Psychopathology, 3,* 461–474.

Kroger, J. (1985). Separation-individuation and ego identity status in New Zealand university students. *Journal of Youth and Adolescence, 14,* 133–147.

Kroger, J., & Haslett, S. J. (1988). Separation-individuation and ego identity status in late adolescence: A two-year longitudinal study. *Journal of Youth and Adolescence, 17,* 59–79.

Kwakman, A. M., Zuiker, F. A. J. M., Schippers, G. M., & deWuffel, F. J. (1988). Drinking behavior, drinking attitudes, and attachment relationships of adolescents. *Journal of Youth and Adolescence, 17,* 247–253.

Lapsley, D. K., Rice, K. G., & FitzGerald, D. P. (1990). Adolescent attachment, identity, and adjustment to college: Implications for the continuity of adaptation hypothesis. *Journal of Counseling and Development, 68,* 561–565.

Mahler, M. S., Pine, F., & Bergman, A. (1975). *The psychological birth of the human infant.* New York: Basic Books.

Main, M., & Goldwyn, R. (1985–1991). *Adult attachment classification system.* Unpublished manuscript.

Main, M., & Hesse, E. (1990). Lack of resolution of mourning in adulthood and its relationship to infant disorganization: Some speculations regarding causal mechanisms. In M. Greenberg, D. Cicchetti, & M. Cummings (Eds.), *Attachment in the preschool years* (pp. 161–182). Chicago: University of Chicago Press.

Main, M., Kaplan, N., & Cassidy, J. (1985). Security in infancy, childhood, and adulthood: A move to the level of representation. In I. Bretherton & E. Waters (Eds.), Growing points of attachment theory and research (pp. 66–104). *Monographs of the Society for Research in Child Development, 50,* (1–2, Serial No. 209).

Main, M., & Solomon, J. (1986). Discovery of a new, insecure-disorganized/disoriented attachment pattern. In T. B. Brazelton & M. Yogman (Eds.), *Affective development in infancy* (pp. 95–124). Norwood, NJ: Ablex.

Main, M., & Solomon, J. (1990). Procedures for identifying infants as disorganized/disoriented during the Ainsworth Strange Situation. In M. Greenberg, D. Cicchetti, & M. Cummings (Eds.), *Attachment in the preschool years* (pp. 121–160). Chicago: University of Chicago Press.

Main, M., van IJzendoorn, M. H., & Hesse, E. (1993). *Unresolved/unclassifiable responses to the Adult Attachment Interview: Predictable from unresolved status and anomalous beliefs in the Berkeley-Leiden Adult Attachment Questionnaire.* Paper presented at the biennial meeting of the Society for Research in Child Development, New Orleans.

Papini, D. R., Roggman, L. A., & Anderson, J. (1991). Early-adolescent perceptions of attachment to mother and father: A test of the emotional-distancing and buffering hypotheses. *Journal of Early Adolescence, 11,* 258–275.

Quintana, S. M., & Lapsley, D. K. (1987). Adolescent autonomy and ego identity: A structural equations approach to the continuity of adaptation. *Journal of Adolescent Research, 2,* 393–410.

Reimer, M. S., Overton, W. F., Steidl, J. H., Rosenstein, D. S., & Horowitz, H. A. (1996). Familial responsiveness and behavioral control: Influences on adolescent psychopathology, attachment and cognition. *Journal of Research on Adolescence, 6,* 87–112.

Reiss, D. (1989). The represented and practicing family: Contrasting visions of continuity. In A. J. Sameroff & R. N. Emde, (Eds.), *Relational disturbances in early childhood* (pp. 191–220). New York: Basic Books.

Resnick, G. (1991). *Attachment and self-representation during early adolescence.* Paper presented at the biennial meeting of the Society for Research in Child Development, Seattle.

Rice, K. G. (1990). Attachment in adolescence: A narrative and meta-analytic review. *Journal of Youth and Adolescence, 19,* 511–538.

Rosenstein, D. S., & Horowitz, H. H. (1996). Adolescent attachment and psychopathology. *Journal of Consulting and Clinical Psychology, 64,* 244–253.

Rosenstein, D. S., & Horowitz, H. A. (1993). Attachment, personality and psychopathology: Relationship as a regulatory context in adolescence. *Adolescent Psychiatry, 19,* 150–176.

Ryan, R. M., & Lynch, J. H. (1989). Emotional autonomy versus detachment: Revisiting the vicissitudes of adolescence and young adulthood. *Child Development, 60,* 340–356.

Smith, J., & George, C. (1993). *Working models of attachment and adjustment to college: Parents, peers and romantic partners as attachment figures.* Paper presented at the biennial meeting of the Society for Research in Child Development, New Orleans.

Sroufe, L. A., & Waters, E. (1977). Attachment as an organizational construct. *Child Development, 48,* 1184–1199.

Steinberg, L., & Silverberg, S. B. (1986). The vicissitudes of autonomy in early adolescence. *Child Development, 57,* 841–851.

Weiss, R. S. (1982). Attachment in adult life. In C. M. Parkes & J. Stevenson-Hinde (Eds.), *The place of attachment in human behavior* (pp. 171–184). New York: Basic Books.

Werner, H. (1957). The concept of development from a comparative and organismic point of view. In D. Harris (Ed.), *The concept of development* (pp. 125–148). Minneapolis: University of Minnesota Press.

Wynne, L., Jones, J. E., & Al-Khayyal, M. (1982). Healthy family communication patterns: Observations in families "at risk" for psychopathology. In F. Walsh (Ed.), *Normal family processes* (pp. 142–164). New York: Guilford Press.

13 / Altered Relations with Peers: Peer-Group Affiliation, Friendships, First Love

Audrey J. Clarkin

Transformations in peer relationships are an important component of adolescence. Volume 2 of this *Handbook* discusses important transformations in interpersonal relationships that occur during the grade-school years. During adolescence, friendships become even more complex and gradually take on the characteristics of adult relationships. A crucial developmental milestone, first love, ordinarily occurs during this period.

Friendships provide important opportunities for adolescents to develop a greater sense of self; at the same time, the nature of these relationships is greatly affected by the self-concept the adolescent already has (Gratevant, 1992). Friendships have both positive and negative aspects; they can be important sources of social support but can also serve as sources of conflict and emotional pain.

CASE EXAMPLE

M.H. is an attractive 15-year-old high school junior, whose parents describe her "as an excellent student, active in many extracurricular activities, and generally cooperative and communicative." Recently M.H. has been dating a college freshman whom she met on her summer job. Her parents are concerned about the relationship as M.H. seems to be neglecting her old friends and certainly is not spending much time at home. Her parents often do not know where M.H. has been, although she is still observing her curfew. M.H. assures her parents that "this relationship isn't serious and I'm doing just as well in my classes." M.H., who is chronologically young for her grade, has always been an easy child to manage, self-motivated, social, and with a wonderful sense of humor. The parents are now uneasy. This relationship could be serious, as M.H., who is popular, has many friends of both sexes but has never paired off with anyone special. College plans are emerging and, for the parents, this is the wrong time for M.H. to be distracted with a special boyfriend and new, older friends.

Adolescence, the transitional period between childhood and adulthood, involves changes and challenges that occur both within and outside the individual. It is a period of self-discovery against a backdrop of interactions with others. Many of the predictable events—the gain in cognitive, verbal, and reasoning abilities; the physical and emotional changes; the same-sex and opposite-sex relationships—impact on social development.

Adolescence can be regarded as a process over time that permits the young person to move from the dependency of childhood to the autonomy of adulthood with all its issues (Compos, Hinden, & Gerhardt, 1995). Adolescents experience changes in relationships with both parents and peers as they progress through this developmental period. Moodiness, regression to more immature behaviors, and overattachment to age mates are typical reactions to the stresses of their subjective experiences.

Viewpoints on Adolescent Social Development

Psychoanalysis seeks to explain behavior by inner wishes and desires and attributes unconscious and subconscious motives to actions. Peer relationships have long been recognized as playing a major role in adolescent development. In psychoanalytic thinking, these relationships have been viewed as defensive in origin, that is, a way of resolving the still remaining conflict over the child's early love affair with the parents. Anna Freud (1958) described the attachments of adolescents to their contemporaries as the vehicle by which adolescents weakened their ties to their "infantile objects," their parents. She differentiated between normal adolescents, in whom this process is gradual, and adolescents who are defending "against

113

their anxiety aroused by the attachment to their infantile objects" by the sudden transference of their attachment to parent substitutes, idealized "leaders," or other adolescents (pp. 268–269).

Psychoanalytic literature (Blos, 1979) has focused on the adolescent struggle to mature, describing it as a period of advancement, regression and reorganization as the individual works through internal conflict and the interpersonal difficulties with parents and others. Because dynamic therapists treat disturbed or at least distressed adolescents, they tend to generalize the turmoil to all adolescents.

Erikson's view of adolescence (1968) is more from the perspective of normative crisis with dramatic fluctuations in ego strength. Identity formation is the primary task of this stage but psychosocial stress exists between personal and social constraints.

A recent study (Hartup, 1993) upholds a more benign view of adolescence, emphasizing the pursuit of self-definition as a necessary separation from parents and family with strong affiliation with peers, but does not view adolescence as crisis. Other studies (Offer, Rostov & Howard, 1981) suggest that simultaneous parent and peer influence is not contradictory and that positive relationships with parents can promote adjustment, autonomy, and independence (as in the case of M.H.). It is when parental role models are absent, when parents are in conflict with each other, or when there is intense conflict between teenager and parent that adolescents seek compensatory satisfaction from peers.

Parents and adolescents do have different perceptions. Teenagers view parents as less influential than they actually are, and parents consider themselves to be more influential than reality would have it. Noller and Callan (1986) report that despite differences in perception, both parents and teenagers acknowledge general satisfaction with family functioning. They conclude that although the normal adolescent transition to adulthood involves some parent-child conflict in the struggle for self-identity and independence, the extreme view of a universal generation gap has been exaggerated. Adolescence demands a redefinition of child-parent relationship, but in healthy families, the connection continues to be nurturing and supportive.

Psychosocial Competence

Normal adolescents think that they have reasonable control over their choices and view change as part of life. They have sufficient knowledge of how to behave in varied social situations, are usually empathetic to others, and are generally in control of their own reactions. Earlier experiences with parents and peers have enabled them to acquire a positive self-image as well as social and communication skills and develop problem-solving and conflict-resolution strategies (Eisenberg, Carlo, Murphy, & van Court, 1995).

Adolescents whose preadolescent development or prior support system, environmental and/or personal, was not adequate will be at risk for maladapted and disturbed behavior (Windle, 1994). While consideration of specific adolescent disorders is considered elsewhere in the text, this chapter describes the implications.

SEPARATION FROM PARENTS

Adolescents respond to the process of separation in a variety of ways as they redefine their relationship with parents. The adolescent female described earlier, M.H., is flattered by the attention of an older male who shares many of her same interests. She sincerely likes this boy, who seems mature and compatible, and is sharing with him and his friends in a way that makes her feel more grown-up. At the same time, M.H. is aware that she is not as available to her parents.

Some adolescents—a minority—cling to parents by overidentification or overdependence, failing to deal with their own wishes or abilities. Others separate from parents more dramatically by distancing (turning exclusively to peers) or by overtly rejecting parental support or by experimenting with behaviors that are objectionable to the parents, such as drugs, stealing, and sex.

One aspect of the separation process is that the adolescent becomes "secretive," no longer revealing feelings, thoughts, or activities to adults, especially to parents. This pattern is normal and expected but engenders anxiety and sometimes self-blame in the parent. Ideally, positive identification with a parental role model accompanied by increasing independence and responsibility contributes to autonomy, increased self-identity, and appropriate adult behavior (Youniss and Smollar, 1989). Valliant and Valliant (1990), in a longitudinal study of Harvard students, substantiated that males who did not experience some adolescent turmoil and testing of authority remained "perennial boys" as adults.

Prototypes of parenting styles—traditional, authoritarian-restrictive, and authoritative—have been associated (Baumrind, 1987) with conforming, problematic, and self-directed adolescent orientations. Supportive family interactions, which permit conflict to exist between parent and adolescents, establish a frame of reference that enables the adolescent to transfer positive interactional skills from the family to the peer group without overconcern about rejection or consequences. When children have not been allowed to make choices or have been totally unsupervised, their resulting behavior becomes problematic.

PEER PROGRESSION

"Peer" is used to describe a homogeneity based on age, sex, social class, or shared leisure activity. Support and acceptance, formerly provided by parents, is now derived from age mates. Often the initial choice of a friend is narcissistic, the desire to seek someone like the self, a "mirror image" to help establish self-identity. Then follows wider experimentation and the gradual realization that different friends can fulfill varied functions— athletic, intellectual, social, instructional—as the adolescent discovers not all expectations can be provided by a single individual. Adolescents seek out peers they would like to resemble, and relationships with these peers form the basis for trial relationships. There occurs a personal synthesis requiring time and integration that often causes stress and distress.

Peers serve as "relevant others" with respect to daily performance in school to psychosocial growth and activities, or on the athletic field. The emphasis in adolescence is on age mates who serve as companions, confidants, consolers, counselors, role models, problem-solvers, and so on (Seltzer, 1989).

The transfer of dependency from parents to peers is part of the developmental process, which allows modeling on a more equitable and recipro-

cal basis with age mates and leads to the gradual recognition of a unique identity. "Who am I?" and "Who will I become?" are the persistent themes of adolescent interactions and are pursued both cognitively and emotionally in exploration with others.

In a study (Adams, 1983) of preadolescents (ages 11 to 12), early and middle adolescents (13 to 15), and older adolescents (17 to 19), greater self-awareness and increasing appreciation for individuality was found with increasing age. Successful social interactions contribute to adolescent adjustment and developmental improvement in social knowledge, self-control, and empathy. Adolescents become more differentiated as persons in their own right as they assume more complicated and adultlike relationships.

CASE EXAMPLE

B.C. is a short, cute-looking blond 15-year-old, who, unlike many of his classmates, will not be shaving for some time. He long ago gave up hopes of being an athlete and would not be mistaken for a "jock." Verbal and sensitive, B.C. has a small group of male friends who spend a lot of time at the computer. They still belong to the Scouts as they enjoy hiking and camping. These boys are not part of the weekend sports activities and do not get invited to coed parties. It used to upset B.C. that popular kids had no time for him, but he is happier now with his computer friends at school and his outdoor friends on weekends. B.C. seldom interacts with individual girls; although he is friendly enough in the presence of girls at school, he seems just not interested.

An important variable is not only the developmental level of an adolescent at a particular point in time but also the timing of physical development—precocious, on time, or delayed—as compared to that of peers. Youngsters who look older often act older and are treated as if they are older so that their actions, self-confidence, and social skills reflect this reinforcement. Female teenagers whose development is proceeding on a par with that of most of their peers feel secure joining their age mates in the shared process of maturing and are glad not to be first or last. Early physical maturation in boys is seen as a positive, and they are esteemed by age mates and often emerge as leaders. Anxiety about bodily changes and fear of embarrassment from peers characterize the late developer who waits impatiently to grow up (as illustrated by B.C.).

Functions of Peer Relationships

Adolescent social interactions can determine social adjustment in numerous ways. As adolescents utilize their improved thinking and verbal and reasoning abilities to deal with social situations, they establish a support system with age mates for their emotional and social needs. It is through peer interactions that adolescents learn to regulate aggressive impulses, develop sexual attitudes and sex-role behaviors, and better define their moral and social values. These critical developmental tasks require exchange between trusted equals where shared feelings and communication help to formulate a person's self-image.

Content analyses of interviews with 1,300 adolescents (Brown, Eicher, & Petrie, 1986) describe the many functions of peer groups and reveal that the consequences of affiliation can be both positive and negative, as represented in table 13.1.

The table summarizes essential contributions of peer affiliation and suggests that positive peer social relationships are critical in shaping the feelings, thoughts and actions of the adolescent as far as self-definition is concerned. When adolescents make good choices in selecting other adolescents to be their friends, the result is a positive one enabling the individuals to complement each other, support each other, and develop unique

qualities because of mutual respect and affiliation (Hartup, 1996). Often interests are shared and expanded. Adolescents who have friends they can depend on and with whom they enjoy themselves experience positive feelings about their relationships and their ability to make such friends, an increased sense of belonging, and more confidence in themselves. When peer relationships are negative, they may provide bonding and social reassurance, but they will impede the adolescent's efforts toward individuation and mature functioning. The reasons for negative affiliation are multiple and include insecurity, intimidation, and aggression; regardless of why such affiliation happens, it deters adolescents from constructive achievements.

Affiliation, competency, and popularity are three important goals for adolescents. As the individual moves away from family dependency, peers become more important for self-understanding, self-esteem, and self-confidence. Acceptance by peers and, more important, having one or more close friends seem critical for adolescents to feel good about themselves (Asher & Parker, 1989). To be socially successful, adolescents need to have acquired skills of listening, carrying on a conversation, cooperating, anger control, problem solving, and conflict resolution, as these determine how a person gets along with peers. These skills can range on a continuum from a minimal level to those that are highly developed.

Recent studies on gangs from a psychological perspective (Goldstein, 1991) reinforce the critical role that affiliation, competency, and popularity can serve when youths turn to negative peer relationships. The number of teenage gangs in urban

TABLE 13.1

Functions and Consequences of Peer Affiliation

Function	Positive Consequences	Negative Consequences
Identity	Defines interests, abilities	Confuses, distracts
Reputation	Improves status and image	Lowers status
Conformity	Provides sense of belonging	Impedes autonomy
Support	Improves confidence	Threatens self
Friendship	Builds and maintains new skills	Restricts, impedes
Activity	Enhances abilities	Inhibits abilities

and suburban communities increase when other support systems are not available or effective.

What does an adolescent look for in a friendship? In early adolescence, most children look for someone similar, someone who likes the same activities and shares the same interests, described by Sullivan (1953) as a chum. The relationship is based on trust and loyalty, and it is the first real sharing of emotions outside the family. Then the circle of peers expands. With increased self-confidence, adolescents realize that they no longer need friends who exactly mirror them. Now choice is prompted by qualities or skills that adolescents would like to possess but do not. A special appreciation for the other person exists. Similarities still are present but there is greater allowance for differences (Cairns, Leung, Buchanan, & Cairns, 1995).

INTIMACY

Intimacy is characterized by a feeling of closeness, connection, and joint belonging. It is the subjective feeling of closeness toward and about another person. Both self-disclosure and shared experiences are important "behavioral paths" to closeness for both boys and girls. In Camarena, Sarigiani, and Peterson's (1990) study of sixth to eighth graders, 'nearly all described a same-sex friend as their closest. Girls differed from boys in terms of the importance of self-disclosure in close friendships, but shared experience was equally important for both groups. As teenagers develop, the ability to share and communicate remains essential. Adolescents place increasing priority on loyalty, trust, and intimacy. Often the relationship becomes exclusive. In late adolescence, friends can be mutually close and intimate yet still grant each other independence. Sensitivity to a friend's needs and wants continues to increase but it is a mutual commitment. As a more autonomous sense of self develops in later adolescence, the need for peer conformity diminishes.

Increasingly, adolescents are exposed to new social situations that require different interactional skills from those of earlier childhood. Family relations are altered and adolescents are faced with many new demands and expectations in situations where parents are no longer available. Academic and social choices in school, dating, part-time employment, and recreation with peers are just a few of these changes. Driving a car, school and nighttime social activities, and associating with friends of friends bring teenagers into a wider circle of age mates where the experience of getting to know each other provides much satisfaction and adolescents make more frequent decisions without adult input.

Requirements for Peer Relationships

Both social competencies and strategies for conflict resolution are needed for adolescents to initiate and maintain relationships with family, peers, and friends. Previously learned social skills and role modeling serve as a basis for the adolescent's decisions in the move toward independence (Gavin & Furman, 1996). Family stresses—such as unemployment, family illness, or divorce—can impact on social development by encouraging too much dependency on age mates or by delaying social progress because of emotional reactions of anger or fear or overattachment to one parent. Single parents who make their children confidants, sharing details of new intimate relationships, can evoke in their adolescents a pseudomaturity or exaggerated sexual interest.

Neglect or abuse, whether physical or sexual, can deter adolescents from positive same-sex or opposite-sex relationships. Socioeconomic and cultural influences also affect whether adolescents move toward or away from peers. A recent phenomena involves talented urban black students who are isolated, scorned, and sometimes abused because peers resent their achievement. Lonely and more socially accepted teenagers do not differ in the frequency of their contacts with peers, but lonely adolescents describe the quality of their peer interactions as less supportive and less intimate (Jones, 1981).

SOCIAL/SEXUAL PEER RELATIONSHIPS

One of the major contributors to our understanding of the importance of peer relationships to adolescent development was Harry Stack Sullivan (1953). Sullivan noted the importance of early same-sex friendships, which he called "chumships," and which provide the opportunity to validate perceptions of the self and to practice for later relationships with opposite-sex peers. He viewed the need for intimacy as fundamental and saw normal development in adolescence as characterized by a shift from intimacy with a similar person to intimacy with a person who is different.

Relative to children, adolescents are more involved and intimate with peers. Teenagers spend much time face to face and on the phone sharing thoughts and feelings. Their conversations with friends are filled with self-disclosures, humor, gossip, problems and possible solutions, social comparisons, and predictions. For many adolescents, school offers the most stable aspect of their lives. It is most important for its social context, the place where they meet and enjoy friends, whether it is walking to class, sitting in a cafeteria, joining a club, or doing homework. When adolescents are socially successful, school connects them with friends. For socially inept adolescents, school can be a place of unhappiness and loneliness (Berndt & Keefe, 1992).

Separation from parents, both physically and emotionally, supports attachment to peers, and affection is transferred from family to age mates and then to age mates of the opposite sex. One such progression is from large-group, structured interactions that are school-, church-, or team-related, to informal smaller coed groups of friends, to paired friends who attend movies and parties together, and eventually to the selection of a particular partner. Sometimes a distant idol is selected or a common crush is shared by the group before a peer of the opposite sex is discovered. Infatuation from a distance is followed by interest in a particular person, which can remain as fantasy. In time, real people emerge as special friends.

Social interactions contribute to an adolescent's sense of self, whether it is with same-sex or opposite-sex peers. Hartup (1983) emphasizes that sexual attitudes and sex-role behaviors are shaped through peer interactions. It is well established that certain configurations of early childhood are reexperienced and reorganized during adolescence. Boys' preadolescent regression is more massive than girls. It is action-oriented and concrete. In its first onset, boys turn away with derision and contempt from the opposite sex. Girls, by contrast, push heterosexual wishes or fantasies into the foreground while regressive tendencies assert themselves peripherally and secretively.

Girls rarely lose themselves in regression as boys do, although aggression and possessiveness dominate their relationship with the opposite sex. It is not unusual for a girl to "forget" her friends when she starts dating. If the new relationship is not successful, reentry into the peer group can be blocked by feelings of resentment on the part of the "forgotten friends." Newly acquired independence is evident in withdrawal from parents, in greater freedom of movement in the community, and in more active social participation with a variety of peers so that opportunities for pairing increase.

Emergence of sexual identity during early adolescence is a precondition for the progression to adolescent heterosexuality. Although social relationships vary by socioeconomic level, culture, and religious background, generally they move from same-sex groups, to group-to-group interactions, to heterosexual groups, to couples. Individual differences exist with adolescents of the same age (Miller & Dyk, 1993). Some are precocious in their social-sexual development. Perhaps they have matured early, perhaps they have been influenced by older siblings, or perhaps adult supervision was lacking. These teenagers are eager to move into serious heterosexual relationships. Socially and emotionally, girls exhibit heterosexual interest and readiness sooner than boys of the same age (Maccoby, 1990).

FIRST LOVE

In the popular culture and often in the opinion of adults, romantic love characterizes adolescence; however, the topic has not been well studied. In a study of 300 teenagers, ranging in age from 14 to 18, Levesque (1993) found many similarities between adolescents' and adults' love relationships. For adolescents, idealism, excitement, and a sense of being meant for each other were strongly correlated with their satisfaction with the other person. Commitment, communication, and passion were not predictive of satisfaction. The adolescents did not focus on how their partners could fit into their future plans. Interestingly, the less the adolescents regarded their relationships heading toward marriage and future commitment, the happier they were as they tended to focus on immediate, positive feelings. Gender differences were not evident.

Levesque's study describes adolescent love relationships as primarily transient and as intense feeling states without the substrates of ongoing and expanding behavioral patterns that allow relationships to endure when experiences are shared and disclosure of self to another is expected.

Some adolescents are socially/emotionally immature or delayed in physical development. They are not as ready for heterosexual interactions and, unlike their age mates, they are uncomfortable with the opposite sex. In other cases, some adolescents experience a disinterest in the opposite sex and are more attracted to the same sex. Some adolescents, who are or would prefer to be homosexual, participate in heterosexual relating and dating because of fear or to gain social acceptance.

Emotional Intensity

Much has been written about the increasing intensity of normal adolescence concomitant with the physiological and psychological changes of this period. Frequent shifts in mood among teenagers and concern over relationships were tracked by ongoing monitoring research (Csikszentmihalyi & Larsen, 1984). Subjects wore beepers and reported day and night on their thoughts, feelings, and actions in an approach called the Experience Sampling Method. Findings indicate that adolescents' moods go up when they have contact with peers and down when parents or teachers are involved. Talking with friends was reported as the most prevalent activity, and adolescents described themselves as *most happy* when doing so. Peer conversations focused on immediate concerns and centered around current activities, music, media, and school events (Hunter, 1985).

Because peer discussions offer opportunities to make comparisons and validate new common experiences, they contribute to the developing self-structure. The many and diverse opportunities for social exchange that occur in adolescence often lead to new friendships and prompt adults to describe adolescents as "forever changing and in constant flux."

Strong, immediate reactions to current interpersonal situations can produce devastation one day for a teenager who verbalizes "she wants to die" and a remarkable recovery when given positive peer attention. Sometimes the loss can involve a best friend or a friend of the opposite sex. Other times it is the loss of a parent, either by divorce or by death. Often previous adjustment determines how the individual will react and predicts how quickly the recovery will take. Because of the immediacy and intensity of the adolescent's emotional response, loss is critical and can prompt high-risk behavior such as excessive drinking, running away, or suicidal ideation. Supportive intervention is frequently indicated for adolescents who have experienced loss, particularly if they have had prior difficulties.

Friendships

Autonomy and intimacy are critical aspects of adolescent psychosocial development that relate to the two major tasks of the period: differentiation and individuation. The first involves moving away from overattachment to parents and from overdependency on peers; the second implies moving toward reciprocal, equal relationships. To be comfortable with one's feelings and responses, to accept the physical and psychological changes that accompany this period, and to be able to express one's opinions and be open to the viewpoint of others provide a vehicle for the adolescent to have a sense of self and to show interest in another who is different.

Adolescents place increasing priority on friendships. As they become more independent, they assume greater responsibility for what happens in a relationship. According to Selman (1980), well-adjusted, adolescents experience friendship in terms of intimate and mutual sharing. The case of Chris and John explicates this close friendship.

CASE EXAMPLE

Chris and John are two high school students who are physically different in appearance. Chris's height and speed have contributed to his position as basketball center, and John's broad and muscular physique makes him ideal as a football lineman. They have known each other since elementary school and share school interests in math and science as well as social compatibility in double dating. There is a comfort level between these two friends that is apparent to parents, teachers, and peers, even though they have a wide circle of friends and are both independent in terms of after-school jobs and prospective colleges. It is not that they always agree, just that things are special between them. Doubtless, there are some adolescents like Chris and John who have reached a level of social development described by Selman as autonomous interdependence.

FRIENDS AND NO FRIENDS

As one would expect, most studies on adolescence focus on friendship maintenance rather than the initiation of relationships. For those individuals who have not found friends before they become teenagers, adolescence is even lonelier and more difficult as peer contacts are critical to everyday living. For this cluster, the more basic task of peer acceptance requires attention to developing skills of knowing how to listen, how to enter a group, and how to carry on a conversation, that their age mates have been practicing for many years. Parents, teachers, and other adults do not play as active a role in encouraging positive social behavior among adolescents as they do when children are younger. Often the isolated adolescent conceals discouragement and depression from adults. Even when adults become alert to such a situation, their personal support can be consoling but does not change peer attitudes.

Peer acceptance and peer rejection are connected to specific yet different responses. Adolescents judge cooperativeness, a sense of humor, sharing common interests or activities, and an attractive appearance as positive qualities. They label verbal and physical aggressiveness, temper outbursts, dependency, and bossiness as offensive behaviors. A teenager who is not accepted by a group is not necessarily rejected. Some adolescents for various reasons—deficits in social skills, anxiety, depression—tend to be ignored or neglected by peers, but they do not receive the negative emotional impact of rejection. Rejection implies that the individual is provocative, noxious, and actively disliked.

Peer Pressure

Peer pressure is widely cited as an important influence on behavior during adolescence. It usually has been regarded in negative terms as a factor in drug and alcohol abuse, delinquency, and early sexual activity. Research studies have found it difficult to quantify peer influences, and results often have been confounded by peer selection; that is, adolescents tend to choose friends who are similar to themselves, so finding that they are engaged in like behaviors does not necessarily mean that the behaviors have resulted from peer contact. A few longitudinal studies show that friends tend to become more alike over time, suggesting that they do influence each other (Kandel, 1978). The relative impact of peer influence at different ages also has been difficult to quantify.

Peer pressure has long been associated with adolescence and usually has a negative implication. Understandably, early adolescents are more susceptible to peer influence than young children, as they are more eager for group entrance and acceptance. Their conformity involves clothes, activities, behavior, and interactions. Peer influences often prompt experimentation with smoking, drinking, drugs, and sex. Only when these behaviors become excessive or debilitating are they considered deviant. Interviews with adolescents on the kinds of peer pressure they experience (Brown, 1982) established that some peers are capable of discouraging antisocial behaviors and can help to orient toward school success, athletic achievement, and responsible behavior.

Peer Groupings

Adolescent peer interactions can be described as dyads, cliques, groups, crowds, and gangs. Friendships—dyads—represent two individuals who are mutually compatible and are distinct from group acceptance or popularity. Cliques number from several to a dozen individuals who understand and appreciate each other. Clique norms develop from within and usually refer to a friendship group but imply an exclusivity greater than that of a group.

If adolescents were asked to name groups that they belong to, they might begin with their daily or weekly routine and describe those who take the same bus, are together in a class, eat lunch each day, are in a school play, on the basketball team, or attend a weekly religious activity. The list can be endless as engaged, involved adolescents make many peer connections. Members of a group do not spend time together exclusively; it is possible to be a member of multiple groups with many different people. Crowds are reputation-based peer groups; the term describes associated attitudes or characteristics—"brains," "nerds," "jocks." Crowd norms are usually imposed, as they suggest a reference group. The forces that promote adolescent groups include similar behavior, socioeconomic level, ethnic background, and value systems. Only a small percentage of students are linked exclusively to one crowd, as academic, athletic, and social events bring many individuals together so that the choices for diverse combinations are numerous.

"Gang" implies a group bound together by some commonality and implies negative or intimidating influence that is asocial or antisocial—neighborhood control or an agreed goal, such as car stealing or group protection based on race or ethnicity. It is currently estimated that more than 4,000 gangs exist in our country with more than 250,000 members, many of whom are adolescents or preadolescents. Previously gangs were associated with big cities, but today their numbers are increasing in all communities and their violent behavior incites fear among residents.

Popularity is a group phenomenon. It depends on how one is viewed by others and implies status within the group. For some teenagers, popularity is measured by how many peers the teenager is acquainted with or vice versa. For others, popularity means being liked by a number of similar age mates or being connected with a high status group. It can be an artificial pseudopopularity that comes from being seen with certain individuals or behaving like a certain group where a person sacrifices choices to accommodate to the group's expectations.

In contrast, well-liked adolescents who have a sense of who they are and what they can do have been positively reinforced by their social interactions since an early age. Not only has experience encouraged them to respect those positive interactions, but it has created a positive reciprocal environment that tends to perpetuate itself. Studies suggest that popularity is different for girls and boys. Popularity can be predicted by the degree of empathy that female adolescents exhibit and by the self-initiative that male adolescents demonstrate. Gender differences both from the viewpoint of psychodynamic factors and related to psychosocial issues are considered in other sections.

Social Behavior Problems

Three groups of troubled adolescents have been identified, (Goldstein, Sprafkin, Gershaw, & Klein, 1980), each exhibiting a distinct cluster of problematic social behaviors. Achenbach and Edelbrock (1981) have described the first group as *externalizers*. They exhibit social excesses, including fighting, disruptiveness, destructiveness, profanity, irritability, defiance, and irresponsibility, with high levels of attention-getting behavior and low levels of guilt. The core of the pattern is aggression and the consequence is conflict with parents, peers, and others.

Social deficits characterize the other two groups. *Internalizers* are inhibited, withdrawn adolescents who are held back from social interactions by fear, anxiety, depression, physical complaints, and expressed unhappiness. Adolescents in the third group, described as immature, fail to meet expectations of self, parents, and teachers. They exhibit a short attention span, clumsiness, passivity, and a preference for younger companions. In time, their adjustment can improve and they can learn prosocial behavior. Table 13.2 details the specific social problems of aggressive, withdrawn, and immature adolescents.

As adolescents deal with increased freedom, more choices, and greater peer influence, the incidence of behavioral difficulties augments and significant sex differences become evident (Rutter & Garmezy, 1983). Girls exhibit less disturbance during childhood than boys, but the pattern is reversed during adolescence (Schonert-Reich & Offer, 1992). Several hypotheses can be offered. Perhaps girls are more emotionally tied to parents and separation is more difficult for them. Perhaps societal or cultural expectations are involved, and reactions to unacceptable behavior are more intense for adolescent girls. Moreover, girls manifest more internalizing symptoms (depression, anxiety) while boys are more prone to externalizing behaviors (aggression, anger).

Peer acceptance has been differentiated from friendship (Inderbitzen-Pisaruk & Foster, 1990)

TABLE 13.2

Social Problem Areas of Adolescents

Externalizers Problems With:	Internalizers Problems With:	Immature Problems With:
Self-control	Conversations	Sharing
Negotiation	Joining in	Handling teasing
Asking permission	Making decisions	Handling failure
Avoiding trouble	Dealing with fears	Goal setting
Dealing with anger	Handling complaints	Concentration

and often is derived from sociometric measures. Adolescents with high peer ratings are comfortable initiating games and activities. They are friendly, outgoing, cooperative, calm reactors and often are viewed as leaders. Teenagers with low peer acceptance fall into the two clusters that are described as externalizers and internalizers (Achenbach & Edelbrock, 1981). Externalizers are aggressive, arrogant, impatient, and often provocative. They often do not understand or care about the goals of the group and simply behave the way they want. Internalizers lack the skills to belong to the group because they are immature, worried, inhibited, easily intimidated, passive, and unable to communicate effectively their thoughts and wishes.

Clinicians who work with adolescents must be cognizant of normal developmental patterns where mood shifts frequently occur and transient social interactions serve a purpose. Learning to modulate responses, to tolerate discrepancies, to acknowledge personal limitations, and to accept others' viewpoints are critical social tasks and vary widely within the range of normal adjustment. Syndromes and pathology characteristic of adolescence are addressed elsewhere in this text.

Although it is known that adolescent boys and girls differ in their degree of intimacy and disclosure, specific research involving gender, socioeconomic, and cultural differences is needed for further understanding of normal adolescent social development.

REFERENCES

Achenbach, T. M., & Edelbrock, C. S. (1981). Behavioral problems and competencies reported by parents of normal and disturbed children aged four through sixteen. *Monographs of the Society for Research in Child Development, 46* (1).

Adams, G. R. (1983). Social competence during adolescence: social sensitivity, locus of control, empathy, and peer popularity. *Journal of Youth and Adolescence, 12,* 203–209.

Asher, S. R., & Parker, J. G. (1989). The significance of peer relationship problems in childhood. In B. H. Schneider, G. Attili, J. Nadel, & R. P. Weissberg (Eds.), *Social competence in developmental perspective* (pp. 5–23). Amsterdam: Kluwer Academic Publishing.

Baumrind, D. (1987). Developmental perspectives on adolescent risk-taking in contemporary America. In C. E. Irwin (Ed.), *Adolescent social behavior and health.* (pp. 93–125). San Francisco: Jossey-Bass.

Berndt, T. J., & Keefe, K. (1992). Friends' influence on adolescents' perceptions of themselves in school. In D. H. Schunk & J. L Meece (Eds.), *Students' perceptions in the classroom* (pp. 51–73). Hillsdale, NJ: Lawrence Erlbaum.

Blos, P. (1970). *The young adolescent: Clinical studies.* New York: Macmillan.

Blos, P. (1979). *The adolescent passage.* New York: International Universities Press.

Brown, B. B. (1982). The extent and effects of peer pressure among high school students: A retrospective analysis. *Journal of Youth and Adolescence, 11,* 121–133.

Brown, B. B., Eicher, S. A., & Petrie, S. (1986). The importance of 'peer group' affiliation in adolescence. *Journal of Adolescence, 9,* 73–96.

Cairns, R. B., Leung, M., Buchanan, L., & Cairns, B. (1995). Friendships and social networks in childhood and adolescence: Fluidity, reliability, interrelations. *Child Development, 66,* 1330–1345.

Camarena, P. M., Sarigiani, P. A., & Peterson, A. C. (1990). Gender-specific pathways to intimacy in early adolescence. *Journal of Youth and Adolescence, 19,* 19–32.

Compas, B. E., Hinden, B. R., & Gerhardt, C. A. (1995). Adolescent development: Pathways and processes of risk and resilience. *Annual Review of Psychology, 46,* 265–293.

Csikszentmihalyi, M., & Larsen, R. (1984). *Being adolescent: Conflict and turmoil in the teenage years.* New York: Basic Books.

Eisenberg, N., Carlo, G., Murphy, B., & van Court, P. (1995). Prosocial development in late adolescence. *Child Development, 66,* 1179–1197.

Erikson, E. (1968). *Identity: Youth and crisis.* New York: Basic Books.

Freud, A. (1958). Adolescence. *Psychoanalytic Study of the Child, 13,* 255–278.

Gavin, L. A., & Furman, W. (1996). Adolescent girls' relationship with mothers and best friends. *Child Development, 67,* 375–386.

Goldstein, A. P. (1991). *Delinquent gangs: A psychological perspective.* Champaign, IL: Research Press.

Goldstein, A. P., Sprafkin, R. P., Gershaw, N. J., & Klein, P. (1980). *Skillstreaming the adolescent.* Champaign, IL: Research Press.

Gratevant, H. D. (1992). Assigned and chosen identity components: A process perspective on their integration. In G. R. Adams, T. B. Gullotta, & R. Montemayor (Eds.), *Adolescent identity formation* (pp. 73–90). Newbury Park, CA: Sage.

Hartup, W. W. (1983). Peer relations. In E. M. Hetherington (Ed.) & P. H. Mussen (Series Ed.), *Handbook of child psychology: Vol. 4 Socialization, personality and social development* (pp. 103–196). New York: John Wiley & Sons.

Hartup, W. W. (1993). Adolescents and their friends. In B. Laursen (Ed.), *Close friendships in adolescence* (pp. 3–22). San Francisco: Jossey-Bass.

Hartup, W. W. (1996). The company they keep: Friendships and their developmental significance. *Child Development, 67,* 1–13.

Hunter, F. T. (1985). Adolescent's perception of discussions with parents and friends. *Developmental Psychology, 21,* 433–434.

Inderbitzen-Pisaruk, H., & Foster, S. L. (1990). Adolescent friendships and peer acceptance: Implications for social skills training. *Clinical Psychology Review, 10,* 425–439.

Jones, W. H. (1981). Loneliness and social contact. *Journal of Psychology, 113,* 295–296.

Kandel, D. B. (1978). Homophily, selection, and socialization in adolescent friendships. *American Journal Sociology, 84,* 427–436.

Levesque, R. J. R. (1993). The romantic experience of adolescents in satisfying love relationships. *Journal of Youth and Adolescence, 22,* 219–251.

Maccoby, E. E. (1990). Gender and relationship: A developmental account. *American Psychologist, 45,* 513–520.

Miller, B. C., & Dyk, P. A. H. (1993). Sexuality. In P. H. Tolan & B. J. Cohler (Eds.), *Handbook of clinical research and practice with adolescents.* New York: John Wiley & Sons.

Noller, P., & Callan, V. (1986). Adolescent and parent perceptions of family cohesion and adaptability. *Journal of Adolescence, 9,* 97–106.

Offer, D., Rostov, E., & Howard, K. I. (1981). *The adolescent: a psychological self-portrait.* New York: Basic Books.

Rutter, M., & Garmezy, N. (1983). Developmental psychopathology. In E. M. Hetherington (Ed.) & P. H. Mussen (Series Ed.), *Handbook of child psychology: Vol. 4. Socialization, personality and social development* (pp. 775–911). New York: John Wiley & Sons.

Schonert-Reich, K. A., & Offer, D. (1992). Gender differences in adolescent symptoms. In B. B. Lahey & A. E. Kazdin, *Advances in clinical child psychology* (pp. 27–60). New York: Plenum Press.

Selman, R. L. (1980). *The growth of interpersonal understanding: Developmental and clinical analysis.* New York: Academic Press.

Seltzer, V. C. (1989). *The psychosocial worlds of the adolescent: Public and private.* New York: John Wiley & Sons.

Sullivan, H. S. (1953). *The interpersonal theory of psychiatry.* New York: W. W. Norton.

Valliant, G. E., & Valliant, C. O. (1990). Natural history of male psychological health, a 45-year study of predictors of successful aging at age 65. *American Journal of Psychiatry, 147,* 31–37.

Windle, M. (1994). A study of friendship characteristics and problem behaviors among middle adolescents. *Child Development, 65,* 1764–1778.

Youniss, J., & Smollar, J. (1989). Adolescent's interpersonal relationships in social context. In T. J. Berndt & G. W. Ladd, *Peer relationships in child development* (pp. 300–316). New York: John Wiley & Sons.

14 / The Loss of Latency Identity

Mohammad Haerian

The period between 6 and 12 years of age has been termed latency by psychoanalysts, juvenile era by Sullivan, age of industry by Erikson, concrete operational stage by Piaget, and school age by Chess and Thomas. Regardless of the terminology, this period is characterized by an extremely active interchange between the child and the environment, laying foundations for autonomy, learning social norms, the capacity for self-reflection, and the gradual growth of morality.

Characteristics of the Latency Period

Latency is described by psychoanalytic theorists as the period of educability, pliability, and calm (Sarnoff, 1976). This period can be achieved by a specific organization of ego mechanisms that enables the child to cope with sexual and aggressive drives. Freud viewed latency as a period of diminished sexual activity (1905/1953), but later (1924/1959) indicated that social forces merely repressed sexual drives in this period. Sexual drives therefore do not diminish during latency years, instead, the personality structure of the child undergoes specific changes that enable him or her to withstand stress and maintain an emotional equilibrium. These changes consist of the development of a protective set of defense mechanisms within the structure of the ego and include fantasy, repression, sublimation, and reaction formation (Sarnoff, 1976). Before entering latency, children are already capable of repression and symbol formation. Latency-age children, however, are able to repress the connection between the symbol and what it represents. As a result, they can use the symbol for the discharge of drives and consequently can protect themselves against oedipal wishes.

Another characteristic of the latency period is the development of a rather harsh and rigid superego and consequent development of guilt. These changes result in an internalization of societal norms and a shift from externally enforced superego to internal control and judgment from within, which make latency-age children's behavior consistent and reliable. Bronstein (1951) divided latency into two periods, the first extending from 5½ to 8 years, and the second from 8 until 10 years. In the first, "the ego still buffeted by the surging impulses is threatened by the new superego which is not only harsh and rigid but still a foreign body" (p. 280). In the second phase, the ego encounters fewer conflicts and the superego becomes less rigid. In addition, there is an increased maturation of cognitive functioning, a gradual shift from fantasy to reality, and a move toward independence. Children gradually distance themselves from the parents with the result of increasing independence, a move toward peers and away from parents, and improvement in reasoning and reality testing.

Borrowing from the physiological knowledge of his time, Freud conceptualized a biological basis for latency. In fact, his view of early libidinal development was influenced by Abraham's early training as an embryologist (Shapiro & Perry, 1976). Although Freud later emphasized the influence of culture in latency, his theory of the biological basis of latency persisted for later generations of psychoanalysts to rethink.

The fact that the age of 7 in various cultures and different times of history has been considered a milestone marking a major shift in the child's capabilities can give credence to the notion that biological changes can have a role in the emergence of latency. If there is controversy about the role of biology in the psychological manifestations of latency, namely resolution of Oedipus complex and superego formation, there is little doubt that biological changes play a major role in children's passage from latency into adolescence. The maturation of the central nervous system along with rapid changes in physical configurations of children set the stage for significant changes in cognitive functioning, capacity for reality testing, body image, self-perception, interpersonal relationships, and eventually adolescents' identity formation. After the age of 7 there is a marked improvement in children's cognitive functioning, enabling them to comprehend cause-and-effect relationships. This lessens the children's reliance on fantasy in problem solving and ushers in the crumbling of latency's defensive structure. In other words, children are no longer calm and reliable; they have an increasing desire for independence, a growing doubt about parental values, and, consequently, more conflict with them. The advent of puberty and its consequent body changes may result in confusion and doubt about one's self. These changes often are more pronounced in girls. In fact, menarche intensifies the psychological trauma of puberty and represents one of the final steps in the feminine body configuration (Sarnoff, 1987). Some researchers believe menarche in girls and the first ejaculation in boys to be the major organizers of personality in this period (Blos, 1962; Kestenberg, 1961, 1967).

Role of the Family

In the preschool years, the family is the central figure in children's lives. It contributes to children's perception, thought processes, fantasies and wishes, and it shapes their perception of themselves. Nowadays many children go to preschool, where they are exposed to outside influences earlier. Therefore, the role of the family as the only source of knowledge and identification becomes somewhat less important. Entry into school brings major changes. Although the family remains important, new figures, namely peers and teachers, introduce new sources of knowledge, identifications, and attachment, and the family is no longer the only and almost absolute source of learning and identification. Normal physical development results in the maturation of motor skills and increased independence from parents. The two major accomplishments of concrete operational thought, namely classification and conservation, enable children to form categories and conceive sameness in the face of apparent differences (Piaget, 1952); this, in turn, better enables children to differentiate fantasy from reality. With these competencies children are ready to enter the world with increasing reliance on their own devices. In the course of entering this new world, children face peers with customs different from their own and a group of adults who evaluate them differently than do their parents. In order to adapt to the new situation, children must recognize a more general and impersonal adult authority. By so doing children learn to evaluate their own behavior and also to critically evaluate their parents' values and their authority (Sullivan, 1953). Children's increased participation in social activities leads to an awareness of their own effect on others; this, in turn, leads to the development of self-evaluation and social awareness. This growing capacity for self-evaluation and objective assessment of others is closely related to development of a sense of morality.

The transition from late latency into adolescence is characterized by the return of overt prelatency fantasy activity. Symbolization and displacement, which are characteristics of fantasy in latency, help the core fantasy to become distorted. The result is a vast distance between the conscious content and the unconscious meaning of the fantasy. In late latency and early adolescence, however, the fantasies are poorly, if at all, disguised. The distinction between conscious content and the unconscious meaning of fantasy gradually gets eroded to the point that it closely resembles the rather "naked" fantasy of prelatency. This is why adolescents have to rework issues related to the Oedipus complex. A consequence of this erosion of latency fantasy is a change in the intensity and direction of object relatedness. According to Sarnoff (1987), "in going from early to late latency there was a shift from thoughts about fantasy objects to thoughts about reality objects" (p. 19). During the transition from late latency to early adolescence, the emphasis on reality objects becomes more intense, and eventually fantasy as object gives way to reality as object, which is a characteristic of adolescence (Sarnoff, 1987).

Separation from earlier attachment figures, the push toward further individuation, and increased autonomy result in a state of restlessness and impulsivity in latency-age youngsters. There is a certain weakening of identifications with the family and other important figures, as well, which finds expression in a variety of developmental features, including feelings of guilt and shame due to conflicts between parental values and the peer-group code prescribing an antiadult direction; loyalty to peers and risk taking in their favor; reluctance to accept adults in official roles openly, even those very much liked by the youngsters; open displeasure with and contempt toward authority figures; tendency to avoid interaction with the opposite sex and finding safety in the same-sex group activities; risk taking, bravado, disregard for own safety and health; tendency to refuse help from adults; and increasing distance from adults as evidenced by gradual decrease in communication with them (Malmquist, 1985). It is important to note that at this stage, the pressures of youngsters' increased sexual and aggressive drives, poorly modulated by a fluid ego and superego, may lead to overt antisocial behavior. For example, this fact may explain some of the antisocial acts committed by youngsters ages 12 to 14 (usually as a group) who have no history of prior delinquent activities.

Another characteristic of children's move from latency to adolescence is the assimilation of their identifications into a broader system, namely identity. Identity and identification have common roots (Erikson, 1968). Identifications have limited usefulness; some have a limited life and exert no real or lasting influence on the personality, whereas a number of identifications begin early in the context of children's attachment and make more lasting contributions (Malmquist, 1985). In spite of this, the sum of children's identifications does not make up their personality. Also, it is important to note that identification does not take place with a person or object per se but rather with the representation of it. The result is that children's developmental level, the internal state, and the level of anxiety contribute to how they perceive and consequently identify with individuals and objects.

The transition to adolescence is marked by cognitive, physiological, psychological, and behavioral changes.

Piaget used the term "hypothetic-deductive thinking" (formal operational) to describe the mental operations of adolescents and adults. Such operations are based on the *form* of a proposition in contrast to the concrete operations of latency-age children, which are based solely on existing reality. Latency-age children are able to reason logically; to organize their thoughts into coherent total structures and to arrange them in hierarchic or sequential relationships. Their reasoning, how-

ever, is based on the concrete, tangible, and existing reality. By age 11 they exhibit a gradual move toward formal operational or hypothetic-deductive thinking. By this Piaget means thinking based on a hypothesis that leads to certain logical deductions. Such a hypothesis may exist only in form (e.g., what would happen if no one ever died?), or it may have conclusions that can be verified on the basis of an existing reality. Children of this age begin to use other abstract propositions, such as implication (if-then), exclusion (either-or), incompatibility (either-or, neither) and the like.

Many changes occur in the transformation of a child's body into that of an adult. The most obvious are physical alterations, an increase in height and weight, changes in body proportion and fat distribution, and the development of secondary sex characteristics. Growth of breasts in girls and increase in the size of the penis and testicles in boys and pubic hair in both coincide with sexual maturation.

Sexual maturation occurs due to secretion of hormones that specifically differentiate the genders. These changes occur approximately within the range of 9 to 14 years and are controlled, integrated, and orchestrated by the central nervous system and endocrine glands. According to a maturational timing, the hypothalamus secretes gonadotrophin releasing hormones, which act on the pituitary to effect the secretion of gonadotrophins. The gonads in turn are activated to produce testosterone in males and estrogen in females.

Girls start to mature about 2 years earlier than boys. Within either sex there is a range of variation in the ages when children reach puberty (Tanner, 1962).

Maturation of the sex organs and development of secondary sex characteristics result in dramatic changes to children's bodies. Budding of the breasts is the first indication of approaching puberty in girls. About the same time there is a rapid growth of vagina and uterus; menstruation starts 2 years later. Coincident with breast development is the appearance of pubic hair.

In boys the first indication of approaching puberty is enlargement of the testes and scrotum. The age when boys start to produce sperm is not clear, but in approximately 50%, sperm may be present after 14 to 15 years of age. The penis starts to grow in length a year or more after the testes and scrotum.

Children have significant psychological reactions to these physiological and physical changes. The hormonal increment exerts a disequilibrating effect on the relatively cohesive personality of latency. The latency structure is loosened and previously repressed impulses and fantasies break through into consciousness.

Identity structures and characterological defenses of latency become fragmented and cease to function effectively. The sense of self as a child and body image become fragmented and blurred, as well. Children become preoccupied with many issues, including their new height, newly developed sexual organs, squeaky voice, wet dreams, and the like. They no longer feel secure and connected with their past. Loyalties and group alliances shift, moving away from the parents and toward the outer world. In addition, there is a shift from playing with the same-sex group to becoming attracted to the opposite sex. These changes result in irritability, touchiness, and sadness. The increasing awareness of sexuality, sexual desires, and sensations often lead to periods of regression to prelatency fantasies and behavior.

Girls deal with the early breast changes by denial and shame or efforts at concealment. The size of breasts becomes of concern to girls, as well. By this age they are keenly aware of the importance of breasts as a symbol of femininity and as one that attracts males.

In boys in particular there is a regression to earlier stage of development manifested by resurgence of dirty jokes and sloppiness. Their encounters with newly developing girls create a mixture of anxiety and curiosity. Boys react to this with behaviors such as peeping, teasing, joking about girls, and making derogatory remarks about them.

At this age boys often hang out with each other. In these private and semiprivate gatherings they often get involved in such games as comparing the length of their urinary stream and the size of their penis, and occasionally group masturbation.

Prominent among preadolescence defenses are narcissism and omnipotence. Narcissism is a defensive measure to cope with inner feelings of low self-esteem, depression, and void. Maturation, according to Sarnoff (1987), is a double-edged sword. While each move toward maturation strengthens youngsters adaptive potential, at the same time their increasingly advanced cognitive functioning reminds them of their limitations.

Therefore, each surrender to the reality of the outside world cuts into youngsters' narcissistic sense of self. Adolescents' narcissism in turn hinders their capacity for establishing a meaningful and mutual relationship with others. Factors that enhance narcissism include persistence of latency style of fantasy and pubertal bodily changes drawing one's attention to self. Factors that enhance object relations include improved reality testing, weakening of the structure of the latency, and social pressures.

Loss of the latency defense structure produces profound changes in the nature of the object relations and perception of the self. These modifications lead early adolescents into deidealization of parental images, instigating a shift to peers and teachers. Latency-age children are able to identify with the same-sex parent and establish and solidify their ego ideal and superego. With the loss of latency identity caused by cognitive maturation and increased interaction with adults, youngsters react to the limitations and faults of the parents with annoyed disappointment. The reaction is to the incongruity between the real parent and the idealized parent image. Many clinicians have listened to latency-age children describing their mothers as the most beautiful and their fathers as the strongest. Several years later the same children talk about the same parents as the ugliest and meanest of all parents.

This deidealization leaves the adolescent character structure temporarily in a state of disequilibrium because the latency superego and ego ideal, as gross and unsophisticated as they may have been, served as an ego control through a sense of calm and satisfaction with the self.

The deidealization of parents appears to be a necessary step in a healthy identity of formation for adolescents in the same way that the first "no" of 2-year-old toddlers serves them to move psychologically toward autonomy and separation from parents.

The coming together of the deidealization of the parents, loosening of the latency-age harsh superego, the uncertainty of a new relationship with peers and others outside of the family circle, the uncertainty about one's changing body, and the sudden surge in sexual drives all contribute to the moodiness, restlessness, and at times confusion of the late-latency, early adolescent.

Anna Freud's assertion (1958) about the normalcy of adolescent turmoil is now thought to hold only in a small percentage of adolescents. Under the stress of the just-mentioned events, the egos of early adolescents are often unable to cope effectively. Of course, those with better-developed coping skills and those who have mastered the developmental tasks of latency will be able to go through this phase of development with less turmoil. This is in keeping with Offer's (Offer & Offer, 1975) findings. In studying a group of normal adolescents, Offer identified 3 categories. The first consisted of those who had had a relatively conflict-free latency and sailed relatively smoothly through the adolescent years. These adolescents (23%) had little conflict with their families with little interruption in their schoolwork, enjoyed their activities, and had meaningful and stable peer relationships. In contrast to this group, about 35% of adolescents suffered from depression and anxiety, were unsuccessful in their studies, and were at odds with their parents. A third group, approximately 21%, experienced periods of anxiety and depression, but these problems did not hamper their adjustment significantly (Offer & Offer, 1975). In his classic Isle of Wight Study (Rutter et al., 1976), Rutter attempted to examine the validity of adolescent turmoil. He found that most parents of 14-year-olds did not perceive their children as alienated from them. Less than 1 in 10 of these parents reported that their child tended to withdraw physically, and only 1 in 6 reported emotional withdrawal or difficulty in communication. In both males and females, these difficulties usually had begun in earlier childhood rather than during adolescence, although communication difficulties were reported more often with boys than with girls.

Rutter also found that the children were not particularly critical of their parents and only a very few rejected them. If there were any conflicts, the majority were about style of clothing or hair, the time for going out and coming in, and the like. Most of the adolescents shared their parents' values on other things and respected the need for restrictions and control. Most cases of alienation were reported as beginnng prior to the age of 10 years.

On the other hand, altercations with parents, depression, and withdrawal were all twice as common among adolescents with psychiatric disorder as in the general population.

The concept of adolescent turmoil, however, is not limited to the alienation from parents but also includes feelings of inner turmoil and affective disturbance. Nearly half of the 14- to 15-year-olds in Rutter's study reported some degree of misery or depression often associated with tearfulness and wanting to get away from everything. Twenty percent reported sleeping problems and about 10% admitted to suicidal feelings.

As many adolescents move away from their parents, their new skills and talents are directed toward obtaining approval and prestige in the peer group. Feelings of being important to others, which result from peer-group acceptance, validate the youngsters' feelings of self-worth and according to Sullivan (1953) are an important feature of the preadolescent intimated friendship— "chumship"—in consensual validation. The self-disclosure typical of chumship leads to affirmation that one's feelings and ideals are accepted, valid, and worthy. With chums, adolescents share, develop altruistic concerns, and correct distortions about themselves. Having a special friendship seems to be much more common for females than for males. Males are more likely than females to associate with several friends at a time rather than with one special friend, and to have more friends and larger activity groups than girls.

In contrast to younger ages, preadolescent friendship becomes more stable and best friends become prominent. Childhood friendships center around play activities and group acceptance. Being a competent friend involves being a fun and nice play partner. In contrast, adolescent friendship demands greater facility in a number of close relationships. It entails being capable of initiating conversations and relationships outside of the classroom and being skilled in appropriately disclosing personal information and providing emotional support to friends (Smallar & Youniss, 1985).

Another change is in the area of self image. Simmons, Rosenberg, and Rosenberg (1973) describe four dimensions of self-image: self-consciousness, which measures the degree of prominence one ascribes to oneself in the perception of others; stability, which describes one's perception of self-image consistently; self-esteem, which indicates the general self-attitude; and perceived self, or how one imagines he or she is viewed by others.

According to Simmons et al., young female adolescents are more self-conscious than their male counterparts and there is a consistent and clearly defined self-image decrement between childhood and early adolescence in both males and females.

Moral Development

A major achievement in late latency and early adolescence is moral development, which is closely related to children's identity formation. Kohlberg (1968, 1976) proposed a comprehensive scheme for moral development. His theory builds on the work of Piaget and identifies three major levels in the attainment of moral understanding, each of which is divided into two stages. Kohlberg's moral levels are: 1—premoral (includes Stages 1 and 2); 2—morality of conventional role—conformity (Stages 3 and 4); and 3—morality of self-accepted (postconventional) (Stage 5 and 6). In Stage 1, children do not consider the interests of others or recognize that they differ from their own. Their reasons for doing right are avoidance of punishment and the superior power of authorities.

In Stage 2, children are aware that everyone has his or her own interests to pursue and that these interests may conflict with others. Children in this stage do right to serve their own needs or interests in a world where it must be recognized that other people have their own interests, as well.

In Stage 3, youngsters are aware of shared feelings, agreements, and expectations that take primacy over their own individual interests. These youngsters do right due to the need to be a good person in their own eyes and those of others.

In Stage 4, youngsters are able to differentiate societal point of view from interpersonal agreements or motives, and the main reason for doing right is to keep the institution going as a whole.

Stage 5 is concerned that laws and duties be based on rational calculation.

Stage 6 is concerned with the validity of universal principles and a sense of personal commitment to them (Kohlberg, 1975).

Young children define "rightness" and "wrongness" in terms of their own subjective feelings. If the self likes something, it is "right"; if the self doesn't like it, it is "wrong." In the intermediate level (Stages 3 and 4), older children and adults continue to define "rightness" and "wrongness" by reference to subjective feelings but to the collective feelings of others and not their own; what is correct is what agrees with the will of authority figures. The concept of rules and regulations of the society become important. During late latency and early adolescence children reach Stages 3 and 4 of moral development.

Gilligan (1982) has argued that "this discussion of moral development takes place against the background of a field where beginning with Freud's theory that tied superego formation to castration anxiety, extending through Piaget's study of boys' conception of the rules of their games, and culminating in Kohlberg's derivation of six stages of moral development from research on adolescent males, the line of moral development has been shaped by the pattern of male experience and thought" (p. 201). According to Gilligan, girls address moral dilemmas quite differently. Their approach points to a greater sense of connection and a concern with relationships. Boys, on the other hand, are concerned with rules. Hence there is a paradoxical conclusion that women's preoccupation with relationships hinders the progress of their moral development. Gilligan concludes ". . . we are attuned to a hierarchical ordering that represents development as a progress of separation, a chronicle of individual success. In contrast, the understanding of development as a progress of human relationships, a narrative expanding connection is an unimagined representation . . ." (p. 209). The tendency to chart the unfamiliar waters of adult development with the familiar markers of adolescent separation and growth leads to an equation of development with separation; it results in a failure to represent the reality of connection in love and in work.

Self-Understanding

Self-understanding and self-differentiation have been addressed by various disciplines from different points of view. Psychoanalytic theory has been the most sensitive to the interplay between the child's cognitive and affective development. Perhaps the most influential psychoanalytic explanation of self-differentiation is Mahler's theory of separation-individuation (Mahler, Pine, & Bergman, 1975). Mahler divides this process into three phases: autism, from 0 to 2 months; symbiosis, from 2 to 6 months; and separation-individuation, from 6 to 36 months. The latter has four subphases:

1. Differentiation, during which infants are more alert and attentive and pull their mother's hair and strain their body from hers.
2. Practicing subphase (12 to 18 months), during which toddlers take the greatest step in human individuation, walking upright, which allows them to explore the world around them and contributes to their growing sense of autonomy and competence.
3. Rapprochement (18 to 24 months). Increasing autonomy due to maturation of neuromuscular apparatus allows more frequent and distant trips away from the mother. This along with the development of more sophisticated cognitive functioning contributes to children's further sense of separateness from the mother. The fear of independence, however, brings with it an awareness of the self's profound limitations.
4. Consolidation, the last subphase of separation-individuation, during which children attain a positive image of self, separate from that of the mother. The development of object permanency and mental representation in Piagetan terms are prerequisites for consolidation of personality.

Children's clear separation from the mother combined with their ability to manage their thoughts and feelings through mental representations allows them to develop an initial image of self that serves as the basis for the development of personality and self-understanding.

Mahler's model, however, has been criticized on a number of grounds. New observations in child development have raised serious questions about the concepts of autism and symbiosis, and the claim that the newborn is an undifferentiated being (Stern, 1985). Furthermore, considering Mahler's overemphasis on mother's reaction and role in different phases, it has been suggested that Mahler's theory reveals more about what the mother does to foster the child's development of self than about the process of self-development. In contrast to Mahler's theory is Kagan's assertion (1981) that initial emergence of self-awareness is mainly due to the infant's inborn biological mechanisms. Kagan strongly deemphasizes the role of social environment in the development of self-awareness. Instead, he believes that there is a direct link between the emergence of self-awareness and maturation of certain brain functions. He suggests that the development of mental representation and the ability to maintain this representation in active memory is directly related to myelinization and the acquisition of mature neural density. Kagan acknowledges that self-knowledge may be effected by the environment; the effect, however, is limited to induce only variations in self-knowledge. According to Kagan, the notion of self-awareness being a lifelong process in just a "Western cultural artifact."

Social cognitive theorists, on the other hand, have advanced the notion that knowledge of the self can be constructed only through social interactions. Baldwin (in Damon & Hart, 1988) believed that one comes to know the self only as one comes to know others. Damon and Hart (1988) argue that although a number of empirical studies have demonstrated that in many respects the knowledge of self and that of the other develop in parallel, there are obvious differences between self and other understanding. They question the role of affect in experiencing the self and also the difficulty of gaining "objective" knowledge about the self. After all, "there may be a profound affective difference between how one receives feedback on the self versus how one receives feedback on others (Damon & Hart, 1982, p. 844).

William James divided the concept of self into two main components, the "me" and the "I." The "me" aspect is "the sum total of all a person can call his" (James, 1892/1961, p. 44), these include all material characteristics, all the social characteristics, and all the spiritual characteristics. The "I," on the other hand, is the "self as knower." This is a subjective aspect of self; the individual becomes aware of it through three types of experiences: continuity, distinctness, and volition. The first two are closely related to and draw heavily upon the objective self ("self as known") for their shape and substance. The sense of volition or agency, on the other hand, underlies one's sense of self-determination. In early childhood, the self is conceived in physical terms and as a process that is totally nonvolitional. Children simply believe that "self" and "mind" are parts of the body and therefore can be described by material dimensions, such as size, color or shape. At this stage, children distinguish themselves from others by their physical appearances. For example, "I am different from my brother because I am smaller," or "I am different from my friend because I have a bike." A 3-year-old asks her twin sister "Are you like me?" and she answers, "No, I have a boat." At this age, children realize that psychological and physical experiences are not the same, but they still believe that the two types of experiences are consistent with one another. At about 8 years of age, children's self-understanding changes. They now begin to understand the volitional aspects of self in their own right and recognize that "self" is not linked to any specific body part. The distinction between mental and physical aspects of self enable children to appreciate the subjective nature of self. This distinction is a necessary requisite to distinguish one's self from others not on the basis of physical and material possessions but because of different thoughts and feelings. "I am different from my friend because I think differently." This shift in the understanding of self applies to all dimensions of self including sexuality, individuality, and continuity. Sexuality refers to a person's sex role. Individuality refers to a person's belief that he or she is unique. Continuity refers to connectness between a person's present, future, and past. In late childhood, all the aspects of self are described more in psychological than in physical terms. In early adolescence, youths become aware of their "self-awareness."

Identity

Self-understanding, self-concept, self-as-subject, and self-other differentiation are all terms that have been used, at times, interchangeably with "identity." While these constructs share many features, they are not necessarily synonymous with identity. (I discussed the concept of self-understanding for it greatly overlaps with that of identity). Identify as defined by Erikson (1968) consists of a sense of inner sameness, continuity over time, being distinct from others, and a sense of inner agency. Blasi (1988), in his essay entitled "Identity and the Development of the Self," describes a

"dialectical relation" between the following elements:

- Identity is an answer to the question "who am I?"; in general, the answer consists of achieving a new unity among the elements of one's past and the expectations about one's future.
- This will give rise to a fundamental sense of sameness and continuity.
- The answer to the identity question is arrived at by a process that includes: realistically appraising one's self and one's past; considering one's culture, particularly its ideology and the expectations that society has for one's self; and at the same time questioning the validity of both culture and society and the appropriateness of other's perceptions and expectations.
- This process of integration and questioning should occur around certain fundamental areas such as one's future occupation, sexuality, and religious and political ideas and should lead to a flexible but durable commitment in these areas.
- This guarantees from an objective perspective one's productive integration in society and, subjectively, a sense of basic loyalty and fidelity.
- These are accompanied by deep preconscious feelings of rootedness and well-being, self-esteem, and purposefulness.
- The sensitive period for the development of identity is the adolescent years. (Blasi, 1988, p. 226)

As such, overall identity gives direction to one's life and provides the person with a framework for organizing behavior across different aspects of life. According to Erikson (1950, 1968), identity formation is the task of adolescence and becomes consolidated in late adolescence. The precursors of identity, however, must be sought in earlier years.

It is interesting to note that in classical psychoanalytic theory, the "formative years" end by resolution of the Oedipus complex. The object relations theorists, however, by emphasizing the centrality of early introjects in the formation of one's self structure, push the formative years back to infancy. Erikson, on the other hand, extends the final significant developmental point upward into adolescence (Marcia, 1988).

Expanding on Erikson's concept of identity, Marcia (1988) has pointed to the importance of two key processes involved in identity formation: exploration of alternatives and commitment to choices. The first process is related to the child's temperament, particularly to his or her sense of curiosity but, more important, to the parents' attitude in allowing the child to become independent and to explore different alternatives from those prescribed by them. Commitment to choices, among other factors, is related to the child's acceptance of him- or herself as a valuable member of the larger society.

Identity formation may occur in a number of different domains (Grotevant, 1987, 1993). These areas include, but are not limited to, occupational, religious, and political ideology; values; sex roles; and views of one's self in friendships and committed relationships. Grotevant views identity formation as occurring within a specific domain. In his model there are interdependencies among different domains, and "individual characteristics" and "contexts of development, i.e., family, peer, culture/society," are the major components shaping one's identity.

Four interrelated personality characteristics are closely related to identity formation, its process, and its final outcome: self-esteem, self-monitoring, ego resiliency, and openness to experience. For example, self-esteem contributes to a person's willingness to take risks and explore alternatives and consider options freely. Self-esteem also is directly related to one's degree of motivation. Self-monitoring refers to that aspect of the self that is capable of adapting its behavior to function harmoniously with the environment. High self-monitoring individuals are sensitive to social cues and are capable of using feedback to modify their behavior in different social contexts, whereas low self-monitoring individuals tend to behave consistently (and rigidly) from one situation to the next. High self-monitoring people capable of using social cues and feedback must be distinguished from those who have very little core sense of identity, changing their attitude and behavior all the time in relation to the changes in the environment.

Ego resiliency refers to a person's flexibility in dealing with new situations. In this sense ego resiliency is closely related to self-monitoring. Openness to experience and information may be regarded as a personality dimension having its roots in a person's temperament and constitutional endowment. It is also closely related to environment's tolerance and sanction for such an attitude. In this context the problems encountered by youngsters brought up in a static and rigid or a totalitarian system should be considered. Socioeconomic status and gender contribute to the context in which identity is formed by controlling what the environment sanctions to be provided for different segments of society. Social norms and ideology also influence the process and outcome of identity formation. Erikson noted that American youth are anti-ideological, glorifying instead a "way of life" and a "comfortable one" (1968).

In referring to the importance of the social context in formation of one's identity, Margaret Mead (1928) points out that in a primitive society, adolescence is a relatively simple task. All young persons growing up in that society, from the time they can pretend roles and expectations, know exactly what is expected of them and what they will become in the future. In a technologically advanced and dynamic society, however, the task of identity formation becomes increasingly difficult. Identity and social roles are not described according to a person's place in the society, or gender or birth order. They have to be achieved. Erikson (1968), making a similar point, states that the primitive man's tool is the extension of his body. "Children in these groups participate in technical and in magic pursuits: to them body and environment, childhood and culture may be full of dangers, but they are all one world. In our world, machines, far from remaining an extension of the body, destine the whole human organization to be extensions of machinery" (pp. 48–49). This point has a much stronger resonance when we consider the explosion of technological knowledge, the narrowing of people's fields of experience and expertise, and the fact that careers, which are a major ingredient of people's identities, may easily become obsolete.

Identity Statuses

Based on a person's degree of *exploration* and *commitment*, Marcia (1966) suggests 4 different identity statuses:

1. Identity Achiever. Youngsters in this category go through a period of exploring available alternatives and options. When an option is chosen, youngsters make a relatively firm commitment to pursue their choice. The result is a sense of confidence, optimism, and stability. As such, identity achievers have resolved their identity crisis.
2. Moratorium. This term is used to define a person who is currently in crisis and is actively seeking

among alternatives in an attempt to arrive at a choice.

Both achievers and moratoriums are involved in self-examination. Achievers have been engaged in self-reflection, whereas moratoriums are currently engaged in an ongoing process of self-examination that involves inferences and hypotheses about one's dispositions and abilities.

3. Identity Foreclosure. Persons in this category have never experienced an identity crisis (and by the same token have not been through self-reflection and self-examination nor through any exploration of options). These people's commitment, however, is firm, and it is usually established fairly early in life. There is a strong sense of identification with parents and other authority figures. Also, a foreclosure's lack of exploration may be due to the parents' style of lack of tolerance for autonomy, the child's own personality style, or the lack of exposure to alternative choices.

4. Identity Diffusion. These individuals are very low in their degree of commitment. They have not arrived at decisions regarding their goals, beliefs, and values, and no self-reflection is involved. Identity diffusion seems to be related to a tendency to avoid facing personal problems, although a lack of consistent role models during the early formative years may be another contributing factor. Individuals in this group make no mental effort to formulate a personal value system. Their behavior is situation-specific and chameleonlike, changing from one situation to another.

Individuals may show a mixture and fluidity of identity statuses in different domains at a given time. For instance, a person may be an identity achiever in the domain of social career but in a diffusion state in the domain of religious and social life (Waterman, 1985). Developmentally, people may move from one identity status to another, depending on the circumstances (experiences, opportunities, and exposures, e.g.). A person with identity diffusion may remain unchanged or may prematurely and without exploration of other alternatives make a firm commitment to a choice and therefore become an early foreclosure; or he or she may become an achiever by exploring other choices and through self-examination. A foreclosure may remain the same or change into moratorium, a situation that may occur when a youngster realizes that an early commitment is challenged in a way that requires exploration of other possibilities. By the same token, a foreclosure may change into identity diffusion, most likely when the person fails in his or her efforts to implement identity

choices and is not psychologically prepared to consider other alternatives. Once a youngster has entered the moratorium status, he or she may advance to achieve a stable identity or may fail to choose from available alternatives and end up with identity diffusion. Adolescents who reach identity achievement status need a social support system for their activities. When such support is lacking, there may be a movement back to moratorium status. It is even possible that an identity achiever, facing "burn out" in attempts to adhere to goals and values, may slip into identity diffusion (Waterman, 1985).

Identity Formation in Girls—Similarities and Differences

The structure of latency, self-understanding, and the process of identity formation is, for the most part, similar in boys and girls. Nonetheless, there are differences between the two genders. Some are related directly to genital and other anatomical differences, and some are secondary to the cultural attitudes and practices of sexual discrimination. The early psychoanalytic views maintained the absence of vaginal awareness in girls until puberty and the centrality of penis envy and the castration complex in female development. Later psychoanalysts reported that girls discover their external genitalia somewhere around 18 months of age and that this discovery is a part of the children's exploration of their bodies. Genital play during this period helps children to form their body image. A girl's genital play at this stage is different from masturbation, for the latter requires a capacity for fantasy, which at this age is absent due to her stage of cognitive development and absence of high levels of sex hormones. This early genital awareness is accompanied by an early sense of femaleness. Whether the child devalues her female genitality and feels inferior to boys has much to do with parental attitudes.

Erikson (1968) believes that psychoanalysis failed to understand the nature of the process of identity formation in girls. He suggested that the existence of an "inner space" set in the center of the female body has much more to do with her body image and identity formation than a missing external organ, namely, the penis. According to Erikson, while there are no sexual differences in the areas of cognitive functioning and abstract reasoning, there is a difference between females and males as to how they arrange space (in play and other activities). He states, ". . . sexual differences in the organization of a play space seem to parallel the morphology of genital differentiation itself. In the male an external organ, erectable and intrusive in character serving the channelization of mobile sperm cells; in the female internal organs with vestilicular access leading to statically expectant ova" (p. 271). Erikson admits that a purely social interpretation would not see anything symbolic about male and female's different use of space. The social theory "takes it for granted that boys love the outdoors and girls the indoors . . ." Neither interpretation can be ignored nor totally accepted.

Sex differences establish a range of attitudes, attributes, and inclinations that "come naturally" to most members of that sex. These differences, however, can be unlearned and relearned. For women the question becomes "how much and which parts of [their] inborn inclinations the women of tomorrow will feel most natural to preserve and to cultivate" (Erikson, 1968, p. 291), with the ever-increasing choices now available. In other words, anatomy is not necessarily destiny.

Other investigators have focused on the issue of "interpersonal relationship" as an organizer for female identity development. While autonomy is the hallmark of a high-achiever male, it is hard for the American culture to regard commitment, fidelity, intimacy, and care for others as meaningful. Josselson (1988; Josselson & Lieblich, 1996) suggests that female development proceeds on an interpersonal track that is not represented in Erikson's scheme. She believes that there is a vast difference in the way women make sense of the world and that this calls for a redefinition of identity. In her model, the self is conceived as intertwined with others.

Conclusion

Identity is a lifelong process that has its roots in children's earliest interactions with the environment. Children's identification and introjects are precursors of the process of identity formation in adolescence. In fact, identity formation starts where the usefulness of identification ends. Although the stage of formal operations is not a necessary requirement for identity formation, it clearly facilitates the process. A significant shift in children's ego structure and cognitive functioning occurs as they transition from prelatency to latency. In the latter stage, children use fantasy reaction formation and repression as their main defense mechanism in order to protect their inner equilibrium. Identification serves as children's main mechanism in learning social norms and values. In their passage from latency to late latency and from the latter to adolescence, this delicate ego structure crumbles, and identification is no longer adequate. Moreover, children begin to doubt their parents' values and standards and gradually pull away from them.

Identity formation is a psychosocial phenomenon and occurs in the context of the family and the larger society. Therefore, these two institutions play an essential role in the process and final outcome of children's identity. Parents' roles are doublefold. On the one hand, they have to foster connectedness in their child; on the other hand, they are required to encourage measured steps toward autonomy, exploration of choices, speaking out, and questioning parental values. A "good enough" relationship with parents promotes the self's sense of cohesiveness.

Parents are essential in modeling and melding children's early identification and in helping them to reevaluate these identifications and, if necessary, to relinquish them later on during adolescence. Children's failure to relinquish their early childhood introjects and identifications or to incorporate them in a cohesive whole leads to disorders of identity in adolescence and adulthood. Overall, any process that would interfere with children's practice of autonomy and attempts at exploring the environment will have a negative impact on their identity formation. Among the many possible factors that may hinder the process of identity formation are children's own temperamental makeup, excessive self-consciousness and shyness, inability to establish stable affective bonds, the parents' lack of tolerance for autonomy (disturbances in separation-individuation in early years and conflict over adolescents' move toward peers and away from parents later on), the society's intolerance for exploration of alternative choices, and the unavailability of those choices. In fact, by providing exposure to a variety of options and opportunities or by denying them, the larger society may facilitate or hinder children's search for identity. By offering a very narrow range of choices, totalitarian societies may significantly limit chil-

dren's actualization of their potential. It is reasonable to presume that a society's tolerance of cultural diversity and its openness and flexibility afford its youths an optimal context to grow and achieve their identity.

REFERENCES

Blasi, A. (1988). Identity and the development of the self." In D. K. Lapsley & F. C. Power (Eds.) *Self ego and identity* (pp. 226–242). New York: Springer-Verlag.

Blasi, A. (1994). Moral identity: Its role in more functioning. In B. Puka (Ed.), *Fundamental research in moral development. Moral development: A compendium* (Vol. 2, pp. 168–179). New York: Garland Publishing.

Blos, P. (1962). *On adolescence*. New York: Macmillan.

Bronstein, B. (1951). On latency. *Psychoanalytic Study of the Child*, 6, 279–285.

Damon, W., & Hart, D. (1992). The development of self-understanding from infancy through adolescence. *Child Development*, 53, 841–864.

Damon, W. & Hart, D. (1988). *Self understanding in Childhood and Adolescence*. Cambridge, MA: Cambridge University Press.

Erikson, E. H. (1950). *Childhood and society* (rev. ed.) New York: W. W. Norton.

Erikson, E. H. (1968). *Identity, youth and crisis*. New York: W. W. Norton.

Freud, S. (1953). Three essays on the theory of sexuality. In J. Strachey (Ed.), *The standard edition of the complete psychological works of Sigmund Freud* (hereafter Standard Edition (Vol. 7, pp. 125–254). London: Hogarth Press. (Originally published 1905.)

Freud, S. (1959). An autobiograhical study. In *Standard edition* (Vol. 20, pp. 7–74) (Originally published 1924.)

Gilligan, C. (1982). New maps of development: New visions of maturity. *American Journal of Orthopsychiatry*, 52 (2), 199–212.

Grotevant, H. (1987). Toward a Process Model of Identity. *Journal of Adolescent Research*, 2 (3), 203–222.

Grotevant, H. D., (1993). The integrative nature of identity: Bringing the sololists to sing in the choir. In J. Kroger (Ed.), *Discussions on ego identity*. Hillsdale, NJ: Lawrence Erlbaum.

Harter, S. (1983). The development of the self and self system. In M. Hetherington, *Handbook of child psychology*, (Vol. 4). New York: John Wiley & Sons.

James, W. (1961). *Psychology: The briefer course*. New York: Harper & Row. (Originally published 1892.)

Josselson, R. (1988). The embedded self: I and thou revisited. In D. K. Lapsley & F. C. Power (Eds.), *Self, ego and identity* (pp. 91–106). New York: Springer-Verlag.

Josselson, R., & Lieblich, A. (1996). *Interpreting experience: The narrative study of lives*. Thousand Oaks, CA: Sage.

Kagan, J. (1981). *The second year of life*. Cambridge, MA: Harvard University Press.

Kestenberg, J. (1961). Menarche. In. S. Lorand & H. I. Schneer (Eds.), *Adolescence*. New York: Hoeher Medical Division, Harper & Row.

Kestenberg, J. (1967). Phases of Adolescence Parts I & II. *Journal of Child Psychiatry*, 6, 426–463.

Kleinman, J. A. (1971). The establishment of core gender identity in normal girls. *Archives of Sexual Behavior*, 1, 103–129.

Kohlberg, L. (1968, 2 Sept.) The child as a moral philosopher. *Psychology Today*, 2 (4), 25–30.

Kohlberg, L. (1976). Moral stages and moralization: The cognitive developmental approach. In T. Lickona (Ed.), *Moral development and behavior: Theory, research and social issues*. (pp. 29–53). New York: Holt, Rinehart and Winston.

Kohlberg, L. (1981). *Essays of moral development* Vol. 1: The philosophy of moral development: Moral stages and the idea of justice. San Francisco: Harper & Row.

Mahler, M., Pine, F., & Bergman, A. (1975). *The psychological birth of the human infant*. New York: Basic Books.

Malmquist, C. (1985). *Handbook of adolescence*. New York: Jason Aronson.

Marcia, J. E. (1988). Common process underlying ego identity, cognitive/moral development, and individuation. In D. K. Lapsley & F. C. Power (Eds.), *Self ego and identity* (pp. 211–225). New York: Springer-Verlag.

Marcia, J. E. (1966). Development and validation of ego identity status. *Journal of Personality and Social Pathology*, 3, 551–558.

Mead, M. (1928). *Coming of age in Samoa*. New York: Morrow.

Offer, D., & Offer J. B. (1975). *From teenage to young manhood*. New York: Basic Books.

Piaget, J. (1952). *The origins of intelligence in children*. New York: International Universities Press.

Rutter, M., et al. (1976). Isle of Wight Studies. *Psychological Medicine*, 6, (2), 313–332.

Sarnoff, C. (1976). *Latency*. New York: Jason Aronson.

Sarnoff, C. (1987). *Psychotherapeutic strategies in late*

latency through early adolescence. Northvale, NJ: Jason Aronson.

Shapiro, T., & Perry R. (1976). Latency revisited. *Psychoanalytic Study of the Child*, 37, 79–105.

Simmons, R. G., Rosenberg, F., & Rosenberg, M. (1973). Disturbance in the self-image at adolescence. *American Sociological Review*, 38 (5), 553–568.

Smollar, J., & Youniss, J. (1985). Parent-adolescent relations in adolescents whose parents are divorced. Special Issue: Contemporary approaches to the study of families with adolescents. *Journal of Early Adolescence*, 5 (1), 129–144.

Stern, D. (1985). *The interpersonal world of the infant*. New York: Basic Books.

Sullivan, H. S. (1953). *The interpersonal theory of psychiatry*. New York: W. H. Norton.

Tanner, J. M. (1962). *Growth at adolescence*. Oxford: Blackwell Scientific.

Tapp, J. L., Kohlberg, L. (1971). Developing senses of law and legal justice. *Journal of Social Issues*, 27 (2), 65–91.

Thomas, A., & Chess, S. (1977): Temperment and Development. New York: Brunner-Mazel.

Waterman, A. (1985). Identity in the context of adolescent psychology. In A. Waterman (Ed.), *Identity in adolescence: Process and contents*. New Direction for Child Development, No. 30. San Francisco: Jossey-Bass, December 1985.

15 / The Self in Adolescence

Richard C. Marohn

Editor's Note

Among the many important transformations that occur during adolescence, the development of the self is certainly one of the most central. The understanding of what exactly the self is and how it is related to other aspects of adolescent development have been the subjects of a vast field of study within psychology. In entering this realm, we are moving beyond what can be explained on the basis of current knowledge of neurophysiology and neuroanatomy. The concept of self implies consciousness of one's own being, and so far no one has been able to explain fully how consciousness arises. Thus, there is an essential mystery to the concept of self, but it is at the same time crucially important to our understanding of development and in our everyday work with adolescents.

Self is based on perceptions of oneself and others and ideas about how others see one. Thus, the development of the self is inextricably bound to the experience that one has with significant others. Both the developing individual and those with whom he or she interacts bring along unique contributions, based on biological substrates as well as many other things, that color their experiences with each other. These experiences begin in the earliest days of life, probably even in utero, and continue throughout life. The individual is forever immersed in a complex web of relationships that define who he or she is. It is with the study of this aspect of being that object relations theorists have concerned themselves. The "objects" are internal images of real, external people, that ". . . constitute a residue within the mind of relationships with important people in the individual's life" (Greenberg & Mitchell, 1983, p. 11).

Object relations theory "designates theories, or aspects of theories, concerned with exploring the relationship between real, external people and in-

ternal images and residues of relations between them, and the significance of these residues for psychic functioning" (Greenberg & Mitchell, p. 12). The term "object relations" refers to "individuals' interaction with external and internal (real and imagined) other people, and to the relationship between their internal and external object worlds" (p. 14).

Many of the object relations theorists began as students of classical psychoanalytic theory but moved away to varying degrees as they saw that it could not explain many important phenomena that they observed in patients, particularly severely disturbed patients. As did other psychoanalytic theorists who were dissatisfied with a narrow drive psychology, Heinz Kohut proposed some revisions of psychoanalytic theory. These revisions became known as self psychology, because of their emphasis on the importance of understanding what happens to the self in normal and psychopathological development and how changes in the self, brought about by psychotherapeutic intervention, can modify psychopathology.

Kohut was a psychoanalyst who developed a conceptual framework for understanding and treating narcissistic and borderline patients in a psychoanalytic mode. He viewed these disorders of personality as the outcomes of various types of pathological development of the self. He termed his theory "the psychology of the self," and it has come to be known as "self psychology." He viewed the self as having a functional role in the life of the individual.

Kohut developed a unique terminology to describe self psychology. He coined the term "selfobject" to describe a concept fundamental to his understanding of development and psychopathology. A selfobject is an intrapsychic structure that is based on interactions with significant others. In the infant's earliest experience with other people, the self and other are not perceived as separate beings, but are fused together in the infant's perception. Thus, selfobjects are internal mental representations of another person who is important in the infant's life; these representations are not yet differentiated from the idea of self; indeed, they might be seen as a combination of self plus other. As development proceeds, there is an increasing awareness of selfobjects as separate from the self. Selfobjects are crucial throughout life although they supply different needs at different phases. They are essential to maintaining self-esteem, regulating affect, and allowing the individual to pursue realistic and meaningful goals. "Selfobject milieu" and "selfobject experience" refer to aspects of the mental life of the individual that always goes on in a context of relationships.

The "grandiose self" and the "idealized parental imago" are terms used to describe immature states in which, in the first case, the idea of the self, and in the second, the idea of the other, are unrealistically inflated. Cohesiveness is a state of good functioning, in which the sense of self is secure. Fragmentation occurs when this state is opposed by threats to self-esteem or overwhelmingly painful affects. Narcissistic rage results as a defensive reaction to try to protect the self against these threats.

The following chapter is an exposition on the development of self in adolescence by a leading proponent of Heinz Kohut's self psychology theory.

LTF

REFERENCES

Greenberg, J. R., & Mitchell, S. A. (1983). Object relations in psychoanalytic theory. Cambridge, MA: Harvard University Press.

Introduction

There has been a long-standing psychoanalytic perspective on adolescent development, psychopathology, and treatment. The concepts associated with the psychology of the self represent recent modifications of this perspective. Many of the formulations of self psychology are similar to other psychodynamic formulations, particularly those of the object relations theorists. Yet, despite similarities, there are important differences (Bacal & Newman, 1990). This chapter does not explicate these distinctions but attempts to summarize the self psychological view of adolescence.

The *self* is a sense of one's inner homeostasis, one's capacity to self-regulate, the importance of fulfilling one's ambitions, the realization of one's talents and abilities, the satisfaction of one's ideals, and the importance of one's relationships with admired others. It includes the sustaining strength of experiences with others who are like oneself and recognizes the abiding, constant presence of an inner sense of initiative. It is not the same as identity. *Identity* describes an appreciation of one's social role, the sense of one's personality, experienced by the person and by others.

The self psychology literature does not provide an explicit explanation for the onset of adolescence. By not discussing how adolescence begins, Kohut and his followers seem to accept Sigmund Freud's (1905/1958) explanation, namely: that the instinctual transformations of puberty and the incest taboo bring on a displacement of libidinal investment from parents to peers. Most self psychologists believe that the drive theory of classical, or Freudian, psychoanalysis is not derived from empirical data or from the clinical experience but is borrowed from other sciences and is no longer a valid inference today (Basch, 1984). In contrast, they adhere to Heinz Kohut's (1959) definition of psychoanalysis as a process informed by introspection and empathy.

If, indeed, adolescence is engendered by the physiological changes of puberty, psychology can only describe those changes and try to understand the attendant transformations of the adolescent phase. As a discipline, psychology cannot explain the onset of this phase.

Developmental Themes

A self psychological perspective is a developmental approach and presents us with three themes, in part reflecting the historical development of Kohut's ideas (Ornstein, 1978, 1990). The themes are: the transformations of narcissism; the cohesion of the self; and the self-selfobject paradigm.

Throughout childhood, in the language of self psychology, the archaic constructs of narcissism, the "grandiose self" and the "idealized parental imago" undergo transformation, in the context of the selfobject experiences with parenting figures. Available, reliable, and consistent parental mirroring responses permit the developing child to modify his or her grandiosity in the direction of mature self-esteem and realistic ambition. Such transformations are set in train before adolescence, and the problems, arrests, and distortions of the preadolescent period influence the further modifications of adolescence. Similarly, the crucial idealization of parents has begun to be displaced and refined into goals, values, and attitudes of respect and admiration for others. In the context of an empathic sustaining selfobject milieu, the maturing self of the child, now becoming an adolescent, can tolerate the many inevitable experiences of selfobject failure. Moreover, provided there is psychological readiness, that self can begin performing certain selfobject functions to enhance its own growth. This shift to function-by-self is not a shift from external to internal, from the "outside" parent to the "inside" internal structure, because the selfobject parent is always experienced as "inside," as part of the self. Rather, the shift is from a selfobject experience to functions that have become part of one's own structure and psychological makeup. How and whether this has happened can be elucidated only by careful evaluation, but it is a crucial measure of preadolescent maturation.

Thus, the person moving into the adolescent period is not faced with the task of "separating" from the "infantile love objects." In fact, that "sep-

aration" process—or better said, transformation process (Marohn, 1987a,b)—has already been progressing in the form of "transmuting internalizations" plus a continuous move toward increased structuralization. Yet adolescence is a most important way station in this continuing process, highlighting as it does by the resurgence of primitive narcissism and associated problems.

FROM PRIMITIVE TO MATURE NARCISSISM

Adolescents are at once brash and grandiose, intimidated and self-depreciating. They are preoccupied with the beauty and ugliness of their bodies, both with their power and grace, and with their "wimpiness" and clumsiness. They aggrandize themselves and hate themselves. They desperately seek others to sustain and to reassure themselves, or they isolate themselves or change friends impetuously. They are fickle in their crushes, friendships, feelings about parents, and in wanting to be alone. They worship others as they once did Mom and Dad but may rapidly transform today's hero or heroine into tomorrow's dud. They no longer relish the music they did last year. Today's crush on the new girlfriend or boyfriend may fade overnight. And their parents worry about the older kids with whom they spend time. Before too long, their fickleness disappears, and they sustain relationships with others on a more intimate and consistent basis. When this happens, the important narcissistic transformations of adolescence have been accomplished. In the view of self psychology, these transformations are more crucial to understanding the developmental process of adolescence than are the changes in libidinal ties (Marohn, 1980).

Kohut (1966) has described other changes in the progress from primitive narcissism to mature narcissism that are important aspects of healthy adult functioning, such as creativity, empathy, wisdom, acceptance of transience, and humor. The clinician often encounters teenagers with unusual abilities in these areas, but how well or how poorly the adolescent patient is progressing usually can be recognized and assessed along these lines of personal growth. Often teenagers do not have an ability to laugh at themselves; they begin to display such a capacity only in late adolescence or young adulthood. Early on, however, they take themselves very seriously. They are filled with dreams and wishes of immortality but are often troubled by a dawning realization of life's impermanence. As they challenge and rework their parental identifications, they begin developing a philosophy of their own, an early step toward achieving adult wisdom. The adolescent's ability to empathize with another, adult or peer, is quite limited in early adolescence, since the youngster is preoccupied with his or her own needs and regulation. He or she lacks the ability to appreciate another's personal psychological life or to recognize the other's having a sense of initiative. Normal adolescent maturation involves an increasing ability to get in contact with the psychological life of another person, which ultimately makes intimacy possible (Erikson, 1950, 1959). Many adolescents find their ability to create coming into full flower in this epoch of life, while others only begin to taste their eventual abilities. As they come into their own, they feel more able to express their inner selves: in poetry, in fiction, in debate, in music, in painting and sculpting, in crafts, and in their dress.

COHESION

One's selfobject parents also assist oneself in achieving self-regulation and self-mastery, which in turn facilitate "cohesion." Cohesion is a state of relative inner homeostasis, always in the context of some inner experienced milieu of sustaining selfobjects. As one matures, cohesion depends less and less on one's parents' functions and more and more on one's own internal psychological structure. In childhood, the actions of one's selfobjects are explicit, obvious, and virtually omnipresent psychologically. As the child matures, the nature of the self-selfobject ties, as experienced psychologically, change. For example, relationships are experienced mainly in terms of physical contact during infancy but through verbal interactions later on. Although the adolescent's decreasing reliance on parental ministrations make it *seem* that "separation" has occurred, in reality, the self-selfobject (adolescent-parent) ties have changed rather than disappeared. Parents are still held as important introjects or parts of silently operating competent psychological structures.

Studies of well-functioning adolescents and youths consistently validate the importance of continuing psychological ties to parents. Adolescents rework these ties and transform them psychologically. They are terrified of primitive narcissistic attachments, and through to-and-fro attachment/ detachment behavior with peers and newly found love relationships, they gradually develop an internal ability to function without the physical presence of the parents, without conscious awareness of their importance, and with primary reliance on adolescents' own psychological skills. Adolescents achieve cohesion, and experience of inner homeostasis, as they modify the nature of their ties to the parents. As time goes on, there is an increasing turning to peers and others for the kind of selfobject sustenance adolescents need. Each individual develops a set of social skills that are used for this purpose. Thus, by later adolescence and young adulthood, a constellation of psychological skills will have been developed that will tend to be used consistently throughout life. The particular array of these skills characterize the person—in other words, form the basis of personality.

FRAGMENTATION

On the negative side, fragmentation represents a threat to such self-sustenance or to the selfobject bonds that sustain a sense of homeostasis. It may be experienced as a sense of "falling apart," or as a sense of inner emptiness, or even as some sort of painful disruption in smooth functioning. Fragmentation is best understood as a disruption of inner psychological homeostasis or as a loss of cohesion. It refers to an internal disarray and not necessarily to a psychotic disintegration. Such fragmentation experiences often are characterized as "adolescent turmoil"; they are part and parcel of the expectable life of the early and middle adolescent, and are seen in various degrees and modes in most adolescents. As psychological competence increases, these states become less frequent and intense but will recur whenever selfobjects fail or as one's ability to regulate the self and self-esteem are attenuated. Thus, most adults suffer minifragmentations or threats of fragmentations, as these experiences are bound to recur throughout life.

Adolescents, who are still learning to rely on their own psychological skills to get what they need from others, and at the same time are faced with coping with changing social demands and biological pressures, have a heightened vulnerability to fragmentation. Accordingly, disturbances in the narcissistic line of development and in maintaining cohesion of the self are inevitable consequences of adolescents' developmental vulnerability. The proper assessment of these disruptions and determination of whether they represent significant psychopathology or tolerable deviations or, indeed, expectable developmental crises has always been one of the most difficult tasks of the adolescent psychiatrist. A diagnostic perspective that focuses on the state of the *self* can be very helpful in distinguishing between normality and pathology.

SUSTAINING POWER OF SELFOBJECTS

The sense of self, of the adolescent and the adult, includes the inner experience of one's selfobjects. These may be primitive and urgent or transformed and silent. Adolescents undergo these transformations, and, as the selfobject ties become increasingly "silent," we know that inner psychological structures are being formed. The adolescents' relations with parents are no longer personalized and consciously felt, but they remain and sustain, partly through the psychological functions that derive from them and partly by the inner sense that they can still be evoked in time of distress. Even after parents die, the inner capacity to resonate intrapsychically with early and primitive self-selfobject experiences continues to bolster the person. For the self psychologist, adult autonomy is not a separateness but a competence, based partly on the abiding ability to recall early experiences with the selfobjects of childhood. And so, when the adolescent's teacher (or the adult's supervisor) nods in approval, the infant's experience of the attuned mother resonating with the baby's initial vocalizations is summoned and enriches the contemporary self experience. Self psychology insists on the value of a continuity with one's past, as opposed to detachment or disengagement from one's history.

Adolescent Vulnerability

Adolescents are almost inevitably subject to narcissistic injuries such as blows to self-esteem or disappointment in another valued person. How well teenagers have been able to sustain themselves with old and new selfobject experiences and with the reliability of their own psychological structures determines how painful and/or how disruptive these injuries, real or imagined, will be. *Rage* results when adolescents' grandiose need to be powerful or when their idealized other's power is thwarted. *Shame* is a parallel experience, when their or the other's exhibitionism is threatened. Both are complex affects, and often include strong somatic responses, such as skin flushing or blushing. In addition, some people with significant self and narcissistic pathology are overstimulated by positive mirroring or idealizing experiences. They cannot tolerate the intensity of their most primitive and deeply repressed wishes being mobilized; they must protect themselves from such inner traumata. And so they reject compliments, they thwart parental praise, they provoke disgust, they avoid intimacy, they treat the ones they love with disdain or indifference. Consequently, adolescent patients may avoid a deep therapeutic engagement, not simply because of the threat of libidinal regression (A. Freud, 1958) but because of the need to protect against being overstimulated by the positive aspects of the relationship with the psychotherapist (Marohn, 1974, 1980).

"ACTING OUT"

The self psychologist recognizes that vulnerable adolescents may be threatened with fragmentation of the self or actually may disintegrate by being injured, or failed, or by being responded to positively, or gratified. These responses are usually precipitated by some real event or interaction, but always carry with them significant transference meaning and definition. Yet the more primitively organized adolescents are, the less "meaning" or symbolism can be found in their behavior. A good deal of adolescent "acting-out" behavior, "conduct disorder," and "delinquency" results from serious deficits in tension regulation or impulse control. Knowing the particular "meaning" of the behavior is less helpful in assessing the adolescent's pathology than is understanding that it stems from the desperate urgency of that adolescent self to reorganize or reconstitute itself. "Acting out" suggests that something "inside" cannot be contained and is expressed "outside" in the form of impulsive behavior. Yet primitively organized or disorganized adolescents do not experience a psychological "inside" and "outside." Instead, they are at one with their environment and make no such psychological distinction (Marohn, 1993). When asked why they "did" something, they reply that they "felt like it." Then clinicians search for the underlying meanings of the behavior and get nowhere. These adolescents are right—their feelings are their thoughts are their behavior. They *do* because they *feel*. Only later, after we as clinicians attempt to help them develop a semblance of inner psychological structure, can we and these adolescents begin to discover wishes and fantasies that their conduct represents.

Treatment Implications

The relationship between adolescent patients and their therapist is a selfobject experience. In itself, without interpretation, it is sustaining, because it provides mirroring and/or idealizing opportunities for the adolescents. Conversely, it is also taxing and potentially threatening, if the mirroring or idealizing aspects are too stimulating and disruptive. The skillful adolescent therapist titrates these issues, so as not to create a situation against which the adolescents must defend and resist. The concept of the therapist as a "twin" or "twinship selfobject" is useful here. This idea refers to an alterego experience of transference in which the sustaining aspects of the experience derive from a sense of the essential similarity to another person. The similarity may be experienced in terms of needs, goals, behavior, or affects. The adolescent therapist recognizes that being a twin and regulating the degree of intense narcissistic transference is often necessary to keep patients in psychotherapy. This is why the relationship with the therapist often takes on more aspects of a "real" relationship in adolescent psychotherapy than it does in adult psychotherapy. Asking questions about school, peers, family, and other experiences, responding directly to questions, and chatting about current events or sports may all help to calm adolescent patients who are in danger of experiencing fragmentation. The self psychologist does not experience "resistance" as an evil to be avoided or elimi-

nated, but recognizes that it is a necessary psychological coping mechanism patients need. Likewise, the inevitable disruptions in the relationship that occur as time goes on serve to increase self-understanding as the breach is understood and repaired.

NEGATIVISM IN PSYCHOTHERAPY

Often, when adolescents seek affirmation and self-enhancement, they present themselves in a disparaging and hostile manner. They may be defending against the emergence of more positive wishes, or they may have already detected a flaw in the therapist or been injured by something, or they may be reexperiencing both past wishes and injuries in the new treatment relationship. Such negativism attests to the presence of a treatment alliance and a transference (Marohn, 1981) and not to an adolescent's untreatability. Such a "negative transference" is not a sign that there can be no treatment, nor that the treatment is doomed, but that the idealizing transference manifestations are being presented in a way most therapists do not like. Therapists prefer agreeable, pleasant patients! The adolescent psychotherapist must be prepared to encounter and help disparaging, hostile, negativistic, and unfriendly patients. Other therapists cannot tolerate an adolescent's demands for special attention, attunement, agreement, and affirmation—or his or her idealization or reverence of the therapist, when such occur. Many therapists are intolerant of such narcissistic enhancement and defend against it; they have been trained to search for the animosity and hatred allegedly "beneath" it, covered over by reaction formation. Self psychology recognizes that rage and hostility do indeed occur in treatment, and they certainly arise in the course of treating adolescents. But they do not simply emerge as defenses are stripped away. Rather, they always result from some injury or disruption in the transference. Cure is enhanced when the patient and therapist together search for the hurt, try to understand it, and achieve a new level of structuralization in the process.

INPATIENT TREATMENT

A discussion of why and when to hospitalize or to refer to residential treatment is not the central task of this chapter, but some thoughts about this subject are in order. Being in psychotherapy is always stressful to the adolescent patient—taxing because of the problems encountered in establishing any bond, taxing because of the specific transferences and deficits that are activated in treatment. If the adolescent's personality structure is relatively sound, he or she can tolerate and master such stresses. Of course, the relationship with the therapist is sustaining, as well, as are relationships with family and peers. But if the adolescent is too damaged, or if there are few or no nourishing relationships in his or her psychological world, inpatient treatment should be considered (Easson, 1969). In the treatment facility, the staff perform important sustaining and modulating selfobject functions—to support the adolescent in psychotherapy, to set limits on behavior, to prepare the patient for the introspection so necessary to a successful psychotherapeutic structuralization. How well or how poorly the adolescent can use staff for selfobject experiences depends, of course, on the youngster's previous selfobject ties and, necessarily, on the staff's empathic capacities. Staff confront the same kinds of countertransference problems as does the psychotherapist; supervision, which facilitates developing introspection and an empathic capacity, is crucial to successful hospital or residential work with teenagers.

CASE EXAMPLES

Nancy: Nancy is a 13-year-old who was hospitalized 2 years and who, prior to admission, had had multiple group placements and psychiatric hospitalizations. She was violent at home, at school, and at other treatment facilities, stole frequently, was often truant from school, and ran away. After admission, she would assault staff without any apparent precipitant, and it was only after several months that the sources of her rage became clear. For a while, there was considerable pressure to think of her as having some kind of biological or hormonal imbalance, because it seemed that her disruptive and assaultive behavior was cyclical and not related to any precipitant. However, the unit chief insisted that the staff hold to its philosophy that all behavior has meaning and can be understood psychologically, and that if the structure of the unit and of the daily program were maintained, the meaning of Nancy's behavior would presently emerge. Eventually, Nancy's rage was brought into the psychotherapy rather than displaced onto others, and she raged at her therapist during their

sessions. She told her therapist that she wanted to strangle her. She expected the therapist would use her for narcissistic gain, so that when the therapist recognized an accomplishment of Nancy's or seemed to be pleased that she was making progress in psychotherapy, Nancy became enraged and felt that her gains had now been turned to "shit." The therapist interpreted the rage as a feeling that the therapist would not permit Nancy to grow up and that she needed to kill the therapist in order to mature. Nancy regained her composure and agreed that there was no way to have a relationship continue once one begins to grow, that people simply will not let one do that.

This dynamic—that adolescents respond with rage or some sort of disruptive behavior when they feel narcissistically exploited—cannot be uncovered by direct observation. We need to have the benefit of the transference experience, often in a safe and controlled environment, to uncover such fantasies. Many of us are accustomed to watching for the narcissistic transference, but we may forget that someone who experiences relationships in a narcissistic mode expects the psychotherapist to be organized in a similar manner. Before she could speak with either the ward staff or with her psychotherapist about her assaults, Nancy needed to move psychologically from a more primitive stage of organization to a more highly developed, structuralized level, at which she could describe and explain the experiences that stimulated her. Her early affective experiences were ill defined, and all she felt before, during, and after a physical assault was numbness, like the somatic reactions of a primitively organized psyche. It was only later that she could rage at and threaten to kill her therapist. Albeit stimulated by primitive narcissistic transference issues, her early violent and rageful behavior was a manifestation of disruption and fragmentation, with no associated mental content. As her therapy progressed and facilitated psychic structuralization, her violent behavior began to look more and more like narcissistic rage driven by specific psychodynamics.

Other adolescents are troubled by parental or therapist attunement for other reasons. They cannot seek mirroring; they seek to disgust the parent. They can no longer idealize; they depreciate.

Karl: Karl was an arrogant and haughty 16-year-old. He seemed to be bright but was failing in school, much to the chagrin of his academically oriented and financially successful parents. Over the years there had been several failed attempts to treat his depressions and behavioral problems. During a diagnostic interview, Karl and his parents talked about previous attempts to help him with his problems; he turned to the psychiatrist and spoke with sarcasm about the "fool" who had treated him before and how playing with puppets wasted his parents' time and money. The therapist was taken aback by his sudden assault, thought for a moment, and then suggested that he must have been terribly disappointed by someone he had admired and that he was angry and disillusioned with whomever that was. Karl was silent for a moment and then spoke about other things. The next day his mother called to say that Karl had talked at length that night about his disappointment with his father. She suggested he could discuss that in another session, and he agreed to another appointment.

At the next session, Karl spoke about how often his father was unavailable to him and how difficult it was for him to reach out to his father, but he was adamant that he did not need therapy. He said that if his parents insisted that he come in "6 times a week," he would have to do so or lose valuable privileges. In effect, Karl was saying that he needed to be seen frequently, but that he would need to save face in the process.

A fledgling therapeutic alliance was established by the therapist's acknowledging the patient's disillusionment with an idealized figure. This emerged when the psychiatrist realized that Karl's verbal assault and characterization of therapists as fools who play with puppets must represent a transference. By countering the patient's assault with an equally firm interpretive stance, the therapist engaged Karl in a therapeutic alliance and a further deepening of the transference relationship. The treatment relationship was threatened later when the psychiatrist asked Karl to add his signature to his father's on a release-of-information form, so that information could be sent to his school to facilitate his placement in a special education program. Although Karl had agreed that he needed to enroll in the program, he gleefully refused to sign the release. Initially, this seemed a resistance, the same kind of obstructive behavior others had complained about, but after several sessions, the idealizing transference surfaced. Karl had become enraged with what he perceived as the therapist's impotence in not being able to send a report without his approval. He experienced a sudden and profound disillusionment and deide-

alization that enraged and paralyzed him and disrupted the treatment alliance.

Conclusion

This chapter attempts to delineate the psychoanalytic psychology of the self as it applies to adolescent development, psychopathology, and treatment. This perspective can be separated thematically into topics such as the transformations of narcissism, the cohesion of the self, and the self-selfobject paradigm. Prior to adolescence, the transformation of the archaic narcissistic structures has already been progressing via transmuting internalizations and the continuous move toward increased structuralization. Yet adolescence is a most important way station in this continuing process, amply highlighted by the resurgence of primitive narcissism and its associated problems. Adolescence is a time of developmental vulnerability, and, consequently, disturbances in the narcissistic line of development and in maintaining cohesion of the self are inevitable.

How to assess properly these disruptions and to determine whether they represent significant psychopathology, tolerable deviations, or expectable crises is the task of the adolescent psychiatrist. Self psychology provides a diagnostic perspective that focuses on how well transformations are proceeding. As selfobject ties become increasingly "silent," we know that inner psychological structures are being formed. The vulnerable adolescent may be threatened with self fragmentation and disintegration by either narcissistic injury or gratification. A self psychological perspective emphasizes the importance of evaluating and treating serious deficits in tension regulation and impulse control. Often these are much more important than uncovering the psychodynamics of a particular behavior.

As selfobject transferences unfold in the treatment relationship, various challenges to the therapeutic alliance and subtle as well as obvious countertransference problems may arise. Self psychology can inform the adolescent psychiatrist's work, in both inpatient and office settings, by elucidating these inevitable problems in psychotherapy.

REFERENCES

Bacal, H. A., & Newman, K. A. (1990). *Theories of object relations: Bridges to self psychology.* New York: Columbia University Press.

Basch, M. F. (1984). The selfobject theory of motivation and the history of psychoanalysis. In P. Stepansky & A. Goldberg (Eds.), *Kohut's Legacy* (pp. 3–17). Hillsdale, NJ: Analytic Press.

Easson, W. M. (1969). *The severely disturbed adolescent.* New York: International Universities Press.

Erikson, E. H. (1950). *Childhood and society.* New York: W. W. Norton.

Erikson, E. H. (1959). *Identity and the life cycle.* New York: International Universities Press.

Freud, A. (1958). Adolescence. *Psychoanalytic Study of the Child, 13,* 255–278.

Freud, S. (1958). The transformations of puberty, in *Three Essays on the Theory of Sexuality,* in J. Strachey (Ed.), *Standard edition of the complete psychological works of Sigmund Freud* (Vol. 7, pp. 132–143). London: Hogarth Press. (originally published 1905.)

Kohut, H. (1959). Introspection, empathy and psychoanalysis: An examination of the relationship between mode of observation and theory. *Journal of the American Psychoanalytic Association, 7,* 449–483.

Kohut, H. (1966). Forms and transformations of narcissism. *Journal of the American Psychoanalytic Association, 14,* 243–272.

Marohn, R. C. (1974). Trauma and the delinquent. *Adolescent Psychiatry, 3,* 354–361.

Marohn, R. C. (1980). Adolescent rebellion and the task of separation. *Adolescent Psychiatry, 8,* 173–183.

Marohn, R. C. (1981). The negative transference in the treatment of juvenile delinquents. *Annual Psychoanalysis, 9,* 21–42.

Marohn, R. C. (1987a, May 9). *A re-examination of Peter Blos' concept of prolonged adolescence.* Paper presented at the annual meeting of the American Society for Adolescent Psychiatry, Chicago, IL.

Marohn, R. C. (1987b, November). *The renaissance of adolescence: reassessment of separation-individuation theory.* Paper presented to the Dept. of Psychiatry Grand Rounds, University of New Mexico School of Medicine, Albuquerque, and as the Joel Handler Memorial Lecture, Chicago Society for Adolescent Psychiatry.

Marohn, R. C. (1993). Rage without content. In A. Goldberg (Ed.), *Progress in self psychology* (Vol. 9, pp. 129–141). Hillsdale, NJ: Analytic Press.

Ornstein, P. H. (1978). Introduction: The evolution of Heinz Kohut's psychoanalytic psychology of the self. In P. Ornstein (Ed.), *The search for the self, Selected writings of Heinz Kohut: 1950–1978* (Vol. 1, pp. 1–106). New York: International Universities Press.

Ornstein, P. H. (1990). Introduction: The unfolding and completion of Heinz Kohut's paradigm of psychoanalysis. In P. Ornstein (Ed.), *The search for the self, selected writings of Heinz Kohut: 1978–1981* (Vol. 3, pp. 1–82). New York: International Universities Press.

16 / Identity Consolidation in Adolescence

Theodore Shapiro and Alexander Kalogerakis

Definition of Identity

"Identity" is a term that has been linked with the phase of life called adolescence. Along with the biological changes of puberty, a wide array of psychosocial events unfold during this second decade of life, and many of these have been subsumed under the umbrella of identity formation. Most students of adolescence agree that one of the tasks of adolescence is consolidation of identity. As with biological maturation, a developmental process is at work.

Erik Erikson, whose name is most closely associated with the term "identity" as a psychological construct, cited two fathers of modern psychology to whom he pays homage in defining the concept. William James wrote of a mental or moral attitude in which a person feels most deeply alive and that this is the real me. Erikson describes this as a subjective sense of an "invigorating sameness and continuity (1968, p. 19). Freud is also noted to have commented on an ethnic sense of inner identity, and this illustrates, for Erikson, the other important contributor to identity: culture (Erikson, 1968).

Others have extended and refined Erikson's conceptions. Kamptner (1988) describes three dimensions of identity: ego identity, self-identity, and the achievement of a sense of meaning or purpose in life. Ego identity includes the development of a worldview, with occupational goals, religious values, and political beliefs. Self-identity is an individual's perception of self, including continuity over time. The third dimension is a personal, philosophical set of aims that, when achieved, adds to the cohesiveness and stability of the individual over time.

Blos (1962) added to these ideas in several ways. Following Erikson, he wrote about the emergence of a stable sense of self as a "sense of identity." At another point, identity formation is considered as roughly synonymous with character formation and the achievement of "irreversible fixity in the ego's relations to the outer world, to the id and the superego" (p. 175).

"Group identity" is another permutation to be considered. In adolescence, groups play an important role in forming individual identity. Subcultural affiliations of adolescents may provide for intense peer interactions and also serve as yardsticks by which teenagers can measure themselves. Group identity may refer to as commonplace a situation as a teenager immersed in adoring a particular rock band (e.g., "Deadheads") or to chilling historical groups such as the Hitler Youth or China's Youth Pioneers (Esman, 1990). In this aspect of identity, the ambient culture plays a major role in defining aims and ideals.

Thus, under the umbrella of "identity," there is an assortment of areas to study: psychoanalytic theories of intrapsychic development, especially pertaining to ego maturation and character; psychosocial theories, which envision active interplay and exchange between the individual and his social milieu; cultural notions, which not only address individual development but also examine the delineation of adolescence as a stage of the life cycle; and family viewpoints, which focus on this particularly potent social institution as a determinant of individual development.

Dynamics of Identity Formation

Anna Freud (1958) summarized psychoanalytic thinking about adolescent development, expanding on previous work. Adolescence is viewed as a time of emotional turbulence, the latter a necessary step toward formation of adult personality. The reason for this "adolescent upset" is the postulated quantitative increase in drive activity and changes in drive quality associated with the biological advent of puberty.

In this conception, the battle between ego and id that ended temporarily in a truce in early latency is reactivated at puberty. The struggle, however, is not merely a replay of the preoedipal and oedipal phase; there are new circumstances. The internal danger is not only due to id impulses but also to the actual existence of the love objects—parents. The libidinal interest in them is reawakened with the additional danger of genital urges that can now be realized. This may lead to a defense Katan (1951) called removal—attempts to change the cast of objects to whom the drives are directed and thus eliminate the threat of incest by "removal" to age-appropriate crushes and romances.

Anna Freud also described other defensive maneuvers used against object ties and impulses. Libido may be displaced from parents to other adults who serve as parent substitutes, to gangs, or to various types of leaders who may represent ideals attractive to youth. Another typical mechanism is reversal of affect. Here, emotions are turned into their opposites. Behaviorally, this may be observed in the uncooperative, hostile adolescent or the adolescent unwilling to accept affection from parents. Pathological variants such as the paranoid adolescent also may develop. Defense by withdrawal of libido to the self may be inferred when grandiosity is seen, or in hypochondriacal states where the adolescent redirects object libido to his or her own body. Regarding the impulses themselves, adolescents may develop the defense of "asceticism"—fighting off all impulses, all pleasures. In this situation, basic bodily needs may be compromised.

These and other ego defenses may be called to action in this prolonged struggle. Anna Freud states that adolescent disharmony—intrapsychic as well as behavioral—is a normal condition; in fact, where it does not appear, clinicians should be suspicious. The payoff, however, is passage to a more stable, mature adaptation as an adult. This is an identity stabilization.

Blos (1962, 1967) shares Anna Freud's view of adolescence as a turbulent period leading to a consolidation of character at its terminus. He describes specific tasks and features of subphases: preadolescence, early adolescence, adolescence proper, and late and postadolescence (1962). He also introduces a view of the entire period of adolescence as a second individuation process (1967). The name of this construct provides a deliberate reference to Mahler's stages of early development. Blos argues that both infancy and adolescence comprise periods where personality organization is vulnerable and psychic structure is altered. What in early childhood is described as "psychological hatching"—developing early autonomy as a toddler—is paralleled in adolescence by a weakening of infantile object ties and the eventual establishment of stable self and object representations.

Blos (1967) defines the second individuation as the process and achievement of the psychological structural changes that allow for giving up infantile objects. Along with this libidinal decathexis, and as a result of it, new attachments to extrafamilial objects can be made. However, there are some difficulties intrinsic to this process. The ego itself is relatively weakened vis-à-vis the increase of drives associated with puberty, and also by the disengagement from parental support. Thus, in this conceptualization, the very task that the developing ego must achieve—libidinal shifting away from infantile object ties—simultaneously weakens the agency entrusted to carry this out.

The danger to ego integrity in adolescence is described as twofold: first, surging drives, and second, the pull of regression. Blos identifies adolescence as the only phase in the life cycle in which ego and id regression may be considered normal: that is, regression in the service of development. A consequence of this regression is the emotional volatility of the age. Examples of regression in adolescence include somatization of conflicts, reexperiencing of traumatic states, idealization of famous people (i.e., from sports, music, movies), and also near-merger states such as intense involvement with philosophical or religious movements.

As loosening of infantile object ties proceeds, ego-restitutive efforts may take the high ground. These efforts are reflected in behaviors such as the need for intense individual experiences, short-lived emotional attachments, and group affiliations. At this point, a stable sense of identity is far from achieved; rather, the adolescent wonders "Who am I?"

Also contributing to this unsettled state of affairs is what Blos describes as the revival of infantile object relations characterized by ambivalence. Infantile rage and sadism typical of ambivalent objects ties may surface as aggressive actions, negativism, or indifference. Another task of adolescence, then, is the development of postambivalent, integrated object relations.

Like Anna Freud, Blos sees turbulence, or in his term regressive phenomena, as normal, and their lack as pathological. Specifically, he warns of a "resistance against regression" that can be as pathological as extremes of regression itself. This type of resistance may be observed in the adolescent who focuses forcefully on the outside world, distancing him- or herself vigorously from parents. The problem with this strategy is that it precludes or limits the reworking of early libidinal ties necessary for what Blos views as normal adolescent development. However, the data to support these formulations rest on clinical experience and not on sample populations of adolescents in the community.

Psychosocial View of Adolescence

While Blos refined classical psychoanalytic concepts of adolescence, Erikson (1950, 1968) created a new developmental schema that shifted the emphasis from a purely intrapsychic description to ego factors and a psychosocial view of this stage of life. For Erikson, the milieu of the individual-family and culture exert a profoundly important influence on development. Erikson's well-known "ages of man" put forth the significant psychosocial tasks of different ages in the life cycle. Identity plays a central role in the epigenetic unfolding, and the task of adolescence is identity vs. *identity confusion* (sometimes also referred to as *role diffusion*).

In this stage, adolescents must reformulate the achievements of earlier development. For Erikson, goals include an ego integration that is "more than the sum of the childhood identifications" (1950, p. 228). The ego must integrate these earlier identifications with new libidinal forces, with developing skills, and with available social roles. Adolescents regularly test a subjective sense of identity by comparing their view of self with how others view them. Along these lines, adolescent love can be conceived of as an attempt to clarify one's own identity by projecting aspects of it onto others and noting the reflections thus derived.

Ideally, the development of identity leads to the possibility of mature love, "intimacy" in Erikson's young-adult stage, and also a vocational role that is consonant with one's internal sense of self and with the social milieu.

The earlier stages each contribute to the form the identity struggle will take. The sense of trust developed as an infant allows for the development of faith—in people, ideas—which is a goal of maturation. Issues of autonomy vs. shame and doubt are replayed in adolescence as youths struggle to make choices among available options, choices that will allow them to avoid shame, particularly vis-à-vis peers. Successful school-age children, in the stage of industry vs. inferiority, bequeath to adolescents a sense of competence, the desire to work, and the ability to value their own work.

Erikson (1968) describes the struggle of adolescence as an "identity crisis." He uses "crisis" in the sense of a turning point or significant moment in development. He regards this crisis as normative, not pathological. However, the *manifestations* of the crisis may vary from the normal to the pathological. Erikson introduces another term, "psychosocial moratorium," which is defined as a kind of second latency: a period of delay when role experimentation is conducted, with a goal of finding a niche in society as adulthood begins. He describes how various cultures have induced such a period of apprenticeship or exploration in their structure.

The issues of ideology and political and philosophical awareness are brought to the fore in Erikson's view of adolescence. The tendency of adolescents to become passionate partisans for various causes is well known. Erikson views this as a psychological necessity of the identity crisis. In fact, he states that ideology is the "guardian of identity" (1968, p. 133). Similarly, "fidelity" is seen as the central quality that youths need to develop and employ.

Individual and Society

Erikson's conceptions thus broadened the scope and shifted the emphasis of the then-popular ego psychology. He asserts that the student of adolescence needs more than a rough cultural awareness—a background upon which to examine intrapsychic forces—but rather a special interest in the relationship between the individual and the society.

The identity concept of adolescence has spawned new and broadly conceived research in the decades since Erikson made his formulations. Four conditions of adolescent identity development or status have been defined: identity achievement, foreclosure, identity diffusion, and moratorium (Marcia, 1980). *Identity achievements* are made by people who have had a crisis or decision-making period and then have established relatively firm commitments. *Foreclosures* are made by people who also are committed to goals, occupation, and values, but these have been chosen for the individual by parents or authority figures. These individuals have not undergone a decision-making phase on their own. *Identity diffusions* are represented in those people who do not have clear occupational or ideological commitments and are not actively trying to form them. *Moratoriums* are suffered by those people who are currently in an identity crisis, trying to arrive at stable choices. Each of these four conditions also can be described by the presence or absence of "crisis" and "commitment," as implied by the preceding definitions. Adolescents and young adults may be categorized within one of the four types at a given time by administration of pen-and-paper test instruments as well as by semistructured interviews (Waterman, 1982). Researchers (reviewed by Marcia, 1980) have tried to relate these identity constructs to other variables, such as moral development, cognitive development, interpersonal relations, college performance and parenting styles. Also, an effort was made to link degree of identity success with success in Erikson's next psychosocial task, intimacy. In most of the areas cited, adolescents who test as "high identity" statuses—identity achievements and moratoriums—tend to do best on other parameters. Although most of these studies are cross-sectional, the few longitudinal designs that have been carried out indicate some stability of identity status over time, especially with low-identity (foreclosure or identity diffusion) statuses. As expected from theoretical considerations, the moratorium status is least stable (Waterman, 1982).

Kamptner (1988), also using cross-sectioned data, developed causal models to relate family and social relations to identity formation. Familial security was found to enhance identity development and adolescents' social involvements. More specifically, parental autonomy predicted familial security, which in turn enhanced adolescents' social confidence and social relatedness. These latter two qualities were found to facilitate identity development. The likely mechanism is that these social skills promote self-knowledge, self-worth, and safe exploration of identity options. Kamptner found some male-female differences, with most of the correlations showing greater strength in males. The question of how valid standard identity measures and theory are for females is controversial (Marcia, 1980; Waterman, 1982).

New Schemes for Identity

Hauser and colleagues (1991) have conducted longitudinal studies on ego development in adolescence, with a special emphasis on family interactions. Hauser uses a model of ego development that focuses on impulse control and moral style, interpersonal style, conscious preoccupations, and cognitive style. The stages run from preconformist through conformist and postconformist types, with substages. For example, a typical conformist would follow external rules; be helpful and superficially nice; be concerned with appearances and acceptability; have conceptual simplicity; and use stereotypes and clichés. A person in the postconformist, autonomous substage would have self-evaluated moral standards and acceptance of inner conflict; would cherish interpersonal relations and respect autonomy; would be concerned with self-fulfillment; see him- or herself in a social context; communicate feelings vividly; and cognitively, would be able to see complex patterns, tolerate ambiguity, and have a broad scope on life issues. These stages are not closely linked to chronological age, although they are viewed as an hierarchical sequence. In empirical tests of this model, most people reach the conformist stage in childhood or adolescence; but many never reach postconformist stages.

Using these stages of ego development, Hauser has identified six paths of ego development in adolescence. These are:

1. Profound arrest. In this path, the adolescent remains steadily in preconformist stages.
2. Steady conformist.
3. Progressive, where the adolescent is moving up the hierarchy.
4. Accelerated. Here the postconformist stage has been reached early and maintained.
5. Moratorium. This path describes the teenager who shows significant up-and-down movement through the hierarchy and corresponds to Erikson's notion of moratorium as a time of experimentation and trying on of roles.
6. Regressive. This path describes a steady move toward lower stages of the hierarchy.

Adolescents and their families were observed, interviewed, and measured by pen-and-paper instruments over a 3-year span. Different patterns of family interactions were observed in each of the 6 paths described. In the profoundly arrested category, parents and teenagers had combative, authoritarian exchanges that were rigid and repetitive. Family members frequently tuned out on one another, and violence was either present or just below the surface. Steady conformist's families were less tumultuous but also showed rigidity that tended to maintain the status quo. Deviation from family values and attempts to explore, differentiate, and change were discouraged. The progressive and accelerated teenagers' families showed better listening skills and tolerance of change and ambiguity. The parents in these families were adept at providing emotional support and the appropriate use of self-disclosure. The authors also emphasize that tolerance of unpleasant emotions is typical of advanced-path families as is the ability of all members to "hang in" during and beyond highly conflictual moments.

The identification of different paths of ego development related to family styles raises a question that was alluded to earlier: whether adolescence is indeed a time of turbulence. Anna Freud, Blos, Erikson, and others have described adolescent turmoil as a normal and necessary state. Offer and colleagues (1975, 1990) have collected longitudinal data on normal adolescents for 3 decades, and their findings question the existence of "normal" adolescent turmoil. Offer and Offer (1975), study-

ing middle-class male teenagers from a midwestern high school for over 10 years, delineated three different adolescent growth patterns: continuous growth, surgent growth, and tumultuous growth. Subjects in each category differed in terms of degree of happiness or psychological pain, extent of trauma in their lives, effectiveness in communication with parents, superego functioning, and other parameters. However, all groups showed roughly equivalent adjustment and overall functioning. The latest report by Offer et al. (1990) includes female teenagers and non-American samples. The authors' conclusions from these studies carried out over many years is that emotional turmoil is not a necessary part of growing up; they provide a concept of adolescence that does not include the necessity for role diffusion, rebellion, and chaotic behavior.

However, the psychoanalytic theoretical views and the empirical data from normal adolescents may not stand in such sharp contrast as it would at first seem. For instance, Erikson (1968) clearly ascribed a "normative" aspect to his "identity crisis" and stated that he did not use "crisis" in a typical behavioral sense. Thus, the "crisis" or turmoil may be more valid when it is considered as an intrapsychic phenomenon that can have a variety of behavioral manifestations. This perspective also acknowledges the different sources of data: material from analytic or other dynamic individual therapy, and questionnaires, structural interviews, and psychological testing. Such disparate sources of data predictably give rise to differences in theory-building.

A final question that should be raised in this exploration of psychological growth in adolescence is that of the impact of culture. Though Erikson placed important emphasis on ethnic background, particularly with his study of specific variant cultures (e.g., Sioux and Yurok Native Americans), a broader question is to consider whether the whole concept of adolescence is culture-bound. Esman (1990), reviewing this issue, reports that social scientists in general concur that adolescence is a product of industrialized societies. Achievement of adulthood varies dramatically in many cultures: initiation rites, progression through stages of changing sexual practice, death of the father—these and other events mark adulthood in disparate societies. Many cultures also have placed significantly different demands on their young men and women seeking adult status.

With these considerations in mind, some qualified conclusions may be drawn. In Western industrialized society, adolescence is a time of growth and change, sometimes marked by emotional turmoil, as youths strive to emerge into adulthood with some sense of self and of a place in the world.

Different models have been developed to explain and categorize these transformations, and place adolescents' growth in a family and cultural context. The multiple available theoretical constructs in this field, in fact, are testimony to the complexity and fascination of the adolescent years. The idea of identity consolidation has been most propitious in producing new knowledge and research.

REFERENCES

Blos, P. (1962). *On adolescence.* New York: Free Press.

Blos, P. (1967). The second individuation process of adolescence. *Psychoanalytic Study of the Child, 22,* 162–186.

Erikson, E. (1950). *Childhood and society.* New York: W. W. Norton.

Erikson, E. (1968). *Identity, youth and crisis.* New York: W. W. Norton.

Esman, A. (1990). *Adolescence and culture.* New York: Columbia University Press.

Freud, A. (1958). Adolescence. *Psychoanalytic Study of the Child, 13,* 279–295.

Hauser, S., Powers, S., & Noam, G. (1991). *Adolescents and their Families: Paths of ego development.* New York: Free Press.

Kamptner, N. L. (1988). Identity development in late adolescence: causal modeling of social and familial influences. *Journal of Youth and Adolescence, 17*(6), 493–512.

Katan, A. (1951). The role of displacement in agorophobia. *International Journal of Psycho-Analysis, 32.*

Marcia, J. (1980). Identity in adolescence. In J. Adelson (Ed.), *Handbook of adolescent psychology* (pp. 159–187). New York: John Wiley & Sons.

Offer, D., & Offer, J. (1975). Three developmental routes through normal male adolescence. In S. C. Feinstein & P. Giovacchini (Eds.), Adolescent psychiatry (Vol. 4, pp. 121–141). New York: Jason Aronson.

Offer, D., Ostrov, E., Howard, K., & Attinson, R. (1990). Normality and adolescence. *Psychiatric Clinics of North America, 13*(3), 377–388.

Waterman, A. (1982). Identity development from adolescence to adulthood: An extension of theory and a review of research. *Developmental Psychology, 18*(3), 341–358.

17 / Consolidation of Gender Identity

Max Sugar

In recent years there have been great advances in genetics and neuroscience, along with the dramatic stimulus of transsexual surgery and the increased awareness of gender disorders in childhood. These have joined to enlarge our understanding of transsexuals and other gender identity disorders as well as of normative gender identity. This chapter presents our understanding of normative gender identity development from infancy on through adolescence.

Gender identity problems were noted by Frankel (1853), Westphal (1870), Krafft-Ebing (1894), Hirschfeld (1936), and Ellis (1936). Since then a large literature has emerged on the development of gender identity and its disorders; works include those by Galenson (1980); Galenson and Roiphe (1974, 1976); Green (1974, 1985, 1987); Meyer (1980, 1982); Meyer and Reter (1979); Money (1980, 1988); Richards (1992); Roiphe (1991); Roiphe and Galenson (1972, 1973a, 1973b, 1981); Stoller (1968, 1975); Tyson (1982, 1994); and Westhead, Olson, and Meyer (1990).

Definition of Terms

Core gender identity has been defined by Stoller (1968) as the inner conviction that one is male or female. Green (1974) considers gender identity as one of three parts of sexual identity, the others being sex preference and the adoption of masculine or feminine sex roles. Money (1980) defined gender identity/role as part of the same concept. Meyer (1980) separated the terms "gender identity" and "sexual identity"; the former refers to the sense of maleness or femaleness while the latter is a pattern of feelings and behaviors, which in any individual may be either masculine or feminine and which evolves throughout life. The term "gender role identity" also has been used to describe gender role, and it refers to the multidimen-sional aspects of personal attitudes and gender-related behaviors (Bem, 1974; Huston, 1985).

In sum, gender identity refers to a subjective awareness of maleness or femaleness, which is partly conscious and partly unconscious, and which gives rise to a conviction of being one or the other. Gender role or gender behavior refers to the outwardly expressed manifestations of gender identity and may or may not be in conformity with anatomy. Normatively, gender identity, sexual identity, and biological anatomical identity all confirm and converge on one another.

Development of Gender Identity

To the casual observer, the development of gender identity appears to be an effortless and uncomplicated process, as if it were an innate given. Gender disturbance correspondingly appears as if it were a deviant biological event. An appreciation of the normative process is necessary in order to understand the vicissitudes of development and the kinds of pathology that may occur. For example, a clinician's awareness of the nature of the early genital and phallic oedipal phases may help him or her to avoid conclusions about nonexisting sexual abuse.

Roiphe and Galenson (1981) and Tyson (1994) consider that the term "bisexuality" as it applies to the development of gender identity refers to the internalized images derived from maternal and paternal—female and male—sources, by means of incorporation, imitation, and identification. Ordinarily, core gender identity is in place by about 30 months of age. Subsequently, an expanded sense of belonging to one sex or the other develops as youngsters imitate and identify with aspects of both mother and father to varying degrees as well as with same- and opposite-sex siblings (Tyson, 1994).

155

Contributions from Infancy

Gender development is a gradual process that evolves over many years. The development of core gender identity begins with the many genetic and chromosomal determinants that come with conception, but it is profoundly affected by sex assignment at birth (Kleeman, 1975)—by the parents' joyous comments "It's a boy" or "It's a girl!" It is then elaborated by the interplay of a host of constitutional, psychological, and environmental factors in complex dynamic flux (Tyson, 1982).

Jones (1927) and Klein (1948) speculated that in girls, genital sensations were present during their early years. In the course of direct observations of infants, Roiphe (1968) and Roiphe and Galenson (1973a) found that sporadic self-stimulation occurs in boys between 7 and 10 months of age and can be observed in girls a few months later. Although this activity increases in frequency until the middle of the second year, it is not continuous, and in boys it is more frequent, focused, and seems to show more intentionality; in girls it is often absent. Roiphe and Galenson (1973b) termed this behavior early genital exploration.

The third stage of the sensorimotor period, from age 4 to 8 months, involves beginning intentionality; the fourth stage of genuine intentionality occurs at 8 to 12 months (Piaget, 1952). These developments seem to be necessary foundations for the early sexual exploration phase at 7 to 10 months and the early genital phase at 15 to 19 months.

Roiphe and Galenson (1981) suggest that the ordinary ministrations by parents as they care for infants provide an anlage of genital stimulation that aids in early genital exploration. Perhaps the infant's discovery of the genitals and the pleasurable feelings derived from manipulating them at about 7 to 10 months also are enhanced by the specific focal stimulation received from caregivers outside of diapering. It has long been known (and used by mothers, caregivers, and nurses) that masturbating will soothe an infant. Whether the same method is applied equally to male and female infants is unknown, but it seems at best a dubious procedure although some professionals have advocated it (Sugar, 1982).

Toddlerhood and the Early Genital Phase

Roiphe and Galenson (1981) found that between 15 and 19 months, there is a heightened genital sensitivity in both sexes; accordingly, they called this epoch the early genital phase. During this phase youngsters display repetitive manual genital self-stimulation or use rocking and thigh pressure to achieve such sensations indirectly. When so engaged, both sexes show erotic arousal with facial expressions of pleasure and accompanying autonomic excitation. In boys, penile erections may occur with or without such accompanying behavior. Lax (1994) feels that the female toddler lubricates during this excited state. During or after such stimulation, the children tend to initiate body contact with the mother. However, after the parent or others discourage it "by various inhibitory behaviors of which they are often quite unaware," this body contact soon ceases and is replaced by an inward gaze (Galenson, 1993). The presence of the "no" gesture at 13 months and speech "no" at 17 months (Sugar, 1982) clearly allows the toddler to appreciate such dissuasion.

Roiphe and Galenson (1981) suggest that the genital and anal sensations are connected, especially for the female infant. Richards (1992) asserts that in girls, urethral and anal sphincter sensations are pleasurable and difficult to isolate from genital sphincter sensations. She notes that "Urinary retention, with tightening and relaxation of the sphincters to release urine, is the prototype of vaginal excitement and orgasm in women" (p. 341). Little girls have sexual pleasure from contracting and relaxing their sphincters (Clower, 1976); they achieve sphincter control earlier than boys; and the girl's sense of mastery is magnified by the sexual pleasure she attains with this control (Richards, 1992). The female infant's sexual sensation is not focused or limited to one site as in the male, but also includes the inner upper thighs, vulva, lower abdomen, and anal area. The girl soon learns that communicating the presence of these sensations is socially inappropriate and enjoys the pleasure without consciously registering it (Richards, 1992).

Richards (1992) feels that girls value their "genitals for the pleasure to be derived from them" (p. 342) and believes with Mayer (1985) that female castration anxiety is a fear of loss of the pleasure that the genitals provide, which is similar for both sexes. Richards (1992) stresses the role of the girl's sphincters in generating body image, since they connect inside and outside. It can be conjectured that the decreased manual masturbation observed in girls after the awareness of the anatomical sex differences may be due to the pleasurable sensations available from contracting and relaxing the sphincters. Ordinarily this is not observable, and therefore it does not arouse negative reactions in parents or other adults.

CASE EXAMPLE

An 18-month-old boy was investigating sex differences with persistent requests to attend both parents in all their functions. He was allowed in the bathroom to observe them brushing teeth and combing hair. The mother otherwise denied him access, while the father made no restrictions and they often showered and urinated together. His interest in father's urinary stream and anatomy was intense but abated after some months.

The Early Castration Reaction of the Early Genital Phase

Between 18 and 24 months, children display visual and tactile curiosity about anatomical sex differences; they make efforts to explore their own and others' genitals, including those of animals and dolls (Roiphe & Galenson, 1981).

In both sexes, with the discovery of the anatomical sex differences, early castration reactions occur and are usually mild. The reactions may involve sleep disturbance, regression in sphincter control (if training has begun or been attained), aggressive behavior, and negativism. The latter reflects the ambivalent relationship to the mother at this time based on increased "dependence and intense aggression mobilized by the threat of object loss" (Roiphe & Galenson, 1981, p. 18); it arises without any triadic implications. Roiphe and Galenson note the presence of a beginning superego that admonishes the toddler, who says to him- or herself almost direct quotes from mother, even

though object constancy has not yet been attained. There is often uneasiness or anxiety about items that suggest castration anxiety, such as broken crayons or toys, and cuts or bruises.

Roiphe and Galenson (1981) stress the significance of the early genital phase and its genital arousal "for the gradual establishment of genital schematization" (p. 33). This implies genital maturation to the level of serving to discharge tension and achieve pleasure, and that the youngster has at the end of this phase become aware of his or her gender. From the beginning of this phase the "infants' major experiences will have a genital reflection." After the early castration reaction, divergent lines of development for males and females can be discerned.

The Latter Part of the Early Genital Phase

Following the early castration reaction, the boy's behavior suggests a profound denial of the anatomical differences between the sexes. He avoids looking at female genitals (a behavior pattern that continues until about 3 or 4 years of age) and displays increased motor activity and intense interest in mobile and transportation toys (Roiphe, 1979).

This differs from the girl's behavior; after the early castration reaction, she now turns to the father with a display of coyness and an increased erotization of her relationship to him. A few weeks after the awareness of sex differences, her direct masturbation diminishes and is replaced by indirect autoeroticism. Usually there is also an increased attachment to dolls and doll play (Roiphe, 1979). It is apparent that both male and female toddlers display a relatively decreased cathexis of mother at this time.

It seems that at 18 to 24 months, the rapprochement subphase of the separation-individuation phase (Mahler, Pine, & Bergman, 1975), with its crisis about loss of narcissistic omnipotence along with fears of loss and the presence of superego precursors, contributes to the early castration reaction. To some extent this may be balanced by the development of object permanence at 18 months

(Piaget, 1952), which signifies that the toddler is aware that objects can be sought and found and that their image can be maintained even though they are physically absent. The symbolic function also begins at 18 months (Spitz, 1965). Age 18 to 24 months appears to be a crucial Rubicon for the youngster's further development; a disturbance in any one of these areas may impinge on, or interfere with, others.

Following the toddler's decreased cathexis of the mother after the early castration reaction, the mother may feel disappointed, experience a sense of loss, and complain that the child does not love her anymore. If the mother tries to cling to the child, this may pose a problem for the child. Alternatively, it may be a stimulus for the mother to become pregnant prematurely. Thus, the child's crisis in coping with these anxieties at 18 to 24 months is matched by a parallel crisis in the mother.

With the early castration reaction, the girl also becomes aware that besides being unlike males, she is also unlike mother due to the absence of breasts. She has difficulty visualizing her genitals, and parents usually do not aid clarification due to their own difficulty in accurately naming specific female genital parts; the tendency is to use one name (e.g., heinie, bottom, vagina, etc.) for everything. Unless there is a sister close to her in age, the girl is likely to feel different from other family members about her body. This may be an impetus for her interest in babies, since they are similarly flat-chested and appear more like herself than mother, father, or brother in body image. She usually has observed her father or male peers during urination and may try to imitate males by standing to urinate. This attention to her own and others' urination may be part of her early castration reaction.

The girl frequently experiences discovery of anatomical differences from the boy as a blow to her omnipotence and hence as a narcissistic injury. However, this is not necessarily the case. Galenson and Roiphe (1976) state that girls who show severe reactions also seem to suffer from a constriction in their fantasy life and general intellectual curiosity.

In some girls, their encounter with penis envy gives rise to a lack of well-being and lowered self-esteem, which reflects a prephallic disturbance in object relations, primarily the relationship with mother. This occurrence may occur as a result of chronic illness or a physical handicap in the child, separation from mother, or mother being emotionally unavailable, any of which may interfere with the youngster's development. Resolution of penis envy allows a girl to identify more fully with the mother's femininity and the female gender role (Galenson & Roiphe, 1976).

CASE EXAMPLES

An 18-month-old female had slowly shifted her attachment from mother to father over the previous month with manifest coyness to, and preference for, him. Then she began to respond to the sound of the arrival of his car by appearing just inside the doorway. Instead of running to greet him as she had done previously, she smiled, assumed a supine position in his path, raised her legs toward him, and reached out to him with her arms. The father responded by greeting her warmly, kneeling beside her, and giving her a hug and a kiss. She beamed but remained supine for several minutes after he walked away. This behavior continued for a number of weeks, after which it was replaced by an upright greeting at the door with the usual smile, embrace and kiss.

An 18-month-old female passenger in a plane who was sitting quite comfortably with her mother (father was absent) tried to attract the attention of the men sitting nearby. She was quickly noticed by women but they did not interest her. When she had the gaze of a man on her, she became openly flirtatious with a broad continuous smile, giggling, squirming, and turning joyfully in her seat. This was followed by her initiation of "peek-a-boo." After the first male responded to her with smiling, greetings, and "peek-a-boo" for about 10 minutes, he withdrew to his reading. She sulked for a few moments, then tried to recapture his interest. Failing that, she turned to another nearby male and smiled broadly when she succeeded in attracting his attention and smiling response.

At that time this little girl was not interested in females, including mother, and specifically sought males for her needs. When in satisfying contact with a male, she had the openness, ease, and glow of joy similar to the 6-month-old infant who is in love with the world.

Symbolic Function

According to Roiphe and Galenson (1981), infants who developed the most severe preoedipal castration reaction displayed delayed and distorted play and language symbolic function. These investigators observed that some girls used language as a defense against fears and anxiety, and some developed temporary language regression in which they avoided using the male pronoun for weeks or months. Other toddlers (male and female) became preoccupied with repetitive and stereotyped forms of play involving a search for the missing phallus. Most of these girls and some of these boys developed an attachment to concrete, phallic-shaped objects.

After the early genital phase, the girl's advance in verbal ability represents an advance in symbol formation and function. Boys demonstrate some interference or delay in these areas due to their denial and avoidance of female genitals. This is observable in the second year of life as their verbal ability comes to lag behind that of girls (Roiphe & Galenson, 1981). It could be speculated that the males' lag in verbal ability compared to females', which is observed from grade school on, stems from this interference or delay in symbol formation and function.

Parens and Pollock (1979) proposed that the wish to have a baby is not necessarily a substitute for a penis; the wish to have a penis and associated distress reactions are not invariable antecedents of the wish to have the baby; indeed, in some girls the wish to have a baby precedes any evidence of the oedipal castration complex. Parens (1990) feels that their findings support the observation by Kesstenberg (1956) that "the little girl singles out the illusion of motherhood as her most cherished, creative experience." He suggests that "the little girl's psyche at this phase of development already is dominated by a heterosexual drive pressure" (p. 271).

It appears that by the time the girl reaches the phallic oedipal phase, primary femininity has been established, the foundations of gender role identity have been laid, and superego development begun. Similarly, the boy now has primary masculinity and the other male attributes.

Girls' Interest in Babies

Based on direct observation, Parens (1990) points out that the girl's interest in babies emerges around 12 months of age; during the first 4 years of life, it evolves in two stages. During the first stage, from about 14 to 24 months, little girls' behaviors and affects suggest the "recognition of baby as baby. Dolls begin to be used, perhaps already as primitively representing babies" (p. 753); and the girls' behavior toward a doll tends to mirror the mother's behavior toward the infant.

A change occurs when the second stage appears around the beginning of the third year. Girls show marked excitement and interest in the baby, which becomes a focus of intense preoccupation. Parens (1990) postulates that in the second stage, the girl's interest in babies expresses inborn factors representing and "complementing component instinctual drive and primary ego dispositions which differentiate at this time."

Preoedipal Sex Role Knowledge

Etaugh and Duits (1990) point out that children's sex role knowledge begins early, with clearly established sex-type toy preferences by age 2 years and a display of knowledge differentiating toys by gender by age 3. Shortly after the second birthday, most toddlers can distinguish between pictures of adults by sex, although accurate differentiation between pictures of girls and boys does not begin regularly until 2½ to 3 years of age.

Two- to 3-year-olds have some beginning gender-related knowledge that influences their behavior even before they can clearly verbalize this. Etaugh and Duits (1990) found that children show a marked shift and are able to provide clear gender labeling of young children at 18 to 37 months, and show knowledge of sex-role stereotypes for toys. The accuracy of gender discrimination increased with age, except on the task involving just toys, with a sharp transition occurring between 27 and 32 months; boys displayed more pronounced sex stereotypes than girls. Gender designation and attributes are taught by parents and others early in childhood; these are elaborated by observation and identification.

The Phallic-Oedipal Phase

In the phallic-oedipal phase, genital masturbation and exhibitionism increase, a preoccupation with the genitals becomes apparent in both sexes, and both sexes mutually explore the differences in their bodies. Boys become curious again, and their attitude during this phase has been termed "being cocky" or showing "penis pride." At this period, it is quite usual for children's play to involve such schemes as "house," "doctor and nurse," or "mother and father."

During the oedipal phase, it is not uncommon for the boy to tell his mother that he is going to be her husband when he grows up, and many a girl at this stage tells her father she will marry him when she grows up. The girl and the boy are now rivalrous with the same-sex parent, but, along with this, there is further identification with that parent. The turning to and interest in the opposite-sex parent is aided by the acceptance and love by the same-sex parent of this development as well as the projected anger the child feels toward the same-sex parent.

Exhibitionism is seen in both little boys and girls, and this helps them to consolidate a narcissistically valued body (Tyson, 1982). Both sexes behave in ways resembling their same-sex parent, imitating and experimenting with their notions of the roles of father or mother, especially in their games of "mother and father" or "doctor and patient." With this practicing and the parents' acceptance of the child's development, the child is given the hope of growing up to be like its same-sex identification model. At the same time, the child continues to elaborate his or her concept of expanding masculinity or femininity, as the case may be, along with gender identity and gender role.

CASE EXAMPLE

When an encopretic boy of 4 was seen for evaluation, he walked on his toes as if wearing women's high-heeled shoes. Inquiry led to the awareness that he still wore mother's shoes at home and walked like her in them and in his own shoes. This had begun at age 3 when he regressed and became encopretic in the context of mother's frequent physical absence and emotional unavailability. As a result of the evaluation, the youngster entered individual therapy, the father became more involved with his son, and the son identified further with the father. After some months, toe-walking ceased. There never was a diagnostic question of gender identity disorder.

Latency Developments

Maturation of adrenal androgen secretion begins at about age 6 to 8 years and peaks in late adolescence. The maturation of gonadal sex steroid secretion in males and females begins at age 9 to 13 and peaks at about midadolescence. These hormones lead to physical masculizing of boys and feminizing of girls (Nottelman, Inoff-Germain, Sussman, & Chrousos, 1990). Puberty may begin in boys as early as 9.5 years and in girls at 8 years of age. Thus, we have a biological basis for the division of latency into early and late (before and after age 8) along with the separation of cognition in latency with the beginning of concrete operations at age 7 (Piaget, 1952). Although less overt than in the oedipal period, autoerotic activity in girls (Clower, 1976) and boys continues in early latency and increases in late latency.

With these data as background we can view the increased gender differentiation with a broader appreciation of the general disparity that develops in latency between boys and girls in musculature, physical abilities, and different choices of play as avenues for discharge of anxieties and developmental needs.

Martin, Wood, and Little (1990) observed that gender stereotypes continue to develop through a series of stages into middle childhood. In the first stage the child learns what kind of things are directly associated with each sex. In the second stage, children age 4 to 6 develop more indirect and complex databases involving information that is relevant to their own sex. At age 8, children move to the third stage, where they learn a great deal more about what is relevant to the opposite sex. Once older children know someone's sex or interests, they make more extreme stereotypic judgments than do younger children, for example: "boys don't jump rope"; "girls don't collect snakes." The associational network that develops is necessarily incomplete but is nonetheless used for information processing. Their play is decidedly and obviously different, boundary maintenance is very significant to the children, and each sex frowns on crossing lines.

Brody, Hay, and Vandewater (1990) noted that among 6- to 12-year olds, girls were more angry at male than at female adults, whereas boys were equally angry at male and female adults. Boys and girls were more hurt and disgusted by opposite-sex than by same-sex children. Girls had more fear in general, but both boys and girls had more fear of adult males than of females. This finding appears to indicate gender-based differences in stereotypes related to fear and anger; and the greater power attributed to the adult male. The latter fits with the well-known fact that boys and girls heed father more readily than mother.

Boys in Latency

As a result of identification with mother from an early age, a certain admixture of femininity might be added to the boy's sense of gender identity and "may be what helps the man in later life to be sensitive and nurturing to his wife and children" (Tyson, 1982, p. 70). Tyson adds that the identification with his father helps the boy and has an enormous influence on the establishment of male gender identity. This nondefensive identification begins in the preoedipal years and serves to consolidate core gender identity. Latency is a period of further elaboration of gender identity and gender roles. The stereotyping of each sex and the need for distance from each other is evident in the rejection of the other sex in children's natural play and groupings.

Girls in Latency

A latency girl's behavior "is often a caricature of femininity yet a variety of preoedipal conflicts, unresolved penis envy, and phallic exhibitionism are also frequently apparent" (Tyson, 1982). For the girl, too, latency is a time for further identification with mother, firming up of gender identity,

and an occasion to practice gender roles. Girls avoid and reject boys at this time as being nasty and dirty.

CASE EXAMPLE

An 8-year-old girl was seen for evaluation because her parents were concerned about her femininity. She wanted to play with the boys in Little League baseball and did not play with dolls spontaneously. With her female peers, however, she did play with dolls as well as engage in the usual girls' games. She collected Teddy bears and other soft and cuddly, furry objects, and enjoyed Brownies. There was no problem in her gender identity, sexual orientation, or gender role, but the parents had difficulty adapting to the changes in society and social roles now allowed girls compared to that of their childhood. From an indirect follow-up much later, it was learned that the girl had been a star athlete in high school and college on girls' teams, and was happily married since early adulthood.

Children's Games

From early in life, a great deal of children's free time is devoted to play, and it becomes especially significant to both genders from latency onward. Accordingly, it is important to consider games in terms of gender distinctions at different developmental phases. Zonal experiences that influence the patterns of play in boys and girls are identifiable (Roiphe & Galenson, 1981) from an early age. For example, at 12 to 15 months, anal zone interest is manifested by concern with the toilet flush and bowl; emptying, filling, scattering, piling, and peg games; smearing; and anal processes as such. With the development of urinary awareness at age 14 to 16 months, infants are fascinated with their peer, parental, animal, and own urinary streams as well as with faucets, hoses, water cans, and other kinds of pouring play. From about 14 months on, the differences in play by gender are clearly observable, with girls building enclosures with blocks and playing inside them, while boys build towers, roads, or houses and play outside them (Erikson, 1950). Table 17.1 lists differences in play due to gender, by age, beginning in toddlerhood.

TABLE 17.1

Children's Games Reflecting Gender

Female Games	Male Games
Toddlerhood	
Doll play	Transportation automobile
Nurturing activities	Logs
	Playdough—pushing it into and through openings
Latency	
Teeter-totter	Ring toss
Jacks	Guns, balls, soldiers
Riding father's knee or ankle	Large doughnut-shaped objects of plastic
Slides	Marbles
Jump rope	Crawling into openings, barrels, pipes, or large toys with openings
Secrets about sex	
Barbie dolls, Ken dolls	Baseball, football, basketball, or stickball
Dancing	Church on fire
Songs (accompanying jump rope and other games) with a direct romantic or disguised sexual theme	Sliding on ice, standing or seated
	Urinating distance contests, especially in winter
Puberty and Early Adolescence	
Horseback riding	Circle jerk
Slumber parties	Diving for rings in swimming pool
Volleyball	Physical activity, bumping & jumping
Running	Baseball, football, basketball
Dancing	Pretend urinating (or spitting) on food (chocolate) = contamination
Gymnastics	
Bike riding	Stickball
Rubbing legs together	

Early Adolescent Developments

The biological and hormonal changes of adolescence lead to normative anxieties that include concerns about the body image, whether that image conforms to one's gender identity (Rosenbaum, 1993), and an upsurge of sexual thoughts (Sugar, 1990; see Chapter 6). With the onset of adolescence there are reactions to a physically changing body, new sexual feelings and fantasies, and the awareness of children's reproductive potential. There also is a push for further individuation and autonomy, simultaneously with regressive wishes. But the fear of fusion with the infantile objects and the revivification of the oedipal issues leads to a move toward same-sex peers for support, acceptance, and anxiety reduction. During this period there may be brief homosexual experimentation and play, which are usually disguised. However, they may be more direct, such as in the "circle jerk"—group masturbation—for boys, or slumber parties for girls, and these may lead to anxieties about sexual orientation.

The development of a mature sexual body obliges the youngster to deal with the reality and irreversibility of being a male or female. Usually this is not perceived as a conflict or even consciously considered, unless there is a gender, or gender-related, problem.

Female Adolescents

Puberty and the onset of menstruation mark the next phase in the development of girls' gender identity (Tyson, 1982). Ritvo (1976) and Tyson (1982) feel that menarche is an important landmark in early adolescence, because it has all the characteristics of a normal developmental crisis (in the sense of a decisive state or turning point). Girls' tomboy behavior just before menarche is considered to be their attempt to deny femininity and have a last fling at phallic fantasies by pretending to be a boy. The fantasy is reinforced by the fact that preadolescent girls are already experiencing their growth spurt; for a while they often exceed age-mate boys in height and athletic prowess. For the normal girl, menarche seems to bring this phase to an abrupt end.

In the girl, breast development and menarche revive prior conflicts but enhance her feminine gender identity (Zilbach, 1993; see Chapter 6). Shopper (1979) points out that the adolescent female's use of a tampon is accompanied by learning to touch and explore her external genitalia and involves a readiness toward fostering autonomy and individuation. The usually prevalent sexual thoughts, fantasies (Sugar, 1990), and autoerotic activities of adolescents—present in over 75% of adolescent females (Masters, Johnson, & Kolodny, 1986) also help to confirm her gender identity.

Although the early adolescent female has issues with her parents about her developing autonomy and individuation, she is not seeking separation but expansion into the larger world, which is accompanied by loosening and expansion of ties to families and others (Zilbach, 1993). With this, she experiences separation anxieties and fears of fusion and regression, along with the bisexual conflicts derived from seeking closeness with, and comfort from, her original love object—her mother. The adolescent female usually manages this bisexual conflict by finding new ego ideals

among peers and older admired females (teachers, coaches, etc.) to emulate. Mother is also a support to her in her identification as a female. Zilbach (1993) emphasizes the adolescent version of primary femininity/active engulfment, as the desire to take in, surround, and contain.

Male Adolescents

With the heightened testosterone levels of early adolescence, there is an increase in erections and masturbation along with accompanying heterosexual fantasies, all of which further confirm a boy's gender identity. Masturbation is phase specific for adolescence, and over 90% of males engage in this practice. The onset of ejaculation is a significant milestone for the male; although it may be traumatic (Sugar, 1974), it also enhances and further confirms his gender identity and is a significant organizer of sexual fantasies, thoughts, and functions.

Blos (1979) felt that the definitive establishment of a masculine gender identity could occur only after adolescence and depended on a resolution of the negative oedipal conflict. For the male, this involves his wish for closeness with his father, which begins in early childhood and recurs in early adolescence. The adolescent male wishes for a special and exclusive relationship with his father and strongly identifies with him. However, this longing for male companionship itself is a source of anxiety, because it is associated with "a dread of homosexuality" (Tyson, 1982, p. 72). By finding male peers and older males (coaches, teachers) with whom to identify, the boy can dilute the intensity of his relationship with his father, while utilizing others as new ego ideals. Thus, a more mature, masculine ego ideal is consolidated that resolves the bisexual conflict.

CASE EXAMPLE

After a 13-year-old boy had one mutual masturbation experience to ejaculation with an older boy, he felt consumed with guilt and anxiety about his sexual orientation and gender identity. Confession, penance, and communion in his parish church failed to relieve him, and when he sought out priests in other churches, they also did not relieve his feelings. One, however, did refer him for clinical evaluation. In the course of the evaluation, it was observed that he suffered from obsessional and not gender identity pathology.

Contributors to Consolidation

A number of additional factors contribute to gender role and help to consolidate gender identity in adolescence.

Peer influence is one of the major contributors to gender role. Although teens conform rigidly to the ideas of their peers, the peer group appears to operate differently for each gender. According to Maccoby (1990), gender-typed behaviors develop in male peer groups whereby competitive and uncooperative behavior becomes normative, while females' peer interactions promote the development of empathy and nurturing. But both groups define what is acceptable for gender role in respect to clothes, music, activities, school achievement, social events, and speech.

Parents consider achievement in mathematics as more important for males than females and frequently view academic achievement as more relevant for their sons than their daughters. Schools promote achievement more in males than in females. Teachers punish, talk to, and listen to males more than females. Teachers and guidance counselors also tend to promote future sex roles by steering students into traditional careers (Berkovitz, 1993).

Consolidation

With adjustment to the physical and hormonal changes of early and midadolescence, the teenager attains the full form and function of being a male or female, and can feel "grown up" as such.

In adolescence, youths begin to revise their ego ideal as they start the shift away from dependence on mother and father and experiment with the different values of peers and adults other than parents. Their heterosexual experimentation helps them confirm their gender identity, gender role,

and sexual orientation. Despite societal changes in the United States in the past three decades, adolescent males still experiment more heterosexually than females (Sugar, 1993). Many adolescents traverse various paths before arriving at a confident sense of their gender identity, as the following cases illustrate.

CASE EXAMPLES

An 18-year-old male presented for evaluation because he felt he was homosexual; he could prove it by the psychiatric books accompanying him, from which he quoted passages. He felt no attraction to females, although he had dated and tried to be romantically involved with them; accordingly, he was certain of his gender identity. Initially he appeared to have a compulsive neurosis, but his perceptions of his gender identity and sexual orientation were correct and he needed help with anxieties associated with his adaptation to his homosexuality.

A 16-year-old female was seen for evaluation and brief therapy due to having a homosexual involvement after she was dropped by her steady boyfriend. She defied parents and friends in their efforts to dissuade her from this relationship. Her shift in sexual orientation was not accompanied by a change in gender identity and arose from her regressive reaction to loss. Many months later, she ended this relationship and resumed dating males. In late adolescence, she married and had a family.

In the usual course of development, by adolescence, the sense of being male or female is firmly settled and is not an issue per se. There may be unconscious gender identity conflicts despite the absence of observable unusual behavior or conscious awareness of such. Ordinarily, by late adolescence consolidation has occurred without conflict for both sexes in respect to gender identity, sexual orientation, and gender role.

The only conscious concerns related to gender that youngsters may experience are feelings of adequacy or inadequacy in their masculinity or femininity. However, these are aspects of gender role. The girl questions how attractive, well developed, appealing, and popular she is, all of which are part of her sense of femininity. For the boy, concerns about his strength, height, and acceptance by peers and girls, are similarly reflections of his sense of masculinity. With late adolescent sexual experiences, the sense of gender becomes further confirmed and consolidated.

REFERENCES

Bem, S. (1974). The measurement of psychological androgyny. *Journal of Consulting and Clinical Psychology, 42*, 155–162.

Berkovitz, I. H. (1993). Effects of secondary school and college experiences on adolescent female development. In M. Sugar (Ed.), *Female adolescent development* (2nd ed., pp. 192–212). New York: Brunner/Mazel.

Bezirganian, S., & Cohen, P. (1992). Sex differences in the interaction between temperament and parenting. *Journal of the American Academy of Child and Adolescent Psychiatry, 31*, 790–801.

Blos, P. (1979). Masculinity: Developmental aspects of adolescence. *Adolescent Psychiatry, 16*, 5–16.

Brody, L. R., Hay, D. H., & Vandewater, E. (1990). Gender, gender role identity and children's reported feelings toward the same and opposite sex. *Sex Roles, 23*, 363–388.

Clower, V. (1976). Theoretical implications in current views of masturbation in latency girls. *Journal of the American Psychoanalytic Association, 24*, 109–125.

Ellis, H. (1936). *Studies in the psychology of sex, Vol. 2, Part II. Eonism.* New York: Random House.

Erikson, E. (1950). *Childhood and society.* New York: W. W. Norton.

Etaugh, C., & Duits, T. (1990). Development of gender discrimination: Role of stereotypic and counterstereotypic gender cues. *Sex Roles, 23*, 215–222.

Frankel, H. (1853). Homo mollis. *Medisine Zeitung, 22*, 102–203.

Galenson, E. (1980). Sexual development during the second year of life. *Psychiatric Clinics of North America, 3*, 37–44.

Galenson, E., & Roiphe, H. (1974). The emergence of genital awareness during the second year of life. In R. C. Friedman (Ed.), *Sex differences in behavior* (pp. 223–231). New York: John Wiley & Sons.

Galenson, E. (1993). Sexuality in infancy and preschool-aged children. *Child and Adolescent Psychiatric Clinics of North America, 2*, 385–391.

Galenson, E., & Roiphe, H. (1976). Some suggested revisions concerning early female development. *Journal of the American Psychoanalytic Association, 24* (5), 29–57.

Green, R. (1974). *Sexual identity conflicts in children and adults.* New York: Basic Books.

Green, R. (1985). Gender identity in childhood and later sexual orientation: Follow-up of 78 males. *American Journal of Psychiatry, 142*, 339–341.

Green, R. (1987). *The "sissy boy syndrome" and the development of homosexuality.* New Haven, CT: Yale University Press.

Greenson, R. (1968). Disidentifying from mother: Its special importance for the boy. In R. Greenson, *Explorations in Psychoanalysis* (pp. 305–312). New York: International Universities Press.

Hirschfeld, M. (1936). *Sexual anomalies and perversions.* London: Alder.

Huston, A. C. (1985). The development of sex-typing: Themes from recent research. *Developmental Review, 5*, 1–17.

Jones, E. (1927). The early development of female sexuality. *International Journal of Psycho-Analysis, 8*, 459–472.

Kestenberg, J. (1956). On the development of maternal feelings in early childhood. *Psychoanalytic Study of the Child, 11*, 257–291.

Kleeman, J. A. (1975). Genital self stimulation in infant and toddler girls. In I. M. Marcus & J. J. Francis (Eds.), *Masturbation from infancy to senescence.* New York: International Universities Press.

Klein, M. (1948). Early stages of the oedipus conflict. In M. Klein, *Contributions to psychoanalysis 1921–1945* (pp. 202–214). New York: Basic Books.

Krafft-Ebing, R. V. (1894). *Psychopathia sexualis* (9th ed.). Stuttgart: Enke.

Lax, R. F. (1994). Aspects of primary and secondary genital feelings and anxieties in girls during the preoedipal and early oedipal phases. *Psychoanalytic Quarterly, 63*, 271–296.

Maccoby, E. E. (1990). Gender and relationships: A developmental account. *American Psychologist, 45*, 513–520.

Mahler, M. S., Pine, F., & Bergman, A. (1975). *Psychological birth of the human infant.* New York: Basic Books.

Martin, C. L., Wood, C. H., & Little, J. K. (1990). The development of gender stereotype components. *Child Development, 61*, 1891–1904.

Masters, W. H., Johnson, V. C., & Kolodny, R. C. (1986). *Masters and Johnson on sex and human loving.* Boston: Little, Brown.

Mayer, E. L. (1985). Everybody must be just like me; observations in female castration anxiety. *International Journal of Psycho-Analysis, 66*, 331–347.

Meyer, J. K. (1980). Body ego, selfness, and gender sense: The development of gender identity. *Psychiatric Clinics of North America, 3*, 21–36.

Meyer, J. K. (1982). The theory of gender identity disorders. *Journal of the American Psychoanalytic Association, 30*, 381–418.

Meyer, J. K., & Reter, D. (1979). Sex reassignment. *Archives of General Psychiatry, 36*, 1010–1015.

Money, J. (1980). *Love and lovesickness.* Baltimore: Johns Hopkins University Press.

Money, J. (1988). Gay, straight and in-between. The sexology of erotic orientation. New York: Oxford University Press.

Nottelman, E. D., Inoff-Germain, G., Sussman, E. J., and Chrousos, G. P. (1990). Hormones and behavior at puberty. In J. Bancroft & J. M. Reinisch (Eds.), *Adolescence and puberty* (pp. 88–123). New York: Oxford University Press.

Parens, H. (1990). On the girl's psychosexual development: Reconsiderations suggested from direct observation. *Journal of the American Psychoanalytic Association, 38*, 743–772.

Parens, H., & Pollock, L. (1979). *The child's wish to have a baby.* [Film.] Reels I and II. Philadelphia: Audio-visual Media Section Eastern Pennsylvania Psychiatric Institute (MCP).

Piaget, J. (1952). *The origins of intelligence in children.* New York: International Universities Press.

Richards, A. (1992). The influence of sphincter control and genital sensation on body image and gender identity in women. *Psychoanalytic Quarterly, 61,* 331–351.

Ritvo, S. (1976). Adolescent to woman. *Journal of the American Psychoanalytic Association, 24* (5), 127–138.

Roiphe, H. (1968). On an early genital phase: With an addendum on genesis. *Psychoanalytic Study of the Child, 23,* 348–365.

Roiphe, H. (1979). A theoretical overview of preoedipal development in the first four years of life. In J. D. Noshspitz (Ed.), *Basic handbook of child psychiatry* (Vol. 1, pp. 118–127). New York: Basic Books.

Roiphe, H. (1991). The tormentor and the victim in the nursery. *Psychyoanalytic Quarterly, 60,* 450–464.

Roiphe, H., & Galenson, E. (1972). Early genital activity and the castration complex. *Psychoanalytic Quarterly, 41,* 344–347.

Roiphe, H., & Galenson, E. (1973a). The infantile fetish. *Psychoanalytic Study of the Child, 28,* 147–166.

Roiphe, H., & Galenson, E. (1973b). Object loss and early sexual development. *Psychoanalytic Quarterly, 42,* 73–90.

Roiphe, H., & Galenson, E. (1981). *Infantile origins of sexual identity.* New York: International Universities Press.

Rosenbaum, M. B. (1993). The changing body image of the adolescent girl. In M. Sugar (Ed.), *Female adolescent development* (2nd ed., pp. 62–80). New York: Brunner/Mazel.

Shopper, M. (1979). The rediscovery of the vagina and the importance of the menstrual tampon. In M. Sugar (Ed.), *Female adolescent development* (pp. 214–233). New York: Brunner/Mazel.

Spitz, R. A. (1965). *The first year of life.* New York: International Universities Press.

Stoller, R. (1968). *Sex and gender* (Vol. 1). New York: Science House.

Stoller, R. (1975). *Sex and gender* (Vol. 2). New York: Science House.

Sugar, M. (1974). Adolescent confusion of nocturnal emissions as enuresis. *Adolescent Psychiatry, 3,* 168–185.

Sugar, M. (1982). *The premature in context.* New York: Spectrum.

Sugar, M. (1990). Developmental anxieties in adolescence. *Adolescent Psychiatry, 17,* 385–403.

Sugar, M. (1993). Adolescent sexuality. *Child and Adolescent Psychiatric Clinics of North America, 2,* 407–413.

Tyson, P. (1982). A developmental line of gender identity, gender role and choice of love object. *Journal of the American Psychoanalytic Association, 30,* 61–86.

Tyson, P. (1994). Bedrock and beyond: An examination of the clinical utility of contemporary theories of female psychology. *Journal of the American Psychoanalytic Association, 42,* 447–467.

Westhead, V., Olson, S., & Meyer, J. K. (1990). Gender identity disorders in adolescence. In M. Sugar (Ed.), *Atypical adolescence and sexuality* (pp. 87–107). New York: W. W. Norton.

Westphal, C. (1870). Die Contrare Sexualempfindung. *Archiv Psychiatriche Nervenkranken, 2,* 73–108.

Zilbach, J. J. (1993). Female adolescence: Toward a separate line of female development. In M. Sugar (Ed.), *Female adolescent development* (2nd ed., pp. 45–61). New York: Brunner/Mazel.

18 / Biological and Social Influences on Gender Identity

Lois T. Flaherty

As explained in Chapter 17, the classical psychoanalytic perspective is a biological one, in that the psychological changes of adolescence are viewed as rooted in the biological developments of that period. Much of adolescent development can be understood in the context of the adolescent's reaction to a physically changing body and to new sexual feelings. However, there is still another biological factor to consider, namely: the possible direct effect of sex hormones on behavior and personality. It is understandable that researchers would look to sex hormones as a possible explanation for gender differences, since these hormones account for nearly all of the physical changes of puberty. The recognition that sex hormones play a role in utero not only on the development of sex organs but on the developing brain itself has led to speculation that a primary sense of gender may be inborn. In fact, there is some evidence that sex hormones influence gender identity. Baucom, Besch, and Callahan (1985) found that females with naturally occurring higher testosterone concentrations perceived themselves as self-directed, action oriented, and resourceful, while women with lower concentrations described themselves more in terms of an expressive role—caring and traditionally socialized. Friedman's more recent and exhaustive review of research on determinants of gender orientation concluded that there is substantial evidence from rat research, and somewhat less clear evidence from human studies, that hormonal influences in utero play an organizing role in brain development that has an effect on sex role behavior and gender identity later on (Friedman & Downey, 1993).

Influence of Sex Hormones

The presence of sex hormones during childhood is necessary for the development of sexual "drives" (Weissman & Barglow, 1980). In experiments of nature, when castration occurs prior to puberty because of illness, such sexual interests do not develop. However, if gonadal loss occurs after puberty, these drives/interests persist. This persistence may be due in part to the ability of the adrenal gland to produce testosterone; this ability partially compensates for the absence of testicular or ovarian function. Another explanation is that the sexuality developed during childhood is potent enough to survive even in the absence (or diminishment) of sex hormones later on. This is of course the case for women in later life, when oophorectomy or menopause does not normally result in diminished sexual interest. From their review of the literature on this subject, Weissman and Barglow (1980) concluded that "the psychologic experience, identifications, mental representations, and conflicts experienced in childhood related to sexuality are not fixed in the mental life of the child unless [the child] has experienced puberty with its accompanying upsurge in sexual hormones" (p. 127).

BRAIN FUNCTION AND GENDER

Much of recent research has focused on biological effects of hormones on brain functioning, especially cognitive functioning. In part, this research has been fueled by studies of early child development that have found consistent superiority of girls over boys in multiple aspects of language development. The development of brain imaging has allowed researchers to observe brain activity and has led to some exciting discoveries. A widely hailed magnetic resonance imaging study compared men's and women's brain activity when they were involved in sounding out words to identify which of a series of nonsense words rhymed. The men's brains showed a localized area of activity in the left inferior frontal gyrus, while women's brains showed a pattern involving the inferior frontal gyri of both hemispheres (Shaywitz et al., 1995). This finding lends further support to earlier data that show a greater tendency toward bilateral hemispheric functioning in women.

It has been speculated that the verbal facility that characterizes girls is related to their apparent increased sensitivity to interpersonal relationships and the emphasis that developing and maintaining relationships receives throughout their lives. The orientation toward relationships is characteristic of female gender role and an important part of gender identity.

TEMPERAMENT AND GENDER

The field of study of temperamental differences between boys and girls represents another attempt to identify what may be innate, biologically determined characteristics. Many of the characteristics associated with the pattern of "difficult temperament" are those typically associated with masculine behavior, such as increased activity level and aggressive behavior. Difficult temperament generally has been found to be more prevalent in boys, and it has been hypothesized that this factor accounts for part of the behavioral gender differences seen as children grow up. However, temperamental characteristics affect and are affected by parenting. It is possible that parents respond more negatively to difficult temperament in girls than they do to similar manifestations in boys; accordingly, parents would exert more control over girls and be more permissive with boys. This control in turn would lead to the behavior effectively being stamped out in girls. This hypothesis of differential parenting was supported by a study that surveyed a cohort of 9- to 18-year-old children and adolescents who had been followed for 10 years. It was found that, although the expected higher prevalence of difficult temperament in boys did exist in childhood, by the time the children became adolescents, there was no sex difference in the distribution of difficult temperament. It appeared that different parental pressures operated on each sex, so that the boys received more discipline (Bezirganian & Cohen, 1992); the net effect was that their difficult temperament was modulated.

Social and Cultural Factors Regarding Gender Identity

THE GENDER INTENSIFICATION HYPOTHESIS

Social and developmental psychologists have been concerned about the influence of social and cultural role expectations on gender identity. The differentiation of gender roles for males and females becomes more complete during adolescence, which occurs, it is hypothesized, because of a culturally mediated "intensification of gender identity," which is defined as an increase both in the awareness of gender roles and in efforts to adhere to these roles. Young children understand identity primarily in terms of physical attributes and do not allow for gradations of maleness or femaleness. (For them that would be akin to having various portions of a penis.) Such an understanding does not allow for much flexibility in their conceptualization of gender roles. As they become older and realize gender is more than physical, children become less rigid in their definitions of what is a boy and what is a girl; but, curiously, as they move into adolescence, they become less tolerant of deviations for sex-typed norms.

PREPUBERTAL DIFFERENCES

Prior to puberty, children of both sexes commonly show some behaviors that are gender-atypical, or characteristic of the opposite sex. Prepubertal girls are given greater latitude than boys in the expression of these gender-atypical behaviors. As a result, young girls commonly show admixtures of masculine and feminine behavior in their play and identifications. For example, it is not considered uncommon for girls to play with toy cars and trucks, whereas boys may be discouraged from playing house. Girls' casual clothes are similar to those of boys, and for a young girl to dislike wearing dresses is not usually considered cause for alarm. The "tomboy" phase, usually occurring during preadolescence, is considered a normative aspect of development for girls.

INSTRUMENTAL VS. EXPRESSIVE ROLES

With increasing age, gender-typical behaviors rise progressively (Sandberg, Meyer-Bahlburg, Ehrhardt, & Yager, 1993; Zucker, 1985). The gender-role differences that are observable in adolescents are similar in many ways to those seen in adults. Sociologists have broadly characterized women's gender role as "expressive," meaning that women are more involved with the emotional side of life, interacting with others primarily by providing care and emotional sustenance. The role of men, on the other hand, has been seen as essentially "instrumental"—acting on the environment to produce tangible products. This gender gap in roles becomes institutionalized in adulthood in terms of division of labor, with men more likely to take on occupational roles that involve competing and taking risks, while women's traditional occupations are characterized by interpersonal orientation involving caring and commitment (Rapoport, 1991).

CONSISTENT FINDINGS OF DIFFERENCES

Galambos, Almeida and Petersen (1990) have summarized the literature on gender identity intensification in early adolescence along with their own research. Among their most consistent findings were that males gain advantage over females in certain areas of mathematics beginning in sixth or seventh grade, the early-adolescent female experiences a decrease in self-image compared to the male, and there is an increase in depression in females in early adolescence. Boys are presumed to be pressured to excel academically, and for them, in sixth and seventh grades, the relationship between school achievement and self-image increases. At the same time, for girls, the pressure is to excel socially, and during this interval there is a decreased relationship between their school achievement and self-image. These authors found that differences in sex-role attitudes are increased in early adolescence compared with childhood. As they develop, early-adolescent girls become more egalitarian while boys become less so. The authors suggested this was due to girls' secondary position in society. Despite perceptions that men's and women's roles have changed drastically, they found little evidence of change in attitudes, preferences, and interests among males and females over the past 25 years.

EFFECT OF PHYSICAL MATURATION

While physical changes of puberty heighten adolescents' awareness of being male or female, and this heightened awareness undoubtedly contributes to gender intensification, it is also true that the child's physical maturation evokes a response from parents and other adults. Behavior that may have been tolerated earlier may now be actively discouraged, with boys and girls guided into traditional gender roles. Parents encourage and expect different things from boys than they do from girls,

and the gap regarding gender socialization widens as the child gets older. For boys, independence, achievement, and competition are emphasized, along with control of affective expression. Boys are punished more often and more severely at home (as well as in school). Girls, in contrast, are more restricted in terms of actions but are punished less and are related to by parents with more warmth and physical closeness (Rapoport, 1991).

SELF-PERCEPTIONS

The differential socialization has effects on the adolescents' own perceptions of themselves; studying these self-perceptions provides an important understanding of male-female differences in gender identity. Williams and McGee (1991) studied 960 adolescents at age 15 from a nonclinical sample in New Zealand; the adolescents were given a list of positive attributes and were asked to check off those that applied to them. While both boys and girls tended to check off multiple positive attributes, indicating that they had generally positive self-perceptions, there were significant differences between the attributes chosen by girls and those chosen by boys. Boys saw themselves as good at sports, confident, popular, attractive, and having lots of hobbies; girls described themselves as reliable, kind, independent, and affectionate. Only 18.4% of the girls saw themselves as attractive, while 34.1% of the boys did so. For girls, their parents' support and their own physical activities were most important in predicting positive responses; for boys, the equivalent predictive factors were part-time jobs (fewer than 10 hours per week), activities, attachment to parents, peers, and school. The findings that girls seem to define themselves in terms of relationships and boys in terms of activities are in keeping with the "expressive" versus "instrumental" dichotomy described earlier.

The process of gender intensification may have deleterious effects on the mental health and functioning of girls. There is a considerable body of literature on androgyny and its importance for self-esteem and achievement, especially in girls. Androgynous teens are more popular, possibly because they have socially valued "masculine" characteristics. Girls may reluctantly adopt traditional feminine behaviors because of cultural expectations (Huston & Alvarez, 1990).

GIRLS' INCREASED VULNERABILITY TO DEPRESSION

The fact that interpersonal relationships seem to be of greater importance to girls than to boys may have some negative effects, in the form of increasing girls' vulnerability to depression. The hypothesized greater importance placed on relationships by girls is one factor that some believe explain the greater prevalence of depression in adolescent girls than boys. (See Chapter 30.) Another possible link is suggested by the fact that others have found positive correlations between self-esteem and self-reported levels of physical activity in high school adolescent girls (Covey & Feltz, 1991). Thus, by not participating in self-esteem–building activities, possibly because they are discouraged from doing so, girls may become more vulnerable to depression.

INTIMACY DEVELOPMENT

Gilligan (1987) noted different patterns of personality development for males and females in accordance with their different gender roles—that of males emphasizes individual achievement and goals (instrumental role); women define their identity in terms of relationships that are judged by a standard of care and responsibility (expressive role) with a focus on the ongoing process of attachment. Intimacy in relationships is thought to be a particularly female feature, and the interest in intimacy development begins in early adolescence. Intimacy is a quality of relationships that is characterized by a feeling of emotional closeness, connectedness to another, and joint belonging; it is the subjective feeling of closeness toward another person. Self-disclosure, or the sharing of personal information about oneself, has commonly been used as a measure of intimacy, and girls have been shown to be much more adept at this than boys. However, when intimacy is defined as a feeling of closeness apart from self-disclosure, these gender differences are not as apparent. Studies of young adolescent boys show that they spend as much time in shared activities with other boys as girls do sharing their feelings; for boys it is the sharing of experiences that defines closeness. For both boys and girls, self-disclosure and shared experiences are important "behavioral paths" to closeness. Girls differ from boys in terms of self-disclo-sure, not shared experience. In brief, as a determinant of closeness, shared experience is more important for boys, self-disclosure for girls (Camarena, Sarigiani, & Peterson, 1990).

ROLE OF FAMILY RELATIONSHIPS

The primary role models for children's gender roles are their parents. In this respect, as their children become adolescents, parents continue to be very important. In addition to identifying with the parent of the same sex, children and adolescents experience their first significant interaction with the opposite sex with their opposite-sex parent. In families with sons, mothers have been noted to become less authoritative when their sons reach adolescence, reinforcing the boy's role as dominant with women. For girls, the reaction of their fathers to their changing physical and social status is crucial in shaping their sense of what it means to be a woman. Older siblings also play an important role as models for identification (in the case of same-sex siblings) and templates for heterosexual interaction (in the case of opposite-sex siblings).

One way in which the importance of fathers has been studied is by examining the effects of loss of a father through death or divorce. Daughters of divorced fathers have been observed to seek male attention, while those whose fathers have died tend to be uncomfortable around males (Hetherington, 1972). It would appear that in the total absence of a father, an adolescent girl has difficulty relating to males, while the partial availability of a father leads to a longing for more male attention.

The more stereotyped the parents' roles in the family, the more rigid the adolescent's gender identity is likely to be. In families where mothers work outside the home, girls have higher career aspirations and children of both sexes have less stereotyped views as well as more positive attitudes about nontraditional roles for women.

PEER INFLUENCES

As it is for so many things, peer influence is also important in the realm of gender identity. The role of the peer group appears to operate differently for boys and girls. Maccoby (1990) notes that gender-typed behaviors develop in male peer groups, as competitive and uncooperative behavior becomes normative. On the other hand, girls' peer interactions promote the development of empathy and nurturing. In addition, peer groups may play a greater role for adolescent girls than for boys. Adolescent males appear to be more tied to home and family than do adolescent females, who have supports both within and outside the family circle (Cooper & Grotevant, 1987). Thus, girls' tendency for greater socialization results in the early development of support networks that have been described as a major factor in women's emotional health.

SCHOOL INFLUENCES

School experiences promote differential academic achievement in girls as opposed to boys. Traditionally, math, science, and computers have been viewed as male domains and writing as a female one. Numerous studies have shown that parents view achievement in mathematics as more important for boys than girls; more than that, they frequently view academic achievement in general to be more relevant for their sons. Schools, too, promote achievement in this area as well as others more in boys than in girls. This fact is generally thought to explain the decline in academic performance seen so frequently in girls once they become adolescents. Teachers and guidance counselors also tend to promote future sex roles, steering students into traditional careers.

The school environment of the junior high school, with its increased size, multiple teachers, and schedule of changing classes, demands much more independence than does the environment of elementary school. This atmosphere is conducive to a style of independent learning, which is more comfortable for boys than for girls. In the school setting, girls start out as more compliant, quieter, more reticent, less openly aggressive and competitive; these characteristics suit them well in elementary school but not in junior high and high school.

MEDIA INFLUENCES

In the lives of adolescents, media, movies, and especially television are very important. Popular television programs often present highly stereotyped images of adult men and women. To date, evidence that television affects behavior is weaker than proof that it affects attitudes. However, both longitudinal and experimental studies support the hypothesis that televised sex roles influence children's sex stereotypes and attitudes. Indeed, a reciprocal interactive effect has been noted, in that adolescents' degree of sex typing influences their choice of programs. Girls who hold more stereotyped views of femininity prefer game shows and soap operas, while boys are more likely to watch action-oriented programs, including those with violence. The stereotypes presented in these programs reinforce the adolescents' ideas of what it means to be male or female. Because the normal developmental process of gender intensification heightens their sensitivity to models for gender-specific behavior, young adolescents may have a particular vulnerability to the influence of sex-typed portrayals. On the positive side, depictions of adults in atypical roles can influence early adolescents in terms of attitudes and possibly in terms of behavior, as well.

TRENDS TOWARD MORE FLEXIBLE GENDER ROLES

In recent years, social and developmental psychologists have moved away from considering rigid distinctions between sex roles to be the norm and have found instead that some degree of androgyny allows for more flexibility in functioning and seems to be associated with increased self-esteem. It is interesting that psychoanalysts, in parallel fashion, have moved toward an understanding of bisexuality as a basic aspect of human nature and a component of mature adult gender and sexual identity.

In today's world, there are many conscious attempts to promote more flexibility in gender roles. Parents commonly encourage their daughters to engage in sports, and high schools and colleges have increasingly emphasized women's athletics. Young boys are given dolls to play with by parents and later are taught cooking in high school. Insofar as cross-gender identifications are associated with better mental health, in terms of both a sense of well-being and happiness with oneself as well as better functioning in relationships and occupations, they are to be encouraged. It appears that cross-gender identifications are in fact increasingly prevalent, perhaps more so than ever before in history.

Conclusion

The mass of research data indicates that adolescence is a time of increasing differentiation according to gender, both in terms of behavior and in terms of how adolescents see themselves and their sense of who they are. Gender identity is extraordinarily complex and rooted in the earliest experiences of life; it subsequently unfolds under multiple influences, biological as well as social. While a core sense of being male or female is essential from very early in life, some flexibility in gender role is growth-enhancing. Socialization is in fact characterized by an interplay of opposing forces, with some tending to promote gender equality and others tending to reinforce stereotypes. During adolescence both biological and social forces act to intensify gender-related development. These forces tend to reinforce many kinds of competency in boys that are related to academic and work roles and to discourage these competencies in girls. Issues of gender identity and gender role remain quite complex and problematic for many adolescents, especially for girls.

REFERENCES

Baucom, D. H., Besch, P. K., & Callahan, S. (1985). Relation between testosterone concentration, sex role identity, and personality among females. *Journal of Personality and Social Psychology, 48,* 1218–1226.

Bezirganian, S., & Cohen, P. (1992). Sex differences in the interaction between temperament and parenting. *Journal of the American Adademy of Child and Adolescent Psychiatry, 31,* 790–801.

Camarena, P. M., Sarigiani, P. A., & Peterson, A. C. (1990). Gender-specific pathways to intimacy in early adolescence. *Journal of Youth and Adolescence, 19,* 19–32.

Cooper, C. R., & Grotevant, H. D. (1987). Gender issues in the interface of family experience and adolescents' friendship and dating identity. *Journal of Youth and Adolescence, 16,* 247–264.

Covey, L. A., & Feltz, D. L. (1991). Physical activity and adolescent female psychological development. *Journal of Youth and Adolescence, 20,* 463–474.

Friedman, R. C., & Downey, J. (1993). Neurobiology and sexual orientation: Current relationships. *Journal of Neuropsychology and Clinical Neurosciences, 5,* 131–133.

Galambos, N. L., Almeida, D. M., & Petersen, A. C. (1990). Masculinity, femininity and sex role. Attitudes in early adolescence: Exploring gender intensification. *Child Development, 61,* 1905–1914.

Gilligan, C. (1987). Adolescent development reconsidered. In C. E. Irwin, Jr. (Ed.), *Adolescent social behavior and health. New directions for child development* (pp. 63–92). San Francisco: Jossey-Bass.

Hetherington, E. M. (1972). The effects of father absence on personality development in adolescent daughters. *Developmental Psychology, 7,* 313–326.

Huston, A. C., & Alvarez, M. M. (1990). The socialization context of gender role development in early adolescence. In R. Montemayor, G. R. Adams, & T. P. Gullotta (Eds.), *From childhood to adolescence: A transitional period?* (pp. 159–179). Newbury Park, CA: Sage Publications.

Maccoby, E. E. (1990). Gender and relationships: A developmental account. *American Psychologist, 45,* 513–520.

Rapoport, T. (1991). Gender-differential patterns of adolescent socialization in three arenas. *Journal of Youth and Adolescence, 20,* 31–51.

Sandberg, D. E., Meyer-Bahlburg, H. F. L., Ehrhardt, A. A., & Yager, T. J. (1993). The prevalence of gender-atypical behavior in elementary school children. *Journal of the American Academy of Child and Adolescent Psychiatry, 32,* 306–314.

Shaywitz, B. A., Shaywitz, S. E., Pugh, K. R., Constable, R. T., Skudlarski, P., Fulbright, R. K., Bronen, R. A., Fletcher, J. M., Shankweiler, D. P., Katz, L., & Gore, J. C. (1995). Sex differences in the functional organization of the brain for language. *Nature, 373,* 607–609.

Weissman, S., & Barglow, P. (1980). Recent contributions to the theory of female adolescent psychological development. *Adolescent Psychiatry, 8,* 214–230.

Williams, S., & McGee, R. (1991). Adolescents' self-perceptions of their strengths. *Journal of Youth and Adolescence, 20,* 325–337.

Zucker, K. J. (1985). Cross-gender-identified children. In B. W. Steiner (Ed.), Gender dysphoria: Development, Research, Management (pp. 75–174). New York: Plenum Press.

19 / Developing a Homosexual Orientation in Adolescence

Max Sugar

In order to appreciate the events leading to the development of a preferred homosexual orientation in adolescence, a review of youngsters' personal histories is basic. This chapter attempts to provide such a review along with an account of some of the youngsters' experiences. It seeks as well to portray their dilemmas on the road to recognizing their orientation and then identifying themselves as homosexual, privately and publicly.

Most adolescents who are troubled about sexual orientation do not seek psychiatric services. For the most part, they are confused, ashamed, and confide in no one; some feel threatened by the idea of seeking help. A number are coerced into psychiatric evaluation by parents; and a few do seek help on their own in an attempt to clarify or to change their orientation.

Some recent research has focused on gender-dysphoric children and their associated gender and sexual identity problems (Brown, 1990; Lothstein, 1980; Sreenivasan, 1985; Westhead, Olson, & Meyer, 1990; Zucker, 1985; Zuger, 1984).

Sexual identity should be viewed as a part of total personality and not as if it were the sum and substance of the individual. If the latter approach prevails, then many serious diagnoses may be overlooked.

Some Pathways to a Homosexual Orientation

Although many biological theories have been presented as the basis for homosexual development, a recent detailed review concludes that the environment explains it (Byne & Parsons, 1993).

Most adolescents who identify as homosexual have a childhood history of feeling different from heterosexual youngsters (Bell, Weinberg, &

Hammersmith, 1981; Saghir & Robins, 1973). Therefore, a review of some aspects of their childhood seems appropriate.

The boy or girl with preoedipal cross-gender identification who will later experience gender dysphoria is likely to display atypical behavior from an early age (Roiphe & Spira, 1991). Such a child may become a social problem in nursery school. About 15% of children seen in a general child psychiatry clinic for conduct disorder and other conditions also have gender identity disorder (GID) or atypical GID (Sreenivasan, 1985).

The incidence of sex abuse of young males, using a broad definition, is considered to be 1 in 3 in Canada (Report of the Commission on Sexual Offences Against Children and Youth, 1984) and may be the same in the United States, but it is probably reported far less frequently than it occurs due to the stigma of homosexuality. It is unknown how many of these victims become homosexual later, but likely many youths seduced by older males, especially relatives, develop a homosexual orientation in adolescence.

Some young females may follow a similar path, their homosexuality deriving from sexual abuse, which may occur to 1 out of 2 (Report of the Commission, 1984). Sixty to 73% of prostitutes have been so victimized (Bagley & Young, 1987, Silbert & Pines, 1983).

The youngster who is sexually abused early in life may experience a pervasive sense of distrust, a marked loss of self-esteem, and difficulty with intimacy. The youngster who is abused repeatedly by a relative or parent in late latency or early adolescence may feel "different" and unsure of gender or sexual orientation. The confusion and a low of self-esteem, which is found on evaluation, appears to be subsumed during the abuse by the sense of acceptance and bribery by the adult. Some of these youngsters develop an erotized mode of relating to everyone indiscriminately.

Some authors consider homosexual development to be a defensive reaction to castration anxiety (Rangell, 1991; Socarides, 1968). Albeit well behaved, these youngsters may appear shy, withdrawn, depressed, and do not have a sense of belonging or a peer group in latency; alternatively, they may be quite popular and/or athletic and accepted all-round. With no history of cross-gender behavior, they nonetheless manifest a homosexual preference in adolescence.

Some youngsters who have a history of cross-dressing or preferential cross-gender play or behavior are eventually diagnosed in adolescence as schizophrenic, manic, or borderline. Among these are many who have participated in precocious and polymorphous perverse sexuality. A large percentage of such borderline cases have a history of early molestation (Lothstein, 1980; Meyer, 1980).

Some Possible Family Contributors

When there is inadequate mothering with threats of separation and abandonment, a little boy may develop cross-gender identification in an effort to manage the ensuing anxieties about abandonment by imitating the mother's dress and behavior and thus retaining a connection with her (Roiphe & Spira, 1991). When there is a deficit in early mothering and fathering with separation threats, losses, and family chaos, such a youngster develops cross-gender interests and identification, becomes gender dysphoric, and typically has additional psychiatric diagnoses (Meyer, 1980, 1982; Westhead et al., 1990).

Some little boys with gender identity disorder have mothers who cannot allow separation due to mother's own pathology. This situation promotes a fear of abandonment and ambivalence about gender identity in the children. An uninvolved or emotionally absent father fosters this development.

The mother of the girl who will have gender identity disorder in the future often regards femininity as inferior and is accordingly distant and rejecting to her daughter. Such a mother is unable to tolerate the normal identification process in early childhood and avoids the little girl. The father may then act as a shield to the child, nurture and protect her against the mother's aggression.

This situation fosters a masculine identification in the girl (Westhead et al., 1990).

Katz and Walsh (1991) found that: the adult male is regarded as powerful and engenders fear in the young male and female; the adult male has considerable persuasive power to have a youngster "engage in atraditional gender activity" (p. 349); and fathers play a more significant role in sex-role socialization than mothers. It seems likely that since adult males are viewed as more powerful in gender socialization than females, the father who is either permissive of or neutral toward cross-gender behavior may thus passively legitimize it.

In the histories of male homosexuals (Saghir & Robins, 1973), 84% had an emotionally or physically absent father who was uninvolved with his son. The boy then identified with his mother and had a negative identification with father. Female homosexuals, on the other hand, felt they identified with the father (77%) or had no parent with whom to identify; many had a dominant mother (53%) with whom they had a poor relationship (67%) but had a closer and more mutual relationship with their father (Saghir & Robins, 1973).

A number of different studies cite a probability, ranging from 50 to 100%, that children who are gender-dysphoric or who persistently behave in a cross-gender manner will develop a homosexual orientation (Bell et al., 1981; Davenport, 1986; Green, 1987; Harry, 1982; Money & Russo, 1979; Westhead et al., 1990; Whitan, 1977; Zuger, 1984).

From a retrospective study of male adults, Hellman, Green, Gray, and Williams (1981) considered that "childhood cross-gender behavior was most prevalent in the transsexual group, moderate among the homosexuals, and least evident in the heterosexual sample. . . . The probability of a homosexual outcome was greatest in subjects with a history in the mid-range of the 'feminine' continuum" (p. 914).

Experiences on the Road to Homosexuality

The details to be presented of these boys and girls in latency and adolescence should provide a fuller view of their experiences.

THE BOY IN LATENCY

Investigations reveal that the gender-atypical male toddler may begin diverging from the usual masculine path at age 2 (Roiphe & Spira, 1991). He is likely to have unpleasant experiences with peers before attaining school age.

In 72% of cases, the boy who is on the road to homosexuality feels different from his same-sex peers beginning in grade school (Bell et al., 1981). Troiden (1989) describes the childhood experience of the homosexual as one of marginality and the perception of being different. For instance, such boys are more interested in the arts than are the other boys; they dislike sports, roughhousing, and boys' games; they never learn to fight; they like ribbons, flowers, and music. They are called sissies, girls, and obscenities by male peers, but most think of themselves as heterosexual.

Before age 12, only 20% feel sexually different from their peers but 31% are sexually interested in the same sex before age 6 (Remafedi, 1987b). Sixty-seven percent were called "sissy," played with girls, had no male buddies, and enjoyed girls' activities (Saghir & Robins, 1973). They showed childhood gender nonconformity, which is a very strong predictor of adult sexual preference.

In recalling their childhood, homosexual men spoke of themselves as very passive and submissive; very few described themselves as being strong. They were aware of the same-sex attraction by age 13 (Troiden, 1989).

THE GIRL IN LATENCY

In their early development, 72% of female homosexuals feel different from other girls during grade school. The girl who becomes homosexual has grown up being disinterested in dolls and boys, interested more in outdoor activities, did not see herself like the others, did not express or show her feelings, and did not enjoy playing hopscotch, jacks, or house like the other girls. In preadolescence 70% were tomboys, and 63% had recurring wishes for cross-gender change and fantasied having a penis (Saghir & Robins, 1973).

Only 20% of them felt sexually different from their peers before age 12. While growing up, the majority of lesbians were very masculine, mostly dominant, and displayed childhood gender non-

conformity. In childhood, 44% of them had homosexual feelings (Bell et al., 1981).

LATENCY EXPERIENCES FOR BOYS AND GIRLS

In latency those with persistent cross-gender behavior are asynchronous with peers, prefer to play with opposite-sex peers, and encounter rejection, ridicule, ostracism, or attacks by same-sex peers. They are usually less active than their peers, withdrawn, and avoid groups. This state of affairs interferes with normal socialization in latency. The cross-gender behavior usually continues until family or social pressures persuade them to hide this. These youngsters may feel quite confused about gender and sexual identity. Collectively, all this interferes with the usual development of character structure in latency.

MALE ADOLESCENT EXPERIENCES

The reports of adults' recollections and of groups of adolescent homosexuals are from selected groups that are not representative of the homosexual population at large. They are helpful in telling us about those who have made a commitment to homosexuality but not about the adolescent who has yet to identify.

At ages 11 to 16, 69% of homosexual adults experienced themselves as feeling sexually different, that is, they were erotically interested in the same sex (Troiden, 1989).

Their first self-identification is at 14 and first homosexual experience to orgasm is age 15 (Remafedi, 1987b). According to Saghir and Robins (1973), Troiden (1989), and Troiden and Goode (1980), the age of homosexual self-identification recalled by adult males was between 19 and 21. The average age of first self-identification as a homosexual according to Boxer and Cohler (1989) and Gerstel, Feraios, and Herdt (1989) is 16.7 years. The difference in these figures are hard to understand, yet they are not explained by the authors. Perhaps it is due to difference in the cohorts, research methods, or more openness about the subject in the last decade.

Roesler and Deisher (1972) noted that 55% of homosexuals had been victims of verbal abuse and 30% of physical assault because of their sexual orientation. They had been discriminated against in employment, housing, and education (37%). Sixty percent had extreme emotional turmoil requiring psychiatric evaluation and/or treatment, and 33% had attempted suicide. Remafedi (1987a) notes the following figures:

extremely marked academic difficulties	80%
mental health problems	72%
substance abuse	58%
runaways	48%
problems with the law	48%
sexually transmitted diseases	45%
truancy	39%
suicide attempts	34%
psychiatric hospitalization	31%
school dropouts	28%
chemical dependency treatment	17%
prostitution	17%

Large numbers also were subjected to verbal and physical abuse.

In high school, 86% tended to be less masculine generally and felt different from age-mate males. More than 80% felt sexually different from their peers during their growing-up years, and they had a negative identification with their father. Before age 14: 78% had a romantic attachment to a male, 76% were sexually aroused by a male, and 65% had romantic or sexual fantasies or imaging of males. Fifty-three percent of them were labeled as homosexual by others before age 19, and the majority were promiscuous and unfaithful before 20 (Saghir & Robins, 1973). Only 10% were labeled by others before they were self-labeled as homosexual.

Before age 19: 95% had been aroused by a male, 62% had been aroused sexually by a female, and 49% of those who had a heterosexual encounter had a positive attitude about it. The first ejaculation was at age 12 or 13, and the adolescents studied had fewer orgasms in their sleep compared to the heterosexual (Bell et al., 1981).

FEMALE ADOLESCENT EXPERIENCES

Before age 14, 80% of lesbians had a romantic attachment to a female, 66% had romantic same-sex fantasies or imagery, and 46% had experienced sexual arousal by a female. Until age 20, 88% of the females studied were faithful (Saghir & Robins, 1973).

Based on adult recall, the women were aware of same-sex attraction between age 14 and 16 (Troiden, 1989); at 17 (Roesler & Deisher, 1972) they first understood the meaning of being homosexual; they engaged in their first homosexual act at 20, and self-defined at 21 to 23. According to Roesler and Deisher (1972), they were 16 to 17 years of age when they first began "coming out" and self-identified at 18. Boxer and Cohler (1989) and Gerstel et al. (1989), indicate that girls come out now at age 16.0. As with the differences in the figures for male "coming out," these differences may be due to different cohorts, research methods, or more openness about the topic in recent years.

Homosexual girls are less often the object of assaults and verbal teasing than homosexual boys since tomboyishness and masculine behavior among girls are more generally accepted than feminine behavior in boys. Girls are also less active sexually than boys, since their sexual activity is based on relationship-seeking, in contrast to the boys', which is sexual gratification-seeking. Schneider (1989) focuses on the special additional problem for the lesbian adolescent in identity, self-esteem, and socialization, which is different from that of the male homosexual due to more confusion and a later onset of feeling same-sex attraction.

The adolescence of homosexual females is markedly different from that of heterosexuals. By age 19, 74% of lesbians saw themselves as different from their same-sex peers. Twenty-one percent of these females were never aroused by the opposite sex, and 12% never had a sexual encounter with the opposite sex (Troiden, 1989). Thus, 88% of lesbian teenagers did have such encounters.

According to Troiden (1989) before age 19, 36% of the girls were labeled as homosexual by others, 73% were sexually aroused by females, and 75% had some sexual encounter with a woman; in 95% of cases, the encounter was physical. These girls were lonely, unhappy, and alienated, and the majority were not dating heterosexually in high school. They had more sexual experiences in the high school years compared to the heterosexual girls, mostly with acquaintances or friends (77%).

For a minority of these girls, their first homosexual encounter was in a group. Troiden (1989) found that homosexual arousal in childhood as well as adolescent homosexual involvement were significant precursors of adult homosexual development.

IDENTIFYING AS A HOMOSEXUAL

Rejected and isolated gay adolescents are among the loneliest people in high school (Tartagni, 1978). Hetrick and Martin (1987) listed isolation, family violence, educational and emotional stresses, shelter seeking, and sexual abuse as the main concerns of homosexual-oriented youth as they seek to cope with a socially stigmatized role. But before they can accept the role, they are faced with innumerable stresses. A recent added stress is the fact that by identifying at an earlier age, as indicated, they do so at a time when they are in a stage of unsettled adolescent development, and they may not be able to cope and adjust as well as they might several years later. In addition, there is now the AIDS epidemic, which may have the opposite effect and help delay their homosexual identification.

Cass (1979) described a theoretical 6-stage model for the homosexual to develop a fully integrated identity. At the outset, a private identity is established first; the final identity is a public one when the two identities become one. This is a process dependent on time, with different durations for males and females and, indeed, for each individual before the final stage is achieved. She felt that while it was "ultimately impossible to achieve the homosexual defining matrix that is totally (cognitively and affectively) congruent, it is possible, however, for incongruency to be reduced to a level both tolerable and manageable" (p. 222).

Troiden (1989) traced a 4-stage model that he felt was more in keeping with the realities of a homosexual developing an identity. The outcome could vary from a marginal type of arrangement to one of acceptance and pride along with commitment. He categorized the stages as: sensitization, identity confusion, identity assumption, and commitment. Briefly, he felt the sensitization stage built on the preceding childhood experiences as a necessary condition.

Confusion begins when the adolescent starts reflecting that he or she could be homosexual. The uncertainty shifts so that by mid- or late adolescence the perception is one of beginning to think "probably homosexual." For the male, the average age when this occurs is 17; for the female, it is 18. With the accumulation of experiences of homosexual and heterosexual arousal and behavior, there comes an altered perception of the self. The stigma about homosexuality becomes apparent along with inaccurate knowledge about homosexuality.

The youngster may handle this confused identity state through denial, trying to eradicate homosexual feelings, getting treatment, avoidance of homosexual behavior, redefining the situation and largely rationalizing it, or accepting that he or she is homosexual and decreasing the isolation. These efforts may go on for years with fluctuations in various directions as the youth struggles to handle his or her situation.

The adolescent who is preferentially homosexual-minded, who is gender-typical in overt behavior, and who is at the same time heterosexually active and homosexually inexperienced, has more confusion about sexual identity because the characteristics are at variance with the prevailing stereotypes. Such a teenager does not know where he or she fits in.

Identity assumption consists of self-definition as a homosexual and presenting oneself to other homosexuals; it is part of "coming out." Coming out occurs much later than actual homosexual encounters or feeling that one is so oriented. Without contact with at least one homosexual, it seems that only a minority of these young people define themselves as such. When assumption of homosexual status does take place, there is identity tolerance and acceptance, regular association with other homosexuals, and experimentation and exploration of the homosexual subculture. For the female, identity assumption occurs between 21 and 23. This is later than the male since for her it is mostly defined in terms of emotional involvement.

A negative contact with other homosexuals may lead to avoiding identity assumption. There may be fear of blackmail, physical attacks, AIDS, stigma, criticism, and discrimination in various areas. To avoid this stigma, some may try to avoid all homosexual activity, which leads to self-hate and despair; or they may "minstrelize," that is, manifest stereotyped gender-inappropriate behavior; they may pass and conceal their behavior and interests from their family and friends; or they may involve themselves in "group alignment," that is, become actively involved in the homosexual community (Troiden, 1989).

In stage 4, Troiden (1989) feels the youngster has made a commitment to a way of life, enters same-sex love relations, and perceives this as a valid, natural self-identity. This occurs for females around age 22 to 23 usually with a first love affair with a same-sex person. For the male, this occurs at age 21 to 24, also via being involved in a love affair with a same-sex person. Disclosure to heterosexuals is more likely to be done first with siblings or close heterosexual friends rather than to parents or employers. Males tell their heterosexual friends between age 23 and 28, and females tell their heterosexual friends around age 28. Since the onset of the AIDS epidemic, homosexuals have been less willing to disclose their sexual orientation to heterosexuals. Both sexes put off telling the family until later still—around age 28 for males and 30 for females (Troiden, 1989).

ADOLESCENT PERSONALITY DEVELOPMENT AND CONSOLIDATION

Isay (1986) indicates that consolidation of sexual identity is delayed in the male homosexual until late adolescence or later, and that its development continues throughout his life. Troiden (1989) maintains that for both males and females, homosexual identity is an emergent organization that spans a lifetime and is never fully determined in a fixed absolute sense. It involves "striving at but never arriving."

The recent public identification of some popular figures as homosexual may provide some positive and ego ideals for homosexual youth, but the AIDS epidemic and the prospect of succumbing to a fatal and frightening disease at an early age counterbalance this new openness.

Unless they identify publicly as homosexual, adolescents on the path to homosexuality have to maintain a double identity. Usually they attempt not to behave overtly like the homosexual stereotype in order to avoid censure, criminal charges, and prejudice in educational, vocational, and social pursuits. These adolescents therefore are very sensitive to the environment; many will try to cover up and behave like heterosexuals. Some also may have heterosexual fantasies, dates, and intercourse parallel with a simultaneous homosexual orientation and yearnings to fulfill their sexual aims with same-sex, like-minded people.

Those on the road to homosexuality usually experience some degree of anxiety and confusion during their early adolescence; others use denial, with the need to hide. Values, identification models, and ego ideals are limited and unclear. Instead of the usual effort to conform to a teenage peer group, these youngsters try to pass as if conforming. Simultaneously they struggle with a sense of being different and perhaps, or probably, homosexual. A stable and realistic self-representation therefore is unavailable at this time. Similarly, self-esteem is difficult to regulate and achieve. Instead of being able to turn to authority figures other than the parents, these youths have to hide their inner selves. They have a problem sharing values with others, identifying with other authorities and their values, and developing a self-critical ego to supplant the self-valuing aspects of the superego. Without the wide choices among ego ideals and socialization opportunities available to the heterosexual adolescent, the homosexual youngster has additional difficulty in pursuing ego and superego development.

Further character formation is a significant part of adolescent development. For this to occur, the youngster has to have some resolution of the second individuation process, deal with residual trauma from childhood, develop ego continuity, and establish a sexual identity. These efforts are all involved in the personality consolidation of late adolescence (Blos, 1979). Where, however, the change from the latency sexual orientation involves a step toward considering oneself homosexual, ego continuity is clearly absent. The trauma that these youngsters may have had in latency related to cross-gender behavior may continue privately or openly in adolescence. Their individuation process involves a negative oedipal solution, and sexual orientation is unsettled. With these problems unresolved, consolidation of personality in adolescence is precluded for the homosexual adolescent.

Conclusion

For youngsters who develop a homosexual identity, their childhood usually is different from that of average children. Such youngsters have a very lonely, frightening, confusing experience in adolescence. The path is also filled with risks—physical, social, legal, educational, and vocational.

With varying stops, detours, and experiences, these youngsters have difficulty learning and then accepting their homosexuality. Sexual identity may be partly consolidated in adolescence or early adulthood; for most, it is an incomplete achievement until later. Consolidation of personality does not occur in adolescence.

REFERENCES

Bagley, C., & Young, L. (1987). Juvenile prostitution and child sexual abuse. *Canadian Journal of Community Mental Health, 6,* 5–26.

Bell, A., Weinberg, M., & Hammersmith, S. (1981). *Sexual preference: Its development in men and women.* Bloomington: Indiana University.

Bieber, I., Dain, H., Dince, P. R., Drellich, M. G., Kremer, M. W., Grand H. B., Grundlach, R. H., Rifkin, A. H., Wilbur, C. B., & Bibber, T. B., (1962). *Homosexuality: A psychoanalytic study.* New York: Basic Books.

Blos, P. (1979). *The adolescent passage.* New York: International Universities Press.

Boxer, A. M., & Cohler, B. J. (1989). The life course of gay and lesbian youth: An immodest proposal for the study of lives. *Journal of Homosexuality, 17,* 315–335.

Brown, G. R. (1990). A review of clinical approaches to gender dysphoria. *Journal of Clinical Psychiatry, 51,* 57–64.

Byne, W., & Parsons, B. (1993). Human sexual orientation. *Archives of General Psychiatry, 50,* 228–239.

Cass, V. C. (1979). Homosexual identity formation: A theoretical model. *Journal of Homosexuality, 4,* 219–235.

Davenport, C. W. (1986). A follow-up of 10 feminine boys. *Archives of Sexual Behavior, 15,* 511–517.

Gerstel, C., Feraios, A. J., & Herdt, G. (1989). Widening circles: An ethnographic profile of a youth group. *Journal of Homosexuality, 17,* 75–92.

Green, R. (1987). *The "sissy boy syndrome" and the development of homosexuality.* New Haven, CT: Yale University Press.

Harry, J. (1982). *Gay children grown up:* gender culture and gender deviance. New York: Praeger.

Hellman, R. E., Green, R., Gray, J. L., & Williams, K. (1981). Childhood sexual identity, childhood religiosity and homophobia as an influence in the development of transsexualism, homosexuality, and heterosexuality. *Archives of General Psychiatry, 38,* 910–915.

Hetrick, E. S., & Martin, A. D. (1987). Developmental issues and their resolution for gay and lesbian adolescents. *Journal of Homosexuality, 14,* 25–43.

Isay, R. (1986). The development of sexual identity in homosexual men. *Psychoanalytic Study of the Child, 41,* 467–489.

Katz, P. A., & Walsh, P. V. (1991). Modification of children's gender-stereotyped behavior. *Child Development, 62,* 338–351.

Lothstein, L. M. (1980). The adolescent gender dysphoric patient: An approach to management and treatment. *Journal of Pediatric Psychology, 5,* 93–109.

Meyer, J. K. (1980). Body ego, selfness, and gender sense: The development of gender identity. *Psychiatric Clinics of North America, 3,* 21–36.

Meyer, J. K. (1982). The theory of gender identity disorders. *Journal of the American Psychoanalytic Association, 30,* 381–418.

Money, J., & Russo, A. J. (1979). Homosexual outcome of discordant gender identity/role longitudinal follow-up. *Journal of Pediatric Psychology, 4,* 29–41.

Rangell, L. (1991). Castration. *Journal of the American Psychoanalytic Association, 39,* 3–24.

Remafedi, G. (1987b). Male homosexuality: The adolescent's perspective. *Pediatrics, 79,* 326–330.

Remafedi, G. (1987a). Adolescent homosexuality: Psychosocial and medical complications. *Pediatrics, 79,* 331–337.

Report of the Commission on Sexual Offences Against Children and Youth. (1984). *Sexual Offences Against Children* (Vol I, p. 175). Ottawa: Canadian Government Publication.

Roesler, T., & Deisher, R. W. (1972). Youthful male homosexuality. *Journal of the American Medical Association, 219,* 1018–1023.

Roiphe, H., & Spira, N. (1991). Object loss, aggression and gender identity. *Psychoanalytic Study of the Child, 46,* 37–50.

Saghir, M., & Robins, E. (1973). *Male and female homosexuality: A comprehensive investigation.* Baltimore: Williams & Wilkins.

Schneider, M. (1989). Sappho was a right-on adolescent: Growing up lesbian. In B. Herdt (Ed.), *Gay and lesbian youth* (pp. 111–129). New York: Haworth.

Silbert, M., & Pines, A. M. (1983). Early sexual exploitation as an influence in prostitution. *Social Work, 28,* 285–289.

Socarides, C. W. (1968). A provisional theory of aetiology in male homosexuality. *International Journal of Psycho-Analysis*, 49, 27–37.

Sreenivasan, M. B. (1985). Effeminate boys in a child psychiatric clinic: Prevalence and associated factors. *Journal of the American Academy of Child Psychiatry*, 24, 689–694.

Tartagni, D. (1978). Counseling gays in a school setting. *School Counseling*, 26, 26–32.

Troiden, R. R. (1989). The formation of homosexual identities. In G. Herdt (Ed.), *Gay and lesbian youth* (pp. 43–92). New York: Haworth.

Troiden, R. R., & Goode, E. (1980). Variables related to the acquisition of a gay identity. *Journal of Homosexuality*, 5, 383–392.

Westhead, V., Olson, S. & Meyer, J. K. (1990). Gender identity disorders in adolescence. In M. Sugar (Ed.), *Atypical adolescence and sexuality* (pp. 87–107). New York: W. W. Norton.

Whitan, F. L. (1977). Childhood indicators of male homosexuality. *Archives of Sexual Behavior*, 6, 89–96.

Zucker, K. J. (1985). Childhood gender disturbances: Diagnostic issues. *Journal of the American Academy of Child Psychiatry*, 21, 274–280.

Zuger, B. (1984). Early effeminate behavior in boys: Outcome and significance for homosexuality. *Journal of Nervous & Mental Disease*, 172, 90–97.

20 / Adolescent Sexuality, Contraception, and Abortion

Sheridan Phillips

Sexual activity among American teenagers has increased dramatically over the past 40 years, largely because sexual intercourse is now initiated at a younger age. National estimates are not available prior to 1970, but Kinsey's data, based on a predominantly white population in the late 1940s, reported that 3% of females and 39% of males had engaged in intercourse by age 15. (See Rodgers, 1992.) By 1979, national estimates for white teenagers reported that 18% of females and 54% of males were sexually experienced by age 15 (O'Reilly & Aral, 1988). Urban rates are even higher: In 1981 and 1982, 35% of white females and 66% of white males in inner-city Baltimore reported being nonvirgins at age 15 (Rodgers, 1992).

The earlier onset of sexual intercourse has resulted in larger numbers of teenagers who are sexually active. National estimates in 1988 indicate that approximately 50% of females and 80% of males have engaged in sexual intercourse by age 19 (Sonenstein, Pleck, & Ku, 1991). Consistent effects of gender and race have been found, with the onset of sexual activity in females lagging behind that of males and black teenagers generally being more sexually precocious than white teenagers (O'Reilly & Aral, 1988).

Gender differences in the onset of intercourse cannot be explained by the age of onset of puberty and thus appear to reflect psychosocial norms, with different expectations for adolescent males and females. The ADSEX survey of junior high and high school students in two metropolitan communities found that approximately 35% of black males and 10% of white males reported prepubertal coitus (at age 9 or younger) whereas virtually no females reported first intercourse below the age of 10 (Rodgers, Billy, & Udry, 1982). While these encounters are different from the typical experience of first intercourse and may be interpreted in several ways, it is clear that prepubertal sexual activity is not well understood and may contribute to gender differences found in sexual activity.

Consistent gender differences in sexual activity do parallel most adolescents' reports of their first experience with intercourse (Kahn, Kalsbeek, & Hofferth, 1988). Both males and females typically had a partner who was older (1 year older for males and 3 years older for females) and who was believed to be sexually experienced; this was especially true for young women's perceptions of their partners. If young women generally are introduced to sexual intercourse by older partners, and subsequently introduce younger males to intercourse, this would account for the greater sexual precocity observed for male adolescents.

Racial differences in sexual experiences may again reflect different psychosocial norms for black and white teenagers (Stanton et al., 1993.) However, they may also represent racial differences in the sequence of sexual experience. The ADSEX survey (Rodgers et al., 1982) reported that white teenagers typically progress from holding hands to kissing to petting and intercourse, moving from necking to feeling breast clothed, feeling breast directly, feeling female sex organs directly, feeling penis directly, and then intercourse. In contrast, black teenagers reported intercourse as occurring before any of the three unclothed petting behaviors. (Black females were particularly inconsistent in their progression through these sexual behaviors.) These differences in the sequence of sexual experiences may at least partly explain the apparently greater sexual precocity of black teenagers.

Although teenagers are drawn to sexual activity, there are consistent reports that the experience is not always satisfactory or even desired. Kahn, Smith, and Roberts (1984) surveyed 288 adolescents (26% of whom had had intercourse) and found that 24% of the females and 16% of the males reported that they had made out, petted, or had coitus with someone when they did not really want to; 38% of females and 19% of males stated that they were unable to refuse when their partners wanted to engage in sexual activities. Kalof's (1995) further analysis of these data indicated that white females were most subject to coercion while black females were the least influenced; for black females, she reports that egalitarian gender role attitudes are inversely correlated with susceptibility to coercive sexual experience. Warzak, Grow, Poler, and Walburn (1995) interviewed 107 female teenagers who had experienced intercourse; according to their findings, 54% had engaged in sexual activity when they did not want to and 45% believed that they lacked effective refusal skills. (No racial differences were reported.) The teenagers rated contexts in which it was particularly difficult to refuse, with the top-rated one being "I had to have unwanted sexual activity with my partner because I love him." The pressure to engage in unwanted sex increased with the couple's history as sexual partners; the fourth-highest context was "Once I became sexually active with a partner, I felt I had to continue . . ." These studies indicate that, while sexual activity can be physically, emotionally, and/or socially gratifying, it is not always satisfactory for sexually active adolescents. The emotional consequences of such experiences are poorly understood.

In summary, while not all teenagers are sexually active, most have engaged in intercourse by age 19. The aggregate extent of this sexual activity has prompted concern about adolescents' potential exposure to sexually transmitted diseases (STDs) and the risk of unwanted pregnancy. Although protection against STDs and pregnancy are clearly interrelated issues, the focus of this chapter is on the potential for pregnancy and its sequelae. In 1985, 1,031,000 teenagers became pregnant; 31,000 of them were under 15 (Henshaw & VanVort, 1989). While pregnancy rates among sexually experienced teenagers actually have declined 19% from 1972 to 1990, the overall teenage pregnancy rate has increased by 23% because the proportion of sexually active teens has grown (Alan Guttmacher Institute, 1994).

Premature pregnancies are a national concern due to the potential adverse consequences for the teenager and her baby (Friedman & Phillips, 1982) as well as for society. Using data from Aid to Families with Dependent Children, Food Stamps, and Medicaid, a cost study from the Center for Population Options assessed the societal cost in 1990 of teenage childbearing (Center for Population Options, 1992). National cost per year for all families started by a teenage birth were $25.1 billion. However, an annual savings of $10 billion could be anticipated if these births could have been delayed until the teenager reached 20. The potential reduction of both social and personal costs has prompted increased scrutiny of adolescent contraception.

Adolescent Sexual Activity and Contraception

Young women are typically introduced to sexual intercourse by a partner who is older, presumed to be more sexually experienced, and is known fairly well (Kahn et al., 1988). Reasons for initiating intercourse vary with the individual teenager and can be quite unrelated to sex per se (Friedman & Phillips, 1982). Generally, however, teenagers cite reasons related to their partner. A significant minority (15%) feel that their partner forced them to engage in intercourse; another 20% say that they wanted to please the partner or avoid hurting him (Rodgers, 1992). The most common reason given is "so that my partner would love me more" (Rodgers, 1992). This first sexual encounter is generally experienced as romantic and spontaneous. It is rarely planned (at least by the young woman) (see Zelnick, Kantner, & Ford, 1981) and often occurs in the context of leisure and summer fun: Approximately half of high school teenagers lose their virginity between May and August (Kahn et al., 1988). It is therefore not surprising that, for many young women, first intercourse is unprotected intercourse.

Data gathered in the late 1970s indicated that more than half of female adolescents did not use any form of contraception at first intercourse (Mosher & McNally, 1991). This fact was of particular concern because one-fifth of teenage pregnancies occurred in the first month after they began intercourse (Mosher & McNally, 1991), and the mean time between first intercourse and pregnancy was 6 months (Kahn et al., 1988). More recent reports, however, are more encouraging. The number of young women who used any form of contraception at first intercourse increased from 48% in 1982 to 65% in 1988 (Forrest & Singh, 1990). This change results almost entirely from increased use of condoms by their partners. It seems clear that there has been a significant change in teenagers' willingness to use condoms, especially among non-Hispanic white adolescents (Mosher & McNally, 1991; Sonenstein et al., 1991). It may be that mass media efforts to educate the public about AIDS have globally enhanced the acceptability of condom use, even though a teenager's use of condoms does not appear directly related to his perception of himself as being at risk for HIV (Brown, DiClemente, & Park, 1992; Pendergast, DuRant, & Gailard, 1992).

While it is encouraging that more teenagers are protected at first intercourse, there are still significant numbers who are not. Teenagers' contraceptive—or noncontraceptive—behavior at first intercourse varies tremendously, reflecting age and demographic differences as well as characteristics of the individual teenager. At one end of the continuum, 17% of women ages 15 to 24 make their first family planning visit *before* first intercourse (Mosher & Horn, 1988). Other young women are protected at first intercourse by their partner's use of a condom, but over one-third are not protected at all.

Demographic analysis of contraceptive use at first intercourse (Mosher & McNally, 1991) indicates that white women were more likely to use some method than black women, with Jewish women most likely and Hispanic women least likely to use any method. Fundamentalist Protestants were less likely to use any method than other Protestants or Catholics. Women were more likely to use some contraception if their mothers had completed high school and if they were older at first intercourse. Aspects of the woman's community (socioeconomic status and employment opportunities) were also significantly related to contraception use, after controlling for individual characteristics.

For one out of five young women, becoming sexually active is a planned experience that includes the conscious decision to use contraception (Zelnik et al., 1981). Such teenagers tend to be older and to come from social backgrounds that promote higher expectations for the future, encourage them to protect themselves from threats to this future, and consider the use of contraception as both common and normal. One key factor is the perception that they have something to lose if they were to become pregnant. This, together with perceived social acceptance of contraception, presumably provides the psychological impetus to take active steps to ensure their protection prior to first intercourse.

For the remaining four out of five young women, one cannot accurately discuss a *decision* to use or avoid contraception. First intercourse is not a planned experience for most young women; it "just happens." Clinical experience suggests that teenagers perceive themselves as "swept away" in an intense tide of romance, emotion, and/or physical pleasure. Methodical planning ahead is the antithesis of this experience, which, for many teenagers, may *need* to be spontaneous and unanticipated. The most promising intervention strategy may be to promote the attitude that (1) young men should keep condoms readily available to show respect and care for a young woman should she become swept away and (2) that a young woman should expect this as a demonstration that her partner cares about her. Because it is still substantially more acceptable for male teenagers to carry condoms than for females (DuRant, Sanders, Jay, & Levinson, 1988), the focus on male responsibility may be more useful, at least with regard to first intercourse.

Following first intercourse, teenagers' sexual activity is erratic (Rodgers, 1992). Over one-quarter of young women report only one instance of intercourse with their first partner. When nonvirgins were asked about intercourse in the past month, 35% of the young women reported none, while 26% had had intercourse at least once per week.

Use of contraception follows an equally varied course. Ten percent of young women make their first family planning visit within 1 month following first intercourse (Mosher & Horn, 1988), joining the 17% who did so prior to intercourse. The remaining 73% of young women wait an average of 23 months after first intercourse before making their first family planning visit (Mosher & Horn, 1988), and 36% of them do so because they suspect they are pregnant (Zabin & Clark, 1981).

Why do so many teenagers wait so long to take active steps to protect themselves against pregnancy? Because female adolescents are hardly a homogeneous group, no single answer applies to all. However, several psychological and social issues appear related to contraceptive behavior. One key issue is the adolescent's *sexual identity*. Acknowledging one's own sexuality is a prerequisite for making an active decision to use contraception. Because the incorporation of sexuality as part of one's identity is one of the developmental tasks of adolescence, teenagers who have not completed this task may deny that they are "sexual beings" and view occasions of sexual intercourse as temporary lapses that will not recur. This may continue until a pregnancy scare or frequent, regular intercourse prompts the teenager to recognize and accept her sexuality and hence the need to take active steps to avoid conception. Indeed, frequency of intercourse has been identified as the primary trigger for the decision to use a systematic method of contraception (DeLamater, 1983; DuRant, Sanders, Jay, & Levinson, 1990).

Another psychological characteristic of adolescents is their sense of *invulnerability,* prompting a variety of risk-taking behaviors. Sexual risk is increasingly being conceptualized as only one of a class of risk behaviors common in adolescence (Jessor, 1991). While risk-taking is heightened in adolescence generally, there also appears to be a subset of teenagers who are likely to engage in more frequent or more serious risk-taking behaviors (Brown et al., 1992). In addition, the use of substances such as marijuana and alcohol has been reported to reduce the likelihood of condom use (Hingson, Strunin, & Berlin, 1990). This sense of invulnerability presumably underlies many of the apparently silly reasons teenagers state for nonuse of contraception, such as: "I didn't think it could happen to me," "I'm too young to be able to get pregnant," and "I don't have sex often enough to get pregnant" (Zabin & Clark, 1981; Zelnik et al., 1981).

Two "cost" factors related to *access* to contraception also influence teenage behavior. The advent of special programs has increased knowledge about and access to contraception, but some teenagers still cite expense and availability as at least contributory to the delay in seeking protection (Zabin & Clark, 1981). Note that the expense of any contraceptive method represents a significantly greater proportion of most teenagers' income than it does for most adults, and must compete with many other more enticing purchases. However, the most important "cost" associated with contraceptive use is teenagers' fear that their parents will learn that they are using contraception: 43% of teenagers cited this as the most important or one of the major reasons why they

delayed making a family planning visit (Zabin & Clark, 1981). A separate study of teenagers attending family planning clinics reported that approximately half of women under 18 believed that their parents knew about their attendance. For patients whose parents did not know, more than half said they would not continue to come if parental notification were required, although few of them (9%) would stop having sex (Torres, Forrest, & Eisman, 1980).

Any form of contraception requires *planning ahead* and taking active steps on *each* occasion of intercourse to prevent a *possible* consequence in the future. Despite their presumably greater awareness of the desirability of prevention, many adults do not engage in systematic behaviors to prevent future health risk. Adolescents have just entered the cognitive stage of formal operations and have less experience with abstract thought about hypothetical future events. Teenagers, especially those in early and midadolescence, are thus not well prepared to engage in systematic prevention. The clinician may be able to prompt a teenager to consider future risks and benefits of contraception by asking "When do you think you'll be ready to have a baby?" Teenagers commonly project an age several years older than their current age, setting the stage for discussion of their own goals and the potential benefit of contraception in achieving them. In an empirical study of this simple intervention, teenagers asked this question were subsequently more likely to say that they would use family planning services than those who were not asked (McDonald, Selmar, & Eitel, 1980).

Planning ahead to ensure protection also generally requires the physical possession of a contraceptive device, with the concomitant challenge of where to keep it so it is both readily available and undetected by parents. Being prepared for protection in advance can also pose concerns when this is the first occasion of intercourse with that partner. A young man carrying a condom may worry about what the young woman will think: Does he do this often and casually? Does he think she will be "easy" and thus is prepared? Has he planned methodically to seduce her this evening? A young woman may protect herself more inconspicuously by taking oral contraceptives routinely or inserting a diaphragm prior to a date, but any admission that she is protected immediately raises the same issues: Is she "easy"? Did she plan for this to happen tonight? Given the importance of romance and spontaneity for teenagers, such concerns can pose a real challenge to an adolescent's social skills.

All current methods of teenagers' contraception have some disadvantages. Concerns about *side effects* of oral contraceptives include fear of weight gain, breakthrough bleeding, amenorrhea, and increased cancer risk (Emans, Grace, & Woods, 1987; Zabin, Stark, & Emerson, 1991). Many young women may be influenced by their mothers' inaccurate perceptions of oral contraceptive side effects that date from their own experiences when doses were higher and side effects were more significant (American Academy of Family Practice Symposium, 1993). Inserting a diaphragm or sponge requires considerable skill. If not inserted prior to a date, insertion involves interruption of lovemaking and inserting the device when the teenager's emotional state and circumstances are hardly ideal for the task. Most women can describe amusing attempts to insert slippery diaphragms even when unhurried and in complete privacy. It is thus understandable that the adolescent novice may elect not to insert the device at the crucial moment even if it is available.

Condoms also require practice if they are to be used effectively and with a minimum of fumbling. Even when used skillfully, they necessitate an interruption in lovemaking and reduce sensation for the young man. Reduced sensation can actually be advantageous in prolonging what is often very brief intercourse in adolescence, but a teenager is unlikely to perceive this as an advantage unless he has learned about gender differences in arousal and orgasmic patterns and is motivated to maximize his partner's pleasure. In general, then, teenagers will be reluctant to use contraception unless they are comfortable with the method they choose and sufficiently skilled to use it with minimal interruption in lovemaking. Such skills involve both mechanics and communication; the best predictor of condom use may be the ability to discuss it with one's partner (Brown et al., 1992).

Levonorgestrel implants (Norplant) and medroxyprogesterone acetate injections (Depo-Provera) have recently provided other options for effective contraception. Despite public controversy regarding the availability of Norplant for teenagers (Bantsky, 1993), some school-based clinics have added it to their contraceptive services. The major advantages of these new methods are (1) they eliminate the need to employ active prevention every day (oral contraceptives) or at each occasion of intercourse (diaphragms and condoms), and (2) they are hidden. One study of adolescent mothers has shown that Norplant is a popular contraceptive option for teenagers who had had a contraceptive failure and pregnancy (Polaneczky, Slap, Forke, Rappaport, & Sondheimer, 1994). A survey by Gold and Coupey (1995) suggests that Depo-Provera may be even more popular than Norplant with young women who are not mothers (62% said they would agree to get an injection every three months to prevent pregnancy vs. 24% who would agree to have subdermal implants inserted). The advantages of Depo-Provera and Norplant must be weighed against the discomfort caused by injection and implantation/removal (removal causes significant pain for one-quarter of Norplant users) and the absence of protection against STDs. Cromer, Smith, Blair, Dwyer, and Brown (1994) also report that 80% of teenagers using Norplant or Depo-Provera had disrupted menstrual cycles (vs. over 80% of oral contraceptive users who maintained regular cycles). Other problematic side effects included nausea, dizziness, and fatigue. Finally, Blair, Cromer, Mahan, Zibners, and Naumovski (1995) suggest that Depo-Provera may suppress the expected skeletal bone mineralization in growing adolescent females. Unfortunately, then, advances in contraceptive technology have not completely resolved the disadvantages of regular contraceptive use.

Adolescents' contraceptive behavior is influenced by the *attitudes* of partners, peers, family, and the larger community. Although parental attitudes and expectations have relatively little effect on sexual behavior per se, they do significantly affect their teenagers' use of contraception (Brown et al., 1992). Given the transition of influence from parents to peers that occurs in mid-adolescence, it is not surprising to find that peer and partner support of contraception is also significantly related to its use (DuRant et al., 1990; Kastner, 1987). In fact, several studies suggest that the recent increase in condom use is more a function of peer attitudes than a teen's own perceived HIV risk (Brown et al., 1992; Pendergast et al., 1992). In the larger community as well,

more pronounced for nonwhites (99.5 per 1,000 in 1977 vs. 89.7 in 1985) than it is for whites (44.1 per 1,000 in 1977 vs. 42.8 in 1985). This decrease in adolescent fertility rates parallels that reported for most other developed countries, although the decline is generally more pronounced than that observed in the United States (Jones et al. 1986).

After the *Roe v. Wade* Supreme Court decision, the number of legal abortions in the United States rose sharply between 1973 and 1980. (See Adler et al., 1992.) For the past decade, approximately 1.5 to 1.6 million abortions have been performed annually (400,000–500,000 annually for teenagers) (Adler et al., 1992; Henshaw & Van Vort, 1989). In the aggregate, it is estimated that 21% of American women of childbearing age have experienced an elective abortion (Tietze, Forrest, & Henshaw, 1988).

Given the large number of women who elect to terminate a pregnancy, remarkably little is known about their decision-making process. Demographically, women who seek abortions tend to be young, unmarried, and nulliparous. (See Adler et al., 1992.) However, demographics do not tell us why one unmarried, nulliparous 18-year-old chooses to have an abortion while another does not. The absence of systematic study of this issue may well reflect the ethical difficulties inherent in investigating a highly emotional and personal process at a stressful time, compounded by the political sensitivity of this topic. One retrospective study of 206 adolescents did compare young women who had had abortions in the preceding 24 weeks with others who were successful contraceptors, currently pregnant, or mothers (Blum & Resnick, 1982). All teenagers completed six paper-and-pencil measures and participated in an interview that focused on critical incidents of sexual decision making. The abortion group was found to have the most developed future time perspective (capacity to understand future consequences), the lowest demand for external approval, and the lowest dependency needs of all four groups. Their comments typically indicated that they were not ready to have a child, and they more frequently discussed how having a baby would interfere with their plans for school and career. Some also noted the potential negative consequences for their babies. As with contraception, then, choosing abortion rather than having a baby may be pivotally related to teenagers' perceptions of the future and

their stage of cognitive development as well as to perceived attitudes of family, partner, and peers.

Substantially more information is available regarding the psychological impact and sequelae of abortion. The early literature, predominantly reporting case studies or findings from self-selected groups, focused on psychopathological responses following abortion (Friedman & Phillips, 1982). While such reports heightened awareness of the psychological distress that may follow an abortion, they are of limited utility in delineating the normative response and sequelae, due to inappropriate generalization from case studies or clinical samples or biased response measures that focus almost exclusively on pathological or negative outcomes (Adler et al., 1992).

More recent research has employed a theoretical framework of stress and coping, conceptualizing unwanted pregnancy and abortion as a potentially stressful complex of life events that can lead to a variety of outcomes, including growth and maturation as well as negative affect and psychopathology. If we consider empirical studies of American women undergoing legal abortions, it does not appear that the procedure poses major psychological hazards for most women (Adler et al., 1992). While mixed emotions are common postabortion, feelings of relief and happiness appear more dominant than those of guilt or sadness. For example, two to three months following a first-trimester abortion, three affective factors were identified for 70 women (Adler, 1975). Positive emotions (relief and happiness) were rated as most intense (mean of 3.96) on a scale from 1 (not at all) to 5 (extremely). Negative emotions that appeared socially based (shame, guilt, and fear of disapproval) had a mean intensity rating of 1.81. Negative emotions that appeared internally based (regret, anxiety, depression, doubt, and anger) had a mean intensity rating of 2.26.

Other investigations have measured psychological functioning and distress, typically reporting improvement from preabortion to just after the abortion and from preabortion or just after to several weeks postabortion (Adler et al., 1992). Longer-term studies compared women who had had abortions 13 months to 8 years previously with others who had not had abortions, and found no negative impact on psychological functioning and self-esteem nor any relationship between self-esteem and time elapsed since the abortion (Adler et al., 1992). A study of 360 black adolescents contrasted teenagers who (1) had a negative test, (2) tested positive and carried to term, and (3) tested positive and elected abortion. Data collected for each group included ratings of self-esteem, locus of control, and state and trait anxiety at the time they requested a pregnancy test and 1 year and 2 years later (Zabin, Hirsch, & Emerson, 1989). No adverse effects of the abortion experience were found; in fact, the abortion group demonstrated higher self-esteem than the negative pregnancy group at 2-year follow-up and higher internal orientation/locus of control than the childbearing group at both 1- and 2-year follow-up.

Overall, these data suggest that the time of greatest psychological distress is prior to the abortion and that most women are unlikely to experience adverse psychological effects after the abortion. Very long-term impact is still unclear. Studies of other stressful life events indicate that those who experience the most distress immediately after the event are those most likely to experience longer-term problems, suggesting that significant negative reactions are unlikely to emerge later for women who are functioning well 1 to 8 years post abortion (Adler et al., 1992). There may, however, be exceptions to this optimistic scenario, such as the woman who elects to have an abortion when young and subsequently is unable to conceive when she is ready to have a child.

While most women appear to cope well following an abortion, some do experience significant distress and other negative reactions. Several factors, many of which are intercorrelated, seem related to psychological outcome postabortion (Adler et al., 1992). Negative outcomes are more likely for women who are younger, nulliparous, and unmarried, and those whose culture or religion prohibits abortion. Psychological difficulties are more common for women who delay abortion until the second trimester; those who do delay are more likely to be black, nulliparous, and in unstable relationships (characteristics also associated with problems following first-trimester abortions). Women who report greater difficulty in making the decision and view the pregnancy as being highly meaningful to them are more likely to experience difficulty postabortion. Perceived social support from parents and partner generally contributes to better postabortion status, although the relationship between perceived and actual support is complex. Finally, women who expect that they will cope well with the abortion typically experience more positive outcomes and lessened negative reactions. The belief in one's ability to cope has been reported to have a causal effect on postabortion status: Counseling intervention that enhanced self-efficacy for coping, combined with standard counseling, was more effective in lowering depressive symptoms postabortion than standard abortion counseling alone (Mueller & Major, 1989).

The findings reported for American women are supported by a Danish study (David, Rasmussen, & Holst, 1981) that tracked psychiatric hospital admissions for 3 months postabortion and postpartum for all women under 50. (Women were excluded if they had had a psychiatric admission within the 15 months prior to abortion or delivery.) The majority of women were either never married or currently married; for this group, the risk of psychiatric admission was approximately the same both for those who had abortions and those who delivered (12 per 10,000 vs. 7 per 10,000). However, those who were separated, divorced, or widowed showed a higher psychiatric admission rate postabortion (64 per 10,000) than postdelivery (17 per 10,000). It may be that this latter group had fewer social supports, with abortion being more stressful without these protective factors. The authors also suggest that these women may experience more ambivalence about carrying their pregnancies to term, increasing the risk of adverse psychological reactions. If never married or currently married, though, Danish women do not appear to experience significant psychological risk as a consequence of abortion.

While abortion will never be an easy decision or process, the advent of "the abortion pill" (RU 486) could make the process simpler and less painful, and potentially avoid confrontations with right-to-life advocates at specialized clinics. In April of 1993, at the instigation of the U.S. Food & Drug Administration, the French manufacturer of RU 486 agreed to license the drug to the U.S. Population Council, based in New York City, which will run a series of clinical trials (Nash, Painton, Simpson, & Skari, 1993). Because the process involves only two sets of pills (RU 486 followed by 400 mg of Cytotec within 48 hours), it would theoretically be possible to administer RU 486 in any doctor's office. Also, European studies indicate that RU 486 is an effective morning-after pill, with fewer side effects than other medication options (Nash et al., 1993). Its use on a morning-after basis would presumably alter some of the psychological aspects of abortion, with RU 486 lying somewhere in between contraception and abortion.

In summary, many American teenagers engage in unprotected intercourse, and some are thus confronted with unwanted pregnancies. Almost half of them elect to terminate the pregnancy by abortion. The risk of adverse psychological se-

quelae is somewhat higher for teenagers because they are young and typically unmarried and nulliparous. In general, however, they are likely to cope well. Negative outcomes are more probable for those who are terminating pregnancies that are wanted and meaningful, perceive a lack of support for their decision from parents or partner, are more conflicted about their decision, are unsure of their coping abilities before the abortion, and/or delay until the second trimester. Identifying teenagers at greater risk enables the clinician to provide them with enhanced anticipatory guidance, a greater focus on self-efficacy and coping, and increased postabortion monitoring.

REFERENCES

Adler, N. E. (1975) Emotional responses of women following therapeutic abortion. *American Journal of Orthopsychiatry, 45,* 446–454.

Adler, N. E., David, H. P., Major B. N., Roth, S. H., Russo, N. F., & Wyatt, G. E. (1992). Psychological factors in abortion: A review. *American Psychologist, 47,* 1194–1204.

The Alan Guttmacher Institute. (1994). *Sex and America's teenagers.* New York: Author.

American Academy of Family Practice Symposium. (1993). Oral contraception: Exploring patient concerns. *Contraception Report, 3,* 4–10.

Bantsky, S. (1993, February 9). Teenagers say decision to use Norplant is theirs alone. *The Evening Sun* (Baltimore, MD), p. 1A.

Bell, C. C., & Jenkins, E. J. (1991). Traumatic stress and children. *Journal of Health Care for the Poor and Underserved, 2,* 175–185.

Blair, J. M., Cromer, B., Mahan, J., Zibners, L., & Naumovski, Z. (1995). Bone density in adolescent girls or Depo-Provera and Norplant (Abstract). *Journal of Adolescent Health, 16,* 164.

Blum, R. W., & Resnick, M. D. (1982) Adolescent sexual decision-making: Contraception, pregnancy, abortion, motherhood. *Pediatric Annals, 11,* 797–805.

Brown, L. K., DiClemente, R. J., & Park, T. (1992). Predictors of condom use in sexually active adolescents. *Journal of Adolescent Health, 13,* 651–657.

Center for Population Options. (1992). *Teenage pregnancy and too-early childbearing: Public costs, personal consequences* (6th ed.). Washington, DC: Author.

Cromer, B. A., Smith, R. D., Blair, J. M., Dwyer, J., & Brown, R. T. (1994). A prospective study of adolescents who choose among levonorgestrel implant (Norplant), medroxyprogesterone acetate (Depo-Provera), or the combined oral contraceptive pill as contraception. *Pediatrics, 94,* 687–694.

David, H. P., Rasmussen, N., & Holst, E. (1981). Post-

partum and post-abortion psychotic reactions. *Family Planning Perspectives, 13,* 88–93.

DeLamater, J. (1983). An intrapersonal and interactional model of contraceptive behavior. In D. Byrne & W. A. Fisher (Eds.), *Adolescents, Sex, and Contraception* (pp. 33–48). Hillsdale, NJ: Lawrence Erlbaum.

DuRant, R. H., Sanders, J. M., Jay, S., & Levinson, R. (1988). Analysis of contraception behavior of sexually active female adolescents in the United States. *Journal of Pediatrics, 113,* 930–936.

DuRant, R. H., Sanders, J. M., Jr., Jay, S., & Levinson, R. (1990). Adolescent contraceptive risk-taking behavior: A social psychological model of females' use of and compliance with birth control. *Advances in Adolescent Mental Health, 4,* 87–106.

Emans, S. J., Grace, E., & Woods, E. R. (1987). Adolescents' compliance with the use of oral contraceptives. *Journal of the American Medical Association, 257,* 3377–3381.

Forrest, J. D., & Singh, S. (1990). The sexual and reproductive behavior of American women, 1982–1988. *Family Planning Perspectives, 22,* 206–214.

Friedman, H. L. (1992). Changing patterns of adolescent sexual behavior: Consequences for health and development. *Journal of Adolescent Health, 13,* 345–350.

Friedman, S. B., & Phillips, S. (1982). Psychosocial risk to mother and child as a consequence of adolescent pregnancy. In E. R. McAnarney (Ed.), *Premature adolescent pregnancy and parenthood* (pp. 269–277). New York: Grune & Stratton.

Gold, M. A., & Coupey, S. M. (1995). Young women's attitudes towards new contraceptive methods (Abstract). *Journal of Adolescent Health, 16,* 150.

Henshaw, S. K., & Van Vort, J. (1989). Teenage abortion, birth and pregnancy statistics: An update. *Family Planning Perspectives, 21,* 85–88.

Hingson, R. W., Strunin, L., & Berlin, B. M. (1990).

Beliefs about AIDS, use of alcohol and drugs, and unprotected sex among Massachusetts adolescents. *American Journal of Public Health, 80,* 295–299.

Irwin, C. E., Jr., Brindis, C., & Brodt, S. (1991). The health of America's youth—A prelude to action. Washington, DC: DHHS, Bureau of Maternal & Child Health.

Jessor, R. (1991). Risk behavior in adolescence: A psychological framework for understanding and action. *Journal of Adolescent Health, 12,* 597–605.

Jones, E. F., Forrest, J. D., Goldman, N., Henshaw, S. K., Lincoln, R., Rosoff, J. I., Westoff, C. F., & Wulf, D. (1985). Teenage pregnancy in developed countries: Determinants and policy implications. *Family Planning Perspectives, 17,* 53–63.

Jones, E. F., Forrest, J. D., Goldman, N., Henshaw, S. K., Lincoln, R., Rosoff, J. I., Westoff, C. F., & Wulf, D. (1986). Teenage pregnancy in industrialized countries. New Haven, CT: Yale University Press.

Kahn, J. R., Kalsbeek, W. D., & Hofferth, S. L. (1988). National estimates of teenage sexual activity: Evaluating the comparability of three national surveys. *Demography, 25,* 189–208.

Kahn, J. R., Smith, K. W., & Roberts, E. J. (1984). *Familial Communication and Adolescent Sexual Behavior.* Final Report of Grant No. APR 000904-01-0 for the Office of Adolescent Pregnancy Programs, United States Department of Health and Human Services. Cambridge, MA: American Institutes for Research.

Kalof, L. (1995). Sex, power and dependency: The politics of adolescent sexuality. *Journal of Youth and Adolescence, 24,* 229–249.

Kastner, L. S. (1987). Ecological factors predicting adolescent contraceptive use: Implications for intervention. *Sexually Active Teenagers, 1,* 85–92.

Litt, I. F., Cuskey, W. R., & Rudd, S. (1980). Identifying the adolescent at risk for contraceptive non-compliance. *Journal of Pediatrics, 96,* 742–745.

McDonald, C. A., Selmar, C., & Eitel, C. (1980). Evaluation of effectiveness of contraceptive counseling (Abstract). *Journal of Adolescent Health Care, 1,* 88.

Mosher, W. D., & Horn, M. C. (1988). First family planning visits by young women. *Family Planning Perspectives, 23,* 108–116.

Mosher, W. D., & McNally, J. W. (1991). Contraceptive use at first premarital intercourse: United States, 1965–1988. *Family Planning Perspectives, 23,* 108–116.

Mueller, P., & Major, B. (1989). Self-blame, self-efficacy, and adjustment after abortion. *Journal of Personality and Social Psychology, 57,* 1059–1068.

Nash, J. M., Painton, F., Simpson, J. C., & Skari, T. (1993, June 14). New, improved and ready for battle. *Time,* pp. 48–51.

O'Reilly, K. R., & Aral, S. O. (1988). Adolescence and sexual behavior: Trends and implications for STD. *Sexually Active Teenagers, 2,* 43–51.

Pendergast, R. A., DuRant, R. H., & Gailard, G. L. (1992). Attitudinal and behavioral correlates of condom use in urban adolescents. *Journal of Adolescent Health, 13,* 133–139.

Polaneczky, M., Slap, G., Forke, C., Rappaport, A., & Sondheimer, S. (1994). The use of levonorgestrel implants (Norplant) for contraception in adolescent mothers. *New England Journal of Medicine, 331,* 1201–1206.

Rodgers, J. L. (1992). Development of sexual behavior. In S. B. Friedman, M. Fisher, & S. K. Schonberg (Eds.), *Comprehensive adolescent health care* (pp. 39–43). St. Louis: Quality Medical Publishing.

Rodgers, J. L., Billy, J. O. G., & Udry, J. R. (1982). The recission of behaviors: Inconsistent responses in adolescent sexuality data. *Social Science Research, 11,* 280–302.

Sonenstein, F. L., Pleck, J. H., & Ku, L. C. (1991). Levels of sexual activity among adolescent males in the United States. *Family Planning Perspectives, 23,* 162–167.

Stanton, B., Romer, D., Ricardo, I., Black, M., Feigelman, S., & Galbraith, J. (1993). Early initiation of sex and its lack of association with risk behaviors among adolescent African-Americans. *Pediatrics, 92,* 13–19.

Terr, L. (1989). Consultation advised soon after child's psychic injury. *Clinical Psychiatry Times, 17,* 5.

Tietze, C., Forrest, J. D., & Henshaw, S. K. (1988). United States of America. In P. Sachdev (Ed.), *International handbook on abortion* (pp. 474–483). Westport, CT: Greenwood Press.

Torres, A., Forrest, J. D., & Eisman, S. (1980). Telling parents: Clinic policies and adolescents' use of family planning and abortion services. *Family Planning Perspectives, 12,* 284–292.

Trussell, J., & Kost, K. (1987). Contraceptive failure in the United States: A critical review of the literature. *Studies in Family Planning, 18,* 237–283.

United Nations. (1988). *Adolescent reproductive behavior: Evidence from developed countries* (no. 109) New York: Population Studies.

Warzak, W. J., Grow, C. R., Poler, M. M., & Walburn, J. N. (1995). Enhancing refusal skills: Identifying contexts that place adolescents at risk for unwanted sexual activity. *Journal of Developmental and Behavioral Pediatrics, 16,* 98–100.

Zabin, L. S., & Clark, S. D., Jr. (1981). Why they delay: A study of teenage family planning clinic patients. *Family Planning Perspective, 13,* 205–217.

Zabin, L. S., Hirsch, M. D., & Emerson, H. R. (1989). When urban adolescents choose abortion: Effects on education, psychological status and subsequent pregnancy. *Family Planning Perspectives, 21,* 248–255.

Zabin, L. S., Stark, H. A., & Emerson, M. R. (1991). Reasons for delay in contraceptive clinic utilization: Adolescent clinic and non-clinic populations compared. *Journal of Adolescent Health, 12,* 225–232.

Zelnik, M., Kantner, J. F., & Ford, K. (1981). *Sex and pregnancy in adolescence.* Beverly Hills, CA: Sage.

21 / Risk-taking Behaviors in Adolescence

Lynn E. Ponton

While an increased propensity for taking risks is part of normal adolescent development, adolescent risk-taking behaviors have serious, sometimes even lethal, consequences. In fact, outcomes associated with risk behaviors are the principal dangers to the health and well-being of adolescents. Sixty-eight percent of all deaths in the under-24 age group are directly attributable to the consequences of risk-taking. One million teenage women become pregnant each year. Eighty percent of all sexually transmitted diseases occur within the 15- to 29-year-old age group. One-quarter of all cases of AIDS are diagnosed in individuals in their 20s, meaning that the disease was contracted during their adolescent years (Haselton & Campana, 1993). These statistics suggest that we need to acquire a better understanding of adolescent risk-taking behavior and work to develop interventions to change it.

This chapter discusses how and why adolescents take risks, highlighting the specific risks for adolescent psychiatric populations. The complex topic of adolescent sexuality is reviewed with an emphasis on aspects that involve unhealthy risk-taking. A rationale is presented for developing interventions (prevention programs) that are both research-based and focus on realistic goals. Sexual risk behaviors are focused on as a specific example, and an intervention developed to target sexual risk behaviors in the adolescent psychiatric population is discussed.

Types of High-Risk Behavior in Adolescence

Risk behaviors have become virtually synonymous with adolescence, reflecting the important role that they play in adolescent's lives and in parent's and society's view of this age group. Their high incidence and serious negative consequences make them important to understand in order to comprehend how adolescents function in today's world. While risk-taking behavior has always been a part of adolescence, teenagers growing up in the United States today face the opportunity for inventive and challenging risk behavior. They have easier access to cars, sex, and drugs than earlier generations of teens (Gelman, 1990). The plethora of risk behaviors include drinking, smoking, and the use of a variety of legal and illegal drugs. Reckless driving of motor vehicles as well as dangerous participation in recreational activities, such as swimming and boating, also carry with them high risks. Teenagers are likely to engage in sexual activity without protection from sexually transmitted diseases or pregnancy. Risky eating behaviors such as harmful dieting, vomiting, or laxative abuse begin to appear during the adolescent years. Mutilating the body in a variety of ways, including cutting and piercing, are considered fashionable by some youngsters. The highest risks of all are associated with violent activities such as rape, robbery, suicide, or murder, all of which rise in prevalence during the teenage years. Finally, many adolescents irresponsibly place themselves in positions where they can be victimized, by running away from home or dropping out of school.

RESEARCH ON WHY ADOLESCENTS TAKE RISKS

Research in the area of adolescent risk-taking has been growing. Jessor (1990), one of the most committed and prolific researchers in the area of adolescent risk behavior, underscores the vast number of risk behaviors available to adolescents. In fact, he notes, large segments of our young people deserve accolades for heroism because they manage to grow up in circumstances with very limited resources and considerable adversity, yet they become active members of our society. Irwin (1989), another researcher committed to the study of adolescent risk behaviors, believes that the basic process of risk-taking is a normal transitional behavior during adolescence. He emphasizes that it is during the teenage years that young people experiment with many aspects of life and begin to understand cause-and-effect relationships; the adolescent mind steadily increases its ability to understand and integrate material. Many believe that the experimentation involved in taking risks and accepting challenges is essential for teenagers, as it contributes to feelings of competency and the ability to think. Irwin believes that it is important to be able to distinguish between behaviors that are developmentally adaptive, even enhancing, to the adolescent and pathological actions in which there are not only no gains but significant risks of danger. Irwin describes the process of risk-taking, noting that it entails an uncertain outcome with possibilities for innocuous as well as harmful consequences. Sexual behavior provides a clear example of this process; an adolescent can derive sexual pleasure from the activity but also can end up a parent-to-be or with a sexually transmitted disease. Irwin defines risk-taking among adolescents as a process whereby young people with limited experience engage in potentially destructive behaviors with or without understanding the consequences of their actions.

Yet Irwin places a limitation on his definition of risk-taking behaviors by excluding behaviors associated with homicide, suicide, or psychiatric disorder, noting that they are characterized by extensive underlying psychopathological processes beyond the control of the young person.

UNDERSTANDING THE PROCESS THROUGH
INDIVIDUAL RISK BEHAVIORS AND THEORETICAL
MODELS

Theoretical frameworks of risk-taking behavior are helpful both to researchers interpreting research findings and to clinicians trying to understand the behaviors of their patients. One of the leading theoreticians in the field, Richard Jessor (1990), conceptualizes adolescent risk-taking as interrelated domains of risk and protective factors affecting both individual adolescents and groups of adolescents. His model explains the lack of effectiveness of overly simplistic approaches, exemplified by the "Just say no" campaign to drugs; this approach was single-focused and failed to take into account the complexity of behavioral patterns. Jessor divides the factors that contribute to adolescent risk-behavior into five areas:

1. Biological or genetic contributions
2. The social environment, which includes factors such as poverty and quality of schools

3. The "perceived environment," which refers to how the adolescent sees his or her own environment. The perceived environment contributes to a teenager's behavior through providing models for both abnormal and conventional behavior.
4. Individual personality factors, including self-esteem, the way a teenager visualizes or fails to visualize the future, the youngster's propensity for risk-taking, and values related to achievement and health
5. Behavioral factors, including school attendance and drinking

Jessor emphasizes the importance of including protective factors, or factors that protect or buffer an adolescent against participation in risk-behavior, in studies of risk.

A second model underscores the importance of adolescent lifestyles in risk-taking. This approach emphasizes the interrelated nature of adolescent behavior. Using this approach, specific behaviors are understood to be embedded in general styles of adaptation that are maintained by complex networks of social and cultural reinforcement (Nutbeam, Aar, & Catford, 1989). This model has obvious clinical and public health implications; both clinical programs oriented to individual patients and larger-scale prevention programs should attempt to influence the lifestyle in which a particular behavior is embedded, as opposed to focusing only on specific kinds of behavior. Feisher, Ziervogal, Chalton, Leger, and Robertson (1993) underscore the importance of using a multivariate methodology for research, a technique that allows relationships between forms of behavior to surface. A recent study conducted by their research group demonstrated that adolescents who are involved in incidents of violent behavior are also likely to smoke cigarettes or marijuana, to have sexual intercourse, and to fail to use seat belts. A study such as this demonstrates that participation in violent activities propels adolescents into multidimensional behavioral patterns.

Risk-taking Behavior and Psychiatric Illness

Adolescents who fall within psychiatric populations present unique and challenging patterns of risk behavior. The interrelationship of risk behavior and psychopathology has important implications for treatment. A great deal of evidence shows that mental disorders or distress often are present at or near the time an adolescent engages in risk behavior. Whether psychopathology is preexistent, develops along with risk behavior, or is one of its consequences is a complex and currently unanswerable question. Examples of the close association between risk behaviors and psychological problems are easily found. For example, depression, a major cause of psychiatric morbidity in adolescents, commonly follows unplanned pregnancy. Substance abuse often predates a suicide attempt. We do not know to what extent psychological problems predate risk behavior in adolescents. Longitudinal studies that examine adolescent risk behaviors over time will help us understand the type of psychological disturbance that adolescents might show before they engage in risky behavior; this knowledge could lead to earlier treatment and prevention efforts.

Even in the absence of such longitudinal studies, it is possible to state that treatment of the mental disorders that so frequently accompany risk behaviors offers an opportunity to short circuit some of the painful cycle of such behavior and avoid serious life-threatening consequences. Early treatment of adolescents with psychological problems is an effective strategy but one that the United States lags shamefully behind in implementing. Adolescents disabled by mental disorders comprise the largest category of disabled young people in this country, approximately 32%, or 630,000, out of a total of 2 million disabled adolescents (Newachek, 1989). This is a population that very much needs help, could benefit from it, and is currently not getting it. A survey of mental health departments in all states, conducted by the Children's Defense Fund, claimed that two-thirds of the serious psychologically disturbed adolescents were not getting any mental health services; adolescents were found to be the most underserved (Knitzer, 1982). It is likely that this untreated population plays a major role in the increasing prevalence of risk behaviors, as teenagers with mental illness are less able to assess risks than are their peers who are psychologically healthy.

Several studies designed to focus on the examination of risk behaviors among adolescents have demonstrated this point. A recent study (DiClemente & Ponton, 1993) looked at risk behaviors that place adolescents at risk for contracting the human immuno-deficiency virus (HIV). Adolescents with mental health problems, specifically those placed in a San Francisco psychiatric hospital, were found to have significantly more risk behaviors than a comparable population of adolescents chosen from a larger population in the San Francisco high schools. The hospitalized adolescents were almost twice as likely to be sexually active and almost twice as likely to report not using condoms during intercourse.

Gruber (1994) has studied the relationship between adolescent risk behavior and psychiatric problems such as depressive illness, substance abuse, and eating disorders. She has reinforced the point that it is important for parents to be aware of the connection between psychological problems and risk-taking, emphasizing that to consign risk-taking behavior to normative adolescence runs contrary to the evidence that repetitious or progressive activity with negative consequences is symptomatic of psychopathology.

Sexuality and Risk-taking

The area of adolescent sexuality has long been associated with risk-taking. Puritanical ideas that restrict discussion, education, and interventions in the sexual arena for adolescents have increased the risk behaviors, highlighted the stigma of adolescent sexual risk-taking, and limited use of interventions. A discussion of adolescent sexuality is important to include in a comprehensive curriculum program because it raises our level of knowledge as mental health professionals working with teens and encourages us to consider how the behavior can be modified. Even aside from the utility of the study of adolescent sexuality, the field is both seductive and fascinating, attracting many researchers.

One of the most important tasks for an adolescent is to learn about his or her sexuality in a way that is socially acceptable, safe, and promotes development. This is not an easy task to achieve. An important part of this task is the continued development of the sexual identity, a process that began in childhood. This development includes the capacity for integration of emotions related to sexuality, a child's experience with masturbation,

195

sexual fantasies, the developing sense of self, and integration of sexual experiences from the childhood period.

A sexual identity includes both a sexual orientation, which can be heterosexual, homosexual, or bisexual, and sexual ideas about oneself. This identity is developed with information acquired through fantasies, masturbation, and sexual relationships with others. The acquisition of a sexual identity is a lifelong process that is begun in childhood and continues throughout adolescence and adulthood, then into later life.

Biological processes that occur in adolescence are an important part of this forming of a sexual identity. Puberty is defined as the developmental process during which both secondary sex characteristics and the capacity for sexual reproduction develop. This is a period when tremendous physical growth is taking place. Fifty percent of ideal adult weight and 20% of linear growth are achieved during this period. The timing of puberty varies, based on the individual and the sex (Irwin & Shafer, 1991). Further discussion of physical aspects of puberty are presented in Chapter 6.

In the United States, the mean age for menarche is currently 12.4 years. Thus, for most adolescent females in this country, puberty and menarche begin during the latency years, not adolescence. The adolescent female is capable of becoming pregnant with the first period. This decrease in the age of puberty and menarche indicates one of the prime reasons why adolescent sexual risk-taking is a growing problem.

Full development through Tanner Stage 5 usually is complete by age 15, which is only the middle phase of the period that we define as adolescence. For males the process of puberty is generally 1½ to 2 years longer, but, as is the case for females, it is initiated in latency or early adolescence.

Most adolescents are ignorant of their achievement of full sexual maturity during early adolescence. Cole and Stokes (1985) report that most adolescents lack basic knowledge about sexuality. Only one-third would consider asking their parents or other adults for information. A majority believe that loving relationships determine permissibility for sexual intercourse and that, by age 14, they are capable of being involved in loving relationships. Younger teens are more susceptible to peer influence than are older adolescents. There is still a double standard; although large numbers of girls are sexually active, many want to be thought of as virgins.

SEXUALLY TRANSMITTED DISEASES

The highest rates of sexually transmitted diseases in this country are found among adolescents in the 15- to 19-year-old age group. Adolescents are susceptible to these illnesses for a number of reasons, including high rates of sexual experimentation, lack of education, multiple partners, failure to employ barrier methods of birth control, and reluctance and difficulty obtaining medical care. Even when they do obtain medical care, they may get inadequate treatment without follow-up. Many adolescent girls have cervical ectropion, the extension of the squamous junction into the vaginal cervix. This condition increases susceptibility to gonorrhea and chlamydia, enhancing the spread of these sexually transmitted illnesses.

The consequences of sexually transmitted diseases are severe in a population that is just beginning its reproductive cycle. Some of the most serious sequelae include sterility secondary to untreated pelvic inflammatory disease, infant mortality from maternally transmitted herpes, and eventual mortality from AIDS. All of these problems provide incontrovertible justification for prevention programs.

SPECIAL PROBLEMS OF HOMOSEXUAL YOUTH

Unquestionably, homosexual adolescents have unique problems. In a study conducted in 1972, Rossler and Diescher found a 31% suicide rate in homosexual males ages 16 to 19 years. They reported that 50% of this population had consulted psychiatrists. Remafidi (1985) found that 31% of gay-identified adolescent males experienced psychiatric hospitalization. Estimates of substance abuse among the adult male homosexual population are also higher than among the general population. These statistics indicate that gay male adolescents are a population at high risk for psychiatric disorders and psychological dysfunction. Recent studies have questioned both the frame and the interpretation of the data reported in these early studies on gay youth (Baumrind, 1995). A study completed on homosexual college students living in an accepting environment with minimal homophobia and retaliation illustrated no differences in self-esteem between homosexual youth and their heterosexual peers (Hershberger & D'Augelli, 1995). Several factors have been found to mitigate psychological dysfunction in a homosexual youth's life, including self-acceptance, family support, and low rates of reported victimization by others.

Many of the studies evaluating psychiatric disorders in the homosexual population were completed before the medical community turned its attention to autoimmune deficiency syndrome, or AIDS. Homosexual adolescents are at higher risk for AIDS as well as for the classic venereal diseases, syphilis and gonorrhea. Two-thirds of reported cases of gonorrhea occur before 25 years of age. Fifty percent of cases of reported syphilis are in homosexual males. This information indicates the importance of recognizing sexually transmitted diseases in this population and developing prevention programs.

The major areas of adolescent sexuality include sexual beliefs, sexual knowledge, role models, and support systems. Homosexual adolescents have more difficulty than their heterosexual peers with all four of these domains. Beliefs are confusing and often conflicted. Knowledge is difficult to obtain and frequently deficient. Role models are hard to find, and peers may be openly hostile. Remafidi (1985) reports that 55% of homosexual adolescents experience verbal abuse from peers and 30% experience assaults.

In reading the results of these studies, it is important to keep in mind the changing perspective from which these questions are being examined. Health care providers are not immune to cultural bias. Many lesbian youths report negative interaction with adolescent health care providers, including disrespect, fear, and being ignored or silenced (Stevens, 1994). Careful examination of our cultural attitudes and bias about homosexual youths is important to research, clinical care, and educative efforts.

One of the earliest and most complex studies on homosexuality was Kinsey's report in 1948 (Kinsey, Pomeroy, & Martin). The study examined the sexual behavior of 6,000 adults and adolescents. Thirty-seven percent of the males studied reported a homosexual experience including orgasm at some point in their lives. Four to 10% reported that their sexual activities were exclusively homosexual for at least 3 years. The mean age awareness of same-sex attractions in the homosexual population was reported to be 13 years. Kinsey's study made an important statement, most notably that adolescence was a crucial period for the development of a homosexual identity. For further discussion of this, see Chapter 19.

A second important concept that emerged from the Kinsey data was that sexual behavior spans a continuum and that the individual's position on the sexual continuum varies at different points in his or her development. The idea is important to a better understanding of sexual orientation. Sexual orientation is a composite of sexual behaviors, sexual fantasies, social role, and an inner sexual identity, and varies at different points in life. It is important to remember that sexual behavior may not be consistent with fantasies or the preferred social role.

Adding to our knowledge in this area, Remafidi (1985) has described, from a retrospective study of homosexuals, four stages of gay identity formation: (1) feeling different from one's peers in early adolescence; (2) awareness of homosexual impulses but defenses against them; (3) talking about sexual preference; (4) commitment. Although homosexual adolescents are forced to examine their sexual object choice in greater detail in adolescence, I believe that heterosexual adolescents, experience the same process, except for stage 2: They feel different from peers when they first experience sexual feelings; then they come to question the feelings, and then they gradually move toward a more serious commitment.

Masturbation is an important part of adolescent sexual development that often goes unmentioned and is still haunted by taboos and mystery. Moore (1975), in a classic work on the subject, noted that masturbation during adolescence has an essential path. He identified masturbation fantasies as complex and significant parts of the psychic life of all humans, most particularly in their contribution to the ego, sexual identity, object relations, and character during adolescence.

According to Coles and Stokes (1985), only 46% of all teen males and only 24% of females report engaging in masturbation. Of that group, only 15% of the boys and 8% of the girls report masturbating without guilt, a very small percentage of adolescents. This is in contrast to the high percentages of adolescents who engage in sexual activity with others, often unprotected. It is quite likely that the sexual behavior of many of these sexually active adolescents is fueled in part by anxiety over masturbatory activity and a belief that sexual intercourse is a more normal activity than is masturbation. It is at least plausible that being more informed might reduce pressures for teenagers to engage in risk-laden sexual behavior.

In the Coles and Stokes study, teens reported that schools and parents were less informative about masturbation than they were about all other areas of sexuality, including reproduction, birth control, and homosexuality. These data underscore the importance of including the topic of masturbation in programs to educate adolescents about sexuality. Yet when a suggestion was made by a former Surgeon General of the United States that adolescents be given appropriate information about masturbation, shock waves were engendered that led to her forced resignation. This event underscored the barriers that still exist in our society to appropriate sex education for adolescents.

STUDIES OF RISK-TAKING BEHAVIOR AND SEXUALITY

The fact that the capacity for risk-taking and participation in sexual activity develop at or close to the same time in an individual's life has enormous implications. This coincidence encourages adolescents to experiment in the area of sexuality. The sexual behavior of adolescents is a complex and fascinating field, often filled with surprises. The outcome of sexual risk behaviors reflects the morbidity and mortality of risk behaviors in general. There are over 1 million teenage pregnancies each year (DiClemente, Hansen, & Ponton, 1996; Stevens-Simon & McAnarney, 1996). Eight percent of young people between the ages of 15 and 29 contract at least one sexually transmitted disease (Haselton & Campana, 1993). One-quarter of all cases of acquired immunodeficiency illness manifest themselves when individuals are in their 20s; many contract it in adolescence.

Psychiatric populations, either inpatient or outpatient, demonstrate more risk-taking behavior in the sexual sphere than nonreferred samples. In a study conducted by DiClemente and I (1993), risk behaviors were examined in an inpatient adolescent psychiatric population and contrasted with a comparable school-based population in San Francisco. Psychiatrically hospitalized adolescents reported a high prevalence of risk behaviors traditionally associated with HIV infection as well as behaviors that were not previously identified as potential routes for HIV transmission. Fifteen percent reported using intravenous drugs, 15% reported sharing intravenous drug needles, 15.8% reported being the sex partner of an intravenous drug abuser, 15.8% reported being the sex partner of a homosexual/bisexual male, and 35% reported having sexual intercourse with someone whose sex history was unknown. Among those adolescents who reported using intravenous drugs, however, all reported sharing needles. These are behaviors commonly linked to HIV risk.

Risk behaviors not previously recognized as associated with HIV transmission were also more prevalent among this population. For example, 60% reported cutting or self-mutilation behavior, 37% reported being sexually abused, and 41% reported having been forced to engage in sexual practices. For those adolescents reporting self-mutilation, approximately 41% shared cutting implements. Of these adolescents, the mean frequency of cutting behavior was 3.4 occasions with a range from 1 to more than 20 times.

High-risk sexual behaviors were also prominent among this population. The majority of the sample (56%) reported being sexually active, with age of sexual onset averaging 10.7 years. Condom use during sexual intercourse was infrequent, however, with almost 67% reporting "never" using condoms. Frequency of sexual intercourse, on the other hand, was quite high, with 45.4% of the adolescents reporting intercourse several times a week and another 18.2% reporting sexual intercourse at least several times a month.

The majority of psychiatrically hospitalized adolescents reported having multiple sex partners, with one-third reporting 9 or more sex partners in the past year. Perhaps as a consequence of these risk behaviors, 15% and 18%, respectively, of psychiatrically hospitalized adolescents reported having had a pregnancy or sexually transmitted disease. Not surprisingly, the 3 girls who reported having been pregnant also reported that their partners never used condoms during sexual intercourse. Of those adolescents who reported being sexually abused, most reported repeated sexual abuse and almost half reported being sexually abused on 3 or more occasions.

Additional analyses identified a differential association between frequency of self-reported risk behaviors and adolescents' primary psychiatric diagnosis. The mean on the Risk Behavior Inventory was 11.1 risk behaviors, with a range from 0 to 26. For conceptual purposes, the diagnostic categories of conduct disorder and personality disorder were combined, and respondents with a diagnosis of "other" were deleted from these analyses. A one-way analysis of variance identified a significant association between psychiatric diagnosis and mean number of reported risk behaviors, with adolescents diagnosed as conduct disorder/personality disorder reporting substantially greater mean risk behaviors than adolescents diagnosed as schizophrenic or with affective disorders.

In subsequent analyses, we dichotomized adolescents' Risk Behavior Inventory scores into "high"- or "low"-risk categories using a median split and examined the relationship between primary psychiatric diagnosis and risk behavior category. Adolescents with psychiatric diagnoses of conduct disorder/borderline personality were more than three times as likely to be classified in the "high"-risk category as adolescents diagnosed as having either schizophrenia or affective disorders.

This study demonstrates several important points about adolescent risk-taking and sexuality. There are a number of risks involved in sexual activity: the risk of sexual victimization, pregnancy, AIDS and sexually transmitted diseases. Second, the ramifications of early exposure to sexual activity are unknown. In 1988, 26% of girls age 15 (increasing to 48% at age 18) reported being sexually active as compared to only 5% in 1970 (Adler, 1994, personal communication). The reported rates of sexual activity are even higher for adolescent males; 60% of all adolescent males at age 18 report having experienced sexual intercourse. Adler questions whether early sexual activity might permanently alter adolescents' responses to sexual activity, leading to jaded 15-year-olds "who have experienced it all."

Whether early sexual activity robs adolescents of the full joy that is possible with a mature sexual relationship or not, it certainly impacts on their present life with the very real concerns of pregnancy, sexually transmitted diseases, and sexual victimization.

A comparative study such as that conducted by DiClementi and I (1993) underscores the needs of a high-risk group such as psychiatrically hospitalized adolescents. It also confirms the point frequently made by youth-at-risk surveys: Comorbidity is the rule. Simply put, risk behaviors exist together. Researchers have yet to understand the complex interrelationships among risk behaviors, but trying to address one risk behavior singly without taking into account other frequently coexisting behaviors is a mistake. This point is addressed more directly in the next section, which focuses on interventions and prevention programs.

Prevention Programs

One of the most important principles regarding interventions which address adolescent risk behaviors is that programs must attempt to change behaviors themselves, not just modify knowledge and attitudes. As social learning theory suggests, adolescents need to believe that they are competent to make decisions and changes in their behaviors. Interventions that include exercises in decision-making skills contribute to adolescents' self-confidence and ability to make decisions for themselves (Ponton, DiClementi, & McKenna, 1991). Role play, peer group discussion, support, and role modeling are techniques that can be used to build decision-making skills in adolescents. A lively presentation style that integrates teen music, video, and peer group interaction often enhances the effectiveness of the intervention. Use of teenagers who have experienced the negative consequences of high-risk behaviors makes adolescents aware that the consequences of the risk behavior could apply to them.

Interventions must be geared to the age, developmental level, and background of the adolescent target audience. As an example, HIV education should not be presented to adolescents who lack a firm grounding in sexual education. Mismatching of intervention and population reduces the effectiveness of the program. Recently I evaluated an HIV education program given to preteens and found that the intervention used was one meant for 18- to 19-year-olds. The mismatch was obvious. The youngsters could not understand the case vignettes used in the study and, as a result, improperly answered the questions.

In developing interventions for psychiatrically impaired adolescents, it is especially important to target their unique risk behaviors (Ponton et al., 1991). Sexual victimization, self-mutilation, and a variety of other risk behaviors are prevalent in those populations and necessitate tailored interventions. Adolescent psychiatric populations also may lag behind in basic knowledge, vocabulary, or reading skills. An awareness of these differences can lead to appropriate modification of the intervention.

Unfortunately, few programs include evaluations of their effectiveness. A research model that includes pre- and posttest measures and an evaluation of the effectiveness of the prevention program is recommended.

In summary, interventions should be based on sound principles and should have as a goal behavioral change, not solely education. They should be tailored to the population at hand with respect to targeted risk behaviors, vocabulary, and teaching materials.

THE ROLE OF THE THERAPIST IN PREVENTION OF HIGH-RISK BEHAVIOR

Work by Wingood and DiClemente (1993) suggests that the therapist is viewed as an important authority figure by many adolescents. This respect means that therapists are in a position to convey basic knowledge about adolescent sexual activity, dispel common misconceptions, and discuss the normal behavior of other teenagers (peer norms, an area of considerable importance to adolescents). A therapist working with adolescents should be knowledgeable about their areas of risk and be able to impart this knowledge to patients in a comfortable, nonthreatening manner. The therapist can reinforce what youngsters already know and discuss their individual obstacles to and/ or strategies for engaging in effective methods of contraception and prevention of sexually transmitted diseases.

Research on developing HIV-prevention programs for adolescents, including those with psychiatric disorders, has increased awareness regarding adolescent risk and the need for education. Conveying values and education in an empathic manner and at the same time working together on a jointly determined focus of the therapy is a complex process. Therapist style, patient diagnosis, overall functioning, and the question of time are all important determinants of this process (Ponton, 1993).

Individual clinicians have an opportunity to help a young person explore his or her own risk-taking process, focusing on both unconscious and conscious motivations for engaging in risky behavior. Behavioral reenactments of early traumatic experience are an example of unconscious factors that may play a large role in an individual adolescent's risk-taking pattern. The clinician is in a unique position to help the adolescent understand such behavior, thereby providing him or her with an important avenue for change.

Parents and teachers need to be better informed about adolescent risk behaviors and to understand how teenagers make decisions. These adults need to be able to talk to youngsters in a way that helps them to develop the ability to assess risks realistically and make appropriate choices. Parents and teachers need to develop a level of comfort for talking with teenagers about these matters. This is not an easy process, and is one that many people shy away from. Through community activities, child and adolescent psychiatrists and other clinicians can play an important role in helping parents and teachers to give more effective guidance to young people.

Conclusion

Behaviors in which adolescents engage that have a significant degree of associated risk, such as drug and alcohol abuse, present tremendous challenges to those who work with young people. Adolescents engage in risk-taking as a normal part of their development, and some amount of risk-taking probably facilitates development into a well-functioning adult. Yet risk-taking behaviors in adolescence have a significant degree of associated morbidity and mortality. Adolescents with psychiatric disorders are much more likely than normal adolescents to engage in high-risk behaviors. Mental health professionals working with adolescents in an office setting can help individual adolescents learn how to accept challenges and take risks responsibly. They can assist adolescents in developing their own process of risk assessment, and often they are in the best position to understand and explain unconscious factors that motivate an adolescent to engage in risk behavior. Mental health professionals also can act as advocates to promote interventions that assess and target risk behavior. Well-constructed, targeted interven-

tions have been shown to be effective in decreasing risk behavior. Such interventions are useful tools to begin to alter this behavior. Professionals must educate themselves and work on decreasing their own biases in this highly charged and stigmatized field.

REFERENCES

Baumrind, D. (1995). Commentary on sexual orientation: Research and social policy implementations. *Developmental Psychology, 31*, 130–136.

Coles, R., & Stokes, G. (1985). *Sex and the American teenager*. New York: Harper & Row.

DiClemente, R. J., Hansen, W. B., & Ponton, L. E. (1996). Adolescents at risk: A generation in jeopardy. In R. J. DiClemente, W. B. Hansen, & L. E. Ponton (Eds.), *Handbook of Adolescent Health Risk Behavior* (pp. 1–4). New York: Plenum.

DiClemente, R., & Ponton, L. (1993). HIV-related risk behaviors among hospitalized adolescents and school-based adolescents. *American Journal of Psychiatry, 150* (2), 324–325.

Feisher, A. J., Ziervogal, C. F., Chalton, D. O., Leger, P. H., & Robertson, B. A. (1993, October 26–31). *Risk-taking behavior of South African high school students: A multi-variate analysis.* Paper presented at the 40th annual meeting of the American Academy of Child and Adolescent Psychiatry, San Antonio, TX.

Gelman, D. (1990, May 17). A much riskier passage. *The New Teens, Newsweek* [Special edition].

Gruber, E. (1994). *Adolescent risk-taking behavior and psychopathology: A review.* Unpublished manuscript.

Haselton, A., & Campana, J. (1993). *Teen sexuality and sexual abuse. Review course in adolescent psychiatry.* San Diego: American Society for Adolescent Psychiatry, 797–802.

Hershberger, S. L., & D'Augelli, A. R. (1995). The impact of victimization on the mental health and suicidality of lesbian, gay and bisexual youths. *Developmental Psychology, 31*, 65–74.

Irwin, C. (1989). Risk-taking behaviors in the adolescent patient; are they impulsive? *Pediatric Annals, 18* (2), 122–133.

Jessor, R. (1990). Risk behavior in adolescence: A psychosocial framework for understanding. In D. Rogers & E. Ginzberg (Eds.), *Adolescents at risk. Medical and social perspectives* (pp. 19–34). San Francisco: Westview Press.

Kinsey, A. C., Pomeroy, W. B., & Martin, C. E. (1948). *Sexual behavior in the human male*. Philadelphia: W. B. Saunders.

Knitzer, R. (1982). *Unclaimed children: The failure of public responsibility to children and adolescents in need of mental health services.* Washington, DC: Childrens Defense Fund.

Moore, W. T. (1975). *Masturbation from infancy to senescence*. New York: Plenum Press.

Newachek, P. W. (1989). Adolescents with special health needs: Prevalence, severity and access to health services. *Pediatrics, 84* (5), 872–881.

Nutbeam, D., Aar, L., & Catford, J. (1989). Understanding children's health behavior: The implications for health promotion for young people. *Social Science Medicine, 29*, 317–325.

Ponton, L. (1993). Issues unique to psychotherapy with adolescent girls. *American Journal of Psychotherapy, 47* (3), 353–373.

Ponton, L. E., DiClemente, R., & McKenna, S. (1991). An AIDS education and prevention program for hospitalized adolescents. *Journal of the American Academy of Child and Adolescent Psychiatry, 30*, 729–734.

Remafidi, G. J. (1985). Adolescent homosexuality: Psychosocial and medical implications. *Pediatrics, 79*, 331–337.

Rossler, D., & Diescher, R. W. (1972). Youthful male homosexuality: Homosexual experience and the process of developing homosexual identity in males aged sixteen to twenty two years. *Journal of the American Medical Association, 219*, 1018–1023.

Shafer, M., & Irwin, C. (1991). The adolescent patient. In A. Rudolph (Ed.), *Pediatrics* (19th ed., pp. 39–81). Norwalk, CT: Appleton and Lang.

Stevens, P. D. (1994). Protective strategies of lesbian clients in health care environments. *Research in Nursing and Health, 17*, 217–229.

Stevens-Simon, C., & McAnarney, E. R. (1996). Adolescent pregnancy. In R. J. DiClemente, W. B. Hansen, & L. E. Ponton (Eds.), *Handbook of adolescent health risk behavior* (pp. 313–332). New York: Plenum.

Tanner, J. M. (1962). *Growth at adolescence* (2nd ed.). Oxford: Blackwell Scientific Publications.

Wingood, G. M., & DiClemente, R. (1993). Cultural and psychosocial factors influencing HIV prevention behavior of Afro-American females. *Ethnicity and Disease, 2*, 381–388.

22 / Adolescent Language and Music

Theodore Shapiro and Alexander Kalogerakis

Adolescence shares characteristics of both childhood and adulthood, but it is also different from each stage. It has been variously defined by observers from social, psychological, and other perspectives (Esman, 1990) and by adolescents themselves in their quest to mold unique personal identities. Two areas in which adolescents often mark their territory are in their use of language and taste in music.

Language in Adolescence

Considering language first, let us imagine the oft-played scenario of parents, exasperated by their teens' seemingly willful neglect of large stores of previously learned English vocabulary, trying vainly to extirpate "like," "you know," and "intense" from their teen's current usage. The parents are working hard against a powerful counterpull—that of the adolescent's wish to create a new language, a sociolect (Shapiro, 1985). In effect, teens are saying that this language is their business, and it separates them from the parents.

Language thus serves a developmental function in line with other changes of adolescence. In our society, puberty and the biological readiness to procreate occur well before the accepted onset of adult life, both in terms of entering the workforce and in starting a new family unit. The current extension of education into the late teens and 20s expands the time span of adolescence. The reworking of oedipal themes (A. Freud, 1959) and the separation and individuation issues that recur at this time (Blos, 1967) are psychological tasks that propel adolescents to change and create the symbols of separateness, rebellion, and adaptation. Adolescents strive to establish new roles in their community that enhance self-esteem and, also most important to them, peer regard. Their use of language in this respect is not dissimilar from the process that occurs in ethnic subgroups trying to maintain their heritage in a sea of homogeneity.

The cultural phenomenon of language or dialect as a group definer is observed most easily in Europe. The former Yugoslavia and Soviet Union, for example, were either formed or greatly altered earlier in this century as political entities. They were comprised of numerous ethnic groups with distinct dialects or languages. Recently these groups have reasserted nationalist political goals, but for much of the century language was the only vehicle for the expression of ethnic identity. Similarly, eastern European Jews who were dispersed through Europe maintained Yiddish as a common tongue, thus differentiating themselves to some degree from their neighbors. A Polish and a German Jew, for instance, sometimes shared a linguistic as well as religious bond that transcended the political boundaries that divided their countries. In the United States also, many ethnic groups maintain their identities as Norwegians, Poles, Greeks, Mexicans, and so forth through social groups, neighborhoods, churches, and schools, all of which promote the use of their language of origin.

Adolescent language serves a similar purpose. Psychological and social separateness are encouraged amid communities that offer other differentiated subcultures, as well—ethnic, religious, socioeconomic, scholastic, professional. Adolescents sharing particular developmental tasks and concerns use a sociolect to provide a common way to express these concerns in a way that is often undecipherable or obscure to adults. The language also serves a normalizing function; that is, a commonly used slang term implies a common concept or activity, as in "jack off" for masturbate. Adolescents also test their creative muscle in these linguistic gymnastics, a subject we will return to in our discussion of pop music as both product and reflection of adolescent culture.

What do adolescents actually do to the language? Linguistically, we can dissect language into several subunits for study. Grammar refers to the relation of words and structure and to the rules of usage that guide sentence formation. Semantics is the study of meaning of words. Pragmatics is the aspect of language that includes the effect of words on people; thus, it includes a social context (Shapiro, 1979).

For the most part, adolescent language preserves standard English grammatical form. However, Munro (1989) has identified some variants. For example, teens may use the definite article "the" in a decidedly indefinite way. For example: "Susan set me up with her big brother. She's the homie."

The sentence roughly means "she's a buddy." It does not imply that Susan is the only homie in the speaker's frame of reference. "The" is used for emphasis rather than as a definite article. Parenthetically, similar usage is found in German and French, perhaps attesting to some universal features of linguistic drift even within language groups.

Another feature identified in slang grammar is the frequent omission of the "to be" form, as in "You crazy." Munro (1989) notes in this usage the influence of another, overlapping subculture, that of black Americans and the well-studied unique dialect, Black English. In fact, this discussion of adolescent language also could be organized around subcultural interdigitations: Black English, surfer's slang, Southern slang, the recent mall language of Vall-speak, and so on. These and other forms influence the teenagers who belong to those groups and often generalize to the population at large, thereby defeating some of the separatist aims of the adolescents' original intent.

Most adolescent argot is differentiated in the area of semantics by using unlikely words in a grammatical fashion. Chomsky's (1965) phrase "John frightened sincerity" (p. 15) illustrates the problem. This is an example of good grammar—adjectives, nouns, and verbs, in correct relation to each other—but poor semanticity. The meaning is nonsense. Here is a similar example taken from adolescent life: "Why did you bite my outfit?" Like Chomsky's example, something seems awry; sincerity cannot be frightened, and one does not bite outfits. But the latter example might be understood by a teen to mean "Why did you steal my idea for an outfit?" (Munro, 1989). Thus, a seemingly nonsensical phrase becomes semanti-

cally "right," given the proper base of extra grammatical knowledge.

This intrusion of extralinguistic knowledge requires us to study the pragmatic or social aspect of language. Popular topics of adolescent slang include sexuality, insults, and bodily function, such as vomiting (Spears, 1991). The use of potentially offending terms is governed by unspoken yet understood rules of conduct. A good example of this is seen in the urban black adolescent argot of the 1960s and 1970s known as "trading dozens" or "soundings." Labov (1975) studied this phenomenon and described the structured manner in which, typically, sexually charged insults were hurled back and forth. Often rhymed couplets were exchanged. They were and are exercises in wit that nevertheless betray raw adolescent concerns: aggression, sexuality, mothers. An example:

"I don't play the dozens and dozens ain't my game. But the way I fucked your momma is a Goddam shame." (Labov, 1975, p. 30)

The form in this example is typical—a disclaiming first line and a contradictory second. Note that this example shares features of an earlier black verbal form, that of the blues lyric, which often repeats a scene-setting first line and then follows with a third, humorous or doleful line.

Along with the perennial adolescent themes such as individuation, sexuality, and aggression, other topics come to the linguistic fore as cultural shifts occur. Drug-related slang has permeated adolescent culture since the 1960s; Vall-speak, the lingo of Valley girls and their cultural cousins elsewhere in malls in the affluent 1980s; various surfer sociolects, prominent in the early 1960s and again now; urban gun-toting teens' lingo in the 1990s. This latter example, reflecting a chilling fact of ghetto life in many urban centers, has spawned yet newer terms (Pooley, 1991, p. 22), such as "Shorty's strapped. He got toast." Translated, this means "Shorty is carrying a gun. He has a machine pistol." The "strapped" teen may have "beef" (a disagreement) with someone and "buck" (shoot) him; may "hose" (spray bullets from an automatic weapon); or "get a body" (kill someone). What may start any of these events is that the youngster was "dissed"—the widely used slang for "disrespected." The latter term is an interesting demotion to street slang from highfalutin adult talk.

The shifting body of adolescent argot moves along several axes: temporal, geographic, and ethnic. For the clinician working with adolescents, it is useful to know some of the reference points as well as the specific meaning of slang words. Adolescents in conversation with adults will also shift between argot and standard English, and these transitions will be of interest to the clinician. Disentangling subcultural phenomena from individual psychology is a difficult task in any age group, but the preceding considerations may aid the persistent older therapist who works with teens (Shapiro, 1985).

Music and Adolescence

As indicated earlier, music—usually what is broadly referred to as popular music—is another prominent preoccupation and diversion of adolescent subculture. Twentieth-century America has seen numerous waves of pop music, from swooning bobby-soxers to Beatle mania, from Elvis to MTV. The latter has combined music with the new technology of video images in a profitable melding of the two largest media, a subject we will return to. In all of these fads and crazes, teens have been major fans, consumers, and often purveyors of the music itself. In much the same way that adolescent argot provides a differentiated form of expression, in pop music teens find a musical genre that is oriented to their concerns. The specific nature of this orientation changes over time. The love songs of the crooners in the 1930s and 1940s portrayed romance in sweet, nonthreatening tones that teens and adults could both enjoy. From Rudy Vallee through Frank Sinatra, this genre took hold of the largest adolescent audiences since recording was possible. With the bumptious, resounding emotion of rock, music became more specialized to adolescent concerns, not only to sexuality and romance but also to autonomy, aggression, and rebellion. The term "rock 'n' roll" itself is euphemistic for sexual behavior, and certainly a "rock 'n' roller," in the earlier days, caused more parental anxiety than a "crooner" did some years earlier. This fact can be observed, for

instance, in the early backlash toward the gyrating Elvis Presley and adults' concerns at the time that rock music was detrimental to youth (Szatmary, 1991). Technological advances, such as television, the transistor radio and boom box, as well as the general upsurge of American consumerism after World War II reaching into the 1960s created a situation in which pop musicians and music entrepreneurs could offer products tailor-made to adolescent tastes and reap substantial profits from this "teen market."

The most instructive early example of this cultural explosion came with the Beatles and their breakthrough onto the American scene. Norman (1981) has provided a detailed account of their "conquering" America, including relevant cultural factors, such as the assassination of President John F. Kennedy. But what was the appeal on an individual level to the teenager? (Note that the fans in the early period of Beatlemania largely consisted of younger teenagers, mostly girls, as were the earlier bobby-soxers, unlike later in the Beatles' career.) The Beatles sang, in early recordings, almost exclusively of romance. Titles of their hit songs ("I Want to Hold Your Hand," "She Loves You," "Please, Please Me") often included personal pronouns, thus creating an intimacy with the fan. The rock beat and enthusiasm with which the songs were performed suggested, although they did not directly assert, the insistence on freedom and autonomy central to youth. (Later material by the Beatles and others made these issues much more explicit.) The new hairstyles the Beatles sported also conveyed a sense of being different and provided a ready, easy method for teens to declare their separateness. As with adolescent argot, the teenager with a Beatle hairdo was making a point—this was the territory of youth, adults were not invited.

The Beatles also were a *group* of four young men. There were groups before, such as the Nat King Cole Trio, The Ink Spots, and The Andrews Sisters, but they were grown-ups. The increased importance of the teen group for adolescence was thus reflected in the format of this pop phenomenon. The Beatles worked as a group, with all members singing and writing the songs (to varying degrees), and *acted* like a group—matching suits, joint appearances, and so on. Their first movie, the documentary-style *A Hard Day's Night* clearly promotes this image, as the Beatles are chased together, play cards together, go out dancing together, and, of course, perform together. In their youth, group function and success mimicked features of adolescence as a stage providing easy identification and hope for similar careers and immediate success.

Larson, Kubey and Colletti (1989) studied fifth through ninth graders' TV watching and music listening habits and illustrated how music and the peer society of adolescence seem to converge. Their findings indicate that latency-age children spend more time than teenagers watching TV; the reverse is true of listening to music. Further, the data indicate that watching TV is more typically done with family, while listening to music among the older subjects was more frequently done alone or with peers. In fact, an adolescent's popularity with peers has been shown to correlate with his or her familiarity and use of popular music. The authors posit that for contemporary youth, this change in media use can be considered a marker for the onset of adolescence. Thus, when youngsters begin to become emotionally involved and interested in pop music, buying discs and developing favorite performers, they are functionally adolescents.

In the 1960s, two genres within pop as a whole appealed to specific developmental and historical-cultural issues of the time. Folk rock and "protest" songs, exemplified by Bob Dylan, reflected a current political mood but also, for teenagers, were expressions of the idealism typical of adolescence. In earlier decades these adolescents' parents listened to folk songs, union songs, and songs of the Spanish civil war. Some of this idealism also was represented in psychedelic rock of the Woodstock era, a genre that also was greatly molded by the burgeoning drug culture of the time. In his exhortation, "turn on, tune in, and drop out," Timothy Leary appealed to three important adolescent activities: experimentation, introspection, and rebellion. All this could be achieved while safely ensconced in a mass peer movement, as was witnessed at Woodstock and other festivals.

In addition to satisfying the increasing peer culture demands of adolescents, pop music also appeals to more individual needs of teenagers. Broadly speaking, pop stars can serve as secondary attachment figures. These fantasied relationships

are significant in adolescent identity development (Greene & Adams-Price, 1990). Along these lines, Esman (1990), Brown and Hendee (1989), and others have noted the subtypes of fans that have grown along with pop music. The "teenybopper" of the 1960s and 1970s is one such example. Typically, a preadolescent or early adolescent girl, the teenybopper would develop "crushes" on one or more male pop stars who may serve as idealized White Knights or equally as frequently as masturbation fantasy objects. These infatuations often would be accompanied by devotion to "teen magazines" and acquisition of various related paraphernalia, such as T-shirts and posters. The acts that most attracted teenyboppers often would be long on "image" and short on musical talent, and this fact corresponded somewhat with the priorities of their young fans.

Older girls who are more musically sophisticated are more interested in soft, romantic music that may be lyrically more adept and musically complex. The ageless themes of romantic longing, friendship, and intimacy purveyed by the "singer-songwriter" find great audience in teenage girls. These softer sounds may provide a soothing backdrop for the anxiety-provoking issues of emerging sexuality for teenage girls in a culture that is less tolerant of such interests in its young women than its young men.

White adolescent males form almost the entire popular base of a different musical genre: heavy metal music. This subset of rock, beginning in the 1970s, has a fairly invariant look and sound. Typically, the heavy metal band is fronted by a long-haired, high-voiced male singer who wears tight leather outfits often with an androgynous look and moves about the stage in an aggressively sexual manner. During the 1960's, one of the earliest precursors to this genre appeared in Greenwich village hangouts in a group explicitly called the Fugs. That group and its progeny, the guitarists in heavy metal bands, dressed similarly and favor long dramatic solos that feature speed rather than other aspects of virtuosity. The guitarist moves his instrument while playing, using it as an overt phallic extension. Lyrics of heavy metal music tend to emphasize sexual needs in an aggressive fashion (especially compared to the singer-songwriters) and youthful rebellion in general. These themes have particular valence for the adolescent boy who, in many ways, is encouraged to be aggressive, to rebel, to be sexually active, but also must begin the transition to a more sublimated, mature adaptation as an adult.

For black adolescents, a number of other genres evolved that, at least initially, had limited appeal to white listeners. Rap, hip-hop, and house music are variants on a highly danceable type of music, sometimes interspersing previously recorded bits of music called "samples" with lyrics spoken rather than sung. Rap, which developed in the 1980s, often carries adamant political messages, with graphic evocations of racial and social concerns and themes of autonomy and independence, which appeal to these developmental strivings of the adolescent.

As in the 1950s, the lyrics and images of rock continue to raise adult hackles. In the mid-1980s, there was much public debate on the effect of rock music on youth, leading to congressional hearings on the topic. Although laden with political issues, the hearings and the related media attention highlighted some of the excesses in recent pop music, with heavy metal singled out as especially meriting parental monitoring. More recently, one rap group has been involved in court proceedings in relation to local obscenity regulations, and some municipalities have sought to prevent the singer Madonna's sexually provocative stage show from coming to town.

What is most clearly demonstrated by such adult reactions to pop music is that, as we have argued, music is a powerful component of adolescent subculture. The nature of the reaction is, in this sense, analogous to xenophobia. What is less clear is whether the specific concern—that excessively sexual or violent music adversely influences youth—has a scientific basis. In a review of the subject, Brown and Hendee (1989) cited data that suggest, for instance, that music preferences are dependent on earlier levels of school achievement. The suggestion is that teens who become interersted in less mainstream genres—such as punk and metal—may self-select based on lower school performance rather than the music *leading* to lower school performance. Other data cited point to the likelihood that adults' interpretations of rock lyrics are quite different from those of adolescents. An example is the lyric of "Born in the USA" a popular Bruce Springsteen song. In a

study of children in the fourth grade through college-age youths, a surprisingly high number of subjects at all age levels incorrectly identified the basic theme of the song. Often a catchphrase, a promotional image of the performer or the song, may be more salient to the teenager than the actual words.

The linking of image to music has spawned a major new medium—the music video. Music videos vary but most can be classified as "concept" videos showing the musician and/or actors in some ministory or set of images while the song plays. More straightforward are the performance type of videos that essentially show the artist in a real or simulated "live" performance of the song. Analyses of concept music videos indicate that a high proportion of them are sexually suggestive and/or violent, and often specifically degrading to women. In these instances, the lyrical content may indeed be secondary, but the images supply the content in a graphic way that may limit individual interpretation. Concerns about the impact of lyrics and especially music videos led the American Academy of Pediatrics (1989) to issue a statement on the object; it opposed censorship but recommended parental supervision and self-restraint in the music industry.

The focus on the deleterious potential of rock music has highlighted an undisputed trend: that of the more explicit sexual and violent imagery in rock as a whole. The question of why this has occurred may be approached from several vantage points. One relevant to this chapter is a developmental one. As rock and its performers have aged, some of its original function as adolescent subculture music has dissipated. Rock music has become big business in the corporate tradition. Perhaps only by pushing the boundaries—sexual, aggressive, racial—can new forms of rock fulfill the wish of adolescents to differentiate "them" from "us."

Another way that rock can maintain its appeal as subculture music is in its use of language. "Vallspeak" in the mid-1980s was presented in a popular rock song of the time with an actual Valley girl doing what might be called a Valley Girl rap—if that is not too confusing. Rap music proper has made extensive use of black and adolescent argot—Young-M.C.'s song "Bust a Move" popularized a slang phrase meaning, roughly, "Go for it" (an older slang phrase that has entered general use). Such verbal inventions (or popularizations) related to music are not new; the Beatles, remember, brought their Liverpudlian language with them—"fab," "gear" and so on. The slew of dances in the late 1950s and 1960s—the "Twist" being the most well known—also reflected the creative use of language in pop music.

During this century the period of life we call adolescence has come into prominence. Associ-ated sociolects and forms of musical expression have developed along with this postchild, preadult phase. Although it is impossible to predict exactly how future adolescents will speak or what type of music they will listen to, we may assume that tomorrow's teens will say things undecipherable to adults and play music that jars adult musical sensibilities. If we accept the premise of the adolescent need to separate, this is as it should be.

REFERENCES

American Academy of Pediatrics, Committee on Communications (1989). Impact of Rock Lyrics and Music Videos on Children and Youth. *Pediatrics, 83,* 314–315.

Blos, P. (1967). The second individuation process of adolescence. *Psychoanalytic Study of the Child, 22,* 162–186.

Brown, E. F., & Hendee, W. R. (1989). Adolescents and their music. *Journal of the American Medical Association, 262,* 1659–1663.

Chomsky, N. (1965). *Aspects of the theory of syntax.* Cambridge, MA: MIT Press.

Esman, A. H. (1990). *Adolescence and culture.* New York: Columbia University Press.

Freud, A. (1959). Adolescence. *Psychoanalytic Study of the Child, 13,* 255.

Greene, A. L. & Adams-Price, C. (1990). Adolescents' secondary attachments to celebrity figures. *Sex Roles, 23,* 335–347.

Labov, W. (1975). *Language in the inner city: Studies in the black English vernacular.* Philadelphia: University of Pennsylvania Press.

Larson, R., Kubey, R., & Colletti, J. (1989). "Changing Channels": Early adolescent media choices and shifting investments in family and friends. *Journal of Youth and Adolescence, 18,* 583–599.

Munro, P. (1989). *Slang U.* New York: Harmony Books.

Norman, P. (1981). *Shout! the Beatles in their generation.* New York: Simon and Schuster.

Pooley, E. (1991, August 5). Kids with guns. *New York Magazine.*

Shapiro, T. (1979). *Clinical psycholinguistics.* New York: Plenum Press.

Shapiro, T. (1985). Adolescent language: Its use for prognosis, group identity, values, and treatment. *Adolescent Psychiatry, 12,* 297–311.

Spears, R. A. (1991). *Contemporary American study.* Chicago: NTA Publishing Group.

Szatmary, D. P. (1991). *Rockin' in time: A social history of rock-and-roll.* Englewood Cliffs, NJ: Prentice-Hall.

23 / Youth Sports and Adolescent Development

Barri Katz Stryer, Steven E. Katz, and Dennis P. Cantwell

I believe that children, like little animals, require play and competition in order to develop. I believe that play is a major agency in civilizing infants. I believe that big-muscle movement helps the infant establish his balance within space in which he will henceforth operate. I believe that competition, reasonably supervised, is essential to the full maturing of the individual.

Children should have the widest possible experience of play—there are "exercises" that even two-month-old infants can be given by their parents—but heavily organized competition with end-of-season championships should not be initiated before the age of twelve, if then.

A sense of competition is natural in children, provides healthy emotional outlets and must not be suppressed; but it should not be exaggerated, either. Adults must not dominate the play of children; practices such as recruiting, redshirting and fake adoption are repugnant.

J. A. MICHENER, *Sports in America*, 1976

Athletics are an integral part of our society, encompassing both spectators and participants, from early childhood through generativity. They are valuable for enhancement of health, disease prevention, and psychological well-being. Exercise and athletics have been reported to decrease anxiety and depression and to increase self-esteem, self-confidence, and self-concept.

Self-concept is formed progressively through development, is multifaceted, and is influenced by a myriad of experiences and interactions with significant others. Children and adolescents define themselves, their abilities, competencies, incompetencies, and self-worth to a great degree by feedback they receive from their environment.

According to Coopersmith (1967), ". . . Self-esteem is the evaluation which the individual makes and customarily maintains with regard to himself. It expresses an attitude of approval or disapproval and indicates the extent to which an individual believes himself to be capable, significant, successful and worthy" (p. 5). Positive self-esteem develops from successful relations and mastery of skills. The most significant influences on the development of self-esteem are family, school, extracurricular activities, and the relationships formed during these interactions.

In childhood and adolescence, sports are the most prevalent extracurricular activity. Prior to the 1900s, children's sports were for the most part organized spontaneously by the participants. In the early 1900s, public schools introduced the first athlethic programs for youngsters. Subsequently, local and national youth agencies began to provide organization and sponsorship of many youth sports. At this time new programs for even younger children are constantly being developed.

Each year an increasing number of youngsters participate in organized sports. In the United States approximately 7 million children between the ages of 6 and 18 participate in school athletic programs; another 20 million, between the ages of 6 and 18, are involved in an organized athletic program, and another 20 million are involved in less structured sports including weekend skiing and neighborhood kickball. Virtually all children, at some time during their development, have some experience with organized sports.

The extent of involvement varies, but by early adolescence many children have already participated in intensive sports training and competition for several years. Athletics are an American obsession in which we risk losing sight of the players as children and people.

This chapter provides an overview of the influence of participation in sports on psychological and emotional development and the interaction between them. The potential positive aspects of athletics for the developing person, the relationship between normal development and sports, the important role models that overlap sports and development, the effects on self-concept and research on youth sports participation are discussed. Finally, proposed recommendations for guidelines in youth sports programs and suggestions for the role of psychiatrists are proposed.

Benefits of Youth Sports

Youth sports provide a healthy outlet and can be very rewarding. They encourage socialization, social competence, and family bonding, and facilitate the development of friendships across racial and ethnic groups, in addition to promoting physical and psychological growth. In a recent study, 65% of black and 45% of white high school athletes stated that athletic participation helped them to avoid drug use, and 32% of whites and 60% of blacks said it helped them avoid alcohol use (*USA Today*, 1993). It is widely accepted that sports have been seen as a vehicle out of poverty and the ghetto throughout most of the 20th century for America's youth. Earlier in the 20th century it was the Irish, Italians, and Jews, and later the blacks and Latinos. As will be discussed later, "this phenomenon" may or may not be beneficial, because for the vast majority of children, including a number of special populations, sports accrue unequivocal benefits. In sports children encounter demands that mirror other life experiences; these afford the children the opportunity to learn leadership skills, cooperativeness, teamwork, self-discipline, coping skills, respect for authority, competitiveness, sportsmanship, self-confidence, success, and failure. Participants have the opportunity for self-evaluation, peer comparison, and healthy competition, which helps to promote the development of positive self-esteem and self-concept.

Good mental health is related to positive self-concept. Positive self-concept is promoted by a sense of belonging, achievement, and normality. Normality, especially to a child, is related to doing what others can do and acquiring a sense of mastery. The more accomplishments children feel they achieve, the greater their sense of self-esteem and belonging. Regular exercise in postcoronary patients improves self-concept and increases acceptance of the disability as well as improving self-competence and self-efficacy. Likewise, participation in sports often has a therapeutic effect for emotionally disturbed and developmentally disabled youngsters. Athletics allows these children social interaction and physical activity while fostering a sense of mastery. Peer, parental, and teacher support facilitate a belief in one's self;

encouraging sport participation can help children to maximize their capabilities. Super and Block (1992) studied 45 men between the ages of 18 and 40 with physical disabilities and found that athletically active disabled men had better self-concept and greater need for achievement than the inactive group. Kapp-Simon, Simon, and Kristovich (1992) looked at self-perception, social skills, overall adjustment, and social inhibition in 45 youngsters 10 to 16 years old with craniofacial anomalies and found social skills and athletic competence to be the best predictors of emotional adjustment. In addition, children whose parents felt they had better skills believed they were more socially accepted. Brook and Heim (1991) did a pilot study looking at 16 asthmatic children and found that those involved in sports had a better self-image, were less anxious, and coped better with their illness than those who were not participating in sports.

Children and adolescents with psychiatric disorders, for example, attention deficit hyperactivity disorder (ADHD) and learning disorders, similarly benefit greatly from athletic participation. Sports can facilitate their development of social skills and peer relations. For those children who have impaired social skills, difficulty maintaining appropriate behavior, or problems with coordination, individual sports are also extremely valuable to provide structure and a sense of accomplishment and success; these are important in the development of physical well-being, self-esteem, and psychological growth. For example, martial arts can be especially beneficial.

The Special Olympics has allowed those children who are so impaired that they cannot participate in the usual competitive leagues an opportunity to experience feelings of mastery, healthy competition, and a sense of belonging, all of which help to maximize their potential psychological growth.

However, the athletic experience can also be detrimentally stressful and potentially devastating. Repeated failure, criticism, poor role models, negative peer interactions, as well as internal and external pressures to perform are fertile ground for the development of psychological disability and poor self-esteem. Responsibility to parents, coaches, and teammates, losing and winning, and inappropriate expectations can negatively affect an individual's functioning, impair a child's ability to reach his or her potential, and promote behaviors detrimental to the athlete's health. In addition, the allure of fame and fortune has at times become so seductive that children and families can become mesmerized by the fantasy of stardom, lose sight of reality, and emphasize sports to the detriment of other important developmental activities. The tragedy is that only an infinitesimal number of these children will ever compete athletically at the elite or professional level. As mentioned, many economically and culturally deprived individuals have seen sports as their ticket to success; when they place all their effort into excelling at sports, they may leave little time for education, socialization, and the development of other necessary skills. When their careers end by natural attrition or are aborted early either by injury or by not making the next tier, these individuals are poorly equipped to function in adult society. It should be noted that this phenomenon is not restricted to the ghetto. Many athletes are recruited before attending or finishing college and forgo a college education and/or a degree in order to compete immediately at the professional level; few of these athletes realize just how few college recruits are successful even in the minor leagues or ever earn high salaries. For every 2,300 high school senior basketball players only 40 will play college basketball and only 1 will play in the National Basketball Association (NBA). Less than 4% of varsity high school football players play college football and less than 1% of college players are even offered a professional contract. Even for those who are talented and fortunate enough to play at the professional level, careers are typically short-lived. The average active tenure in the National Football League (NFL) is 3.2 years—yet one must be in the NFL for 4.5 years to qualify for a pension and be 55 years old to draw on it. Unfortunately, the average lifespan of a professional football player is 54 years (Edwards, 1993). In the United States, 2 million children and adolescents participate in competitive gymnastics per year and only 7 or 8 participate in the Olympic games every 4 years. These findings illustrate why we have an obligation to attempt to ensure that even children with superior athletic talent have a well-rounded developmental experience. No mat-

ter how much they achieve in sports, they must be prepared for life.

Development and Sports

With respect to development and sports, organized athletic participation may start as early as the preschool years. Not infrequently, however, young children lack the physical development necessary to acquire the skills for some sports, the emotional maturity necessary to cope with the demands of competition, and the cognitive development to fully understand and interpret the rules. Eyesight, for example, does not fully mature until ages 6 or 7. Until that time children remain farsighted and have more difficulty tracking moving objects such as baseballs.

Prior to 10 years of age, children depend significantly on adult feedback and reinforcement, but with increasing age there is a progressive shift to dependence on peer comparison, the ability to follow rules, and reliance on conscience. During early adolescence peer evaluation becomes the more valued source of competence assessment (Weiss & Bredemeier, 1990). During later adolescence, the importance of peer comparison decreases as the impact of nonparental adult role modeling increases. Adolescence is characterized by the development of abstract thinking, an increased desire for autonomy, conflict between independence and dependence, the struggle to find a social niche and to define one's identity, as well as meeting the demands of increased new interests and responsibilities. These are stressful demands, and adolescents characteristically crave greater independence, control, and autonomy than the hierarchical and winning nature of structured and competitive sports can provide and coaches can tolerate. These athletes are children first; sport participation is only one of many necessary and important developmental experiences. Despite the changing developmental needs and cognitive capacities characteristic of moving from childhood through adolescence, nurturance, support, encouragement, consistency, and understanding of the athlete as a person are necessary.

Significant Adults

PARENTS

Children learn best and internalize most by role modeling. Parents' and coaches' attitudes and behavior significantly impact athletes' participation, enjoyment, attitudes, values, beliefs, stresses, and perceptions of achievement, demands, and capabilities. Most parents take pride in their children and all identify with them to some degree, but sometimes they lose sight of the developmental needs of their children. Some parents contribute significantly to the potentially detrimental aspects of sports and are at times the greatest source of stress for their children and others.

A six-year-old struck out and his coach, trying to console him, tells him that Pete Rose, who had the most hits in all of baseball history, struck out more than 1000 times. The child said "Yeah but Pete doesn't have to ride home with my dad" (*San Diego Union*, 6/25/91).

The father of a six-year-old threatened to sue his son's little league coach for jeopardizing the boy's major league future by using a reduced injury factor ball (*San Diego Union*, 6/25/91).

The parents of a seven-year-old figure skater remind her several times a week to keep up her athletic excellence as it will pay for college.

At times children are recognized only for their athletic endeavors and grow up believing their self-worth is primarily dependent on their athletic prowess. Some parents encourage their children not to rest when they are injured or deny their children time to heal to comply with the schedule of competition. Children have been held back a year in school in order to be physically larger than classmates in an effort to increase athletic advantage; it has even been reported that parents have requested surgical procedures on healthy children in an effort to improve their performance. In addition, at the intramural prepubescent level, parents frequently "pull strings" and attempt to change their children's teams or determine All Stars by unfair methods. Parents may react with anger when their child makes a mistake, is ready to stop a sport, or wants to take a break; not infrequently they are unable to listen to reason, to be empathic or supportive, and can only remind the child of the time and money they have invested in his or her athletic endeavors. In

a small number of cases, a parent's self-worth becomes so dependent on the successes and failures of the child in sports that the pressure the parent places on the child becomes his or her most significant stressor. Parents provide crucial role models for development. Children long for the approval of their parents and readily identify with and internalize their attitudes and values both constructive and maladaptive.

Two ten-year-old little league teams watch as the police break up a fight between coaches and parents (*San Diego Union*, 6/25/91).

A father runs onto the soccer field and pummels the referee (*Reporters Dispatch*, Westchester County, 11/94).

It has been hypothesized that adolescent Swedish ice hockey players behave more aggressively than their peers because they are taught to win at all costs (*L.A. Times*, 9/12/94).

COACHES

Coaches, the other important adults for athletes, significantly influence the development of social behavior and self-perception (Weiss & Bredemeier, 1990). In community programs, most coaches are volunteers without formal training, and the training of school coaches is highly variable. Despite the fact that some coaches either instinctively or through training are idealized role models and teachers for children, typically coaches have little knowledge of physiological or psychological development or of the research demonstrating the best ways to enhance motivation, performance, and development on and off the playing field. In addition, they typically lack the knowledge and skill necessary for tactful communication and education for parents. The situation may be further complicated by the fact that, especially in adolescence, coaches may minimize or denigrate the influence of parents on their children if the coaches' attitudes and values are in conflict with those of the parents. At the high school, college, and professional levels, a coaching style characterized by low warmth, communication, and nurturance and high expectations of socially mature behavior dominate; this style tends to be perpetuated by winning (Weiss & Bredemeier, 1990). Coaches, like parents, have been known to make children feel bad unless they win, to favor certain players, and to show inappropriate, unsportsmanlike behavior to parents, officials, spectators, and players.

A seven-year-old T-ball player watches his coach knock his mother unconscious (*San Diego Union,* 6/25/91).

Burton, Tannehill, Martens, and Gould (1987) observed 22 community youth basketball coaches and found criticism employed 20 times more often than praise and punishment 4 times more often than reward. Coaches may use negative reinforcement, sarcasm, not acknowledge the positives, patronize children, and even encourage negative peer interactions.

Athletes may feel misunderstood by their coaches, who frequently lose sight of the developmental level of their athletes and the important role of sports other than the score and outcome. They may forget or minimize the importance of family, friends, and school in the young athlete's life. Even when confronted with these realities, some coaches may not or cannot respond to their athlete's pleas. As with parents, some of these difficulties result from the coaches' personal investment in the athlete's success; this investment puts coaches at risk of creating increased pressure as they become vicariously involved in the athlete. In these cases the coaches' personal goals may make it difficult to promote the child's needs. In keeping with the adage, "No pain, no gain," parents, coaches, and society may encourage young athletes to compete with injuries.

PROGRAM COORDINATORS

Formal sports programs usually are organized by adult program coordinators and consequently modeled after adult and professional sports. The goal of professional sports is to provide entertainment and financial profit, which makes winning more crucial. The developmental needs of children and adolescents often are lost to the strong emphasis on outcome.

Research on Motivation, Enjoyment, and Attrition

Scientific studies demonstrate that positive reinforcement, encouragement, and sound technical instruction within a supportive environment are the best ways to facilitate motivation, morale, enjoyment, performance, physical competence, and group cohesion in sports (Horn, 1985; Smith, 1993; Smith, Smoll, & Curtis, 1979). Motivation in sports, for boys and girls 8 to 18 years old, is related to improvement of skills, having fun, learning new skills, being challenged, and being physically fit (Smith, Zane, Smoll, & Coppel, 1983). A healthy goal is to encourage desired behaviors with positive reinforcement and to instill motivation and a desire to achieve as opposed to a fear of failure.

Enjoyment is a major reason youngsters play sports; lack of enjoyment is related to attrition. Scanlan and Lewthwaite (1986) found a positive correlation between enjoyment and desire for continued participation. The same investigators looked at predictors of enjoyment in competitive wrestlers 9 to 14 years old and demonstrated more pleasure for boys who perceived: greater satisfaction with their performance from coaches and parents; less pressure from their mothers; fewer negative reactions from their mothers; more spontaneous positive involvement and interaction from adults; and themselves as "more able."

In addition, there is an inverse relationship between the amount of pleasure received from participating in a contest and level of postcompetition stress, independent of game outcome. It has also been demonstrated that children like sports less and derive less pleasure from them when they perceive: their coaches as punitive and critical; greater negative interactions with their mothers; less satisfaction from parents and coaches with their performance; and themselves as having less skill (Scanlan and Lewthwaite, 1986; Smith, Smoll, & Curtis, 1978; Wankel & Kreisel, 1985).

ATTRITION

Regular physical exercise gradually decreases between childhood and adolescence. Seventy-five percent of youngsters who begin organized sport participation by 7 years of age quit before they are 15 years old, and 25 to 50% of youth involved in sports quit each year. Starting earlier in childhood leads to quitting earlier, but it does not increase the chances of making the Olympics. Earlier in life the relative lack of coordination secondary to children's development can prematurely portray them as "bad athletes" or "klutzy kids," leading to a negative experience and lack of continued interest in participation. These early experiences may contribute to an increasingly sedentary lifestyle with age, which is a significant public health concern with respect to physical and emotional well-being. Sedentary lifestyle has been linked to increased incidence of coronary artery disease, hypertension, diabetes mellitus, obesity, and other chronic medical conditions. In addition, the incidence of obesity in the population has increased in recent years coincident with the decrease in physical activity. These findings make the significant attrition rates of youth sports of great concern. In addition, the problem is heightened by the decreasing financial resources for school systems resulting in the discontinuation or limiting of physical education and scholastic sport programs. Inadequately informed school board members and administrators frequently argue that physical education is not an essential part of the total developmental experience. Physical education programs that are enjoyable, instructive in the benefits of exercise, and self-esteem-enhancing are most likely to increase future exercise behavior. Students are more likely to say that they plan to exercise in the future if they had positive feelings about physical education (Ferguson, Yesalis, Pomrehn, & Kirkpatrick, 1989).

Studies of attrition in youth sports often relate it to negative sport experiences, including not playing, overemphasis on competition, too much pressure, boredom, dislike of the coach, lack of pleasure, and competitive stress. Burton and Martens (1986) studied 8- to 17-year-old wrestlers and related dropout to an athlete's perceived potential being consistently threatened by failure. Thirty-three percent of 10- to 15-year-old soccer players related quitting to too much pressure and criticism from coaches and emphasis on competition (Pooley, 1980). More than 50% of 10- to 18-year-old former swimmers reported not liking the coach and the pressure as at least somewhat important in relation to dropping out (Gould et al., 1985). Similarly, swimmers attributed their teammates' attrition to pressure, conflict with coaches, and insufficient successes (McPherson et al., 1980). Robinson and Carron (1982) looked at 98 high school football players and found 26 dropouts who felt, in comparison with those who continued to play, less a part of the team, that their poor performance was related to ability, less support

for playing from their fathers, less pleasure from participation, and that the coach was a dictator. On the other hand, Durant, Pendergrast, Donner, Seymore, and Gaillard (1991) looked at adolescent withdrawal from school-sponsored sports and found it due to, in descending order: injury, being cut from a team for academic or other reasons, unspecified reasons, necessity of working, inconvenient schedule, and too much schoolwork. However, they also noted less intent to participate in organized sports in the future when withdrawal was linked to not playing, feeling less able, or not having enough free time and if the athlete was black, female, or older. In addition, and perhaps most important, athletes whose withdrawal was self-initiated (quit as opposed to being cut or injured) were least likely to think they would be involved in nonorganized sports in the future. These authors also noted that for scholastic sports, the reasons for withdrawal were not the same across different sports.

Although many studies link attrition to negative sport experiences, it is also a widely held impression that some children's interest and participation in organized sports decline as they become adolescents and increasingly social members of society. At that time they are faced with balancing social activities, academics, athletics, and other organized activities. When this competes with the increased time desired for peer relations and necessary for school, involvement in sports at competitive levels often decreases. Children who make this choice consciously or unconsciously may be making a healthy choice for reasons of socialization. However, learning how to balance some regular activity and commitment with these other demands and interests is important and beneficial. In fact, many well-known adolescent elite athletes have complained about wanting to be more regular people. Andrea Jaeger cited this as her reason for leaving tennis at 18 years old; at one point in her career, Kim Zemeskal had reportedly considered quitting for similar reasons, but after a break she resumed her athletic career. Traditionally, leaving sports for increasing social interests during and after puberty has been reported to be more common in girls. It is likely, however, that the reason for this is more complicated and related to differential encouragement, respect, availability, and greater emphasis on male participation and excellence in sports from society as a whole that influences coaches, schools, peers, and parents.

With the introduction of Title IX and the increasing emphasis on physical fitness for physical and psychological well-being, it will be interesting to see whether this pattern will be altered. Title IX mandates that for colleges and universities with both women's and men's sports programs, total funding for mens' sports must be equal to that allocated for women's sports in relation to percent of the student population. Thus, if 50% of students are women, 50% of funding for athletics must be for women's sports.

Stress and Athletics

Despite the aforementioned research on the benefits of youth sports and how to maximize enjoyment, motivation, and self-esteem, there is great concern that the pressure involved with youth sports is sometimes more than children are developmentally prepared to handle.

Youngsters' participation in youth sports falls on a continuum from experimenting with several sports once a week to intramural, interscholastic, and private club associations. Within the competitive arenas, there are further subdivisions of "intensive" training at various levels from beginner, local to countrywide competition to elite, national, and international competition. The amount of pressure and stress as well as enjoyment the children experience from their involvement is influenced by the interactions of a multitude of internal and external factors, including the child's genetic predisposition and temperament. Regardless of the parameters, however, the sport experience does place some children under high levels of unnecessary and/or unhealthy stress. Smoll and Smith (1990) suggest that for most children, sports are not very stressful and that some degree of stress may better prepare them for other life experiences.

Stress occurs when demands exceed available resources. It is further related to the person's perception of the situation, his or her abilities, and the outcome or perceived outcome if the demand is not met (Smoll & Smith, 1990). It should be acknowledged that children have different capacities for stress. For the vast majority of children, a moderate amount of stress and anxiety are important developmental experiences and can motivate performance. In sports stress is more determined by the setting, past experiences, social learning, and perceived family and social pressure than the competition (Magill, Ash, & Smoll, 1982). Thus, for each individual or athlete, what is stressful and pathologically stressful depends on previous experiences, expectations, and perceptions that have shaped his or her belief systems, self-worth, self-concept, self-esteem, and character. Some athletes perceive winning as everything; their identity, love, support, and respect from family and coaches all are dependent on their sport participation and performance. Being bored and unchallenged with minimal demands and feeling misunderstood by parents and coaches can also be stressful and decrease gratification.

Early studies evaluated stress in terms of physiologic measures, but this did not prove helpful. Current studies utilize self-report measures of stress, anxiety, self-esteem, expectations, etc., to measure state and trait anxiety. Trait anxiety is defined as one's permanent personality predisposition whereas state anxiety represents one's reaction to a specific situation at a specific point in time (Cratty, 1983; Morris, 1984). Martens (1978b) defined competitive trait anxiety (CTA) as one's permanent personality disposition representing the tendency to feel threatened and experience stress during athletic competitions. He developed a self-report instrument, the Sport Competition Anxiety Test, which measures the frequency with which athletes experience anxiety symptoms during sport competition. Lewthwaite and Scanlan (1989) modified this to allow separation of cognitive and somatic anxiety symptoms, with cognitive anxiety meaning worries about performance, failure, and others' perceptions, and somatic anxiety relating to autonomic arousal and affective or physiological responses.

Simon and Martens (1979) compared state of anxiety of 9- to 14-year-old boys with respect to four common activities: group and solo band performances, scholastic tests, and athletic competition. Sleep disturbance in anticipation of a performance was lowest before an athletic event. Band soloists experienced the greatest anxiety, and individual sport competitors reported more anxiety than team competitors. For all athletes, anxiety was slightly higher during the season than preseason, and wrestlers were the only athletes reporting more anxiety than students taking examinations.

Studies indicate that the development of test anxiety is related to negative interactions and feedback and unrealistic expectations by parents and teachers as well as self-induced pressure and expectations of other students. These studies are noted because of the parallels to athletic participation. Major predictors of anxiety in youth sports include: negative parental and coach interactions, fears and worries about losing, fear of failure, and amount of fun experienced, which is inversely correlated with anxiety independent of game outcome (Gould, Horn, & Spreeman, 1983; Passer, 1983). However, game outcome is important for postcompetition anxiety. Major predictors of postcompetition anxiety include: victory vs. defeat and amount of fun experienced (Scanlan & Passer, 1978, 1979). Both male and female soccer players and male wrestlers who lost their events report greater postgame anxiety than winning participants. Having won decreased anxiety levels lower than pregame levels, and having lost increased it above pregame levels. Children complaining of less fun reported greater postcompetition anxiety. State anxiety for most 10- to 12-year-old boys and girls playing soccer was only slightly increased during the season compared with the preseason except for the significant 20-point increase seen in a few children (Scanlan & Passer 1978, 1979). Similarly, Simon and Martens (1979) noted a small number of athletes whose state anxiety prior to competition was extremely high.

Lewthwaite and Scanlan (1989) looked at competitive trait anxiety in 9- to 14-year-old competitive wrestlers and demonstrated lower self-esteem, more upset with poor performance, and more preference for avoiding competition in athletes with a higher frequency of somatic competitive trait anxiety (SCAT) symptoms. Boys with more frequent cognitive anxiety showed greater personal upset with respect to poor performance, and perceived: (1) greater coach and parental shame and disappointment with a poor performance; (2) negative feedback and interactions from adults; and (3) more parental pressure to participate.

Passer (1983) followed 10- to 15-year-old recreational soccer players and demonstrated that high-SCAT players compared to low-SCAT players expected poorer performances and greater shame and negative feedback, criticism, and punishment from coaches and parents in relation to a poor performance. Gould, Horn, and Spreeman (1983)

found the expectation of lower tournament finishes and less confidence in high-SCAT compared to low-SCAT 13- to 19-year-old elite national wrestlers.

Finally, competitive stress also can increase the risk of injury, cause sleep disturbances, decrease performance after a certain critical point and decrease enjoyment. Twenty-one percent of children in the Michigan Youth Sports Study reported sleep disturbances related to athletic performance. Forty-six percent of children complaining of sleep disturbances reported worrying about a performance, and 25% reported being upset about losing as a contributing factor.

Potential Adverse Effects of Youth Sports and Intensive Training

POTENTIAL ADVERSE PSYCHOLOGICAL EFFECTS

In addition to the aforementioned potential negative short-term effects, there are less acute potentially long-term problems subsequent to intensive sport participation. Developmentally individuals benefit from a balanced life encountering a variety of experiences. Some young athletes are involved in their sport to such a degree that they live and breathe the sport and thereby suffer from a lack of other important developmental experiences and social isolation. One forgets that most of these young people will not grow up to be world-class or Olympic athletes; even if they do, virtually all will leave their sport by about age 30 to 35. Some of these youngsters leave their parents' home very early or families relocate to train with the "best" coach, and many at any competitive level begin traveling extensively and staying in hotels before the age of 14. World-class gymnasts are expected to be adults between 12 and 14 years old. In certain sports, such as tennis and golf, significant sums of money may cause added pressure. Likewise, pressures are significant in numerous scholastic sports, where entrance and financial tickets to college and later professional contracts may be at stake. This is an interesting twist in a society in which a large percentage of our youth have significantly extended adolescence through their 20s. It is as if we are promoting being an athlete at the expense of childhood. Even in those athletes who remain with their families, the entire family may revolve around the sport, encouraging the child to perceive his or her self-worth and concept as dependent on participation and performance in athletics. In some situations children's success in sports has been known to be a significant source of income for families. For some of these adolescents, schooling, parties, even family outings are dependent on their coaches and their athletic schedule. If a youngster wants to quit the sport, he or she may feel extreme guilt with respect to his or her parent's commitment of time and money and the commitment to coaches.

Excess stress, decreased performance, or inability to participate because of injury has been seen to lead to dysthymia, depression, chronic fatigue, substance abuse, conversion disorders, and eating disorders. In the general population, the prevalence of eating disorders has been consistently reported as 1% for anorexia and 1 to 3% for bulimia. In female athletes, the prevalence of disordered eating has been reported between 15 to 62% (Nattiv, Agostini, Drinkwater, & Yeager, 1994). Increased vulnerability to eating disorders is also related to cognitive distortions, which can develop secondary to intense sports participation. Sports emphasizing lean physique and low body weight for peak performance (swimming and distance running) as well as those where aesthetics influence scores (gymnastics and figure skating) are associated with an increased vulnerability to eating disorders in the athlete (Nattiv et al., 1994). In 1992 the University of Washington found 32% of 182 female college athletes and 62% of female college gymnasts engaged in at least one disordered eating behavior (vomiting, laxative abuse, diet pills, etc.) (Ryan, 1995). In extreme cases the stress of a youngster's participation in sports may lead to a belief that there is no way out. In these situations, malingering or purposeful injury has been used to escape competition (Nash, 1987).

Finally, burnout or staleness, due to overtraining, often referred to as overtraining syndrome, can lead to medical and emotional disorders. This syndrome contains many physiological signs and symptoms as well as psychological signs and symptoms akin to depression. Many of the signs and symptoms of burnout may be characteristic of other serious medical and psychiatric disorders; these other conditions must be ruled out, especially if the effects are interfering with areas of the child's life besides athletics. Psychologically, burnout causes many high-level athletes to quit before they achieve their potential. Burnout is the sequelae of "'working too hard'" under too much pressure "'for too long'" (Maslach, 1982 from Feigley, 1984), coincident with the "'progressive loss of idealism, energy and purpose'" (Freudenberger & Richelson, 1981 from Feigley, 1984). Overtraining is the primary cause of chronic fatigue and depression in both high school and college athletes, but one must not forget to rule out other possible causes (Lidstone, Amundson, & Amundson, 1991; Puffer & McShane, 1991).

POTENTIAL PSYCHOPHYSIOLOGICAL EFFECTS

All the physiological manifestations of stress have been seen in athletes, including stress-related gastrointestinal distress and dermatologic conditions. Stress can manifest itself as pain, injury, or diffuse weakness, muscle soreness, or objective signs and symptoms of pain without identifiable physiologic cause. Pain and injury can be a seemingly acceptable way to quit or decrease expectations, or to escape high-pressured competition without losing face. Being injured is not equivalent to quitting, and an injured teammate is still part of the team (Nash, 1987).

Marks and Goldberg (Thornton, 1991) reported on 25 athletes, all diagnosed by family practitioners, pediatricians, or orthopedists with relatively minor or common orthopedic problems that are usually self-limited and not particularly distressing or incapacitating, who presented to the authors with severe incapacitating pain. The primary caregiver referred these children to special orthopedists for a second opinion because the continued complaints were so severe that there was concern that the physicians were missing a more serious condition. Intensive medical workups, including magnetic resonance imaging (MRI) scans, confirmed the original somatic diagnosis as well as an adjustment disorder with disproportionate pain motivated unconsciously to escape the pressure associated with the sport. Young athletes may exaggerate minor injuries and complain of pain weeks after injuries should have healed to escape the pressure of their sport.

Reflex sympathetic dystrophy (RSD) is well documented in adults but was first described in children in 1977 by Fermaglick. This is an exaggerated response of the sympathetic nervous system to a minor trauma so that the athlete develops severe, recurrent, chronic pain affecting an entire extremity accompanied by autonomic nervous system changes and dystrophy of the bone, skin, and soft tissue. Muscle atrophy, bone demineralization, and contractions result from inactivity and inadequate treatment. Very few children exhibit this syndrome. Lyle Micheli saw more than 20 cases between 1982 and 1985; as of 1995, more than 100 cases had been seen at the Sports Medicine Clinic at Boston Children's Hospital (personal communication, Lyle Micheli). The majority are participants in intensive athletic training and stressful competition, especially in individual sports. Psychological stress has been suggested to be important in reflex sympathetic dystrophy. Gymnasts, dancers, and figure skaters who are also high academic achievers from middle- to upper-class demanding families seem to be at greatest risk (Nash, 1987; Pillemer & Micheli, 1988).

Finally, in the overall area of risk, safety, and lifestyle, Nattiv and Puffer (1991) compared health risk behaviors in athletes and nonathletic peers. They found college athletes to have a significantly higher proportion of risky lifestyle behaviors when compared to nonathletes with respect to alcohol use; driving under the influence of drugs and alcohol; getting into a car with an impaired driver; use of seat belts; use of helmets on bikes, mopeds, or motorcycles; use of contraception; number of sexual partners and sexually transmitted diseases. It can be speculated that such behaviors are related to the need to prove oneself, feel more comfortable socially by increasing self-esteem, gain peer acceptance and decrease anxiety to escape feelings of isolation and being alone, to demonstrate competence outside of one's sport, and to defend feelings of invulnerability.

Interventions

COACHES EFFECTIVENESS TRAINING

In the 1970s Smith et al. developed the Coaches Behavior Assessment System (CBAS) (Smith, Smoll & Curtis, 1978). They studied 51 Little League baseball coaches in 202 games. The coaches were evaluated by trained coders,

coaches' self-perceptions of their own behaviors, and data collected from 542 players after the season. The results were analyzed for several parameters and indicated that players respond best to supportive, instructional coaches. In addition, players on teams with a supportive environment liked each other more. The team's record was not related to how much the players liked the coach or whether they wanted to retain the same coach. However, players on winning teams believed their parents liked their coaches more than players on losing teams. Winning was not of great importance to the players, but they were aware of its importance to their parents. The importance of winning increased after the age of 12 but remained less important than coaching behaviors. Other studies also have reported the greater importance of winning to adults than children. Most children would rather play on a losing team than sit on the bench of a winning team. However, it is important to note that with increasing age, winning becomes increasingly important during adolescence, although having fun also continues to increase in importance (Martens, 1978). Finally, there was a significant interaction between athletes' self-esteem and coach supportiveness, which is defined as positive reinforcement for effort, participation, and desirable performance and efforts to respond to mistakes with encouragement and constructive noncritical instruction. Participants with low self-esteem were especially responsive to fluctuations in positive technique.

Subsequently, Smith et al. (1979) developed Coaches Effectiveness Training (CET), which is a cognitive-behavioral approach to educate coaches to provide a positive, supportive environment for their teams. This program was tested by randomly assigning 31 Little League baseball coaches to an experimental and a control group. The experimental group was educated regarding the research that prompted the development of CET, then underwent CET; thereafter feedback and self-monitoring were used to increase the coaches' self-awareness and encourage them to use the information learned. During the season, trained observers collected data on the coaching behaviors of every coach and after the season data was collected from 325 children. The win-lose records of the two groups were not significantly different. However, trained coaches were better liked, were considered better teachers, and their players liked each other more and enjoyed participating more. Perhaps most important was the significant increase in self-esteem from the previous year for children who played on experimental teams compared with the insignificant change for control group players.

Smoll et al. replicated this study and the results in 1989. With respect to self-esteem, the increase in self-esteem for experimental players was specific to those who initially were rated as having low self-esteem. In addition, the authors evaluated competitive anxiety and saw lower levels in players on the teams of trained coaches when compared to those on the teams of untrained coaches.

In 1992, Barnett, Smoll, and Smith demonstrated a 26% dropout rate for control players, which is comparable to attrition rates in other studies of youth sports, but only a 5% attrition rate of experimental players. Control group dropouts reported that not returning was associated with a negative sport experience that previous season.

Conclusions and Recommendations

Sports play a prominent role in the lives of many youngsters. They are influential across several domains and at all developmental levels regardless of the athlete's degree of involvement. Sport participation and talent, when approached sensitively, with continuing awareness of the developmental needs of the youngster as a human being, not just an athlete, should enhance a child's development. However, for this to be the expected outcome, all levels of participation should be reexamined. The vast majority of youngsters involved in sports are not going to make it a career or be Olympic, world-class, or professional athletes. Even for those who reach these lofty levels, participation at the competitive level usually ends at a relatively young age, and athletic talent and participation alone do not promote a healthy, well-balanced individual who is prepared to face the world in other arenas. Regardless of how superior a child's athletic talent is, if participation interferes with his or her personal development, we are doing the child a disservice. Adults must help facilitate a balance to ensure that the emphasis on

athletics does not interfere with school or family relations or prevent adequate socialization and the introduction and enjoyment of other activities. Children are not miniature adults, and youth sports, even at the elite level, should not emulate professional sports.

The American Academy of Pediatrics has recognized some of the problems inherent in youth sports and has endorsed several of the following observations and recommendations.

To begin with, it is important to understand the value of unstructured play and a variety of diverse experiences. Children need to learn how to relax and what to do with free time. These activities are important since they promote the growth of ingenuity, problem solving, spontaneity, curiosity, information for making choices, and creativity. Youngsters should be supported in experimenting with various sports and encouraged to find at least one sport they enjoy and can comfortably make a commitment to. If support and gentle encouragement are not sufficient, they should not be forced to persevere. Participation should be a choice without intimidation, bribery, or pressure.

With maturation, athletes should be encouraged to participate and take responsibility for setting goals and making choices involving scheduling practices and other important activities. Guidance and encouragement should be provided in a nonjudgmental, supportive manner for the benefit of the athlete, not the coach, the team, or the family. This will allow the sports arena to enhance the adolescent's evolving identity and promote autonomy. If motivation and enjoyment are going to be enriched and facilitate positive psychological growth, coaches and parents must tailor their interactions to the development level of each athlete.

Adults should not look at the goals of youth sports as winning a game or being a star athlete. Children need short-term goals with reasonable, realistic expectations. They must be secure in the belief that love and identity are not contingent on athletics. The ultimate goal should always be to promote the development of a healthy, well-balanced, and well-adjusted person with positive self-esteem and a good self-concept. Thus, enjoying the process and reducing stress is of utmost importance. The magnitude of stress, when it can be controlled, should be moderated; at all times the athlete's developmental age must be borne in mind, and the goal should be attempting to ensure, not to compromise, functioning and development of self-concept.

The philosophy of learning play and having fun should be key elements in establishing short-term goals. Positive reinforcement and role modeling are the most effective means of producing desired behaviors. Likewise, bad attitudes, poor sportsmanship, and disrespect for teammates and officials are behaviors that provide poor role models. If the emphasis is on process, game outcome will automatically become less significant. Competition and stress are inevitable in life and need to be mastered, but in youth sports they should be learned in settings where fun and gaining new skills remain primary.

Stress may become detrimental when competition becomes the primary focus. Smoll and Smith (1990) point out that adults can facilitate a healthy perspective with respect to competition by clearly communicating to children that neither winning nor losing has any bearing on their value or the affection adults have for them. Success is achieved by striving for victory or trying one's hardest, but that it is not equivalent to winning and losing is not equivalent to failure (Smoll & Smith, 1990). Baseball teams and basketball teams may lose more than 40% of their games and still win the championship or the World Series. We are all going to lose some competitions. Coaches and parents must make clear that losing or making a mistake is acceptable as long as one is trying. Children must experience success and failure. They must learn to win and lose with equanimity and to feel comfortable with competition without experiencing pathological anxiety and fear of failure.

Parents and coaches must establish communication and respect for each other, for players, and for officials, and must understand their roles in relation to the child's sport. Parents should show interest but not be overly involved or sideline coaches. They should understand the basics of their child's sport and place emphasis on having fun and enjoying participation rather than outcome. If these goals are promoted, it seems logical that athletes at all levels will experience greater enjoyment, less anxiety, and less stress. Simultaneously, they should be emotionally better adjusted, experience fewer negative sequelae, and benefit from a more well-rounded sense of self. Those

youngsters with innate potential and drive to be superior athletes can still succeed.

Unfortunately, despite the wealth of information available, most coaches and parents remain unaware of the stress and pressure placed upon youth athletes. Critical coaching with an emphasis on winning remains the norm, and fun and promoting self-esteem are often secondary. Many adults involved with youth sports, including coaches, parents, and program coordinators, are unaware of the harm they can cause and often appear to forget or ignore that their young athletes are developing people before they are sports stars. Education is the obvious starting point. All adults who participate in youth sports, and athletes when appropriate, need to be informed of the seriousness of the potential problems, recommendations for healthy change and marked potential benefits. Organized youth sports should be tailored to the athletes' developmental and chronological capacity. Numerous suggestions to facilitate these goals have been made, including adapting equipment and rules to meet the physical and psychological abilities of the children, making expectations predictable, decreasing uncertainty, and, at least prior to adolescence, allowing all children equal playing time. With sport participation as the vehicle, children can benefit from learning cognitive coping, relaxation, and stress management techniques that will be useful in many of life's arenas.

In addition, in order to better stress reinforcement for effort and participation especially prior to 13 years old, restructuring of the end of the season should deemphasize or even eliminate playoffs, All Stars, significant media attention, and elaborate championship ceremonies recognizing individuals. Such events should recognize all participants. Even after age 13, deemphasizing specific games, decreasing media attention, and decreasing perceived expectations will usually decrease anxiety.

Similarly, during the early years, an alternative model for organized sport participation is to utilize adults solely as facilitators to teach skills and rules and to maintain safety, fairness, and respect. It should be recalled that for generations children did very well on their own playing in schoolyards, streets, and playgrounds without adult involvement. At the youngest ages, especially preschool and kindergarten, focus should be on basic skills, not on playing games. One possible model would be for children to play different positions, with different teammates, each with equal playing time during a game. There would be no running win-lose record, since the teams would change continually. Playing with the same peers at some point can have advantages for more complicated cooperative play.

Other important considerations exist at the more competitive levels. First, some authorities feel that it is unhealthy for children under age 12 to 13 to be competing at highly competitive levels. This chronological age clearly will vary with the individual's emotional maturity, ability to cope with competition, and reaction to stress. It has even been suggested that rules be made regarding children not competing outside the local intramural level until a certain age and that children be ineligible for national, international, and Olympic competition until a predetermined age. In the upcoming Olympic games (2000) female gymnasts will have to be 16 years old. In some instances, professional and international competition should be reserved for adults 21 and older. In addition guidelines should be set for the hours of practice per day and number of practices per week to increase productivity, energy, focus, and psychological as well as physical well-being. Coaches and parents must continue to give positive reinforcement for effort during the learning process. As proficiency increases and improvement becomes more subtle, athletes need to understand that refinement is the same as acquisition of a new skill was previously.

It has been shown that coaches can be taught to interact more effectively and positively with youngsters and that understanding psychological principles is beneficial. CET is available, and more than 7,600 coaches had been trained by 1992. This kind of training should be mandatory for all youth sport coaches. Similarly, parents can be educated with respect to their roles in making the youth sport experience positive and healthy. After education, reinforcement and monitoring is necessary to ensure continued appropriate coaching behaviors. Parents and coaches should also be educated to identify young athletes who experience dangerous levels of competitive stress. Parents are in a position to make healthy choices and set necessary limits for children, if they can separate their own needs from their child's. Officials must learn to address inappropriate and unsportsmanlike behavior of coaches, athletes, and spectators. Once coaches are educated, we can only hope that they will be able to intervene sensitively to protect the child in families where parents continue to place undo stress on the child and others. Early prevention is preferable to later psychiatric intervention.

ROLE OF PSYCHIATRY

The onus is on health care professionals to promote safe, healthy, and balanced athletic participation. Preseason physicals are required prior to competing. These physicals present an opportunity for parents and coaches to be educated about mental health issues and stress. In some programs, preparticipation physicals are conducted by a multidisciplinary team of sports physicians. Child psychiatrists should be team members and play a salient role with respect to education and screening. Given the opportunity and encouragement, children will discuss their concerns. In this setting, untreated depression, attention deficit hyperactivity disorder, eating disorders, risk-taking behavior, and parent-child or coach-child problems can be identified and interventions can follow that likely would not have occurred until the detrimental consequences of sports participation had become more serious.

As psychiatrists, we should be involved in the educational process and take some initiative in preventing the problems and promoting the benefits of youth sports. We should educate other professionals involved with youth sports regarding screening questions, when a psychiatric evaluation is indicated, and how to make an appropriate referral. This is extremely important, as many sports-related problems are seen initially by primary care physicians or orthopedists. In our practice of child psychiatry, we should pay special attention to evaluating the role of sports in the life of each of our patients. Such an evaluation can be therapeutic as long as the proper setting is utilized and appropriate developmental and psychiatric principles are followed. On the other hand, presenting symptoms that seem related to sport participation or initial complaints about participation or performance problem may be indicative of other problems. Serious performance problems are often indicative of deeper psychological issues. In addition to the customary comprehensive psychiatric history, a developmental and family history of the child's involvement in sports should be undertaken for athletic patients. At a minimum, the following issues should be explored:

When and how the child became involved in sports and the specific sport?

Did/does the child participate in more than one sport?

What is the meaning of sports to the patient and family?

What are the expectations and aspirations for athletics for the patient, family, and coach?

What are the athlete's and family's level of involvement in the sport?

What was his or her participation schedule and how has it changed to date?

How many days and hours does he or she practice?

What is his or her school schedule, hours of unstructured time, and how does athletics interfere with other activities?

What feelings about competition, practice schedules, coaches, and parental involvement does the athlete have?

How are family relations and peer relations effected by sport participation?

What is the athletic participation of family members currently and previously (e.g., was mother/father or grandmother/grandfather an elite/aspiring elite or professional athlete or coach?)?

Psychiatrists can also play an important role when athletes are injured or when they cease playing a sport. At higher competitive levels, athletes should be prepared for the time when they will withdraw because of natural attrition, injury, or other causes. Termination is an extremely stressful event for most athletes.

Youth sports can be very beneficial for children at all levels, including the most competitive levels, but it may take professional intervention and significant attitudinal change to ensure that the benefits exceed the risks. Guidelines have been published for youth sports, many of which have been discussed in this chapter. Although abundant room for more research exists, the available body of knowledge supports the premise that structured youth sports need improvement. It is unfortunate that despite the aforementioned information, few substantive changes at the local, national, or international levels have been made.

REFERENCES

Barnett, N. P., Smoll, F. L., & Smith, R. E. (1992). Effects of enhancing coach-athlete relationships on youth sport attrition. *The Sport Psychologist, 6,* 111–127.

Boys who play hockey found to behave worse. (1994, September 12). *Los Angeles Times.*

Bradley, E. (1993, November 9). "Survey: Sports foster racial unity." *USA Today.*

Brook, U., & Heim, M. (1991). A pilot study to investigate whether sport influences psychological parameters in personality of asthmatic children. *Family Practice, 8* (3), 213–215.

Burton, D., & Martens, K. (1986). Pinned by their own goals. An explanatory investigation into why kids drop out of wrestling. *Journal of Sports Psychiatry, 8,* 183–195.

Burton, D., Tannehill, D., Martens, R., & Gould, H. (1987, April 17). *Developing better youth sport coaches: An evaluation of the level 1 American Coaching Effectiveness Program.* Paper presented at the annual conference of the American Association for Health, PE, and Dance, Las Vegas, NV.

Carroll, F. Pressure parents exert can negate value of youth leagues. (1991, June 25). *San Diego Union.*

Coopersmith, S. (1967). *The antecedents of self-esteem.* San Francisco: W. H. Freeman.

Cratty, B. (1983). *Psychology in contemporary sports.* Englewood Cliffs, NJ: Prentice-Hall.

Durant, R. H., Pendergrast, R. A., Donner, J., Seymore, C., & Gaillard, G. (1991). Adolescents' attrition from school sponsored sports. *American Journal of Diseases of Children, 145,* 1119–1123.

Edwards, H. (1993). From Demyaneko 9/3–9/93 Doc of the Bay, Professor Harry Edwards discusses the off-field conflicts which confront NFL players. *LA Village View,* pp. 28–30.

Feigley, D. (1984). Psychological burnout in high level athletes. *Physician and Sports Medicine 12* (10), 109–119.

Ferguson, K. J., Yesalis, C. E., Pomrehn, P. R., & Kirkpatrick, M. B. (1989). Attitudes, knowledge and beliefs as predictors of exercise intent and behavior in schoolchildren. *Journal of School Health, 59* (3), 112–115.

Fermaglick, D. R. (1977). Reflex sympathetic dystrophy in children. *Pediatrics, 60* (6), 881–883.

Freudenberger, H. J., & Richelson, G. (1981). *Burnout: How to beat the high cost of success.* New York: Bantam.

Gould, D. (1993). Intensive sport participation and the prepubescent athlete. Competitive stress and burnout. In B. R. Cahill & A. J. Pearl (Eds.), *Intensive* participation in children's sports (pp. 19–38). Champaign, IL: Human Kinetics.

Gould, D., Horn, T., & Spreeman, J. (1983). Sources of stress in junior elite wrestlers. *Journal of Sport Psychology, 5,* 159–171.

Gould, D., Feltz, D., Horn, T., & Weiss, M. (1982). Reasons for attrition in competitive youth swimming. *Journal of Sport Behavior, 5,* 155–165.

Horn, T. S. (1985). Coaches' feedback and changes in children's perceptions of their physical competence. *Journal of Educational Psychology, 77,* 174–186.

Kapp-Simon, K. A., Simon, D. J., & Kristovich, S. (1992). Self-perception, social skills, adjustment and inhibition in young adolescents with craniofacial anomalies. *Cleft Palate—Craniofacial Journal, 29* (4), 352–356.

Lewthwaite & Scanlan. (1989). Predictors of competitive trait anxiety in male youth sport participants. *Medicine and Science in Sports and Exercise, 21* (2), 221–229.

Lidstone, J. E., Amundson, M. L., & Amundson, L. H. (1991). Depression and chronic fatigue in the high school student and athlete. *Primary Care, 18* (2), 283–296.

Magill, R. A., Ash, M. J., & Smoll, F. C. (Eds.). (1982). Children in sport (2nd ed.). Champaign, IL: Human Kinetics.

Martens, R. (1978a). *Joy and sadness in children's sports.* Champaign, IL: Human Kinetics.

Martens, R. (1978b). *Sport competition anxiety test.* Champaign, IL: Human Kinetics.

Maslach, C. (1982). Understanding burnout: Definitional issues in analyzing a complex phenomenon. In W. S. Paine (Ed.), *Job stress and burnout: Research, theory, and intervention perspectives* (pp. 29–40). Beverly Hills, CA: Sage.

McPherson, B., Marteniuk, R., Tihany, J., & Clark, W. (1980). The social system of age group swimmers: The perception of swimmers, parents and coaches. *Canadian Journal Applied Sport Science, 4,* 142–145.

Michener, J. A. (1976). *Sports in America.* New York: Random House.

Morris, A. (1984). *Sports medicine. Prevention of athletic injuries.* Dubuque, IO: Brown Publishers.

Nash, H. L. (1987). Elite child athletes: How much does victory cost? *Physician and Sports Medicine, 15* (8), 129–133.

Nattiv, A., Agostini, R., Drinkwater, B., & Yeager, K. (1994). The female athlete triad: The interrelatedness of disordered eating, amenorrhea, and osteoporosis. *Clinics in Sports Medicine, 13* (2), 405–418.

Nattiv, A., & Puffer, J. (1991). Lifestyles and health risks of collegiate athletes. *Journal of Family Practice, 33* (6), 585–590.

Passer, M. W. (1983). Fear of failure, fear of evaluation, perceived competence and self-esteem in competitive trait anxious children. *Journal of Sport Psychology, 5,* 172–188.

Pillemer, F. G., & Micheli, L. J. (1988). Psychological considerations in youth sports. *Clinics in Sports Medicine, 7* (3), 679–689.

Pooley, J. C. (1980). Dropouts. *Coaching Review, 3,* 36–38.

Puffer, J. C., & McShane, J. M. (1991). Depression and chronic fatigue in the college student-athlete. *Primary Care, 18* (2), 297–308.

Reporters dispatch. (1994, November 10). Gannet Newspapers Local Sports News in Brief.

Robinson, T., & Carron, A. (1982). Personal and situational factors associated with dropping out versus maintaining participation in competitive sport. *Journal Sport Psychology, 4,* 364–378.

Ryan, J. (1995). *Little girls in pretty boxes: The making and breaking of elite gymnasts and figure skaters.* New York: Doubleday.

Scanlan, T. K. (1986). Competitive stress in children. In M. R. Weiss & D. Gould (Eds.), *Sport for Children and Youths* (pp. 113–118). Champaign, IL: Human Kinetic Press.

Scanlan, T. K., & Lewthwaite, R. (1986). Social aspects of competition for male youth sport participants. IV. Predictor of enjoyment. *Journal of Sport Psychology, 8,* 25–35.

Scanlan, T. K., & Passer, M. W. (1978). Factors related to competitive stress among male youth sport participants. *Medicine and Science in Sports, 10* (2), 103–108.

Scanlan, T. K., & Passer, M. W. (1979). Factors influencing the competitive performance expectancies of young female athletes. *Journal of Sport Psychology, 1,* 212–220.

Simon, J. A., & Martens, R. (1979). Children's anxiety in sport and nonsport evaluative activities. *Journal of Sport Psychology, 1,* 100–169.

Skolnick, A. A. (1996). Health pros want new rules for girl athletes. *Journal of the American Medical Association, 275,* 22–24.

Smith, R. E. (1993). A positive approach to enhancing sport performance: Principles of positive reinforcement and performance feedback. In J. M. Williams (Ed.), *Applied sport psychology; Personal growth to peak performance* (pp. 25–35). Mountain View, CA: Mayfield Publishing Co.

Smith, R. E., Smoll, F. L., & Curtis, B. (1978). Coaching behaviors in little league baseball. In F. L. Smoll & R. E. Smith (Eds.), *Psychological perspective in youth sports* (pp. 173–201). Washington, DC: Hemisphere.

Smith, R. E., Smoll, F. L., & Curtis, B. (1979). Coaches effectiveness training: A cognitive-behavioral approach to enhancing relationship skills in youth sport coaches. *Journal of Sport Psychology, 1,* 59–75.

Smith, R. E., Zane, N. W. S., Smoll, F. L., & Coppel, D. B. (1983). Behavioral assessment in youth sports: Coaching behaviors and children's attitudes. *Medicine Science Sports Exercise, 15* (3), 208–214.

Smoll, F. L., & Smith, R. E. (1989). Leadership behaviors in sport: A theoretical model and research paradigm. *Journal of Applied Social Psychology, 19,* 1522–1551.

Smoll, R. L., & Smith, R. E. (1990). Psychology of the young athlete: Stress-related maladies and remedial approaches. *Pediatric Clinics of North America, 37* (5), 1021–1046.

Super, J. T., & Block, J. R. (1992). Self-concept and need for achievement of men with physical disabilities. *Journal of General Psychology, 119* (1), 73–80.

Thornton, J. S. (1991). Springing youth athletes from the parental pressure cooker. *Physicians and Sports Medicine, 19* (7), 92–99.

Tofler, I., Katz Stryer, B., Micheli, L., & Herman, L. (1996, July 25). Physical and emotional problems of elite female gymnasts. *New England Journal of Medicine, 335* (4), 281–283.

Wankel, L. M., & Kreisel, P. S. J. (1985). Factors underlying enjoyment of youth sports: Sport and age group comparisons. *Journal of Sport Psychology, 7,* 51–64.

Weiss, M. R. (1993). Psychological effects of intensive sport participation on children and youth: Self-esteem and motivation. In B. R. Cahill & A. J. Pearl (Eds.), *Intensive participation in children's sports* (pp. 39–70). Champaign, IL: Human Kinetics.

Weiss, M. R., & Bredemeier, B. J. (1990). Moral development in sport. *Exercise Sport Science Review, 18,* 331–377.

24 / Bar and Bat Mitzvah

Irving H. Berkovitz, Neil Comess-Daniels, Toby Comess-Daniels,
Douglas Hollan, and Leonard J. Comess

Editor's Note

Rites of passage have existed since antiquity to provide formal, socially defined markers that denote movement from one stage of life to another. They are particular ways in which the changing identity of a person is recognized by the individual, the family, and the community. Rites of passage often involve ceremonies with religious meaning. The milestone of achieving adult rights and privileges is one of the most meaningful to the individual as well as to his or her social group. In traditional societies organized around hunting and gathering, the achievement of physical maturity, including reproductive capacity, is sufficient for the individual to be able to fulfill culturally defined male and female adult roles. In societies that are more dependent on technology, in which adult roles are assumed more gradually and variably, rites of passage also are more variable and less likely to be marked by an elaborate social ceremony. Indeed, for American teenagers, important milestones such as gaining a driver's license or graduating from high school are more likely to be celebrated mainly with peers rather than with the extended family and community, and in a purely secular manner. In our secular society, menarche retains almost no religious significance, although negative attitudes toward it may be understood as remnants of earlier religious taboos. Bar and Bat Mitzvah represent exceptions to this trend in that they are, first and foremost, religious ceremonies, even though the social events that usually accompany them have been influenced by the secularization of American society. The ceremonies of Bar and Bat Mitzvah are examples of socially defined rites of passage that have been carefully maintained as a way of affirming and underlying the individual's attainment of adult status in the Jewish community. In the United States, as in many other Western countries in which Jews live in varying degrees of assimilation, the ceremonies retain a central core of affirmation of a unique identity. Thus, an understanding of Bar and Bat Mitzvah can assist us in our appreciation of the role of rites of passage in adolescent development LTF.

For hundreds of years, Bar Mitzvah has been a ceremony that Jewish boys have experienced around their 13th birthday. Bat Mitzvah, a comparable ceremony for girls, has been introduced in the 20th century. Both ceremonies have developmental significance for the individual adolescents and their families. The ceremony for the boys is the more traditional and the better known.

Review of the Literature

The Bar Mitzvah ritual is closely related to the ceremonies so richly described in anthropologic and psychoanalytic literature pertaining to the transition from childhood to biological and sexual maturity among non-Western peoples. In spite of this fact, the ritual has received relatively little attention in the psychiatric literature. Arlow (1951) emphasized the significance of Bar Mitzvah as "connected with the conflicted relations between the father and son and their respective generations" (p. 354). His findings were derived from a group of adult men undergoing psychoanalysis in the late 1940s. The Bar Mitzvah ceremonies of Arlow's patients took place at least 20 to 30 years earlier, and the sociocultural customs associated with them would have been special for that era. Nonetheless, his study provides us with a psychoanalyst's insights into the psychological meaning of Bar Mitzvah.

We wish to thank Janet Hadda, Ph.D., Randi Markowitz, M.Sc., and Max Sugar, M.D., for contributions. Also, the class of the 1992 summer institute for Jewish Educators, University of Judaism, Los Angeles, California, provided several comments that helped make this account more contemporary.

Arlow described the Bar Mitzvah ritual as an "institutionalized form of initiation rites" (p. 355) serving at least 5 goals. These include first, integrating" the youth with the social patterns of the community and with the traditions and values of his forebears" (p. 372) and, second, enabling him "to master the feelings which arise out of Oedipal rivalry" (p. 371). Arlow states that this juncture can become the occasion for rebellion against the parents, by the boy's refusal to participate. More usually it can begin the process of peaceful detachment from the authority of his father. Some boys may then begin a "renewed submission to an exalted father image—God" (p. 372). Third, the ritual serves "to separate the young boy from his mother and rupture the passive attachment to her" (p. 372); and fourth, "to discharge the fear and hostility which the older generation harbors toward the developing younger generation" (p. 354). An element of imposed performance anxiety exists in the ceremony. The initiate fears public humiliation should he fail to pronounce the blessings correctly or falter in the delivery of his speech. Thus, finally, the ritual indicates that the boy has attained a certain level of maturity so that a higher degree of responsibility and performance is expected. Arlow feels that the Bar Mitzvah "serves as a sharp reminder to the boy of his new biological status and forces him to reexamine his attitude toward his masculinity" (p. 360).

Although Arlow's hypotheses were derived from Bar Mitzvah memories of more than 50 years ago, some of his conclusions are still generally applicable. For example, in one of the men, during "this transition to independence and equality the rabbi served in the role of a temporary intermediary, whose acceptance as a superior father substitute constituted for the patient a socially sanctioned repudiation of the father and therefore was less fraught with guilt" (p. 363). In the more recent era of more prevalent divorces and absent fathers, many boys have been helped and appreciate the empathic male rabbi as a supportive father figure. This appreciation may be less likely when the rabbi is too strict and demanding. Such an attitude also may lead to the boy's later repudiation of participation in synagogue activities.

Pollens (1970–71) published his own son's Bar Mitzvah speech to demonstrate the turnabout of a son who had initially rebelled against "the 'canned garbage' speech the Rabbi wrote for all the Bar Mitzvah boys" and then wrote his own speech where he found new meaning in being a Jew.

Schoenfeld (1990) focuses on the meaning of the Bar/Bat Mitzvah to the family as expressed in the social events that surround the ritual. He interviewed 20 families who had or were to have Bar/Bat Mitzvah at a large Reform temple. It was an "intense emotional experience for the family, one to be shared with those who are emotionally close" (p. 279), with reunions of family members and out-of-town friends and relatives attending.

Pogrebin (1991) writes that the first Bat Mitzvah ceremony occurred in 1922 "when Rabbi Mordecai Kaplan, founder of the Reconstructionist Movement conducted the Bat Mitzvah of his daughter Judith. Reform congregations soon followed suit, and the Conservative branch came around in the early Fifties" (p. 131). Orthodox Rabbis accepted this in the 1980s. Pogrebin feels that a more activist identity is exemplified by several of the women described in the Talmud and deserves greater emphasis. She feels that the role of active, accomplished women in Jewish history has been neglected and that the Bat Mitzvah ceremony should emphasize this and offer the young girl the possibility that she could be a leader for her people. To have told a 13-year-old girl in the 1950s "today you are a woman" would have meant motherhood and marriage, rather than an "activist" concept of womanhood, such as "to become a judge, a prophet or a conqueror" (p. 134). In the 1990s the activist message in becoming Bat Mitzvah may be finding acceptance in more congregations and families.

The Training

In liberal forms of Judaism in the United States (the Reform, Conservative, and Reconstructionist denominations), which constitute the majority of Jewish affiliation in the country, training in Hebrew schools to attain the status of Bar/Bat Mitzvah begins in the fourth or fifth grade (9 or 10 years old) and usually continues until somewhere in the seventh-grade year when the student turns 13 years of age (at which time the ceremony takes place). This training, whose major focus is to acquire a modicum of facility with the Hebrew language, may or may not have been preceded by attendance at "religious" or "Sunday" school once each week since kindergarten (5 years of age). The focus of "Sunday" school is "Judaica" background—history, culture, rites, rituals and liturgy.

Hebrew school takes place either two or three times each week, usually occupying an afternoon or two during the week and/or on Sunday mornings, 2½ to 3 hours per session. Each day's curriculum is a mixture of Hebrew language instructions and/or Judaica. Hebrew language instruction usually is focused on prayer book and biblical Hebrew rather than modern conversational Hebrew.

Toward the end of Hebrew school, often about 6 months prior to the 13th birthday, the student will begin specific Bar/Bat Mitzvah training. Usually this means weekly meetings with the cantor (in the larger congregations), rabbi, or a Bar/Bat Mitzvah tutor. Here the student focuses on the specific skills and requirements of the service at which she or he becomes Bat/Bar Mitzvah. These requirements can vary widely from synagogue to synagogue.

In the Orthodox view, a central aspect of the Bar/Bat Mitzvah is the assumption by the youngster of adult responsibility for all of his or her behavior between self and God. However, this is modified somewhat for women, since they are not obligated for all the 613 deeds and restrictions that apply to men. Once he is Bar Mitzvah, as an overt sign of the change in status, the young man has the obligation to wear a prayer shawl and phylacteries daily (except on Sabbath) during morning prayers. Women are not required to wear these items.

Several psychosocial elements are relevant to understanding the impact of the training on the child. How does the commitment to attend Hebrew school several days each week in a pluralistic society affect the youth? The demographics of the child's neighborhood must be taken into account. What is the tenor of the parental commitment to the training process? What is the level of Jewish practice of the parents and of the household? Is the youth from an interfaith household (practicing another religion in addition to Judaism) or interbackground household (parents are of different religious upbringing but have chosen to practice Judaism)? How much of the training is a matter of rote memorization and how much is process oriented, soliciting and eliciting the stu-

dent's perspectives on the moral, philosophical and ethical underpinnings of that which he or she is learning? Are there different familial, communal, or institutional expectations for boys versus girls? Is attaining of Bar/Bat Mitzvah status seen as the "end" of Jewish education and perhaps the end of active participation in the synagogue and/or synagogue affiliation? All of these factors will affect the quality of the training period and the personality of the Jewish identity that results from it.

The Service

Most often the training will have prepared the youth to lead the congregation during all or some of the prayers for the Sabbath morning (sometimes afternoon, rarely evening) service (sometimes read but usually chanted); to read some number of verses of the Torah (Pentateuch) portion of the week from the Torah scroll itself (a text without musical markings) and often with the traditional chant (either memorized from a recording or learned from the ancient musical notation system). Since the Torah scroll lacks vowels and musical notes, only a scholar can read and chant it easily. (The Torah is read through according to an ancient weekly cycle that takes a year to be completed.) Thus, a Bar/Bat Mitzvah has to study to learn the passages for a specific segment. In addition, the celebrant reads the attendant blessings and some designated verses from the Haftorah (prophetic books of the Jewish Bible) portion of the week (which has a different chant) and its attendant blessings. Members of the family—parents, grandparents, and siblings—may be on the bimah (the platform from which the service is performed) and also read the blessings preceding and following the chanting of portions of the Torah.

In Orthodox services, once the chanting of the Torah and the blessings is completed, the Bar Mitzvah is showered with nuts and candies by the women congregants. This practice has been followed by some Conservative and a few Reform congregations. Although seen as an expression of warmth and affection, it could also be understood as a message heralding and signifying the male's entrance into the reproductive mode of adulthood. (In Conservative and Reform congregations, it signals the female's entrance.) After the readings, just before the end of the service, the Bar/Bat Mitzvah delivers a short interpretive speech that usually has to do with the weekly texts that were read. The speech can deal with the meaning of the portion of Torah, movement into puberty ("Today I am a man or woman"), or on the entrance into the corpus of Judaism. Often the speech is written by the rabbi. Occasionally a more individualistic youth may choose to write his or her own speech, perhaps with some monitoring by rabbi and parents. At times, the youth may include political overtones and social criticism. "Thanks were extended to parents and teachers. And high hopes expressed for the future. Parental pride and satisfaction would be a meaningful presence felt by everyone; and gifts would be showered on the youth by family and friends" (Noshpitz, 1979, p. 278).

After the readings and speech, lunch can be served, with general merriment and congratulations. Often there may be a party later in the evening with as lavish features as the means and taste of the parents and child will allow. There may be a dinner at the synagogue or at a hotel. Adult friends or business associates of the parents may predominate and/or adolescent friends may predominate at a party. Many of these parties include entertainment and dancing. Some include candle-lighting ceremonies, videotaping, and photography (Schoenfeld, 1990). Occasionally the family and/or youth will choose to perform the ceremony in Israel, as a reconsecration of the Jewish heritage.

Thus, the Bar and Bat Mitzvah involve both religious ceremony and social celebration. "Through staging this sequence of ritual and social events, parents are communicating how they have come to terms with the role of Jewish identity in their lives . . . The celebration is a dramatization to their children that they expect them to make the choice also" (Schoenfeld, 1990, p. 297). Sklare (1971) noted that the style of celebrating Bar/Bat Mitzvah borrows from Jewish wedding celebrations, suggesting that this "serves the purpose of communicating to the child the importance of a future endogamous marriage" (p. 195).

In the latter half of the 20th century in the United States, less than 25% of Jews belong to synagogues. Nevertheless, when the son in the family reaches 11 to 12 years, many of these nonaffiliated families do think of Bar/Bat Mitzvah for various reasons, including tradition, pleasing grandparents, and/or atoning for nonaffiliation. Some have said they "want the kid to know where he came from." Many will then join a synagogue to allow beginning of preparation for Bar/Bat Mitzvah. Doing so does not always indicate a full return to the practice of Judaism.

Bat Mitzvah is often considered more optional. Girls who chose to become Bat Mitzvah two or three decades ago demonstrated a strong personal resolve and commitment to engage in the requisite study and resulting rite of passage. Girls of the 1980s and 1990s feel they have more of a choice and bring a sense of involvement and special significance to this bridge in their lives. Many adult women are performing a Bat Mitzvah ceremony to strengthen their Jewish identity (Schoenfeld, 1988).

"The year of Bar/Bat Mitzvah is for many a year of party dresses and suits, of learning and practicing social skills, of fitting into the social cliques which teenagers seem to need as part of their strategy of coping with the many uncertainties and insecurities of adolescence" (Schoenfeld, 1990, p. 284).

Thus, it can be seen that a variety of motives determine the decision to prepare a youth to be Bar/Bat Mitzvah. In most families, the religious motives probably predominate. Because so much hard work is required to prepare for it, the youngster who does not have a strong religious commitment may be motivated by other factors. The prospect of receiving presents motivates some youths. Some youngsters do it as an act of respect for their grandparents. Families likewise have many reasons for wanting their children to go through with it. Some grandparents will even "bribe" a youth to begin and persevere through the arduous preparation. Some parents see the event as an opportunity to show the synagogue community their affluence, eminence, or devotion to the rabbi, especially during the course of the subsequent party.

These complex motivations, the lengthy time required, and the expense incurred by families can make the preparation for Bar or Bat Mitzvah, as well as the event itself, a focus of family conflict. In some families, the style of the party after the ceremony provokes a conflict of generational tastes. There may be a conflict between the taste and preferences of the teen and that of the parents or grandparents in choice of music (heavy metal, rock, rap, etc.), entertainment, and decorations. The ability of the family to negotiate differences is tested. In more affluent families, large monetary or material gifts may be bestowed on the youth; indeed, a large bank account may accumulate. In some instances, this may give the 13-year-old a feeling of power that may, in turn, fuel later argument or defiance of parental authority. Usually the teen is given limited access to the use of these funds. Some families will use this money as the beginning of teaching the youngster how to save, begin charitable giving, spend wisely or invest. Some synagogues and/or families require, or encourage, charitable giving, called "tzedaka."

This may be

a time when many of these youngsters experiment with changes in the form of their religiosity. The Orthodox youth shifts from mere observance to joining the ranks of the mystics; or he goes in the opposite direction and becomes secular; contrariwise, the child of the Reform family may turn Orthodox. Or the identity conflict may drive a youth into conversion; he abandons Judaism for a kind of secularism or atheism, or he goes through a formal ceremony and embraces some variety of Christianity. . . . a particular youth may turn to Zionism and become actively engaged . . . with return of Jews to Israel. Or, he may . . . become a critic of Zionism and a defender of the Palestinian Arabs." (Noshpitz, 1979, p. 279)

Special Conditions

In recent years, more female rabbis and cantors are involved in preparing males for Bar Mitzvah. Often males of this age feel anxious about continuing a close relation with an adult female, especially if the boys have entered puberty. In many synagogues, however, this situation has not posed a problem.

Some parents have a strong need for their offspring to excel and bring them glory, or give them "nakhes," the Yiddish term for parental pride. Although they may be willing, some of these youths may not be capable to endure and excel in the task assigned to them. Synagogues that have Bar/ Bat Mitzvah counselors may be able to detect which parents are overzealous and perhaps com-

peting with other parents through their children. Tactful counseling, usually by the cantor or rabbi, may be able to lessen the likelihood of a child's experiencing the event as a failure.

In cases where the parents are divorced, there may be a dilemma and/or conflict as to which set of parents will be on the bimah. Occasionally this situation reexposes the teen to the conflicts and choices involved in the original divorce. The youngster may have the opportunity to reexamine past emotions and perhaps come out with a new understanding of the parents. Alternatively, in some reconstituted families, the parents may take the opportunity to include in their speech a reaffirmation of their unified devotion and love for the adolescent. In less happy circumstances there may be a repeat of the family trauma and subsequent depression and withdrawal, vitiating the positive developmental possibilities of the occasion.

Sociocultural Perspectives

Bar/Bat Mitzvah, like all other "rites of passage" (Van Gennep, 1909/1960), both mark and promote a transition from one status to another—in this case, from child into adolescent and young adult, and in some cases, to becoming a more committed Jew. For both boys and girls, the ceremonies mark social, psychological, and physiological changes.

Structurally, Bar and Bat Mitzvah resemble many other rites of passage. They begin with rites of separation, which clearly distinguish initiates from both the young adults they are about to become and the children they are leaving behind. This is followed by a transitional or "liminal" period (from the Latin *limen*, meaning threshold) during which old identities are loosened or erased and the foundations for new ones are begun.

In many cultures, the liminal period often is characterized by danger and ambiguity—as the initiate is left dangling between two statuses (one more familiar and secure, the other at once enticing and hazardous). It may involve rituals of exclusion or ordeal that dramatize for the initiates the importance and significance of the developmental step they are about to take. The liminal period of Bar/Bat Mitzvah ceremonies does not involve physical danger, but it does involve a certain degree of social isolation and the challenge, if not the ordeal, of mastering new linguistic, cultural, and religious knowledge.

The ceremony concludes with rites of incorporation, which dramatically symbolize that the liminal period has come to an end. The initiate has now fully assumed his or her new status as a young adult. Like other initiation rites, this final stage is the most elaborated culturally and symbolically.

Some authors question if Bar/Bat Mitzvah is truly a rite of passage, since full adult status is not achieved. Also, in many other rites, adults are involved in every part of the ceremony. In Bar/Bat Mitzvah the youth may have his or her own party, occasionally without adults. Some prefer the designation "definitional ceremony" (Schoenfeld, 1992, personal communication). Also, it is of interest that in many cultures, the confirmation, initiation, or circumcision ritual usually involves a group of participants (Turner, 1967, 1972). The Bar/Bat Mitzvah ritual is one of those where the individual adolescent receives the concentrated attention and concern of the family and elders. Occasionally, owing to the synagogue's scheduling requirements, two or three ceremonies may occur on the same morning, but this situation usually is avoided. The solo performance probably contributes to some of the youth's anxiety but also may indicate the special valuing and expectation of the future achievements of the youth as an individual.

When the Therapist Attends a Patient's Bar/Bat Mitzvah Ceremony

The therapist who is treating a youngster of this age group may be invited by the youth or the parents to attend the Bar/Bat Mitzvah ceremony.

Attending any major event in a patient's life, whether it is a wedding, graduation, or stage performance, can have significant effects on the treatment relationship and its effectiveness. The therapist needs to consider whether to attend in terms of its consequences for the therapy relationship.

If the therapist does attend, there is the opportunity to witness firsthand the dynamics of the extended family more vividly than has been encountered in the office. He or she may witness the impact of parents, siblings, and extended family members on the patient and his or her coping skills with these persons who may or may not have been described in the sessions. This information can advance the therapy and enrich the relationship with the youth. Rejection of the invitation may inflict hurt. An expeditious solution is for the therapist to attend the ceremony as part of the audience but not to attend the party. The party may involve more compromising social/familial ramifications; family members often ask questions about the therapy that cannot be answered without betraying confidentiality.

Conclusion

Bar and Bat Mitzvah have many features in common with rites of passage into adolescence throughout history. How these ceremonies and the preparations for them, as well as the social celebrations that follow them, are played out will be reflective of the individual youngster and family. The experience of becoming a Bar or Bat Mitzvah can have a salutary effect on the youngster's emotional growth. On the whole, this ceremony and celebration does represent a significant and happy passage into adolescence for many Jewish boys and girls and their families.

REFERENCES

Arlow, J. A. (1951). A psychoanalytic study of a religious initiation rite Bar Mitzvah. *Psychoanalytic Study of the Child, 6*, 353–374.

Noshpitz, J. D. (1979). The Jewish child. In J. D. Noshpitz (Ed.), *Basic Handbook of Child Psychiatry* (Vol. 1, pp. 278–279). New York: Basic Books.

Pogrebin, L. C. (1991). *Deborah, Golda and me. Being female and Jewish in America.* New York: Crown Publishers.

Pollens, B. (1970–71). A special Bar Mitzvah. *Psychoanalytic Review, 57*, 554–557.

Schoenfeld, S. (1988). Integration into the group and

sacred uniqueness: An analysis of adult Bat Mitzvah. In W. Zenner (Ed.), *Persistence and flexibility: Anthropological perspectives on the American Jewish experience* (pp. 117–135). Albany: State University of New York Press.

Schoenfeld, S. (1990). Some aspects of the social significance of Bar/Bat Mitzvah celebration. In S. Fishbane & J. N. Lightstone (Eds.), *Essays in the social scientific study of Judaism and Jewish society* (pp. 278–304). Quebec, Montreal, Canada: Dept. of Religion, Concordia University.

Sklare, M. (1971). *America's Jews*. New York: Random House.

Turner, V. (1967). *The forest of symbols*. Ithaca, NY: Cornell University Press.

Turner, V. (1972). *Drama, fields and metaphors: Symbolic action in human society*. Ithaca, NY: Cornell University Press.

Van Gennep, A. (1960). *Rites of passage*. Chicago: University of Chicago Press. (Originally published 1909.)

25 / Junior High/Middle School and High School Life

Irving H. Berkovitz

Transition to Junior High/ Middle School

In moving from the smaller, usually neighborhood elementary school to the junior high school (grades 7 to 9, ages 12 to 14) or the middle school (grades 6 to 8, ages 11 to 13), the child is traversing an important part of development, from the smaller, familylike setting to the less personalized, larger group setting, from childhood to adolescence. If the move is simply one to a middle school on the same campus as the elementary school, then this transition is not as threatening. The peer group will remain the same and access to previous teachers will be easily available. However, in larger cities, often the child will have to move to a larger campus, farther from the home school, frequently requiring bus or car transportation.

Certainly the child will feel pleasure, anticipation, and a sense of accomplishment in moving on from the elementary school. Yet many children also are apprehensive and have often exaggerated fears of what will happen to them in the middle school. These fears may reflect what are regarded as the risks of entering a wider, bigger, less familiar world. In the elementary school of 300 to 600 students, these youngsters had negotiated the issues of dealing with adults outside the family circle, bigger peers who may bully or nurture them, and intellectual tasks that they had mastered, to one degree or another. Their sense of worth, or lack thereof, had been established, giving some measure of security.

In the middle/junior high, they imagine being assailed by new, bigger, more dominating peers, bullies, gangbangers, and dope pushers. There usually is a bigger campus, 800 to 1,500 students, 5 to 6 teachers instead of the previous 2 to 3, classes with as many as 30 to 40 students, a larger cafeteria, lockers, and more homework. If they have siblings who have already been to the same middle school, they may be offered a measure of reassurance. If, however, the sibs are of the bullying variety, fears may be aggravated. For some children the move away from the elementary school personnel will entail a serious loss, especially in cases in which the personnel have served as nurturing parent surrogates. Such children may pay frequent visits to the elementary school in an attempt to keep in touch with these earlier supports.

Over and above these external fears, the processes of puberty will have begun for many, but not all, of these 11- to 12-year olds. Puberty is destabilizing to their sense of internal security. With the secondary sexual bodily changes, new disquieting feelings occur. Previous casual physical affection from loving friends or family members (of the same or opposite sex) are now disturbing rather than reassuring. New impulsive actions occur. Previous controls are weakened and the sense of the dependability of one's actions is lessened. A physical twitchiness appears and rapidly oscillating emotions of love and hate prevail, which collectively can confound the young person as well as the parents and teachers (Martin, 1972). Some have described youngsters this age as "hormones with legs."

As a result, the middle school/junior high school campus is often tumultuous, bubbling with activity and noise, with children running, screaming, and embracing. This situation is very different both from the former grade school milieu and from the high school campus scene to come. This younger, middle school period is one of the crucial transition points that determines the future strength and depth of attachment to peer group, adults, and educational process as well as motivation and values for the future. While undoubtedly a basic pattern was established in earlier years, it becomes more apparent, tested, and possibly modifiable at this stage.

The Junior High School/Middle School Experience

In the words of an educator, "For many students the middle grades represent the last chance to develop a sense of academic purpose and personal commitment to educational goals. Those who fail at the middle grade level often drop out of school and may never again have the opportunity to develop to their fullest potential." Some educators feel "young adolescents are not ready for the atomistic independence foisted on them in secondary schools." They feel that this is one of the causes of the behavior problems endemic to many junior high schools.

> Behavior problems lead to omnipresent control mechanisms, resulting in the dissonant combination of an overdose of both unearned independence and overbearing regulations. Young adolescents are told, incorrectly, that they are adults, and then infantilized when they do not measure up. (Lipsitz, 1984, p. 189)

For many teachers, control measures become the major issue.

To meet with these crucial opportunities and dangers, more educators and other interested community groups have been focusing on how to make the middle school experience more conducive to promoting positive development for all youths, but especially for those already showing or at risk for developing problems. The need for extra attention to the developmental and psychological needs of this age group has been realized for a long time. The Carnegie Council on Adolescent Development (1989) recommends several features for junior high/middle schools. These include:

1. Create small communities for learning that will "ensure that every student is known well by at least one adult" (p. 36)
2. Teach a core academic program
3. Ensure success for all students
4. Empower teachers and administrators to make decisions about experiences of middle grade students
5. Select staff who are expert at teaching young adolescents
6. Foster the health and fitness of young adolescents by providing a health coordinator in every middle school

7. Reengage families by giving them meaningful roles in school governance
8. Connect schools with communities through identifying service opportunities and using community resources to enrich the instructional program and provide constructive after-school activities

"Research findings suggest that students whose parents and friends value education highly tend to have more success and fewer discipline problems in school" (California State Dept. of Education, 1987, p. 20). While positive family values are certainly desirable (although not always available), the quality of the school is also of importance. An exemplary school culture is considered to include: "a sense of order and purpose . . . classrooms organized for efficiency . . . student centeredness . . . an attitude of optimism and high expectations among both students and teachers. Teachers who like adolescents . . . organizational health, where leadership is in evidence" (Roueche & Baker, 1986, pp. 24–34). A study (George & Oldaker, 1985/1986) of the school culture in effective middle schools showed that "students who feel valued by teachers and view school as more than just a place to meet friends tend to show respect for their schools." The exemplary schools "developed programs that demonstrated persistent caring for students as young people . . . students' attitudes toward school and feelings about teachers became moderately or strongly positive." There was "greater student participation in special interest activities, [and] . . . better school attendance" (p. 81).

Because of the conflicts occasioned by the strong ambivalent emotions, less effective intellectual controls and distractions in handling the sexual conflicts (Blos, 1972), some advocate single-sex schools at this period. However, most schools are coed. In schools for girls only, there appears to be more opportunity for the girls to develop initiative, self-confidence, and competitive skills. By ages 15 to 16, the age of formal operations according to Piaget, there is often sufficient personality development for youths to maintain academic and personal goals despite the vicissitudes of coed classes. Miller (1970) makes the point that young people are not given enough opportunities in schools to discuss their pressing bodily and social changes so as better to adapt to them.

It is hoped that these personal needs can be recognized while attending to their academic needs. Some of the important curricular tasks include attention to acquisition of knowledge, developing capacities for critical thought and effective communication, character development, and learning to learn. Side by side with these tasks, for example, the language arts/social studies curriculum could address the developmental questions: "Who am I? What do I want to be? What is important?" These questions need to receive attention in the course of teaching all the subjects of the core curriculum.

Transition to High School

Entry into high school, usually ninth grade, brings with it some of the same pleasure and pride of moving on developmentally as did entry into junior high/middle school. Yet it can also raise some of the same anxieties. Once again the young person is leaving a familiar and somewhat more nurturant setting for a larger, more threatening place and group. Having mastered the transition to middle school may lessen the anxiety for many children. The high school usually is two or three times as big as the middle school, both in population (800 to 3,000) and, possibly, in area. There are many more interest groups and activities, such as athletic teams, drama, newspaper, and debating team. These activities can provide new opportunities for finding expression and affiliation; alternatively, they can present a baffling array of demanding choices and possibilities for feeling excluded. Some high schools try to create smaller units of 600 to 800 students by dividing into schools within the school.

More children of this age group, 14 to 17 years, have reached puberty, so that usually this complicating part of the separation process has been mastered. However, now the conflict moves to issues around exclusion or inclusion into the right peer group, concern about popularity, good looks, physical prowess, party invitations, and prom dates.

For some youths, part of the conflict may begin aboard the buses on the way to school. Cliques and antagonisms as well as friendships may coalesce first thing in the morning and often continue for the four years of shared transportation. Where a long ride is involved, conflict between students and driver may occur. Some districts have installed videotape monitors on buses for educational and recreational programs, to make use of the time for learning or to lessen the amount of conflict. In some cases, destructive acts have occurred.

The High School Experience

In the high school peer group, some consolidation of and experimentation with identities is occurring. There are at least three to four identifiable student groups: the popular ones, the athletic ones or the jocks, the studious ones, and the drug/alcohol-abusing ones. In different parts of the United States there may be subgroups, such as surfers, dopers, soshes, gangbangers, grinds, nerds, heavy metal freaks, punkers, and grunges. In all schools there exist those students who feel isolated and still unsure about affiliation. Some get a feeling of affiliation from a particular interest group, drama, newspaper, chorus, or athletic teams. Loners may gravitate to the library or seek to escape to a neighborhood arcade, lunchroom, or lawn in front of the school, unless there is a closed campus policy. Some areas can get marked out as the upperclass quad, the gang hangout, or ethnic/racial self-segregation areas, to satisfy the need for small-group attachment in the larger, more crowded setting.

One study of nonclinical teenagers, ages 13 to 18, in school found "greater difficulty in personality functioning during early than during middle adolescence." Of interest was the finding that 47.5% of the subjects were considered "clear of personality function disturbance" and that 13% had improved in competence from age 13 to 16 (Golombek, Marton, Stein, & Korenblum, 1987, p. 376). Competence was considered to be "an increased ability to test reality regarding self and others, to communicate, to maintain identity in varied relationships and circumstances, and to demonstrate improved self-esteem" (p. 374). Those who were angry and alienated from peers—24.6%—remained disturbed.

For many teenagers, the high school period is fraught with joy and pain, discovery and disappointment. Theatrical media and literature of all types present vivid tragic and humorous portrayals of the major and minor crises, triumphs and defeats of this epoch. While the high school teenagers' motility is less active than during earlier adolescence, the internal swings of feeling can be even more intense. Some researchers question presence of universal adolescent turmoil, but hints of overt and covert turmoil are widely evident. The tension around getting good grades and Scholastic Achievement Test scores to qualify for better colleges, or to make other plans after graduation, is compelling. Many distract and/or soothe themselves with abuse of drugs or alcohol, or sexual activity. Some "bury themselves" in the books to avoid peer group temptations or to develop work or college aspirations.

The majority of teenagers are not symptomatic but go through whatever turmoil they are experiencing in a contained unobtrusive way. Building on data from a 10-year study of "normal adolescent males," Offer and Offer (1975) distinguished three groups: (1) a continuous growth group (23%), which "progressed throughout adolescence and young manhood with a smoothness of purpose and reassurance . . ." (p. 40); (2) a surgent group (35%), which showed developmental spurts, a cycle of progression and regression, and more psychopathology than the first group; and (3) a tumultuous growth group (21%), which showed internal turmoil manifested by "overt behavioral problems in school and in the home" (p. 45). Other studies find that approximately 20% of youths are disturbed (Offer, Howard, Schonert, & Ostow, 1991). Possibly at least that percentage have transient adjustment disorders; in some instances these resolve. In others they become a part of the individual's character structure.

Despite the shrinking financial support and the escalating problems in most of today's public high schools, in many there are still young persons receiving significant encouragement and training from dedicated teachers and administrators. Academic decathalons, seniors taking college courses, science fairs, and community service programs are but a few of the positive indications (Berkovitz, 1995). Notwithstanding this, the high dropout rate and the 20% who are disturbed deserve more attention.

Therapeutic opportunities for disturbed teenagers are never sufficient, despite the fact that most high schools have full-time psychologists and nurses. Counselors usually have a load of 300 to 500 students. Peer counseling is available in some schools. The adolescents who are training to be peer counselors often will get as much, or more, benefit as the counselees. More group counseling programs do exist in the high schools, conducted by counselors and even outside consultants (Berkovitz, 1987). School-based clinics are becoming more prevalent in high schools and occasionally in junior high schools. These clinics are seen as instilling a new sense of personal responsibility for health in young people as well as discovering neglected health needs. While physical health is the clinic's prime concern, at least 20% of patients are seeking, and at times receiving (when available), mental health assistance (Lear, Gleicher, St-Germaine, & Porter, 1991).

Some therapeutic, as well as maturing, influences will occur in a variety of programs. High school sex and family life education classes are franker about adolescent issues than discussions in earlier grades. Concern about the AIDS epidemic has made these classes more relevant. The greater occurrence of suicides in high schools has led to the introduction of suicide prevention programs that sensitize students to mental health considerations in general as well as to depression and ways to deal with it. There has been some disagreement about the value of in-school suicide prevention programs. For example, out of a group of high school students exposed to an in-class presentation lasting 1½ hours, 2.5% reported having made a (first) suicide attempt during the 18 months follow-up compared with 2.7% of the control group (Vieland, Whittle, Garland, Hicks, & Shaffer, 1991). Yet a number of students who have contemplated suicide do feel prompted to seek help after such programs. Posttraumatic stress disorder has been reported in peers of adolescent suicide victims (Brent et al., 1995).

Concern about alcoholism, drug abuse, gang membership, and smoking prevalence has led to the introduction of programs to reduce these activities (Webb, Baer, & McKelvey, 1995). Some campuses provide counseling for gay/lesbian students to lessen the frequent damaging reactions to harassment and stigmatization that these individuals often encounter. Due to concern about high dropout rates, dropout prevention programs have been introduced for these and other students.

The RAND Corporation investigated the problems of high schools serving disadvantaged minority youth in eight inner-city New York high schools and five other New York and Washington, D.C., high schools (Hill, Foster, & Gendler, 1990). The primary challenge facing all these schools was how to motivate the unmotivated. The authors found that successful schools, especially the parochial and special-purpose public schools (termed FOCUS schools),

concentrated on student achievement, "social contracts" that communicate reciprocal responsibilities between students and staff, aggressive molding of student attitudes and values, and basic curricula that all students eventually complete even though their preparation and initial coursework may vary. The neighborhood [non-FOCUS] schools emphasize program delivery and compliance with regulations rather than outcomes, prefer to let staff and students define their own school roles, see themselves as delivering information and skills rather than influencing students' outlooks and offer fundamentally different curricula to students in different tracks.

According to this study, "FOCUS schools unhesitatingly placed burdens on their low-achieving students" (p. 44), namely to improve achievement. In the neighborhood public schools, on the other hand "adults agree not to demand too much in return for the students' agreement not to cause trouble" (p. 43). Rutter, Maugham, Mortimore, and Oustan (1980) describe conditions in 12 London (England) high schools where programs similar to those in the FOCUS schools achieved better academic and personal results for students.

In many districts, special types of alternative high schools have been developed to accommodate the varied needs of students and the demands of some parents. On the other hand, many districts provide continuation high schools for poorly adjusted students. Often these are located separate from the larger high school and serve only 100 to 200 students. They offer the poorly adjusting student an opportunity to find a smaller milieu in which to receive individualized academic support and/or nurturance away from the distraction of the larger high school group.

Special interest elementary or secondary magnet schools exist in many districts serving 100 to 300 students. They were developed in order to promote racial desegregation as well as to increase student-parent-staff interest and enthusiasm, much as described in the FOCUS schools of the RAND project. Magnet schools may be oriented to science, business, the performing arts, or gifted

students. In larger districts, even more specialized interests may be offered, such as medicine or fashion.

Those youths who are able to attend private high schools will find smaller classes and usually more concentrated attention to academics. Some may miss the opportunities provided in the larger, more socially and economically diverse student body of the public high school. Some students may alternate periods of time in public and private schools. Drug use, experimentation, and abuse, poor motivation, and depression probably occur everywhere. In the larger schools, those youths who feel overwhelmed and alienated may escape notice, whereas in a smaller school, they may receive more rapid intervention from peers or staff.

If a high school has sufficient budget and interest, besides the usual athletic teams, a plethora of extracurricular clubs and organizations will be available. In the various extracurricular activities, as much or more learning can take place as in the academic classes, especially in regard to social skills and self-discipline. Young persons learn to develop ability to express feelings, to achieve some understanding for others, to acquire tolerance for differences, to find ways to achieve safe intimacy, and to come to an appreciation of their own skills and limitations in comparison to others. Many also will learn to manipulate, exploit, and control others. The initiative to try many different interests will lay the groundwork for later sublimations and even career interests.

Impact on Individual Development

A majority of adolescents will develop positively during this period, whatever the deficiencies present in the school system. Familial, genetic, and other assets can help children thrive. Many youngsters who were damaged by childhood traumata and/or deprivation may experience aggravation of their disabilities. Peer group and/or school personnel insensitivity, scapegoating, or exploitation may intensify feelings of failure, rage, and helplessness. Fortunately, during this period many adolescents do find supportive relationships and experiences or a new therapeutic input that can ameliorate previous handicaps. In both public and private secondary schools, some sensitive, caring faculty member, or other adult, often recognizes an at-risk, needy young student and tries to provide a positive surrogate parenting experience.

In addition, "Learning, in adolescence, becomes an essential aspect of beginning to regard oneself as an effective and competent person who can become independent and selfreliant" (Berlin, 1980, p. 2694). The peer group can serve as a support system in sharing problems and troubles and in attempting to find ways of solving these issues. At times the peer group also can have a negative influence. Learning social skills is a major developmental task and often "requires organized opportunities for activities under the guidance and help of adults" (Berlin, 1980, p. 2695). At this time, too few schools provide this opportunity. In some schools group counseling is available for those with manifest problems (Berkovitz, 1987). Some schools provide groups for youth with "normal" developmental issues. Needless to say, both types of groups should be a more available feature of all secondary schools.

Adolescent depression, or the prevalence of actions and or drug/alcohol abuse to mask depression, have been seen by many clinicians. Hormonal, familial, and interpersonal events have been implicated as primary causative factors. However, this question may be raised: To what degree do school experiences aggravate or ameliorate these factors? Certainly the progressively increasing interpersonal and academic difficulties associated with each advancing grade level can aggravate previous feelings of inadequacy and alienation and increase an existing level of depression and poor self-esteem. Possibly latent depressive tendencies may become more overt. It is conceivable that several factors may well contribute to a greater prevalence of depression, masked and overt: These include the needs for students to master an increasing load of information, technical and otherwise, in today's high school curricula; the increase of class size in many schools; and other fiscal stringencies reducing supportive services for both emotional and academic needs.

Violence in Schools

The high schools of the 1980s and 1990s are unique in the unfortunate amount of aggression, violence, and danger on campus (Berkovitz, 1985). This fact is especially true in the inner city, but violence is present even in suburban areas. Incidents between students and students and between students and faculty are not uncommon. Occasionally incidents arise where faculty members assail students. Gang rivalries are present. Some teens join gangs for protection as well as affiliation. The presence of weapons on campus is not uncommon, and many deaths have occurred.

Some high schools have become like fortresses with security guards, metal detectors, locked doors and identification necessary. The need for constant vigilance interferes with the development of a calm educational atmosphere. Teachers may hesitate to challenge or discipline some violence-prone students, or may do it in a way that aggravates the situation. Unfortunately, teacher training has not always included learning verbal ways to deal with adolescent anger or confrontation (DeCecco & Richards, 1974). Knowledgeable, cautious students soon learn which peers to avoid or not to alienate. Students in violence-prone high schools often suffer posttraumatic stress disorder symptoms even though they were not directly involved in the violence.

Ethnic and racial self-segregation may prevail in many schools. Counterphobic adolescents may challenge domineering peers and risk violent retaliation. Some schools have introduced a peer mediation program, which involves peer intervention into student to student friction. Intervening peers receive training much like in other peer counseling programs, but with a special focus on conflict resolution.

Special Education

Special education offers an opportunity for the disabled 10% of the school population to attend smaller classes and receive specialized attention. Public Laws 94–142 and 101–476 provide federal financing, with some state supplementation. Segregated classes, while providing small-group security, at times foster stigmatization by nondisabled students. Special schools for the deaf, blind, and seriously emotionally disturbed (SED) raise special developmental issues. Reintegration into classrooms and schools with the less disabled—"mainstreaming"—requires liaison with and support of the receiving teacher as well as some discussion with the new peers to build acceptance of differences.

Special Factors Affecting Female Adolescents

For many years educational opportunities for female students in schools were not on a par with those for male students. Title IX of the Higher Education Act passed in 1972 and 1975 (Title IX, 1988) mandated more equitable provisions for females in schools. As a result, several changes in school practices have occurred. Females have now entered courses once considered unusual for their sex, such as, architectural drafting, industrial arts, auto mechanics, and carpentry. Reciprocally, boys have entered homemaking, cooking, and cosmetology. More high schools have allowed pregnant girls to stay in school and provide special aids, such as nursery care of the infant during class hours and classes in child care for the mothers and occasionally the fathers. In colleges, women now receive recognition for abilities in sports once considered the exclusive domain of men—sailing, crew, basketball, and distance running (Berkovitz, 1991).

A recent study raised questions about the possible effects of schooling on self-esteem in early teenage girls (American Association of University Women [AAUW], 1991). The survey found that at age 8 to 9, 60% of the girls were confident, assertive, and felt positive about themselves. However, by the time they reached 10th grade, at age 14 to 15, only 29% still felt that way. Boys, on the other hand, moved from 67% to 46%. Ten percent more girls declined in self-esteem than boys.

There are several possible explanations for this decline. Physical appearance is most important for girls in middle school, the time of the greatest decline. Boys viewed the adolescent physical changes positively; they see themselves getting bigger and stronger. Girls believed that their changes were leading in a negative direction. Also, the higher self-esteem of the boys translated into more grandiose career dreams, and they were somewhat more likely than girls to believe that their career dreams would come true (AAUW, 1991).

An additional influence could well be menarche and its social concomitants. This physical change contributes positively to the self-esteem of many girls but negatively to some. "Early developing girls especially will have rounder, nonpreferred shapes" (Petersen, Sarigiani, & Kennedy, 1991, p. 249). Of major concern to most adolescent girls at this time are such questions as: "Whom to date? How to handle the sexual overtures of the boys? Which boys to trust? When to have sexual relations? How far to go?" Only a few schools provide a nonjudgmental group format in class or in group counseling in which these and other issues can be clarified through discussion by boys as well as girls (Berkovitz, 1987).

The school's contribution to the lesser self-esteem of girls could be related to the finding that girls ages 8 to 14 were thought not to be good at math and science. When the girls learned that, their sense of self-worth and aspirations for themselves deteriorated (AAUW, 1991). While true for boys, too, this situation is more prevalent in girls. Female students often failed to achieve their academic potential in the areas of math and science (Wentzel, 1988). In one study, the greater male enrollment in math courses seemed related to the finding that the males had "greater confidence in themselves as learners of math, more positive perceptions of the attitudes of mother and father toward them as learners of math and greater perceived usefulness of math" (Sherman & Fennema, 1977, p. 161). The small number of female math or science teacher role models in high schools also may be a factor (Stake & Noonan, 1985). The AAUW study (1991) claimed that girls often are less computer proficient and have less access to computers. Yet where college women were specifically instructed and encouraged, and, in fact, required to use computers, they were as competent and as confident as male students (Arch & Cummins, 1989). This finding confirms the fact that girls are no poorer than boys in math skills.

Often the extracurricular part of campus life is very influential in perpetuating gender-related stereotypes. In many middle and high schools, male athletic events are the main social events. Both male athletes and female cheerleaders have considerable visibility and are members of an elite group. Often the male athletes are achievement oriented, competitive, and aggressive, while the females are encouraged to smile and be concerned about their appearance. These values then become incorporated into the informal peer culture (Eder & Parker, 1987).

Some believe that "girls, more than boys, were likely to rate being popular as more important than doing things well" (Simmons & Rosenberg,

1975, p. 231) including achieving in school. However, "girls were more likely to report they studied with friends, boys reported spending more time involved in sports and organizations" (Schneider & Coutts, 1985, p. 50). Thus, girls may be better able to satisfy simultaneously their affiliative and achievement needs. Women's studies courses have become a feature in some high schools and in many colleges. These courses have been seen to raise the self-esteem of many women. In one course, which included men, as well, each group was better able to learn about the stereotypes each had of the other (Harris, 1983).

Dropping Out of School

A major concern in most American high schools is the high dropout rate, especially for Hispanic and African American youths. In 1987–1988 in Brooklyn, Bronx, and Manhattan, only 63% of expected high school graduations occurred (Hill et al., 1990). Many factors are involved, including the family's placing low value on education, school programs that do not attain significant involvement or offer relevancy, and social service needs that interfere with appropriate attention to school attendance or studying, among others. The student's dropping out represents an individual limitation of opportunity as well as a loss to society.

Several preventive programs have been attempted. A prime one is to improve the education in earlier grades so that involvement in educational programs becomes important all through a child's school career. Other programs begin in the secondary school years, especially junior high/middle school years. A major thrust of such programs is to give more in-school individualized attention to the program planning for each student. Many families often lack the knowledge, time, energy, or interest to help a child explore and plan available future options. In some schools, budget has been provided for extra counseling.

More colleges and even professional schools are developing outreach programs in high schools to interest youths in pursuing higher education. High-achieving high school juniors are eligible to begin college courses in their senior year. A privately funded project (Focus on Youth, 1989) provided for representatives of community social service agencies to go into the high school to work with school personnel to help students considered to be at risk for dropout. This program provided material basics, such as food and clothing, as well as counseling. At the end of 1 to 2 years, the number of students staying to complete high school increased significantly.

The adolescent who neglects school, feels unsuccessful, and then drops (or flunks) out may be reacting to a depression about family conflicts, personal assets, poor interpersonal relations, or psychopathology. In some families education has low priority and dropout bears no stigma. However, for many youngsters, dropping out may be seen as a form of self-damage, akin to nonlethal suicide. Psychotherapy or adventitious encouragement from an interested adult or mentor may arouse more constructive energies. The General Educational Degree (GED) is available in most school districts to provide the student with a high school diploma, without requiring completion of course credits. The awarding of this degree is based on the student's ability to pass a test of basic skills. With proper coaching and preparation, most dropout students do pass this. The boost to self-esteem as well as for improved employment opportunities fostered by receipt of this degree can be impressive and crucial.

Transition from High School to College

The transition from high school to college is similar in some ways to the previous two transitions—entry into middle school and later into high school—in that a familiar, manageable setting is being surrendered and a new, challenging setting is being entered. However, entry into college differs in that the peer group is now being divided according to ability more than in the previous two transitions. Families, friends, and lovers may find their closeness severed geographically. The ambivalence and sorrow about leaving the closely knit high school peer group can be poignant. The battles that go on in many families when the youngster procrastinates in completing college applications can reflect the youngster's reluctance to relinquish dependencies and leave the nest. Choice of college is a painful reckoning day; in some instances youngsters are forced to confront reality, with a penalty for the previous years of devaluing studies being exacted.

Going to a college in another city represents a severe stress for some adolescents, as it involves the loss of previous friendships, familiar geography, and familial supports. Some families are emotionally unable to release the adolescent. The youth may have been important to maintaining a family equilibrium, which will have difficulty surviving without him or her. After the youth's departure, family strife may increase. Parental divorce may occur. Some families immediately redo the departed student's room, to avoid grief feelings and perhaps to retaliate for the feelings of desertion.

The student may return to the family home on visits with warmth and nostalgia or, at times, new friction. New, possibly critical insights about relationships in the family or new divergent philosophical/political beliefs may have been learned. He or she may attempt to reconstruct the family members to conform to the new ideals. Some families can appreciate and incorporate these new values and even make changes in response, confirming the youth's new budding adult maturity. Thus, the student can become, or remain, a new participating, though now more provocative, family member.

Conclusion

The period of ages 12 to 20 (or 22), the junior (middle)/senior high and college years, are significant developmental years. Self-esteem, cognitive abilities, social skills, career and relationship choices, sexual identity, and many other personality traits reach full development in these years. Schools, agencies second in influence only to the family, can offer a significant contribution to this development, positively or negatively. This influence is imparted through both the qualities of the individual educators and the structure of, and values transmitted by, the particular school system and the peer group. Occasionally childhood problems become aggravated. The potential is present also for individual psychological development to be enhanced and previous problems to be lessened.

Each of the transition points—elementary school to junior high/middle school, junior high/middle school to high school, high school to college—is a focus for stress. Accordingly, it may be accompanied by anxiety and/or pride, advances in development and skills, or aggravation of pathology. The move to junior high/middle school also occurs at the same time as pubertal stress and is considered especially crucial in the youth's developing future goals and commitments, both behaviorally and academically. In high schools, these choices can be consolidated and new interests and social skills developed. At times, a dropout path can be intensified. Opportunities for correction of some previous problems are available in some high schools, either by deliberate intervention from adults or peers or by developmental changes. Many more schools could provide additional attention to behavioral and emotional issues for average as well as at-risk adolescents, without undue extra expense. Psychiatric/psychological consultation toward this goal is described in other chapters.

REFERENCES

American Association of University Women (1991). *Shortchanging Girls, Short Changing America*. Washington, DC: Author.

Arch, E. L., & Cummins, D. E. (1989). Structured and Unstructured exposure to computers: Sex differences in attitude and use among college students. *Sex Roles, 20* (5/6), 245–253.

Berkovitz, I. H. (1985). The many places of anger in the school setting. In I. H. Berkovitz & J. S. Seliger (Eds.), *Expanding mental health interventions in schools*, Dubuque, IA: Kendall/Hunt.

Berkovitz, I. H. (1987). Value of group counseling in secondary schools. *Adolescent Psychiatry, 14,* 522–545.

Berkovitz, I. H. (1991). Effects of secondary school and college experiences on adolescent female development. In M. Sugar (Ed.), *Female adolescent development* (2nd ed., pp. 192–212). New York: Brunner/Mazel.

Berkowitz, I. H. (1995). The adolescent in the schools: A therapeutic guide. *Adolescent Psychiatry, 20,* 343–364.

Berkovitz, I. H., & Seliger, J. S. (Eds.). (1985). *Expanding mental health interventions in schools.* Dubuque, IA: Kendall/Hunt.

Berlin, I. N. (1980). Psychiatry and the school. In H. I. Kaplan, A. M. Freedom, & B. J. Sadow (Eds.),

Comprehensive textbook of psychiatry III. (3rd ed., pp. 2693–2706). Baltimore: Williams & Wilkins.

Blos, P. (1972). The child analyst looks at the young adolescent. In J. Kagan & R. Coles (Eds.), *12 to 16—Early adolescence* (pp. 55–72). New York: W. W. Norton.

Brent, D. A., Perper, J. A., Moritz, G., Liotus, L., Richardson, D., Cannobio, R., Schweers, J., and Roth, C. (1995). Posttraumatic stress disorder in peers of adolescent suicide victims: Predisposing factors and phenomenology. *Journal of the American Academy of Child and Adolescent Psychiatry, 34,* 209–215.

California State Department of Education. (1987). *Caught in the middle; Educational reform for young adolescents in California public schools.* Sacramento: Author.

Carnegie Council on Adolescent Development. (1989). *Turning points, Preparing American youth for the 21st century.* New York: Carnegie Corporation.

DeCecco, J. P., & Richards, A. K. (1974). *Growing pains, uses of school conflict.* New York: Aberdeen Press.

Eder, D., & Parker, S. (1987). The cultural production and reproduction of gender: The effect of extracurricular activities on peer-group culture. *Sociology of Education, 60,* 200–213.

Freud, A. (1946). *Ego and mechanisms of defense.* New York: International Universities Press.

George, P. S., & Oldaker, L. L. (1985/1986). A national survey of middle school effectiveness. *Educational Leadership, 43,* 79–85.

Golombek, H., Marton, P., Stein, B., & Korenblum, M. (1987). Personality functioning status during early and middle adolescence. *Adolescent Psychiatry, 14,* 365–377.

Harris, R. M. (1983). Changing women's self-perceptions: Impact of a psychology of women course. *Psychological Reports, 52,* 314.

Hill, P. T., Foster, G. E., & Gendler, T. (1990). *High schools with character.* Santa Monica, CA: RAND Corporation.

Honig, W. (1987). Foreword to *Caught in the middle: Educational reform for young adolescents in California public schools.* Sacramento: California State Department of Education.

Lear, J. G., Gleicher, B. H., St. Germaine, A., & Porter, R. J. (1991). Reorganizing health care for adolescents. The experience of the school-based health care program. *Journal of Adolescent Health, 12,* 450–458.

Lipsitz, J. (1984). *Successful schools for young adolescents.* Arlington, VA: Transaction.

Los Angeles Educational Partnership. *Focus on Youth, Evaluation Report.* (1989). Unpublished manuscript.

Martin, E. C. (1972). Reflections on the early adolescent in school. In J. Kagan & R. Coles (Eds.), *12 to 16—Early Adolescence.* New York: W. W. Norton, pp. 180–196.

Miller, D. (1970). Adolescents and the high school system. *Journal of Community Mental Health, 66,* 483–491.

Offer, D., & Offer, J. B. (1975). *From teenage to young manhood.* New York: Basic Books.

Offer, D., Howard, K. I., Schonert, K. A., & Ostrov, E. (1991). To whom do adolescents turn for help? Differences between disturbed and non-disturbed. *Journal of the American Academy of Child and Adolescent Psychiatry, 30,* 623–630.

Petersen, A. C., Sarigiani, P. A., & Kennedy, R. E. (1991). Adolescent depression: Why more girls? *Journal of Youth & Adolescence, 20* (2), 247–272.

Roueche, J. C., & Baker, G. A. III (1986). *Profiling excellence in America's schools.* Arlington, VA: American Association of School Administrators.

Rutter, M., Maugham, B., Mortimore, P., & Oustan, J. (1980). *Fifteen thousand hours.* Cambridge, MA: Harvard University Press.

Schneider, F. W., & Coutts, L. M. (1985). Person orientation of male and female high school students: To the educational disadvantage of males? *Sex Roles, 13* (1/2), 47–63.

Sherman, J., & Fennema, E. (1977). Study of mathematics by high school girls and related variables. *American Educational Research Journal, 14,* 159–168.

Simmons, R. G., & Rosenberg, F. (1975). Sex, sex roles and self image. *Journal of Youth and Adolescence, 4,* 229–258.

Stake, J. E., & Noonan, M. (1985). The influence of teacher models on the career confidence and motivation of college students. *Sex Roles, 12,* 1023–1031.

Title IX: A Practical Guide to Achieving Sex Equity in Education. (1988). National Coalition for Women and Girls in Education. (Available from National Women's Law Center, 1616 P Street, NW, Washington, DC, 20036.)

Webb, J. A., Baer, P. E., & McKelvey, R. S. (1995). Development of a risk profile for intentions to use alcohol among fifth and sixth graders. *Journal of the American Academy of Child and Adolescent Psychiatry, 34,* 772–785.

Wentzel, K. R. (1988). Classroom goals and academic competence in adolescence. *Journal of Educational Psychology, 8* (2), 131–142.

Vieland, V., Whittle, B., Garland, A., Hicks, R., & Shaffer, D. (1991). *Journal of the American Academy of Child and Adolescent Psychiatry, 30,* 811–815.

26 / The End of Adolescence: Transition to Young Adulthood

John G. Looney and Lois T. Flaherty

While by no means the end of development, the end of adolescence can be considered the ultimate end of childhood. The transition from adolescence to young adulthood, unlike that from childhood to adolescence, is not marked by such an easily identifiable event as puberty, with its dramatic physical changes that force major psychological readjustments. This transition, perhaps more so than any other in the life cycle, is influenced to a great extent by social and cultural expectations for independent functioning. From an economic standpoint, the transition to adulthood is characterized by a shift from a primary mode of consuming society's resources to a mode of producing or to accumulating further knowledge toward a goal of producing. While contemporary society does not have formal ceremonies to mark the entrance into the threshold of adulthood, certain experiences typically occur during this period of life that are equivalent in some ways to rites of passage. These experiences vary for different adolescents and different families, but almost always, some significant event marks the entrance into the threshold of adulthood. Moving into one's own quarters, a first job, graduation from college, the first serious sexual experience associated with commitment, marriage, or military service can all serve as markers.

By the late adolescent years, physical development has been completed and cognitive capacities have matured, but many of the developmental tasks of adolescence are not fully resolved and they continue to be worked on actively as part of the process of transition to the young adult phase of life. Just as childhood developmental delays may manifest themselves as adolescent problems, failure to resolve the key developmental tasks of adolescence results in young adult problems. Because of this fact, it is critical, in the assessment of young adults, to look for developmental issues that are part of the adolescent period but often linger into the transitional period. These initial adolescent tasks are detailed elsewhere in this volume. It is very important to consider the manner in which unresolved issues during these key developmental stages of adolescent development can impede normal young adult development.

Stages of Development in Adolescence

These stages often are described as occurring within three phases. The first phase, the pubertal or early adolescent phase, is marked by the onset of puberty and lasts approximately 2 years. Boys and girls appear to handle differently increased sexual and aggressive drive pressures. Boys seem to avoid an active masculine position during this period and regress to pregenital concerns. They appear to behave in a way that is reminiscent of the anal period. They are often messy in their dressing and grooming, and their jokes and language often refer to excretory functions; their topics of conversation are sometimes quite smutty. At this age, boys tend to group together closely. They often derogate girls and want nothing to do with them. Girls, on the other hand, seem to take an opposite position. Although they also get together in groups, their concern usually is focused on making themselves attractive to boys and pursuing boys. During this period of adolescence, adults often find teenagers difficult to communicate with. Their interests are often remote from those of their parents, and they commonly exhibit little interest in their studies.

The second phase, a transitional period, begins approximately 2 years after the onset of puberty, lasts about 2 years, and involves important shifts. One change is the beginning development of a capacity for abstract thinking. Although a capacity is present, effective usage often is not. Adolescents in this phase sometimes seem to play with abstract thought much as a younger child would play with toys. They might explore a wide variety of what-if propositions, some of them frankly bizarre. During this phase, adolescents seem to be widely searching for identities and for idealistic models with whom they can identify. They sometimes seem to be changing their identities as if trying on clothing. Their idealism may lead to experimentation with value systems other than those conveyed by their parents. During this transitional phase, adolescents often reduce their previously intense level of involvement with same-sex peer groups and form a special friendship with one person of the same sex. These relationships are often very special, very private, and very intense. They enable adolescents to practice an intense relationship with a member of the same sex prior to attempting such a relationship with a member of the opposite sex.

Late adolescence, or the period most identified in the popular culture with adolescence, begins approximately 4 years after the onset of puberty and continues to an indefinite end in the next 2 or 3 years. It is a period of very strong feelings and emotions. There is a decisive turn to intense relationships with members of the opposite sex, which often begins with "going steady." Although these steady relationships are sometimes very serious, most do end, sometimes quite painfully. Often these relationships seem to be chosen on the basis of marked similarity to, or dissimilarity from, the opposite-sex parent. When a similar person is chosen and the relationship breaks down, the next partner is often quite different from the previous one. Sometimes there is a series of these relationships before an adolescent is able to transition into a young adult choice of a partner. Adolescents in this period usually demonstrate some practicality in their use of abstract thinking. They can project into the future about college, marriage, and a profession.

Researchers' Contributions

Our knowledge of child and adolescent development was first informed by clinical studies, subsequently by studies of small, nonclinical populations, and later by larger-scale studies. We are just beginning to accumulate knowledge about young adult development. Understanding of this phase of the life cycle has proceeded slowly, beginning with the awareness that it is, indeed, a distinct stage of life.

Anna Freud (1958) was one of the first to write about theoretical developmental constructs based on observations of children, both patients and normal children. Her concept of multiple parallel developmental lines is well known to students of child development, but it offers an equally valid framework within which clinicians who work with adolescents and young adults can assess development according to how these different lines are modified or completed. Erik Erikson (1950) similarly developed theoretical constructs from observations of patients and normal youth, and we shall describe how these constructs have molded some relevant empirical research about young adult development. Until recently, the body of knowledge about this period of life consisted mainly of theoretical ideas drawn from observation of patients or natural observation methods with normal youth. Our study of young adult development is just beginning to spawn empirical research using larger samples of normal youth, which allows for testing of these hypotheses.

Keniston (1970) studied college students under stress and identified youth as a separate stage of development that occupied a place in between adolescence and adulthood. He postulated that this stage had emerged as a distinct phase as societies evolved toward more technologically based economies, prolonging the time necessary for individuals to acquire skills that enabled them to become independent wage earners. He pointed out the disparate pathways that development might take at this stage, based on the individual's intellectual endowment and the opportunities (or lack thereof) available to him or her. The most restricted avenue is that of foreclosure, in which the young person settles upon a philosophy of life that is basically an unquestioning acceptance of the cultural traditions he or she has grown up with. This mode is usually associated with concrete operational thinking and conventional moral reasoning (Kolberg, 1964). This way of being in the world is the most prevalent, and always has been, as the vast majority of the world's youth lack capacity and, sadly, opportunities to actualize their capacity for higher levels of development.

At the other end of the spectrum, and more

prevalent (although by no means universally so) on elite college campuses such as Yale and Harvard, where Keniston and Kolberg respectively worked, are youths who preoccupy themselves with developing an ideology, or worldview, that can serve as a guide to life. These youths are the ones who ponder the meaning of life and the origins of good and evil, who stay up all night in their dormitory rooms discussing their ideas, and who are able to maintain themselves in what Erikson termed a "moratorium" while they work out who they are and what they want to do. Writing during the era of the counterculture movements of the 1960s, Keniston (1970) was impressed with the ways in which late adolescents and young adults used membership in these groups to further develop an identity and work out the inevitable tensions that exist between the ideals of the individual and the realistic possibilities of society.

Gould was one of the first to study young adult psychiatric patients. He noted persistent themes that arose in psychotherapy groups of patients of this age (1978). These motifs included a sense of feeling established in life, autonomous, and separated from family. He extrapolated that these feelings were established in an incremental fashion during the transition period, because groups of mid to late adolescents are just beginning to contemplate these issues.

Other authors have approached the task of understanding the transition to young adulthood by intensive studies of small populations of nonpatients. Levinson (1978) carried out an in-depth study of 40 men between the ages of 35 and 45. Levinson's most remarkable finding was the discovery that adult life evolves through relatively orderly sequences, with stages of stability alternating with unstable transitional periods usually lasting 3 to 5 years. During these transitional periods, individuals must question the pattern of their existing life, reappraise it, and move on to new directions. Levinson's "novice" phase (a period of learning to be an adult) consists of three stages. He describes the first stage as the early adult transition stage, and unstable transitional stage that occurs between the ages of 17 and 22. Levinson sees this stage as a time of profound change:

The early adult transition presents two major tasks. One task is to terminate the adolescent-like structure and leave the pre-adult world. A young [adult] has to ques-

tion the nature of that world and [his/her] place in it. It is necessary to modify existing relationships with important persons and institutions, and to modify the self that formed in pre-adulthood. Numerous separations, losses, and transformations are required. The second task is to make a preliminary step into the adult world: to explore its possibilities, to imagine oneself as a participant in it, to make and test some tentative choices before fully entering it. The first task involves a process of termination, the second a process of initiation. Both are essential in a transitional period. (P. 73)

The tasks of termination and initiation just described must be completed in order to accomplish the following basic goals of the novice phase, which are to: (1) evolve a life dream, (2) achieve a relationship with a mentor, (3) make a solid occupational choice, and (4) work out a love relationship. These accomplishments do not have to be achieved in this precise order.

George Vaillant (1977) has added to our knowledge of young adult development through his study of adult men who first were identified as research subjects many years earlier when they were students at Harvard. Vaillant used a hierarchy developed by Semrad and colleagues (1973) of mechanism of defenses as a way of assessing their manner of coping with adult life. He found that those men who were doing well in life tended to use higher-order defense mechanisms, such as sublimation and humor, and had supportive relationships. Although Vaillant did not actually know these subjects when they were college students, the implication is that they had, or were developing, effective coping mechanisms as young adults.

Looney and colleagues (1980) studied a large cohort of young physicians making the transition from training in psychiatry to careers. Although these individuals were at the far upper end of the period of young adult development in age, their prolonged educational track appears to have kept them within the young adult group regarding psychological development. These young physicians experienced stress of alarming propositions, and some developed psychiatric symptoms. Yet most traversed this period well, establishing enduring vocational direction and personal commitments. Those with the greatest tendencies to affiliate with others appeared to fare best, establishing strong supportive personal networks.

Women's Differing Pathways

Authors such as Gilligan (1982) point out the male bias of many developmental studies and suggest that women may have different, but equally well-defined, developmental processes. She has focused on the moral development of women, pointing out that women's moral decisions are guided by concern for relationships, while men's tend to be determined by adherence to precepts. Others have looked at ways in which women learn to think and the difficulty they have in developing their own "voices," or ability to think for themselves (Belenky, Clinchy, Goldberger, & Tarule, 1988). Students of women's development agree that familial and societal pressures often combine to inhibit women's actualization of their full intellectual potential. The period of transition to young adulthood is one in which young women often are confronted for the first time with the dilemmas they will face throughout life with regard to self versus others. They frequently perceive that they are forced to make major decisions about careers versus families in a way that pits their internalized values of selfless giving against self-actualization (Flaherty, 1982).

Inadequacies of Current Knowledge

Despite the richness and the unquestioned contribution of these studies to our knowledge, there are some deficiencies. One problem is that most of the studies ascertain critical tasks in the phase of transition to adulthood only retrospectively. A second problem is that they often involve only small groups of subjects from socioeconomic groups that are ethnically and culturally homogeneous. Most studies have not included young women. Exactly how young men and young women differ during this period of transition to young adulthood needs further clarification. Third, many of the studies do not involve measurement with clearly defined and well-accepted research instruments; rather they are based on data from unstructured interviews and/or observations, which, while meaningful, are subject to observer bias. These landmark, pioneering studies must be followed by more systematic studies, using standardized measurements, of a large population from different socioeconomic, ethnic, and geographic segments of youths who are at the time in the process of this transition. Much further study is needed to understand these complex forces and how best to intervene in promoting healthy psychological development.

Essential (Developmental) Tasks of Adolescence

Despite the limitations on the current state of our knowledge, a significant body of knowledge is emerging about the transition from adolescence to young adulthood. Distilling the work of a number of authors in this area, Arnstein (1989) has identified the key developmental tasks of the adolescent period that must be completed in order for the individual to approach mature psychological adulthood. These tasks are as follows:

1. Separation from parents
2. Ego synthesis or identity formation
3. The development of a capacity for intimacy
4. The achievement of genital primacy
5. Change in object relations
6. Stabilization of character structure
7. Development of a time perspective
8. Development of a capacity for friendship
9. Commitment to a set of life goals encompassing vocation and work role
10. Achievement of an effective moral code

Space constraints prohibit an in-depth review of each of Arnstein's young adult developmental landmarks, and the reader is referred to his excellent work in this area. We offer here a brief review of several of these tasks that are particularly important and reflect the ideas of Levinson and others in this field.

SEPARATION FROM PARENTS

The achievement of actual physical separation from parents by moving out of the parental home is an important milestone during the transition into young adulthood. Young people usually leave home by the end of high school, typically for college but in some instances for military service or vocational pursuits. The ability to separate and to meet day-to-day stresses on one's own is a significant developmental accomplishment at this phase of life.

Levinson (1978) confirms earlier ideas about the importance of differentiation of self from parents as well as actual separation from parents. Although people change the quality of attachment to parents throughout life, in fact, he believes, people never completely separate psychologically from the parents. Another task he notes in the period from 17 to 22 years of age is making the first step into the adult world. This step often means making a transition into a form of life different from that of one's parents. Living apart is an important milestone of this developmental epoch.

For many young people, the experience of living away from parents comes for the first time with going away to college or joining the military. By and large, young people do not have adequate societal support for this step. They are sent off to college or the military with well-meaning advice from parents. This advice is of limited use, however, because the college and military environments are so different now from how they were in the past when parents may have experienced them. External rules, in the forms of curfews, strictly enforced bans on alcohol, and chaperoning of social events are nearly nonexistent. Drugs, as well as the money to buy them, are readily available. And there are indications that today's youths experience more stress than did those of yesteryear. For example, alcohol usage is substantially different now (Center on Addiction and Substance Abuse, 1994). College students now binge drink with alarming frequency. Forty-two percent of students imbibe five or more drinks in one setting every 2 weeks (Presley & Meilman, 1992). Women are drinking at least three times harder than in the past, and they are catching up with men in binge-drinking patterns (Presley & Meilman, 1992). Ninety-five percent of arrests for violence on campus occur in drunken students, and in 90% of alleged or proven sexual assaults, one or both people were using alcohol (Presley & Meilman, 1992).

In the past, college students socialized to have fun and used alcohol to enhance pleasurable experiences and as a social lubricant to reduce anxiety. Sometimes they became intoxicated in the course of social activity, but this was not usually their goal. Along the way, young people learned to manage alcohol within the context of young adult development. Now the pattern is for students to get drunk first and then see what there is to do.

One does not have to look far to find sources of stress for today's college students. The list of the things they must manage is truly daunting: time, money, separating from their parents, relationships with their professors, general social relationships, intimate social relationships, new ethnical dilemmas, alcohol, and more. Young people's preparation for college, however, is parental advice combined with a week or less of college orientation. They have no gradual indoctrination but are plunged quickly into a different world. Just as alcohol serves as a stress reliever for many adults, it is understandable that college students also use it for this purpose. Quite likely the anxiety associated with so many demands for new ways of functioning, plus very limited institutionalized support, is a factor in the prevalent use of alcohol on college campuses.

College students' anxieties are undoubtedly magnified even further by the trend toward increasing vocational competition. Young people no longer expect to exceed their parents' vocational accomplishments. Yet they have little actual preparation for the intense competition for jobs they will face upon college graduation. It probably should not be surprising that so many young people do not succeed. The data show that more college graduates become alcoholic than achieve master's degrees and doctorates combined.

By way of comparison, we may consider what is involved in another route to leaving the parental home: the military. In contrast to college, the military systematically teaches young people the critical skills they will need to succeed, at least within the confines of the military environment. The mechanism for this teaching is an extended indoctrination and training program that begins with boot camp and continues thereafter. For a large segment of American youth, the military provides an important avenue to adulthood. Traditionally it has served as a means of education and training for disadvantaged youth and those who would otherwise have very limited options in adult society. Succeeding in the military environment involves learning important skills, such as working with others, getting along with those in charge, following rules and regulations, and practicing self-discipline. Drug screening is done routinely. The military has evolved these structures in response to its specific needs and goals, which are to have a fit and capable workforce—very different objectives from those of our colleges and universities. But neither is it in the best interest of educational institutions to turn out dysfunctional graduates, and colleges could benefit from adapting some of the institutionalized supports used successfully in the military. Indeed, some schools have developed special programs to prepare disadvantaged students to remediate deficiencies in basic skills and to survive in the college environment, out of the recognition that these students may be doomed to failure without this help. There is evidence that colleges are beginning to pay more attention to the need for more extensive orientation and preparation for meeting the increased demands for autonomous functioning. In addition, they are beginning to put in place alcohol and drug education and treatment programs.

IDENTITY FORMATION

The formation of a stable identity has been generally viewed as one of the most important developmental tasks of the last adolescent period. Although Erik Erikson (1950) described the process of identity formation as taking place throughout the life cycle, he recognized it as the defining developmental task of the late adolescent period. Identity can be defined as a sense of who one is, in relation to oneself, to others, and to the world as a whole. A secure identity is dependent on continuity of this sense over time. Although the awareness of who one is can be said to begin in infancy and to evolve throughout life, during adolescence the most intensive work on this important developmental task takes place, and during late adolescence a kind of integration of past, present, and future identities takes place that serves as a foundation for the rest of the life cycle. If childhood can be said to involve the absorption of elements of identity and adolescence can be characterized by the reorganization of identity, the transition to young adulthood can be viewed as involving a consolidation of identity. This consolidation involves the weaving together of hitherto disparate elements, elements that in the past may have seemed irreconcilable, into a coherent whole that allows the individual to become a generative adult.

Building on Erikson's landmark work, Marcia (1966) has studied the issue of identity formation in young adulthood, using an empirical interview approach to study nonclinical populations. From her research on a nonpatient population of late adolescents, it appears that identity formation plays an important role in subsequent emotional health and has practical value in the individual's functioning in later life. The research paradigm is based on the concepts of crisis in previously held ideals with commitment to new ideas and new definitive choices. Marcia defined four groups on the basis of the presence or absence of a crisis, followed by a new commitment:

1. *Identity achievement* characterized the group that, having explored life's options, decided on a way of being.
2. *Foreclosure* was defined as commitment in the absence of a searching or crisis phase, leading to a premature identity formation.
3. *Moratorium* described a group that was actively in a crisis or testing phase, struggling to make a commitment.
4. *Diffusion* occurred in those who were found to be experiencing neither crisis nor commitment, and were in a state of drifting and avoiding identity formation tasks.

A key finding of Marcia's research was that achievement of a stable identity is not always reached in the transition from adolescence to young adult life. Those who accomplished this task appeared to be healthier, more mature young people. They had higher self-esteem, higher resistance to conformity pressure, and a greater sense of self-direction.

Arnstein (1989) approached the topic of transition to young adulthood both from the study of patients and from naturalistic observation of a normative (although somewhat atypical) population, Yale undergraduates. He agrees that the evolution of an identity at the end of adolescence and into this transition period is a major task of this period of life. The hallmark of successful completion of this task is the ability to define who one is and understand how others see one. Sometimes this definition appears to be smoothly achieved and well established by age 17. In other cases, the process of identity formation involves many twists and turns and continues to evolve through the 20s.

THE DEVELOPMENT OF A CAPACITY FOR INTIMACY

Another key task during this period of transition is the development of the capacity for true psychological and sexual intimacy. Although in contemporary American society sexual activity usually begins during adolescence, much more is involved in an intimate relationship than sexual performance. The achievement of a relationship that involves intimacy and real caring on the part of both partners must be mastered during this transition period if the person is to be able to sustain a lasting relationship of support and mutuality with another person. The capacities for sharing, for negotiation, and for true friendship are critical.

There is evidence that the issues of identity and intimacy are linked, and in different ways for males and females. Women tend to define themselves in terms of relationships. Whereas, for males, identity precedes intimacy, for females, identity and intimacy appear to be fused together. Dyk and Adams (1990), who studied this, found that females who are more traditionally feminine in gender role orientation also had more of what they called "fused identity/intimacy development." They were waiting to be in a relationship with a male to complete their identity development. Those women who had more of a cross-sex role orientation had higher correlations between identity formation and intimacy. They concluded that a more encompassing sex role orientation may enhance resolution of the identity crisis and help women move on to intimacy formation in ways that did not eclipse their individuality. Belenky, Clinchy, Goldberger, and Tarule (1988) presented detailed accounts of ways in which women who had their identity defined very early in their lives by becoming wives and/or mothers, later struggled to expand their notion of who they were by taking on other roles, as they learned to think in different ways about themselves and the world. For further discussion of this issue, see Chapters 17 and 18.

COMMITMENT TO A SET OF LIFE GOALS ENCOMPASSING VOCATION AND WORK ROLE

Arnstein (1989) believes that the establishment of a set of life goals is an extremely critical task in this transitional phase of development. He states, ". . . there is a general need to establish life goals, which task encompasses vocation and anticipated work role, presumes the capacity for commitment and the achievement of an acceptable moral code, and requires sufficient confidence and self-esteem to permit the individual to pursue the goals chosen" (p. 133). Obviously, this process will be determined to a large degree by what options are available. These options are vastly different for the college-educated youth than for the high school dropout. This process has been described as one that entails, for some young people, a sense of limitless opportunities and their own limitless potential, or omnipotentiality. They are intoxicated by the apparent vast array of possibilities open to them; they may be unable to make a commitment to pursue a single path, because choosing one possibility means eliminating others. Although a normative experience during the young adult stage, for some youths, this sense of omnipotentiality is the beginning of a psychotic condition, with manic features of grandiosity and expansiveness.

CASE EXAMPLE

A 25-year-old man who had vowed to himself to "make a million and retire by the time I'm 35" found himself intoxicated with possibilities for business ventures after he attended a high school reunion and met many of his friends and began talking with them about his interests in starting a business. Later that night he was unable to sleep and found his thoughts coming so fast that it frightened him. He remained in a hypomanic state for the next several weeks.

It is during the young adult stage of life that having a mentor, an older person who encourages and guides career development, can be crucial experience that has a defining influence on later life. Mentoring has been identified as critical in the lives of many individuals who become successful in their careers. A mentor can be a college professor, a boss, an athletic coach, or an army platoon leader. It is a person who has knowledge and skills to be successful in a field of work, and shares these to help a junior colleague grow and develop. The relationship with a mentor is often an intense one that involves many elements of a therapeutic relationship. Like therapy, the mentorship usually ends or is transformed into a much more attenuated relationship once the protégé outgrows his or her need for it.

Clinical Implications

The clinician who works with late adolescent and young adults must first consider how well the tasks of adolescent development have been accomplished. The next consideration is the social and cultural context, for pathways to adulthood will vary greatly according to the opportunities available and the expectations and demands of family, teachers or supervisors, and peers. Finally, what may be pathological for older adults frequently is normative for the young adult who is not ready to make a commitment to pursue a single set of goals or lifestyle, or is still working out identity issues.

Conclusion

There appears to be no clear demarcation between the end of adolescence and the period of transition to young adulthood. Graduation from high school is probably the closest approximation to such a demarcation. At the end of high school, some peo- ple will still be working on resolution of a large number of these; some on only a few. Several distinct new tasks come into view, the first of which is the achievement of physical separation from parents. Even though psychological separation may be reworked constantly throughout life, a physical separation, contemplated to be permanent, needs to take place. Another important change is that the young person leaving high school may engage in very different pursuits: full-time work, military service or further education. During adolescence, the young person may have developed the ability to contemplate a variety of future possibilities for his or her life. However, this transitional period demands that these possibilities be explored in a more practical way and that a process of a commitment to one choice begun. A sense of identity—who one is and who others think one is—is an important issue to be resolved in this transitional phase. Combining sexuality with true mutuality and commitment to the other is a critical source of concern of youths in this phase of development.

With time, increasingly sophisticated research studies will lend more to our understanding of this phase of development for both young men and young women.

REFERENCES

Arnstein, R. L. (1989). Overview of normal transition to young adulthood. In S. C. Feinstein (Ed.), *Adolescent psychiatry* (Vol. 16, pp. 127–141). Chicago: University of Chicago Press.

Belenky, M. F., Clinchy, B. M., Goldberger, N. R., & Tarule, J. M. (1988). *Women's ways of knowing: The development of self, voice and mind.* New York: Basic Books.

Center on Addiction and Substance Abuse at Columbia University. (1994). *Rethinking rites of passage: Substance abuse on America's campuses.* New York: Columbia University.

Dyk, P. H., & Adams, G. R. (1990). Identity and intimacy: An initial investigation of three theoretical models using cross-lag panel correlations. *Journal of Youth and Adolescence, 19,* 91–110.

Erikson, E. H. (1950). *Childhood and society.* New York: W. W. Norton.

Flaherty, L. (1982). To love and/or to work: The ideological dilemma of young women. *Adolescent Psychiatry, 10,* 41–51.

Freud, A. (1958). *Adolescence. Psychoanalytic Study of the Child, 13,* 255.

Gilligan, C. (1982). *In a different voice.* Cambridge, MA: Harvard University Press.

Gould, R. L. (1978). *Transformations.* New York: Simon & Schuster.

Keniston, K. (1970, Autumn). Youth: A "new" stage of life. *The American Scholar,* pp. 631–654.

Kohlberg, L. (1964). Development of moral character and moral ideology. In M. Hoffman (Ed.), *Review of child development research* (Vol. 1, pp. 383–432). New York: Russell Sage.

Levinson, D. J. (1978). *The Seasons of a man's life.* New York: Alfred A. Knopf.

Looney, J. G., Harding, R. K., Blotcky, M. J., & Barhart, F. D. (1980). Psychiatrists' transition from training to career: Stress & mastery. *American Journal of Psychiatry, 137* (1), 32–36.

Marcia, J. E. (1966). Development and validation of ego identity status. *Journal of Personality and Social Psychology, 3,* 551–558.

Presley C. M. (1992). *Alcohol and drugs on American college campuses: A report to college presidents.* Carbondale, IL: Southern Illinois University.

Semrad, E. V., Grinspoon, L., & Feinberg, S. E. (1973). Development of an ego profile scale. *Archives of General Psychiatry, 28,* 70–77.

Vaillant, G. E. (1977). *Adaptation to life.* Boston: Little, Brown.

SECTION II
Syndromes of Adolescence

27 / Psychiatric Classification and Diagnosis in Adolescence

Glen T. Pearson, Jr.

Introduction, Overview, and History

Psychiatry has experienced a renewal of interest in nosological issues over the past decade. The publication of the third edition of the American *Diagnostic and Statistical Manual of Mental Disorders (DSM-III)* (American Psychiatric Association [hereafter APA], 1980) was attended by an outpouring of praise, criticism, and debate on theoretical, clinical, political, and interprofessional grounds. More important, *DSM-III* provided for the first time a more or less reliable basis for the empirical study of nosological issues generally and for the classification of disorders of childhood and adolescence specifically. Previous editions of this work (APA, 1952, 1968) had given scant attention to disorders of youth; the vastly increased coverage of these disorders in the official nosology stimulated researchers to produce a flood of empirical studies and challenged clinicians of varying theoretical persuasions to reconcile the descriptive diagnostic categories and the emerging findings of empirical research with their clinical experience (and with their enriched beliefs about psychopathology in young people).

In the context of this flurry of nosological activity, many authors (Achenbach, 1985; Klerman, 1986; Rutter, 1985, 1986; Rutter & Tuma, 1988; Werry, 1988) surveyed the field of classification efforts historically, currently, and with a view toward an improved taxonomy in the future. The history of the systematic classification of psychiatric disorders prior to 1980 was marked by almost total neglect of the disorders of childhood. Although this neglect began to be redressed in *DSM-III* (APA, 1980) *DSM-III-R* (APA, 1987) and *DSM-IV* (APA, 1995), and although the official nomenclature now lists as a major heading those disorders "usually first evident in infancy, childhood, or adolescence," most of the categories in the section refer to disorders whose onset is in prepuberty, with the result that adolescence now appears to occupy the same unenviable position of nosological neglect that characterized childhood and adolescence prior to 1980.

This chapter addresses principles and issues of psychiatric classification, diagnosis, and the diagnostic process from the perspective of adolescence as a unique developmental phase, distinct not only from adult life but also from earlier childhood.

HISTORICAL PERSPECTIVES ON CLASSIFICATION

Conceptual Nosologies: In a brief account of the history of psychiatric classification, Menninger (Menninger, Hoeper, Hankin, & Hewitt, 1963) identifies two traditions: Hippocratic and Linnean. The Hippocratic tradition is characterized by clinically oriented description, an emphasis on similarities (in Havens's [1973] term, "lumping"), and a pragmatic, humane approach. The Linnean tradition is a scientific and academic one, with an emphasis on differentiation, or "splitting" (Havens, 1973). Bemporad and Schwab (1986) point out that clinical practitioners have tended to follow the Hippocratic tradition, while academicians and researchers have followed the Linnean. They cite the fascinating example of Pinel, who as an academic physician spent years devising an elaborate classification, with eight pages devoted to psychiatry. The year after his classification was published, he left academic life and went to the Saltpetriere Hospital; there, after three years of actually treating patients, he reduced his complex classification of mental illness to only four basic types (Bemporad & Schwab, 1986, p. 149). This theme of cyclical alternation between Linnean and Hippocratic approaches pervades the long history of medical taxonomy; in a trenchant commentary on the hasty revision of *DSM-III*, Werry (1988) recounts the practical destruction of "the brilliant clinical classifications of Hippocrates, then Sydenham in the 17th century, by ideological meddlers like Aristotle and the 18th century 'humoralists' who tried to impose evermore ideological and dissected taxonomies."

The modern classification of psychiatric disorders began in the 19th century with Kraepelin (1883), who succeeded not only in isolating syphilis as the cause of general paresis but also in differentiating among the major psychiatric disorders of adult life—schizophrenia, affective disorders, and neuroses (Achenbach, 1985). In so doing, he reduced a Linnean "mess of potage to usable simplicity" (Werry, 1988), thereby returning classification to the clinical tradition of Hippocrates. Kraepelin believed that psychiatry would progress from clinical description to the discovery of organic etiologies, an expectation that has "helped embed the organic disease model in the vocabularies of mental health workers" (Achenbach, 1985). Kraepelinian concepts have dominated the official nomenclatures that began to emerge at about the same time.

Official Nosologies: In Europe, the 1893 International Statistical Institute updated a classification of causes of death originally promulgated in 1853 by the International Statistical Congress. In the early 20th century, this effort came under the wing of the League of Nations, and the classification underwent several revisions, until 1948, when the newly formed World Health Organization (WHO) published the sixth edition of *International Classification of Diseases* (*ICD-6*). By this time, the classification had evolved from a list of diseases for noting causes of death to a categorization briefly describing reasons for hospitalizing patients (Schwab-Stone, Towbin, & Tarnoff, 1991). Although it contained an expanded section on mental disorders, *ICD-6* was considered unsuitable for descriptive statistical needs in the United States. A seventh edition, published in 1955, was essentially unchanged but heralded the beginning of a development project, sponsored by WHO, that led in turn to the publication in 1968 of *ICD-8.*

In the United States, official psychiatric nosology began with a classification prepared by the New England Psychological Society in 1880 for the Census Bureau (Schwab-Stone, Towbin, & Tarnoff, 1991). The American Psychiatric Association began in 1917 to collect statistics on hospitalized patients; this preliminary classification was revised in 1935 and remained in use until the publication of the first *Diagnostic and Statistical Manual* in 1952 (APA, 1952). *DSM-I* was largely based on a classification developed by William Menninger and used by the U.S. military and Veteran's Administration. Relying on psychoanalytic theory and the Meyerian concept of reaction types, it offered little or nothing for the classification of child or adolescent psychiatric disorders (Schwab-Stone, Towbin, & Tarnoff, 1991).

A trend toward convergence of the American and European systems of classification began in 1968 with the contemporaneous publication of *ICD-8* (WHO, 1969) and *DSM-II* (American Psychiatric Association, 1968). Despite ongoing dialogue and joint planning, so far no unified classification has resulted. *ICD-8* was followed by a 10-year research project that culminated in the publication of *ICD-9* (WHO, 1977); *DSM-III* was published three years later, the product of a broad-based effort encompassing several landmark features: an overall conceptualization of mental disorder, comprehensive descriptions of disorders, specific operational diagnostic criteria, a hierarchical organization of diagnostic classes, a multiaxial system, and a section entitled "Disorders First Evident in Infancy, Childhood, or Adolescence," which contained four times as many categories as *DSM-II* (Schwab-Stone, Towbin, & Tarnoff, 1991). American psychiatry was so pleased with *DSM-III* that it immediately set about to revise it (Pearson, 1990).

The revised third edition of the *Diagnostic and Statistical Manual* (*DSM-III-R*, PA, 1987) was published somewhat hastily, purportedly in order to "fine-tune" the classification in the light of empirical research. Yet the relatively brief interval between *DSM-III* and *DSM-III-R* prompted an outcry of protest, primarily from empirical researchers, who complained that the revision was not so much a fine-tuning as a whole new classification system, particularly in the child and adolescent arena (Werry, 1988; Werry, Reeves, & Elkind, 1987). Authorities who had rejected criticism of *DSM-III* as "the outcome of large-scale committee work, designed not so much to ascertain truth as to reconcile different power groups" (Eysenck, 1986) felt compelled to accept the same argument with respect to *DSM-III-R* (Cantwell & Baker, 1988).

The tenth edition of the *International Classification of Diseases, Injuries, and Causes of Death* (*ICD-10*, WHO, 1988) is expected to be the last of the series of decennial revisions of the entire system. Mechanisms will be specified for adding, deleting, or revising categories in the future. The now-current official American nosology, *DSM-IV*, was published in 1994. The areas of convergence between the two systems are generally thought to be greater than the dissimilarities.

The two major areas of difference between *ICD* and *DSM* lie in the degree to which criteria for diagnosis are specified and operationalized and in their assumptions about comorbidity (Schwab-Stone, Towbin, & Tarnoff, 1991). *ICD* provides guidelines for diagnosis rather than operational criteria, thus offering clinicians more flexibility than the *DSM*. *ICD* assumes that there is usually one psychiatric syndrome and that, in general, co-occurring disorders will be rare. *ICD* has mixed categories and discourages multiple diagnoses; *DSM* has no mixed categories and encourages multiple diagnoses. In addition, the *DSM-III-R* and *DSM-IV* eliminated some hierarchical exclusion rules that were present in *DSM-III*, thus increasing the likelihood that multiple diagnoses will be made.

Alternative Nosologies Designed for Youths: Impelled by the conviction that no classification of adult psychopathology can ever be applicable to children and adolescents, many workers in the field have proposed alternative diagnostic schemes for youths. Some two dozen such classifications, including those in the textbooks of Kanner (1935) and Chess (1959), are cataloged in the appendix of the diagnostic manual of the Group for the Advancement of Psychiatry (GAP) published in 1966. The product of years of research and debate by the GAP Committee on Child Psychiatry, the GAP manual discussed theoretical considerations and proposed a classification with a developmental and biopsychosocial framework. The major categories were hierarchically arrayed from least to most serious ("Healthy response" is the first category) and permitted clinicians to classify children with developmental deviations and "transient reactive disorders," which would not qualify them for a diagnosis under *DSM*. The value of this approach was illustrated in a study of GAP diagnoses given to over 300 clinic-referred children and adolescents, which found that 9% were healthy responses, 15% had developmental deviations, and 20% had transient reactive disorders; thus, nearly 44% had conditions that could not be called "mental disorders" in the *DSM* sense (Bemporad, Pfeifer, & Bloom, 1970). The GAP manual was widely circulated and was used in child psychiatry training centers and child guidance clinics. Its authors presumed that its developmental orientation made it equally applicable to children and adolescents; however, it contains no theoretical discussion of adolescence as a unique developmental phase, and even in its exhaustive symptom list the focus appears to rest almost exclusively on the clinical pictures presented by preschool and latency-age children.

Other authors have argued that adult diagnostic criteria are inappropriate for children and adolescents and have proposed diagnostic classifications. Anna Freud (1965) believed strongly that the adult criteria of distress and dysfunction could not be applied to children, because they often do not experience distress and their functional levels normally fluctuate. For Freud, only the interruption of developmental processes constituted disorder, and she proposed a metapsychological diagnostic profile based on her concept of developmental lines (Freud, 1963). Using this instrument, a psychoanalytically oriented clinician could describe an individual child's current functioning along several developmental parameters. The result was a rich ideographic portrait of the individual that was of no use in a statistical classification. Freud's diagnostic profile was widely read and used in some training centers as an organizing principle for drawing inferences from clinical observations in diagnostic assessments. It, too, gave scant attention to the clinical presentations of adolescents.

A number of investigators have been pursuing the dream of a rational classification of child and adolescent psychopathology through quantitative empirical methods (Achenbach, 1980, 1985, 1988; Achenbach, Conners, Quay, Verhulst, & Howell 1989; Quay, 1986). This research has been ongoing for over 40 years but has greatly accelerated recently with the development of more powerful computers. Multivariate statistical methods such as factor and cluster analyses are applied to behavioral data from large representative samples to identify covarying attributes or syndromes. Achenbach (1980) recognizes the importance of developmental variables in behavioral symptomatology. He addresses that issue in sample selection by dividing age cohorts, and finds some differences in the behavioral presentations of adolescents compared with younger children. Advocates of these empirical methods believe a statistically derived classification would avoid the many pitfalls of the traditional, clinically derived categorical approach (Quay, 1986), but it is difficult to imagine how a system that ignores clinical intuition would be useful to a clinician in everyday practice.

Theoretical Issues

Embedded in the history of psychiatry's attempts to classify disease are a number of issues of theoretical significance. These range from theories of development, psychopathology, and classification, to the theory of science itself. An exigetical discussion of any, let alone all, of these is obviously beyond the scope of this chapter; however, in order to assess the strengths and liabilities of systems of classification, and their relevance to adolescent clinical populations, at least a surface acquaintance with the various theoretical issues, the interface among them (together with the tensions that inhere in the interface), and some of the data that have been adduced in various studies are needed. The definitions commonly used and misused terms seems in order to begin.

Taxonomy is the science of classification. *Nosology* is the classification of disease. Authors who favor nonmedical, nondisease models of classification (Achenbach, 1985; Eysenck, 1986; Quay, 1986; Salzinger, 1986) eschew "nosology" and often refer to a classification as a "taxonomy" of psychopathology. A *nomenclature* is a list of approved terms for describing and recording clinical observations; it must be extensive, so that any condition (no matter how rare) can be recorded accurately. Kramer (1988) has provided a concise explanation of the inherent tension in official nosologies that are intended both as a nomenclature and as a *statistical classification*. A statistical classification must be confined to a limited number of categories chosen to facilitate the statistical study of phenomena; it must encompass the entire range of conditions with a few categories. The exhaustive specificity of a nomenclature militates against its usefulness as a statistical classification. (The alert reader will have noticed that the official American nosology is intended to serve both purposes.) Quoting from the *ICD-9* (WHO, 1977), Kramer

(1988) concludes: "a specific entity should have a title in a classification only when its separation is warranted by the frequency of its occurrence or its importance as a morbid condition."

ISSUES FROM CLASSIFICATION THEORY

A number of authors currently active in the field have described various approaches to classification. Achenbach (1985) lists three major "taxonomic paradigms": Kraepelinian, psychodynamic, and multivariate. The Kraepelinian paradigm is a categorical way of organizing presumed medical disease entities; the psychodynamic paradigm is a categorical way of organizing inferred psychological abnormalities; and the multivariate paradigm is a dimensional approach, grouping individuals by covarying attributes derived from statistical analysis. Volkmar (1991) describes three "models of classification": categorical, dimensional, and ideographic. The categorical model assumes that disorder is either present or absent; if present, the similarities with other similarly diagnosed cases outweigh the differences, and the associated features are similar. The dimensional model statistically assesses dimensions of function (or dysfunction) by reducing phenomena to dimensions along which an individual can be placed. The ideographic model rejects simple labels and focuses on the total context of the individual's life to formulate the case (the formulation may be theory-driven or eclectic).

The overlap between Achenbach's "taxonomic paradigms" and Volkmar's "models of classification" is obvious. Innumerable other conceptual models have been proposed, most of which reflect the same areas of overlap and divergence that are represented in the foregoing example. Issues from conflicting theories of psychopathology, as well as professional rivalries, appear to influence the conceptual approaches favored by various authors. The two major questions at issue concerning the conceptual approach to classification are the following: (1) Is classification better served by listing mutually exclusive categories, defined by a small set of features that are "singly necessary and jointly sufficient" (Cantor, Smith, French, & Mezzich, 1980), by appraising dimensions of functioning throughout a population, or by some other approach? (2) What should be the basis of the classification? If categorical, should it be etiology, phenomenology, or some other basis? If dimensional, what dimensions of function or dysfunction should be used as the basis for classification? We shall return to these vexing questions following a brief consideration of the issues presented by theories of psychopathology, science, and development.

ISSUES FROM THEORIES OF PSYCHOPATHOLOGY AND SCIENCE

What do we believe about the underlying causes of psychiatric disorder? In the introductory chapter (Klerman, 1986) of a remarkable volume that he coedited (Millon & Klerman, 1986), Gerald Klerman examines the current scene of American beliefs about psychopathology and attempts to place the debate about nosology in a historical context, both of the prevailing "schools" of psychopathology and of the history of science. Klerman invokes Kuhn's (1970) theory of scientific progress as a framework for understanding the current status of the field of psychopathology.

It is Kuhn's thesis that the history of any scientific field will be marked periodically by a "revolution," in which will emerge a new "paradigm" to enable restructuring of the ways in which the field defines its problems and organizes its data. A paradigm encompasses both cognitive and communal components; "cognitive" refers to theories, hypotheses, and ideas that define the field, and the rules of research and evidence evaluation; "communal" refers to the community of scientists who share the values and acknowledge the particular form of "truth." Whenever one paradigm attains dominance in a field, that field becomes defined and disputes are resolved, ushering in what Kuhn calls a period of "normal science" (Klerman, 1986; Kuhn 1970).

Klerman (1986) has characterized the American landscape as comprising five major schools of psychopathology: biological, psychoanalytic, interpersonal, social, and behavioral/cognitive. This formulation is similar to that of Havens (1973), and while Klerman excludes the "existential" school described by Havens as having insufficient impact on clinical practice to qualify as a competitor for dominance, he acknowledges his debt to Havens and to existentially oriented workers. In terms of the theory of scientific progress (Kuhn, 1970), the presence of multiple competing paradigms indicates that no one paradigm has emerged as dominant, and thus the field of psychopathology is currently "preparadigmatic," or, in a word, prescientific. One could argue, as Havens probably would, that any unifying paradigm in psychopathology will encompass contributions from all of these schools, and quite possibly others, rather than an unscathed emergence into dominance of one of the current schools.

To say that "*DSM-III* potentially embodies a new paradigm for American psychiatry" (Klerman, 1986) seems to ask a great deal of a classification. Rather, since the concepts embodied in *DSM-III* (separate syndromes, diagnosed by operational criteria, on multiple axes) are intellectually compatible with most of the American schools of psychopathology, perhaps the nosology could become the vehicle for the eventual convergence of the schools in a unifying paradigm.

ISSUES FROM DEVELOPMENTAL THEORY

If it is axiomatic that "a child is not a little grown-up," then it is also true that an adolescent is neither simply an overgrown child nor an immature adult. Psychiatric disorders in the young are characterized by developmental considerations, and there has been considerable debate concerning the extent to which adolescence constitutes a "special stage requiring singular diagnostic attention" (Rapoport & Ismond, 1990). Our knowledge of the continuities and discontinuities from childhood through adolescence to adult life is far outweighed by our ignorance, not only of disorder but also of normal development. Rutter (1985) considers existing psychoanalytic, trait-stabilization, cognitive, social, temperamental, and attribution theories of personality development both jointly and severally inadequate. He concludes that "there are a variety of helpful concepts about different facets of personality functioning, but that, still, these fall far short of any clear conceptualization of how personality is organized." Yet many studies point to developmental trends both in normality and in psychopathology. Because of nosological, conceptual, and methodological limitations, large quantities of data have produced very modest findings, and no grand conclusions are possible.

In reviewing a number of these studies, Graham and Rutter (1985) have summarized the changes in patterns of psychiatric disorder from childhood to adolescence. The manifestations of emotional disorders in childhood are protean and diffuse; in adolescence they become more differentiated and similar to their counterparts in adulthood. The prevalence of conduct disorders changes little in the transition from childhood to adolescence, but there is a marked increase in the range of delinquent activities. In childhood, conduct disorders are strongly associated with learning difficulties, whereas those originating in adolescence bear no such relationship. Although it is rare for seriously criminal behavior to begin for the first time in adult life, the converse is not true, and many delinquent juveniles will give up their antisocial pursuits when in their 20s. Anorexia nervosa, alcoholism, drug abuse, and affective disorders all show a marked rise in frequency in adolescence. And concerning the affective disorders, the sex-ratio changes from predominantly male in prepuberty to predominantly female in adolescence and adult life. It has been suggested that depression in adolescent and adult males may be concealed by the presence of antisocial behavior and that, when this is taken into account, the sex-ratio is more nearly equal (Graham & Rutter, 1985).

Developmental variables may influence not only the prevalence of manifest psychiatrc disorder but also our ability to diagnose it. A broad range of research on both nonclinical and referred children and adolescents documents that some of the variables on which the reliability and validity of clinical interviews rest, such as attitudes about the patient and helping-professional roles, rapport, and trust, undergo developmental progression throughout childhood and adolescence (Kovacs, 1986). Kovacs noted that the *DSM-III* criteria for diagnosis of depression "make few accommodations for the patient's developmental stage" and urges that the examiner of children and adolescents be knowledgeable about the developmental variability of relevant attitudes and competencies.

Normal development across the course of adolescence also has been empirically studied. A number of adolescent developmental tasks that have been described by various authors (Blos, 1967; Erikson, 1963; Lewis, 1991) aggregate concisely

into three developmental subphases of adolescence, characterized by three corresponding core issues. In a review of their own and others' empirical research on normal adolescent development, Offer and Boxer (1991) have portrayed these as follows: In early adolescence (ages 12 to 14), the youngster must learn to accept his or her growing and changing body, including an understanding of the self. During middle adolescence (ages 14 to 16), the teenager must separate psychologically from the internalized figure of the parent and venture out of his or her own family world to seek social and affectional relationships. In late adolescence (ages 16 to 19), the struggles of the individual are organized around the issue of identity and its psychological, social, sexual, vocational, and spiritual ramifications (Offer & Boxer, 1991).

The process of identity development itself has been empirically studied. Erikson's (1963) theory of psychosocial development, as it relates to the formation of personal identity, postulates that identity comprises a clear sense of self-definition, commitments regarding values and beliefs, activity directed toward the implementation of commitments, the consideration of a range of identity alternatives, some extent of self-acceptance, a sense of personal uniqueness, and confidence in one's personal future. These features of identity have been operationalized in assessment instruments for research purposes (Waterman, 1982).

Identity development is characterized along two dimensions: crisis and commitment. A crisis is a period of struggle, or active questioning, toward arriving at aspects of personal identity such as vocational choice and ideological beliefs. Commitment involves making a firm decision in such areas and engaging in appropriate implementing activities. Four outcomes or identity "statuses" are possible: achievement, moratorium, foreclosure, and diffusion. Identity achievement indicates that the individual has gone through a period of crisis and emerged, having developed relatively firm commitments. Moratorium indicates that the individual is currently in crisis and is actively seeking alternatives in an attempt to arrive at a choice. Foreclosure indicates that the individual has never experienced a crisis but has nevertheless made enduring commitments, which usually reflect the wishes of parents or other authorities. Identity diffusion characterizes an individual who may or

258

may not have experienced a crisis but who has no commitments and is not actively seeking alternatives.

In a review of the empirical research literature on identity development, Waterman (1982) found that movement from adolescence to adulthood involves changes in identity "status" that could be characterized as progressive developmental shifts: from diffusion to either foreclosure or moratorium, from foreclosure to moratorium, from moratorium to either achievement or diffusion, and from achievement either to sustained achievement or, regressively, to moratorium or diffusion.

This brief overview of issues from theories of development should serve to highlight the inherent complexities of developmental considerations in the classification of psychiatric disorders in adolescence. As we shall see, these developmental issues of adolescence weigh heavily in the clinical pictures presented by adolescents with psychiatric disorders.

CHARACTERISTICS OF AN
ADEQUATE CLASSIFICATION

Returning to the fundamental questions concerning whether classification should be categorical or dimensional, and whether it should be based on etiology or phenomenology, we find no simple answer to either question. Although Kraepelin believed that psychiatry would progress from careful clinical description to the establishment of organic etiologies (Achenbach, 1980), his classification itself was largely descriptive, since etiology was known for only a minority of disorders. Current psychiatric nosologies, which have followed the Kraepelinian tradition, find themselves more or less in the same position concerning our knowledge of etiologies. In any case, etiology is not necessarily the best basis for classification (Cantwell, 1988). In our present state of knowledge, there is no right or natural way to classify psychiatric disorders of children and adolescents; there is no natural scheme "out there" waiting to be discovered (Cantwell, 1988; Rutter & Gould, 1985).

The characteristics required of an adequate classification of child and adolescent psychiatric disorder have been delineated by a number of authors (e.g., Cantwell, 1988; Carlson and Garber,

1986; Cohen, Leckman, & Volkmar, 1988; Quay, 1986; Rutter, 1986; Rutter & Gould, 1985; Volkmar, 1991) commencing with the publication of *DSM-III* and converging, with the publication of *DSM-IV*, toward broad-based agreement on the following.

1. The classification should be *based on facts, not concepts*, so that it is usable by workers of different theoretical orientations. This lowest-common-denominator approach has been a source of frustration to clinicians with dearly held theoretical views (Volkmar, 1991).
2. *Disorders, not individuals, are classified.* Understanding of this characteristic is a potential source of relief for some of the aforementioned frustrated theoreticians.
3. There should be *provision for developmental variability* in the expression of disorders, although there should not be separate classifications for different age periods (Rutter & Gould, 1985).
4. The classification must be *reliable;* different clinicians seeing similar disorders should agree on the applicability of the taxonomic terms to cases.
5. The categories must have *validity*, a measure of the extent to which they in fact define what they purport to describe. (Subtypes of validity are discussed later.)
6. *Differentiation,* the extent to which differing cases are provided categories separating them from one another, must be adequate.
7. There must be adequate *coverage* so that important disorders are not omitted. The concepts of coverage and differentiation have been most aptly stated by Stengel (1989); classification terms should be "jointly exhaustive and mutually exclusive."
8. The system must be *logically consistent*, based on constant principles.
9. The classification must be *clinically relevant* and assist in decision making.
10. It must be *usable in ordinary clinical practice*, requiring only such information as is likely to be routinely available (Rutter & Gould, 1985).

The remaining question of whether our classification shall be categorical or dimensional seems to be implicitly answered in the foregoing list of generally accepted requirements. We like to think categorically, and categories we shall have. Dimensional approaches may be helpful in shedding additional light on known disorders that are categorically defined, and some disorders may be better defined along dimensions of dysfunction. In addition, for some disorders, multivariate dimensional studies may provide an avenue to establishing the external validity that is currently in exceedingly short supply.

RELEVANCE OF CURRENT NOSOLOGY TO ADOLESCENCE

With their vastly expanded coverage of disorders of childhood, the *DSM-III, III-R,* and *IV* have resulted in correspondingly increased attention to psychopathology in children. As we have seen, while most of the categories are supposed to be applicable to adolescents, with very few exceptions the descriptive narrative and criteria for the disorders reflect the clinical pictures presented by preadolescent children. Criteria for adult disorders may, of course, be applied to adolescents; however, while it is true that major disorders occurring in adolescence exhibit more continuity of form with the same disorders in adult life (Rutter, 1985), it is also true that adolescents are less likely than adults to present classical clinical pictures.

Criticisms of *DSM* as a classification of child and adolescent psychiatric disorders have focused on a number of deficiencies, most having to do with such problems as lack of validity for many of the categories (Cantwell, 1988; Quay, 1986; Rapaport & Ismond, 1990; Rutter & Gould, 1985; Rutter & Tuma, 1988). In fact, it was decided in the interest of coverage to include any disorder for which face validity could be established; that is, if clinicians could agree that a category captured the consent of a disorder that they consensually believed to exist, the category was included. This is the lowest common denominator of validity measures, and it is widely accepted that while most *DSM-III-R* categories do have face validity, only a minority have descriptive or construct validity, and very few have predictive validity (Cantwell, 1988; Volkmar, 1991). In response to this criticism, it has been pointed out that the decision to take a "splitter" approach in *DSM-III* was intentional, with a view to providing adequate coverage, in the hope that empirical research would adduce evidence of validity and data that might better differentiate the categories (a sort of "split now, lump later" plan). These criticisms (and those concerning such related issues as reliability and field trial methodology) have been submitted by a large

number of authors, most of whom have a pronounced research orientation.

Not surprisingly, authors professing primarily a clinical orientation who have offered criticisms of the current *DSM* are far less numerous than the researchers. A major complaint is that the classification itself seems to have taken shape in response to epidemiological rather than clinical needs (Cohen, Leckman, & Volkmar, 1988). *DSM* lends itself to simple, "clean" diagnostic cases, not to the complex admixture of psychopathological features presented by the majority of real patients; it sacrifices clinical relevance for measurability (Bemporad & Schwab, 1986).

The most telling criticism of the *DSM,* and the most relevant to our consideration of diagnosis in adolescence, has been voiced by both researchers and clinicians of every theoretical stripe (Bemporad & Schwab, 1986; Cantwell & Baker, 1988, 1989; Carlson & Garber, 1986; Rutter, 1988; Volkmar, 1991). It is that for adolescents, as for children, psychopathology must be considered in the context of development. The lack of a developmental framework for the diagnosis of psychiatric disorder in the young is the *DSM's* most serious shortcoming. The manual does attempt to address this deficiency in two ways: first, by providing a separate section for child and adolescent psychiatric disorders; and second, by making passing reference in the narrative (and sometimes in the criteria) to developmental variations in the presentation of particular symptoms. This approach is minimally successful with regard to children and not at all successful concerning adolescents. The "split now, lump later" strategy informed the approach to anxiety in the young so fulsomely in *DSM-III-R* that in *DSM-IV* most of the Anxiety Disorders of childhood and adolescence were consolidated with their (presumably) equivalent categories in adulthood (Shaffer et al., 1989). Disorders of mood, which are surely as prevalent in youth as anxiety disorders, were not accorded the same "splitting" distinction, and the cursory attention the manual pays to developmental variability refers only occasionally to children and not at all to adolescents. Finally, the manual contains no provision for identifying and recording the many manifestations of adolescent personality dysfunction that often underly and maintain the common "state" disorders diagnosed on Axis I. Although (with one appropriate exception) the *DSM* does not specifically prohibit the diagnosis of personality disorder in adolescence (or, for that matter, in childhood) both its formal structure and its narrative content discourage the user from considering variables of characterological functioning when diagnosing young patients. In addition, the *DSM* narrative and criteria for personality disorders contain no references to developmental variations in adolescence (or childhood).

ISSUES OF PSYCHIATRIC CLASSIFICATION IN ADOLESCENCE

Identity Disorder: This category appeared in the official nosology for the first time in *DSM-III*. Its appearance implied that clinical experts in the field agreed that such a disorder existed and was adequately described by the defining criteria (had face validity). The criteria, in turn, seemed to represent an attempt to operationalize Erikson's (1963) psychosocial theory with regard to the adolescent developmental "crisis." Many clinical psychiatrists with an interest in adolescence were involved in the work to establish identity disorder as a category in *DSM-III*. By the time the nomenclature began to be revised a few years later, the empirical researchers were in the ascendancy and identity disorder was recommended for deletion from *DSM-III-R* in 1986. The basis for this recommendation was that the diagnosis was seldom used and that no empirical studies of the category had been published. In short, both construct and predictive validities of identity disorder were called into question; and since most of the cases were within the purview of college mental health professionals, who had no opportunity to evaluate or report on the long-term outcomes of their patients, no data were available to support the retention of the category in the nosology (Rapoport & Ismond, 1990).

Identity disorder was retained in *DSM-III-R* in consequence of a political decision when its recommended deletion was rejected by the Assembly of the American Psychiatric Association in December 1986. Within a year following the publication of *DSM-III-R* in 1987, the APA Task Force on *DSM-IV* was appointed, and the work group on child and adolescent disorders was dominated by academic psychiatrists with a strong empirical orientation, half of whom were researchers

in pediatric psychopharmacology (Rapoport & Ismond, 1990). Identity disorder was given to a subcommittee on anxiety disorders, which proposed to review the extent to which the diagnosis was used by clinicians and whether there was any empirical evidence to support its retention in *DSM-IV* (Shaffer, et al., 1989). The work group surveyed attendees at the October 1989 meeting of the American Academy of Child and Adolescent Psychiatry and found that 80% of respondants used the diagnosis of identity disorder in adolescents (Rachel G. Klein, 1990, personal communication); however, there was still no published empirical studies of the disorder. Some three dozen clinical case reports of identity disorder compiled by the Committee on Diagnosis and Assessment of the American Society for Adolescent Psychiatry (Pearson, 1990) were submitted to the work group; but this documentation was thought unsuitable to the requirements of empirical validation, because the outpatient cases were too idiographically described and the inpatient cases all had other "comorbid" diagnoses. Identity disorder appears in *DSM-IV* as a condition not attributable to mental disorder but requiring attention or treatment.

Personality Disorders: The diagnosis of personality pathology in adolescence is controversial on a number of levels. Conceptually, the field is experiencing difficulty in making the shift from theoretical formulations of personality "organization" or "structure" to the atheoretical, phenomenological approach required by the *DSMs*. An interesting example is the inferred relationship between identity disorder in adolescence and borderline personality disorder in adult life, which is mentioned in both *DSM-III* and *DSM-III-R*. The criteria for identity disorder reflects aspects of Erikson's theory of identity, and the category first appeared during a period when Kernberg's (1984) theories of personality organization were very influential in psychodynamic circles. The lack of an integrated identity is a cardinal feature of Kernberg's construct of borderline personality structure, and the *DSM* criteria for borderline personality disorder include "identity disturbance" as one of several features of generalized instability (none of which is essential). Although the incidence of identity is the only symptomatic feature in identity disorder, the *DSM-III-R* narrative implies that identity disorder may be a forme fruste of borderline personality disorder. The influence of theory, from Erikson, to Kernberg, to the *DSM*, is unacknowledged but seems clearly apparent.

The diagnosis of personality disorder is also controversial on grounds of labeling or stigmatization of young patients. Some clinicians believe that the *DSM*'s prohibition of the use of antisocial personality disorder prior to age 18 does, or should, extend to other disorders of personality. Opposed to this sentiment are the findings of the Toronto Longitudinal Study of personality dysfunction (Korenblum, Marton, Golombek, & Stein, 1990), which clearly show that personality dysfunction, severe enough to qualify for diagnosis by *DSM-III* criteria, is quite prevalent in a nonclinical population of adolescents. Although the form of disorder changes developmentally across the course of adolescence, the prevalence remains high. The Toronto group postulates that both the entry into and exit from adolescence represent at-risk periods for the genesis of character pathology. Avoidance of "labeling" adolescents on Axis II may lead to repeated treatment failures because of inadequate diagnostic formulations that focus on "state" disorders while ignoring more pervasive characterological features. Evolving disorders of personality function can be treated successfully in adolescence because it is a period of dynamic flux; the identity is not yet consolidated; the building blocks of character have not been cemented into place.

Depression: Most practitioners who work extensively with adolescents believe that mood disorders often present not with emotional sadness but with behavioral disturbance. Empirical researchers and epidemiologists continue to assert that depressive disorders can be diagnosed in childhood and adolescence using the same criteria as are applied to adult life, and that there is no research evidence that depression in adolescents appears different from the same disorder in adults. While this is undoubtedly true, it seems to beg the question whether depression might have other symptomatic presentations, as well. All the relevant research has been conducted using *DSM* (or research diagnostic) criteria that assume isomorphy among child, adolescent, and adult versions of the disorder. Yet there is abundant evidence from epidemiological studies (Rutter, 1988) and developmental studies of psychopathology (Kovacs, 1986; Rutter, 1986) of age differences in depressive phenomena. The problem is that until

we know what phenomena in each age period are equivalent to those in other periods, we cannot construct reliable and valid measures of depressive symptomatology that will apply across age groups; and without those measures we cannot investigate the developmental trends (Rutter, 1988).

Clinical Issues: The Diagnostic Process in Adolescence

In the years since the advent of *DSM-III*, a generation of psychiatrists has been trained in the atheoretical, phenomenological approach to diagnosis. The same generation has also witnessed an explosive growth of new knowledge in biological psychiatry. The confluence of these two processes makes it ever more difficult for students of the field to assimilate information about psychopathology in any way other than the minimally required phenomenological classification of disorder. But diagnosis in psychiatry is more than the selection of an appropriate label or assignment to a coded classification; it is a "continuing process of investigation and clinical understanding," in which the issues of classification are but one important aspect (Cantwell, 1985).

In no other age period is the process of clinical understanding more crucial to the psychiatrist's ability to help patients than in adolescence. Because of the developmental tasks with which the adolescent patient is struggling, he or she is exquisitely sensitive to the inquiring authority of the psychiatrist. It is perhaps uniquely important to teenagers that they be acknowledged as a person. (Adults may take it for granted that they are, while children may take it for granted that they aren't.) An approach that obviously probes for symptoms (as required by the classification) is likely to be taken as evidence that the psychiatrist is seeing the patient as a "case" and not as a person. Adolescents need to experience the psychiatrist as a person who is interested in knowing them as people and not just as bearers of psychopathology.

A humane, respectful approach to the personhood of the adolescent patient is necessary not only for accurate diagosis but for treatment, which is integral to the diagnostic process. Treatment depends on the relationship between psychiatrist and patient, and an adolescent patient who is not engaged in a relationship with the therapist will defeat any and all attempts at therapeutic intervention. The effectiveness of almost any treatment approach depends much more on the personal characteristics of the patient and the quality of the therapist-patient relationship than on the nature of the "disorder."

If nosology classifies disorders, not children, psychiatrists cannot treat disorders without also treating children as persons. A psychiatric diagnosis is necessary but not sufficient information on which to base a treatment plan; the diagnosis can tell us only a small part of what we need to know. A *clinical formulation,* in which data about the disorder is integrated with one's understanding of the patient as a person (Shapiro, 1989), as a participant in the therapeutic relationship, and as a member of his or her family and other relevant social systems (Pearson, 1991), provides the foundation upon which effective treatment can be based. The clinical formulation combines categorical, dimensional, developmental, and functional or process models of diagnosis (Cohen, Leckman, & Volkmar, 1988) in organizing a broad range of information about the adolescent and his or her world, gathered by the psychiatrist in the process of participating in a relationship with the youngster.

Here we as psychiatrists cannot afford to be "atheoretical." We need a set of organizing principles to bring order to the mass of information we acquire about patients and their worlds as well as their disorders. Our beliefs about the nature of man and theoretical convictions about human behavioral science, development, and psychopathology are more or less automatically (one might say "unconsciously") brought to bear on the data, because as human beings, we require order and meaning. It is therefore crucial for psychiatrists to acknowledge, examine, and make explicit their own beliefs, convictions, and theories, and to be prepared to utilize them as instruments of clinical understanding.

Shapiro (1989) has called for a renewal of attention to the psychodynamic formulation and its central importance to any therapeutic endeavor. The ability to formulate a case requires the clinician to hold, at a minimum, four fundamental "convictions": (1) there is unconscious mental functioning; (2) symptoms may be driven by internalized conflict or by developmental deviance based on deprivation; (3) symptoms have meaning to the child and affect his or her adaptation to the environment by how they are construed; and (4) the therapeutic relationship ("transference") has a critical role in undoing repetitive maladaptive behaviors and symptoms. The psychodynamic formulation is constructed from the viewpoints of ego psychology, development (Freud, 1963), and object relations theory; thus it portrays the child in depth in terms of his or her temperament, drives, defenses, coping mechanisms, developmental attainments, and relationships.

This detailed portrait of the patient must then be placed in the context of his or her real relationships with family, peers, adults, authorities, and others in the community. Adolescence is characterized by a geometric expansion of the individual's social horizon. Systems theory offers the clinician a framework for understanding the boundaries and interfaces among the many social systems in which adolescents have membership and the ongoing impact of these systems on the youngster's life and "disorder." The psychiatrist must enlist the adolescent patient's help in identifying the social systems in which the patient lives and moves. Together they must sketch the boundaries, interfaces, and rules of interaction in and among these systems. The psychiatrist may then listen to the patient's material with a "fourth ear," attuned not only to evidence of impact on the adolescent of family or peer-group systems issues but also to opportunities for the adolescent to become the agent of beneficial changes in his or her family, peer group, or community systems (Pearson, 1991).

TECHNICAL CONSIDERATIONS IN THE APPROACH TO ADOLESCENT PATIENTS

The initial task of the diagnostic process is to engage adolescent patients in a relationship in which they experience respect for and interest in themselves as persons. In the context of this relationship, adolescents allow access to their psychological and social worlds and, finally, to their "disorder." Participation in the relationship permits the psychiatrist to formulate a comprehensive understanding of adolescents and their social systems, which in turn sets the stage for helping interventions. The diagnostic process is not limited to clinical understanding and treatment planning; it incorporates measured steps of relationship-building activity by the therapist that initially engages adolescents, then holds them in a deepening attachment, and finally goes on to establish a working therapeutic alliance.

It is important to distinguish among engagement, attachment, and alliance, because the concept of "alliance" has been invoked so often for such a long time that it is increasingly misused to refer to attachments and even to compliant resistances. *Alliance* means that the patient has, by identification with the nonjudgmental, inquiring, and examining functions of the therapist, established his or her own self-examining functions ("observing ego"), which can then "ally" with those of the therapist in the work of treatment. Developmental variables in adolescence strongly influence the form and stability of the alliance. *Attachment* simply means a state of affectionate regard by the adolescent for the psychiatrist. In the steps the clinician takes toward encouraging attachment, both positive and negative feelings must be acknowledged and accepted. If the attachment is to be useful for therapeutic purposes, it must be secure enough to contain the patient's ambivalence toward the therapist. *Engagement* is the initial process of involving the adolescent in an interactional dialectic, an opening gambit in the diagnostic process. The adolescent is engaged by evoking, provoking, or otherwise attracting his or her interest in the psychiatrist and the process. Engagement is obviously prerequisite to attachment, which, in turn is a necessary, but not a sufficient, condition for an alliance eventually to develop. It is engagement that concerns us in the diagnostic process.

How do psychiatrists engage an adolescent? Concisely put, they must somehow understand "where" the child is and "meet him or her there." "Somehow" encompasses empathically processing verbal and nonverbal communications from the adolescent and using clinical intuition to identify the issues that are most salient *from the youngster's point of view* and then communicating that

understanding in a context of interest and respect. An explanation of how this is done is a formidable, perhaps impossible, task. Nevertheless, some features of the psychiatrist's approach to the adolescent, and to the process, can be helpful to consider.

Personal Style: Some adults, including some psychiatrists, are "kid" people. They like adolescents, enjoy working with them, and naturally and spontaneously convey their respect and appreciation of them as people. If such an orientation can be learned, it would behoove psychiatrists who work with adolescents to learn it. If not, they must remind themselves that genuineness and honesty are the cardinal virtues for adults working professionally with teenagers. Genuineness extends to letting the child know the clinician as a person, not only as an adult professional (we are, after all, asking the child to let us know him or her as a person). This means acknowledging the feelings the clinician has concerning the adolescent and his or her issues in the treatment relationship, not disclosing the clinician's personal life outside the treatment; although, occasionally, the judicious use of self-disclosure based on relevant past experience can enhance the yougster's sense of the importance of the relationship and of feeling understood (Pearson, 1991).

Control of the Relationship: Most adolescents will not engage meaningfully in a relationship in which they feel they have no control. Ideally, teenagers should feel that they have chosen their doctor or therapist. This is a goal to work toward even when, as is usually the case, youngsters had no part in the decision to begin treatment. The clinician earns the job of chosen therapist by respecting the autonomy of the adolescent in any way that does not jeopardize treatment, often by actively removing him- or herself from the medical authoritative role and by honestly acknowledging personal limitations. Giving the adolescent control of the relationship also extends to how the treatment time is spent, what kind of material is produced, and how the material is to be responded to by the therapist (Lewis, 1987)

Technical Neutrality: Therapists must keep themselves equidistant from the opposing forces that codetermine the adolescent patient's conflicts. Neutrality does not mean passivity or a remote, distant, unemotional attitude. It means tol-

264

erating both poles of the youngster's ambivalence; taking in with equal interest and acceptance both the libidinal (loving) and the aggressive (hating) derivatives with which the child invests the therapist.

Transference: Once an adolescent is engaged and is beginning to attach to the therapist, as the transference develops, it should be handled in a way that allows for a real relationship. It is not necessary or desirable to "safeguard" the transference; transferences are ubiquitous, robust, and sturdy. Clinicians must remain genuine, forthcoming, and active; and there will remain more transference than we could ever hope to clarify or interpret (Lewis, 1987).

Conclusion

The current classification of psychiatric disorders is an imperfect but serviceable instrument, somewhat better suited to the need of epidemiology and statistical reporting than to those of clinical diagnosis. The attention paid in *DSM-III, DSM-III-R,* are *DSM-IV* to disorders of childhood has increased awareness of psychopathology in youth and stimulated much research activity. However, the lack of an overall developmental framework continues to be the classification's most serious shortcoming. Adolescence, a unique developmental phase distinct from both childhood and adult life, remains almost totally neglected. It will be important for future editions of the nosology to address the issue of developmental variations in the clinical presentation of disorder in all ages, including adolescence.

Developmental issues in adolescence influence the symptomatology of psychiatric disorders during the teen years and call for special knowledge and skills on the part of psychiatrists working with adolescents. The diagnostic process is much more than the assignment of a label and a classification code, and treatment effectiveness depends more on the personal characteristics of the child and the quality of the physician-patient relationship than on the nature of the disorder. If they hope to reach a clinical understanding adequate for providing effective treatment, mental health professionals must approach adolescents with genuine honesty and with interest in and respect for the patient as a person. If an adolescent is meaningfully engaged in a relationship with a psychiatrist, the diagnostic process cannot only provide clinical understanding but also pave the way for the establishment of the therapeutic alliance, which is pivotal for treatment success.

REFERENCES

Achenbach, T. M. (1980). DSM-III in light of empirical research on the classification of child psychopathology. *Journal of the American Academy of Child Psychiatry, 19,* 395–412.

Achenbach, T. M. (1985). *Assessment and taxonomy of child and adolescent psychopathology.* Newbury Park, CA: Sage Publications.

Achenbach, T. M. (1988). Integrating assessment and taxonomy. In M. Rutter, H. Tuma, & I. S. Lann (Eds.), *Assessment and diagnosis in child psychopathology* (pp. 300–339). New York: Guilford Press.

Achenbach, T. M., Conners, C. K., Quay, H. C., Verhulst, M., & Howell, R. (1989). Replication of empirically derived syndromes as a basis for taxonomy of child/adolescent psychopathology. *Journal of Abnormal Child Psychology, 17* (3), 299–323.

American Psychiatric Association. (1952). *Diagnostic and statistical manual of mental disorders.* Washington, DC: Author.

American Psychiatric Association. (1968). *Diagnostic and statistical manual of mental disorders* (2nd ed.). Washington, DC: Author.

American Psychiatric Association. (1980). *Diagnostic and statistical manual of mental disorders* (3rd ed). Washington, DC: Author.

American Psychiatric Association. (1987). *Diagnostic and statistical manual of mental disorders* (3rd ed., rev.). Washington, DC: Author.

American Psychiatric Association. (1994). *Diagnostic and statistical manual of mental disorders* (4th ed.). Washington, DC: Author.

Bemporad, J. R., Pfeifer, C. M., & Bloom, W. (1970). Twelve months' experience with the GAP classification of childhood disorders. *American Journal of Psychiatry, 125,* 658–664.

Bemporad, J. R., & Schwab, M. E. (1986). The DSM-III and clinical child psychiatry: In T. Millon & G. L. Klerman (Eds.), *Contemporary directions in* psychopathology: Toward the DSM-IV (pp. 135–150). New York: Guilford Press.

Blos, P. (1967). The second separation-individuation of adolescence. Psychoanalytic Study of the Child, 22, 167–186.

Cantor, N., Smith, E., French, R., & Mezzich, J. (1980). Psychiatric diagnosis as prototype categorization. Journal of Psychology, 89, 181–193.

Cantwell, D., & Baker, L. (1988). Issues in the classification of child and adolescent psychiatric psychopathology. Journal of the American Academy of Child and Adolescent Psychiatry, 28, 691–700.

Cantwell, D., & Baker, L. (1989). Stability and natural history of DSM III childhood diagnoses. Journal of the American Academy of Child and Adolescent Psychiatry, 28, 691–700.

Cantwell, D. P. (1985). Classification. In R. Michels & J. Cavenar (Eds.), Psychiatry (Vol. 2). Philadelphia: Lippincott.

Cantwell, D. P. (1988). DSM-III studies. In M. Rutter, A. H. Tuma, & I. S. Lann (Eds.), Assessment and diagnosis in child psychopathology (pp. 3–36). New York: Guilford Press.

Carlson, G. A., & Garber, J. (1986). Developmental issues in the classification of depression in children. In M. Rutter, C. Izard, & P. Read (Eds.), Depression in young people (pp. 399–433). New York: Guilford Press.

Chess, S. (1959). An introduction to child psychiatry. New York: Grune & Stratton.

Cohen, D. J., Leckman, J. F., & Volkmar, F. R. (1988). The diagnostic process and classification in child psychiatry: Issues and prospects. In J. E. Mezzich & M. von Vranach (Eds.), International classification in psychiatry: Unity and Diversity (pp. 284–297). Cambridge: Cambridge University Press.

Erikson, E. H. (1963). Childhood and society. New York: W. W. Norton.

Eysenck, H. J. (1986). A critique of contemporary classification and diagnosis. In T. Millon & G. L. Klerman (Eds.), Contemporary directions in psychopathology: Toward the DSM-IV (pp. 93–98). New York: Guilford Press.

Freud, A. (1963). The concept of developmental lines. Psychoanalytic Study of the Child, 18, 245–265.

Freud, A. (1965). Normality and pathology in childhood. New York: International Universities Press.

Graham, P., & Rutter, M. (1985). Adolescent disorders. In M. Rutter & L. Hersov (Eds.), Child and adolescent psychiatry: Modern approaches (pp. 351–367). Oxford: Blackwell Scientific Publications.

Group for Advancement of Psychiatry. (1966). Psychopathological disorders in childhood: Theoretical considerations and a proposed classification (Report No. 620). New York: Author.

Havens, L. (1973). Approaches to the mind. Boston: Little, Brown.

Kanner, L. (1935). Child psychiatry. Springfield, IL: Charles C Thomas.

Kernberg, O. F. (1984). Severe personality disorders: Psychotherapeutic strategies. New Haven, CT: Yale University Press.

Klerman, G. L. (1986). Historical perspectives on contemporary schools of psychopathology. In T. Millon & G. L. Klerman (Eds.), Contemporary directions in psychopathology: Toward the DSM-IV (pp. 3–28). New York: Guilford Press.

Korenblum, M., Marton, P., Golombek, H., & Stein, B. (1990). Personality status changes through adolescence. Psychiatric Clinics of North America.

Kovacs, M. (1986). A developmental perspective on methods and measures in the assessment of depressive disorders: the clinical interview. In M. Rutter, C. Izard, & P. Read (Eds.), Depression in young people: Developmental perspectives (pp. 435–465). New York: Guilford Press.

Kraeplin, E. (1983). Compendium der Psychiatrie. Leipzig: Abel.

Kramer, M. (1988). Historical roots and structural bases of the International Classification of Diseases. In J. E. Mezzich & M. von Cranach (Eds.), International classification in psychiatry: Unity and diversity (pp. 3–29). Cambridge: Cambridge University Press.

Kuhn, T. (1970). The structure of scientific revolutions (2nd ed., Vol. 2, No. 2). Chicago: University of Chicago Press.

Lewis, M. (1991). Psychiatric assessment of infants, children and adolescents. In M. Lewis (Ed.), Child and adolescent psychiatry: A comprehensive textbook (pp. 447–463). Baltimore: Williams & Wilkins.

Lewis, O. (1987). The paranoid-schizoid position and pathologic regression in early adolescence. Journal of the American Academy of Psychoanalysis, 15 (4), 503–519.

Menninger, K., Hoeper, E., Hankin, J., & Hewitt, K. (1963). The vital balance. New York: Viking Press.

Millon, T., & Klerman, G. (1986). Contemporary directions in psychopathology: Toward the DSM-IV. New York: Guilford Press.

Offer, D., & Boxer, A. (1991). Normal adolescent development: Empirical research findings. In M. Lewis (Ed.), Child and adolescent psychiatry: A comprehensive textbook (pp. 266–278). Baltimore: Williams & Wilkins.

Pearson, G. T. (1990, October 6). Introduction to DSM-IV diagnostic issues in adolescence. Paper presented to the American Society for Adolescent Psychiatry. Minneapolis, MN.

Pearson, G. T. (1991). Social systems contributions to adolescent psychotherapy. In M. Slomowitz (Ed.), Adolescent psychotherapy (pp. 57–79). Washington, DC: American Psychiatric Association Press.

Quay, H. (1979). Classification. In H. C. Quay & J. S. Werry (Eds.), Psychopathological disorders of childhood (2nd ed., pp. 1–42). New York: John Wiley & Sons.

Quay, H. (1986). A critical analysis of DSM-III as a taxonomy of psychopathology in childhood and adolescence. In T. Millon & G. L. Klerman (Eds.), *Contemporary directions in psychopathology: Toward the DSM-IV* (pp. 151–165). New York: Guilford Press.

Rapoport, J. L., & Ismond, D. R. (1990). *DSM-III-R training guide for diagnosis of childhood disorders.* New York: Brunner/Mazel.

Rutter, M. (1985). Psychopathology and development: Links between childhood and adult life. In M. Rutter & L. Hersov (Eds.), *Child and adolescent psychiatry: Modern approaches* (pp. 720–739). Oxford: Blackwell Scientific Publications.

Rutter, M. (1986). The developmental psychopathology of depression: Issues and perspectives. In M. Rutter, C. Izard, & P. Read (Eds.), *Depression in young people: Developmental perspectives* (pp. 3–30). New York: Guilford Press.

Rutter, M. (1988). Depressive disorders. In M. Rutter, A. H. Tuma, & I. S. Lann (Eds.), *Assessment and diagnosis in child psychopathology* (pp. 347–376). New York: Guilford Press.

Rutter, M., & Gould, M. (1985). Classification. In M. Rutter & L. Hersov (Eds.), *Child and adolescent psychiatry: Modern approaches* (pp. 304–321). Oxford: Blackwell Scientific Publications.

Rutter, M., & Tuma, A. H. (1988). Diagnosis and classification: Some outstanding issues. In M. Rutter, A. H. Tuma, & I. S. Lann (Eds.), *Assessment and diagnosis in child psychopathology* (pp. 437–445). New York: Guilford Press.

Salzinger, K. (1986). Diagnosis: Distinguishing among behaviors. In T. Millon & G. L. Klerman (Eds.), *Contemporary directions in psychopathology: Toward the DSM-IV* (pp. 115–134). New York: Guilford Press.

Schwab-Stone, M., Towbin, K. E., & Tarnoff, G. M. (1991). Systems of classification: ICD-10, DSM-III-R, and DSM-IV. In M. Lewis (Ed.), *Child and adolescent psychiatry: A comprehensive textbook* (pp. 422–434). Baltimore: Williams & Wilkins.

Shaffer, D., Campbell, M., Cantwell, D., et al. (1989). Child and adolescent psychiatric disorders in DSM-IV: Issues facing the work group. *Journal of the American Academy of Child and Adolescent Psychiatry, 28,* 830–835.

Shapiro, T. (1989). The psychodynamic formulation in child and adolescent psychiatry. *Journal of the American Academy of Child and Adolescent Psychiatry, 28,* 675–680.

Stengel, T. (1989). The classification of mental disorders. *Bulletin of the World Health Organization, 21,* 601–663.

Volkmar, F. R. (1991). Classification in child and adolescent psychiatry: Principles and issues. In: M. Lewis (Ed.), *Child and adolescent psychiatry: A comprehensive textbook* (pp. 415–421). Baltimore: Williams & Wilkins.

Waterman, A. S. (1982). Identity development from adolescence to adulthood: An extension of theory and a review of research. *Developmental Psychology, 18,* 311–358.

Werry, J. (1988). In memoriam—DSM-III. *Journal of the American Academy of Child and Adolescent Psychiatry, 27,* 138–139.

Werry, J. S., Reeves, J. C., & Elkind, G. S. (1987). Attention deficit, conduct, oppositional, and anxiety disorders in children: I. A review of research on differentiating characteristics. *Journal of the American Academy of Child and Adolescent Psychiatry, 26,* 133–143.

World Health Organization. (1969). *Manual of the international statistical classification of diseases, injuries: and causes of death* (8th rev.). Geneva: Author.

World Health Organization. (1977). *Manual of the international statistical classification of diseases, injuries: and causes of death* (9th rev.). Geneva: Author.

World Health Organization. (1988). Mental, behavioral and developmental disorders, clinical descriptions and diagnostic guidelines. In *Tenth revision of the International Classification of Diseases.* Geneva: Author.

28 / Personality Disorder in Adolescence

Glen T. Pearson, Jr.

Background and History

Personality refers to habitual ways of relating to others and adapting to the environment. It involves thinking, feeling, and behavior; it expresses itself in nearly every facet of functioning. In many ways, personality can be considered to be the essence of the person, that which is unchanging despite changes in role or in affective states. The notion that personality constitutes something enduring about an individual is an old one. Early theories emphasized the biological basis of personality; the theory of the four humors is an example. This early theory emphasized the importance of mood and the tendency of mood to be persistent: the choleric individual, for example, is quick to anger, and the phlegmatic one is unemotional.

Yet personality is, in essence, not a physical entity but a theoretical construct. It may be best understood as a system, or type of organization, that defines how an individual exists within his or her environment. The notion of development of personality becomes important, as it can be seen that as life proceeds, the ways in which a person exists become progressively more organized and more adapted to the particular circumstances in which he or she lives. Alternatively, maladaptive functioning may be the outcome of various influences that produce interferences with development or deviations to it. These influences may be biological, social, or cultural. Understood in this way, personality disorder is a type of dysfunction that interferes with competence in one or more domains—social, affective, or cognitive. While not always the case, personality dysfunction also may cause subjective distress.

The notion of personality is closely linked to that of identity. Identity is the stability of patterns of thinking, feeling, and behavior that contribute to an internal sense of being the same person from one day to the next—having a stable identity. Thus, from a developmental perspective, both change and constancy are involved in the evolution of personality.

For the adult, personality is usually conceptualized as a relatively unchanging phenomenon. Likewise, disturbances of personality are seen as relatively resistant to change. According to the fourth edition of the *Diagnostic and Statistical Manual of Mental Disorders (DSM-IV)*; American Psychological Association [APA]; 1994, "A Personality Disorder is an enduring pattern of inner experience and behavior that deviates markedly from the expectations of the individual's culture, is pervasive and inflexible, has an onset in adolescence or early adulthood, is stable over time, and leads to distress or impairment" (p. 629).

Adolescence generally has been considered the period during which significant consolidation of many aspects of personality occurs. We have seen how affect becomes more differentiated and also more intense, how expectations for role functioning become more complex, and how the idea of the self develops as an outcome of integrative mental functioning that incorporates both of these along with the perceptions of bodily changes that are part of puberty. How then can personality during adolescence be considered? From a theoretical point of view, if we postulate that there must be some enduring substrate that persists from early childhood throughout the life cycle, then of course personality exists during adolescence. The difficulty comes in measuring it, in differentiating between that which is transient, a reaction to the experience of adolescence in whatever context it is experienced, and that which is constant. An equally challenging question is: To what extent can personality dysfunction, when it appears in adolescence, be modified by experience?

The diagnosis and treatment of personality disorder in childhood and adolescence has been a controversial and poorly understood area, and is a relatively neglected area of study. *DSM-III-R* and *DSM-IV* discourage clinicians from diagnosing personality disorder in adolescents; in fact, an informal survey in 1989 showed that a large number of clinicians believed—incorrectly—that the diagnostic criteria for personality disorder exclude children and adolescents (Pearson, 1989). Notwithstanding the neglect of the topic, an important body of knowledge does exist about the diagnosis and treatment of personality disorders in adolescence. This chapter discusses the diagnosis, treatment, outcome, and intercurrent economic issues.

To summarize: (1) personality disorders not only occur, but commonly present in adolescence; (2) adolescent personality disorder constitutes a public health and social problem of considerable magnitude; (3) personality diagnoses can be reliably made in adolescence; and, finally, (4) adolescence is a unique developmental phase during which personality disorders can be treated successfully.

DSM Diagnostic Classification

DSM-IV provides criteria (really lists of symptoms) that, in theory, can be used for any age group. Using these purely descriptive criteria, personality disorders can be diagnosed in childhood and adolescence. Descriptive diagnosis is one level of assessment and is generally necessary for uniform reporting for third-party payors and for statistical and research purposes. However, such descriptive diagnoses are of limited help to the clinician in understanding the patient or in planning and carrying out treatment. For these purposes, a psychodynamic formulation including a structural assessment of personality is needed. Thus, we may consider that there are really two parallel systems of diagnosis: descriptive (DSM-IV) and dynamic/structural.

The personality disorders in the two most recent Diagnostic and Statistical Manuals (3rd ed.–4th ed.) are grouped in three "clusters" of topology, illustrated in Table 28.1.

However, evidence for validity of these groupings is not strong, and alternative ways of clustering them have been suggested. Masterson and Klein (1989) have proposed an alternate grouping for these 11 disorders so as to designate most of them under the heading of borderline personality disorder, with a separate category for narcissistic and antisocial personality disorders. The eccentric cluster is left intact.

The various DSMs have addressed the difficulty of diagnosing adolescent personality dysfunction by providing diagnostic categories for children and adolescents that are in some ways counterparts to the adult personality disorders. According to DSM-IV, antisocial personality disorder cannot be diagnosed before age 18. Conduct disorder is the child/adolescent diagnosis corresponding to antisocial personality disorder. Follow-up studies of conduct disorder have shown that most children or adolescents with conduct disorder do not go on to develop antisocial personality disorder, although a high-risk subgroup does.

In DSM-III and DSM-III-R, borderline personality disorder also had a counterpart in adolescence, identity disorder. Its existence had been a matter of controversy, and it was not retained in DSM-IV as a specific disorder but was renamed "identity problem" and moved to the category of "V codes," or conditions that may be a focus of clinical attention without constituting separate disorders by themselves. Many psychiatrists, especially those who work with college students, have maintained that identity disorder is a valid diagnosis and is quite common in their clinical populations. It seems unlikely, however, that identity disorder, as it was understood in DSM-III-R and by these clinicians, is related to borderline person-

TABLE 28.1

The Personality Disorders in DSM-IV "Clusters" of Typology

A. Odd/eccentric	Paranoid, schizoid, schizotypal
B. Dramatic/emotional/erratic	Antisocial, borderline, narcissistic, histrionic
C. Fearful/anxious	Avoidant, dependent, obsessive-compulsive

ality disorder in the same way that conduct disorder is related to antisocial personality disorder, as a precursor; rather, it may be a phase-specific problem of the late adolescent period.

Except for borderline and narcissistic personality disorders, most of these diagnoses are seldom applied to adolescents. Most adolescents who qualify for a personality disorder diagnosis are in Cluster B (dramatic/emotional), and it is these adolescents who pose the greatest challenges for treatment programs.

Adolescents who meet the descriptive criteria for schizoid or schizotypal personality are sometimes seen in outpatient settings but are more likely to be described as having "traits" of these disorders than to be given an Axis II diagnosis. They usually do not require hospitalization, and many of them probably never come to clinical attention. Although many youngsters with borderline and/or narcissistic disorders have paranoid features, rarely do they meet the criteria for paranoid personality disorder, and usually it is not the paranoid symptoms that lead to their being identified as disturbed.

Histrionic features frequently dominate the clinical picture in borderline adolescent females, and occasionally patients are seen who meet the criteria for both personality diagnoses.

Avoidant personality disorder has a corresponding diagnosis in the disorders first appearing in childhood or adolescence. Adolescents with this disorder occasionally are seen in outpatient practice.

Although obsessive-compulsive illness and other Axis I anxiety disorders are fairly common in childhood and adolescence, children and adolescents probably rarely if ever meet the criteria for obsessive-compulsive personality disorder. The fact that the criteria for passive-aggressive personality disorder (in *DSM-III* and *III-R*) could be used to describe the average teenager underscored a lack of developmental considerations in these criteria and led to the exclusion of this category from *DSM-IV*.

Thus, the utility of *DSM* personality disorder criteria in adolescence is mainly for borderline and, to a lesser extent, narcissistic personality disorders. Table 28.2 is a list of *DSM-IV* criteria. Adolescents who qualify for personality disorder diagnoses other than borderline are usually, if not always, psychodynamically and structurally similar

TABLE 28.2

DSM-IV *Criteria for Borderline Personality Disorder*

Includes five of the following:
1. Frantic efforts to avoid real or imagined abandonment
2. A pattern of unstable and intense interpersonal relationships characterized by alternating between extremes of idealization and devaluation
3. Identity disturbance: markedly and persistently unstable self-image or sense of self
4. Impulsivity in at least two areas that are potentially self-damaging (e.g., spending, sex, substance abuse, reckless driving, binge eating)
5. Recurrent suicidal threats, gestures, or behavior, or self-mutilating behavior
6. Affective instability due to a marked reactivity of mood (e.g., intense episodic dysphoria, irritability, or anxiety usually lasting a few hours and only rarely more than a few days)
7. Chronic feelings of emptiness or boredom
8. Inappropriate, intense anger or difficulty controlling anger (e.g., frequent displays of temper, constant anger, recurrent physical fights)

to the borderlines. Most adolescents with personality disorders will have at least 5 of the 8 symptoms in the borderline list. However, the understanding of the patient and treatment approach will be based on the psychodynamic formulation and structural assessment.

Epidemiology

The prevalence of Axis II disorders in adolescent general populations is unknown. In a community-based sample of adolescents followed over a 2-year period, Bernstein et al. (1993) found a prevalence of any dramatic cluster personality disorder at time of initial study of 14.6%, with a prevalence of any Axis II disorder of 31.2%. They found generally low rates of persistence of personality disorder diagnoses over 2 years. For moderate and severe borderline personality disorder, persistence rates were 29% and 24%, respectively. Six years later, prevalence data for the subjects at ages 17 to 26 years showed only 5.6% met criteria for borderline personality disorder. Prevalence of all Axis II disorders decreased with age, presumably as the identity instability and turbulence of adolescence subside.

These investigators found that subjects who were identified as cases of borderline personality disorder showed significantly greater dysfunction than those identified as noncases on 11 of 12 measures of distress and functional impairment. Examples of these measures are short duration of friendships, lack of romantic relationships, problems at work, dropping out of school, low enjoyment of others, and depressive symptoms.

Golombek and Martin (1992) examined behavioral patterns, attitudes, and emotional states of a nonclinical sample of adolescents in Toronto who were studied during early, middle, and late adolescence. These researchers conceptualize personality in terms of functioning and refer to "personality functioning." They measured personality functioning in 7 areas: identity, reality testing, relatedness, verbal communication, self-esteem, identity, and role adequacy, and rated adolescents as either "dysfunctional" or "clear of dysfunction" with regard to each area. Functioning tended to improve over time as judged by improved mental status and coping mechanisms. There was also a direct correlation between degree of disturbance and conduct problems. Personality characteristics tended to remain stable from middle to late adolescence. Both prominent hatred and depression, both indicative of dysphoric mood states, were predictive of poorer functioning (Stein et al., 1987).

These investigators use their own instruments, which, although not equivalent to *DSM* criteria, clearly differentiate between normality and pathology. They speak of personality function and disturbance rather than personality per se. This fact highlights the understanding that what is being studied is really the functioning of individuals, a dynamic quality, rather than a static entity. At their initial data point, 16% of the 13-year-olds showed marked disturbance of personality functioning, while another 30% displayed mild to moderate disturbance. These data suggest that personality dysfunction is fairly common in adolescence. At the same time, findings of this study suggest

that a given individual's pattern of personality functioning may change over time. The degree to which change was likely varied with the category of personality dysfunction, with schizoid being the most stable and histrionic the least. Interestingly, antisocial traits tended to disappear with increasing age.

The prevalence for personality disorders in early to midadolescence is higher than that for adults, but for late adolescents these rates are comparable to rates obtained for adults in epidemiological studies. A number of recent studies confirm the magnitude of the problem of personality disorder in adults. Zimmerman and Coryell (1989) studied approximately 800 first-degree relatives of normal controls and of patients with a variety of psychiatric disorders in Iowa and found that more than a sixth of the sample received a personality disorder diagnosis; rates were similar for the relatives of patients and the relatives of normal controls. As part of the National Institute of Mental Health Epidemiologic Catchment Area Program, a survey of 810 adults in East Baltimore was done using structured interviews and *DSM-III* criteria for personality disorders. Of this sample, 5.9% were found to have personality disorders (Samuels, Nestadt, Romanski, Folstein, & McHugh, 1994). Other epidemiological studies have shown prevalence rates in adults of 6 to 9% (Reich, Yates, & Nduaguba, 1989).

Among clinical populations, the prevalence of adolescents who meet diagnostic criteria for personality disorders, especially borderline personality disorders, is fairly high. This is especially true with respect to inpatients and incarcerated delinquents (Eppright, Kashani, Robison, & Reid, 1993; McManus, Lerner, Robbins, & Barbour, 1984). In Wisconsin, an analysis of records of 180 children and adolescents referred to a Learning Disabilities Service revealed that 16% met the criteria for borderline, 11% for passive-aggressive, and an additional 4% for other personality disorders (Westman, Ownby, & Smith, 1987).

Thus, some degree of personality dysfunction is common in adolescents, but rates fall with increasing age to approximate the prevalence in adults. In terms of causes of psychiatric morbidity, personality disorder ranks especially high in adolescent populations and is a relatively common condition in adults.

Structural Diagnosis

In contrast to the descriptive criteria of the *DSMs*, theoretical views of personality disorder form the basis for diagnostic thinking based on a structural view—that is, a hypothetical understanding of how personality is formed by experience.

Object relations theorists have contributed much to the understanding of severe personality pathology. Theories are ways of thinking that help the clinician to understand patients. The relevance of theory is in how useful it is in organizing clinical data. The good clinician will use whatever aspects of each given way of thinking are relevant to understanding an individual adolescent in a given situation at a particular point in time. Similarities among the major theories of Kernberg (1975), Masterson (1976), Rinsley (1982), Adler (1989), and most others are great, and the differences are mostly technical. Campbell (1982) compared the major theorists in a concise review.

Bowlby (1988) postulated the existence of an internal psychological organization within personality that includes representational models of the self and attachment figures. He held that various types of attachment were related to enduring behavioral and emotional patterns around relationships that formed the substrates of the adult personality. For a fuller discussion of the relevance of attachment theory in adolescence, see Chapter 12.

One of Rinsley's (1982) important concepts is that the failure or arrest of both the separation and individuation processes of development may be present in schizophrenia, major affective disorders, and borderline personality disorder. Rinsley and Masterson contributed the concept of abandonment-depression. They described a subjective state that involves an early experience of the loss of the maternal protection against both internal and external stimulation and that also leaves the individual subject to feelings of abandonment and sadistic superego pressures. This abandonment-depression involves the affective expression of profound emptiness, estrangement, derealization, and meaninglessness (Rinsley, 1980, 1982). Masterson (1976, 1989) emphasizes that the pathological defenses subserve avoidance of the depression caused by the libidinal unavailability of the object during rapprochement. Subsequent development incorporates these deficits and fixations in the evolving structure of the personality.

Kernberg (1975, 1984) sees most, if not all, personality disorders as the clinical expression of an underlying borderline personality organization. He uses the term "borderline" not only because of tradition, but because the personality structure is developmentally intermediate between neurotic and psychotic personality structures. According to this view, borderline conditions arise from a developmental failure in the rapprochement phase of separation-individuation, under the influence of a high level of pregenital aggression. A failure to achieve libidinal object constancy results, and primitive defense mechanisms persist, especially splitting, denial, projection, and projective identification, as do pathological relations with internalized objects. In Kernberg's formulation, splitting persists in order to protect the good object from the destructive effects of the child's aggression. Kernberg differentiates neurotic, borderline, and psychotic personality structures by reference to three key variables: identity integration, defense mechanisms, and reality testing.

Differentiation of Borderline Personality Structure from Psychotic and Neurotic Personality Structures

REALITY TESTING

Borderline structures can be differentiated from psychotic ones on the basis of the presence of primary process thinking in the clinical situation. Most of the literature on structural diagnosis in personality disorder is written from the perspective of the psychotherapy of adult outpatients. In that setting, "the clinical situation" means the consulting room interview for evaluation and therapy. Most adolescents with personality disorders will not permit themselves to be evaluated, let alone treated, in that setting, and most of their communications, certainly the most important ones, are behavioral, not verbal. Therefore, it is usually necessary to utilize observations made in other settings, such as a hospital, day

273

treatment program, or special school. Placement of the child in one of these settings may be necessary even to conduct an evaluation. In the clinically oriented milieu, behavioral communications can be observed and translated into secondary process verbalizations for diagnostic and therapeutic purposes.

IDENTITY

The presence of an integrated identity differentiates neurotic character structure from borderline and psychotic ones. In borderline conditions, self and object representations are differentiated enough to maintain ego boundaries, but good and bad self and object representations are split and cannot be integrated into wholes; hence, the patient lacks an integrated identity. In psychotic structure, not only identity but ego boundaries are compromised. However, the notion of a "lack of integrated identity" must be applied with caution in adolescence, since some degree of identity diffusion is normative.

Neurotic character structure presents a defensive hierarchy organized around repression and other mature mechanisms; borderline and psychotic structures, in contrast, show primitive mechanisms, especially splitting. The concept of splitting is crucial, for it also characterizes object relations and hence interactions with others. It is the phenomena of interactions that can be observed and form the basis for making inferences about intrapsychic functioning.

Other factors that can be used to help identify borderline structures include such nonspecific manifestations of ego weakness as lack of anxiety tolerance, impaired impulse control, and absence of capacity for sublimation. Poorly integrated superego functioning is likewise seen in borderline patients.

Clinical Presentation

The presentation of adolescents with personality disorder is often dramatic, as the following cases illustrate.

CASE EXAMPLES

Jenny: Jenny a 12-year-old girl is brought to the State Hospital Adolescent Center for admission, escorted by three workers from the Juvenile Department, who are relieved to have her under lock and key, and relinquish her gladly. Her small size and early pubertal status contrast with her heavy makeup, which is smeared as a result of physical struggling and tears of rage. Not only the makeup, but a hardened, bitter look suppress her natural attractiveness. The referral information indicates that she had run away from home and was picked up by the authorities after being on the streets for 2 weeks. She has been involved in drug and alcohol use, stealing, promiscuous sex, and violent fighting with her mother and other adults.

She opens, and closes, the admission interview by saying "I told those bastards that I'm not talking to any more goddamned mother-fucking shrinks." Later—much later—when some rapport has been established, she begins to share some of the experiences that led up to her admission:

"My momma calls me bitches and whores, just bitches and whores, all the time." (Her use of plurals suggests every episode of name-calling has multiplied her sense of inner badness.) When asked by the interviewer, with some hesitancy for fear of seeming critical, about what about her own behavior might have led to her mother's accusations, she replied, "Well, man, I was fuckin' these dudes and she came home early from work, and I was so high I didn't give a shit, just kept on fuckin' this dude, and she went off on me and jumped my shit and we got in a big fight so I left."

Eric: Eric was a handsome, affable, and charming 15-year-old boy who was transferred to a private, inpatient adolescent unit from another hospital's adolescent service. He arrived in an ambulance, in four-point restraint, and the referral information indicated that he was returned to his former hospital after eloping by tearing a hole in the ceiling and going out through the roof. He grinned infectiously when asked about his elopement. Since age 12 he had been on the run, from school, from parents, from authorities. In the next year and a half, while being treated in the hospital, he succeeded in eloping for extended periods three more times and eventually was discharged against medical advice, while absent without leave. By the age of 18, he had lost an eye to a gunshot wound, become addicted to cocaine and alcohol, been given probation for burglary, and ended up doing time in jail for violating his probation.

Both of these cases illustrate the presence of conduct disorder and antisocial features so often seen in adolescents with severe personality disturbances. As is clear from these examples, the issue of personality disorder in adolescence presents thorny issues for the field of adolescent psychiatry.

Etiology and Pathogenesis

Research findings have increasingly pointed toward abuse and parental psychopathology, mediated biologically and environmentally, as likely contributors to the etiology of personality disorder. Much of the evidence for this is based on retrospective reports of adult patients, but high rates of abuse also have been found among children with borderline personality disorder (Goldman, D'Angelo, & DeMaso, 1993).

Higher rates of depressive disorders, antisocial disorders, and substance abuse disorders have been found in the families of adults with borderline personality disorder. Similar findings have emerged from the more limited number of studies on adolescents (Goldman et al., 1993; Ludolph et al., 1990). Goldman et al., in a study of outpatient children and adolescents diagnosed with borderline personality disorder, found that 70% were raised in environments where there was serious psychopathology in at least one parent. This finding could be explained on the basis of biological vulnerability or the impact of familial psychopathology on the developmental experiences of these children.

Links et al. (1990) and others have speculated that biparental failure (defined as both parents failing to carry out their parental functions) may be an etiologic factor, particularly when it is coupled with earlier abuse. These failures may be the result of or associated with primary psychiatric disorders or may exist independently.

Bezirganian and colleagues (1993) studied mother-child interaction, father-child interaction, and maternal personality in relation to adolescent diagnoses of personality disorders on two occasions, 2.5 years apart, in a random sample of 776 adolescents. They found that a combination of maternal inconsistency and overinvolvement predicted a persistence or an emergence of borderline personality disorder, but not of any other Axis II disorder.

McManus et al. (1984) found that 25 to 26% of the adolescents with borderline personality disorder in their study had a coexisting major affective disorder. In their study of adolescent inpatients with borderline personality disorder, Garnet and colleagues found Axis I comorbidity was high: 18 (86%) of the 21 patients had a concurrent baseline diagnosis of major depression, and 9 (43%) had a diagnosis of dysthymia. Conduct disorder was diagnosed in 11 (52%) of the patients (Garnet, Levy, Mattanah, Edell, & McGlashan, 1994). Many studies of adult borderline patients have focused on the comorbidity of borderline personality disorder and affective disorder. A review of these studies by Gunderson and Elliott (1985) suggested that the signs and symptoms of borderline conditions and affective disorders overlap. The result is that many patients meet both sets of diagnostic criteria. This finding is in contrast to the hypothesis that one disorder was secondary to the other, or that they simply coexisted by coincidence.

This finding is very much in keeping with clinical experience with adolescents, which supports a strong correlation between borderline personality pathology and mood disorders. The majority of borderline adolescents, who typically present with egregious behavioral symptoms and little evidence of depression, will eventually meet the criteria for major depression after treatment is begun and their behavioral resistances are contained. Their affective symptoms are also responsive to pharmacotherapy with antidepressants or mood-stabilizing drugs.

Suicide and suicide attempts are a risk in borderline personality disorder. Clarkin has found that the subjects in their study of adolescent and young adult inpatients who had concurrent major depressive disorder and borderline personality disorder had histories of more frequent and more lethal suicide attempts than the subjects with depression alone. Brent and others have extensively studied risk factors for adolescent suicide using retrospective methods for assessing psychopathology in suicide victims. They found personality disorder was more prevalent among suicide victims than among controls, and in particular, Cluster B disorders were more common in completers than in controls. Rates for borderline personality disorder were not as high as those that have been reported for young adult suicide victims, however.

Some disorders first evident in childhood or adolescence appear to carry a significant risk for the development of personality disorder in adolescence. These include the entire group of disruptive behavior disorders, including attention deficit hyperactivity disorder, conduct disorder, and oppositional-defiant disorder. A childhood history of these disorders is often found in borderline adolescents. Specific developmental disorders, especially learning disabilities, are also overrepresented in any sample of personality-disordered adolescents. And many, if not most, of the adolescents with personality disorder also qualify for one or more diagnoses of substance abuse or dependence.

Eppright et al. (1993) assessed 100 incarcerated juvenile offenders ages 11 to 17 using structured interviews. The majority of these youngsters (87%) met criteria for conduct disorder. Twenty-seven percent of the total group met criteria for borderline personality disorder and 75% for antisocial personality disorder. Among those diagnosed as having conduct disorder, the only comorbid personality disorder that was present with significant frequency was antisocial personality disorder. The other comorbid personality disorder diagnoses that appeared most frequently were the borderline, narcissistic, paranoid, passive-aggressive, and dependent types. Borderline personality disorder was observed more frequently in the females than in the males with conduct disorder.

Studies of combat veterans with posttraumatic stress disorder have found high rates of comorbid personality disorders. While borderline personality disorder is the most prevalent, avoidant, paranoid, and obsessive-compulsive disorders are also common. While it lis likely that preexisting psychopathology plays a role in the development of posttraumatic stress disorder, it is also plausible that the experience of trauma and its enduring psychological sequelae lead to alterations in personality function. It is possible that changes in personality functioning could occur in response to the highly disruptive reexperiencing and physiologically based symptoms typically seen in the disorder. The understanding of personality disorder as a functional adaptation explains how this could occur. It also can help to explain the lack

of stability of personality diagnoses over time in the adolescent populations studied. Thus, personality function—whether healthy or pathological—can be seen as a dynamic process that is subject to a variety of influences at least into adulthood and perhaps throughout the life cycle.

Prognosis

Garnet and others (1994) attempted to identify diagnostic criteria that are specific for borderline personality disorder as well as predictive of future borderline personality disorder during adolescence. They studied 21 adolescent inpatients with *DSM-III-R* borderline personality disorder 2 years after hospitalization. Seven of these patients (33%) met criteria for borderline personality disorder at follow-up. Even for this subgroup of patients, symptom patterns changed over time, although chronic feelings of emptiness or boredom and inappropriate, intense anger were highly persistent. Affective instability (71% agreement), identity disturbance (71% agreement), and suicidal behaviors (67% agreement) also tended to continue. The least stable symptoms were unstable, intense relationships (50% agreement) and impulsiveness (57% agreement). It might be argued that the latter are more features of the adolescent period than they are signs of psychopathology.

The authors concluded that adolescents may have features of borderline personality disorder transiently "without signaling the presence of an enduring syndrome" (Garnet et al., 1994). They suggested that identity disorder or conduct disorder may be more useful terms for these patients. Stability of the borderline diagnosis in adults, while greater, is not complete either. Links, Mitton, and Steiner (1993) found that 60% of adult inpatients diagnosed with borderline personality disorder had a stable diagnosis after 2 years.

These data are in keeping with the Toronto group's finding that various types of dysphoric mood seemed to be among the most enduring dysfunctions among their sample; they pointed to the importance of depression as a significant risk factor for morbidity in adolescence.

These research findings also support the views of psychoanalytic theorists who have described the adolescent as in a state of flux in terms of ego functions, drive and defense equilibria, self-system cohesiveness, and object relations. In short, the personality structure of the adolescent is still evolving. Even if some maladaptive patterns of behaving and relating have become stable in adolescence, they have usually not endured long enough to be entrenched. Blos (1962) maintained that it is not until late adolescence that character consolidation takes place, at which time the "infantile conflicts are rendered specific and become centered within the self-representation."

Treatment

PRINCIPLES OF TREATMENT

Context: A secure context is essential for treatment of adolescents with severe personality disorders (Rose, 1987). This usually means a hospital or residential treatment setting. Context means more than just the ability to restrain the child from running away or doing physical damage to self, others, or property. Context also implies the express mandate of the parents and other significant social systems for the program to provide treatment to the child. It requires a consensus about who is responsible for the child now, who will assume responsibility for him or her upon release from residential treatment, what the goals for treatment are, and what the responsibilities of all the parties to the treatment plan are.

Hospitalization or residential treatment is the treatment of choice for most of these adolescents. Residential treatment programs not only provide controls for externalizing behavioral symptoms but also give the treatment staff control of important therapeutic variables having to do with relationships. There are some case reports of successful outpatient psychoanalytic treatment, extending over several years, of adolescents whose defenses are more internalizing and whose clinical presentation is more schizoid or schizotypal.

Engagement: Engagement, like context, is an ongoing issue that must be worked on from the beginning to the end of treatment. First, the therapist has to find a way to engage the patient in a relationship. Then the task is to help the adolescent generalize this to engagement with others in

the treatment program. The final step is to help him or her use what has been learned in treatment in relationships outside the treatment program.

For engagement to occur, the therapist must understand where the child is and meet him or her there, as illustrated in the following case example.

Mike was 13 and had been in residential treatment programs and hospitals several times and improved, only to regress after discharge; he was small for his age and could still be controlled physically by an adult male; he had a therapist who loved him and a staff that hated him. He hit people, and his behavior had landed him in his room with no privileges to interact with his peers or his staff. The psychiatrist interviewed him for 30 minutes without getting any eye contact or more than a monosyllabic, flat response. Finally, grasping that hitting was the only way Mike knew to make contact with people, the psychiatrist said:

D: You know what I'd do if I was your doctor?
M: What?
D: I'd pick a fight with you.

Mike looked up for the first time, showing some affect, and said:

M: You'd get fired.
D: No, I wouldn't, because I wouldn't hit you back, and anyway, I wouldn't let you hurt me.
M: (with excitement) You couldn't stop me.
D: You wanta bet?

The therapist succeeded in beginning to engage Mike in relationship by understanding where he was and meeting him there. He explained to Mike's treatment team that hitting people was the only way the boy knew to make contact with them. It was suggested that they meet him at that level by being prepared to counter his attempts to hit them and talk with him about his need to hit (make contact with others).

Commitment: Commitment refers to the therapist's assurance to the patient early on that he or she will be available to the patient for as long as necessary. This assurance may need to be repeated many times. If treatment is successful, the adolescent will internalize the therapist as his or her first whole-object image. One consequence is that as the youngster moves out into the real world, he or she will need to be able to check back with the therapist. It is helpful at each of the nodal points of separation in treatment—discharge from the hospital, termination of outpatient therapy—to say something like "Although I won't be your therapist any more, I'll always be glad to hear from you." The patient may be invited to write or call; the therapist should answer letters and phone calls.

Control: It seems almost self-evident that control must be maintained over the patient's behavior. Behavioral control is necessary not only to ensure safety but also to deprive the patient of action as a mechanism for externalizing his or her pain. Control has to be asserted by the treatment authority in the beginning, but it also has to be progressively handed back over to the patient across the course of treatment. Many long-term treatment failures in good treatment programs are related to the failure ever to get beyond the level of a control struggle with a difficult adolescent.

Regression and Reconstruction: Regression and reconstruction characterize the entire treatment program for adolescents with personality disorder. When the adolescent's behavioral defenses against inner pain are taken away, he or she regresses. The treatment program must meet him or her at that level and, by clarification, interpretation, and working through in the context of a network of therapeutic relationships and opportunities for more normative developmental experiences, reconstruct the adolescent's personality development along healthier lines. In an excellent paper on pathologic regression in early adolescence, Owen Lewis (1987) formulates early adolescent regression in terms of the paranoid-schizoid position of Melanie Klein, and says that probably even normally developing adolescents show at least transient regression to that primitive level of object relationship. This is a parsimonious explanation for a variety of observations that others have made about the psychoanalytic therapy of adolescents.

Continuity: Continuity means continuity of care. The key treatment figures in a child's treatment program need to continue active treatment with the child and family after discharge from residential care. Therapists are not interchangeable parts.

Systems Involvement: To treat these adolescents, the therapist must be involved with a variety of social systems. First and foremost of these is the child's family, and the interface and boundaries between the treatment of the child and the management of the family constitute an issue of major proportions, one that by itself can either facilitate or doom a treatment program. The therapist also has to learn how to manage involvement with a number of other social systems: schools, child service agencies such as child welfare, and juvenile justice or adult correctional systems. Being involved effectively with those agencies while maintaining a proper therapeutic relationship with the child can be very difficult.

TREATMENT MODALITIES

Psychotherapy: Psychotherapeutic approaches can be incorporated into the treatment in many ways. The principles of psychoanalytic therapy can be incorporated programmatically in the milieus of residential programs. Individual and group psychotherapies also are usually prescribed for inpatient adolescents. Most of the early and middle stage work of confrontation, working through resistances, establishing alliance, and beginning clarification is done in the group treatment setting. The individual therapist becomes progressively more central as a treatment figure during the middle and late stages of inpatient treatment, and carries the work forward with the patient after discharge. There is a rich literature on the analytically oriented psychotherapy of adult borderline patients; many of these principles apply to the treatment of borderline adolescents.

Important contributions to the technique of therapy with severely disturbed adolescents have been made by Kernberg (1975, 1984), Masterson (1976, 1989), Campbell (1982), and Lewis (1987). These include the following principles of technical neutrality and *control of relationship.*

For the therapist, technical neutrality does *not* mean being passive, reflective, like the stereotype of the analyst behind the couch. It does mean keeping oneself equidistant from the opposing forces that determine the patient's conflicts. This means taking in with equal acceptance and interest both the libidinal and aggressive derivatives with which the child invests the therapist.

An adolescent cannot be meaningfully engaged in therapy if he or she has no control. This is Lewis's idea, based on a well thought out analysis of the state of object relationship in early adolescence (1987). Adolescent patients referred for therapy should be told to evaluate the therapist, just as the therapist is evaluating them. If the therapist concludes that he or she can be helpful to a particular child, an offer to become the therapist will be made, but it will be entirely up to the adolescent to accept. Furthermore, the patient can fire the therapist any time. (If a patient threatens to fire later in treatment as a resistance, the therapist should insist that it be understood like anything else, rather than gratified; but this also should be explained to the child up front. A therapist who has succeeded in engaging the child initially is extremely unlikely to be fired later on.) Giving the adolescent control over the relationship also extends to how the hours are spent, what kind of material is produced, and how it is handled by the therapist.

The therapist must be more active with adolescents than with adults. Therapists cannot sit back and wait for the adolescent to talk, and long silences are counterproductive. Experience treating younger children in the playroom is very helpful in sensitizing therapists to how much of an adolescent's communication is behavioral rather than verbal. At times it is helpful to respond to adolescents' behavioral communications in kind rather than by immediately translating them into verbal content. Doing so has the advantage of maintaining or enhancing engagement with the child, and as clarification proceeds, the material can be translated into words.

P: (slouches in chair)
T: (slouches in chair)
P: (makes facial grimace)
T: (mirrors facial grimace)
P: What?
T: You tell me, you started this conversation.

The degree of object relationship impairment in the adolescent determines how much emphasis there can be on confrontation and on the interpretation of defenses. These processes of psychoanalytic therapy are incorporated in the milieus of effective residential programs, where they can be delivered consistently on a very intensive basis. Lewis (1987) believes interpretive work with the adolescent can begin when evidence appears that he or she has entered the "depressive position" as described by Melanie Klein, which usually does not occur until late adolescence.

Reality Testing: Specific interventions designed to help the patient with reality testing are needed throughout the course of treatment. These may include sharing opinions, giving advice, setting

limits, acknowledging the child's parents' mistakes (and the therapist's own), endorsing the parents' or other authorities' right and responsibilities to make rules for the child, and frequently clarifying the difference between what a given situation "feels like" to the child and what it "really is."

Family Therapy: Family therapy is an essential part of the treatment of these adolescents. The family must be considered to be part of the treatment team and not as a nuisance (Jones, Pearson, & Dimperio, 1989). Parent-blaming is to be avoided; it is all too common. The family therapist has to be a full member of the treatment team, empowered to represent the treatment program to the family and vice versa. Through the family therapist, the treatment team forms an executive coalition with the patient's parents, and the parents learn about optimal family functioning by seeing how the team responds to their child. Dysfunctional patterns of communication are addressed in family therapy during the middle stage of treatment, and the family is helped to negotiate with their child concerning his or her reintegration into the family as the time for discharge approaches. The integration of object-relations theory and family systems theory in the treatment of adolescent personality disorder has been described (Jones et al., 1989). One of the most common mistakes residential programs make in the area of family work is that they unwittingly endorse a family's expectation in the beginning of treatment that the program is accepting sole responsibility for "fixing" the child, to the parents' specifications, with no expectation of collaborative work or change in the family.

Pharmacotherapy: Drug treatment is appropriate for diagnosed comorbid conditions in adolescents with personality disorder and sometimes for specific target symptoms. Lithium and antidepressants are useful in bipolar disorder and depression; stimulants and tricyclic antidepressants in attention deficit hyperactivity disorder and low-dose potent neuroleptics to address psychotic regression or low-grade paranoid symptoms. For the borderline adolescent, medication is only an adjunct to treatment and never the primary treatment. It should be prescribed only in the context of an active alliance with the child, with the therapist recognizing what medication means to the patient and with the patient understanding that he or she is still 100% responsible for his feelings and behavior.

Behavior Therapy: Behavior therapy is an integral part of any residential treatment program for adolescents. There is no question that behavior therapy does change behavior. But if behavior is changed without engaging the child meaningfully around issues of internalized object relationships, the change will not be maintained after discharge from the program.

Treatment of Comorbid Conditions: In addition to concurrent mood disorders, psychotic symptoms, and attention deficit hyperactivity disorder, frequently other comorbid conditions are seen that require treatment. Specific learning disabilities call for special educational approaches that are available both in inpatient schools and through the public schools for outpatients. Adolescents with comorbid substance abuse and dependency present an especially difficult problem. Twelve-step programs, although effective with adults, include requirements that may be insurmountable obstacles for adolescents with personality disorders. Steps 1 and 2, which call on the patient to acknowledge powerlessness and to embrace a Higher Power, are unsuitable goals for younger adolescents. A minority of older adolescents are able to make a commitment to recovery and do very well in these programs. Continued involvement in Alcoholics Anonymous or Narcotics Anonymous can provide an ongoing network of positive peer relationships following inpatient treatment.

Collaboration with Community Agencies: Many of these adolescents will have ongoing involvement with child welfare and or juvenile justice authorities. Others need help with getting appropriate educational services. Collaboration with systems outside the treatment program should be undertaken only with the adolescents' and parents' knowledge, and with careful attention to boundaries, confidentiality, and the therapist's role. Adolescents who have a background of delinquent behavior should be advised that the therapist's role is not to get them out of trouble but to help them understand why they need to get in trouble, so they can change the behavior that gets them there.

Milieu Treatment: The treatment milieu is the sine qua non of residential programs. A milieu is made up of the physical space the children live in, the people they interact with, and the activities and events they participate in and experience around the clock. The 24-hour nature of the milieu makes it a more potent force than any specific treatment modality. It is crucial that this force be utilized to therapeutic advantage. The hospital is not merely a place where children live while receiving treatment; rather, the children's experience of living in the hospital *is* the basic treatment.

Safety must be assured. This means security from outside and inside the group, and from outside and inside each child. The system of human relationships is the most important factor in safety.

The basic physical and emotional needs of each child must be met in a manner that is nurturing. Not only meals, but timely snacks are important to adolescents. The emotional atmosphere on the unit has to be warm; direct-care staff should be selected not only on the basis of job skills but because of their personal characteristics. They should have respect and healthy affection for adolescents.

Clarity of rules, roles, responsibilities, boundaries, and values is an ongoing concern. Therapeutic objectivity, meaning attitudes that are nonjudgemental and nonpunitive, is essential. Open group process among the staff keeps each member alert to the possibility of unconscious negative countertransference. Libidinal countertransference is also a significant problem and is best dealt with in individual supervision.

The milieu must achieve a balance between flexibility and consistency, a challenge for any staff. A milieu is consistent in its rules and expectations and flexible in responding to the individual child by taking account of his or her changing needs and fluctuating capacities.

The milieu has to provide for identification of problems and ongoing means for working toward solutions. It communicates an expectation that problems are to be solved through active efforts of the individual, working in concert with others.

Group process is at the heart of residential treatment, especially for adolescents. Group process will go on among the adolescents whether the staff are aware of it or not, and it is likely to be the most single most powerful influence on the individual. The staff's aim should be to manage the patient group process with the active participation of the staff, so as to safeguard the treatment group as a cohesive, process-oriented system of therapeutic relationships, where the experiencing and reporting of inner conflict is safe, where identified problems can be clarified, interpreted, and ultimately worked through. This is done by beginning and ending every treatment day with a meeting of the group. The group's therapeutic attention focuses on everything going on with each adolescent. The child brings unique strengths and deficits into the group, "lives them out" there, and participates in interpretive work and working through.

Developmental progression is another important component of the therapeutic milieu. Every program has to have some orderly way of assigning patients their responsibilities and privileges. Strictly behavioral programs tie increases in privileges to the child's achievement of behavioral goals. In a program for adolescents whose personality disturbance is the result of developmental deficits, a level system should accommodate the fluctuations of their developmental progression. Three areas are key: mastery of anxiety, impulse control, and relationships with others, in particular their level of engagement with staff. Adolescents should be evaluated frequently in an attempt to assign them to the highest level that they can handle. The lower levels address the needs of adolescents with poor control of anxiety, poor control over impulses, and unstable or impaired relationships with caregivers. As the adolescent progresses through higher levels, his or her treatment program recapitulates the developmental sequence from early childhood to adolescence, which is basically one of the adults taking most of the responsibility for the young child, to the teenager's taking most of the responsibility for the self.

It is essential that a residential treatment program for adolescents have a school as an integrated part of the comprehensive treatment program. Teachers must be included as team members for treatment planning, implementation, and review. Specialized classes are needed for children at different levels of development and for specific learning problems. Adolescents' school problems are made a focus of both academic and therapeutic intervention, and their functioning in school is an important part of decision making in their treatment.

A virogous program of therapeutic activities rounds out the adolescents' milieu. These activities involve normative and developmental goals: exercise, outdoor play, fun, perceptual and motor skills development, basic socialization, teamwork, and leisure skills. Specific therapeutic issues are also addressed in activities: attitudes toward self and others, capacity for enjoyment, sublimated expressions for aggressive drive derivatives, initiative, competition, and sexuality.

Adjunctive components of the treatment setting include the ongoing modeling and active teaching of social skills and activities of daily living that the staff provide to individual adolescents, as needed. Behavioral programming is routinely a part of all milieu therapy and includes a wide variety of positive reinforcements for all the adolescents, such as checks and stars, extinction and time-out procedures, and the like. Individual programs of behavior modification including token economies are also designed as needed.

Stages of Treatment

Adolescents in long-term residential treatment usually pass through three or four identifiable phases (Pearson, 1987). These include an "intake phase," during which not only must the acute needs of the patient be addressed, but the groundwork laid for development of a longer-term relationship. Resistance is an issue throughout treatment, although it is heightened during the next phase, the "resistance phase," during which the adolescent reenacts his or her problems in relationships with staff and other patients. This is the phase during which a long-term plan should be developed that includes continuation of treatment following discharge; ideally, the therapist makes a commitment to be available as long as is necessary. What I have termed the "hospital thereapeutic phase" involves a continual reworking of issues of attachment, separation, idealization, devaluation, dependency, autonomy, hatred and love. Finally, during the posthospitalization phase of treatment, the adolescent struggles to generalize what he or she has learned about the self in the hospital to life in the real world.

The ultimate goal of treatment is developmentally phase-adequate emotional, behavioral, and social functioning. A renegotiation of separation-individuation is necessary to achieve this. A related goal is object constancy, or the establishment of whole-object relatedness. This is the ability to see oneself and others realistically, which carries with it the capacity to tolerate ambivalence and integrate identity. If treatment is successful, the youngster will rely less on primitive defenses, such as splitting, denial, projection, projective identification, and omnipotence.

Outcome

There are no controlled studies of treatment outcome in adolescents with personality disorders. Those studies that have been done all emphasize the importance of continuity of care and long-term treatment in determining a favorable outcome (Gossett, Lewis, & Barnhart, 1983; Masterson & Costello, 1980).

In 1985, I retrospectively reviewed 1,400 consecutive admissions to Terrell State Hospital Child and Adolescent Services (in Texas) over the 10-year period from 1973 to 1983 and found long-term follow-up and outcome data on 140, 10% of the total (Pearson, 1987). Of the group of 140 patients, the most common diagnoses at the time of their hospitalization were borderline personality disorder (23%), schizophrenia (18%), and major affective disorder (17%). A mixed group of characterological, family, and behavioral problems was fourth at 16%. However, the majority of all four of these groupings was composed of adolescents we would now classify as personality disorders.

Outcome was judged on the basis of whether the young person had achieved an age-appropriate level of functioning and was without significant symptoms; these two dimensions were rated independently. Thus, there were four possible levels of outcome based on these ratings; a fifth category was added for those who were so impaired that they were chronically or intermittently institutionalized. Unequivocally favorable outcomes (either 1 or 2) were found in 41.4%. Eighteen percent were placed in the third level, which meant that they were functioning fairly well but required support of living with families or in structured living situations. Twenty-one percent were functioning poorly in similar supportive living arrangements (level 4), and 16% were chronically or intermittently institutionalized. Of those whose primary diagnosis had been borderline personality disorder, 72% were doing well at follow-up. Outcomes were also favorable for two other groups, with 80% of those with affective disorders and 86% of the mixed group in the highest two categories.

An analysis of the treatment of the patients with successful outcome pointed unequivocally to the importance of a long-term, stable therapeutic relationship. The fact that these patients kept in touch for so many years after their treatment is an indication that this relationship was an important and enduring part of their lives.

Issues of Economics and Public Policy

In the 1980s, the number of private psychiatric hospital beds available for adolescents grew explosively, and the marketing of medical services in order to fill for-profit beds was undoubtedly a factor in the increasing utilization of these hospitals. This trend waned in the face of regulatory legislation in many states and the implementation of increased cost controls on the part of third-party payers. Although some adolescents were hospitalized unnecessarily, the dramatic increase in utilization was in part fueled by increased availability and accessibility of inpatient treatment to many adolescents who needed it. Today, very few benefit plans provide for residential care long enough to effectively treat personality disorders. The result is that many of these youngsters are eventually treated in the public sector or have their treatment financed by public funds, such as Medicaid.

The growth in private psychiatric hospitals has actually contributed to an increased demand for public hospital beds, at a time when planning in the public sector is emphasizing community treatment and hospital funding is being diverted to nonhospital alternatives. Aggressive marketing of inpatient treatment by hospitals has increased demand for it on the part of families, but managed care has increasingly limited lengths of stay. The result is increasing numbers of "referrals" made to state hospitals, which typically are already at capacity with children and adolescents and are attempting to develop community alternatives for the ones they already have. The intake team for the public agency tries to deflect these referrals into community-based alternatives, but the families have been "sold" on hospital care as the only reasonable and safe option for their children.

The high per-diem cost and long duration of residential treatment programs make payers question whether their money is well spent. There are few data to answer this question. In an early 1980s attempt to quantify the relative cost of treatment versus incarceration, the federal Law Enforcement Assistance Administration (LEAA) compared the costs of providing treatment to incarcerated juvenile delinquents to the estimated social costs of providing only incarceration, and found that for every dollar spent on treatment, two dollars were returned in savings on future social expenditures. With the advent of managed care and in the current service delivery environment, studies are beginning to be done to quantify treatment costs in the context of other social expenditures. These methods are being developed not only in order to maximize efficiency but also in recognition of the fact that when treatment costs are merely shifted to other systems, such as juvenile justice, child protection, and adult criminal justice, overall expenditures actually increase, and at a terrible human cost to youth and society.

Managed care has fueled the attempt to develop alternatives to longer-term residential treatment for personality disorders in adolescence. This is now the world in which we must practice. The bad news is that we have had to give up the more stringent controls we used to have over symptomatic behavior. The good news is that we are having to learn how to engage difficult youngsters in long-term therapeutic relationships without those controls. If we are successful, the child no longer has to start all over after discharge from treatment, because the adoption of new modes of emotional, social, and behavioral functioning has occurred in the setting of his or her "real" life. In the meantime, conscientious therapists must have an almost limitless capacity for tolerating the anxiety that the chaotic behaviors these youths engender.

Conclusion

In summary, the problems of personality disorder in adolescence are complex, from the standpoint of both diagnosis and treatment. Personality disorder does exist and can be effectively treated in adolescents. Because of the fluidity of personality function in adolescence, this developmental phase presents us with unique opportunities for the effective treatment of these disorders. If youngsters receive effective treatment before the final establishment of identity and consolidation of character structure, both they and society can be spared the years of misery that they will otherwise experience and inflict. The histories of adolescents with personality disorders are often tragic; as patients, these adolescents are extremely difficult; but they also can be very rewarding to work with. Given that we do not yet have all the answers to these problematic patients, and no one theory can satisfactorily explain the full range of clinical experience, an eclectic approach that uses concepts from a variety of theoretical points of view according to their utility in a particular situation is most appropriate. A long-term commitment on the part of the therapist is essential. Treatment, to be effective, needs to be intensive and long term, and is difficult to sustain in today's climate of cost containment. However, the social costs of failure to treat are high. There are few fields in medicine in which both the challenges and the opportunities are as great as they are in this one.

REFERENCES

Adler, G. (1989). Narcissistic personality disorder. *Treatments of psychiatric disorders,* pp. 2736–2741. Washington, DC: American Psychiatric Association.

American Psychiatric Association. (1987). *Diagnostic and statistical manual of mental disorders,* 3rd ed. rev. Washington, DC: Author.

American Psychiatric Association. (1994). *Diagnostic and statistical manual of mental disorders*, 4th ed. Washington, DC: Author.

Bernstein, D. P., Cohen, P., Velez, C. N., Schwab-Stone, M., Siever, L. J., & Shinsato, L. (1993). Prevalence and stability of the DSM-III-R personality disorders in a community-based survey of adolescents. *American Journal of Psychiatry, 150*, 1237–1243.

Bezirganian, S., Cohen, P., & Brook, J. S. (1993). The impact of mother-child interaction on the development of borderline personality disorder. *American Journal of Psychiatry, 150*, 1836–1842.

Blos, P. (1962). *On adolescence: A psychoanalytic interpretation*. New York: Free Press.

Bowlby, J. (1988). *A secure base: Clinical applications of attachment theory*. London: Routledge.

Campbell, K. (1982). The psychotherapy relationship with borderline personality disorders. *Psychotherapy Theory, Research, and Practice, 19*, 166–193.

Eppright, T. D., Kashani, J. H., Robison, B. D., & Reid, J. C. (1993). Personality disorders in an incarcerated juvenile population, *American Journal of Psychiatry, 150*, 1233–1236.

Garnet, K. E., Levy, K. N., Mattanah, J. J. F., Edell, W. S., & McGlashan, T. H. (1994). *American Journal of Psychiatry, 151*, 1380–1382.

Goldman, S. J., D'Angelo, E. J., & DeMaso, D. R. (1993). Psychopathology in the families of children and adolescents with borderline personality disorder. *American Journal of Psychiatry, 150*, 1832–1835.

Golombek, H., & Marton, P. (1992). Adolescents over time: A longitudinal study of personality development. *Adolescent Psychiatry, 18*, 213–284.

Gossett, J., Lewis, S., & Barnhart, D., (1983). *To find a way*. New York: Brunner/Mazel.

Gunderson, J. G., & Elliott, G. R. (1985). The interface between borderline personality disorder and affective disorder. *American Journal of Psychiatry, 142*, 277–288.

Jones, J. M., Pearson, G. T., & Dimperio, R. (1989). Treatment of the hospitalized adolescent and family: An integrated systems-theory approach. *Adolescent Psychiatry, 16*, 449–487.

Kernberg, O. F. (1975). *Borderline conditions and pathological narcissism*. New York: Jason Aronson.

Kernberg, O. F. (1984). *Severe personality disorders: Psychotherapeutic strategies*. New Haven, CT: Yale University Press.

Lewis, O. (1987). The paranoid-schizoid position and pathologic regression in early adolescence. *Journal of the American Academy of Psychoanalysis, 15*, 503–519.

Links, P. S., Boiago, I., Huxley, G., Steiner, M., & Mitton, J. E. (1990). Sexual abuse and biparental failure as etiologic models in borderline personality disorder. In P. S. Links (Ed.), *Family environment and borderline personality disorder*. Washington, DC: American Psychiatric Press.

Links, P. S., Mitton, M. J., & Steiner, M. (1993). Stability of borderline personality disorder. *Canadian Journal of Psychiatry, 38*, 255–259.

Ludolph, P. S., Westen, D., Misle, B., Jackson, A., Wixom, J., & Wiss, F. C. (1990). The borderline diagnosis in adolescents: Symptoms and developmental history. *American Journal of Psychiatry, 147*, 470–476.

Masterson, J. F. (1976). *Psychotherapy of the borderline adult*. New York: Jason Aronson.

Masterson, J. F., & Costello, J. (1980). *From borderline adolescent to functioning adult: The test of time*. New York: Brunner/Mazel.

Masterson, J. F., & Klein, R. (Eds.). (1989). *Psychotherapy of disorders of the self*. New York: Brunner/Mazel.

McManus, M., Lerner, H., Robbins, D., & Barbour, C. (1984). Assessment of borderline symptomatology in hospitalized adolescents. *Journal of the American Academy of Child Psychiatry, 23*, 685–694.

Pearson, G. T. (1987). Long-term treatment needs of hospitalized adolescents. *Adolescent Psychiatry, 14*, 342–357.

Pearson, G. T. (1989). Unpublished manuscript.

Pearson, G. T. (1991). Social systems contributions to adolescent psychotherapy. In M. Slomowitz (Ed.), *Adolescent psychotherapy* (pp. 57–79). Washington, DC: American Psychiatric Association.

Reich, J., Yates, W., & Nduaguba, M. (1989). Prevalence of DSM-III personality disorders in the community. *Social Psychiatry and Psychiatric Epidemiology, 24*, 12–16.

Rinsley, D. B. (1980). *Treatment of the severely disturbed adolescent*. New York: Jason Aronson.

Rinsley, D. B. (1982). *Borderline and other self disorders*. New York: Jason Aronson.

Rose, M. (1987). The context for psychological change in a therapeutic community for adolescents. *Residential Treatment for Children & Youth, 5*, 29–47.

Samuels, J. F., Nestadt, G., Romanski, A. J., Folstein, M. F., & McHugh, P. R. (1994). DSM-III personality disorders in the community. *American Journal of Psychiatry, 151*, 1055–1062.

Stein, B., Golombek, H., Marton, P., & Korenblum, M. (1987). Personality functioning and change in clinical presentation from early to middle adolescence. *Adolescent Psychiatry, 14*, 378–393.

Westman, J., Ownby, R., & Smith, S. (1987). An analysis of 180 children referred to a university hospital learning disabilities service. *Child Psychiatry and Human Development, 17*, 275–282.

Zimmerman, M., & Coryell, W. (1989). DSM-III personality disorder diagnoses in a nonpatient sample: Diagnostic correlates and comorbidity. *Archives of General Psychiatry, 46*, 682–689.

29 / Adolescent Impulse Control Disorders: Eating Disorders and Substance Abuse

Robert L. Hendren and Claudia K. Berenson

Introduction

Impulse control disorders include such behaviors as fire setting, gambling, paraphilia, trichotillomania, and violence. More recently the concept of impulse control disorder has been used to explain the etiologies of psychiatric disorders commonly occurring in adolescence such as substance abuse, disruptive behavior disorders, suicidal attempts associated with depression, and eating disorders. The basis for this conceptualization rests not only on the associated symptom clusters that lead to a psychiatric diagnosis but also on neurobiological markers and response to psychiatric treatment and to psychotropic medication. Understanding the etiology of impulse control disorders goes beyond simply a diagnosis and can help guide assessment and effective treatment.

The recent editions of the *Diagnostic and Statistical Manual of Mental Disorders* (*DSM*) are based on statistically reliable clusters (American Psychiatric Association, (1980, 1987, 1994). Diagnoses based on DSM-IV therefore do not reflect an underlying psychologic, biologic, or cultural etiology. The strength of the DSM-IV symptom-based diagnoses lies in their reproducibility across settings and clinicians. The weakness of this classification is evident in the increasing recognition of comorbidity. Comorbidity suggests an underlying etiology in the overlapping symptom clusters that is not identified by the symptoms themselves. It has been suggested that these different comorbid subgroups may have differing risk factors, clinical courses, and pharmacologic responses (Biederman, Newcorn, & Sprich, 1991).

Recent studies have found considerable comorbidity of attention deficit hyperactivity disorder with conduct disorder, oppositional defiant disorder, mood disorders, anxiety disorders, learning disabilities, Tourette's syndrome, and borderline personality disorder (Biederman et al., 1989). De-

pression and suicide in adolescence are shown to be highly correlated with drug use, delinquency, and eating disorders (Apter et al., 1995; Kandel, Raveis, & Davies, 1991). Common to all of these comorbid disorders is an underlying problem with impulse control.

Biologic abnormalities are increasingly found to be associated with poor impulse control. One of the most replicated findings in biological psychiatry is an association between a low cerebrospinal fluid (CSF) level of the serotonin metabolite 5-hydroxyindoleacetic acid (5-HIAA) in patients who have attempted suicide compared with those who have not (Linnoila, 1988). Because of an association between low CSF 5-HIAA and violent suicide attempts, it has been suggested that low CSF 5-HIAA results in violent behaviors (Linnoila, DeJong, & Virkkunen, 1989). However, low CSF 5-HIAA levels also are found to be related to higher scores of impulsiveness (Linnoila et al., 1989). Low CSF 5-HIAA is found in arsonists regardless of the presence of violence (Linnoila et al., 1989); & in alcoholics (Ballenger, Goodwin, Major, & Brown, 1979) and depressed relatives of alcoholics who are not themselves alcoholic (Rosenthal, Davenport, Cowdry, Webster, & Goodwin, 1989); and among individuals with poor impulse control (Virkkunen et al., 1994).

Evidence for a serotonergic impulse control disorder model also comes from pharmacologic studies. Drugs that reduce serotonin turnover or function, such as ethanol and benzodiazepines, also produce disinhibition, impulsivity, and aggression. Antidepressants that enhance central serotonin neurotransmission such as imipramine, fluoxetine, buspirone, and lithium carbonate are reportedly of benefit in the treatment of drive-dysregulation syndromes such as bulimia nervosa, kleptomania, paraphilia, compulsive gambling or sexual behaviors, and obsessive-compulsive disorder (Pearson, 1990). Thus, various lines of evidence suggest that abnormality in serotonin systems may be associated with poor impulse control that may manifest itself in a variety of associated disorders.

Altered platelet monoamine oxidase (MAO) activity is also associated with impulsivity. Low MHPG levels, a measure of norepinephrine metabolism, are inversely related to sensation seeking and impulsivity (Gabel, Stadler, Bjorn, Shindledecker, & Bowen, 1994). Both high and MAO levels correlate with disruptive behavior disorder (Staff et al., 1989). Poor impulse control is also associated with low blood glucose concentration during the oral glucose tolerance test (GTT) (Linnoila et al., 1989). Individuals with an impulse control disorder have a distinct psychological style. Cognitively they often are selective in the information they process, have difficulty with abstraction, and are catastrophizing, overgeneralizing, and personalizing (Lee & Prentice, 1988). They are sensation and novelty seeking, harm avoidant, not particularly reward dependent, and frequently have a short attention span (Gabel et al., 1994). Depression is common (Riggs, Baker, Mikulich, Young, & Crawley, 1995). Self-soothing mechanisms have not been developed to relieve uncomfortable symptoms. Their families have a high incidence of depression and impulse control disorders. These impulse control disordered young people and their families make frequent use of lower-level defenses. Socially, these young people are likely to come from an environment that sanctions impulsive behavior, does not include a nuclear family, and has a high level of stress and geographic mobility.

It is important to note that the etiology of impulse control disorder is related to the additive effect of multiple factors. For instance, birth complications combined with early maternal rejection to predict violent crime at age 18 years. Neither of the risk factors were predictive alone (Raine, Brennan, & Mednick, 1994). Self-regulation at 4 years could be predicted by maternal ratings of the child's impulsivity and attention span, an objective measure of delay ability, and maternal negativity at 24 months of age (Silverman & Ragusa, 1993).

Thus, these biological and psychological findings support an underlying problem with impulse control for disorders such as eating disorders, substance abuse, and disruptive behavior disorders. The remainder of this chapter examines two disorders common among adolescents, eating disorders

and substance abuse, and describes how this impulse control disorder conceptualization can elucidate the etiology and effectively guide treatment.

Substance Abuse

Substance use and abuse among adolescents are major public health problems in Western cultures and are often associated with other psychiatric disorders. Prevalence of substance use in adolescence differs markedly for different drugs, with more socially accepted drugs being the most widely used. Among high school seniors, lifetime prevalence for alcohol use has remained around 90% over the past 20 years. Use of other drugs, such as marijuana, cocaine, hallucinogens, and stimulants, showed an increase in prevalence in the 1970s and 1980s with a decrease in recent years. (See Table 29.1) Thus, the major drug used and abused by young people today is alcohol.

Substance abuse is best viewed as a continuum, with nonuse and causal experimentation on one end and compulsive, regular, heavy use on the other. Most young people are at the less serious end of the continuum, and most adolescents "mature out" of substance abuse (Kandel & Logan, 1984).

The greatest risk for adolescents generally is created by the combination of the psychiatric disorders associated with substance abuse and actual substance use. Adolescents, particularly those with any type of depressive disorder, who abuse psychoactive substances appear to be the group at highest risk for suicidal behavior (Crumley, 1990; Levy & Deykin, 1989). Two recent studies clearly demonstrate this association. In San Diego County, California, substance abuse was the main psychiatric diagnosis in 53% of 133 consecutive young suicides (Fowler, Rich & Young, 1986). In Allegheny County, Pennsylvania, the proportion of adolescent suicide victims who had detectable blood alcohol levels rose from 12.9% between 1968 and 1972 to 46% between 1978 and 1983 (Brent, Perper, & Allman, 1987).

A relationship among depression and suicide and adolescent substance abuse, delinquency, and eating disorders has also been noted among high school students (Kandel et al., 1991). Conduct

TABLE 29.1

Trends in Annual Lifetime Prevalence of Various Types of Drugs for 12 Graders

	Class of													
	1980	1981	1982	1983	1984	1985	1986	1987	1988	1989	1990	1991	1992	1993
Marijuna/Hashish	60.3	59.5	58.7	57.0	54.9	54.2	50.9	50.2	47.2	43.7	40.7	36.7	32.6	35.3
Inhalants Adjusted	17.3	17.2	17.7	18.2	18.0	18.1	20.1	18.6	17.5	18.6	18.5	18.0	17.0	17.7
Amyl & Butyl Nitrites	11.1	10.1	9.8	8.4	8.1	7.9	8.6	4.7	3.2	3.3	2.1	1.6	1.5	1.4
Hallucinogens Adjusted	15.6	15.3	14.3	13.6	12.3	12.1	11.9	10.6	9.2	9.9	9.7	10.0	9.4	11.3
LSD	9.3	9.8	9.6	8.9	8.0	7.5	7.2	8.4	7.7	8.3	8.7	8.8	8.6	10.3
PCP	9.6	7.8	6.0	5.6	5.0	4.9	4.8	3.0	2.9	3.9	2.8	2.9	2.4	2.9
Cocaine	15.7	16.5	16.0	16.2	16.1	17.3	16.9	15.2	12.1	10.3	9.4	7.8	6.1	6.1
Crack	NA	NA	NA	NA	NA	NA	NA	5.4	4.8	4.7	3.5	3.1	2.6	2.6
Other Cocaine	NA	NA	NA	NA	NA	NA	NA	14.0	12.1	8.5	8.6	7.0	5.3	5.4
Heroin	1.1	1.1	1.2	1.2	1.3	1.2	1.1	1.2	1.1	1.3	1.3	0.9	1.2	1.1
Other Opiates	9.8	10.1	9.6	9.4	9.7	10.2	9.0	9.2	8.6	8.3	8.3	6.6	6.1	6.4
Stimulants	26.4	32.2	27.9	26.9	27.9	26.2	23.4	21.6	19.8	19.1	17.5	15.4	13.9	15.1
Crystal Meth. (Ice)	NA	NA	NA	NA	NA	NA	NA	NA	NA	NA	2.7	3.3	2.9	3.1
Sedatives	14.9	16.0	15.2	14.4	13.3	11.8	10.4	8.7	7.8	7.4	7.5	6.7	6.1	6.4
Barbiturates	11.0	11.3	10.3	9.9	9.9	9.2	8.4	7.4	6.7	6.5	6.8	6.2	5.5	6.3
Methaqualone	9.5	10.6	10.7	10.1	8.3	6.7	5.2	4.0	3.3	2.7	2.3	1.3	1.6	0.8
Tranquilizers	15.2	14.7	14.0	13.3	12.4	11.9	10.9	10.9	9.4	7.6	7.2	7.2	6.0	6.4
Alcohol	93.2	92.6	92.8	92.6	92.6	92.2	91.3	92.2	92.0	90.7	89.5	88.0	87.5	87.0

Source: L. D. Johnston, P. M. O'Malley, & J. G. Bachman (1994). *National survey results on drug use from The Monitoring the Future Study, 1975–1993, Vol. 1. Secondary School Students.* Rockville, MD: U.S. Department of Health and Human Services.

disorder, major depressive episode, and the combination of attention deficit, hyperactivity, and impulse disorder were the most prevalent diagnoses after detoxification among a group of adolescents in an inpatient treatment facility (DeMilio, 1989). High school females who met criteria for bulimia and purging reported higher rates of drunkenness, marijuana use, cigarette use, and greater levels of depressive symptomatology (Killen et al., 1987a,b). The association of alcohol abuse and bulimia suggests a general lack of impulse control in these students (Timmerman, Wells, & Chen, 1990). Thus, there is a strong association between those psychiatric disorders that are accompanied by poor impulse control and the impulsive and problematic use of psychoactive substances.

ETIOLOGY OF SUBSTANCE ABUSE

Biologic Factors: A family history of alcoholism is one of the most powerful predictors of alcoholic risk. Sons and daughters of alcoholics are four times more likely to develop alcohol-related problems than offspring of nonalcoholic parents (Goodwin, 1983). However, the extent of the genetic predictor is variable. Schukit (1986) noted that the identical twin of an alcoholic has a 60% risk of developing alcoholism, while a fraternal twin has only a 20 to 30% risk. In a study of male and female twins, Pickens et al. (1991) found significant differences between monozygotic and dizygotic male twins for the diagnosis of alcohol abuse and/or dependence, but not for female twins. One study suggests that alcoholism is associated with the dopamine D_2 receptor gene marked by the A_1 allele, a gene linked with the neural mechanism for reward and for depression (Blum et al., 1990). This finding has not been consistently replicated, but one of the confirming studies found the A_1 allele to be significantly more common in patients with Tourette's disorder, attention deficit hyperactivity disorder, autism, and posttraumatic stress disorder (Comings et al., 1991). Based on these findings, the authors suggest that the A_1 allele may be a marker for some personality trait associated with a number of different disorders in addition to alcoholism—a kind of restless, impulsive, somewhat compulsive behavior.

Individuals at risk for becoming alcoholic because of inherited factors are biologically and behaviorally different from individuals who have

few or no inherited factors that predispose them to alcoholism. For instance, in one study of violent offenders and impulsive fire setters, those subjects who had alcoholic fathers had a lower mean cerebrospinal fluid 5-hydroxyindoleacetic acid (5-HIAA) concentration and were more often impulsive than subjects without alcoholic fathers (Linnoila et al., 1989). In another study, the sons of familial alcoholics were found to have significantly higher basal thyrotropin levels and peak thyrotropin levels than control boys (Moss, Guthie, & Linnoila, 1986). Low levels of the serotonin metabolite 5-HIAA have been implicated in the enhanced thyrotropin response.

On the basis of adoption studies, Cloninger (1987) has proposed a classification scheme whereby a subgroup of patients with a high genetic loading for alcoholism, an early onset of alcoholism, a severe course, and coexisting psychiatric problems are classified as type 2. Type 1 patients do not have the genetic loading or the early onset of substance abuse and behavioral problems. In support of this classification system, Buydens-Branchey, Branchey, and Noumair (1989) and Buydens-Branchey, Branchey, Noumair, and Lieber (1989) found that patients who started abusing alcohol in their teens were three times more likely to be depressed and four times as likely to have attempted suicide as patients with a later onset of alcohol abuse. They also were more likely to have been incarcerated for crimes involving violence. Further study of serotonin precursor availability in this group of subjects supports an interpretation that subjects with an early onset of alcoholism have a preexisting serotonin deficit that could manifest itself by increased alcohol intake early in life.

Neuropsychological Factors: Neuropsychological traits such as attention problems, behavioral overactivity and aggression, sensation seeking, and low sociability comprise features of a vulnerability to alcoholism (Tarter, Laird, Kabene, Bukstein, & Kaminer, 1990). Aggressive behavior as early as 6 years of age has been shown to predict heavy substance use in adolescence, particularly for males (Flannery, Vazgonyi, Torquati, & Fridrich, 1994; Kellam et al., 1989). The aggressive behavior noted in these younger children seemed to be the result of attention problems. Delinquent male adolescents at high risk for substance abuse demonstrated deficits in information processing in a noisy environment as assessed by auditory event-related potential (ERP) techniques (Burke, Burke, & Rae 1994; Herning, Hickey, Pickworth, & Jaffe, 1989). This deficit in information processing is suggested to be a marker for other central nervous system functions, including impulse and mood regulation. In a study of temperamental traits, substance-abusing adolescents were discriminated from normal controls on a variety of temperamental scales closely linked to behavioral activity regulation (Tarter et al., 1990). Drug use severity was associated with high activity level.

A strong link exists between senation seeking and drug use. Sensation seeking is a personality trait defined by the need for novel and complex sensations and experiences, and a willingness to undergo risks to have such experiences (Pedersen, Clausen, & Lank, 1989). In a normal nonclinical adolescent population, scores on the sensation-seeking scales of disinhibition and experience seeking are found to be moderate to strong predictors of drug use (Pederson et al., 1989). In fact, sensation seeking is a better predictor than is social class, self-esteem, mental health, and several items referring to social bonding theory.

Other factors that may precede or coincide with early drug use include aggressiveness, poor school performance, and personality traits such as low self-esteem, depressive mood, and rebelliousness (Flannery et al., 1994). Earlier psychopathology, such as hostility, paranoid ideation, depression, and obsessive-compulsive symptoms, has been found to predict substance use 17 months later, and earlier substance use has been found to predict later psychopathology (Friedman & Glickman, 1987). Thus, there appears to be an additive or cumulative affect of psychopathology and substance use.

Psychosocial Factors: Social and cultural factors are strong predictors of whether an adolescent will use substances and may affect whether the vulnerable adolescent will become a substance abuser. Both parental values and peer influences are found to be important predictors. Adolescents are more likely to use substances if their parents are users or if they are perceived to be users (Fawzy, Coombs, & Gerber, 1983). A permissive parental attitude is found to be as or more important than actual parental substance use in determining adolescent substance use (McDermott, 1984). Children of alcoholics are more likely to become alcoholic themselves if family rituals such as meals, weekends, and holidays were disrupted during the period of heaviest parental drinking (Wolin & Bennett, 1980). Peer drug association is found to be a better predictor of substance use than emotional distress variables except for anger (Swain, Oetting, Edwards, & Beavais, 1989).

The larger social context also has been shown to be an important influence. For instance, a survey of youths in France and Israel, countries with very different cultural attitudes toward substance abuse, revealed that while the overall sequence in the use of legal and illegal substances is similar, the French youths reported greater use and involvement (Kandel & Logan, 1984). Another example is that prevalence studies of drug use by American Indian youth reveal higher levels of use in certain tribes (May, 1982). Use within a tribe appears to be related to the user's degree of acculturation; in cases where tribe culture did not condone substance abuse, greater use occured among those youth not connected to the tribal culture.

RECOGNITION, ASSESSMENT, AND
DIAGNOSTIC ASSESSMENT

Assessment of most drug-related problems requires a careful, comprehensive history. The primary factors interfering with the diagnosis of chemical dependency in adolescents are the patient's and the family's tendencies to deny the illness. Adolescents typically minimize their drug use or even lie about the role it plays in their lives. At the same time, adolescents may give indirect evidence of the problem in their concern about themselves and their hope that someone will be able to help them. They may broach the subject of drugs indirectly through discussion of friends who use drugs or theoretical discussions about the overreaction of the adult world to adolescent drug use. At other times the approach may be more direct—such as appearing drunk or "high" on drugs—in situations in which they are likely to be caught.

In order for clinicians to understand fully both past and current drug use, it is critical to assess family functioning, parental drug use, and parental attitudes toward drug use. Failure to assess these factors may lead to unsuccessful interventions or treatment, as one or more family members may sabotage efforts to provide help.

Drug Use History: Adolescents often need prompting and need to be asked direct questions to provide a complete drug use history. Specific questions should be asked about each drug category as well as the context in which the drug use occurs. Polydrug use is more prevalent among teens than among adult substance abusers. The parents also need to be asked about direct and indirect evidence of drug use and their reactions to these findings. Adolescents usually will not deny drug use if the effects are obvious, but they may use a great deal of rationalization, minimization, and various explanations to defend the sometimes obvious drug involvement.

Indirect evidence of drug abuse includes a change in friends, deterioration of adaptive functioning in school and at home, a wide variations in mood, communicativeness, and level of consciousness. More subtle manifestations include a loss of interest in previous constructive activities such as academics or extracurricular activities and organizations. While adolescents usually rationalize these changes as a simple change in interest patterns, if the activities are not replaced by other constructive ones, this explanation should be viewed with some skepticism. Adolescents' intense degrees of felt and expressed anger toward parents in the face of relatively benign parental behavior also is indicative of possible drug involvement. Clinicians also may seek additional direct and indirect evidence from teachers, counselors, friends, and others who had had recent contact with the adolescents.

Laboratory Evaluation: In a routine assessment, often it is impractical to test urine, blood, or gastric aspirate. However, such testing is imperative in acute emergencies such as drug overdose, suicide attempt, accidental injuries, or other medical or psychiatric problems. A toxicologic evaluation is also helpful when adolescents deny apparent intoxication or when assessing abstinence in treatment programs. Other laboratory evidence demonstrating the effects of drugs on body systems may provide supporting evidence of a drug abuse problem, especially alcoholism, but these changes are not commonly seen in adolescents.

Diagnosis: The various editions of the Diagnostic and Statistical Manual do not have different criteria for childhood, adolescent, and adult substance abuse, although *DSM-IV* does discuss specific culture, age, and gender features for each type of substance-related disorder. The degree of dysfunction necessary to meet the diagnostic criteria for adults would be equivalent to extreme deterioration in young people. As a result, *DSM* criteria are of limited value for making the diagnosis in children and adolescents (Bailey, 1989). In diagnosing adolescent substance abuse, clinicians must realize that while some amount of experimentation may be within normal limits, certain adolescents are at greater risk of a substance abuse disorder based on the factors listed previously. Structured interviews and rating scales may be of some benefit in this assessment process.

Treatment: Prevention and treatment of adolescent drug use will be more effective if the underlying motivational forces that contribute to the drug use can be addressed. Problems of impulse control are foremost among the biopsychosocial factors etiologically related to the development of substance abuse problems. These problems include an underlying biologic/genetic predisposition to substance abuse and poor impulse control, individual personality characteristics of emotional disorder, and a social context that is conducive to the underlying vulnerabilities that express themselves as a substance abuse disorder. Effective treatment, therefore, should address each of these vulnerabilities while creating an environment that helps each adolescent control his or her impulses.

The first step in effective treatment is the engagement of the adolescent substance abuser and family in treatment. A strategic structured system approach is effective in establishing this engagement (Szapocznik et al., 1988). In this approach, the family and the substance-abusing adolescent are viewed as being resistant to change. The family is organized to maintain the disordered structure, and the symptom is viewed as a means of self-regulation. The intervention is aimed at the resistance to change rather than focusing on change itself. In Szapocnik et al.'s 1988 study, 93% of families were engaged with this approach and 77% completed treatment controls.

To determine the most appropriate treatment setting, clinicians must assess the response of the adolescent and the family to the evaluation as well as the severity of the impulse control risk factors. Outpatient therapy is indicated when there is (1) an acceptance of the problem and the need for help, (2) a willingness to abstain from all mood-altering substances and to cooperate with random urine screens, and (3) a commitment to regular attendance at therapy and support groups. Indications for inpatient treatment include (1) acute or chronic medical or psychiatric problems that preclude outpatient treatment, (2) continued association with substance-abusing peers, (3) a lack of motivation, and (4) previous failure in an outpatient program. Residential and day treatment are indicated for adolescents with additional psychiatric, behavioral, social, or family problems who have been or are likely to be unsuccessful with only outpatient or inpatient treatment.

Family, siblings, and significant others in the patient's life should have a basic understanding of the etiology and treatment of impulse control disorders and substance abuse. They should become familiar with ways in which they may help or hinder the patient's progress and should be encouraged to participate in the treatment and aftercare of the adolescent. Specific approaches for working with the family are reviewed by Bry (1988) and include how to "join" the family, focusing on concrete behavior, and restructuring and reframing techniques. When the adolescent's family is not available, one-person family therapy can allow the adolescent to explore the dynamics in his or her family.

Several psychotherapeutic approaches can be effective with substance-related disorders in adolescents. Behavior techniques are aimed at helping the adolescent control the addictive behavior and impulsiveness. Educational and group interventions can explore the reasons for substance use and choice of substances. Social skills and assertiveness training might include teaching drug users to find other and less dangerous ways of obtaining novel and stimulating experiences. Cognitive behavioral approaches link cognitive assumptions and distortions with dysfunctional behavior that reinforces the assumptions and distortions. Psychodynamic approaches explore underlying personality and social factors associated with substance abuse and aid identity development. Other aspects of treatment include experienced-based life skills enrichment, relaxation training, expressive therapies, and vocational counseling. The 12 Step Program of Alcoholics Anonymous can provide a structure to support the adolescent's effects to control his or her substance use and can more generally help contain impulses.

The common goals of all these interventions are to increase self-esteem, to foster open and honest communication abilities, and to attain a greater measure of self-confidence as well as coping and developmental skills. Adolescents with psychiatric disorders comorbid with substance abuse should complete a thorough evaluation including family history and chronology of symptom onset. Subgroups of adolescents with coexisting disorders could then have a specific program designed for them based on the psychiatric disorder and the substance abuse (Bukstein, Brent, & Kaminer, 1989).

Pharmacologic treatment of disorders comorbid with substance abuse in adolescence should always be considered. Treatment of attention deficit hyperactivity disorder (ADHD) with stimulant medication can reduce impulsivity. If stimulant abuse is a concern, certain antidepressants, such as desipramine and bupropion, are often useful. Treatment of depression with serotonin reuptake inhibitors and other serotonergic drugs (fluoxetine, buspirone) may benefit the depression and has shown some ability to decrease alcohol intake, as well (Schatzberg & Cole, 1991). Desipramine may be able to reduce cocaine craving during rehabilitation.

Outcome: Longitudinal follow-up studies indicate that children and adolescents who abuse drugs have a higher rate of problems continuing into young adulthood (Holmberg, 1985). Most of these problems are the result of the combination of psychopathology, impulsive behaviors, and substance abuse. Poor outcome includes such measures as continued treatment for psychiatric disorders and substance abuse, early childbirth and pregnancy, school dropout, and trouble with the law.

It is difficult to evaluate studies of treatment efficacy due to the widely varying definitions of the patient population, treatment programs, and outcome variables. Family involvement (Weidman, 1987) and court pressure (Pompi & Resnick, 1987) are effective in reducing treatment dropout. Peer influences and family and religious support are also associated with positive outcome (Barrett, Simpson, & Lehman, 1988). Factors predicting cessation of drug use include conventionality in social role, unfavorable social context, and degree of prior involvement. Those who use drugs in response to social influence are more likely to stop using them than those who also use drugs for psychological reasons (Kandel & Raveis, 1989). Thus, outcome is to some extent related to the ability to control impulses.

Prevention: Most prevention programs for substance abuse among children and adolescents focus on the social factors that may be deficient in containing the uncontrolled use of substances. Thus, effective programs are directed toward family involvement and improved functioning, social skills enhancement, improved decision-making skills, and role modeling. Within the larger social context, effective programs have involved changing social attitudes, including peer tolerance of substance abuse. These programs have worked through the media, public health policy, and the cooperation of community programs. Facts about drug and alcohol use can be taught so that abuse is perceived as an unacceptable means of coping with everyday life (Morrison, 1990). Certain programs involve high-risk youths, such as children of alcoholics, school dropouts, and behavior-disordered children. It seems clear that all children with a psychiatric disorder known to coexist with substance abuse, especially when there is an underlying defect in impulse control, should be involved in early education programs along with their families.

Eating Disorders

ETIOLOGY

In the *DSM-IV* classification of eating disorders, anorexia nervosa and bulimia nervosa have been linked in their clinical presentation, treatment, and research. A significant percentage of patients meet criteria for both disorders. Controversy continues to exist in the literature about whether the disorders represent subtypes with a common biologic vulnerability or frequently comorbid disorders with a distinct etiology. Other syndromes such as binge eating in obese patients (Spitzer et al., 1993) and rumination in a group of adolescents without esophageal motility problems (Lucas, 1991), share symptoms of bulimia nervosa. Most recent studies divide patients into several subgroups using food restriction, binge eating, purging, and weight criteria as markers defining specific subtypes. Impulsive behaviors seem to correlate more often with those adolescents who meet criteria for bulimia. However, a considerable number of youth may meet criteria for either bulimia or anorexia at a given time during the longitudinal course of their eating disorders (APA, 1993).

Typically, anorexia and bulimia have their onset in adolescence with a 10:1 female-to-male ratio. Males are reported to have a later age of onset. Homosexuality or asexuality have been described as risk factors for males with eating disorders (Carlat & Camargo, 1991). The disorders have been reported both in prepubertal children and in the elderly. The specific etiology remains unclear, although most research points to a multifactorial paradigm that includes interacting sociocultural, biologic, and psychologic risk factors. Garfinkel and Garner (1982) have proposed a useful model that considers the interaction of these risk factors in the etiology and pathogenesis as well as the persistence of these eating disorders.

EPIDEMIOLOGY

According to Lucas's population-based studies of inhabitants of Rochester, Minnesota, the prevalence of anorexia nervosa is 0.3% for females and 0.02% for males. In the 1980s, the annual incidence rate was estimated to be 5 per 100,000. There is some suggestion that incidence is increasing in younger patients (10 to 19 years old) but is remaining stable in those over 21 (Lucas, 1991). In an analysis of 25 studies that considered time trends, Fombonne (1995) concluded that there was no evidence for a secular increase in incidence of anorexia nervosa. Evidence is also lacking for an increase in the incidence of bulimia over the past 25 years, the time encompassing definition of the disorder (Fombonne, 1996).

In a net analysis of 42 published studies (Sullivan, 1995), the mortality rate associated with anorexia nervosa for patients with the disorder was calculated as 5.9%. Sullivan notes that this death rate is considerably higher than that reported for all female psychiatric inpatients, a fact that underscores the gravity of this disorder.

The prevalence rate of bulimia nervosa has been less thoroughly studied but is estimated to be between 2 to 3% of high school and college girls

(Lucas, 1991). In community-based studies, males account for between 10 to 15% of all identified bulimics (Carlat & Camargo, 1991).

Clusters of eating-disorder symptoms, including preoccupation with weight and dieting, compulsive exercise or occasional purging for weight control, body image distortion and the use of cocaine or amphetamines for anoretic effects, have been reported in females who do not meet full criteria for either anorexia or bulimia (Johnson & Connors, 1987).

BIOLOGICAL FACTORS

The role of genetics in either anorexia or bulimia has not been clarif   Family studies (Garfinkel & Garner,   82; Gershon, Schneiber, & Hamourt, 1983; Kassett et al., 1989; Strober, Lampert, Morrell & Burroughs, 1990), have pointed to substantial heritability in the eating disorders. Differential concordance in monozygotic as compared to dizygotic pairs has been reported in several twin studies of anorexic and bulimic pairs (Fitchner & Noegel, 1990; Holland, Hall, Murray, Russell, & Crisp, 1984; Hsu, Chesler, & Santhouse, 1990; Kendler et al., 1991).

The regulation of mood, appetite, hunger, and satiety is complex and controlled by a variety of interrelated biologic mechanisms. Recent studies have documented aberrations in neurotransmitter and neuroendocrine systems that link mood to feeding behavior and impulse control, although no study is conclusive.

Both anorexic and bulimic patients have exhibited dysfunction in serotonin, a neurotransmitter implicated in regulation of mood, impulse, and appetite behavior. Hyposerotonergic function has been documented in anorexic and bulimic patients (Jimerson, Lesem, Kaye, & Brewerton, 1992; Kaye, Ebert, Gwirtsman, & Weiss, 1984; Kaye, Ebert, Raleigh, & Lake, 1984). The low rate of serotonin found in anorexia nervosa is hypothesized to be a result of malnutrition and insufficient dietary tryptophan (Clippen et al., 1976). There is evidence that individuals with bulimia nervosa and depression also exhibit decreased serotonin levels when measured by their response to a specific serotonin agonist, chlorphenylpiperazine (Brewerton, Brandt, Lesem, Murphy, & Jimerson, 1990).

Dysfunction in norepinephrine transmitter sys-

tems are documented in eating disorders. Low norepinephrine levels similar to those noted in depression are found to persist in weight-restored anorectics. Reduced cerebrospinal fluid norepinephrine concentration (Kaye et al., 1990) and possible increased alpha-2-adrenoceptor activity (Heufelder, Warnoff, & Pirke, 1985) are found in bulimic patients.

Additional neuropeptide disturbances are reported in both anorexia and bulimia. Although endogenous opiates seem to be altered, conflicting reports have characterized the research. Cholecystokinin (CCK), a peptide, secreted by the gastrointestinal system and related to satiety, is impaired in some bulimic patients (Geracioti & Liddle, 1988).

Many of the neuroendocrine abnormalities documented in patients with anorexia nervosa are the result of malnutrition. However, the hypothalamic-pituitary ovarian dysfunction resulting in amenorrhea may be a primary dysfunction unrelated to weight loss. One-third of anorectic patients cease to menstruate before appreciable weight loss occurs, and the menstrual disorder may persist even after adequate weight restoration (Halmi, 1974; Morgan & Russell, 1975). The etiology of the menstrual irregularities in anorexia may be the result of specific hypothalamic dysfunction (Walsh, 1980). Reestablishing a regular menstrual cycle has been associated with improved psychological functioning (Falk & Halmi, 1982).

Increased rates of affective disorders, substance abuse disorders, anxiety disorders, and cluster B and C personality disorders are reported in eating-disorder patients. Cluster B personality disorders as grouped in the *DSM-IV* include antisocial, borderline, histrionic, and narcissistic disorders. Cluster C encompasses avoidant, dependent, and obsessive-compulsive disorders. Although certain depressive symptoms are a result of starvation and weight loss, studies support an increased incidence of affective disorder in anorexia and bulimia (Halmi et al., 1991; Laessle, Kittl, Fichter, Whittchen, & Pirke, 1987; Laessle, Whittchen, Fichter, & Pirke, 1989). An increased rate of both bipolar and unipolar affective disorder is reported in first-degree relatives of bulimic patients (Kassett et al., 1989; Mitchell, Hatsukami, Pyle, & Eckert, 1986; Pyle, Mitchell & Eckert, 1981; Strober & Katz, 1987). Studies exploring the relationship between sexual abuse and eating disorders have resulted in conflicting data (Conners &

Morse, 1993; Folsom et al., 1993; Garfinkel et al., 1995; Pope & Hudson, 1992; Rorty, Yager & Rossotto, 1994). The relationship between traumatic events and deficits in self-regulation, which may result in impulsivity, is an area for future investigation.

In an investigation of risk factors based on premorbid psychopathology, 58% of 24 recovered anorectic women reported the presence of one or more childhood anxiety disorders approximately 5 years before the onset of anorexia nervosa symptoms (Deep, Nagy, Weltzin, Rao, & Kaye, 1995). In contrast, depressive symptoms occurred only 1 year prior to anorexia. The authors propose that a biologic vulnerability for anorexia may be expressed earlier in development by the presence of significant anxiety symptoms.

Substance abuse has been closely linked with bulimia (Beary, Lacey, & Merry, 1986; Jonas, Gold, Sweeney, & Pottash, 1987; Lacey & Moureli, 1986; Peveler & Fairburn, 1990). Studies include trends linking purging with drunkenness in 10th-grade girls (Killen et al., 1987a) and increased rates of alcoholism in relatives of bulimics (Kassett et al., 1989).

Although not systematically studied, bulimic patients, but not anorectics, more often exhibit impulsive behaviors such as shoplifting, overspending, and sexual promiscuity. Obsessive-compulsive traits are found more often in the anorectic population. In a review of 11 studies of patients with anorexia nervosa, Rothenberg (1990) asserts that obsessive-compulsive patterns unrelated to eating are common and second only in frequency to affective disorder symptoms in these patients. He further postulates that the typical style of perfectionism, orderliness, cleanliness, rigidity, scrupulousness self-righteousness, and obsessional ruminations frequently seen in these patients lead to a consideration of anorexia nervosa as a variant of obsessive-compulsive disorder. However, many of the studies investigating comorbidity have not been directed specifically to the adolescent population.

NEUROPSYCHOLOGIC FACTORS

No specific personality type characterizes either anorectic or bulimic patients. Both cluster B (antisocial, borderline, histrionic, and narcissistic) and C (avoidant, dependent, obsessive-compulsive)

personality organizations have been reported (Swift & Wonderlich, 1988). Some studies support borderline personality organization in disorders. Object relations theorists and self psychologists have underscored defects in early formation of the self and difficulties in negotiating appropriate separation individuation (Yates, 1989). The oral phase of development marred by oral gratification and tension reduction surrounding oral functions is a critical area for understanding the roots of eating-disorder pathology. The helplessness, lack of mastery, inability to tolerate affective states, defects in self-regulation, and disturbance in body image and concept seem to be rooted in the earliest phase of development. In addition, the primitive defenses of splitting, projection, and denial can be understood from the vantage point of a regression to or fixation in the oral phase of development. Many of these features are explicated in the classic works of Bruch (1973, 1978).

The Offer Self Image Questionnaire (OSIQ), an instrument designed to describe adolescents' feelings about their psychological world in a number of salient areas (Offer, Ostrov, Howard, & Atkinsons, 1990), has been administered to 30,000 normal and psychiatrically disturbed teenagers in a number of national and cross-cultural studies. The parameters studied include facets of adolescent psychosocial development divided into the following aspects of the self: psychological, social, sexual, familial, and coping. Teenagers with eating disorders demonstrate a typical profile with difficulties in many of the OSIQ categories. Further, in a study comparing eating-disordered adolescents to other psychiatric patients and healthy controls, parental discord, hostility, overprotection, and inappropriate pressure were identified as significant perceptions of the eating-disordered girls as distinguished from the two other groups (Horesh et al., 1996).

Social insecurity, overcompliance, dependency, and faulty autonomy are often seen in anorectic patients and may be predisposing factors (Strober, 1985). Bulimic patients more often exhibit traits related to disregulation of affect and impulse. They also have problems in self-regulation, high achievement expectation, and rejection sensitivity (Johnson & Conners, 1987). Correlating dimensions of temperament with vulnerability for eating disorders has received minimal focus in the reseach literature to date. A recent study

(Bulik, Sullivan, Weltzin, & Kaye, 1995) evaluated temperament in 32 eating-disordered women utilizing the Tridimensional Personality Questionnaire (TPQ), an instrument developed by Cloninger and based on his theoretical constructs. Restrictive anorectic patients displayed qualities of high reward dependence. High novelty seeking was typical of bulimic patients; they seemed similar to youths at high risk for alcohol and substance abuse. Mixed anorectic-bulimic patients displayed a harm avoidance profile. Decreased capacity for self-control has been reported in a group of college women who were similar in profile to bulimic patients (Heilbrun & Bloomfield, 1986). The symptoms of overachieving and relentless exercising are categorized as obsessional, whereas cycles of overeating and associated anxiety and guilt are considered to be aspects of impulse discontrol. One study has linked type A personality traits to anorexia in terms of cardiovascular reactivity and elevated hostility scores on a structured interview (Brunner, Maloney, Daniels, Mays, & Farrell, 1989).

The significance of cognitive distortions in body size estimation, although prominent in anorectic patients, has not been determined. Instability in perception of body image has been noted in both anorexia and bulimia. Specific cognitive distortions such as overgeneralization, superstitiousness, and dichotomous thinking have been described as common features in both disorders (Fernandez, 1984; Garner, 1985).

Research is being conducted with taste preference and attention to satiety in an effort to determine deficits in the eating disorders (Heilbrun & Worobow, 1991; Sunday & Halmi, 1990).

SOCIOCULTURAL FACTORS

Traditionally, eating disorders are most common in young, middle and upper socioeconomic families of industrialized nations. Rowland (1970) notes that Jewish, Italian, and Catholic populations have an increased risk of developing the disorder. Yates (1989), in a comprehensive review of eating disorders, asserts that the development of eating disorders in Native American or Hispanic minorities may be related to displacement or removal from traditional values and settings in conjunction with upward socioeconomic mobility. To date there have been few studies of the incidence of eating disorders among American minority groups. In a recent review of the research, Crago (Crago, Shisslak, & Estes, 1996) indicates that the risk for African American and Asian American girls seems to be relatively less compared to Caucasian and Hispanic females. Native American girls seem to carry relatively higher risk for the development of eating disorders.

The influence of the media in promoting thinness and equating this with beauty or desirability has been cited as a significant contributor to the development of eating disorders in a vulnerable group. Models, dancers, and gymnasts are noted for having a high incidence of eating disorders. Additionally, abnormal eating behaviors and attitudes toward food, as well as an increased trend in eating disorders, have been reported in groups of athletes of both sexes, such as runners, divers, male wrestlers, or boxers, in whom weight is a factor in competitiveness or classification (Stoutjesdyk & Jevne, 1993).

DIAGNOSIS, ASSESSMENT, AND TREATMENT

Diagnosis: Diagnosis is made on the basis of the clinical interview, family history, physical examination, and laboratory studies. Although many patients alternate between bulimic and anorectic symptoms (Casper, Eckert, Halmi, Goldberg, & Davis, 1980; Garfinkel, Moldofsky & Garner, 1980; Kassett, Gwirtsman, Kaye, Brandt, & Jimerson, 1988; Mitchell, Pyle, & Eckert, 1985), current diagnostic nomenclature makes a distinction between the two disorders. Aside from the weight-loss criteria, the patients with anorexia nervosa should demonstrate amenorrhea for 3 months, an intense fear of gaining weight, and body image distortion. Bulimia is characterized by binge eating, fears of a lack of control in eating, and concerns with weight and body shape. A variety of methods of purging are seen in this disorder. Although not validated in children and younger adolescents (APA, 1993), a number of self-report instruments are helpful adjuncts in assessment of the eating disorders. (See Table 29.2).

The Diagnostic Interview Schedule for Children, 2nd edition (DISC-2.1) was found to have good sensitivity in establishing a diagnosis of eating disorders in this younger group (Fisher et al., 1993). Anorexia and bulimia have been reported in individuals with insulin-dependent dia-

TABLE 29.2

Self-report Instruments for Eating Disorders

Title	Author	Year
Eating Disorders Inventory (EDI)	Garner, Olmstead, and Poivy	1983
Diagnostic Survey for Eating Disorders (DSED)	Johnson	1985
Eating Disorders Questionnaire	Mitchell, Hatsukami, and Pyle	1985
Self-Rating Scale for Bulimia (BITE)	Henderson and Freeman	1987
Stanford Eating Disorders Questionnaire	Agras	1987
Eating Disorder Examination (EDE-Q)	Fairburn and Beglin	1994

betes, cystic fibrosis, and chronic illnesses in which food metabolism is an aspect.

Because of youths' secretive attitude toward their disordered eating, their families, who have no knowledge of their children's disorder, may refer them to medical specialists for one or more of the signs and symptoms. The pediatrician may be consulted for fatigue and weight loss, or the initial referral may be to the gynecologist for amenorrhea or menstrual irregularities. Symptoms of tooth sensitivity due to periomolysis (loss of enamel and dentition) or toothache related to dental caries from high carbohydrate intake may result in a dentist's being the initial professional to see an eating-disordered adolescent.

Assessment: In evaluating the parameters of an eating disorder, the clinician should review the patient's current and longitudinal eating habits; food preferences and oddities; weight and attitudes toward weight; profile of food restriction; self-induced vomiting, use of purgatives including ipecac and baking soda or medications used for weight control including diuretics, laxatives, and diet pills; obsessive-compulsive rituals relating to food and eating or weighing; exercise patterns; attitudes and affect changes in conjunction with restricting; binging or purging episodes.

Evaluation for comorbid disorders, particularly affective, anxiety, or substance abuse disorders, should be included. Attention should be directed to a history of sexual abuse. A complete developmental history, including loss and separation and the quality of object relations, should be obtained. Cognitive style, coping strategies, personality traits, and impulse control are part of the comprehensive evaluation of an eating disorder. An evaluation of family functioning with attention to specific dysfunctional styles and current secondary gains for the eating-disordered patients should be an aspect of assessment.

Physical signs and symptoms are legion and complex, reflecting disordered metabolism and the sequelae of specific aspects of purging. Thorough medical investigation including laboratory tests are mandatory. Semistarvation may be associated with fatigue, dry skin, orthostatic hypotension, syncope, hypothermia, edema, short stature, osteoporosis, gastrointestinal motility disturbance, cognitive changes, and seizure activity. Bingeing behavior may result in parotid gland enlargement, striae from quick weight change, polyuria, polydyspia, yellowish skin particularly on the palms and soles, and toothache. Purgatives including laxatives and diuretics or self-induced vomiting may result in palpitations, bloody diarrhea, bruises over the knuckles, conjunctival hemorrhages, dry mouth or mouth pain, shortness of breath, and a variety of fluctuating mineral and fluid imbalances (APA, 1993; Powers, 1984).

Laboratory Evaluation: Standard initial laboratory studies include a complete blood count and differential, urinalysis, thyroid profile, chemistry panel, and electrocardiogram. Other diagnostic tests should be selected for specific signs and symptoms displayed by the individual patient. Serial monitoring of mineral or electrolyte parameters is important. However, clinically significant hypokalemia has been demonstrated to be a rare phenomenon in eating-disordered patients and has been documented as occurring only in low-weight patients who are purging at least daily (Greenfield, Mickley, Quinlan, & Roloff, 1995). Specific studies such as serum amylase, estradiol level, leutinizing hormone, follicle stimulating hormone levels, bone mineral densitometry, and a magnetic resonance imaging (MRI) or computed tomography (CT) scan may be useful in certain patients. However, the abnormalities frequently demonstrated on CT or MRI scans of the head have not been documented as having prognostic significance (APA, 1993; Powers, 1984).

Treatment: Treatment of the eating-disordered adolescent should be comprehensive, multimodal, and targeted to specific symptom constellations. To date, no single treatment regime has proven superior as the optimal approach to these chronic, frequently relapsing disorders. There seems to be promise in using techniques designed to remediate defective impulse control particularly targeted to bulimic symptomatology.

Outpatient treatment is the method of choice in bulimia. Approximately 75% of anorectic patients require hospitalization for weight restoration and modification of their low motivation for change.

In treatment of the anorectic patient, an initial goal should be directed to restoration to a weight of 90 to 100% of ideal body weight. More specifically, the target weight should be at a level where reproductive function in the adolescent resumes. Nutritional counseling and individual and family supportive psychotherapy should be early intervention strategies, and behavior modification techniques are also helpful for improving weight gain. However, strict behavioral contingencies do not have a significant advantage over loose behavior programs in weight restoration. Studies to date have supported both approaches to the achievement of weight gain (Nusbaum & Drever, 1990).

In uncomplicated anorexia nervosa, no psychotropic medications have particular value. Cyproheptadine (Halmi, Eckert, Ladee, & Cohen, 1986) has been of some benefit in increasing appetite. The outpatient treatment of anorexia should be individualized and multimodal. Individual, group, and family therapy and cognitive-behav-

ioral strategies have all been efficacious although poorly studied. Psychodynamic or interpersonal therapies directed to issues of adolescent development, defects in ego, and pathologic defenses have been clinically useful and in some cases may achieve more durable results in youths with eating disorders (APA, 1993). Once adequate nutritional balance is achieved, medications may be useful in relieving symptoms of specific comorbid disorders, such as affective or anxiety disorders. Fluoxetine has been reported to improve weight maintenance after weight restoration as well as to reduce obsessionality (Kaye, Weltzin, Hsu, & Bulik, 1991).

Most patients with bulimia nervosa can be managed effectively as outpatients. Group therapy, cognitive-behavioral techniques, and psychodynamic and interpersonal therapy have each been demonstrated to lead to improvement in various controlled and uncontrolled studies as well as in clinical reports. Cognitive-behavioral therapy using self-monitoring techniques aimed at normalizing dietary intake, altering distortions of body shape and weight, and removing rigidity and rules about foods and eating is an efficacious treatment modality in many controlled studies (Fairburn, 1988). Several recent reports, however, endorsed the use of interpersonal therapy that did not address eating as a therapeutic issue (Agras, 1991). This finding supports the thesis that the antecedents of personal stress and dysphoria are etiologically significant in the development of an eating disorder and, if remediated, will effectively reduce symptoms. Double-blind placebo-controlled studies have demonstrated that all antidepressants, including tricyclic antidepressants, MAOIs, and fluoxetine, are effective in reducing the binge/purge cycle in bulimics. Both depressed and nondepressed patients with bulimia respond with improvement (Walsh, 1991).

Conclusion

Certain adolescents who develop substance abuse and eating disorders share underlying etiologic factors related to poor impulse control. These factors include a common biologic vulnerability evidenced in genetic predisposition and neurotransmitter function especially noted in serotonin regulation and in psychological traits such as low self-esteem and depression. The outcome of these vulnerabilities may be determined by characteristics within the family and in the culture. The social context of the vulnerable individual may help to contain or support some young people, while it may direct others to such disorders as substance abuse and/or eating disorders.

Treatment of impulse control disorders also shares commonalities across specific disorders. Biologic vulnerabilities should be recognized and discussed, as they help to explain ways of behaving and feeling. Altered neurotransmitter function can be treated with agents that primarily affect the dysfunctional system. Psychological interventions, such as behavioral programs and cognitive treatments, help to contain impulses and develop coping skills. They are particularly useful in the early to middle phases of treatment. Psychodynamic approaches help the adolescent understand underlying drives that lead to greater internal control. Family therapy and environmental examination and restructuring help to contain and redirect dysfunctional behavior.

While the concept of impulse control dysfunction is useful in understanding the etiology and guiding the treatment for many adolescents with substance abuse and eating disorders, we are not proposing this as a model for all adolescents with these disorders. Certain adolescents may develop these disorders without having poor impulse control as the major dysfunction. For those who do have impulse control problems, however, the conceptualization is useful and meaningful.

REFERENCES

Agras, W. S. (1987). The eating disorders: Assessment. In *Eating disorders: Management of obesity, bulimia and anorexia nervosa* (pp. 16–28). New York: Pergamon Press.

Agras, W. S. (1991). Nonpharmacologic treatments of bulimia nervosa. *Journal of Clinical Psychiatry 52* (suppl.) 29–33.

American Psychiatric Association. (1980). *Diagnostic and statistical manual of mental disorders* (3rd ed.). Washington, DC: Author.

American Psychiatric Association. (1987). *Diagnostic and statistical manual of mental disorders*, (3rd ed., rev.). Washington, DC: Author.

American Psychiatric Association. (1993). APA practice guideline for eating disorders. *American Journal of Psychiatry, 150,* 212—228.

American ,Psychiatric Association. (1994). *Diagnostic and statistical manual of mental disorders* (4th ed.). Washington, DC: Author.

Apter, A., Bleich, A., Plutchik, R., Mendelsohn, S., & Tyano, S. (1988). Suicidal behavior, depression, and conduct disorder in hospitalized adolescents. *Journal of the American Academy of Child and Adolescent Psychiatry, 27,* 696–699.

Apter, A., Gothelf, D., Orbach, I., Weizman, R., Ratzoni, G., Har-Even, D., & Tyano, S. (1995). Correlation of suicidal and violent behavior in different diagnostic categories in hospitalized adolescent patients. *Journal of American Academy of Child and Adolescent Psychiatry, 34* (7), 912–918.

Bailey, G. W. (1989). Current perspectives on substance abuse in Youth. *Journal of the American Academy of Child and Adolescent Psychiatry, 28,* 151–162.

Ballenger, J. C., Goodwin, F. K., Major, L. F., Brown, G. L. (1979). Alcohol and central serotonin metabolism in man. *Archives of General Psychiatry, 36,* 224–227.

Barrett, M. E., Simpson, D. D., & Lehman, W. E. (1988). Behavioral changes of adolescents in drug abuse intervention programs. *Journal of Clinical Psychiatry, 44,* 461–473.

Beary, M., Lacey, J., & Merry, J. (1986). Alcoholism and eating disorders in women of fertile age. *British Journal of Addiction, 81,* 685–689.

Begleiter, H., & Porjesz, B. (1986). Potential biological markers in individuals at high risk for developing alcoholism. *Alcoholism, 12,* 488–493.

Biederman, J., Baldessarini, R. J., Wright, V., et al. (1989). A double-blind placebo controlled study of desipramine in the treatment of ADD: I. Efficacy. *Journal of American Academy of Child and Adolescent Psychiatry, 28,* 777–784.

Blum, K., Noble, E. P., Sheridan, P. J., Montgomery, A., Ritchie, T., Jagadeeswaran, P., Nogami, H., Briggs, A. H., & Cohn, J. B. (1990). Allelic association of human dopamine D_2 receptor gene in alcoholism. *Journal of the American Medical Association, 263,* 2055–2060.

Brent, D. A., Perper, J. A., & Allman, G. T. (1987). Alcohol, firearms and suicide among youth: Temporal trends in Allegheny County, Pennsylvania, 1960–1983. *Journal of the American Medical Association, 257,* 3369–3372.

Brewerton, T. D., Brandt, H. A., Lesem, M. D., Murphy, D. L., & Jimerson, D. C. (1990). Serotonin in major psychiatric disorders. In E. F. Coccaro and D. L. Murphy (Eds.), *Serotonin in major psychiatric disorders* (pp. 153–184). Washington, DC: American Psychiatric Press.

Bruch, H. (1973). *Eating disorders: Obesity, anorexia*

nervosa and the person within. New York: Basic Books.

Bruch, H. (1978). *The golden cage: The enigma of anorexia nervosa.* Cambridge, MA: Harvard University Press.

Brunner, R. L., Maloney, M. J., Daniels, S., Mays, W., & Farrell, M. (1989). A controlled study of type A behavior and psychophysiologic responses to stress in anorexia nervosa. *Psychiatry Research, 30,* 223–230.

Bry, B. H. (1988). Family-based approaches to reducing adolescent substance abuse: Theories, techniques, and findings. *NIDA Research Monograph, 77,* 39–68.

Bukstein, O. G., Brent, D. A., & Kaminer, Y. (1989). Comorbidity of substance abuse and other psychiatric disorders in adolescence. *American Journal of Psychiatry, 146,* 1121–1141.

Bulik, C. M., Sullivan, P. F., Weltzin, T. E., & Kaye, W. H. (1995). Temperament in eating disorders. *International Journal of Eating Disorders, 17,* 251–261.

Burke, J. D., Burke, K. C., & Rae, D. S. (1994). Increased rates of drug abuse and dependence after onset of mood or anxiety disorders. *Hospital and Community Psychiatry, 45,* 451–455.

Buydens-Branchey, L., Branchey, M. H., & Noumair, D. (1989). Age of alcoholism onset I. Relationship to psychopathology. *Archives of General Psychiatry, 46,* 225–230.

Buydens-Branchey, L., Branchey, M. H., Noumair, D., & Lieber, C. S. (1989). Age of alcoholism onset II. Relationship to susceptibility to serotonin precursor availability. *Archives of General Psychiatry, 46,* 231–236.

Carlat, D. J., & Camargo, C. A. (1991). Review of bulimia nervosa in males. *American Journal of Psychiatry, 178* (7), 831–843.

Casper, R. C., Eckert, E. D., Halmi, K. A., Goldberg, S. C., & Davis, J. M. (1980). Bulimia, its incidence and important in patients with anorexia nervosa. *Archives of General Psychiatry, 37,* 1030–1044.

Clippen, A. V., Gupta, R. K., Eccleston, E. G., Wood, K. M., Wakeling, A., & De Sousa, V. F. A. (1976). Plasma tryptophan in anorexia nervosa. *Lancet, 1,* 962.

Cloninger, C. R. (1987). Neurogenic adaptive mechanisms in alcoholism. *Science, 236,* 410–416.

Comings, D. E., Comings, B. G., et al. (1991). The dopamine D2 receptor locus as a modifying gene in neuropsychiatric disorders. *Journal of the American Medical Association, 266,* 1793–1800.

Connors, M. E., Morse, W. (1993). Sexual abuse and eating disorders: a review. *International Journal of Eating Disorders, 13,* 1–11.

Crago, M., Shisslak, C. M., & Estes, L. S. (1996). Eating disturbances among American minority groups: A review. *International Journal of Eating Disorders, 19,* 239–248.

Crumley, F. E. (1990). Substance abuse and adolescent suicidal behavior. *Journal of the American Medical Association, 263,* 3051–3056.

Deep, A. L., Nagy, L. M., Weltzin, T. E., Rao, R., & Kaye, W. H. (1995). Premorbid onset of psychopa-

thology in long-term recovered anorexia nervosa. *International Journal of Eating Disorders, 17,* 291–297.

Demilio, L. (1989). Psychiatric syndromes in adolescent substance abusers. *American Journal of Psychiatry, 146,* 1212–1214.

Devor, E. J., & Cloninger, C. R. (1989). Genetics of alcoholism. *Annals of Reviews of Genetics, 23,* 119–136.

Fairburn, C. G. (1988). The current status of psychological treatments of bulimia nervosa. *Journal of Psychosomatic Research, 32,* 635–645.

Fairburn, C. G., & Beglin, S. J. (1994). Assessment of eating disorders: Interview or self report questionnaire? *International Journal of Eating Disorders, 16,* 363–370.

Falk, J. R., & Halmi, K.A. (1982). Amenorrhea in anorexia nervosa. *Journal of Biologic Psychiatry, 17,* 799–806.

Fawzy, F. I., Coombs, R. H., & Gerber, B. E. (1983). Generational continuity in the use of substances: The impact of parental substance use on adolescent substance use. *Addictive Behaviors, 8,* 109–114.

Fernandez, R. C. (1984). Disturbances in cognition: Implications for treatment. In P. S. Powers & R. C. Fernandez (Eds.), *Current treatment of anorexia nervosa and bulemia* (pp. 133–142). New York: Karger.

Fisher, P. W., Shaffer, D., Piacentini, J. C., Lapkin, J., Kafantaris, V., Leonard, H., & Herzog, D. B. (1993). Sensitivity of the Diagnostic Interview Schedule for Children, 2nd edition (DISC-2.1) for specific diagnoses of children and adolescents. *Journal of the American Academy of Child and Adolescent Psychiatry, 32,* 666–673.

Fitchner, M. M., & Noegel, R. (1990). Concordance for bulimia nervosa in twins. *International Journal of Eating Disorders, 9,* 255–263.

Flannery, D. J., Vazgonyi, A. T., Torquati, J., Fridrich, A. (1994). Ethnic and gender differences in risk for early adolescent substance abuse. *Journal of Youth and Adolescence, 23,* 195–213.

Folsom, V., Drahn, D., Nairn, K., Gold, L., Demitrack, M. A., & Silk, K. R. (1993). The impact of sexual and physical abuse on eating disordered and psychiatric symptoms: A comparison of eating disordered nd psychiatric inpatients. *American Journal of Psychiatry, 13,* 249–257.

Fombonne, E. (1995). Anorexia nervosa. No evidence of an increase. *British Journal of Psychiatry, 166,* 462–471.

Fombonne, E. (1996). Is bulimia nervosa increasing in frequency? *International Journal of Eating Disorders, 19,* 287–296.

Fowler, R. C., Rich, C. L., & Young, D. (1986). San Diego suicide study II. Substance abuse in young cases. *Archives of General Psychiatry, 43,* 962–965.

Friedman, A. S., & Glickman, N. W. (1987). Effects of psychiatric symptomology on treatment outcome for male drug abusers. *Journal of Nervous and Mental Diseases, 175,* 419–424.

Gabel, S., Stadler, J., Bjorn, J., Shindledecker, R., & Bowden, C. L. (1994). Sensation seeking in psychiatrically disturbed youth: Relationship to biochemical parameters and behavior problems. *Journal of American Academy of Child and Adolescent Psychiatry, 33* (1), 123–129.

Garfinkel, P. E., & Garner, D. M. (1982). *Anorexia nervosa: Multidimensional perspective.* New York: Brunner/Mazel.

Garfinkel, P. E., Lin, E., Goering, P., Spegg, C., Goldbloom, D. S., Kennedy, S., Kaplan, A. S., & Woodside, D. B. (1995). Bulimia nervosa in a Canadian community sample: Prevalence and comparison of subgroups. *American Journal of Psychiatry, 152,* 1052–1058.

Garfinkel, P. E., Moldofsky, H., & Garner, D. M. (1980). The heterogeneity of anorexia nervosa. *Archives of General Psychiatry, 37,* 1036–1040.

Garner, D. M. (1985). Cognitive therapy for bulimia nervosa. *Annals of Adolescent Psychiatry, 13,* 358–390.

Garner, D. M., Olmstead, M. P., & Poivy, J. (1983). Development and validation of a multidimensional inventory for anorexia nervosa and bulimia. *International Journal of Eating Disorders, 2,* 15–34.

Geracioti, T. D., & Liddle, R. A. (1988). Impaired cholecystokinin secretion in bulimia nervosa. *New England Journal of Medicine, 319,* 683–688.

Gershon, E. S., Schneiber, J. L., & Hamourt, J. R. (1983). Anorexia nervosa and major affective disorders associated in families: A preliminary report. In S. B. Guze, F. Earls, and J. E. Barrett (Eds.), *Childhood psychopathology an development* (pp. 279–284). New York: Raven Press.

Goodwin, D. W. (1983). The genetics of alcoholism. *Hospital and Community Psychiatry, 34,* 1031–1034.

Greenfield, D., Mickley, D., Quinlan, D. M., & Roloff, P. (1995). Hypokalemia in outpatients with eating disorders. *American Journal of Psychiatry, 152,* 60–63.

Halmi, K. A. (1974). Anorexia nervosa: Demographic and clinical features in 94 cases. *Psychosomatic Medicine, 36,* 18–26.

Halmi, K. A., Eckert, E., Ladee, T. J., & Cohen, J. (1986). Anorexia nervosa: Treatment efficacy of cyproheptadine and amitriptyline. *Archives of General Psychiatry, 43,* 177–181.

Halmi, K. A., Eckert, E., Marchi, A., Sampugnaro, V., Apple, R., & Cohen, J. (1991). Comorbidity of psychiatric diagnoses in anorexia nervosa. *Archives of General Psychiatry, 48,* 712–718.

Heilbrun, A. B., & Bloomfield, D. L. (1986). Cognitive differences between bulimia and anorexic females: Self control deficits in bulimia. *International Journal of Eating Disorders, 5,* 209–222.

Heilbrun, A. B., & Worobow, A. L. (1991). Attention and disordered eating behavior: Disattention to satiety cues as a risk factor in the development of bulimia. *Journal of Clinical Psychology, 47,* 3–9.

Henderson, M., & Freeman, C. P. L. (1987). A self rating scale for bulimia, the BITE. *British Journal of Psychiatry, 150,* 18–24.

Herning, R. I., Hickey, J. E., Pickworth, W. B., & Jaffe, J. H. (1989). Auditory event-related potentials in adolescents at risk for drug abuse. *Biological Psychiatry, 25,* 598–609.

Heufelder, A., Warnoff, M., & Pirke, K. M. (1985). Platelet alpha 2 adrenoceptor activity and adenylate cyclase in patients with anorexia and bulimia. *Journal of Clinical Endocrinology and Metabolism, 61,* 1053–1060.

Holland, A. J., Hall, A., Murray, R., Russell, G. F., & Crisp, A. H. (1984). Anorexia nervosa: A study of 34 twins pairs and one set of triplets. *British Journal of Psychiatry, 145,* 414–419.

Holmberg, M. G. (1985). Longitudinal studies of drug abuse in a 15-year-old population, 2: Antecedents and consequences. *Acta Psychiatrica Scandinavica, 71,* 80–91.

Horesh, N., Apter, A., Ishai, J., Danziger, Y., Miculcinar, M., Stein, D., Lepkifker, E., & Minouni, M. (1996). Abnormal psychosocial situations and eating disorders in adolescence. *Journal of the American Academy of Child and Adolescent Psychiatry, 35,* 921–927.

Hsu, K. G., Chesler, B. E., & Santhouse, R. (1990). Bulimia nervosa in eleven sets of twins: A clinical report. *International Journal of Eating Disorders, 9,* 275–282.

Jimerson, D. C., Lesem, M. O., Kaye, W. H., & Brewerton, T. D. (1992). Low seratonin and dopamine metabolite concentrations in cerebrospinal fluid from bulimic patients with frequent binge episodes. *Archives of General Psychiatry, 49,* 132–138.

Johnson, C. (1985). Initial consultation for patients with bulimia and anorexia nervosa. In D. M. Garner & P. E. Garfinkel (Eds.), *Handbook for psychotherapy for anorexia nervosa and bulimia.* (pp. 19–54). New York: Guilford Press.

Johnson, C. L., & Connors, M. E. (1987). *The etiology and treatment of bulimia nervosa.* New York: Basic Books.

Jonas, J. M., Gold, M. S., Sweeney, D., & Pottash, A. L. (1987). Eating disorders and cocaine abuse: A survey of 259 cocaine abusers. *Journal of Clinical Psychiatry, 48,* 47–50.

Kandel, D., & Logan, J. (1984). Patterns of drug use from adolescence to young adulthood. I. Periods of risk for initiation, continued use, and discontinuation. *American Journal of Public Health, 74,* 660–666.

Kandel, D. B., & Raveis, V. H. (1989). Cessation of illicit drug use in young adulthood. *Archives of General Psychiatry, 46,* 109–116.

Kandel, D. B., Raveis, V. H., & Davies, M. (1991). Suicidal ideation in adolescence: Depression, substance use and other risk factors. *Journal of Youth and Adolescence, 20,* 289–309.

Kassett, J. A., Gershon, E. S., Maxwell, M. E., Guroff, J. H., Kazuba, D. M., Smith, A. L., Brandt, M. A., & Jimerson, D. C. (1989). Psychiatric disorders in the first degree relatives of probands with bulimia nervosa. *American Journal of Psychiatry, 146,* 1468–1471.

Kassett, J. A., Gwirtsman, H. E., Kaye, W. H., Brandt,

300

H. A., & Jimerson, D. C. (1988). Pattern of onset of bulimic symptoms in anorexia nervosa. *American Journal of Psychiatry, 145,* 1287–1288.

Kaye, W. H., Ballenger, J. C., Lydiard, R. B., Stuart, G. W., Laraia, M. T., O'Neil, P., & Fossey, M. D. (1990). CSF monoamine levels in normal weight bulimia: Evidence for altered noradrenergic activity. *American Journal of Psychiatry, 147,* 225–229.

Kaye, W. H., Ebert, M. H., Raleigh, M., & Lake, R. (1984). Abnormalities in CSF monoamine metabolism in anorexia nervosa. *Archives of General Psychiatry, 41,* 350–355.

Kaye, W. H., Ebert, M. H., Gwirtsman, H. E., & Weiss, S. R. (1984). Differences in brain serotonergic metabolism between bulimic and nonbulimic patients with anorexia nervosa. *American Journal of Psychiatry, 141,* 1598–1601.

Kaye, W. H., Weltzin, T. E., Hsu, L. K., & Bulik, C. M. (1991). An open trial of fluoxetine in patients with aneroxia nervosa. *Journal of Clinical Psychiatry, 52,* 464–471.

Kellam, S., Ialongo, N., Brown, H., Laudolff, J., Mirsky, A., Anthony, B., Aheram, M., Anthony, J., Edelsohn, G., & Dolan, L. (1989). Attention problems in first grade and shy and aggressive behaviors as antecedents to later heavy or inhibited substance use. *NIDA Research Monograph, 95,* 368–369.

Kendler, K. S., MacLean, C., Neale, M., Kessler, R., Heath, A., & Eaves, L. (1991). The genetic epidemiology of bulimia nervosa. *American Journal of Psychiatry, 148* (12), 1627–1637.

Killen, J. D., Taylor, C. B., Telch, M. J., Robinson, T. N., Maron, D. J., & Saylor, K. E. (1987a). Depressive symptoms and substance abuse among adolescent binge eaters and purgers: A defined population study. *American Journal of Public Health, 77,* 1539–1541.

Killen, J. D., Taylor, C. B., Telch, M. J., Robinson, T. N., Maron, T. O., Saylor, K. E. (1987b). Evidence for an alcohol stress link among normal weight adolescents reporting purging behavior. *International Journal of Eating Disorders, 6,* 349–356.

Lacey, J., & Moureli, E. (1986). Bulimic alcoholics: Some findings of a clinical subgroup. *British Journal of Addiction, 81,* 389–393.

Laessle, R. G., Kittl, S., Fichter, M. M., Whittchen, M. U., & Pirke, K. M. (1987). Major affective disorder in anorexia nervosa and bulimia: A descriptive diagnostic study. *Psychiatry, 151,* 785–789.

Laessle, R., Whittchen, H., Fichter, M. M., & Pirke, K. M. (1989). The significance of subgroups of bulimia and anorexia nervosa: Lifetime frequency of psychiatric disorders. *International Journal of Eating Disorders, 8,* 569–574.

Lee, M., & Prentice, N. M. (1988). Interrelations of empathy, cognition, and moral reasoning with dimensions of juvenile delinquency. *Abnormal Child Psychology, 16,* 127–139.

Levy, J. C., & Deykin, E. Y. (1989). Suicidality, depression, and substance abuse in adolescence. *American Journal of Psychiatry, 146,* 1462–1467.

Linnoila, R. A. (1988). Suicidal behavior, impulsiveness and serotonin. *Acta Psychiatrica Scandinavica, 74,* 529–535.

Linnoila, M., DeJong, J., & Virkkunen, M. (1989). Family history of alcoholism in violent offenders and impulsive fire setters. *Archives of General Psychiatry, 46,* 613–616.

Lucas, A. R. (1991). Eating disorders. In J. M. Werner (Ed.), *The comprehensive textbook of child and adolescent psychiatry* (pp. 573–583). Washington, DC: American Psychiatric Press.

Martin, K. P., & Coleman, E. (1991). Serotonin and paraphilias: The convergence of mood, impulse and compulsive disorders. *Journal of Clinical Psychopharmacology, 11* (3), 224 (1982).

May, P. A. (1982). Substance abuse and American Indians: Prevalence and susceptability. *International Journal of Addictions, 17,* 1185–1209.

McDermott, D. (1984). The relationships of parental drug use and parents' attitudes concerning adolescent drug use to adolescent drug use. *Adolescence, 19,* 89–97.

Mitchell, J., Hatsukami, D., & Pyle, R. (1985). Eating Disorders Questionnaire. *Psychoparhmocology Bulletin, 21,* 1025–1043.

Mitchell, J., Hatsukami, D., Pyle, R., & Eckert, E. D. (1986). Bulimia with and without a family history of depressive illness. *Comprehensive Psychiatry, 27,* 215–219.

Mitchell, J. E., Pyle, R. L., & Eckert, E. D. (1985). Bulimia. In E. Hales & A. Frances (Eds.), *American Psychiatric Association Annual Review* (Vol. 4, pp. 464–480). Washington, DC: American Psychiatric Press.

Morgan, H. G., & Russell, G. S. M. (1975). Value of family background and clinical features as predictors of long term outcome in anorexia nervosa. *Psychological Medicine, 5,* 355–371.

Morrison, M. A. (1990). Addiction in adolescents. In Addiction Medicine (Special Issue), *Western Journal of Medicine, 152,* 543–546.

Moss, H. B., Guthie, S., & Linnoila, M. (1986). Enhanced thyrotropin response to thyrotropin releasing hormone in boys at risk for development of alcoholism. *Archives of General Psychiatry, 43,* 1137–1142.

National Institute on Drug Abuse. (1990). *High school senior drug use 1975–1989.* Rockville, MD: Author.

Nusbaum, J. G., Drever, E. (1990). Inpatient survey of nursing care measures for treatment of patients with anorexia nervosa. *Issues in Mental Health Nursing, 11,* 175–184.

Offer, D., Ostrov, E., Howard, K. I., & Atkinsons, R. (1990). Normality and adolescence. *Psychiatric Clinics of North America, 13* (3), 377–388.

Pearson, H. J. (1990). Paraphilias, impulse control, and serotonin. *Journal of Clinical Psycholpharmacology, 10* (3), 233.

Pedersen, W., Clausen, S.-E., & Lavik, N. J. (1989) Patterns of drug use and sensation seeking among adolescents in Norway. *Acta Psychiatrica Scandinavica, 79,* 386–390.

Peveler, R., & Fairburn, C. (1990). Eating disorders in women who abuse alcohol. *British Journal of Addiction, 85,* 1633–1638.

Pickens, R. W., Svikis, D. S., McGue, M., Lykken, D. T., Heston, L. L., & Clayton, P. J. (1991). Heterogeneity in the inheritance of alcoholism: A study of male and female twins. *Archives of General Psychiatry, 48,* 19–28.

Pompi, K. F., & Resnick, J. (1987). Retention of court-referred adolescents and young adults in the therapeutic community. *American Journal of Drug and Alcohol Abuse, 13,* 309–325.

Pope, H. G., & Hudson, J. I. (1992). Is childhood sexual abuse a risk factor for bulimia nervosa? *American Journal of Psychiatry, 149,* 455–463.

Powers, P. S. (1984). Therapeutic use of symptoms, signs and laboratory data. In P. S. Powers & R. D. Fernandez (Eds.), *Current treatment of anorexia nervosa and bulimia* (pp. 215–235). New York: Karger.

Pyle, R. L., Mitchell, J. E., & Eckert, E. D. (1981). Bulimia: A report of 34 cases. *Journal of Clinical Psychiatry, 42,* 60–64.

Raine, A., Brennan, P., & Mednick, S. A. (1994). Birth complications combined with early maternal rejection at age 1 year predispose to violent crime at age 18 years. *Archives of General Psychiatry, 51,* 984–988.

Riggs, P. D., Baker, S., Mikulich, S. K., Young, S. E., & Crowley, T. J. (1995). Depression in substance-dependent delinquents. *Journal of the American Academy of Child and Adolescent Psychiatry, 34* (6), 764–771.

Rorty, M., Yager, J., & Rossotto, E. (1994). Childhood sexual, physical and psychological abuse in bulimia nervosa. *American Journal of Psychiatry, 151,* 1122–1126.

Rosenthal, N., Davenport, Y., Cowdry, R., Webster, M., & Goodwin, F. (1989). Monoamine metabolites in cerebrospinal fluid of depressive subgroups. *Psychiatry Research, 2,* 113–119.

Rothenberg, A. (1990). Adolescence and eating disorder: The obsessive-compulsive syndrome. *Psychiatric Clinics of North America, 13,* 469–488.

Rowland, C. (1970). Anorexia and obesity. *International Psychiatry Clinics, 1,* 37–137.

Roy, A., Virkkunen, M., & Linnoila, M. (1987). Reduced central serotonin turnover in a subgroup of alcoholics? *Progress in Neuropsychopharmacology and Biological Psychiatry, 11,* 173–177.

Schatzberg, A. F., & Cole, J. O. (1991). *Manual of clinical psychopharmacology* (2nd ed.). Washington, DC: American Psychiatric Press.

Schukit, M. A. (1986). Genetic and clinical implications of alcoholism and affective disorders. *American Journal of Psychiatry, 143,* 140–147.

Silverman, I. W., & Ragusa, D. M. (1993). A short-term longitudinal study of the early development of self-regulation. *Journal of Abnormal Psychology, 20* (4), 415–435.

Spitzer, R. L., Yanovski, S., Wadden, T., Wing, R., Marcus, M. D., Stunkard, A., Devlin, M., Mitchell, J., Hasin, D., & Horne, R. L. (1993). Binge eating disorder: Its further validation in a multisite study. *International Journal of Eating Disorders, 13,* 137–153.

Stoff, D. M., Friedman, E., Pollock, L. Vitiello, B., Kendall, P. C., & Bridger, W. H. (1989). Elevated platelet MAO is related to impulsivity in disruptive behavior disorders. *Journal of the American Academy of Child and Adolescent Psychiatry, 28,* (5), 754–760.

Stoutjesdyk, D., & Jevne, R. (1993). Eating disorders among high performance athletes. *Journal of Youth and Adolescence, 22,* 271–282.

Strober, M. (1985). Personality factors in anorexia nervosa. *Pediatrics, 2,* 134–138.

Strober, M., & Katz, J. L. (1987). Do eating disorders and affective disorders share a common etiology? *International Journal of Eating Disorders, 6,* 171–180.

Strober, M., Lampert, C., Morrell, W., & Burroughs, J. (1990). A controlled family study of anorexia nervosa: Evidence of familial aggregation and lack of shared transmission with affective disorders. *International Journal of Eating Disorders, 9,* 239–253.

Sullivan, P. F. (1995). Mortality in anorexia nervosa. *American Journal of Psychiatry, 152,* 1073–1074.

Sunday, S. R., & Halmi, K. A. (1990). Task perceptions and hedonics in eating disorders. *Psychologic Behavior, 48,* 587–594.

Swain, R. C., Oetting, E. R., Edwards, R. W., & Beavais, F. (1989). Links from emotional distress to adolescent drug use: A path model. *Journal of Consultation and Clinical Psychology, 57,* 227–231.

Swift, W. J., & Wonderlich, S. A. (1988). Personality factors and diagnoses in eating disorders: Traits, disorders and structures. In D. M. Garner & P. E. Garfinkel (Eds.), *Diagonstic issues in anorexia nervosa and bulimia nervosa* (pp. 112–165). New York: Brunner/Mazel.

Szapocznik, J., Perez-Vidal, A., Brickman, A. L., Foote, F. H., Santisteban, D., & Hervis, O. (1988). Engaging adolescent drug abusers and their families in treatment: A strategic structural systems approach. *Journal of Consulting and Clinical Psychology, 56,* 552–557.

Tarter, R. E., Laird, S. B., Kabene, M., Bukstein, O., & Kaminer, Y. (1990). Drug abuse severity in adolescents is associated with magnitude of deviation in temperament traits. *British Journal of Addiction, 85,* 1501–1504.

Timmerman, M. G., Wells, L. A., & Chen, S. (1990). Bulimia nervosa and associated alcohol abuse among secondary school students. *Journal of the American Academy of Child and Adolescent Psychiatry, 29,* 118–122.

Virkkunen, M., Rawlings, R., Tokola, R., Poland, R., Guidotti, A., Nemeroff, C., Bissette, G., Kalogeras, K., Karonen, S. L., & Linnoila, M. (1994). CSF biochemistries, glucose metabolism, and diurnal activity rhythms in alcoholic, violent offenders, fire setters, and healthy volunteers. *Archives of General Psychiatry, 51,* 20–27.

Walsh, B. T. (1980). The endocrinology of anorexia nervosa. *Psychiatric Clinics of North America, 3,* 299–312.

Walsh, B. T. (1991). Psychopharmacologic treatment of bulimia nervosa. *Journal of Clinical Psychiatry, 52* (suppl.), 34–38.

Weidman, A. A. (1987). Family therapy and reductions in treatment dropout in a residential therapeutic community for chemically dependent adolescents. *Journal of Substance Abuse and Treatment, 4,* 21–28.

Wolin, S. J., & Bennett, L. A. (1980). Disrupted family rituals: A factor in the intergenerational transmission of alcoholism. *Journal of Studies on Alcohol, 41,* 199–214.

Yates, A. (1989). Current perspectives on the eating disorders: History, psychological and biological aspects. *Journal of the American Academy of Child and Adolescent Psychiatry, 28,* 813–828.

30 / Mood Disorders in Adolescents

Rebecca Rendleman and John T. Walkup

Over the last 20 years much research has been done to identify the phenomenology of mood disorders in children and adolescents (Kovacs & Gatsonis, 1989; Ryan et al., 1987; Strober & Carlson, 1982). Studies have validated mood disorder diagnoses by demonstrating that children and adolescents can reliably meet diagnostic criteria for a variety of mood disorders and that mood disorders can be differentiated from other psychiatric disorders by the clinical presentation, natural course of symptoms, family history, risk for comorbid conditions, and outcome.

Early-onset mood disorders are not transient, benign conditions but pose an increased risk for chronicity, for the development of more severe forms of mood disorders, such as bipolar disorder, and for the development of comorbid psychiatric disorders. Evidence from family aggregation studies (Puig-Antich, 1987). and longitudinal studies (Kovacs & Gatsonis, 1989) suggest that early-onset mood disorders are seen with increased frequency within families and are continuous with mood disorders in adulthood.

Mood disorders in children and adolescents are often unidentified when presenting with other psychiatric disorders or medical problems or viewed as expected reactions to difficult life circumstances. As a result, mood disorders in children and adolescents, like those in adults, are often underdiagnosed and inappropriately treated. In this chapter we review the current literature and provide a guide to the treatment and management of children and adolescents with mood disorders.

Major Depression

NOSOLOGY

The absence of an accepted definition of the term "depression" accounts for much of the controversy surrounding the diagnosis of major depression in children and adolescents (Angold, 1988). Depression can refer to a symptom of low or sad mood, a syndrome encompassing a group of individual symptoms that consistently cluster together, or a disorder distinguished by a distinct course of illness, family history, treatment response, or outcome (Carlson & Cantwell, 1980). While the first two concepts may or may not be pathological entities, the third represents a disorder or disease.

The great advances in the past 20 years in the identification and validation of major depression in children and adolescents reflect the increased rigor and specificity of the nosology used in research studies. This chapter focuses on the concept of major depression as a disorder. The current operational criteria for major depressive disorder in children and adolescents are the same as for adults and are outlined in the fourth edition of the *Diagnostic and Statistical Manual of Mental Disorders* (*DSM-IV*) (American Psychiatric Association, 1994). (See Table 30.1.)

EPIDEMIOLOGY

Prevalence studies of depression in children and adolescents have been fraught with a number of methodological problems, resulting in widely varying prevalence rates. Problems that have been identified include sample characteristics, method of ascertainment, source of information, and diagnostic criteria (Angold, 1988; Kashani, & Sherman, 1988). Lower prevalence rates are seen in studies that utilize: parental interviews alone rather than those relying on child reports or combined child and parent reports, semistructured interviews rather than questionnaires or rating scales, and community samples rather than patient populations.

Studies that utilize strict diagnostic criteria and semistructured interviews report prevalence rates for major depression that increase with age. The rate is quite low, at 0.3%, in preschool children (Kashani & Sherman, 1988) and increases to 1.8%

TABLE 30.1

Criteria for Major Depressive Episode

A. Five (or more) of the following symptoms have been present during the same 2-week period and represent a change from previous functioning: at least one of the symptoms is either (1) depressed mood or (2) loss of interest or pleasure.

Note: Do not include symptoms that are clearly due to a general medical condition, or mood-incongruent delusions or hallucinations.

   (1) depressed mood most of the day, nearly every day, as indicated by either subjective report (e.g., feels sad or empty) or observation made by others (e.g., appears tearful). **Note:** In children and adolescents, can be irritable mood.

   (2) markedly diminished interest or pleasure in all, or almost all, activities most of the day, nearly every day (as indicated by either subjective account or observation made by others)

   (3) significant weight loss when not dieting or weight gain (e.g., a change of more than 5% of body weight in a month), or decrease or increase in appetite nearly every day. **Note:** In children, consider failure to make expected weight gains.

   (4) insomnia or hypersomnia nearly every day.

   (5) psychomotor agitation or retardation nearly every day (observable by others, not merely subjective feelings of restlessness or being slowed down)

   (6) fatigue or loss of energy nearly every day

   (7) feelings of worthlessness or excessive or inappropriate guilt (which may be delusional) nearly every day (not merely self-reproach or guilt about being sick)

   (8) diminished ability to think or concentrate, or indecisiveness, nearly every day (either by subjective account or as observed by others)

   (9) recurrent thoughts of death (not just fear of dying), recurrent suicidal ideation without a specific plan, or a suicide attempt or a specific plan for committing suicide

B. The symptoms do not meet criteria for a Mixed Episode. . . .

C. The symptoms cause clinically significant distress or impairment in social, occupational, or other important areas of functioning.

D. The symptoms are not due to the direct physiological effects of a substance (e.g., a drug of abuse, a medication) or a general medical condition (e.g., hypothyroidism)

E. The symptoms are not better accounted for by Bereavement, i.e., after the loss of a loved one, the symptoms persist for longer than 2 months or are characterized by marked functional impairment, morbid preoccupation with worthlessness, suicidal ideation, psychotic symptoms, or psychomotor retardation.

Note: From *Diagnostic and Statistical Manual of Mental Disorders*, 4th ed., American Psychiatric Association, 1994. Washington, D.C.: Author, p. 327. Copyright 1994 by the American Psychiatric Association. Reprinted with permission.

in school-age children (Kashani et al., 1983). The most dramatic increase occurs during adolescence. A conservative estimate in 14- to 16-year-olds (Kashani, Carlson, et al., 1987) of 4.7% is similar to prevalence rates estimated in adult populations. Some investigators report prevalence rates during late adolescence to be much higher (15–28%) than in adulthood (Kandel & Davies, 1982).

Sex ratios also change as a function of age in major depression. Males and females appear equally affected during preadolescence. The proportion of females experiencing major depression tends to increase following puberty. By late adolescence, sex ratios approximate the female preponderance described in adult studies (Weissman & Myers, 1978).

To date, studies have not reliably shown race and socioeconomic factors to influence prevalence rates for major depression in children and adolescents. However, most community-based studies that rigorously diagnosed major depression had small sample sizes and were unable to clearly detect the contributions of racial or socioeconomic factors to the prevalence rates. A recent comparison of Anglo, African, Mexican, and other Hispanic Americans found increased rates of depressive symptoms in Mexican American males and females compared to their same-sex counterparts, even when adjusted for confounding variables. Females report more symptoms of depression than males in every ethnic group (Roberts & Sobhan, 1992).

CLINICAL PRESENTATION—SIGNS, SYMPTOMS, AND SUBTYPES

The careful study of the phenomenology of major depression in children and adolescents is a relatively recent endeavor. Traditionally, practitioners have been reluctant to make the diagnosis, viewing major depression in children and adolescents as impossible due to developmental immaturity, not diagnosable using adult criteria, or disguised or "masked" by various externalizing symptoms such as somatic complaints, conduct problems, or school refusal.

A problem unique to the study of the phenomenology of major depression in childhood is posed by the vast developmental changes that occur from infancy through adolescence. Most investigators have addressed the problem by first using strict adult diagnostic criteria to identify children with major depression and then comparing symptom profiles in various age groups. The majority of these studies have relied upon cross-sectional data and reported few fundamental differences between symptom presentations in children and adolescents (Kovacs, & Gatsonis, 1989; Mitchell, McCauley, Burke, & Moss, 1988; Ryan et al., 1987).

The presentation of major depression in children and adolescents includes a prominent mood change, either sad or irritable, for a sustained period of time. A change in mood is the core feature of the disorder. Associated symptoms tend to differ from individual to individual, creating quite variable clinical presentations. However, symptoms do appear to organize loosely into a few broadly defined presentations or types. One study identified 5 factors based on a component analysis of depressive symptoms in a large sample of children and adolescents who met Research Diagnostic Criteria for major depression. The factors included an endogenous factor, a negative cognitions factor, an anxious factor, an appetite-weight factor, and a conduct factor. The identification of an endogenous and an anxious factor in children and adolescents with major depression mirrors the findings in studies of subtypes of major depression in adults (Ryan et al., 1987). (See Table 30.2.)

Specific comparisons of symptom profiles between children and adolescents with major depressive disorder (Ryan et al., 1987) show subtle but significant differences in symptoms. Prepubertal children have more somatic complaints, depressed appearance, psychomotor agitation, and hallucinations than teenagers. Even though clini-

TABLE 30.2

Principal Component Factor Analysis of Depressive Symptoms in Children and Adolescents with
Major Depression

Endogenous Factor: Anhedonia, fatigue, psychomotor retardation, social withdrawal, depressed mood, hypersomnia, decreased weight, anorexia, and diurnal mood change

Negative Cognitions Factor: Negative self-image, hopeless/helpless, suicidal ideation, brooding/worry, depressed mood

Anxiety Factor: Separation anxiety, insomnia, somatic complaints, psychomotor agitation, hallucinations and brooding/worry

Appetite-weight Factor: Increased appetite and weight

Conduct Factor: Conduct disorder, anger/irritability, psychomotor agitation, suicidal ideation

---

Adapted from N. D. Ryan, J. Puig-Antich, P. Ambrosini, H. Rabinovich, D. Robinson, B. Nelson, S. Iyengar, & J. Twomey (1987). The clinical picture of major depression in children and adolescents. *Archives of General Psychiatry, 44,* 859. Reprinted with permission.

cians often rely heavily on depressed appearance to make the diagnosis, depressed appearance is not as frequently observed as other depressive symptoms, such as somatic complaints. Adolescents report more hopelessness, greater anhedonia, increased need for sleep, and weight changes than children and are even less likely than children to appear depressed. Suicidal ideation is common in both children and adolescents. The frequency of suicidal ideation, the corresponding level of suicidal intent, and the rates of suicide attempts are similar in children and adolescents with depression. Adolescents tend to resort to more lethal methods in actual suicide attempts than do children, a fact that may be related to children's relative inability to conceptualize more effective methods of suicide compared to adolescents (Ryan et al., 1987).

Despite the high prevalence of major depressive disorder, the various presentations in children and adolescents can be subtle and the diagnosis may not be obvious upon initial assessment. Children, adolescents, and their parents do not often present with a chief complaint of a disturbance in mood. Most often children and teenagers present for care when one or more of the symptoms of depression cause impairment in daily living. For example, a teenager may present with a chief complaint of disturbed eating behavior, weight loss, sleep problems, separation problems, obsessions and compulsions, behavior problems, somatization, inattention, poor concentration, overactivity, or social withdrawal. In the presence of such complaints, without a careful and systematic assessment of mood and related symptoms of major depressive disorder, these symptoms may be attributed to another psychiatric disorder or even to a nonpsychiatric medical problem. This tendency for depressed children and adolescents to present with other symptoms and not to complain of a disturbance in mood as the primary problem led in the 1960s to the concept of "masked depression." Central to the idea of masked depression was that these other symptoms represented a manifestation of an underlying depression that had to be inferred indirectly (Cytryn & McKnew, 1972). The flaw in this early notion of depression was that a clinically significant change in mood was not necessary for the diagnosis. Recent studies of the phenomenology of major depression in children suggest that de-

pression is not truly "masked" but may not be immediately apparent without a thorough assessment for a primary change in mood. In addition to identifying this primary change in mood, clinicians should consider a mood disorder in the differential diagnosis when the patient presents with a strong family history of mood disorder, an abrupt change in behavior or functioning, or an episodic or seasonal pattern of dysfunction.

CLINICAL PRESENTATION—
DEVELOPMENTAL CONSIDERATIONS

Although limited in conceptual ability, preschool children can develop major depression. Such children will appear sad in demeanor or report sad feelings as well as experience appetite loss, changes in sleep patterns, and fatigue. Somatic complaints are also very common and distinguish depressed preschoolers from other disturbed preschoolers (Kashani & Carlson, 1987).

As school-age children have better-developed verbal capacity as well as greater ability to discriminate emotional states, self-report measures begin to be reliable in this age group. Additionally, information gained from children's self-reports may differ from information provided by adults. Specifically, children provide needed information about internal symptoms, of which adults often are not aware. Teachers and parents provide important information on behavioral and neurovegetative symptoms, which children tend to report less accurately. Furthermore, children have difficulty identifying the time course or episodic nature of their mood disorders, making it necessary to rely on parental reports to determine the longitudinal course of symptoms.

School-age prepubertal children with major depression tend to report feelings of sadness and appear sad in demeanor. They regularly present with irritability, loss of interest in pleasurable activities, poor concentration, insomnia, social withdrawal, and psychomotor agitation. Like their preschool counterparts, they commonly report somatic complaints that may follow a pattern of diurnal variation similar to mood with somatic symptoms worse in the morning. In fact, somatic complaints can be so severe and disabling that parents may not attend to the signs and symptoms of major depression. Depressed children with somatic complaints may present first to their pediatrician. If the depression is not identified, patients may undergo extensive medical evaluations or have extended absences from school. Interestingly, as children mature, somatic complaints decrease in frequency, suggesting that increased capacity for abstract thinking allows children to discriminate between feeling sad and feeling physically ill.

As in adults, psychotic symptoms may be part of the pattern of major depression in children and adolescents. In a study of 95 children and 92 adolescents with major depressive disorder, Ryan and colleagues (1987) found that 30 of the children and 17 of the adolescents had either hallucinations or delusions. The presence of psychotic symptoms was associated with greater severity of depression in both children and adolescents. In the adolescent group, psychotic symptoms were also frequently associated with drug and alcohol use.

Caution is necessary in the evaluation of psychotic symptoms and in the inferences drawn from a child's report of unusual sensory experiences. In school-age children, the rates of psychotic disorders are very low, yet clinically it is not uncommon for children to report hearing voices, seeing things that are not there, or having strongly held bizarre beliefs. Often young children's description of unusual experiences appear similar to hallucinations, but they usually are more transient, situationally mediated, and/or responsive to redirection. In one study of depressed children, auditory hallucinations were much more common than depressive delusions. The auditory hallucinations were seen most frequently in conjunction with anxious symptoms. While hallucinations were observed frequently in this study, interviewers felt that only a small percentage of these phenomena were clinically consistent with true auditory hallucinations (Ryan et al., 1987). Cognitive immaturity plus anxiety, and not psychosis, may better explain children's frequent reports of unusual experiences.

Adolescents' mental capacities are developed to the point that they are able to give fuller descriptions of the cognitive symptoms of major depression such as hopelessness and worthlessness. Teenagers also can better differentiate their normal functioning from their functioning during a depressive episode. However, the same enhanced capacities also facilitate teenagers' ability to dis-

guise and deflect attention away from their abnormal mood states. Clinically, depressed teenagers defend against the change in mood, the resulting impairment, and the sense of being different. Often depressive symptoms in teenagers appear stylized and may reflect an attempt to normalize the depression-related changes. This behavioral adaptation can be subtle, as in the accentuation of certain personality characteristics such as introversion or affective instability, or more global, as in the development of lifestyles involving depressive themes. For instance, depression, anhedonia, and social withdrawal can present as a persona of boredom, indifference, and disaffection. Similarly, as peer relationships suffer during a depressive episode, depressed teenagers may present as disaffiliated or may join peer groups that have developed around mood-congruent rebellious and morbid themes. Substance abuse, common in these peer groups, may serve as another mechanism by which depressed teenagers cope with their symptoms. Often substance abuse complicates and obscures the clinical presentation and can lead to delays in diagnosis and treatment.

CLINICAL PRESENTATION—NATURAL HISTORY

Longitudinal studies offer the unique advantage of studying the patterns of symptom development within individuals, providing the essential linkages between the various cross-sectional presentations described earlier. In the early 1980s Kovacs and colleagues began a longitudinal, naturalistic study of latency-age children identified as having major depression. This landmark study documented the course of prepubertal affective disorder into adolescence and young adulthood. The children, 8 to 13 years old, were diagnosed by *DSM-III* criteria with major depressive disorder, dysthymic disorder, and adjustment disorder with depressed mood. They were followed over time to document their clinical course, patterns of comorbid conditions, and outcome with respect to the development of a new episode of major depression and a first episode of bipolar disorder, anxiety disorder, or conduct disorder (Kovacs, Feinberg, Crouse-Novak, Paulauskas, & Finkelstein, 1984; Kovacs, Feinberg, Crouse-Novak, Paulauskas, Pollock, et al., 1984).

The natural history of a major depressive episode as delineated by Kovacs is distinct from other depressive disorders and contradicts the popular notion that major depression in children and adolescents is a transient, benign condition. While there is great variability in episode length, on average major depression lasted 9 to 10 months in contrast to adjustment disorder with depressed mood, which lasted 4 to 5 months, and dysthymic disorder, which lasted more than 3 years. Spontaneous recovery was much more likely to occur early in the course of an episode of major depressive disorder but became improbable after 18 months. In contrast, in dysthymic disorder, the rate of recovery was gradual over time. Children with earlier ages of onset were more likely to have a protracted recovery from both major depressive disorder and dysthymic disorder. The risk of recurrence of a major depressive episode increased with time. Approximately 25% of the children had a recurrence within 1 year of recovery, 40% within 2 years, and 72% within 5 years. Strikingly, bipolar disorder developed in 20% of children within 2 years of recovery from a major depressive episode (Kovacs, Feinberg, Crouse-Novak, Paulauskas, & Finkelstein, 1984; Kovacs, Feinberg, Paulauskas, Pollock, et al., 1984).

COMORBID CONDITIONS

The nature of the relationship between major depression and other psychiatric disorders is variable and at times complex. Clearly, depression can independently co-occur with any variety of medical and psychiatric disorders. Patients with sickle cell disease, Crohn's disease, Tourette's disorder, and somatoform, eating, and elimination disorders can all have a mood disorder, but not invariably so. Depression can develop secondarily as a complication of another primary disorder, such as schizophrenia, obsessive-compulsive disorder, or learning disabilities (so-called secondary depression). Depression also can serve as a risk or etiologic factor in the development of other disorders. According to longitudinal studies, the course of depression may include the development of other disorders, including recurrent depressive episodes, dysthymia, bipolar disorder, the disruptive behavior disorders, or substance abuse. Last, symptoms of major depression can cluster and overlap with other disorders such that individuals with major depression can be misdiagnosed. These complicated relationships make the study of major depression and its comorbid conditions difficult.

Based on longitudinal studies, most children and adolescents with a mood disorder meet criteria for an additional psychiatric diagnosis at the time of first presentation and/or go on to develop additional disorders over the course of their illness. The most common co-occurring conditions are the anxiety disorders, conduct disorder, and dysthymic disorder (Kovacs, Feinberg, Crouse-Novak, Paulauskas, & Finkelstein, 1984).

Anxiety Disorder: Up to 50% of children with depressive disorders—major depressive disorder, dysthymic disorder, or adjustment disorder with depressed mood—will be diagnosed with an anxiety disorder. In preadolescent children with depressive disorders, 41% present with anxiety disorders, the most common being separation anxiety disorder; next in occurrence is overanxious disorder. By the age of 19, the cumulative risk for developing a comorbid anxiety disorder is 0.47. In Kovacs's study, the anxiety disorders predated the onset of the depressive disorder in two-thirds of the cases and were associated with an earlier onset of depressive disorder. Anxiety disorders remained after the remission of the depressive disorder in 50% of children with major depressive disorder and in 75% of children with dysthymic disorder. High levels of maternal psychopathology and poor maternal health, increase the risk of a child having a comorbid anxiety disorder (Kovacs, Gatsonis, Paulauskas, & Richards, 1989); this fact suggests that psychosocial factors are also important in the formation and maintenance of anxiety disorders in these patients.

Conduct Disorder: There is considerable overlap between children with conduct disorder and children with major depression. Many conduct-disordered children and adolescents endorse depressive symptoms; likewise, many depressed children have symptoms of conduct disorder.

Between 15 and 37% of psychiatrically referred children with major depression have conduct problems at the time of their initial presentation. In the majority of these cases, the onset of depression precedes that of the conduct disorder (Kovacs, Paulauskas, Gatsonis, & Richards, 1988; Puig-Antich, 1982), suggesting that mood disorders may play a role in the development of certain conduct problems. The conduct disorder typically seen in depressed children (including major depressive disorder, dysthymic disorder, and adjustment disorder with depressed mood) differs from conduct disorder in the general population in that boys and girls are equally represented, the course is frequently episodic, and 21% go on to develop bipolar disorder (Kovacs et al., 1988). While having comorbid conduct disorder does not appear to influence the severity of depressive symptoms, recovery from major depression, or risk for a subsequent episode, a comorbid conduct disorder is associated with poorer long-term functioning as indicated by increased runaway behavior, contact with police and the juvenile court system, and school suspensions. The presence of co-occurring conduct problems also interferes with the diagnosis and treatment of a mood disorder in these youngsters. Symptom identification, the development of a treatment alliance, and countertransference issues are all more complicated in youngsters with depression and comorbid conduct disorder.

The results of treatment interventions also provide information on the relationship between mood disorders and conduct disorders. Children with major depression and conduct disorder can experience a remission of both disorders following treatment with imipramine (Puig-Antich, 1982), suggesting that pharmacologic interventions may be useful in decreasing conduct disorder symptoms in children with mood disorders, improve the long-term prognosis of children with mood disorders, or even impact on patients with ongoing conduct disorder. No longitudinal study of children treated for their mood disorder has been undertaken to identify whether comorbid conditions such as conduct disorder can be prevented.

PATTERNS OF INTERPERSONAL RELATIONSHIPS

As in adults, psychosocial functioning is found to be impaired in children and adolescents with major depression. Depressed preadolescent inpatients have significantly less social activity and affective expression than nondepressed peers (Kazdin, Esveldt-Dawson, Sherick, & Colbus, 1985). Preadolescent depressed children demonstrate significant impairment in overall functioning, including academic achievement, school behavior, peer relations, and family relations, although this functioning is not significantly different from that of nondepressed psychiatric controls (Puig-Antich et al., 1985a). Depressed children

also tend to have the poorest interpersonal relationships with poorer communication between mother and child, greater difficulty maintaining best friends, and more teasing by peers than nondepressed psychiatric outpatients. At the time of recovery from depression, school function appears to normalize but deficits in interpersonal relationships improve only partially (Puig-Antich et al., 1985b), suggesting that there is a risk for long-term social impairment even though the core depressive symptoms are no longer present. This fact may be related to, as some children have described, difficulty rejoining their peers after they have been depressed. Alternatively, the perceptions of other persons involved with the child may have changed dramatically over the course of the depressive episode such that barriers develop impeding the return to more normal functioning.

Few studies specifically address the psychosocial functioning of adolescents with major depressive disorder; however, adolescents identified with depressive symptoms on symptom surveys consistently had problems in family functioning, peer relationships, social competence, and academic achievement (Kandel & Davies, 1982; Kovacs & Goldston, 1991). In a recent study of adolescents diagnosed with major depressive disorder, similar impairments were noted (Puig-Antich et al., 1993). During a depressive episode these teenagers had marked disturbance in their relationships with parents, siblings, and peers and in their academic performance.

ETIOLOGY

The advances in the evaluation, phenomenology, and natural history of major depression in children and adolescents have made it possible to study hypotheses concerning the etiology of major depression in these age groups. The impact of development and maturation on the symptoms and course of major depression may make difficult, the direct comparison of adult studies with child and adolescent studies, yet most child and adolescent researchers have designed studies based on hypotheses developed to study adult depressive disorders. As in adult studies, investigators generally have attempted to validate a single explanatory model while making little effort to integrate the many findings from other models (McCracken, 1992). In addition, most researchers have not used adequate control groups to assess the specificity of their findings (McCracken, 1992). As a result, our understanding of the etiology (or etiologies) of depression in children and adolescents remains rudimentary both in terms of the integration of the multiple and varied findings from research and the specificity of these findings to depression. The following sections present the various etiologic models.

Genetic Model: Studies that support the genetic hypothesis of affective disorders fall into three distinct types: twin and adoption studies, family aggregation studies, and genetic linkage studies.

Twin and adoption studies are useful in providing evidence for the role of both genetic and nongenetic factors in the etiology of affective illness. To date, no twin or adoption studies have utilized child or adolescent probands. However, an analysis of adult twin studies reveals concordance rates of from 0.58 to 0.74 in monozygotic twins and from 0.17 to 0.29 in same-sex dizygotic twins (Tsuang & Faraone, 1990).

Family studies identify an individual with a given disorder and then complete diagnostic assessments of relatives in an effort to assess the role of genetics in the familial transmission of that disorder. In families the affected individual or proband can be a child (so-called bottom-up approach) or an adult (so-called top-down approach). Family study data can be analyzed in a variety of ways, including segregation analyses that attempt to identify specific genetic patterns of transmission.

Family studies clearly show an increased risk for major depression in family members of depressed probands. In spite of differences in methodology, control groups, and statistical assumptions between the various studies, the risk for depression increases for family members as the age of the proband decreases, suggesting that early-onset depression may represent a more heritable form of the disorder (Puig-Antich, 1987). Specifically, the age-corrected lifetime risk for major depression is lowest (0.17) for first-degree relatives of adult probands (Weissman, Gershon, et al., 1984). The risk increases (0.37) with adolescent probands and is highest (0.53) with prepubertal probands (Puig-Antich et al., 1989). The higher concordance rate for monozygotic versus dizygotic twins plus the results of family studies suggests the likelihood that at least some forms of major depression in children and adolescents are strongly mediated by genetic factors.

Clearly, psychosocial risks are conferred upon children with depression when one or more of their parents are also depressed. Children and teenagers of depressed parents have a threefold increase in risk for *any DSM-III* disorder despite being most at risk for major depression (Weissman, Prusoff, 1984). They tend to have an earlier onset of depression when compared to depressed children and adolescents of nondepressed parents and are more likely to have substance abuse, poor social functioning, and school problems (Weissman et al., 1987). Children and teens of depressed parents with comorbid anxiety disorders are at the highest risk for the development of depression and an anxiety disorder (Weissman, Leckman, Merikangas, Gammon, & Prusoff, 1984). Depressed parents, especially those with anxiety disorders, are more likely to have secondary alcoholism, which imposes an additional risk to their children.

While a number of linkage studies have been done to date, the results have not provided clear and convincing evidence of a specific genetic locus for any affective disorder. Some investigators have reported evidence implicating various loci for bipolar disorder, but these results have not been replicated by other investigators. Methodologic differences between studies are often cited as reasons for the inability to replicate linkage findings, but the concept of genetic heterogeneity of the affective disorders is an equally compelling argument (Tsuang & Faraone, 1990).

Biologic Models: The effectiveness of tricyclic antidepressant therapy in adults with major depression in the 1960s stimulated the initial interest in biological hypotheses of major depression. Perhaps one of the most studied and persistent of these hypotheses is that depression results from the disregulation in the catecholamine neurotransmitter system. In support of this hypothesis, depressed adults demonstrate alterations in levels of peripheral catecholamines and their metabolites, abnormal response to neuroendocrine and pharmacologic challenges, and disruptions in circadian rhythms, all thought to be mediated through the catecholamine system. Although studied much less, depressed children and adolescents also demonstrate biologic changes. In the pursuit of biological markers of depression in children and adolescents, investigators have discovered both similarities and dissimilarities among depressed children, adolescents, and adults. Due to the paucity of studies examining biologic hypotheses in the child and adolescent population, the small numbers of children in the studies, and the absence in many instances of needed control groups, it is difficult to draw conclusions from this work. In general, these studies lend support to the idea that childhood- and adolescent-onset depression is continuous with adult depression but also highlight the impact of developmental or maturational changes on the manifestation of depression throughout the life cycle.

Although studies in depressed adults have systematically shown a decrease in catecholamine metabolites in urine, plasma, and cerebrospinal fluid, the research is incomplete in children. Decreased urinary 3-methoxy-4-hydroxyphenylglycol (MHPG) was identified in prepubertal depressed children compared to normal controls (McKnew & Cytryn, 1979) but not in a sample of adolescents (deVilliers et al., 1989).

Abnormalities in the hypothalamic-pituitary axis (HPA) as demonstrated by 24-hour cortisol hypersecretion and nonsuppression of cortisol response to the dexamethasone suppression test (DST) have been demonstrated in a subgroup of depressed adults and are thought to be mediated in part by the catecholamine system. Cortisol hypersecretion has not been observed in either prepubertal depressed children (Birmaher et al., 1992) or depressed adolescents (Dahl et al., 1991). Age effects have been postulated to account for this finding, as age is positively correlated to cortisol hypersecretion in adult depression (Puig-Antich, 1987). Although some studies found that DST response did not discriminate among depressed prepubertal outpatients, nondepressed prepubertal outpatients, or normal controls (Birmaher et al., 1992), other studies do report discriminative power of the DST in prepubertal populations (Casat, Arana, & Powell, 1989). In adolescent populations, the sensitivity and specificity of the DST approaches that in adult studies (Goodwin & Jamison, 1990) with pooled estimates of 47.1% and 80.2% respectively (Casat et al., 1989). In children and adolescents as with adults, the rate of DST nonsuppression is higher among inpatients than outpatients and varies with stress level (Casat et al., 1989).

Growth hormone (GH) secretory patterns, which are in part mediated by the catecholamine system, have been an area of extensive research in childhood and adult depressive disorders. Physiologic challenges of GH secretion, including the insulin tolerance test and the acute administration of desipramine and clonidine, demonstrate growth hormone hyposecretion in depressed prepubertal children, adolescents, and adults compared to controls. However, studies of GH secretion in depression also show important developmental differences. Growth hormone secretion during sleep, a potent stimulator of GH, changes dramatically with age such that prepubertal depressed children show hypersecretion and depressed adults show hyposecretion compared to controls (Puig-Antich, 1987). Depressed adolescents do not show any abnormality in sleep-related GH secretion except in a subgroup of suicidally depressed adolescents; they have a pattern of hyposecretion similar to that of depressed adults (Dahl et al., 1992). It is postulated that age and developmental effects on sleep regulation may account for the variability in sleep-related growth hormone secretion in these studies (Dahl et al., 1992).

Melatonin, which is also in part mediated by the catecholamine system, has not been adequately studied in children and adolescents. In the single published study, children with major depression ($N = 10$) had decreased sleep-related melatonin secretion compared to short-statured controls (Cavallo, Holt, Hejazi, Richards, & Meyer, 1987). The study's results are similar to studies of adult depressed patients who also demonstrate decreased sleep-related melatonin secretion. Studies of the thyroid axis in children and adolescents have failed to reproduce the positive findings in adult studies. Specifically, only adults with major depression have a blunted response of thyroid stimulating hormone (TSH) to thyrotropin releasing hormone (TRH) (Puig-Antich, 1987). Possible explanations for the lack of a response to TRH include age effects of TSH response or diagnostic imprecision and heterogeneity in study samples.

Psychological Models: Psychological models of major depression have developed along many different paths and have taken into account observations about children such as cognitive style or self-esteem, characteristics of the environment including stressful life events, and qualities of the parent-child relationship. Empiric confirmation through systematic study is rare and has been technically difficult.

It is likely that psychological issues in individuals with major depression are both causes and consequences of the depression. Intuitively, when people think badly of themselves, others, and the world in which they live, it seems logical that they would feel depressed. However, it also appears clear that when people are depressed, it is difficult for them to perceive themselves or the world in positive terms. Most psychological models do not address the direction of the interaction and consider depression symptoms to be the result of a psychological deficit. Treatment, therefore, is directed toward the psychological deficit in an effort to eliminate the depression. An alternative conceptualization of depression suggests that the perceived psychological deficits are actually symptoms of an underlying disease and thus treatment should be directed at eliminating the disease itself. Successful treatment of the disease would then correct the psychological deficits. Since it is likely that major depression is a heterogeneous disorder, it is also likely that both conceptualizations play a role in etiology.

Child psychoanalytic literature for a long time did not consider that depression in children was the same condition as depression in adults (Rie, 1966; Sandler & Joffe, 1965). Adult depression was viewed as the result of the loss and subsequent incorporation of an ambivalently loved object. Aggressive and hostile feelings toward the lost object were turned against the self causing self-hatred and depression. Children and to a lesser extent adolescents were viewed as having inadequate ego maturity to allow the development of mature or adult-type depression.

Bowlby (1988) expanded the etiologic conception of depression in childhood by focusing on parental loss and disrupted attachment. He described the stages in a child's reaction to prolonged separation from the primary caregiver as progressing from protest to despair to detachment. Such processes occur even in very young children and can result in depressive symptoms. Bowlby saw the disruption in the development of normal attachment behaviors as critical to later functioning and suggested that early loss and disturbed attachment was an important vulnerability to the development of depression later in life. His development of attachment theory fueled the field of

infant psychiatry and led to the operationalization and longitudinal studies of attachment behaviors. However, prospective studies of children with secure and insecure attachment have not shown that early attachment behavior is a strong predictor of future functioning let alone the development of mood disorders (Lamb, Nash, Teti, & Bornstein, 1991).

Studies on the role of parental loss during childhood in the development of depression complements the attachment theories. Criticisms of the "parental loss" literature concern the lack of a rigorous definition for the term "loss" and the lack of prospective studies. Prospective studies are particularly vital in that important competing and associated variables can occur both before and after the loss (Tennant, 1988). The term "loss" has been variably defined as parental death and/or parental separation/divorce. Parental death by itself has not been demonstrated to be a risk factor for major depression. Furthermore, studies of parental separation have identified the presence of family discord and inadequate postseparation parenting rather than parental loss itself as a risk factor for adult depression (Tennant, 1988).

Other studies specifically focusing on parenting indicate that inadequate parenting is a specific risk factor for depression. This finding is supported by research in several different areas. The frequency of affective disorders in children born to affectively disordered parents is much higher than that seen in the general population (Weissman, Prusoff, et al., 1984). Lack of affection, uninvolvement, and detachment, which can occur in the relationship of depressed parents with their children, contribute to subsequent childhood depression (Weissman, Paykel, & Klerman, 1972). While it is difficult to identify the role of genetic factors in these studies, it is clear that depressed parents do demonstrate impairment in the quality of their parenting, which may contribute to the development of anxiety and depression in their children.

Cognitive-behavioral models of depression emphasize the impact of negative cognitions on an individual's affective, motivational, and behavioral states. These negative cognitions can include negative views of oneself, the world, and the future (Beck, 1967). Whether negative cognitions are causes or consequences of depression remains controversial. Clearly treatment addressed at changing these cognitions has demonstrated benefit in adults.

The concept of learned helplessness complements some of the tenets of Beck's cognitive model of depression. The concept was derived from experiments in dogs exposed to inescapable electric shocks that went on to develop a pattern of depressionlike maladaptive responses to aversive stimuli. Its application toward a model of depression rests on the assumption that exposure to uncontrollable life events leads to a state of hopelessness, which in turn results in the motivational, cognitive, and emotional impairments seen in depression. In an effort to account for variation in symptoms between individuals, the model was revised to include individual attributional styles as a modifier of the impact of uncontrollable life events (Seligman & Peterson, 1986). Few studies have been done in children to test this hypothesis. As with the cognitive model of depression, it is difficult to ascertain whether the observed deficits are causes or consequences of depression.

EVALUATION

Clinical experience in identifying mood disorders is one of the most important tools in evaluating depression. Traditionally, it has been difficult for practitioners to acquire such experience as the child and adolescent mental health field has not been specifically oriented toward the identification of mood disorders as primary impairing conditions. The evaluative task is somewhat clearer when clinicians are familiar with the base rate of the disorder, the variability in presentation at different ages and developmental levels, and understand symptom overlap with other childhood disorders. Clinician bias regarding etiology, phenomenology, and treatment of depression can readily influence recognition of the disorder.

Obtaining information on depressive symptoms from more than one source is essential. Information provided by the patient, parents, and even teachers often is necessary to establish the diagnosis. Relying on parental reports exclusively will result in an underestimation of depressive symptoms.

Self-report and parent-report measures are available to screen for affective illness or to monitor treatment. It should be noted, however, that self-report scales may not be as reliable in children under 8 years old and thus should be used cautiously in this age group. A number of structured and semistructured interviews have been developed in the last 10 years that can be employed to aid in diagnosis. Such instruments can be very useful for practitioners with little experience in making the diagnosis of depression in children and adolescents.

Medical Evaluation: Children and adolescents who present with symptoms of depression should have a full medical evaluation as well as a psychiatric evaluation. This evaluation should include a full medical history, review of systems, a list of current and recent medications, and a thorough physical examination. Additionally, a substance use history is essential as substance abuse can mimic depression.

Specific laboratory investigations will be dictated by the individual case. However, the assessment of thyroid function has become nearly routine in the medical assessment of depressive symptoms. In teenage populations, screens for pregnancy and illicit substance use are important in the evaluation as teens can be less candid about their activities in these domains.

Psychological Testing: Often it is best to defer cognitive testing of severely depressed children or teenagers, as their performance may be impaired by the depression itself. As children recover, cognitive testing may be a useful adjunct to treatment planning and disposition, particularly when there are concerns regarding significant academic impairment or social deficits. The presence of learning disabilities or intellectual deficits will clearly affect treatment recommendations, especially if more verbal and cognitive forms of psychotherapy are being considered. While projective testing may help elicit depressive themes in children who have a difficult time describing their moods, they are no substitute for the clinical exam. The interpretation of projective tests is based on psychological models; thus, depressive themes elicited on projective tests must be viewed in this context. Caution is warranted in using the results of projective testing to establish diagnosis, etiology, and treatment recommendations.

PSYCHOLOGICAL TREATMENTS

Psychological treatments of adult depression have received serious attention in the last 10 years and have been the subject of prospective controlled studies. Perhaps the largest study of 239 nonbipolar, nonpsychotic depressed adult outpatients demonstrated that for treatment of moderate to severe depression, both cognitive and interpersonal therapies are superior to placebo (Elkin et al., 1989). Very few studies of the effectiveness of psychological treatment for depression in children and adolescents have been undertaken, despite the fact that individual therapies are the most widely prescribed treatment by practitioners. Preliminary results from a pilot study on the use of interpersonal psychotherapy in depressed adolescents are promising (Mufson et al., 1994). Cognitive-behavioral therapies have been subject to more rigorous evaluations in children and adolescents, although these studies are also limited in number. Results tend to support the notion that treatment aimed at increasing self-control, interpersonal skills, and problem solving, either in groups or individually, helps bring about a reduction in depressive symptoms (Kazdin, 1990). Despite the lack of rigorous study, it is likely that specific interpersonal and cognitive treatments are useful in the treatment of childhood and adolescent depression as they have been demonstrated in adults. However, psychotherapy should not be prescribed without consideration of the goals of treatment and should not be an "automatic" recommendation because the clinician is reluctant to utilize other treatment modalities. As has been found in adult studies, a combination of pharmacologic and psychological therapy may be the most effective treatment of depression in children and adolescents.

The role of family work in the treatment of depression also has been anecdotal. Parental education about depression and its treatment is essential. With proper guidance, parents can be keen observers of their children and can help provide needed structure and supervision to depressed children and teens. There has been a tendency to exclude parents from the treatment of children and adolescents; doing so loses a valuable resource and promotes in parents a feeling of helplessness. There is great need to evaluate the efficacy of family involvement, given the evidence that parenting problems are a risk factor for depression (Tennant, 1988).

PHARMACOLOGIC TREATMENTS

Tricyclic Antidepressants: Although the use of tricyclic antidepressants in depressed children dates back to the 1960s, the published studies

dating before the 1980s are plagued by methodological problems, particularly poor experimental design, unclear inclusion criteria, unspecified response criteria, and inadequate dose of medication and duration of treatment (Ambrosini, Bianchi, Rabinovich, & Elia, 1993). More recent studies have attempted to define these variables rigorously, following guidelines derived from adult studies of tricyclic antidepressant efficacy.

Despite the increased rigor in design, studies have failed to provide convincing evidence of the efficacy of tricyclic antidepressant treatment in children and adolescents. However, methodological problems continue to limit any conclusions made from these studies regarding the efficacy of tricyclic antidepressants. Problems include diagnostic heterogeneity, the presence of comorbidity, inadequate sample size, the presumption of comparability between different tricyclic antidepressants, the difficulty in evaluating treatment response, and the reliability and validity of instruments used to measure depression (Conners, 1992). Interestingly, an unintended result of these studies has been the polarization of clinicians who use medications from those who do not. Because of their positive clinical experience, many clinicians, even some involved in negative treatment trials, use pharmacologic agents to treat major depression in children and adolescents. Other clinicians less disposed toward using medications often cite the negative studies as support for their use of psychological formulations and treatments.

Three published double-blind, placebo-controlled studies exist that examine tricyclic antidepressant responsiveness in prepubertal children with major depression. Puig-Antich and colleagues (1987) found no significant difference in overall response rate between subjects receiving imipramine and the placebo control group (56% versus 68%). The lack of a placebo washout period and the lack of follow-up of the placebo responders for possible recurrence of depression are of particular concern in this study. It is important to note that in the group that responded to imipramine, a significant relationship existed between medication plasma level and clinical response. The high placebo response rate appears to distinguish this study from published adult studies, although some adult studies evince similar high placebo response rates (Klein, Gittelman, Quitkin, & Rifkin, 1980). Another study using imipramine with a plasma level fixed in the range 125 to 250 nanograms per milliliter (ng/ml) demonstrated superiority of imipramine to placebo. Furthermore, DST nonsuppression was correlated to clinical response to imipramine (Preskorn, Weller, Hughes, Weller, & Bolte, 1987).

A third study using nortriptyline showed a poor response rate in both the active and placebo groups (30.8% versus 16.7%) (Geller et al., 1992). A major drawback to this study is that the subjects were a more chronically depressed group of children (94% had major depression for greater than 2 years, 50% had major depression for greater than 5 years) with significant comorbid anxiety and conduct disorder (Geller et al., 1992). It is not surprising that a poor response from single-drug treatment is found in severely depressed children and adolescents, as adults with severe, chronic depression often fail to respond to single-drug treatments.

There have been fewer rigorous studies in adolescent populations. One double-blind, placebo-controlled study using amitriptyline in a fixed dosage of 200 milligrams per day (mg/day) with no plasma determination showed no significant difference between the amitriptyline group and the placebo group (Kramer & Feiguine, 1981). Another study using nortriptyline showed a poor response in both the treatment and placebo group despite therapeutic levels (Geller, Cooper, Graham, Marsteller, & Bryant, 1990). As in the authors' study of prepubertal children with depression, adolescent subjects were more chronically ill with major depression. In an open study of imipramine in adolescents with major depression, only 44% of subjects responded. In contrast to the preadolescent studies of imipramine, no relationship was found between response and plasma drug level (Ryan, Puig-Antich, Cooper, Rabinovich, Ambrosini, Davies, et al., 1986). In using any pharmacologic agent in children and adolescents, it is important to know the pattern of drug response and side effects as well as differences between children and adults in medication metabolism. The pharmacokinetics of tricyclic antidepressants are particularly noteworthy in children and adolescents. There is an inverse relationship between rate of metabolism and age, with preschool-age children having the highest rate of metabolism (Ryan, 1990). Children's increased rate of drug metabo-

lism is thought to be related to increased first-pass metabolism and decreased protein binding, leading some to suggest that twice-a-day dosing may be necessary. In adolescent populations, plasma levels of imipramine are similar for single versus divided dosing schedules, which makes once-daily dosing more feasible (Ryan, Puig-Antich, Cooper, Rabinovich, Ambrosini, Fried, et al., 1986). As in adults, there is wide individual variation in plasma level with a given dose. Given the great interindividual variation in drug metabolism, plasma level determinations are useful to monitor for safety and compliance, and to determine whether an adequate dose of medication has been utilized in a patient not responding as expected.

Current guidelines based on the limited research in prepubertal children suggest that imipramine should be titrated upward to reach a level from 125 to 250 ng/ml (Preskorn, Weller, & Weller, 1982; Puig-Antich et al., 1987). A therapeutic window has not been demonstrated, although higher plasma levels of imipramine are associated with toxicity and delirium and should be avoided (Preskorn, Weller, Hughes, & Weller, 1988). Studies in adolescent populations have not demonstrated a clear relationship between plasma level and clinical response to imipramine. However, sustained imipramine levels of 200 ng/ml are important to determine definitively whether a patient has clearly failed a treatment trial (Ambrosini et al., 1993). Nortriptyline is titrated to a level of 50 to 150 ng/ml as in adults. Adequate studies examining clinical response to plasma level have not yet been performed.

The common side effects of tricyclic antidepressants stem from their anticholinergic activity and include dry mouth, constipation, blurred vision, and tachycardia. Orthostatic hypotension, which is a function of the alpha-adrenergic activity of antidepressants, is also common but is rarely associated with symptoms. Mild changes in the electrocardiogram, including prolongation of the PR interval, widening of the QRS interval, and prolongation of the QTc, are common and rarely symptomatic. Uncommon side effects include the development of cardiac conduction abnormalities or arrhythmias. Hypertension also has been observed in children and can be a reason for drug discontinuation. Hypertension caused by tricyclic antidepressants resolves upon removal of the drug. Seizures have been described and usually are seen in children with preexisting seizure disorders or with abnormal electroencephalograms. Other side effects, such as rashes, gynecomastia, and galactorrhea, are rarer.

Delirium can be seen in children and may be confused with worsening of an affective disorder. An assessment of cognitive status is necessary whenever a deterioration in a child's mental state is evident. Delirium is usually associated with higher antidepressant plasma levels (Preskorn et al., 1988) or drug combinations.

Induction of mania is a clear risk for patients of all ages on antidepressants. Children and adolescents without documented bipolar disorder may develop hypomania or mania for the first time during a trial of antidepressants (Geller, Fox, & Fletcher, 1993). This can be clinically confusing as the change can be rapid and markedly inconsistent with the presenting complaint. It is not uncommon for patients who have become hypomanic on antidepressants to be clinically misunderstood as "transference cures," "flight into health," or "hysterical acting out" (Akiskal, Khani, & Scott-Strauss, 1979). Patients with bipolar depression are more at risk for the development of antidepressant-induced mania or hypomania. It appears that all antidepressants have a similar tendency to promote shifts in polarity in those patients vulnerable to such changes. Antidepressants also have been noted to induce rapid cycling in adult bipolar patients, although similar clinical outcomes have not been reported in children and adolescents.

Recently there has been increased concern regarding the cardiotoxicity of tricyclic antidepressants due to several case reports of sudden death in prepubertal children receiving desipramine ("Sudden Death in Children . . ." 1990). Whether the deaths were related to use of desipramine is not entirely clear, but caution is warranted. A careful assessment of cardiac status, including family history of sudden death (not related to coronary artery disease), nonvasovagal syncope, and a baseline electrocardiogram are essential. Further, it is recommended that this potential risk be explained to parents when obtaining informed consent (Riddle et al., 1991). When discussing this risk with parents, it may be useful to have a comparison. The risk of sudden death in children on tricyclics is estimated at 7 per million, while the risk of unexplained sudden death in children and adolescents is estimated at 4 per million. Clearly

the risk is greater on tricyclic antidepressants, but these numbers need to be placed into perspective with other everyday risks, such as the risk of death from a car ride to the doctor's office, which is estimated at 70 per million (Biederman, 1993).

Serotonin Reuptake Inhibitors: Serotonin reuptake inhibitors have been increasingly used as the first-line medication for major depressive disorder in children and adolescents due to their greater margin of safety, more agreeable side effect profile, and ease of administration compared to tricyclic antidepressants. Despite their popularity, serotonin reuptake inhibitors have not been widely studied in younger populations. Fluoxetine has received the most attention and is the focus of this section.

Fluoxetine, whose structure and pharmacologic action are distinct from the tricyclic antidepressants, is a highly selective serotonin reuptake inhibitor (SSRI). Although its use in children and adolescents is becoming more popular, there are very few studies of its efficacy, dosing requirements, and side effect profile in this age group. To date the only double-blind, placebo-controlled study published showed no difference in response between depressed adolescents and normal controls (Simeon, Dinicola, Ferguson, & Copping, 1990). One open study of fluoxetine in treatment-refractory depressed adolescents, however, reports a response rate of greater than 60% with doses of 5 to 40 mg over a 6- to 8-week observation period. Most subjects did not tolerate the initiation of fluoxetine at 20 mg but did better with starting doses of 5 to 10 mg. The most common complaints were tremor and dry mouth (40%); decreased appetite, sweating, and nausea (33%); and restlessness and drowsiness (27%). Blood pressure, laboratory investigations, and electrocardiogram parameters remained the same before and during treatment. One person dropped out of the study following the development of a skin rash. One out of the 15 subjects developed mania necessitating the discontinuation of the medication (Boulos, Kutcher, Gardner, & Young, 1992).

Concern regarding the development of suicidal ideation and self-injurious behavior in adults on fluoxetine prompted an increased awareness of such symptoms in children and adolescents. Similar findings have been documented in 6 out of 42 children and adolescents with obsessive compulsive disorder or Tourette's disorder treated with between 20 and 60 mg fluoxetine (King et al., 1991). In five out of the six cases, the onset of symptoms occurred within 3 weeks of the onset of fluoxetine treatment or a dose increase. Pharmacologically induced hyperserotonergic states may be responsible for the mental status changes seen in some patients on fluoxetine. (See Sternbach, 1990, for review.)

Although studies are few, results to date suggest that children and adolescents may be more sensitive to fluoxetine than adults both with respect to response and to adverse side effects using adult dosing schedules. No electrocardiogram or specific baseline laboratory investigations are essential before beginning fluoxetine. Dosing should begin at 5 to 10 mg/day with gradual titration upward under close psychiatric supervision. Fluoxetine usually is given in the morning but may be shifted to the evening if drowsiness is experienced. Once-a-day dosing is sufficient because of fluoxetine's very long half-life. In studies in which they are available, blood levels do not appear to correlate with drug response and thus do not need to be obtained routinely. Fluoxetine may be a good choice for patients who are very fearful of blood drawing or who do not have good venous access. Peak dosage is not expected to exceed 20 to 40 mg. As in adults, mania can be a complication of fluoxetine treatment in children and adolescents.

Other serotonin reuptake inhibitors that are being used for the treatment of major depressive disorder in children and adolescents are sertraline and paroxetine. The shorter half-life of these agents theoretically makes them attractive alternatives to fluoxetine in that they are more quickly cleared from the body in the event of adverse behavioral side effects. However, there has been no published data to establish efficacy, guide administration, or outline adverse effects in younger populations; thus these drugs should be used with caution.

Combining other medications with the serotonin reuptake inhibitors, especially tricyclic antidepressants, can result in unusually high medication plasma levels due to the inhibition of the cytochrome P450 drug metabolism system by the serotonin reuptake inhibitors. Levels of desipramine can be elevated more than 300% when combined with either fluoxetine 20 mg/day or paroxetine 20 mg/day. Sertraline can have similar but less dramatic effects on desipramine levels. Sertraline

50 mg/day increased desipramine levels approximately 30%, although the latter was not a clinically significant increase (Preskorn, 1994).

Monoamine Oxidase Inhibitors (MAOIs): There have been no published controlled trials using MAOIs in children and adolescents for depression. One published chart review of adolescents treated with MAOIs reported 74% response in tricyclic-refractory depression. Only 57% of these patients demonstrated both positive clinical response and dietary compliance. These results suggest that MAOIs may be useful in refractory depression but that the dietary compliance of patients and families is a limiting factor (Ryan, Piug-Antich, et al., 1988).

Lithium: Lithium has been found to augment tricyclic antidepressant response in adults with major depressive disorder. A chart review of 14 adolescents with major depressive disorder who received lithium augmentation of antidepressants revealed a response in 6 patients. Of those who responded, improvement was gradual over the first month (Ryan, Meyer, et al., 1988). One prospective study has looked at lithium augmentation in adolescents who had an inadequate response to imipramine (Strober, Freeman, Rigall, Schmidt, & Diamond, 1992). Results suggest that a number of patients did experience an augmentation response and that it was gradual over the course of a month. In contrast to experience with adults, lithium levels must be higher in the range of 0.5 to 1.1 (milliequivalent per liter (mEq/L) in order to achieve an augmentation response in children and adolescents.

Lithium also may be useful as a first-line medication in depressed children or adolescents with a family history of bipolar disorder, particularly in patients who have a history of mania. For unipolar depression, lithium alone is less useful than other antidepressant treatments.

Bipolar Disorder

As with major depression, the recognition and research in bipolar disorder in childhood and adolescence is a relatively recent phenomenon. Older conceptual models of mania postulated that mania was a defense against depression. As the superego during latency was considered too rudimentary for the development of depression, it was believed unlikely that children, and to a lesser extent adolescents, could have mania. However, it has long been observed in studies of adults with bipolar disorder that the onset of illness frequently can be traced to childhood and adolescence (Kraeplin, 1921). In 1960, Anthony and Scott published an important paper in which they proposed stringent criteria for juvenile manic-depressive illness, thereby establishing a clear working definition in prepubertal children (Anthony & Scott, 1960). Up to the time of their review of the literature, very few case reports of prepubertal children with mania existed. Since then many more cases have been described in the literature, and research data bases are being developed.

The cardinal feature of mania, first identified by Kraepelin in the early 20th century, is an elevation in mood, characterized as either euphoria or irritability. Other symptoms include inflated self-esteem or grandiosity, decreased need for sleep, increased talkativeness, pressured speech, racing thoughts, flight of ideas, distractibility, increased activity or psychomotor agitation, and uncharacteristic involvement in activities with strong potential for painful consequences. The current working definition of mania in adults is described in the *DSM-IV* manual and is unmodified for children and adolescents (APA, 1994). Impairment in adaptive functioning is a necessary feature for diagnosis. (See Table 30.3.)

EPIDEMIOLOGY

In a community sample of 150 adolescents ages 14 to 15 years assessed for psychiatric disorders (*DSM-III* criteria) and impairment in adaptive functioning, the point prevalence of bipolar disorder was 0.7% (1/150) (Kashani, Beck et al., 1987). If impairment in adaptive functioning was not included, the prevalence rate rose to 7.3% (Carlson & Kashini, 1988). If the duration of ill-

TABLE 30.3

Criteria for Manic Episode

A. A distinct period of abnormally and persistently elevated, expansive, or irritable mood, lasting at least 1 week (or any duration if hospitalization is necessary).

B. During the period of mood disturbance, three (or more) of the following symptoms have persisted (four if the mood is only irritable) and have been present to a significant degree:

   (1) inflated self-esteem or grandiosity

   (2) decreased need for sleep (e.g., feels rested after only 3 hours of sleep)

   (3) more talkative than usual or pressure to keep talking

   (4) flight of ideas or subjective experience that thoughts are racing

   (5) distractibility (i.e., attention too easily drawn to unimportant or irrelevant external stimuli)

   (6) increase in goal-directed activity (either socially, at work or school, or sexually) or psychomotor agitation

   (7) excessive involvement in pleasurable activities that have a high potential for painful consequences (e.g., engaging in unrestrained buying sprees, sexual indiscretions, or foolish business investments)

C. The symptoms do not meet criteria for a Mixed Episode. . . .

D. The mood disturbance is sufficiently severe to cause marked impairment in occupational functioning or in usual social activities or relationships with others, or to necessitate hospitalization to prevent harm to self or others, or there are psychotic features.

E. The symptoms are not due to the direct physiological effects of a substance (e.g., a drug of abuse, a medication, or other treatment) or a general medical condition (e.g., hyperthyroidism).

Note: Manic-like episodes that are clearly caused by somatic antidepressant treatment (e.g., medication, electroconvulsive therapy, light therapy) should not count toward a diagnosis of Bipolar I Disorder.

Note: From *Diagnostic and Statistical Manual of Mental Disorders*, 4th ed., American Psychiatric Association, 1994. Washington, D.C.: Author, p. 332. Copyright 1994 by the American Psychiatric Association. Reprinted with permission.

ness criteria is not specified, as was the case with *DSM-III-R*, then the prevalence rises to 13.3%. Lifetime prevalence rates in adult populations is around 1.0%. There are no studies of the prevalence of mania in prepubertal children, and the prevalence rate is thought to be quite low. The influence of age, race, and sex on prevalence of bipolar disorder in children and adolescents is not known.

AGE OF ONSET

Studies of adult bipolar inpatients indicate that at least 20% of patients become symptomatic before age 20, with most developing symptoms between the ages of 15 and 20 years (Joyce, 1984; Loranger & Levine, 1978). Prospective determinations of the age of onset of bipolar disorder is complicated by the difficulty clinicians have in recognizing the disorder in children and adolescents. Factors that contribute to physician underrecognition of early-onset bipolar disorder include: (1) the low base rate of the disorder, which leads to inadequate clinician exposure and experience; (2) the variability in presentation; (3) the symptom overlap with other childhood disorders (e.g., hyperactivity); and (4) the developmental change in symptom presentation (Bowring & Kovacs, 1992).

CLINICAL PRESENTATION

When mania presents in its full syndrome, there can be little confusion as to the diagnosis. Numerous clinicians and investigators have documented the full syndrome as seen in adults in prepubertal children and adolescents. However, the impact of development and age of onset on the core features of mania has not been well delineated and may alter symptom presentation.

Young children with bipolar disorder (earlier than 9 years old) present with more irritability and emotional lability than older children, who have more euphoria, elation, and grandiosity. However, hyperactivity, pressured speech, and distractibility do not appear to vary. As in depression, certain cognitive aspects of mania, such as grandiosity, may vary as a function of development (Carlson, 1983). While inferring a diagnosis from drug response is generally not appropriate, the specificity and effectiveness of lithium treatment

for bipolar disorder may be an exception. In a large group of children with various treatment-refractory behavioral disorders, those who responded to lithium demonstrated "cyclic affective extremes, especially hateful hostile anger, and manic overexcitement, a family history of effective disorder especially bipolar disorder, aggressiveness and prominent neurovegetative disorders, especially hyperphagia, hyperdipsia, salt cravings, and encopresis" (Delong & Aldershof, 1987, p. 394). Both Carlson's and Delong's observations are based on retrospective studies. No prospective, longitudinal, or at-risk studies have been performed to assess bipolar disorder symptomatology across development.

It is not likely that a clear manic syndrome is the first evidence of psychiatric disturbance in children and adolescents with bipolar disorder. A number of behavioral disturbances, in addition to depression, have been described as antecedent to the development of bipolar disorder; these include school phobia (Hassenyeh & Davison, 1980), anorexia nervosa (Hsu, Holder, Hindmarsh, & Phelps, 1984), and conduct disorder (Kovacs et al., 1988). Attention deficit hyperactivity disorder (ADHD) also has been described in the history of some children and adolescents who present with bipolar disorder. Whether these presenting disorders are distinct from bipolar disorder or represent prodromal or subsyndromal presentations of mania is not clear and is subject to controversy at the present time (Carlson, 1990a). What is clear is that most follow-up studies of anorexia, school phobia, ADHD, and conduct disorder do not show bipolar disorder as a frequent outcome. Bipolar disorder should be considered in the differential diagnosis of children with episodic conduct disorder, ADHD refractory to standard treatment, late-onset conduct disorder or ADHD, or a family history of bipolar disorder (Carlson, 1990a, 1990b).

One published study has attempted to determine predictors of bipolar outcome in adolescents whose initial presentation is one of major depression. In a prospective study of 60 adolescents hospitalized for major depressive disorder, within 3 to 4 years follow-up 20% ultimately developed mania. Predictors for bipolarity were: (1) depressive episode characterized by rapid onset, psychomotor retardation, and mood-congruent psychotic features; (2) strong family history of bipolar disorder and affective illness spanning multiple generations; and (3) pharmacological induction of mania by tricyclic antidepressants (Strober & Carlson, 1982).

Psychotic presentations in childhood and adolescence introduce further diagnostic uncertainty. While the presence of psychotic symptoms limits the differential to schizophrenia, mood disorder (psychotic depression and bipolar disorder), delirium, or the organic psychoses including drug-induced psychoses, it is difficult at times to make the appropriate diagnosis. Numerous investigators have commented on the problems in distinguishing schizophrenic psychoses from affective psychoses during the acute phase of illness (Ballenger, Reus, & Post, 1982; Hassenyeh & Davison, 1980; Horowitz, 1977; Joyce, 1984). Early-onset bipolar disorder is associated with more "schizophreniclike" symptoms, which makes the distinction from schizophrenia difficult (Ballanger et al., 1982). Over 50% of children and adolescents diagnosed with bipolar disorder at long-term follow-up were misdiagnosed with schizophrenia when initially seen (Werry, McLellan, & Chard, 1991). Early age of onset and psychotic presentation were correlated with a misdiagnosis of schizophrenia in patients with early-onset bipolar disorder (Joyce, 1984). Misdiagnosing bipolar disorder as schizophrenia has significant clinical consequences, including: (1) the underutilization of appropriate medications for affective illness, such as lithium; (2) unnecessary disability from an untreated mood disorder; (3) exposure of young mood disorder patients to the side effects of neuroleptics including tardive dyskinesia and neuroleptic malignant syndrome; and (4) the psychological burden of the poorer prognosis and the more onerous diagnosis of schizophrenia. Particularly helpful in establishing the diagnosis of bipolar disorder are the episodic nature of symptoms, a clear change in activity and affect from baseline, a family history of bipolar disorder (Carlson, 1990b), and importantly, an awareness of diagnostic bias against mania and toward the diagnosis of schizophrenia in the United States.

Special mention should be given to bipolar presentations in mentally retarded children and children with pervasive developmental disorders, populations that are even more likely to be misdiagnosed. In the moderately to severely mentally retarded patient, the fact that it is very difficult to ascertain internal states in a clear and unambiguous way forces clinicians to rely more heavily on behavioral observation (McCracken & Diamond, 1988) as well as a positive family history for bipolar disorder. Clearly an abrupt change in functioning in a developmentally disabled child should prompt consideration of the new onset of an affective disorder, including bipolar disorder.

TREATMENT

Lithium: As in adults, lithium is considered the first-line treatment of mania in children and adolescents. It should be noted, however, that there have been no double-blind, placebo-controlled studies examining the efficacy of lithium in this population. Most of the literature consists of case studies. Delong and Aldershof in 1987 presented their findings in treating over 150 children and adolescents with refractory behavior disorders with lithium. Of the 59 patients who were retrospectively diagnosed as having bipolar disorder, 66% (39/59) were considered responders in a 12- to 84-month follow-up period. There were no significant differences in treatment response in children and adolescents. Preliminary evidence regarding lithium prophylaxis in adolescents with bipolar disorder suggests that lithium may be useful in preventing future episodes of bipolar disorder. Of 37 adolescents treated acutely for mania with lithium and followed for 18 months, a threefold increase in relapse was seen in 12 of 13 (92.3%) adolescents who prematurely discontinued lithium treatment compared to the 9 of 24 adolescents who relapsed while on lithium (Strober, Morrell, Lampert, & Burroughs, 1990). The patients who discontinued lithium often relapsed within 6 months of discontinuation.

Prior to the initiation of lithium therapy, baseline investigations including an electrocardiogram, complete blood count, electrolytes, kidney function tests, and thyroid function tests are recommended. Renal disease is a relative contraindication to the initiation of lithium. The desired range of lithium levels is the same as for adults, 0.7 to 1.2 mEq/L. Children tend to clear lithium more quickly than adults due to their increased renal clearance and may require higher doses to maintain a therapeutic level (Jefferson, 1982). Dosing schedule based on weight allows for safe and quick achievement of therapeutic levels in prepubertal children (Weller, Weller, & Fristad, 1986). Lithium levels should be checked on a regular basis to assure that dosage remains in the therapeutic range and, most important, to avoid toxicity. Although in adults the regular determination of creatinine clearance and serum creatinine has been challenged (Schou, 1988), some clinicians may continue to check these on a regular basis until the effects of lithium in children and adolescent have been more thoroughly studied.

Lithium is generally well tolerated in children and adolescents, and side effects are mild. The most common side effects appear to be weight gain, decreased motor activity, excessive sedation, irritability, stomachache, pallor, vomiting, tremor, and headache (Campbell, Perry, & Greene, 1984). A special consideration in this age group is the potential development of acne and alopecia. In addition, an occasional child or adolescent may develop nocturnal enuresis as a complication of lithium-induced polyuria. Lithium accumulates in the bone and has been shown to inhibit bone size experimentally in rats (Jefferson, 1982). How this may impact growth in children is unclear, and there are no published reports of retarded growth related to lithium. Cognitive impairment on performance tasks may be evident and may impact on school performance. As with all medications, side effects must be balanced with therapeutic efficacy (Jefferson, 1982).

Carbamazepine: Carbamazepine has been used to treat bipolar disorder successfully in adults who are lithium nonresponders or are unable to tolerate lithium. While there is much experience with the use of carbamazepine in children, its efficacy for the treatment of bipolar disorder has not been well established. It is considered a second-line treatment in children and adolescents with bipolar disorder. Baseline complete blood counts and liver function tests should be obtained and followed at regular intervals to observe for granulocytopenia and drug-induced hepatitis. Current guidelines suggest that drug dosage should be balanced between clinical response and side effects; thus the therapeutic range may extend from 4 to 12 micrograms per liter (Post, Trimble, & Pippenger, 1989). Common side effects include dizziness, ataxia, sedation, diplopia, and rash. A number of case reports in the literature indicate that some children and adolescents treated with carbama-

zepine with acceptable drug levels develop a manic syndrome that disappears with discontinuation of medication (Myers & Carrera, 1989; Pleak, Birmaher, Gavrilescu, Abichandani, & Williams, 1988; Reiss & O'Donnell, 1984). It is presumed that the development of mania is related to the tricyclic structure of carbamazepine.

Valproic Acid: Valproic acid is increasingly being used as a second-line treatment of bipolar disorder. Research in adults suggests that valproic acid is a useful agent for patients who cycle rapidly, are refractory to lithium, or experience mixed states (Calabrese & Woyshville, 1995). Some clinicians now use valproic acid as a first-line medication. Its major advantages over lithium and carbamazepine are its more favorable side effect profile and its ability to be rapidly titrated to therapeutic levels over 24 hours (Keck, McElroy, Tugrul, & Bennett, 1993). Valproic acid is generally well tolerated, which may lead to increased compliance. Presently there are no published studies on the use of valproic acid in children and adolescents with bipolar disorder. In the absence of controlled trials in children and adolescents, it is most useful to do rigorous, sequential pharmacologic trials in these often complex patients.

Clozapine: Clozapine as a treatment for psychotic mania refractory to traditional treatments deserves mention. Studies in adults demonstrate that clozapine is effective in the short term and maintenance treatment of bipolar disorder and has mood-stabilizing properties (Zarete, Tohen, & Baldessarini, 1995). Experience with clozapine in children and adolescents with schizophrenia is positive although the research is limited (Remschmidt, Schulz, & Martin, 1994). There is no literature on the use of clozapine in children and adolescents with bipolar disorder. Nevertheless, it should be considered in the medication algorithm of children and adolescents with severe refractory bipolar disorder, especially those with chronic psychotic symptoms, as these patients tend to be on high doses of neuroleptic medication for extended periods of time and have increased risk of tardive dyskinesia.

Clonazepam: Clonazepam is also used for the treatment of bipolar disorder and has been demonstrated to decrease the intensity of manic episodes but to have a lesser effect on the actual cycling process of bipolar patients. Many clinicians use clonazepam instead of neuroleptics for the acute management of manic agitation and as an adjunct to other mood-stabilizing medications.

Conclusion

Over the last two decades, significant developments in our knowledge of child and adolescent mood disorders have occurred. We are increasingly aware of developmental influences on the clinical presentation of depression and bipolar disorder and the continuity of childhood mood disorders with those in adulthood. Not only can major depression and bipolar disorder occur early in development, but early-onset mood disorders are associated with greater severity and chronicity and place children with mood disorders at increased risk for other psychiatric disorders during their lifetime. As we are more knowledgeable about the important role of both genetic and psychosocial factors in the etiology and course of the mood disorders, thinking simplistically and reductionistically is increasingly difficult.

Recognition that untreated mood disorders are associated with serious morbidity in children and adolescents is leading to increasing pressures in clinical practice to identify and treat mood disorders as well as to new research and advocacy efforts. In an effort to address the increasing clinical need, practitioners appear to be diagnosing and treating child and adolescent patients more aggressively. Yet they do so in a scientific vacuum. Research focusing on the underlying neurobiology of the mood disorders offers real promise as methodologic improvements are occurring rapidly in genetics and the neurosciences. Published treatment studies have not provided the definitive results to guide the clinician, although large controlled trials of psychopharmacologic agents are under way. In addition, new treatment study methodologies are being developed to address the methodologic limitations identified in previous pharmacologic treatment trials. Advances in psychological treatments will be critical as they are the most commonly utilized and least well studied treatments child psychiatrists use today. There is increasing federal grant support for the standardization of various psychological treatments and for the use of these approaches in controlled trials.

Perhaps most important, there has been an increase in awareness among those who suffer with mood disorders, their families, and their friends, resulting in decreased stigma, increasing personal support, and political and scientific advocacy.

REFERENCES

Akiskal, H., Khani, M. & Scott-Strauss, A. (1979). Cyclothymic temperamental disorders. *Psychiatric Clinics of North America, 2* (3), 527–554.

Ambrosini, P. J., Bianchi, M. D., Rabinovich, H., & Elia, J., (1993). Antidepressant treatments in children and adolescents I. Affective disorders. *Journal of American Academy of Child and Adolescent Psychiatry, 32,* 1–6.

American Psychiatric Association. (1987). *Diagnostic and statistical manual of mental disorders* (3rd ed., rev.). Washington, DC: Author.

American Psychiatric Association. (1994). *Diagnostic and statistical manual of mental disorders* (4th ed.). Washington, DC: Author.

Angold, A. (1988). Childhood and adolescent depression I. Epidemiological and aetiological aspects. *British Journal of Psychiatry, 152,* 601–617.

Anthony, J., & Scott, P. (1960). Manic-depressive psychosis in childhood. *Child Psychology and Psychiatry, 1,* 53–72.

Ballenger, J. C., Reus, V. I., & Post, R. M. (1982). The "atypical" clinical picture of adolescent mania. *American Journal of Psychiatry, 139,* 602–606.

Beck, A. (1967). *Depression: Causes and treatment.* Philadelphia: University of Pennsylvania Press.

Biederman, J. (1993). *Cardiac side effects of tricyclic antidepressants.* Paper presented at the midyear Institute of the American Academy of Child and Adolescent Psychiatry, San Juan, Puerto Rico.

Birmaher, B., Ryan, N. D., Dahl, R., Rabinovich, H., Ambrosini, P., Williamson, D. E., Novacenko, H., Nelson, B., Sing Lo, E., & Puig-Antich, J. (1992). Dexamethasone suppression test in children with major depressive disorder. *Journal of the American Academy of Child and Adolescent Psychiatry, 31,* 291–297.

Boulos, C., Kutcher, S., Gardner, D., & Young, E. (1992). An open naturalistic trial of fluoxetine in adolescents and young adults with treatment-resistant major depression. *Journal of Child and Adolescent Psychopharmacology, 2,* 103–111.

Bowlby, J. (1988). Developmental psychiatry comes of age. *American Journal of Psychiatry, 145,* 1–10.

Bowring, M. A., & Kovacs, M. (1992). Difficulties in diagnosing manic disorders among children and adolescents. *Journal of the American Academy of Child and Adolescent Psychiatry, 32,* 611–614.

Calabrese, J. R., & Woyshville, M. J. (1995). A medication algorithm for treatment of bipolar rapid cycling? *Journal of Clinical Psychiatry, 56* (suppl 3), 11–18.

Campbell, M., Perry, R., & Green, W. (1984). Use of lithium in children and adolescents. *Psychosomatics, 25,* 91–106.

Carlson, G. A. (1983). Bipolar affective disorders in childhood and adolescence. In D. P. Cantwell & G. A. Carlson (Eds.), *Affective disorders in childhood and adolescence* (pp. 61–84). New York: S. P. Medical and Scientific Books.

Carlson, G. A. (1990a). Annotation: Child and adolescent mania—diagnostic considerations. *Journal of Child Psychology and Psychiatry, 31* (3), 331–341.

Carlson, G. A. (1990b). Bipolar disorder in children and adolescents. In G. A. Carlson & E. B. Weller (Eds.), *Psychiatric disorders in children and adolescents* (pp. 21–36). Philadelphia: W. B. Saunders.

Carlson, G. A., & Cantwell, D. P. (1980). A survey of depressive symptoms, syndrome and disorder in a child psychiatric population. *Journal of Child Psychology and Psychiatry, 21,* 19–25.

Carlson, G. A., & Kashani, J. H. (1988). Manic symptoms in a non-referred adolescent population. *Journal of Affective Disorders, 15,* 219–226.

Casat, C. D., Arana, G. W., & Powell, K. (1989). The DST in children and adolescents with major depressive disorder. *American Journal of Psychiatry, 146,* 503–507.

Cavallo, A., Holt, K. J., Hejazi, M. S., Richards, G. E., & Meyer, W. J. (1987). Melatonin circadian rhythm in childhood depression. *Journal of the American Academy of Child and Adolescent Psychiatry, 26,* 395–399.

Conners, C. K. (1992). Methodology of antidepressant drug trials for treating depression in adolescents. *Journal of Child and Adolescent Psychopharmacology, 2,* 11–22.

Cytryn, L., & McKnew, D. H. (1972). Proposed classification of childhood depression. *American Journal of Psychiatry, 129,* 149–155.

Dahl, R. E., Ryan, N. D., Puig-Antich, J., Nguyen, N. A., Al-Shabbout, M., Meyer, V. A., & Perel, J. (1991). 23-hour cortisol measures in adolescents with major depression: A controlled study. *Biological Psychiatry, 30,* 25–36.

Dahl, R. E., Ryan, N. D., Williamson, D. E., Ambrosini, P. J., Rabinovich, H., Novacenko, H., Nelson, B., & Puig-Antich, J. (1992). Regulation of sleep and growth hormone in adolescent depression. *Journal of the American Academy of Child and Adolescent Psychiatry, 31,* 615–621.

Delong, G. R., & Aldershof, A. L. (1987). Long-term experience with lithium treatment in childhood: Correlation with clinical diagnosis. *Journal of the Ameri-*

can Academy of Child and Adolescent Psychiatry, 26, 389–394.

de Villiers, A. S., Russell, V. A., Carstens, M. E., Searson, J. A., van Zyl, A. M., Lombard, C. J., & Taljaard, J. F. (1989). Noradrenergic function and hypothalamic-pituitary-adrenal axis activity in adolescents with major depressive disorder. *Psychiatry Research, 27,* 101–109.

Elkin, I., Shea, T., Watkins, J. T., Imber, S. D., Sotsky, S. M., Collins, J. F., Glass, D. R., Pikonis, P. A., Leber, W. R., Docherty, J. P., Fiester, S. J., & Parloff, M. B. (1989). National Institute of Mental Health treatment of depression collaborative research program. *Archives of General Psychiatry, 46,* 971–982.

Geller, B., Cooper, T. B., Graham, D. L., Fetner, H. H., Marsteller, F. A., & Wells, J. M. (1992). Pharmacokinetically designed double-blind placebo-controlled study of nortriptyline in 6- to 12-year-olds with major depressive disorder. *Journal of the American Academy of Child and Adolescent Psychiatry, 31,* 34–44.

Geller, B., Cooper, T. B., Graham, D. L., Marsteller, F. A., & Bryant, D. (1990). Double-blind placebo-controlled study of nortriptyline in depressed adolescents using a "fixed plasma level" design. *Psychopharmacology Bulletin, 26,* 85–90.

Geller, B., Fox, L. & Fletcher, M. (1993). Effect of tricyclic antidepressants on switching to mania and on the onset of bipolarity in depressed 6- to 12-year-olds. *Journal of the American Academy of Child and Adolescent Psychiatry, 32,* 43–50.

Goodwin, J. K., & Jamison, K. R. (1990). *Manic-depressive illness.* New York: Oxford University Press.

Hassanyeh, F., & Davison, K. (1980). Bipolar affective psychosis with onset before age 16 years: Report of 10 cases. *British Journal of Psychiatry, 137,* 530–539.

Horowitz, H. A. (1977). Lithium and the treatment of adolescent manic depressive illness. *Diseases of the Nervous System, 6,* 480–483.

Hsu, G., Holder, D., Hindmarsh, D., & Phelps, C. (1984). Bipolar illness preceded by anorexia nervosa in identical twins. *Journal of Clinical Psychiatry, 45,* 262–266.

Jefferson, J. W. (1982). The use of lithium in childhood and adolescence: An overview. *Journal of Clinical Psychiatry, 43,* 174–177.

Joyce, P. R. (1984). Age of onset in bipolar affective disorder and misdiagnosis as schizophrenia. *Psychological Medicine, 14,* 145–149.

Kandel, D. B., & Davies, M. (1982). Epidemiology of depressive mood in adolescents. *Archives of General Psychiatry, 39,* 1205–1212.

Kashani, J. H., Beck, N. C., Hoeper, E. W., Fallahi, C., Corcoran, C. M., McAllister, J. A., Rosenberg, T. K., & Reid, J. C. (1987). Psychiatric disorders in a community sample of adolescents. *American Journal of Psychiatry, 144,* 584–589.

Kashani, J. H., & Carlson, G. A. (1987). Seriously depressed preschoolers. *American Journal of Psychiatry, 144,* 348–350.

Kashani, J. H., Carlson, G. A., Beck, N. C., Hoeper,

E. W., Corcoran, C. M., McAllister, J. A., Fallahi, C., Rosenberg, T. K., & Reid, J. C. (1987). Depression, depressive symptoms, and depressed mood among a community sample of adolescents. *American Journal of psychiatry, 144,* 931–934.

Kashani, J. H., McGee, R. O., Clarkson, S. E., Anderson, J. C., Walton, L. A., Williams, S., Silva, P. A., Robins, A. J., Cytryn, L., & McKnew, D. H. (1983). Depression in a sample of 9-year-old children: Prevalence and associated characteristics. *Archives of General Psychiatry, 40,* 1217–1223.

Kashani, J. H., & Sherman, D. D. (1988). Childhood depression: Epidemiology, etiological models, and treatment implications. *Integrative Psychiatry, 6,* 1–21.

Kazdin, A. E. (1990). Childhood depression. *Journal of Child Psychology and Psychiatry, 31,* 121–160.

Kazdin, A. E., Esveldt-Dawson, K., Sherick, R. B., & Colbus, D. (1985). Assessment of overt behavior and childhood depression among psychiatrically disturbed children. *Journal of Consulting and Clinical Psychology, 53,* 201–210.

Keck, P. E., McElroy, S. L., Tugrul, K. C., & Bennett, J. A. (1993). Valproate oral loading in the treatment of acute mania. *Journal of Clinical Psychiatry, 54,* 305–308.

King, R. A., Riddle, M. A., Chappell, P. B., Hardin, M. T., Anderson, G. M., Lombroso, P., & Scahill, L. (1991). Emergence of self-destructive phenomena in children and adolescents during fluoxetine treatment. *Journal of the American Academy of Child and Adolescent Psychiatry, 30,* 179–186.

Klein, D., Gittelman, R., Quitkin, F., & Rifkin, A. (1980). *Diagnosis and drug treatment of psychiatric disorders: Adults and children.* Baltimore: Williams & Wilkins.

Kovacs, M., Feinberg, T. L., Crouse-Novak, M., Paulauskas, S. L., & Finkelstein, R. (1984). Depressive disorders in childhood. I. A longitudinal prospective study of characteristics and recovery. *Archives of General Psychiatry, 41,* 229–237.

Kovacs, M., Feinberg, T. L., Crouse-Novak, M., Paulauskas, S. L., Pollock, M., & Finkelstein, R. (1984). Depressive disorders in childhood. II. A longitudinal study of the risk of a subsequent major depression. *Archives of General Psychiatry, 41,* 643–649.

Kovacs, M., & Gatsonis, C. (1989). Stability and change in childhood-onset depressive disorders: Longitudinal course as a diagnostic validator. In L. N. Robins & J. E. Barrett (Eds.), *The validity of psychiatric diagnosis* (pp. 57–75). New York: Raven Press.

Kovacs, M., Gatsonis, C., Paulauskas, S. L., & Richards, C. (1989). Depressive disorders in childhood. IV. A longitudinal study of comorbidity with and risk for anxiety disorders. *Archives of General Psychiatry, 46,* 776–782.

Kovacs, M., & Goldston, D. (1991). Cognitive and social cognitive development of depressed children and adolescents. *Journal of American Academy of Child and Adolescent Psychiatry, 30,* 388–392.

Kovacs, M., Paulauskas, S., Gatsonis, C., & Richards, C. (1988). Depressive disorders in childhood. III. A longitudinal study of comorbidity with and risk for conduct disorders. *Journal of Affective Disorders, 15,* 205–217.

Kraepelin, E. (1921). *Manic-depressive insanity and paranoia.* Edinburgh: Livingstone.

Kramer, A. D., & Feiguine, R. J. (1981). Clinical effects of amitriptyline in adolescent depression. A pilot study. *Journal of the American Academy of Child and Adolescent Psychiatry, 20,* 636–644.

Lamb, M. E., Nash, A., Teti, D. M., & Bornstein, M. H. (1991). Infancy. In M. Lewis (Ed.), *Child and adolescent psychiatry. A comprehensive textbook* (pp. 222–256). Baltimore: William & Wilkins.

Loranger, A. W., & Levine, P. M. (1978). Age at onset of bipolar affective illness. *Archives of General Psychiatry, 35,* 1345–1348.

McCracken, J. T. (1992). Etiologic aspects of child and adolescent mood disorders. *Child and Adolescent Psychiatric Clinics of North America, 1,* 89–109.

McCracken, J. T., & Diamond, R. P. (1988). Bipolar disorder in mentally retarded adolescents. *Journal of the American Academy of Child and Adolescent Psychiatry, 27,* 494–499.

McKnew, D. H., & Cytryn, L. (1979). Urinary metabolites in chronically depressed children. *Journal of the American Academy of Child Psychiatry, 18,* 608–615.

Mitchell, J., McCauley, E., Burke, P., & Moss, S. (1988). Phenomenology of depression in children and adolescents. *Journal of the American Academy of Child and Adolescent Psychiatry, 27,* 12–20.

Mufson, L., Moreau, D., Weissman, M., Wickramaratne, P., Martin, J., & Samoilov, A. (1994). Modification of interpersonal psychotherapy with depressed adolescents (IPT-A): Phase I and II studies. *Journal of the American Academy of Child and Adolescent Psychiatry, 33,* 695–705.

Myers, W. C., & Carrera, F. (1989). Carbamazepine-induced mania with hypersexuality in a 9-year-old boy. *American Journal of Psychiatry, 146,* 400.

Pleak, R. R., Birmaher, B., Gavrilescu, A., Abichandani, C., & Williams, D. T. (1988). Mania and neuropsychiatric excitation following carbamazepine. *Journal of the American Academy of Child and Adolescent Psychiatry, 27,* 500–503.

Post, R. M., Trimble, M. R., & Pippenger, C. E. (1989). *Clinical use of anticonvulsants in psychiatric disorders.* New York: Demos Publications.

Preskorn, S. H. (1994). Targeted pharmacotherapy in depression management: Comparative pharmacokinetics of fluoxetine, paroxetine, and sertraline. *International Clinical Psychopharmacology, 9* (Suppl 3), 13–19.

Preskorn, S. H., Weller, E., Hughes, C., & Weller, R. (1988). Relationship of plasma imipramine levels to CNS toxicity in children. *American Journal of Psychiatry, 145,* 897.

Preskorn, S. H., Weller, E. B., Hughes, C. W., Weller, R. A., & Bolte, K. (1987). Depression in prepubertal children: Dexamethasone nonsuppression predicts differential response to imipramine vs. placebo. *Psychopharmacology Bulletin, 23,* 128–133.

Preskorn, S. H., Weller, E. B., & Weller, R. A. (1982). Depression in children: Relationship between plasma imipramine levels and response. *Journal of Clinical Psychiatry, 43,* 450–453.

Puig-Antich, J. (1982). Major depression and conduct disorder in prepuberty. *Journal of the American Academy of Child Psychiatry, 21,* 118–128.

Puig-Antich, J. (1987). Affective disorders in children and adolescents: Diagnostic validity and psychobiology. In H. Y. Meltzer (Ed.), *Psychopharmacology: The third generation of progress* (pp. 843–859). New York: Raven Press.

Puig-Antich, J., Goetz, D., Davies, M., Kaplan, T., Davies, S., Ostrow, L., Asnis, L., Twomey, J., Iyengar, S., & Ryan, N. D. (1989). A controlled family history study of prepubertal major depressive disorder. *Archives of General Psychiatry, 46,* 406–418.

Puig-Antich, J., Kaufman, J., Ryan, N. D., Williamson, D. E., Dahl, R. E., Lukens, E., Todak, G., Ambrosini, P., Rabinovich, H., & Nelson, B. (1993). The psychosocial functioning and family environment of depressed adolescents. *Journal of American Academy of Child and Adolescent Psychiatry, 32,* 244–253.

Puig-Antich, J., Lukens, E., Davies, M., Goetz, D., Brennan-Quattrock, J., & Todak, G. (1985a). Psychosocial functioning in prepubertal major depressive disorders. I. Interpersonal relationships during the depressive episode. *Archives of General Psychiatry, 42,* 500–507.

Puig-Antich, J., Lukens, E., Davies, M., Goetz, D., Brennan-Quattrock, J., & Todak, G. (1985b). Psychosocial functioning in prepubertal major depressive disorders. II. Interpersonal relationships after sustained recovery from affective episode. *Archives of General Psychiatry, 42,* 511–517.

Puig-Antich, J., Perel, J. M., Lupatkin, W., Chamber, W. J., Tabrizi, M., King, J., Goetz, R., Davies, M., & Stiller, R. L. (1987). Imipramine in prepubertal major depressive disorders. *Archives of General Psychiatry, 44,* 81–89.

Reiss, A. L., & O'Donnell, D. (1984). Carbamazepine-induced mania in two children: Case report. *Journal of Clinical Psychiatry, 45,* 272–274.

Remschmidt, H., Schulz, D., & Martin, M. (1994). An open trial of clozapine in thirty-six adolescents with schizophrenia. *Journal of Child and Adolescent Psychopharmacology, 4* (1), 31–41.

Riddle, M. A., Nelson, C., Kleinman, C. S., Rasmusson, A., Leckman, J. F., King, R. A., & Cohen, D. J. (1991). Sudden death in children receiving norpramin: Review of three reported cases and commentary. *Journal of the American Academy of Child and Adolescent Psychiatry, 30,* 104–108.

Rie, H. E. (1966). Depression in childhood: A survey of some pertinent contributions. *Journal of the American Academy of Child Psychiatry, 5,* 653–685.

Roberts, R. E., & Sobhan, M. (1992). Symptoms of depression in adolescence: A comparison of Anglo, African, and Hispanic Americans. *Journal of Youth and Adolescence, 21,* 639–651.

Ryan, N. D. (1990). Heterocyclic antidepressants in children and adolescents. *Journal of Child and Adolescent Psychopharmacology, 1,* 21–31.

Ryan, N. D., Meyer, V., Dachille, S., Mazzie, D., & Puig-Antich, J. (1988). Lithium antidepressant augmentation in TCA-refractory depression in adolescents. *Journal of the American Academy of Child and Adolescent Psychiatry, 27,* 371–376.

Ryan, N. D., Puig-Antich, J., Ambrosini, P., Rabinovich, H., Robinson, D., Nelson, B., Iyengar, S., & Twomey, J. (1987). The clinical picture of major depression in children and adolescents. *Archives of General Psychiatry, 44,* 854–861.

Ryan, N. D., Puig-antich, J., Cooper, T., Rabinovich, H., Ambrosini, P., Davies, M., King, J., Torres, D., & Fried, J. (1986). Imipramine in adolescent major depression: Plasma level and clinical response. *Acta Psychiatrica Scandinavia, 73,* 275–288.

Ryan, N. D., Puig-Antich, J., Cooper, T. B., Rabinovich, H., Ambrosini, P., Fried, J., Davies, M., Torres, D., & Suckow, R. F. (1986). Relative safety of single versus divided dose imipramine in adolescent major depression. *Journal of the American Academy of Child and Adolescent Psychiatry, 26,* 400–406.

Ryan, N. D., Puig-Antich, J., Rabinovich, H., Fried, J., Ambrosini, P., Meyer, V., Torres, D., Dachille, S., & Mazzie, D. (1988). MAOIs in adolescent major depression unresponsive to tricyclic antidepressants. *Journal of the American Academy of Child and Adolescent Psychiatry, 27,* 755–758.

Sandler, J., & Joffe, W. G. (1965). Notes on childhood depression. *International Journal of Psychoanalysis, 46,* 88–96.

Schou, M. (1988). Effects of long-term lithium treatment on kidney function: An overview. *Journal of Psychiatric Research, 22,* 287–296.

Seligman, M. E., & Peterson, C. (1986). A learned helplessness perspective on childhood depression: Theory and research. In M. Rutter, C. Izard, & P. Read (Eds.), *Depression in young people: Developmental and clinical perspectives* (pp. 223–249). New York: Guilford Press.

Simeon, J. G., Dinicola, V. F., Ferguson, H. B., & Copping, W. (1990). Adolescent depression: A placebo-controlled fluoxetine treatment study and follow-up. *Progress in Neuro-Psychopharmacology and Biological Psychiatry, 14,* 791–795.

Sternbach, H. (1990). The serotonin syndrome. *American Journal of Psychiatry, 148,* 705–713.

Strober, M., & Carlson, G. (1982). Bipolar illness in adolescents with major depression. Clinical, genetic, and psychopharmacologic predictors in a three- to four-year prospective follow-up investigation. *Archives of General Psychiatry, 39,* 549–555.

Strober, M., Freeman, R., Rigall, J., Schmidt, S., & Diamond, R. (1992). The pharmacotherapy of de-

SECTION II / SYNDROMES OF ADOLESCENCE

pressive illness in adolescence: II. Effects of lithium augmentation in nonresponders to imipramine. *Journal of the American Academy of Child and Adolescent Psychiatry, 31*, 16–20.

Strober, M., Morrell, W., Lampert, C., & Burroughs, J. (1990). Relapse following discontinuation of lithium maintenance therapy in adolescents with bipolar I illness: A naturalistic study. *American Journal of Psychiatry, 147*, 457–461.

Sudden death in children treated with a tricyclic antidepressant. (1990). *The Medical Letter, 32*, 53.

Tennant, C. (1988). Parental loss in childhood. *Archives of General Psychiatry, 45*, 1045–1050.

Tsuang, M. T., & Faraone, S. V. (1990). *The genetics of mood disorders.* Baltimore: Johns Hopkins University Press.

Weissman, M., & Myers, J. K. (1978). Affective disorders in a US urban community: The use of research diagnostic criteria in a epidemiological survey. *Archives of General Psychiatry, 35*, 1304–1311.

Weissman, M., Gammon, D., John, K., Merikangas, K., Warner, V., Prusoff, B. A., & Sholomskas, D. (1987). Children of depressed parents. Increased psychopathology and early onset of major depression. *Archives of General Psychiatry, 44*, 847–853.

Weissman, M. M., Gershon, E. S., Kidd, K. K., Prusoff, B. A., Leckman, J. F., Dibble, E., Hamovit, J., Thompson, D., Pauls, D. L., & Guroff, J. J. (1984). Psychiatric disorders in the relatives of probands with affective disorders. The Yale University-National Institute of Mental Health collaborative study. *Archives of General Psychiatry, 41*, 13–21.

Weissman, M. M., Leckman, J. F., Merikangas, K. R., Gammon, G. D., & Prusoff, B. A. (1984). Depression and anxiety disorders in parents and children. Results from the Yale family study. *Archives of General Psychiatry, 41*, 845–852.

Weissman, M. M., Paykel, E. S., & Klerman, G. L. (1972). The depressed woman as mother. *Social Psychiatry, 7*, 98–108.

Weissman, M. M., Prusoff, B. A., Gammon, G. D., Merikangas, K. R., Leckman, J. F., & Kidd, K. K. (1984). Psychopathology in the children (aged 6–18) of depressed and normal parents. *Journal of the American Academy of Child Psychiatry, 23*, 78–84.

Weller, E. B., Weller, R. A., & Fristad, M. A. (1986). Lithium dosage guide for prepubertal children: A preliminary report. *Journal of the American Academy of Child Psychiatry, 25*, 92–95.

Werry, J., McLellan, J., & Chard, L. (1991). Childhood and adolescent schizophrenia, bipolar and schizoaffective disorders: A clinical and outcome study. *Journal of the American Academy of Child and Adolescent Psychiatry, 30*, 457–465.

Zarate, C. A., Tohen, M., & Baldessarini, R. J. (1995). Clozapine in severe mood disorders. *Journal of Clinical Psychiatry, 56*, 411–417.

328

31 / Dissociative Disorders in Children and Adolescents

Joyanna L. Silberg, Desanka Stipic, and Fereidoon Taghizadeh

Introduction

Psychiatric interest has returned to the study of dissociation, a phenomenon that stimulated the interest and writings of the forefathers of modern psychiatry a century ago. Charcot and Janet's descriptions of patients suffering from amnesia, fugue, and "successive" personalities in the late 19th century paralleled Freud and Breuer's interest in hypnotic and dissociative states in *Studies on Hysteria* (1895) (Ellenberger, 1970). Both Janet and Freud recognized that the "hysterical symptoms" of their patients, which often included dissociated memories and "split" personalities, were associated with childhood trauma. However, Freud's initial stance that many of his patients' symptoms originated in sexual "seduction" as children was replaced by a theory that considered these "recollections" to be based on fantasy. Despite the interest of Americans William James and Morton Prince in dissociative phenomena in the early part of the 20th century, the tide of scientific and psychoanalytic inquiry shifted away from dissociation, as psychoanalytic concepts emphasizing "repression" and Kraepelinian concepts of schizophrenia predominated. The tide may be shifting again due to the wealth of clinical investigation over the last two decades into the dissociative spectrum of disorders, particularly multiple personality disorder (MPD), now termed dissociative identity disorder (DID). This resurgence of interest in dissociative disorders and related posttraumatic stress disorder (PTSD) has been spurred, in part, by the increasing recognition of the combat-related disorders of Vietnam veterans and the number of trauma survivors of domestic violence, particularly victims of child abuse (Kluft, 1991b; Putnam, 1989).

According to the fourth edition of the *Diagnostic and Statistical Manual of Mental Disorders* (*DSM-IV;* American Psychiatric Association [APA], 1994), dissociative disorders are characterized by "a disruption in the usually integrated functions of consciousness, memory, identity or perception" (p. 487.) Dissociation has been viewed as a normative capacity for absorption and involvement in internal fantasy (Putnam, 1989), a psychobiological process (Ludwig, 1983), a psychological defense (Rapaport, 1942), and more recently an adaptive response to trauma (Putnam, 1989; Spiegel, 1991). Studies of variations in individual hypnotizability (a phenomenon related but not identical to dissociation) and studies of normative dissociative experiences in nonpsychiatric populations support the notion that dissociative capacity is a trait that is distributed in the general population (Putnam, 1989). Individuals with a high capacity for normal dissociation are seen as easily "lost in thought" particularly when engaged in automatic behaviors, such as driving. Ludwig (1983) has suggested that dissociative processes are a psychobiological survival strategy that allow the organism to preserve functional, energy-conserving survival behaviors when faced with overwhelming traumatic experience or conflict. In addition, the dissociative processes allow the organism to isolate unpleasant memories and affects. Rapaport (1942) has viewed dissociation as a psychological defense similar to "repression" but that involves removing from conscious awareness "a set" of unacceptable "affects" or "strivings." The contemporary view of pathological dissociation is as an adaptive response to trauma that may initially have survival benefits during the period of trauma but remains as a maladaptive defensive style after the trauma has passed (Putnam, 1989; Spiegel, 1991). Pathological dissociation may be manifest in disturbances of personal identity, which may take the form of fugue or alternating identities, and disturbances in memory (Nemiah, 1991).

The application of these concepts to the field of child and adolescent psychiatry has remained preliminary. Beginning data suggest that normative dissociative capacity is high in childhood and early adolescence and that abused children demonstrate more dissociative symptomatology than normal children (Putnam, 1991a). The relationship of the concept of dissociation to the preschooler's well-developed capacity for absorption in fantasy play is unclear. Preliminary case studies and research on abused children with dissociative symptoms suggest that early fantasy-proneness may be an important substrate on which dissociative defenses are built (Albini & Pease, 1989; Lynn, Rhue, & Green, 1988). The contemporary interest in dissociative disorders provides an opportunity for researchers and clinicians in the field of child and adolescent psychiatry to explore the nature of consciousness, identity, and personality, the process by which psychological defenses may emerge, and how normal developmental patterns may be disrupted in response to trauma.

This chapter reviews the nosology of dissociative disorders and then addresses the prevalence, clinical presentation, diagnosis, and treatment of each of the *DSM-IV* dissociative disorders as they apply to children. The heaviest emphasis will be on dissociative identity disorder (multiple personality disorder), about which there is the most information.

Nosology

The first *Diagnostic and Statistical Manual*, published in 1952, differentiated between "conversion reaction" and "dissociative reaction" as two important pathological manifestations of "hysterical" symptomatology. In 1968, the *DSM-II* subsumed these two conditions under the nomenclature "hysterical neurosis." In 1980, in recognition of the emerging descriptive literature about dissociative disorders, *DSM-III* divided the category of "hysterical neuroses" into two diagnostic entities—dissociative disorders and conversion disorders (APA, 1980). The third edition of the *Diagnostic and Statistical Manual* (*DSM-III-R*, APA, 1987) and the World Health Organization *International Classification of Diseases* (1990, [*ICD-10*]) continued this distinction.

The *ICD-10* classification system differentiates among neurotic, somatoform, and stress-related dissociative disorders, thus recognizing the dissociative component of many somatoform disorders. *DSM-III-R* defined five dissociative disorders:

multiple personality disorder (MPD), psychogenic amnesia, psychogenic fugue, depersonalization disorder, and dissociative disorder not otherwise specified (DDNOS). *DSM-IV* has continued to revise our understanding of these conditions through significant name changes and the addition of descriptive criteria (APA, 1994).

Most significantly, multiple personality disorder has been renamed dissociative identity disorder, the essential feature of which is "two or more distinct identities or personality states that recurrently take control of behavior" (APA, 1994, p. 484). These personality states appear to have independent memories, a distinct sense of self and personal history, and separate patterns of cognitive, interpersonal, and perceptual attributes. An additional criteria added for *DSM-IV* includes memory difficulties as part of the diagnostic criteria.

Depersonalization disorder is a condition characterized by "a feeling of detachment or estrangement from one's self" (APA, 1994, p. 488). During these experiences, reality testing is intact and these repeated experiences cause marked distress. Psychogenic amnesia has been renamed dissociative amnesia and is characterized by an episode or more of disturbance in the ability to remember personal information usually of a stressful nature.

Psychogenic fugue has been renamed dissociative fugue, which is a condition involving "sudden unexpected travel away from home or one's customary place" and "assumption of a new identity" or "confusion about personal identity" (APA, 1994, p. 488).

DDNOS is a residual category that includes dissociative manifestations not meeting the above-described criteria. DDNOS is a particularly important category for children and adolescents, many of whom display dissociative phenomena that do not meet the strict criteria for adult disorders. In particular, children and adolescents may have symptoms resembling dissociative identity disorder, but amnesia may not be present. Some children and adolescents describe hallucinated presences or voices that influence their behavior, but switches to alternate identities may not be observed. DDNOS also includes dissociative trance disorders, which are aberrant altered states of consciousness common to many cultures.

The current classification of dissociative disorders in children and adolescents relies on the adult nosology just described. As this classification system continues to be revised and broadened in light of new research on clinical symptomatology, it is hoped that developmental considerations will begin to become part of the descriptive nosology. Peterson (1991) has proposed introduction of the category of childhood "dissociation identity disorder" (later renamed "dissociation disorder of childhood"), as many youngsters display symptoms that are precursors to adult dissociative disorders that are not well described by the current classification system. Currently, within *DSM-IV* these youngsters fall under the category DDNOS. Initial research suggests that the criteria for dissociative disorder of childhood describe a unique population not captured as well by the DDNOS category (Peterson & Putnam, 1994).

Many other unresolved controversies in nosology remain including the relationship of PTSD phenomena (such as acute stress disorder) (Spiegel, 1991), conversion disorders (Nemiah, 1991), and the subgroup of parasomnias with traumatic origins (i.e., sleepwalking disorder) to the dissociative spectrum.

Dissociative Identity Disorder (Multiple Personality Disorder) and Dissociative Disorder Not Otherwise Specified

The inclusion of multiple personality disorder as a diagnostic category in *DSM-III* in 1980 ushered in a decade of productive research and case descriptions of the adult syndrome of DID (MPD) (Kluft, 1984b; Putnam et al., 1986; Ross, 1989). Although etiological theories all presume the condition to arise in early childhood, as a consequence of severe abuse, reports of childhood and adolescent DID (MPD) remain comparatively sparse.

The earliest description of a case of childhood DID (MPD) has been attributed to Despine in 1840 (Fine, 1988). Despine recounts the case of Estelle, an 11-year-old patient suffering from paralysis, who was helped though a hypnotic treatment that uncovered a "choir of angels" with various names who could control Estelle's behavior.

Through the help of these "angels," Estelle regained movement of her legs and was able to access dissociated feeling states. As Fine points out, Despine unknowingly used most of the treatment techniques recognized today as essential components in the treatment of DID (MPD).

The first reported case of adolescent DID (MPD) was described by Dewar in 1823 and reviewed by Bowman (1990). Between 1823 and 1926, 5 additional cases of adolescent DID (MPD), characterized by conversion symptoms, amnesias, and "switching" while in sleep states, were reported in the literature (Bowman, 1990).

Despite these early and consistent case reports, the study of child and adolescent DID (MPD) remains in its infancy. The study of pediatric DID (MPD) has been hailed as "an important opportunity for the application of preventive psychiatry" (Kluft, 1990, p. 1), yet until very recently the published case reports were limited to a few case series (Dell & Eisenhower, 1990; Fagan & McMahon, 1984; Hornstein & Putnam, 1992; Hornstein & Tyson, 1991; Kluft, 1985) and a few case reports (Albini & Pease, 1989; Bowman, Blix, & Coons, 1985; LaPorta, 1992; Malenbaum & Russell, 1987; Riley & Mead, 1988; Weiss, Sutton, & Utecht, 1985). Currently this meager literature is undergoing rapid expansion with larger case series (Putnam, Hornstein, & Peterson, 1996), more focused analysis (Coons, 1994; 1996; Goodwin, 1996; Yeager & Lewis, 1996), beginning prognostic data (Silberg & Waters, 1996), case studies highlighting diagnostic complexity (Jacobsen, 1995), and the development of assessment and research tools (Lewis, 1996; Putnam, Helmers, & Trickett, 1993; Silberg, 1996c; Steinberg & Steinberg, 1995.) The authors' collective experiences as diagnosticians, therapists, and community consultants at our 72-bed child and adolescent inpatient psychiatric facility suggest that the time is right for psychiatric research to keep pace with the rapid increase in the diagnosis of DID (MPD) and the related DDNOS in clinical settings.

EPIDEMIOLOGY

Ross (1991) reported a preliminary finding of a prevalence rate of 1% for multiple personality disorder and 5 to 10% for dissociative disorders in the city of Winnipeg. This study, with a sample of 1,055 adult respondents, may have had methodological difficulties in the sampling, follow-up, or instruments used but represents the first large epidemiological study in the field. Previous estimates are much more conservative—1 to 100,000 estimated by Coons (1984) in the city of Indianapolis.

When prevalence data on the incidence of child abuse, commonly found in the history of DID (MPD) victims, is examined, the higher prevalence estimates appear more plausible. The U.S. Department of Health and Human Services (1988) uncovered a conservative prevalence of 1.6 million youth, or 25.2 per 1,000, who were sexually, physically or severely emotionally abused from birth to age 17, based on reported cases in 1988.

Among populations at high risk for abuse, which, according to these figures, is a significant percentage of the population, the prevalence of dissociative disorders is probably even higher than Ross's 1% prevalence finding. Children of DID (MPD) mothers are a group at particular risk, due to possible biological factors or potential for repeated traumatization. Coons (1985), Kluft (1985), Braun (1985), and Malenbaum and Russell (1987) report on mother-child pairs; Coons calculates a 9% prevalence rate for dissociative disorders among these children. Yeager and Lewis (1996), starting with a population of 11 children with DID (MPD) or DDNOS, uncovered significant dissociative pathology in a majority of the parents and siblings.

Similarly, theoretical speculations would suggest that in general populations of abused children, the prevalence would be high as well. An initial exploratory study of 122 child abuse victims suggested a prevalence of 30% for dissociative symptoms that appeared predominantly in the youngsters who had been abused before age 6 (Rodberg, Bagly, & Welling, 1990.) In the largest sample to date of abused children systematically evaluated for dissociation, Waterbury (1991) found a 73% prevalence of dissociative disorders among 231 severely traumatized inner city children and adolescents in a crisis shelter.

Estimates of the prevalence of dissociative disorders among adult inpatients have ranged from 0.5 to 2% (Kluft, 1991b) to 5% (Ross, 1991). As skill in diagnosis among child clinicians has improved, initial studies suggest that prevalence rates in child psychiatric settings are at least as high. In a general adolescent inpatient cohort, 23% of patients reported dissociative symptoms as well as a child abuse history (Sanders & Giolas, 1991). Hornstein and Tyson (1991) report a 5% prevalence rate for DDNOS and DID (MPD) combined and 3% for DID (MPD) among consecutive admissions to the children's inpatient unit at the University of California at Los Angeles. Similarly, among 498 consecutive admissions to the child and adolescent inpatient services at Sheppard-Pratt in 1991, 5.2% were diagnosed with dissociative disorders (primarily, DDNOS) (Silberg, 1991). Interestingly, these initial findings using *DSM-III-R* criteria parallel Proctor's (1958) finding of a 3% prevalence rate for dissociative disorders in a child psychiatric admission cohort, using older definitions.

Although in adult DID (MPD) populations the ratio of females to males is 9:1 (Kluft, 1991b), in adolescent populations it appears closer to 2:1 (Dell & Eisenhower, 1990) while in some child populations more equal representation of both sexes is reported (Putnam et al. 1996; Vincent & Pickering, 1988). The reasons for this developmental trend of more female cases in older ages may be due to cultural factors in identification of the disorder—more male cases may be in legal rather than psychiatric settings, and female cases may be easier to diagnose. Goodwin (1996) presents case histories of boys with DID who may mask symptoms or abuse secrets in an effort to reject the shame associated with the role of victim.

In summary, the beginning epidemiological data indicate that DID (MPD) and DDNOS are more common than once thought, particularly within at-risk populations—offspring of DID (MPD) mothers, child abuse victims, and child and adolescent psychiatry inpatients. As these disorders are more completely described and increasingly recognized by the child psychiatry community, further research is needed to help validate these initial trends and provide more complete prevalence information.

CLINICAL PRESENTATION

DSM-IV describes the DID (MPD) patient as having at least two identities or personality states with "enduring patterns" of relating to the world. These distinct personality manifestations, termed "alternate personalities" or "alters," may have widely differing attitudes, perceptions, and behavioral styles. Although the media has tended to characterize these alter presentations as flamboyant and dramatic, the DID (MPD) patient more typically presents with subtle symptomatology, as the patient uses this defensive style as a kind of camouflage to blend into the environment (Kluft, 1991b). Detection of the DID (MPD) phenomenology is difficult because dissociative patients present multiple symptoms that may make distinguishing them from children and adolescents with a wide spectrum of disturbances difficult. The information regarding childhood and adolescent DID (MPD) presentation gathered from case series, case reports, and clinical experience creates a consistent picture of patients with polysymptomatic presentations who initially show fluctuating behavior, forgetfulness, and an observed dazed state. Many display behavioral disruptiveness, severe family conflicts, and may complain of depressive symptoms, hearing voices, nightmares, flashbacks, and puzzling, fluctuating skills that may cause school problems. Some may present with self-mutilating behavior, sometimes of a sexual nature, and adolescent girls may be involved in abusive relationships with the opposite sex. In younger children, self-injurious masturbatory behavior may be observed (Albini & Pease, 1989; Fagan & McMahon, 1984; Riley & Mead, 1988). Aggressive behavior in younger dissociative children may take the form of unpredictable tantrums of surprising intensity, which appear to be out of context (Riley & Mead, 1988). Suicidal ideation and suicide attempts are common (Hornstein & Putnam, 1992) and may lead to repeated hospital admission. Frequently, the most disruptive symptoms to the patient and family are the posttraumatic symptoms, which can result in significant sleep problems. Multiple physical complaints, particularly headaches, may be reported, or somatic complaints associated with details of abuse histories. Table 31.1 lists important symptoms that may alert the evaluator to a DID (MPD) or DDNOS diagnosis.

The child or adolescent with DID (MPD) or DDNOS presents with a range of dissociative symptomatology that reveal a facility with the induction of autohypnotic state changes. These

TABLE 31.1

Dissociative Symptoms and Their Description

Symptom	Description
Trance states and amnesia	Concentration and attention difficulties, brief amnestic episodes, denial of observed behavior
Behavioral fluctuations	Variability in skills/academic performance/personal styles, dangerous and impulsive behaviors, including sexual promiscuity and disturbed eating patterns
Affective symptoms	Depression, including suicidal states; volatile, angry, and agitated states
Pseudopsychotic features	Hallucinatory phenomena—auditory/visual; passive influence experiences; thought process disturbances with "switching"
Somatoform symptoms	Chronic headaches, multiple physical complaints and pseudoseizures, and other conversion symptoms
Anxiety	With posttraumatic features—sleep disturbance, nightmares, hypervigilance, flashbacks, panic states, phobic avoidance
Disturbance of personal identity	Feels like more than one person, uses several names, has sensory distortions about self or body image, depersonalizes

symptoms may include vivid dreaming, depersonalization phenomena, and skill in self-induction of trance states. Although some dissociative behavior may fall along a normal continuum, the level of dissociative activity in these patients suggests the pathological development of dissociation for defensive purposes.

When DID (MPD) is diagnosed and alternate personalities (alters) have presented themselves, the therapist or evaluator may get a glimpse of the complex internal world of these patients. The alternate personalities appear to take control of the child or adolescent and may have independent memories, behavior patterns, or cognitive skills. Studies have shown that these alternate personalities in adult patients may have distinct physiological characteristics, such as autonomic nervous system reactivity, vision changes, and differing visual-evoked potentials, and may manifest independent state-dependent learning and retrieval (Putnam, 1991c). The process during which the patient changes from one alter state to another, which may be accompanied by eye rolls or gestures, is termed "switching." Dell and Eisenhower's (1990) adolescent cohort had a mean number of alters of 24. All patients in their sample showed angry alters, child alters, scared alters, and depressed alters, and most had persecutors, internal helpers, and opposite-sex alters. Silberg and Waters (1996) so have described "laughing" alters whose role is to deny pain and "parental alters" who take over internal parental functions and may be competitive with adoptive or foster parents. Alters may have the names of family members or abusers but also may have fantasy names and be based on cartoon characters, TV heros, or imaginary companions, particularly in children and younger adolescents. Retrospective patient reports suggest that the alters are created at particular moments of abuse, when youngsters may feel the need to escape an aversive situation. Once the dissociative defenses used in the creation of alters is developed, new alters may be created readily to serve particular functions or as adaptation to added psychosocial stressors (Dell & Eisenhower, 1990). Patients with DID (MPD) may show wide variations in amnestic patterns among the alter states for past and current events.

The DDNOS patient may display many of the same symptoms as the DID (MPD) patient, but distinct alter states are not observed. Many of these patients report "alterlike" presences whom they perceive as attempting to influence their behavior. Comparisons between DID (MPD) patients and patients with DDNOS suggest that the DDNOS subgroup is, as a whole, less sympathetic (Putnam et al., 1966) with less evidence of amnesia (Hornstein & Putnam, 1992; Putnam et al., 1996; Silberg, 1996a,b,c). However, a subgroup of severely disorganized DDNOS patients with extremely chaotic environments or underlying cognitive impairments also has been described (Hornstein, 1996; Silberg, 1996a,b,c).

DEVELOPMENTAL COURSE OF DID (MPD) AND DDNOS

A beginning developmental understanding of the course of DID (MPD) and DDNOS is emerging from preschool case reports (Albini & Pease, 1989; Fagan & McMahon, 1984; Riley & Mead, 1988), childhood case reports (Malenbaum & Russell, 1987; Weiss et al., 1985), and cohorts of school-age children and adolescents (Hornstein & Putnam, 1992; Hornstein & Tyson, 1991; Kluft, 1985; Putnam et al., 1996; Yeager & Lewis, 1996). Preschool dissociative disorder may most frequently take the form of "incipient multiple personality disorder" (Fagan & McMahon, 1984) as alter systems are not clearly developed, but precursors to alter systems may appear as dissociated aspects of the self projected onto imaginary friends or transitional objects. In childhood, DID (MPD) symptomatology appears to emerge more frequently than in the preschool years, but many childhood cases of dissociative disorders are diagnosed DDNOS, as they do not fully meet *DSM-IV* criteria for DID (MPD). The DDNOS childhood cases are characterized by hallucinated internal voices that criticize, command, argue, or provide helpful advice rather than discrete alter personalities that take full control of the child. Preliminary case reports suggest that childhood cases of DID (MPD) are characterized by fewer alter personalities than adolescents (Vincent & Pickering, 1988; Yeager & Lewis, 1996). The youngest patient described in the literature meeting full criteria for DID (MPD) is a 3-year-old with 2 alter presentations, each uniquely adapted to 2 disparate households (Riley & Mead, 1988). Adolescent patients tend to be more symptomatic than childhood dissociative patients, with increasing amnesia, self-destructiveness, eating disorders, and somatic symptoms (Putnam et al., 1996). In many ways the adolescents with DID (MPD) begin to present in a fashion more similar to adult DID (MPD) presentation. Alter systems appear to be crystallizing, organizing, and becoming more complex. The number of alters more closely resembles adult samples, and the percentage of patients who present with more classic DID (MPD) symptomatology rather than DDNOS continues to increase (Dell & Eisenhower, 1990; Hornstein & Putnam, 1992; Hornstein & Tyson, 1991). The ratio of females to males also increases, as is more typical with adults (Dell & Eisenhower, 1990; Putnam et al., 1996).

Adolescent Subtypes: Kluft (1991b) has offered a beginning topology to characterize subgroups of adolescent patients. He describes a set of adolescent male DID (MPD) patients who show aggressive and violent behavior, who are contrasted with male DID (MPD) cases who are more passive and depressed and from those who show predominantly homosexual concerns. Kluft (1985) also identifies subtypes of adolescent girls including a withdrawn, childlike, and classically depressed type and a group with florid and dramatic switching who appear to have rapid-cycling disorders, or PTSD variants (Kluft, 1991b). Kluft (1985) comments on the turmoil, instability, and lack of safety of this adolescent patient sample who are involved in sexual promiscuity, drugs, and chaotic living situations.

THEORETICAL CONSIDERATIONS

The syndrome of DID (MPD) and the related DDNOS present a challenge to psychoanalytic and developmental theory, as these patients have clearly progressed along an atypical developmental course, not readily open to classical interpretations. Their internal sense of "dividedness," with multiple, coexisting behavioral styles, affects, and memories has been explained as an initially adaptive, pathological development of dissociative defenses in the face of overwhelming life trauma. However, the coexisting developmental levels contained in alter systems of varying ages may seem to contradict developmental theory, which presupposes a natural progression from less mature to more mature ego development. This quandary has yet to be fully explored within the DID

(MPD) field. Armstrong (1994) has proposed that DID (MPD) theory consider Werner's postulation (Werner & Kaplan, 1963) that development progresses through a process of increasing differentiation and integration. Within this context the DID (MPD) patient, with multiple dissociated identities, may have progressed along a dimension of increasing differentiation without the accompanying integration. Developmental theoreticians such as Stern (1985) and Greenspan (1989), who stress the significance of predictable interactive patterns between children and adults for development of consistent identity and healthy bonding, may provide a working model for the development of further explanations of the DID (MPD) phenomenon.

Within a classically psychoanalytic theoretical context, dissociation may be seen as a "splitting of the ego" described by Freud as a way of holding two contradictory beliefs when wished-for events and reality collide. Within Winnicott's developmental framework, the personality has split off, and the individual alters can be viewed as transitional objects (Marmer, 1980).

The multiple behavioral anomalies seen in the DID (MPD) patient may be understood within psychoanalytic theory as defects in ego functioning resulting from the identification with and introjection of abusive parental models. The abused individual develops an identity consistent with viewing him- or herself as a victim or an aggressor, and may seek to reenact traumatic events and relationships.

Initial theoretical constructs for understanding DID (MPD) are preliminary; the challenge remains for future scholars to more completely "integrate" the "differentiated" field of multiple personality disorder and dissociative disorders into the overall body of contemporary theories of development and psychopathology.

ETIOLOGY

Although controversy may exist regarding its prevalence or relation to established developmental theories, there is a general consensus concerning the basic etiology of dissociative identity disorder (multiple personality disorder). Retrospective patient accounts strongly suggest that the disorder is a consequence of severe forms of trauma including physical and sexual abuse during childhood (Putnam et al., 1986). However, understanding the mechanism by which these traumatic events lead to the unique configuration of DID (MPD) presents a challenge for psychiatric research and theory. Kluft (1984a) has organized observations and speculations about the etiology of DID (MPD) around four factors:

1. Predisposition for dissociation
2. Intense trauma during childhood
3. Internal and external shaping influences
4. Unavailability of environmental soothing

These factors provide an organizing framework for the following discussion.

The patient who develops a dissociative disorder is presumed to have a predisposition to dissociate and to use dissociation defensively. This capacity for dissociation may be transmitted genetically, as suggested by the transgenerational incidence of dissociative disorders (Braun, 1985; Coons, 1985; Yeager & Lewis, 1996), but is apparently also enhanced by traumatic experience (Sanders & Giolas, 1991). Research has begun to explore how repeated trauma may induce a state of chronic hyperarousal or underarousal that may lead to alterations in the serotenergic and endogenous opiate system in the brain (van der Kolk, 1987). How these neurophysiological changes may relate specifically to the defensive activity that we term "dissociation" is an important question for future research. Putnam (1991c) has suggested that research on state-dependent learning and on the self-regulation of state changes in infants may be a fruitful direction for further inquiry into the psychophysiological basis of dissociation.

The second etiological factor for the development of DID (MPD) is the presence of significant abusive events in the patient's early life. Putnam et al.'s classic study (1986) clearly demonstrated the prevalence (97%) of severe forms of abuse, including incest, ritualistic abuse, and physical abuse, frequently of a bizarre and sadistic nature, in these patients' reported histories. In child and adolescent populations, where documentation of abuse is more available, researchers have found 91 to 100% of cases with corroborating evidence of child abuse (Coons, 1994; Dell & Eisenhower, 1990; Hornstein & Putnam, 1992; Silberg & Waters, 1996).

Traumatic histories of sadistic abuse suffered in rituals in religious cults have been reported in adult DID (MPD) patients (Young, Sachs, Braun, & Watkins, 1991); based on the authors' clinical experience, this is evident in children and adolescents as well. Nonabusive forms of traumatization in the adolescent patient's history are occasionally reported, including multiple surgical procedures (Dell & Eisenhower, 1990) or repeated losses (Weiss et al., 1985). Of note, the early 20th century adolescent DID (MPD) cases reviewed by Bowman (1990) rarely include mention of sexual or physical abuse as precipitating events but do include nonabusive forms of trauma.

Retrospective adult and adolescent studies date memories of trauma to the preschool years between the ages of 2 to 5 (Dell & Eisenhower, 1990; Kluft, 1984a). Developmental theory would suggest that traumatic relationships within the preschool years would be particularly disruptive to identity formation. Stern's (1985) integration of research on the development of self suggests that the concept of "the core self" emerges through a complex cognitive and interpersonal process whereby affirming reactions of an interested caregiver help the emerging youngster revise and modify "theories" about consistent selfhood. If the same caregiver provides contrasting abusive and nurturing experiences (as is true in many abusive households) or if different caregivers provide vastly different experiences, it is easy to see how this pattern of identity formation could be profoundly disrupted.

Kluft proposes that the next important factors in the etiology of DID (MPD) are shaping influences, both internal—such as intrapsychic characteristics of the patient—and external—such as an environment of contradictory parental demands—that offer possible substrates for the development of alters. More recent studies of dissociative children have helped provide data that support this theory. Hornstein and Tyson (1991) report that dissociative children come from chaotic environments characterized by multiple placements as well as significant psychiatric illness among the parents. The experience of dichotomous and frequently changing environments, or pathology within the parents, including substance abuse, DID (MPD), paranoia, sexual perversion, antisocial disorder, or explosive disorder (Goodwin, 1989) may help shape the course of a developing dissociative disorder. The violent and often unpredictable shifts within the family environment are mirrored in the youngster's pathology.

Finally, Kluft proposes that the youngster who turns to the dissociative process used in DID (MPD) lacks the soothing from the environment necessary to process the traumatic material; the self-soothing and split-off parts of the self assume that role. Perhaps this factor determines a pathological course of dissociative disorder rather than a posttraumatic stress disorder for the youngster exposed to extreme trauma. A youngster with PTSD may relive the trauma again and again, but in a functional family is helped to process this eventually in play and dialogue with significant others (Terr, 1988). The youngster for whom the traumatic experiences are repetitive and environmental soothing is lacking has no chance for processing the experience by working through the trauma. This child may be forced to project parental qualities on to imaginary playmates or dolls, which become important transitional objects and may be the beginnings of alter personalities.

In summary, current research indicates that DID (MPD) and DDNOS develop as adaptive reactions to traumatic environments. These disorders are characterized by the pathological development of dissociative defenses that apparently serve to protect the youngster from psychological disintegration in a traumatic environment. Dissociation provides a means of escaping reality, providing detachment and offering a method for self-soothing when soothing is absent from the environment. The dissociative defenses preserve the youngster's capacity to relate to an abusing caregiver by shielding from consciousness traumatic memories associated with the abuse. Current theory suggests that this defensive activity is encouraged by chaotic and changeable environments in which the youngster must become intensely self-reliant.

It is rare in psychiatry to be able to make definitive statements about etiology. Unanswered questions remain, however, concerning the biological, social, and developmental factors that lead the child into this particular strategy for coping with trauma.

DIAGNOSIS

Dissociative disorders, especially DID (MPD), are probably the most underdiagnosed and misdiagnosed disorders in childhood and adolescence. The difficulty in diagnosis of DID (MPD) has

been well documented in the adult literature—the average number of years the patient is in treatment until a correct diagnosis is made is reported to be 6.8 (Putnam, Guroff, Silberman, Barban, & Post, 1986). In adolescent populations, the difficulty in diagnosis is compounded by the adolescent's secretiveness, the fact that many of the symptoms can suggest other psychiatric conditions of lesser controversy, and the general unfamiliarity of most child clinicians with this diagnosis. Most pediatric DID (MPD) patients have had previous diagnoses—1.36 previous diagnoses in Dell and Eisenhower's (1990) adolescent sample; 2.7 in Hornstein and Putnam's (1992) childhood sample. Attention to careful history-taking, sensitive clinical evaluation, and knowledge of the related differential diagnoses can help increase accuracy in early identification of DID (MPD) and DDNOS.

History-Taking: Interviewing a knowledgeable caregiver about the patient's history is an essential preliminary step. History of previous psychiatric treatment is of particular importance, as these patients have been historically refractory to other treatment attempts and this may be an important diagnostic clue. Family history should include gathering information regarding previous placements and living arrangements. Uncovering history regarding abusive experiences, both physical and sexual, is essential, but this is a sensitive and difficult matter, particularly if it is suspected that the informant may be the abuser. This information may be sketchy at first but is usually gathered over time through patient recollections and family disclosures as the treatment alliance is secured and treatment progresses. Clearly, if current abuse is suspected, evaluators needs to follow state reporting guidelines. Questioning about trauma should include inquiry into any medical procedures or hospitalizations as well as witnessing violence within the family. Careful history-taking should include questioning the informant about observed symptoms specifically related to dissociation—amnesia; fluctuation in skills, behaviors, or moods; observed trance behaviors; sleep disorders; and somatic complaints. The interviewer should also ask about unusual drawings or notes for which the patient has no memory, samples of differences in handwriting, and other ancillary evidence that point to dissociative phenomena. Questions about dissociative symptoms may be adapted from a variety of behavioral checklists developed for dissociative children and adolescents (Dean, 1989; Fagan & McMahon, 1984; Goodwin, 1989; Kluft, 1985; Peterson, 1991; Putnam, Helmers, & Trickett, 1993; Reagor, Kasten & Morelli, 1992). The Child Dissociative Checklist (Putnam et al., 1993) is a reliable observer-report instrument with established discriminant validity that may be valuable as an initial screening tool.

Clinical Interview: The clinician should be sensitive to the fact that these dissociative children and adolescents do not trust adults, value their privacy highly, and may be reluctant to acknowledge symptoms that they feel make them seem "weird." Particularly, adolescents may attempt to rationalize and minimize symptoms in an effort to present in a normal manner. Past drug use, Satanic possession, boredom, or an overly vivid imagination may be offered as explanations for some of their dissociative symptoms. Younger children may believe that their internal voices are ghosts, spirits, or alien life-forms (Silberg, 1996b).

The diagnostic interview may be facilitated with structured interview scales for dissociative disorders developed by Ross et al. (the Dissociative Disorders Interview Schedule, 1989) or Steinberg (1986) (the Structured Clinical Interview for *DSM-III-R* Dissociative Disorders). Steinberg and Steinberg (1995) have piloted the SCID-D with adolescents with some success. The Bellevue Dissociative Disorders Interview for Children (Lewis, 1996) presents a flexible interview format for young children, including questions about imaginary friends and transitional objects. Common symptoms reported by dissociative patients include depression, school problems, auditory hallucinations, and amnesia. The interviewer is encouraged to ask extensive questions about trauma-related experiences, flashbacks, dreams, visions, and hallucinations—both visual and auditory. Specific content of the hallucinations is important as it may reveal important details about alter systems. The authors have found that questions about transitional phenomena such as imaginary friends, stuffed animals, or treasured personal possessions may help to open up a discussion of the patient's inner fantasy life. To minimize the patient's concern about the "weirdness" of the symptoms, the interviewer is encouraged to explain in matter-of-fact, nontechnical language how dissociative defenses help people cope with frightening memo-

ries (Silberg, 1996b). While conducting the interview, the clinician should be observant of the subtle behaviors associated with autohypnotic state changes. Signs of "switching" may be subtle in children and adolescents, and may be signaled by eye-rolls, subtle posture changes, or hand and body movements. When "switching" is not observed and alternate personalities are not accessed but other dissociative phenomena are present, the diagnosis of DDNOS may be warranted.

The clinical interview with younger children utilizes observation of play as well as direct questioning. When observing the fantasy play of the young child, astute clinicians looking for dissociative symptomatology should attend to the presence of traumatic themes accompanied by sudden shifts in affect, as the child tries to deny or magically escape in fantasy. The dissociative younger child has difficulty leaving the boundaries of fantasy play and may rigidly cling to imaginative identities even when the play is terminated. Frequent fantasy identities of animals or cartoon characters, which may be precursors to alters, are seen in dissociative preschool children. As young children are extensively involved in imaginative fantasy play, the differentiation between pathological and nonpathological absorption in fantasy material may be a very difficult one to make. Whereas normal children can move readily between fantasy and reality constraints easily and reestablish appropriate reality boundaries when necessary, preschoolers with dissociative disorders may respond with defensive anger at interpretations of their behavior as "pretend play." On other occasions, these youngsters may be extremely secretive about fantasy projections, and this too is pathognomonic. The normal youngster is delighted to share his or her imaginary world of play with an interested adult. Imaginary playmates in normal children are not perceived as threatening, are experienced as make-believe, and usually disappear by age 6 or 7 (Silberg, 1996b; Trujillo, Lewis, Yeager, & Gidlow, 1996). In contrast, dissociative children perceive their imaginary compansions as real, may find them frightening and controlling, and perceive a group of imaginary companions in conflict (Silberg, 1996b; Trujillo et al., 1996).

Psychological Testing: The DES, the Dissociative Experiences Scale, is a self-report rating scale with a comprehensive list of dissociative and post-traumatic stress disorder symptoms including losing time, depersonalization, flashbacks, nightmares, and amnesia (Bernstein & Putnam, 1986) that may be helpful in disclosing the range and frequency of dissociative experiences for adults. Another scale for self-report of dissociative experiences is the Children's Perceptual Alteration Scale (CPAS) (Evers-Szoztak & Sanders, 1992).

Recent research suggests that traditional psychological testing may be useful particularly if the evaluator is sensitive to the shifts in style of responses and changing patterns of relatedness that may be observed during the testing procedures (Silberg, 1996c). A diagnostic clue in the testing profile may be wide fluctuations in performance between and within subtests that do not appear consistent with known neuropsychological disorders. Projective test findings on children and adolescents with DID (MPD) or DDNOS may include intensely morbid imagery, forgetting, sleeping, or pretending presented as a defense, emotional confusion, themes of good and evil,

images of multiplicity, themes of magical transformation, and depersonalized imagery. These youngsters frequently respond to the test setting with highly charged affective responses of fear, aggression, or traumatic memory and may give indications of dividedness and amnesia with multiple, conflicting responses and denial of responses (Silberg, 1994, 1996c). A new test measure, the Dissociative Features Profile, may be used along with traditional psychological testing to identify and score these dissociative features (Silberg, 1996c).

Differential Diagnosis/Rule-Outs: The typical dissociative patient presents with multiple symptomatology suggesting a variety of diagnoses. Generally, Putnam (1991a) suggests that the dissociative disorder be viewed as a superordinate diagnosis, superseding other existing conditions. However, when a coexisting diagnosis presents consistent symptoms, multiple diagnoses may be appropriate. All patients in Dell and Eisenhower's

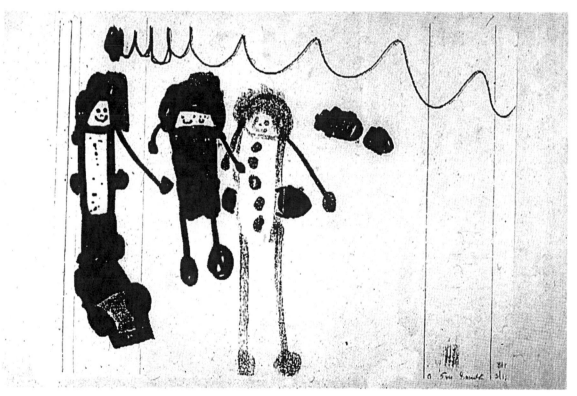

FIGURE 31.1

This drawing by a 5-year-old with DID (MPD) shows a figure with two faces. Multiple body parts on drawings may be a diagnostic indicator of childhood dissociative disorders.

TABLE 31.2

Symptoms of MPD and DDNOS and Associated Differential Diagnoses

Symptom	Differential Diagnoses
Trance states and amnesia	Psychomotor/absence seizures Attention deficit disorder with hyperactivity/developmental learning disorders Psychogenic amnesia/psychogenic fugue Substance abuse
Behavioral fluctuations	Conduct disorder Oppositional defiant disorder Personality disorder—Antisocial, borderline Malingering Selective mutism Eating disorders
Affective symptoms	Affective disorders—major depression, bipolar (including rapid cycling) Personality disorders—Borderline Conduct disorder
Pseudopsychotic features	Psychotic disorder—schizophrenia, schizophreniform, brief reactive Organic mental disorders—substance induced Atypical developmental disorder Atypical psychosis
Somatoform features	Organic medical disorders Somatoform disorders/conversion disorder Tic disorders
Anxiety symptoms	Primary anxiety disorder, including panic disorder Posttraumatic stress disorder (uncomplicated) Parasomnia/Sleepwalking Disorder
Disturbance of personal identity	Gender identity disorder Bipolar disorder Eating disorders Depersonalization disorder

(1990) adolescent cohort qualified for at least one other *DSM-III-R* diagnosis besides DID (MPD). Thus, differential diagnosis requires knowledge of comorbidity as well as an awareness of DID (MPD) symptoms which are typical of other conditions. Table 31.2 depicts some common symptoms of childhood and adolescent DID (MPD) or DDNOS with a comprehensive list of the other diagnoses these symptoms may suggest.

The trancelike spells of these patients may be mistaken for the absences of attention found in ADHD or seizure disorders. We have seen many patients who appear to have both attention and dissociative disorders, a finding reported by others as well (Graham, 1996; Hornstein, 1996; Nemzer,

1996; Peterson, 1996). The differential diagnosis between DID (MPD) and seizure disorders, particularly temporal lobe epilepsy, is complicated by the fact that a small percentage of dissociative patients may also have seizure disorders (Loewenstein & Putnam, 1988). A careful neurological workup is encouraged to help identify the contribution of neurological dysfunction to the patient's behavior especially in the face of a past history of trauma.

The aggressive, antisocial behavior of these patients may lead to conduct disorder or oppositional disorder diagnoses (Dell & Eisenhower, 1990; Putnam et al., 1996). DID (MPD) patients may have alters who are impulsive, promiscuous, and engage in illegal acts, but this behavior pattern may fluctuate with more prosocial behavior of other alternate personalities. Severely disturbed eating patterns may be evident in adolescent patients with DID (MPD) or DDNOS (Putnam et al., 1996), with both anorectic and bulimic features.

Mood disorders may be the most common initial diagnoses given to DID (MPD) patients (Dell & Eisenhower, 1990; Putnam et al., 1996), before the dissociative disorder is identified. The rapid affective changes and associated switching may be seen as rapid-cycling bipolar disorder with psychotic decompensation (Kluft, 1991b; Steingard & Frankel, 1985). Self-destructive and suicidal behaviors are common symptoms of dissociative patients that are consistent with affective disorder diagnoses.

The hallucinatory phenomena, passive influence experiences, and thought process disturbances of these patients may suggest a schizophrenia diagnosis. In schizophrenia, the patient's hallucinations tend to be vague and heard from outside the head, whereas the DID (MPD) patient's experience is usually more coherent. Similarly, the schizophrenic's delusional system is more disorganized, while the DID (MPD) patient's belief system about his or her multiple selves is consistent and well elaborated. In addition, schizophrenic patients have poor relatedness and flat affect, while the dissociative patient has better interpersonal relatedness, although it may fluctuate.

Confused thinking, depersonalization experiences, and fluctuating attention may also suggest substance abuse disorders. In this case the differential diagnosis is complicated by the fact that many dissociative patients may have alters who abuse drugs and may use a variety of drugs as self-medication for their hallucinatory phenomena, PTSD symptoms, or underlying mood disorders. In these cases, accurate diagnosis may be impossible until the adolescent is drug-free.

Headaches or other somatic complaints associated with past physical or sexual abuse may suggest somatoform disorders. DID (MPD) patients frequently report headaches accompanying "switches" of alters. The high level of posttraumatic anxiety symptoms, including sleep disorders, nightmares, and phobias, may suggest anxiety disorder diagnoses. Posttraumatic stress

disorder does tend to co-occur with dissociative disorders (Dell & Eisenhower, 1990; Hornstein & Putnam, 1992).

The stormy interpersonal relationships, treatment resistance, and self-destructive propensities of these patients may lead to personality disorder diagnoses. The relationship between borderline personality disorder and DID (MPD) is a controversial issue (Clary, Burstin & Carpenter, 1984). Fink (1991) suggests that there may be many disorders on Axis II that can coexist with Axis I dissociative disorders, but these diagnoses should be given only if the personality disorder traits seem to exist across "the whole" person.

The diagnosis of DID (MPD) and DDNOS is a challenging task for even the most experienced clinician. Diagnostic sensitivity is improving, as evidenced by the increasing number of cases identified over the last few years. As research provides more information on comorbidity and varying clinical presentations, clinical accuracy in diagnosing dissociative disorders in children and adolescents will be enhanced.

TREATMENT

Although treatment outcome varies, more favorable results are reported when parenting is consistent and the treatment course is not interrupted (Silberg & Waters, 1996). Treatment length may be as rapid as several sessions (Kluft, 1985) or as long as 7 years (Silberg & Waters, 1996). Treatment is reported to be very rapid for younger children with precursors to DID (MPD) symptomatology who are living in stable family environments. However, even after the dissociative barriers have dissolved in treatment, the youngster may be left with a multitude of problems and deficits in ego functioning from having lived in an abusive environment.

In contrast to the frequently reported rapid remission and treatment success with preschool or child cases (Fagan & McMahon, 1984; Kluft, 1985), adolescent cases of DID (MPD) may be more refractory and difficult to treat (Dell & Eisenhower, 1990; Kluft & Schultz, 1993). This difficulty may be due to adolescents' limited motivation for treatment, their difficulty in establishing alliances, and their entrenchment in dysfunctional families that may interfere with therapeutic progress. In fact, if the adolescent is still living in an abusing family system, the dissociative defenses are probably functional and promised protection from adults has never materialized. As part of the normative adolescent stage of identity consolidation, the alternate personalities may become more invested in asserting their independence and goals of personality consolidation may be difficult to achieve. Despite this pessimistic picture, Dell and Eisenhower (1990) report successful treatment with 55% of their sample.

Individual Treatment: The effective treatment of dissociative disorders and DID (MPD) begins with careful assessment of the individual symptomatology, a review of history, and an evaluation of the family environment, as described in the previous section. As the psychotherapeutic techniques useful in the treatment of DID (MPD) and DDNOS are very specific, the need for accurate diagnosis is particularly important.

The first step in treatment is always to ensure the patient's safety (Hornstein & Tyson, 1991; Kluft, 1985; Waters & Silberg, 1996b). Involving protective service agencies to help gain a safe living environment for a youngster still living in an abusive environment is essential. The therapist may need to establish a liaison with legal authorities when reporting of abuse results in prosecution, and the adolescent is required to testify.

The next step in treatment is to secure a therapeutic alliance (Hornstein & Tyson, 1991; Waters & Silberg, 1996b). During the initial phase of treatment, the dissociative patient may be quite resistant to the diagnosis. The authors have found that a gentle, exploratory approach is helpful in the early stages of treatment, enlisting the patient's help in trying to unravel some of the mysteries of disturbing memory lapses or erratic behavior.

Although a dissociative disorder is strongly suspected, it may take many months in the therapeutic process before the therapist recognizes alter states. Therapists are often unprepared for the first presentation of an alter. The patient's "switch" may be dramatic with changes in posture, voice quality, and facial presentation. However, more commonly, the patient has switched to various alters on many occasions without the therapist picking up the subtle signs that a switch has occurred. After alter personalities have begun to be identified, the treatment follows a similar course as is recommended in adult work with DID

(MPD). Subsequent stages of treatment include developing an alliance between alter personalities, processing the trauma, moving toward integration (the removal of barriers and eventual consolidation of the alters), and encouraging age-appropriate coping (Waters & Silberg, 1996a,b).

For the younger child, play therapy techniques that gradually allow the playing out of the traumatic memories are useful (Fagan & McMahon, 1984; Riley & Mead, 1988). As some traumatic memories may be preverbal, it is not uncommon for symbolic reenactment to occur in play that cannot be expressed verbally (Terr, 1988). Helping the youngster to represent split-off parts of the self with play-dough, drawings, puppets, or dolls is useful. If the youngster has no words or internal labels for the state changes observed, providing temporary labels may be helpful so that language can become a working metaphor for the therapeutic work. As these parts are described and understood by the child and split-off traumatic memories worked through either in language or in symbolic form, the integration of identity may occur naturally. In some cases, suggestive imagery of two personalities "hugging" or "walking together" may be needed to encourage integration of identities (Fagan & McMahon, 1984). As in adult work with DID (MPD), the therapist must be openly accepting of all split-off parts, voices, hallucinations, or behaviors, and frame these as important elements that are there for protection of the patient. The therapist may encourage concrete expression of the acceptance of other parts by having the child make a "thank you card" for a "voice" or "alter" that helped the child deal with trauma (Silberg, 1996a).

Techniques particularly useful with adolescents include hypnotherapy (Bowman et al., 1985; Dell & Eisenhower, 1990; Williams & Velazquez, 1996), contracting with the patient and alters to reduce self-destructive risks, and encouraging writing, drawing, and other creative expressions. The therapist must be familiar with principles of psychodynamic psychotherapy for adolescence and enhance ego functioning while exploratory work proceeds. Therapy sessions should ideally occur at least twice weekly and more often during stressful periods.

The treatment tends to progress very slowly, with numerous setbacks and regressions. These setbacks may be caused by internal conflicts between alters or outside circumstances, such as visits by the abuser or legal battles in which the adolescent must confront the abuser.

Kluft (1991b) has identified several schools of thought regarding therapy with DID (MPD) patients. The authors suggest that the "integrationist" school, focusing on eventual unity of the personality, is the most appropriate for children and adolescents, as this approach has the most potential for reversing the severe course that this disorder takes in adulthood. Integration techniques for children include concrete play activities that illustrate the process of parts coming together (Waters & Silberg, 1996a). After the patient has achieved a state of personality consolidation, follow-up therapy to solidify gains and check that dissociative defenses have not returned is strongly encouraged (Dell & Eisenhower, 1990; Kluft, 1991b; Waters & Silberg, 1996a). For a more complete discussion of individual therapeutic issues in the treatment of DID (MPD), the reader is referred to several texts on adult treatment (Putnam, 1989; Ross, 1989 or child treatment (Shirar, 1996; Silberg, 1996a).

Therapists treating their initial DID (MPD) cases should receive supervision and ongoing consultation with clinicians with expertise in dissociative disorders, as treatment dilemmas abound, and these patients arouse intense countertransference reactions. It is easy for the novice therapist to become intrigued, enamored, and protective of newly diagnosed DID (MPD) patients, and therapeutic boundaries may be crossed inadvertently.

The authors have found that work with the DDNOS child or adolescent is equally difficult. The therapist must help the patient to explore, understand, and accept dissociated feeling states. In the absence of distinct alter personalities, the therapist can help the patient to identify dissociated feeling states in ways that promote psychological understanding and unity of the personality.

Family Treatment: The treatment problems of the patient with dissociative disorders are compounded by the difficult family work that must progress side by side along with the individual treatment. Dell and Eisenhower (1990) and Fagan and McMahon (1984) have classified three types of families of DID (MPD) patients: nurturant, rejecting, and abusive. The "nurturant" type of family, which may not be the environment of original abuse, is most easily engaged in therapy and

the prognosis is good. However difficult, work with the family is essential to inform parents about the nature of the dissociative disorder and to encourage consistency in relating and responding to the patient. In many cases, dissociative pathology among the parents may be uncovered during family treatment. Ideally, the parent is treated as a partner in the treatment, learning modified treatment techniques for managing anger outbursts, flashbacks, and "switches" (Waters, 1996).

In our setting, we have found it helpful to have parents or foster parents "meet" alter identities to provide reassurance that they are loved and accepted by the parents. Dissociative children in foster homes may have alters that are attached to the abusive parent. This loyalty ot the family of origin may sabotage the placement if oppositional alters are not addressed directly in family therapy.

Inpatient Treatment: The hospital may become a safe haven for the patient involved in self-destructive or dangerous behavior, may provide a protective environment for difficult abreactive work, and may help diffuse family crises at sensitive points in treatment (Hornstein & Tyson, 1991). Inpatient treatment of adolescents is frequently complicated by countertransference issues of the treatment team toward the family or adolescent, staff splitting over belief and nonbelief in the disorder, and the patient's own potential for manipulation and splitting of the treatment team. Experience with adults has shown that treatment usually progresses more rapidly on specialized DID (MPD) units (Kluft, 1991a), but no data on adolescents are available.

Multidisciplinary Approaches: Educational programming for the DID (MPD) student best occurs within an environment where teachers have some familiarity with the diagnosis and can be sensitive to therapeutic issues. Issues such as whether to call patients by their alter names or whether to adjust academic expectations during "switches" are difficult and best addressed in a careful, individualized fashion. In our setting, educating teachers about the traumatic triggers for a child or adolescent, judicious use of "the quiet room" for alter presentations who cannot handle the academic setting, and active processing with the patients about the roots of specific disruptive behaviors have been helpful in the educational environment of students with DID (MPD) and DDNOS. Limited self-hypnotic strategies to decrease anxiety and assist in focusing on the here-and-now may also be helpful. The educational staff must be alert to the dissociative patient's tendency to involve others in reenactments of abusive scenarios when disruptive outbursts need to be controlled. The consulting psychiatrist can assist the staff in processing their own countertransferential reactions to these events. Waterbury (1996) has described techniques for helping dissociative students identify feeling states and predict their changeable behavior. She also suggests use of a "relaxation box" stocked with various stress-relieving objects for the child to manipulate during stressful times.

Homogeneous group therapy of DID (MPD) patients has been reported to be helpful with adults (Coons & Bradley, 1985) and dissociative adolescents (Brand, 1996). In the authors' experience, psychoeducational groups focusing on techniques for managing flashbacks or disruptive switches and providing education about dissociation can be particularly helpful. We have found that adolescent DID (MPD) patients can benefit from heterogeneous group therapy only during the most stable periods of their treatment. At times, in a heterogeneous group, other patients may resent the DID (MPD) patient; seeing him or her as monopolizing time and attention.

DID (MPD) patients are particularly receptive to art therapy (Sobol & Schneider, 1996), movement therapy, and music therapy as the creative arts allow for the dramatization and expression of the unconscious affects and motivations of their alter systems. Collaborative work between ancillary therapists can be extremely helpful in assisting patients to work through trauma and explore identity issues.

Psychopharmacological Therapy: Experts in the treatment of adolescent and adult patients with dissociative disorders support the importance of intensive psychotherapy and hypnotherapy over somatic treatments (Dell & Eisenhower, 1990; Kluft, 1991b; Putnam, 1989; Nemzer, 1996).

Target symptoms for medication treatment of dissociative patients should be those that appear across the "whole person" as much as possible (Loewenstein, 1991b). Unfortunately, no one medication appears to impact specifically on the dissociative constellation of amnesias, trance phenomena, and other autohypnotic features. Nonetheless, the posttraumatic stress symptoms of DID

(MPD) patients have been treated with benzodiazepines, clonidine, and propranolol with mixed response (Loewenstein, 1991b). Of these, only propranolol (Famularo, Kinscherff, & Fenton, 1988; Nemzer, 1996) and clonidine (Kinze & Leung, 1989; Nemzer, 1996) have been reported to be used for PTSD symptomatology in pediatric populations. The authors have had some preliminary success treating PTSD symptomatology in dissociative adolescents with buspirone.

Loewenstein, Hornstein, and Farber's research (1988) suggests that clonazepam (Clonopin) may be particularly useful for the treatment of sleep problems, anxiety, and flashbacks in PTSD accompanying DID (MPD). Although its use is known in the treatment of other anxiety disorders of childhood and adolescence (Bernstein & Borchardt, 1991; Biederman, 1987), treatment should proceed conservatively with dissociative patients who have substance-abusing alters. Antihistaminic sedatives may be a safer choice for decreasing agitation and anxiety in prepubertal children and in sleep induction with adolescents.

Patients with comorbid depressive symptoms may respond to tricyclic antidepressants or the new serotonergic agents such as fluoxetine (Loewenstein, 1991b; Nemzer, 1996). Fluoxetine, with fewer side effects and less abuse potential, may be a safe choice when treating the affective symptomatology of dissociative patients, especially those with eating disorders and a propensity for self-mutilation.

Many dissociative youngsters have been previously misdiagnosed with conduct disorders and have been treated with neuroleptics to control aggression or psychostimulants for associated attentional problems. Dissociative auditory hallucinations do not respond to neuroleptics (Putnam, 1989), but the patient may experience subjective improvement due to a decrease in agitation. Putnam (1989) recommends discontinuing the neuroleptics slowly, especially if patients have used them for long periods. Some dissociative patients appear to respond to psychostimulant medication (Nemzer, 1996; Graham, 1996) but it is unknown to what frequency dissociative disorders tend to co-occur with attention deficit disorders. Clinical experience suggests that buspirone may be helpful for attentional problems that stem from anxiety and posttraumatic experiences.

The use of lithium for dissociative patients is

recommended only when comorbid bipolar disorder is present or the patient shows significant explosive behavior (Nemzer, 1996). Similarly, anticonvulsives such as carbamazepine and valproic acid may be beneficial for controlling intense aggressive episodes or comorbid bipolar disorder (Nemzer, 1996).

Currently, psychopharmacological recommendations for dissociative youngsters are based solely on clinical experience; multicenter, double-blind studies comparing responsiveness to these somatic treatments are needed so that effective psychopharmacological treatment guidelines can be delineated.

Prognostic Considerations: Although long-term prognostic information on treated children and adolescents is unavailable, the difficulty in treating DID (MPD) patients in adulthood is well documented—they require intensive, several-times-a-week therapy for many years (Kluft, 1991b). Kluft (1991c) has suggested that good prognostic indicators for adults are the patient's intellectual level, minimal impulsivity, family support, capacity for relatedness, availability of community resources, and the capacity for higher-order defenses. In a study of childhood treatment, Silberg and Waters (1996) report consistent parenting and length of treatment as two factors most closely predictive of improvement. Positive prognostic indicators specific to adolescents include the family's availability and motivation for treatment as well as its nurturing potential (Dell & Eisenhower, 1990). In addition, Dell (personal communication) has noted that the more successful adolescent treatment cases are those displaying more symptomatology of anxiety rather than aggressive, impulsive behavior. Although beginning therapy earlier rather than later is ideal, some patients may be too deeply entrenched in dysfunctional families, too rejecting of the diagnosis, or too involved in antisocial behavior to be available to treatment in their teen years. Current theory and clinical experience suggest that treatment of the DID (MPD) adolescent is a challenging task that may yield significant benefit as it may help to deter the especially morbid course of the disorder in adulthood and its intergenerational perpetuation. Diagnosis and treatment of dissociative patients at younger ages offers clinicians the opportunity to have a profound impact on a patient's life course.

CASE EXAMPLE

Anna: Anna was 14 years old when she was admitted to a long-term psychiatric unit under the care of one of the authors. She had had a long history of self-mutilation, depressive episodes, sexual masochistic activity, and suicide attempts. This was her fourth psychiatric admission, and she had been in outpatient treatment intermittently since age 7. Early medical history included a third-degree burn at the age of 11 months, a hospitalization for an adenoidectomy at 16 months, and viral discitis at 22 months. Her early history included sexual abuse by a baby-sitter, alleged sexual abuse by her father, and a rape at age 13 by her former boyfriend.

Hospital evaluation uncovered the following symptoms: time loss, psychogenic amnesia, fluctuation in skills and habits, nightmares, flashbacks, and an eating disorder. Within 2 months of her hospitalization, she presented an angry alter who threatened physical harm to Anna. At this point, the diagnosis of DID (MPD) was made. Approximately 10 additional alters were identified in the subsequent course of treatment, including angry alters, child alters, protective alters, a mature teenage alter, and a male alter.

Anna experienced great distress at the emergence of these alters, and the course of her hospitalization was stormy with severe suicidal and self-mutilating behaviors, requiring quiet room, isolation, and occasional use of cold, wet-sheet packs. She was managed with nortriptyline, lorazepam, and later clonazepam.

As therapy progressed, Anna began to recall further details about physical and sexual abuse and history about the development of her alters. She recalled the emergence of alters during specific abusive events in her childhood. During therapy, she was encouraged to explore her alters' beliefs, feelings, and functions and was encouraged to see them as helpers who needed to collaborate for her sake.

Anna was discharged to a residential treatment center and subsequently continued in outpatient therapy with the treating hospital therapist. The patient's individual therapy was augmented with family sessions, during which the mother was invited to deal with family conflicts or to meet and provide reassurance to a frightened child alter. As a result, the relationship between the patient and her mother improved dramatically. During the family therapy, mother was encouraged to help Anna achieve autonomy while still providing nurturance for Anna's child alters. Through this process Anna began to deal with her overwhelming feelings of rejection and abandonment.

She is now 17 years old, is maintained on a therapeutic dose of doxepin, and continues in outpatient treatment two times a week. She reports no hallucinations and little switching but has not yet achieved integration. She still experiences occasional mood swings and eating disorder symptoms, particularly during transition periods. Although Anna's therapeutic work is not completed, she has progressed significantly. She attends a community school, and successfully holds a job. She has found a creative outlet in writing and has received recognition for her work.

CASE EXAMPLE

Dennis: Dennis was a 5-year-old youngster who was referred for a consultation by his therapist in a social service agency who had been seeing him in therapy for several months. The therapist noted changeable behavior and lack of progress in therapy, and the foster mother was requesting he be moved to another family as she found him "distant and unreachable." He had been removed from his home due to ongoing physical abuse of his older sister by the father. The mother was chronically depressed and had allowed the father to assume most caretaking functions before the children were removed from the home. The therapist reported that when he interacted with his mother, his language and behavior deteriorated and he assumed a babyish, whiny disposition. The foster mother reported that following visitation with his father, he would take off his clothes and wander around the house in an unresponsive daze. She would overhear him having long conversations with himself using different voices when she was in another room. When left alone with peers, he would quickly begin to initiate oral genital contact, and he had frequent wetting accidents both day and night. His kindergarten teacher reported that Dennis was a loner with erratic school performance and evidence of much higher potential. On evaluation, Dennis presented as an articulate child who was small for his age. He alternated between an aggressive, threatening posture with the evaluator and inappropriate seductiveness, at one point trying to remove his pants and asking to play "sex games." When asked about inner experiences, Dennis reported that two "tiger people" lived in his brain who told him what to do and what to say to people. As he began to describe these "tiger people" in more detail, his affect suddenly switched, and he denied memory of having talked about this. Based on this consultation, Dennis was diagnosed with DDNOS, and the recommendation was for residential treatment. Following this evaluation, physical evidence of ongoing sexual abuse was found, and visitation with the father was legally terminated. He was transferred to a residential treatment center where play therapy continued. In this setting, Dennis's behavior was less erratic, and he began to reenact some of the abusive experiences in play. As therapy progressed, Dennis spoke of the "tiger people" less frequently. Changeable, regressive behavior was still observed during visitation with mother, which is a current focus of therapeutic intervention.

Depersonalization

In contrast to the evolving body of descriptive information concerning DID (MPD) and the related DDNOS, the literature on depersonalization disorder among adolescents is meager. Among adolescents, depersonalization phenomena may appear along a continuum of severity ranging from common, mild experiences (Dixon, 1963); transient symptoms in response to stressors (Elliott, Rosenberg, & Wagner, 1984); to a chronic disorder causing marked distress (Meyer, 1961; Steinberg, 1991).

Adolescent depersonalization, which most commonly presents after age 15 (Nemiah, 1989), may have its roots in depersonalization experiences of childhood (Shimizu & Sakamato, 1986). These children may experience a sense of loss of reality without loss of reality testing, feelings of "deadness" estrangement from the environment (Fast & Chetnik, 1976), and visual perceptual distortions or "metamorphopsia" (Salfield, 1958). Children describe the experience as unpleasant, accompanied by severe anxiety, and distinct from other feeling states. In adolescents, this subjective sense of depersonalization may also include feelings of derealization and the sense of watching oneself from a distance, which appears linked to the developmental capacity for self-awareness (Fast & Chetnik, 1986). Depersonalization experiences may also include feelings of "inauthenticity," a factor associated with intense self-criticism (Jacobs & Bovasso, 1992).

Mild depersonalization symptoms during adolescence are common (up to 46% of college students [Dixon, 1963]) and may result from sleep deprivation, illness, psychosocial stressors, and drug-induced states (Steinberg, 1991). Even small amounts of marijuana may trigger depersonalization, which may persist and become intensified as a convenient defense mechanism (Szymanski, 1981). Depersonalization symptoms peak at 30 minutes following marijuana intoxication (Mathew, Wilson, Humphreys, Lowe, & Weithe, 1993). Intoxication from hallucinogens, mescaline, cocaine, and alcohol can trigger these reactions, as well (Steinberg, 1991). Benzodiazepine withdrawal has also been reported to stimulate depersonalization symptoms (Terao, Yoshimura, Terao, Abe, 1992).

Transient depersonalization episodes are found in response to life-threatening danger as in war (Kozavic-Kovacic, Folnegovic-Smalc, Skinjaric, Szajnberg & Marusic, 1995), cult indoctrination, severe illness and pain states, as part of the traumatic response to abuse and rape (Steinberg, 1991), or following head trauma (Gigsby & Kaye, 1993). Adolescents may also present at times of domestic disasters with depersonalization in response to anxiety, loss, separation, and dangerous experiences (McKellar, 1978). The experience of transient identity loss is least likely to occur in teens with positive global self-esteem and a stable self-concept (Elliott et al., 1984).

Depersonalization disorder is distinguished from these mild or transient symptomatic presentations by the persistence of these symptoms, their interference with social or occupation functioning, and their causing marked distress. The prevalence of depersonalization disorder among adolescents is unknown. The use of the Structured Clinical Interview for Dissociative Disorders, may assist in the documentation of the prevalence of this disorder (Steinberg, 1986). Meyer (1961) has reported on a cohort of adolescents who show acute onset of symptoms, a prolonged course, slow remission, and a favorable outcome. *DSM-IV* has assisted in clarifying the core diagnostic features and associated symptoms of derealization, disturbances in time perception and visual perception, and symptoms of anxiety (APA, 1994).

Current etiological theories for depersonalization phenomena range from biologically based theories implicating temporal lobe dysfunction (Sedman, 1970), changes in central benzodiazepine receptors (Stein & Uhde, 1989) or serotonergic dysfunction (Simeon, Stein, & Hollander, 1995) to psychological theories stressing trauma-related, psychodynamic, or developmental antecedents. Putnam (1989) and Shader and Sharfman (1989) conceptualize depersonalization as an adaptive response to trauma that becomes maladaptive in the absence of ongoing stress. Psychodynamic etiologies propose that depersonalization is a defense against painful affects, anxiety, and conflict. The split between the observing and the experiencing self creates a distancing from one's body with subsequent dampening of emotions and sensations (Steinberg, 1991). From a developmental framework, the feelings of estrangement of the vulnerable adolescent attempting to define his or her identity within a social context can result in feelings of depersonalization (Meares & Grose, 1978; Meyer, 1961). Younger adolescents who are passive, have poor frustration tolerance and feelings of inferiority may be particularly vulnerable to feelings of depersonalization (Shimizu & Sakamato, 1986).

Depersonalization symptoms may also appear among a variety of other diagnoses—posttraumatic stress disorder, panic disorder, affective disorders, schizophrenia, substance abuse, head injury, seizure disorders, tremors, migraines, obsessive-compulsive disorder, and evolving personality disorders. In addition, depersonalization experiences are commonly reported among patients with DID (MPD) and DDNOS, and careful diagnostic evaluation for these conditions should be part of the differential diagnosis. Evaluation of adolescents through skillful interviewing, self-reports, and structured clinical interviews (the SCID-D; Steinberg & Steinberg, 1995) may assist in clarifying the differences between the mild and transient forms of depersonalization, the symptom associated with other disorders, and depersonalization disorder itself.

Treatment for depersonalization is indicated when there is significant distress or dysfunction (Steinberg, 1991). Adolescent treatment strategies have included individual therapy, group therapy, family therapy, and pharmacotherapy. Individual therapy techniques include psychodynamic therapy (Torch, 1987), hypnotherapy that encourages an increased sense of control (Steinberg, 1991), and supportive therapy with removal from danger (McKellar, 1978). Meares and Grose (1978) stressed the importance of expressive group therapy using painting and self/body-image-enhancing techniques as a means of confirming and solidifying identity in depersonalizing teens. There is one report of combined family therapy and behavior modification using a reward contingency plan to treat adolescent depersonalization disorder (Dollinger, 1983). The use of pharmacotherapy may include antidepressants and anxiolytics especially in cases of comorbidity with depression and panic disorders (Noyes, Kuperman, & Olson, 1987). Although not adequately tested in pediatric populations, ferotonin reuptake blockers (fluoxetine) may alleviate symptoms in adults (Fichtner, Horevitz, & Braun; 1992; Hollander et al., 1990; Ratliff & Kerski, 1995).

A review of the sparse literature on depersonalization in adolescence leaves many questions unanswered. The relationship of the spectrum of depersonalization phenomena to sexual trauma and self-mutilation is an important area for future study (Putnam, 1991c; Raine, 1982). Future studies will need to standardize diagnostic criteria more carefully, as many of the cases described in the literature might currently fall under the DDNOS or DID (MPD) categories if rediagnosed with contemporary criteria and improved diagnostic methods.

Dissociative Amnesia and Fugue

Dissociative amnesia and dissociative fugue remain a very poorly studied subset of dissociative disorders in adult and adolescent psychiatry (Loewenstein, 1991a). A review of the adolescent literature on these conditions consists of a few early case studies (Bornstein, 1946; Geleerd, Hacker & Rapaport, 1945) or case series that include a few older adolescents (Coons, 1996; Coons & Milstein, 1992). Conclusions regarding adolescents have historically been extrapolated from studies of adult populations that have had major methodological and diagnostic difficulties (Loewenstein, 1991a).

As research has begun to investigate traumatic memory processes, old conceptions of dissociative amnesia as a discrete condition of sudden onset have been brought into question. The current *DSM-IV* description of "dissociative amnesia" defines a disturbance of "one or more episodes of inability to recall important information" (APA, 1994, p. 481) and omits the reference to sudden onset that helped define the former condition termed "psychogenic amnesia" (APA, 1987). In addition, the *DSM-IV* definition emphasizes the frequent traumatic nature of the material forgotten.

Emerging retrospective research suggests that traumatic forgetting is in fact quite common in the general population. Elliot and Briere (1995) found that 23% of a general population reported a history of sexual abuse and, of these, 42% described a time in which they had forgotten all or part of this memory. At least one prospective study, which followed emergency room child abuse victims into their adult years (Williams,

1995), suggests a similar frequency of traumatic forgetting for these events (38%). Retrospective research has begun to suggest factors that increase the likelihood that traumatic events, particularly child abuse, will be forgotten. Traumatic amnesia is most likely to occur following traumatic events occurring at earlier ages (Briere & Conte, 1993; Herman & Schatzow, 1987), involving violence or threats (Elliot & Brierè, 1995; Herman & Schatzow, 1987), and for which there is an unavailability of maternal support (Elliot & Briere, 1995).

Experimental studies of children's memory suggest that previous knowledge and information about an event and frequent exposure to event information enhance their memory, while stress experienced during an event may impair recall (Ornstein, 1995). Extrapolation from these experimental studies might suggest that sexual abuse events, which come as a surprising and unfamiliar experience, which are clouded in secrecy due to threats or lack of environmental support, and which are highly stressful, might be particular prone to be forgotten.

Beginning physiological research has begun to document the connection between stress and brain anatomy, suggesting that dissociative amnesia may have a neurophysiological basis. Stress may lead to anatomical changes in the brain such as reduced hippocampal size, and it is known that neurotransmitter or neuropeptides that are released during stress play a role in memory function (Bremner, Krystal, Southwick, & Chaing, 1995).

The diagnosis of dissociative amnesia may be distinguished from common amnestic reactions to stressful events when the impaired recall is a source of significant distress to the individual or results in significant interference in functioning. There are currently no good data on the prevalence of this form of dissociative amnesia in adolescents. Studies are needed to clarify the adolescent clinical presentation, associated symptoms, and past psychiatric and family history. Coons (1996) describes a case of a teenage girl with acute memory loss following a kidnapping during which she was tortured. Symptoms also included hallucination, derealization, memory loss for the particular event (localized amnesia), and memory loss for traumatic childhood events as well (selective amnesia). The comorbid conditions is this case included PTSD and major depression.

Precipitants to dissociative amnesia have been identified as child abuse (Coons & Milstein, 1992), death of a loved one (Coons & Milstein, 1992; Domb & Beaman, 1991), marital conflict and disavowed behavior (Coons & Milstein, 1992) or criminal assaults (Coons, 1996; Sengupta & Saxona, 1993). In reported adolescent cases, amnesia has followed kidnapping and torture (Coons, 1996) or death and family illness (Keller & Shaywitz, 1986). Kopelman (1995) has suggested that cases of dissociative amnesia tend to have three associated predisposing factors: a stressful event, a history of depressed mood, and a transient organic amnesia due to head trauma, intoxication, or seizure activity. Thus, Kopelman emphasizes that an underlying organic disposition may underlie many cases that appear to be exclusively psychologically based. Loewenstein (1991a) has suggested that psychological conflict may underlie cases of dissociative amnesia characterized by sudden onset, while traumatic experience more often accounts for the chronic form.

Adolescents with amnesia should receive a thorough psychological and medical evaluation. When the amnesia is recurrent, the evaluator should have a high index of suspicion for DID (MPD) and DDNOS, especially in patients who have histories of childhood abuse and trauma (Loewenstein, 1991a). Other causes of amnesia to be considered in the differential diagnosis include concussion, seizures, alcohol-induced amnesia, or substance abuse intoxication (Keller & Shaywitz, 1986). In organic causes of amnesia, there may be more obsessive questioning and less frequent identity confusion (Kopelman, 1995). In the assessment of amnesia, the evaluator should detail the duration of the amnesia and the extent of memory preservation before and after the event (Kopelman, 1995). Psychological assessment can include memory tests that help to discriminate malingering from true amnesia. Malingerers may tend to have lowered IQs, disproportionate impairment for autobiographical information, and impairment on recognition memory tasks. The Autobiographical Memory Interview (the AMI: Kopelman, Wilson, & Baddely, 1990), may be used to help assess episodic and semantic memory.

Treatment for dissociative amnesia should involve establishing a therapeutic alliance and recognizing the adaptive nature of the defense (Loewenstein, 1991a). Hospitalization may be necessary to assure safety and alleviate underlying anxiety (Linn, 1989). Supportive psychotherapy to assist in clarifying traumatic events and hypno-therapy to support abreactive work around the events preceding the memory loss may be helpful. Although narcoanalysis—that is, amytal use—in dissociative and conversion reactions in children has been documented in the literature (Proctor, 1958), its contemporary use has been less popular in dissociative states of childhood and adolescence.

The *DSM-IV* category of psychogenic fugue involves sudden travel that may begin abruptly following an episode of great distress or trauma. The adolescent has amnesia or confusion about his or her past identity, and there may be a change in behavior inconsistent with the old identity. The change may be heralded by a stuporous state of consciousness (Venn, 1984).

Cases of dissociative fugue have been described in childhood and adolescence (Akhtar & Brenner, 1979; Bornstein, 1946; Geleerd et al., 1945; Venn, 1984) but appear to be extremely rare. In a review of 133 cases (Akhtar & Brenner, 1979), only 1 occurred in a child under 10, and several occurred among adolescents.

Like dissociative amnesia, dissociative fugue has been understood as a reaction to trauma (Loewenstein, 1991a) or psychological conflict (Ford, 1989).

The differential diagnosis of dissociative fugue should include DID (MPD) (Ford, 1989) and depression, psychotic illness, dementia, and mental retardation (Akhtar & Brenner, 1979). Organic causes of fugue to be ruled out include alcohol- and drug-related states, epilepsy, cerebrovascular accidents, migraine, brain tumors, head trauma, steroid toxicity, uremia, and hypoglycemia (Akhtar & Brenner, 1979). It is suggested that in childhood, these organic causes are the most likely diagnosis (Akhtar & Brenner, 1979).

Ford (1989) recommends that treatment of dissociative fugue in adolescents include supportive therapy with suggestive interventions such as visual imagery, progressive relaxation, and automatic writing as a means of revealing the underlying conflict. There is one report of family therapy used in the treatment of adolescent dissociative fugue using paradoxical techniques and a family systems interpretation (Venn, 1984). However, the lack of clarity in the diagnosis of this treatment case makes generalization difficult.

Amnesia and fuguelike states may be more common symptoms than the sparse literature on these disorders suggests, particularly in populations of traumatized children and adolescents (Loewenstein, 1991a). The authors' experience is that clinical populations of children and adolescents frequently report amnesia related to a traumatic event or ongoing memory gaps for a period of time in their personal history. Fuguelike states with identity confusion, but without assumption of a new identity, have been described in adolescent runaways from abusive environments (Goodwin, 1989; Loewenstein, 1991a). The expanded *DSM-IV* definition of "dissociative fugue," which includes identity confusion in the criteria, should set a framework for future data collection on these traumatized adolescents.

Dissociative amnesia and dissociative fugue are the least understood of the dissociative disorders. Patients with these disorders, like the more frequently described DID (MPD) patients, suffer blackouts, amnesia, personality changes, and spontaneous trances. Many clinical presentations of adolescents with these dissociative disorders and with depersonalization disorder as well cite an association with traumatic events (frequently of a sexual nature), high hypnotizability, and difficulty in direct expression of anger within the family system (Dollinger, 1983; Venn, 1984). Ongoing research is needed to clarify whether the etiological pathways and clinical syndromes of dissociative amnesia and dissociative fugue are in fact distinct or whether they and depersonalization disorder, dissociative identity disorder (multiple personality disorder), and DDNOS are closely related manifestations of the same pathogenetic process.

Future Directions

Although more is known about the dissociative disorders in children and adolescents now than a decade ago, what remains unknown presents an overwhelming challenge. As the study of dissociation has moved away from research that simply documents the validity of the DID (MPD) diagnosis, fruitful directions for further research abound. Of particular importance will be studies on the neurophysiology and neuroendocrinology of trauma and dissociative disorders to help identify the biological underpinnings of the clinical manifestations of dissociation. A related area of inquiry will be biological treatments and how they may differentially affect the nervous system of a traumatized individual. The continuing uncovering of childhood and adolescent cases of depersonalization, dissociative amnesia, fugue, dissociative identity disorder, and DDNOS through careful diagnostic assessment will be important for accurate clinical descriptions and developing nosology. Longitudinal studies of at-risk abused youngsters will need to be undertaken to help answer questions about etiology and the biological and environmental determinants that result in a youngster developing a dissociative disorder. These longitudinal studies should include an evaluation of environmental and biological family factors that relate to dissociation and should track the intergenerational prevalence of these disorders. Finally, further study of varying patient responses to treatment will be essential, so that the next generation of child psychiatrists will be better equipped to provide adequate treatment for patients with these perplexing and difficult-to-treat disorders.

It is hoped that research findings will progress along with parallel advances in the theoretical understanding of dissociative symptomatology and what these diagnoses may reveal about important developmental issues. As Freud's preliminary concepts are revisited through 21st-century methodology, we may gain a more comprehensive understanding of the "unconscious mind" that he described a century ago.

REFERENCES

Akhtar, S., & Brenner, I. (1979). Differential diagnosis of fugue-like states. *Journal of Clinical Psychiatry,* 40, 381–385.

Albini, T. K., & Pease, T. E. (1989). Normal and pathological dissociations of early childhood. *Dissociation,* 2 (3), 144–149.

American Psychiatric Association. (1952). *Diagnostic and statistical manual of mental disorders.* Washington, DC: Author.

American Psychiatric Association. (1968). *Diagnostic and statistical manual of mental disorders.* (2nd ed.). Washington, DC: Author.

American Psychiatric Association. (1980). *Diagnostic and statistical manual of mental disorders* (3rd ed.). Washington, DC: Author.

American Psychiatric Association. (1987). *Diagnostic and statistical manual of mental disorders* (3rd ed., rev.). Washington, DC: Author.

American Psychiatric Association. (1994). *Diagnostic and statistical manual of mental disorders* (4th ed.) Washington, DC: Author.

Armstrong, J. G. (1994). Reflections on multiple personality disorder as a developmentally complex phenomenon. *Psychoanalytic Study of the Child, 49,* 349–364.

Armstrong, J. G., Putnam, F. W., Carson, E., & Libero, D. (1996). The adolescent Dissociative Experience Scale. In J. L. Silberg (Ed.), *The dissociative child: Diagnosis, treatment and management* (pp. 337–340). Lutherville, MD: Sidran Press.

Bernstein, E., & Putnam, F. W. (1986). Development, reliability and validity of a dissociation scale. *Journal of Nervous and Mental Disease, 174* (12), 727–735.

Bernstein, G. A., & Borchardt, C. M. (1991). Anxiety disorders of childhood and adolescence: A critical review. *Journal of the American Academy of Child and Adolescent Psychiatry, 30* (4), 519–532.

Biederman, J. (1987). Clonazepam in the treatment of prepubertal children with panic-like symptoms. *Journal of Clinical Psychiatry, 48* (suppl.), 38–41.

Bornstein, B. (1946). Hysterical twilight states in an eight-year-old child. *Psychoanalytic Study of the Child, 2,* 229–239.

Bowman, E. S. (1990). Adolescent MPD in the nineteenth and early twentieth centuries. *Dissociation, 3* (4), 179–187.

Bowman, E. S., Blix, S. F., & Coons, P. M. (1985). Multiple personality in adolescence: Relationship to Incestual experience. *Journal of the American Academy of Child and Adolescent Psychiatry, 24* (1), 109–114.

Brand, B. (1996). Supportive group psychotherapy for adolescents with dissociative disorders. In J. L. Silberg (Ed.)., *The dissociative child: Diagnosis, treatment and management* (pp. 223–237). Lutherville, MD: Sidran Press.

Braun, B. G. (1985). The transgenerational incidence of dissociation and multiple personality disorder: A preliminary report. In R. P. Kluft (Ed.), *Childhood antecedents of multiple personality disorder* (pp. 127–150). Washington, DC: American Psychiatric Press.

Bremner, J. D., Krystal, J. H., Southwick, S. M., & Chaing, D. S. (1995). Functional neuroanatomical correlates of the effects of stress on memory. *Journal of Traumatic Stress, 8,* 527–553.

Briere, J., & Conte, J. (1993). Self-reported amnesia for abuse in adults molested as children. *Journal of Traumatic Stress, 6,* 21–31.

Clary, W. F., Burstin, K. J., & Carpenter, J. S. (1984). Multiple personality and borderline personality disorder. *Psychiatric Clinics of North America, 7* (1), 89–99.

Coons, P. M. (1984). The differential diagnosis of multiple personality. A comprehensive review. *Psychiatric Clinics of North America, 7* (1), 51–85.

Coons, P. M. (1985). Children of parents with multiple personality disorder. In R. P. Kluft (Ed.), *Childhood antecedents of multiple personality disorder* (pp. 151–165). Washington, DC: American Psychiatric Press.

Coons, P. M. (1994). Confirmation of childhood abuse in childhood and adolescent cases of multiple personality disorder and dissociative disorders not otherwise specified. *Journal of Nervous and Mental Disease, 182,* 461–464.

Coons, P. M. (1996). Clinical phenomenology of 25 children and adolescents with dissociative disorders. *Child and Adolescent Psychiatric Clinics of North America, 5* (2), 361–375.

Coons, P. M., & Bradley, M. D. (1985). Group psychotherapy with multiple personality patients. *Journal of Nervous and Mental Disease, 173* (9), 515–519.

Coons, P. M., & Milstein, V. (1992). Psychogenic amnesia: A clinical investigation of 25 cases. *Dissociation, 5,* 73–79.

Dean, G. (1989). Dean Adolescent Inventory Scale. In B. James (Ed.), *Treating traumatized children: New insights and creative interventions* (pp. 237–246). Lexington, MA: Lexington Books.

Dell, D. F., & Eisenhower, J. W. (1990). Adolescent multiple personality disorder: A preliminary study of eleven cases. *Journal of the American Academy of Child and Adolescent Psychiatry, 29* (3), 359–366.

Dixon, J. C. (1963). Depersonalization phenomena in a sample population of college students. *British Journal of Psychiatry, 109,* 371–375.

Dollinger, S. J. (1983). A case report of dissociative neurosis (depersonalization disorder) in an adolescent treated with family therapy and behavior modification. *Journal of Consulting and Clinical Psychology, 51* (4), 479–484.

Domb, Y., & Beaman, K. (1991). Mr. X—A case of amnesia. *British Journal of Psychiatry, 158,* 423–425.

Ellenberger, H. F. (1970). *The discovery of the unconscious: The history and evolution of dynamic psychiatry.* New York: Basic Books.

Elliot, D. M., & Briere, J. (1995). Posttraumatic stress associated with delayed recall of sexual abuse: A general population study. *Journal of Traumatic Stress, 8,* 629–648.

Elliott, G. C., Rosenberg, M., & Wagner, M. (1984). Transient depersonalization in youth. *Social Psychology Quarterly, 47* (2), 115–129.

Evers-Szostak, M., & Sanders, S. (1992). The Children's Perceptual Alteration Scale (CPAS): A measure of children's dissociation. *Dissociation, 5* (2), 91–97.

Fagan, J., & McMahon, P. P. (1984). Incipient multiple personality in children. *Journal of Nervous and Mental Disease, 172,* 26–36.

Famularo R., Kinscherff, R., & Fenton, T. (1988). Propranolol treatment of childhood posttraumatic stress disorder, acute type: A pilot study. *American Journal of Diseases of Children, 142,* 1244–1247.

Fast, I., & Chetnik, M. (1976). Aspects of depersonalization—derealization in the experience of children. *International Review of Psycho-Analysis, 3,* 483–490.

Fichtner, C. G., Horevitz, R. P., & Braun, B. (1992). Fluoxetine in depersonalization disorder. *American Journal of Psychiatry, 149,* 1750–1751.

Fine, C. G. (1988). The work of Antoine Despine: The first scientific report on the diagnosis and treatment of a child with multiple personality disorder. *American Journal of Clinical Hypnosis, 31* (1), 33–39.

Fink, D. (1991). The co-morbidity of multiple personality disorder and DSM-III R, axis II disorders. *Psychiatric Clinics of North America, 4* (3) 547–566.

Ford, C. (1989). Psychogenic fugue. In American Psychiatric Association, *Treatments of psychiatric disorders. A task force report of the American Psychiatric Association* (vol. 3, pp. 2190–2196). Washington, DC: Author.

Geleerd, E. R., Hacker, F. J., & Rapaport, D. (1945). Contribution to the study of amnesia and allied conditions. *Psychoanalytic Quarterly, 14,* 199–220.

Goodwin, J. (1989). *Sexual abuse: Incest victims and their families* (2nd ed.). Chicago: Year Book Medical Publishers.

Goodwin, J. (1996). Childhood DID: The male population. In J. L. Silberg (Ed.), *The dissociative child: Diagnosis, treatment and management* (pp. 69–84). Lutherville, MD: Sidran Press.

Graham, D. B. (1996). The pediatric management of the dissociative child. In J. L. Silberg (Ed.), *The dissociative child: Diagnosis, treatment and management* (pp. 301–318). Lutherville, MD: Sidran Press.

Greenspan, S. (1989). *Development of the ego: Implications for personality theory, psychopathology and the psychotherapeutic process.* Madison, CT: International Universities Press.

Grigsby, J., & Kaye, K. (1993). Incidence and correlates of depersonalization following head trauma. *Brain Injury, 7,* 507–513.

Herman, J. L., & Schatzow, E. (1987). Recovery and verification of memories of childhood sexual trauma. *Psychoanalytic Psychology, 4,* 1–14.

Hollander, E., Liebowitz, M. R., Decaria, C., Fairbanks, J. Fallon, B., & Klein, D. F. (1990). Treatment of depersonalization with serotonin reuptake blockers. *Journal of Clinical Psychopharmacology, 10,* 200–203.

Hornstein, N. L. (1996). Complexity of psychiatric differential diagnosis in children with dissociative symptoms and disorders. In J. L. Silberg (Ed.), *The dissociative child: Diagnosis, treatment and management* (pp. 27–45). Lutherville, MD: Sidran Press.

Hornstein, N. L., & Putnam, F. W. (1992). Clinical phenomenology of child and adolescent dissociative disorders. *Journal of the American Academy of Child and Adolescent Psychiatry, 31* (6), 1077–1085.

Hornstein, N. L., & Tyson, S. (1991). Inpatient treatment of children with multiple personality/dissociation disorders and their families. In *Psychiatric Clinics of North America 4*(3), 631–648.

Jacobs, J. R., & Bovasso, G. B. (1992). Depersonalization and its association with affective and cognitive dysfunctions. *Journal of Personality Assessment, 59,* 352–365.

Jacobsen, T. (1995). Case study: Is selective mutism a manifestation of dissociative identity disorder? *Journal of the American Academy of Child and Adolescent Psychiatry, 31,* 1077–1085.

Keller, R., & Shaywitz, B. A. (1986). Amnesia or fugue state: A diagnostic dilemma. *Journal of Developmental and Behavioral Pediatrics, 7* (2), 131–132.

Kinzie, J. D., & Leung, P. (1989). Clonidine in Cambodian patients with posttraumatic stress disorder. *Journal of Nervous and Mental Disease, 177,* 546–550.

Kluft, R. P. (1984a). MPD in childhood. In *Psychiatric Clinics of North America 7,* 121–134.

Kluft, R. P. (1984b). Treatment of multiple personality disorder: A study of 33 cases. *Psychiatric Clinics of North America, 7,* 9–29.

Kluft, R. P. (1985). Childhood multiple personality disorder: Predictors, clinical findings and treatment results. In R. P. Kluft (Ed.), *Childhood antecedents of multiple personality* (pp. 167–196). Washington, DC: American Psychiatric Press.

Kluft, R. P. (1990). Thoughts on childhood MPD (editorial). *Dissociation, 3* (1), 1–2.

Kluft, R. P. (1991a). Hospital inpatient treatment of multiple personality disorder. *Psychiatric Clinics of North America, 14* (3), 695–719.

Kluft, R. P. (1991b). Multiple personality disorders. In A. Tasman & S. M. Goldfinger (Eds.). *Review of Psychiatry* (10th ed., pp. 161–188). Washington, DC: American Psychiatric Press.

Kluft, R. P. (1991c, September). *Natural history of MPD.* Paper presented at the meeting on diagnosis and treatment of MPD: A Developmental Perspective, The Sheppard and Enoch Pratt Hospital, Baltimore, MD.

Kluft, R. P., & Schultz, R. (1993). Multiple personality in adolescence. In S. L. Feinstein & R. Majron (Eds.), *Adolescent psychiatry* (Vol. 19, pp. 259–279). Chicago: University of Chicago Press.

Kopelman, M. D. (1995). The assessment of psychogenic amnesia. In A. D. Baddely, B. A. Wilson, F. N. Watts (Eds.), *Handbook of memory disorders* (pp. 427–450). West Sussex, UK: John Wiley & Sons.

Kopelman, A., Wilson, B. A., & Baddely, A. D. (1990). *Autobiographical Memory Interview.* Bury St. Edmunds, Suffok, UK: Thames Valley Test Company.

Kozaric-Kovacic, D., Folgenovic-Smalac, V. Skinjaric, J., Szanberg, N. M., & Marussic, A. (1995). Rape, torture, and traumatization of Bosnian and Croation women: Psychological sequelae. *American Journal of Orthopsychiatry, 65,* 428–433.

LaPorta, L. D. (1992). Childhood trauma and multiple personality disorder: The case of a 9-year-old girl. *Child Abuse & Neglect, 16,* 615–620.

Lewis, D. D. (1996). Diagnostic evaluation of the child with dissociative identity disorder/multiple personality disorders. *Child and Adolescent Psychiatric Clinics of North America, 5* (2), 303–332.

Linn, L. (1989). Psychogenic amnesia. In American Psychiatric Association, *Treatments of psychiatric disorders. A task force report of the American Psychiatric Association, 3* (pp. 2186–2190). Washington, DC: Author.

Loewenstein, R. J. (1991a). Psychogenic amnesia and psychogenic fugue: A comprehensive review. In A. Tasman & S. M. Goldfinger (Eds.), *Review of psychiatry* (pp. 189–221). Washington, DC: American Psychiatric Press.

Loewenstein, R. J. (1991b). Rational psychopharmacology in the treatment of multiple personality disorder. *Psychiatric Clinics of North America, 14* (3), 721–740.

Loewenstein, R. J., Hornstein, N., & Farber, B. (1988). Open trial of clonazepam in the treatment of posttraumatic stress symptoms in multiple personality disorder. *Dissociation, 1,* 3–12.

Loewenstein, R. J., & Putnam, F. W. (1988). A comparison study of dissociative symptoms in patients with complex partial seizures, MPD, and posttraumatic stress disorder. *Dissociation, 1,* 17–22.

Ludwig, A. M. (1983). The psychobiological functions of dissociation. *American Journal of Clinical Hypnosis, 26,* 93–99.

Lynn, S. J., Rhue, J. W., & Green, J. P. (1988). Multiple personality and fantasy proneness: Is there an association or dissociation? *British Journal of Experimental and Clinical Hypnosis, 5,* 138–142.

Malenbaum, R., & Russell, A. T. (1987). Multiple personality disorder in an eleven-year-old boy and his mother. *Journal of the American Academy of Child and Adolescent Psychiatry, 26* (3), 436–439.

Marmer, S. S. (1980). Psychoanalysis of multiple personality. *International Journal of Psycho-analysis, 61,* 439–459.

Mathew, R. J., Wilson, W. H., Humphreys, D., Lowe, J. V., & Weithe, R. E. (1993). Depersonalization after marijuana smoking. *Biological Psychiatry, 33,* 431–441.

McKellar, A. (1978). Depersonalization in a 16-year-old boy. *Southern Medical Journal, 71* (12), 1580–1581.

Meares, R., & Grose, D. (1978). On depersonalization in adolescence: A consideration from the viewpoint of habituation and identity. *British Journal of Medical Psychology, 51,* 335–342.

Meyer, J. E. (1961). Depersonalization in adolescence. *Psychiatry: Journal for the Study of Interpersonal Process, 24,* 357–360.

Nemiah, J. C. (1980). Dissociative disorders. In H. I. Kaplan, A. M. Freeman, & B. Sadock, (Eds.), *Comprehensive textbook of psychiatry* (3rd ed., pp. 1544–1561). Baltimore: Williams & Wilkins.

Nemiah, J. C. (1989). Dissociative disorders, hysterical neurosis; dissociative type. In H. I. Kaplan & B. J. Sadock (Eds.), *Comprehensive textbook of psychiatry* (5th ed., pp. 1028–1044). Baltimore: Williams & Wilkins.

Nemiah, J. C. (1991). Dissociation, conversion and somatization. In A. Tasman & S. M. Goldfinger (Eds.), *Review of psychiatry* (pp. 248–260). Washington, DC: American Psychiatric Press.

Nemzer, E. D. (1996). Psychopharmacologic interventions for children and adolescents with dissociative disorders. In J. L. Silberg (Ed.), *The dissociative child: Diagnosis, treatment, and management* (pp. 239–273). Lutherville, MD: Sidran Press.

Noyes, R., Kuperman, S., & Olson, S. B. (1987). Desipramine: A possible treatment for depersonalization disorder. *Canadian Journal of Psychiatry, 32* (9), 782–784.

Ornstein, P. A. (1995). Children's long-term retention of salient personal experiences. *Journal of Traumatic Stress, 8,* 581–605.

Peterson, G. (1991). Children coping with trauma: Diagnosis of "dissociation identity disorder." *Dissociation, 4,* 152–164.

Peterson, G. (1996). Diagnostic taxonomy: Past to future. In J. L. Silberg (Ed.), *The dissociative child: Diagnosis, treatment and management.* Lutherville, MD: Sidran Press.

Peterson, G., & Putnam, F. W. (1994). Preliminary results of the field trial of proposed criteria for dissociative disorders of childhood. *Dissociation, 7,* 209–220.

Proctor, J. T. (1958). Hysteria in childhood. *American Journal of Orthopsychiatry, 28,* 394–406.

Putnam, F. W. (1989). *The diagnosis and treatment of multiple personality disorder.* New York: Guilford Press.

Putnam, F. W. (1991a). Dissociative disorders in children and adolescents: A developmental perspective. *Psychiatric Clinics of North America, 14* (3), 519–531.

Putnam, F. W. (1991b). Dissociative phenomena. In A. Tasman & S. M. Goldfinger. (Eds.), *Review of psychiatry* (vol. 10, pp. 145–160). Washington, DC: American Psychiatric Press.

Putnam, F. W. (1991c). Recent research of multiple personality disorder. *Psychiatric Clinics of North America, 14* (3), 489–501.

Putnam, F. W., Guroff, J. J., Silberman, E. K., Barban, L., & Post, R. M. (1986). The clinical phenomenology of multiple personality disorder: Review of 100 recent cases. *Journal of Clinical Psychiatry, 47,* 285–293.

Putnam, F. W., Helmers, K., & Trickett, P. K. (1993). Development, reliability, and validity of a child dissociation scale. *Child Abuse and Neglect, 17,* 731–741.

Putnam, F. W., Hornstein, N., & Peterson, G. (1996). Clinical phenomenology of child and adolescent dissociative disorders: Gender and age effects. *Child and Adolescent Psychiatric Clinics of North America, 5* (2), 351–360.

Raine, W. J. (1982). Self-mutilation. *Journal of Adolescence, 5* (1), 1–13.

Rapaport, D. (1942). *Emotions and memory.* Baltimore: Waverly Press.

Ratliff, N. B., & Kerski, P. (1995). Depersonalization treated with fluoketine, *American Journal of Psychiatry, 152,* 1689–1690.

Reagor, P. A., Kasten, J. D., & Morelli, M. A. (1992). A Checklist for Screening Dissociative Disorders in Children and Adolescents. *Dissociation, 5* (1), 4–19.

Riley, R. L., & Mead, J. (1988). The development of symptoms of multiple personality in a child of three. *Dissociation, 1* (3), 41–46.

Rodberg, G., Bagly, C., & Welling, D. (1990, November). *Dissociative disorders and abused children.* Proceedings of the 7th International Conference on Multiple Personality/Dissociative States, Chicago.

Ross, C. A. (1989). *Multiple personality disorder: Diagnosis, clinical features, and treatment.* New York: John Wiley & Sons.

Ross, C. A. (1991). Epidemiology of multiple personality and dissociation. *Psychiatric Clinics of North America, 14* (31), 503–517.

Ross, C. A., Heber, S., Norton, G. R., Anderson, D., Anderson, G. & Barchet, P. (1989). The Dissociative Disorders Interview Schedule: A structured interview. *Dissociation, 2,* 169–189.

Salfield, D. (1958). Depersonalization and altered disturbances in childhood. *Journal of Mental Science, 104,* 472–476.

Sanders, B., & Giolas, M. H. (1991). Dissociation and childhood trauma in psychologically disturbed adolescents. *American Journal of Psychiatry, 148* (1), 50–54.

Sedman, G. (1970). Theories of depersonalization: A reappraisal. *British Journal of Psychiatry, 11* (7), 1–14.

Sengupta, S. J., & Saxona, S. (1993). Generalized dissociative amnesia. *Australian and New Zealand Journal of Psychiatry, 27,* 699–700.

Shader, R. I., & Scharfman, E. L. (1989). Depersonalization disorder. In American Psychiatric Association, *Treatments of psychiatric disorders. A task force report of the American Psychiatric Association* (vol. 3, pp. 2217–2222). Washington, DC: Author.

Shimizu, M., & Sakamoto, S. (1986). Depersonalization in early adolescence. *Japanese Journal of Psychiatry and Neurology, 40,* 603–608.

Shirar, L. (1996). *Dissociative children: Bridging the inner and outer worlds.* New York: W. W. Norton.

Silberg, J. L. (1991, November). *Differential diagnosis of dissociative disorders in children.* Paper presented at the 8th International Conference on Multiple Personality/Dissociative States, Rush Presbyterian— St. Luke's Medical Center, Chicago.

Silberg, J. L. (1994, November). *Psychological testing features associated with dissociative diagnoses in children and adolescents.* Paper presented at the 11th International Conference on Multiple Personality/ Dissociative States, Rush Presbyterian—St. Luke's Medical Center, Chicago.

Silberg, J. L. (Ed.). (1996a). *The dissociative child: Diagnosis, treatment and management,* Lutherville, MD: Sidran Press.

Silberg, J. L. (1996b). Interviewing strategies for assessing dissociative disorders in children and adolescents. In J. L. Silberg (Ed.), *The dissociative child: Diagnosis, treatment and management* (pp. 47–67). Lutherville, MD: Sidran Press.

Silberg, J. L. (1996c). Psychological testing with dissociative children and adolescents. In J. L. Silberg (Ed.), *The dissociative child: Diagnosis, treatment and management* (pp. 75–100). Lutherville, MD: Sidran Press.

Silberg, J. L., & Waters, F. S. (1996). Factors associated with positive therapeutic outcome. In J. L. Silberg (Ed.), *The dissociative child: Diagnosis, treatment and management* (pp. 103–112). Lutherville, MD: Sidran Press.

Simeon, D., Stein, D. J., & Hollander, E. (1995). Depersonalization disorder and self-injurious behavior. *Journal of Clinical Psychiatry, 56* (suppl. 4), 36–39.

Sobol, B., & Schneider, K. (1996). Art as an adjunctive therapy in the treatment of children who dissociate. In J. L. Silberg (Ed.), *The dissociative child: Diagnosis treatment and management* (pp. 195–222). Lutherville, MD: Sidran Press.

Spiegel, D. (1991). Dissociative disorders. In A. Tasman & S. M. Goldfinger (Eds.), *Review of psychiatry* (vol. 10, pp. 261–275). Washington, DC: American Psychiatric Press.

Stein, M., & Uhde T. (1989). Depersonalization disorder: Effects of caffeine and response to pharmacotherapy. *Biological Psychiatry, 26,* 315–320.

Steinberg, M. (1986). The structured clinical interview for DSM-III-R Dissociative Disorders. New Haven, CT: Department of Psychiatry, Yale University School of Medicine.

Steinberg, M. (1991). The spectrum of depersonalization: Assessment and treatment. In A. Tasman & S. M. Goldfinger (Eds.). *Review of psychiatry* (vol. 10, pp. 223–247). Washington, DC: American Psychiatric Press.

Steinberg, M., & Steinberg, A. (1995). Using the SCID-D to assess dissociative identity disorder in adolescents: Three case studies. *Bulletin of the Menninger Clinic, 59,* 221–231.

Steingard, S., & Frankel, F. M. (1985). Dissociation and psychotic symptoms. *American Journal of Psychiatry, 142* (8), 953–955.

Stern, D. (1985). *The interpersonal world of the infant.* New York: Basic Books.

Szymanski, H. V. (1981). Prolonged depersonalization after marijuana use. *American Journal of Psychiatry, 138* (2), 231–233.

Terao, T., Yoshimura, R., Terao, M., & Abe, K. (1992). Depersonalization following nitrazapan withdrawal. *Biological Psychiatry, 31,* 212–213.

Terr, L. (1988). What happens to early memories of trauma? A study of 20 children under age 5 at the time of documented traumatic events. *Journal of the American Academy of Child and Adolescent Psychiatry, 27* (1), 96–104.

Torch, E. (1987). The psychotherapeutic treatment of depersonalization disorder. *Hillside Journal of Clinical Psychiatry, 9,* 133–143.

Trujillo, K., Lewis, P. O., Yeager, C. A., & Gidlow, B. (1996). Imaginary companions of school boys and boys with dissociative identity disorder; A normal to pathological continuum. *Child and Adolescent Psychiatric Clinics of North America, 5,* 375–391.

U.S. Department of Health and Human Services.

(1988). *Study findings: Study of national incidence and prevalence of child abuse and neglect* (DHHS contract no. 105-85-1702). Washington, DC: National Center on Child Abuse and Neglect.

van der Kolk, B. (1987). *Psychological trauma.* Washington, DC: American Psychiatric Press.

Venn, J. (1984). Family etiology and remission in a case of psychogenic fugue. *Family Process, 23,* 429–435.

Vincent, M., & Pickering, M. R. (1988). Multiple personality in childhood. *Canadian Journal of Psychiatry, 33,* 524–529.

Waterbury, M. (1991, November). *Dissociative disorders in 170 abused inner city children.* Paper presented at the 8th International Conference on Multiple Personality Dissociative States, Rush Presbyterian—St. Luke's Medical Center, Chicago.

Waterbury, M. (1996). School interventions for dissociative children. In J. L. Silberg (Ed.), *The dissociative child: Diagnosis, treatment and management* (pp. 319–333). Lutherville, MD: Sidran Press.

Waters, F. S. (1996). Parents as partners in the treatment of dissociative children. In J. L. Silberg (Ed.), *The dissociative child: Diagnosis, treatment and management* (pp. 277–299), Lutherville, MD: Sidran Press.

Waters, F. S. & Silberg, J. S. (1996a). Promoting integration in dissociative children. In J. L. Silberg (Ed.). *The dissociative child. Diagnosis, treatment and management* (pp. 171–194). Lutherville, MD: Sidran Press.

Waters, F. S. & Silberg, J. S. (1996b). Therapeutic phases in the treatment of dissociative children. In J. L. Silberg (Ed.), *The dissociative child: Diagnosis, treatment and management* (pp. 139–169). Lutherville, MD: Sidran Press.

Weiss, M., Sutton, P. J., & Utecht, A. J. (1985). Multiple personality in a 10-year-old girl. *Journal of the American Academy of Child and Adolescent Psychiatry, 24* (4), 495–501.

Werner, H., & Kaplan, B. (1963). *Symbol formation.* New York: John Wiley & Sons.

Williams, L. (1995). Recovered memories of abuse in women with documented child sexual victimization histories. *Journal of Traumatic Stress, 8,* 639–674.

Williams, D. T., & Velazquez, L. (1996). The use of hypnosis in children with dissociative disorders. *Child and Adolescent Psychiatric Clinics of North America, 5,* 495–508.

World Health Organization. (1990). Draft version of *International Classification of Diseases*—revision (10th ed.). Geneva: Author.

Yeager, C. A., & Lewis, D. O. (1996). The intergenerational transmission of violence and dissociation. *Child and Adolescent Psychiatric Clinics of North America, 5,* 393–430.

Young, W. C., Sachs, R. G., Braun, B. G., & Watkins, R. T. (1991). Patients reporting ritual abuse in childhood: A clinical syndrome. Report of 37 cases. *Child Abuse and Neglect, 15,* 181–189.

32 / Psychoses in Adolescence

Lois T. Flaherty

Although psychotic disorders make up a small proportion of all psychiatric illnesses seen in adolescents, they account for significant morbidity. This chapter discusses the varied presentations of these disorders in adolescents and their diagnosis and management.

History

Since the advent of modern psychiatry in the early part of the 20th century, both schizophrenia and affective disorders with psychotic symptoms have been recognized as occurring in the adolescent period. Kraeplin (1919) described schizophrenia as an illness typically having an onset during the adolescent and young adult stages of life and characterized by a deteriorating course and significant cognitive impairment. He saw the essential feature of the illness as the destruction of the inner unity of the mind and the weakening of volition and drive. The term "thought disorder" originated with Eugen Bleuler (1911/1950) and has often been used interchangeably with schizophrenia, although disturbances of thinking are seen in other illnesses, as well.

Traditionally, psychoses have been classified either as functional, or having no known organic etiology, or organic, caused by some demonstrable agent. With the discovery of alterations in brain structure and metabolism in disorders such as schizophrenia, this distinction is becoming less meaningful. At the same time, evidence is growing that environmental factors also play an important role, not only as precipitants of illness in vulnerable individuals but in course and outcome.

Epidemiology

Onset of schizophrenia occurs before the age of 25 in approximately 60% of those affected; onset of manic-depressive illness occurs between the ages of 10 and 19 in approximately 30% of cases. Although the incidence of drug-induced psychoses during adolescence is unknown, clinical evidence suggests that they occur frequently during the adolescent years. Patients diagnosed as having psychotic disorders generally make up a minority of those hospitalized on adolescent psychiatric inpatient units, even units devoted to the treatment of severely disturbed adolescents. Data from a recent study in a university setting in which all adolescents admitted were diagnosed according to rigorous criteria yielded a 7% prevalence of psychotic disorders among the patients studied (Mattanah, Becker, Levy, Edell, & McGlashan, 1995). In a recent review of adolescent hospital admissions, the prevalence of bipolar illness was found to be 7.6%, with the majority of the patients with this disorder manifesting mood-congruent psychotic symptoms during their hospitalization (Ghadirian & Roux, 1995). A long-term follow-up study of 31 adolescents treated at Timberlawn Hospital, a long-term private inpatient center, included 8 with psychotic disorders, or about 25% (Gossett, Lewis, & Barnhart, 1983). Another follow-up study of 140 adolescents hospitalized at Terrell State Hospital cited 18% with schizophrenia and 17% with "major affective disorders" (Pearson, 1987). Presumably some of the latter group had psychotic disorders. Thus, percentages for psychotic disorders are likely to be highest in long-term treatment settings, but still make up a minority of diagnoses of adolescent inpatients.

CLINICAL PRESENTATION

These disorders rarely manifest themselves completely at the outset, and their presentations are often atypical when considered in light of adult diagnostic criteria. The course of these illnesses, especially schizophrenia, frequently is characterized by a long prodromal period during which symptoms first appear in relatively mild form and are nonspecific. In one careful follow-up study of high-risk children born to a schizophrenic parent, the mean length of time between the onset of first symptoms and the appearance of a full-blown schizophrenic disorder was 7 years; the mean age of onset of symptoms was 14 (Mirsky, Silberman, Latz, & Nagler, 1985).

Schizophrenia: Because of the diversity of manifestations and variability in course and outcome of schizophrenia, it is likely that there are multiple forms of this illness, perhaps with different pathological mechanisms. Current diagnostic criteria emphasize a constellation of psychotic symptoms associated with functional impairment. The cardinal symptoms, described more fully later, involve delusions and hallucinations, disorganized speech and behavior, and blunted, flat, or inappropriate affect. The fourth edition of the *Diagnostic and Statistical Manual of Mental Disorders* (*DSM-IV*; American Psychiatric Association [APA], 1994) recognizes paranoid, disorganized, catatonic, undifferentiated, and residual subtypes; these distinctions are often difficult to make in adolescent patients and may not have the stability that they do in adults.

The case histories of adults with schizophrenia often show a pattern of symptom onset during adolescence. One pattern is typified by an adolescent who appears to have been well functioning prior to her illness, as illustrated by the following example.

A 36-year-old woman described herself as having been an outstanding student in high school. She was selected to go to a 6-week journalism camp during the summer. She received a D on her first written assignment with the terse comment "Try harder next time." She felt like a complete failure and was miserable for the remainder of the camp, telling no one about the experience. During the succeeding year, her increasing depression was compounded by her parents' separation, and she began to have suicidal thoughts. Gradually she developed paranoid delusions involving her family; she thought that her brother had been kidnapped and killed by the mafia and replaced by a look-alike. Over the years, the delusions became progressively more systematized.

Psychosis in Bipolar Illness: Bipolar, or manic-depressive, illness is an underdiagnosed condition during adolescence, with many of these severely disturbed teenagers being labeled schizophrenic (Carlson, Fennig, & Bromet, 1994). Psychotic symptoms most commonly include grandiose delusions and/or auditory hallucinations. Manic epi-

sodes characteristically involve distinct periods of elevated, expansive, or irritable moods associated with hyperactivity, distractibility, insomnia, increased energy, reduced sleep, flight of ideas, and loud, pressured, and rapid speech. Adolescents in a manic phase may exhibit intrusive social behavior, calling friends at all hours of the day and night, and manifest an unceasing and unselected enthusiasm for social interaction. They joke, are superlively, and may be somewhat theatrical and behave in an unusually sexually provocative fashion. A euphoric high exists in spite of reality. They may go on wild buying sprees.

These manic behaviors may alternate rapidly with periods of severe depression, or each may last for several days or weeks. A positive family history for manic-depressive illness usually is elicited, and in many cases the onset of the illness can be related to a specific environmental stress, particularly major separations within the family.

Major Depressive Episodes with Psychotic Features: Depression may be so severe as to be accompanied by profound alterations in functioning and psychotic thought processes. Instead of the extreme psychomotor retardation seen in adults with major depressive episodes, adolescents with this disorder may be simply hypoactive. The key feature is an extreme preoccupation with feelings of guilt and worthlessness. These preoccupations may take the form of delusions about imagined wrongs committed or self-blame for harm suffered by others, for example, death of a parent. Hallucinations, usually in the form of auditory accusatory voices telling the patient he or she is bad or worthless, may be present. These psychotic features are termed mood-congruent because they are in keeping with the patient's mood of depression and hopelessness and low self-esteem. Such patients often feel they and others would be better off if they were dead, and think about, plan, and in some cases attempt suicide.

At times in either depressed or manic phases, the content of patients' delusions or hallucinations may be not directly related to their mood and are more like those of schizophrenic patients, for example, delusions about being persecuted, or controlled by outside forces.

Drug-induced Psychoses: Drug abuse can produce acute psychotic reactions as well as those with a more insidious onset. Acute toxic psychoses can result from amphetamines, marijuana, and the hallucinogenic drugs, most notably lysergic acid (LSD) and phencyclidine (PCP) (Patterson, Logan, & Vandewalle, 1982). The hallmarks of an acute toxic psychosis are confusion, disorientation, anxiety, agitation, and disturbances of perception, reason, and judgment. In their most severe form, these reactions can be associated with extremely bizarre behavior, based on the user's extreme distortion of reality, such as jumping out of a window in the belief that one can fly. The characteristic alterations differ somewhat depending on the responsible drug; an amphetamine-induced psychosis, for example, is classically characterized by paranoid delusions while hallucinogenic drugs tend to produce various visual alterations, such as seeing rainbows or flashes of color. One of the most disturbing changes is that occasionally produced by PCP with serious distortions in perception and thinking along with a release of primitive kinds of aggressive behavior. This type of dissociative reaction occasionally is responsible for bizarre assaults or murders. PCP is one of the most widely used recreational drugs in the US and is an especially popular drug among adolescents; the average age of first use is 14 years (Young, 1987).

Drugs vary in their psychotogenic effects. It seems likely that marijuana is capable of inducing psychosis only in susceptible individuals, since few users of this widely used drug become psychotic. Phencyclidine, on the other hand, seems to produce psychotic states relatively frequently; thus, its effects may not be dependent on individual susceptibility. Amphetamines can induce a psychotic state that is indistinguishable from schizophrenia; the fact that this is so raises intriguing questions about how the pathophysiology of schizophrenia and drug-induced psychoses may be related.

It should be kept in mind that adolescents who are emotionally disturbed frequently turn to drugs in an attempt to control their distress by "self-medication." The use of hallucinogens by schizophrenic youngsters is not uncommon. Thus, drug use can significantly obscure the clinical picture.

Brief Psychotic Disorder: According to *DSM-IV*, brief psychotic disorder is an illness that has an acute onset of positive psychotic symptoms, lasts less than 1 month, and involves complete recovery (APA, 1994). It is not a grouping that has been well studied, and is relatively uncommon. Postpartum psychoses, which may be seen in ado-

lescents, fall into this category. Obviously, this illness cannot be distinguished from the more enduring psychotic disorders at the time of its onset. It is likely that adolescents whose brain functioning is already compromised may be more likely to develop transient psychotic disorders; for example, Chess (1977) found a high incidence during adolescence among a group of mentally retarded children followed into this period.

Schizophrenia-Spectrum Disorders: Schizotypal personality disorder, considered a condition related to schizophrenia, involves disturbances of thinking, bizarre fantasies and preoccupations, and may include perceptual distortions such as illusions and paranoid ideation. Extreme discomfort in social situations is often part of this syndrome. Schizoid personality disorder, also one of the schizophrenia spectrum disorders, involves a pervasive pattern of social isolation, often accompanied by lack of emotional expressiveness, and resembles the deficit syndrome or negative symptom pattern seen in schizophrenia. Both of these conditions have been described in children and adolescents, and schizoid personality is sometimes a premorbid state of schizophrenia (Meijer & Treffers, 1991; Wolff & Chick, 1980). Schizotypal personality disorder does not seem to progress to schizophrenia and does not involve the deterioration in habit functioning or negative symptoms seen in the latter, although it can be quite disabling; it is considered by some to be a mild form of schizophrenia.

Studies of biological relatives of persons with schizophrenia have shown an increased prevalence of schizophrenia spectrum disorders in the relatives. This research finding supports the concept of an inherited vulnerability that expresses itself variably under different conditions.

PSYCHOTIC SYMPTOMS

Disturbances of Thinking: Thinking involves many functions, including memory, perception, and the integration and classification of information taken in from the environment. Thought disorders are characterized by primary disturbances in either the form or the content of thinking. Disturbances in thought content are manifested by difficulty in distinguishing reality from fantasies, fears, or preoccupations. In mild form these kinds of disturbances may appear in the form of excessive hypochondriasis or convictions about ugliness or physical deformity, as in the case of a 16-year-old girl who believed that the presence of a few dark hairs on her breast meant that she was completely deformed. The disturbances may be seen in an adolescent's excessive preoccupation with what others are thinking or saying about him, along with the attribution of his own worrisome thoughts about himself to others. One girl, for example, was convinced that a female teacher on whom she had a crush believed that she was homosexual. Another patient repeatedly worried that he had run over pedestrians while driving his car, and had to check constantly in his rearview mirror to see if this had, in fact, happened.

In their more blatant form, disturbances of thought content appear as hallucinations, delusions, and ideas of reference. Delusions and hallucinations are the hallmark of a psychotic disorder. When they are florid, they are obvious to everyone, but they may be subtle and their unreality is sometimes difficult to guage. More florid delusions will involve obviously fantastical underpinnings, such as a belief that one's body has been taken over by Martians. Others are more difficult to distinguish from frequent adolescent concerns, as in the case of an adolescent who is convinced others are talking about her at school. Hallucinations are more obviously either present or absent. They can involve any sensory modality; auditory and visual are the most common. Olfactory and tactile hallucinations are more likely to be associated with identifiable brain lesions than are the other kinds of perceptual distortions, but they also occur in psychotic disorders that are not secondary to a medical condition. The distinction between an affective disorder and schizophrenia-spectrum disorder has been made on the basis of whether the content of the delusions and hallucinations is mood-congruent—that is, in keeping with the mood disturbance. Examples are the delusion that one is unbearably ugly in association with depression and a hallucinated voice telling one that one is bad and deserves to die. In practice, this distinction is often difficult with adolescents and may not be altogether reliable, although the clinician should attempt to make it. For example, the delusion that one is God or sent by god could be part of manic grandiosity or a schizophrenic idea.

Other delusional symptoms include ideas of reference, which refer to the belief that one is receiving special messages from the media or other environmental cues. Thought broadcasting is the belief that one can put one's thought into the minds of others; and thought insertion, that others can control one's thinking.

Obsessions, intrusive and unwanted thoughts that are troublesome and disturbing, are another type of thought disturbance but are distinguished from psychotic thoughts in that the person who has them recognizes they do not make sense and struggles to keep them at bay. However, severe obsessions and compulsions may be difficult to distinguish from psychotic symptoms. For example, a 16-year-old boy with obsessive-compulsive disorder described "a voice in my head, like a god's voice" telling him to carry out various compulsive rituals. His awareness of the absurdity of this experience and the absence of any other psychotic symptoms ruled out the existence of a psychotic disorder; what he was describing was the force of his compulsions. To make matters more complicated, obsessions and compulsions are sometimes present in schizophrenia (McClellan & Werry, 1994).

Formal Thought Disorder: Disorders in the form of thinking range from mild disorganization and difficulty maintaining a focus in conversation, to total unintelligibility. When loosening of association is less severe, the flow of speech may be comprehensible, although difficult to follow. When loosening of associative thought is severe, speech is irrational, incoherent, disconnected, and bizarre. Consider this case example.

A 16-year-old girl commented, "Why can't I go out? The world is cold, old, bold; never again. My hair is a mess. No wonder he does like me, summer, sun and salt. Oh God, if birds could fly why oh why can't I? Soft skin is important, you know, snow, milk, stale, pale hospitals. Needles, knives, Christ died for your sins, will I die? Will you die? Nope, no, absolutely not. Why can't I go out?" (Flaherty & Sarles, 1981)

Thought disorder has been shown to be present in manic-depressive illness as well as in schizophrenia and other psychotic disorders (Marengo & Harrow, 1985). Although the type of disturbance is not exactly the same (Andreason & Powers, 1976), from a practical clinical point of view, the presence or absence of thought disorder is not necessarily a helpful sign in distinguishing between mood disorder and schizophrenia or schizophrenia-spectrum disorders, especially in adolescents. It has been suggested that thought disorder is primarily an indicator of the severity of psychotic illness rather than of diagnosis. It has been seen as a consequence of deficits in information processing, involving a failure to comprehend the listener's needs, inability to focus on a train of thought, and other problems with use of connecting forms of language (Caplan, 1994).

The inability to organize one's thinking interferes with goal-directed behavior. The result may be a pervasive difficulty "getting one's act together" that goes beyond the occasional bouts of regressive disorganization common during this period. The adolescent may drift through school and other activities, barely managing to avoid flunking out, or may indeed fail. An extreme difficulty with focusing on relevant tasks may occur, so that homework assignments are never completed. There is an inability to make rational decisions, weighing pros and cons and considering consequences. An adolescent boy, for example, having forgotten his homework assignment, cut class rather than accept the consequences of being unprepared, even though the consequence of cutting was suspension from school. These adolescents tend to do better in very structured tasks and school subjects that leave little to the imagination, such as history and geography. They have more difficulty with more abstract subjects such as literature, advanced mathematics, or creative art. Sports participation becomes difficult, involving as it does both the ability to react to constantly changing circumstances and the use of the body in space. The adolescent may drop out of athletic activities, rationalizing nonparticipation by saying that he or she has lost interest.

Disturbances in Mood and Affect: By definition, mood symptoms are prominent in affective disorders with psychotic features. In schizophrenic disorders, although it is the aberrant thinking that is the primary disturbance, disturbances in mood and affect are also present. In adolescent schizophrenia, mood symptoms are likely to be prominent and may be the presenting symptoms. Emotional expression may be blunted and flattened, with mood varying from apathetic states to periods of intense anxiety and irritation. Moods and affect are often also inappropriate for a particular context, for example, smiling may occur when suicidal thoughts are mentioned. Opposite wishes, ideas,

and feelings may be expressed simultaneously, as in concurrent love-hate feelings for the same person or object. In some cases depressed or elevated mood may be quite prominent. This is illustrated by the case of a 19-year-old male patient whose current clinical picture is consistent with schizoaffective disorder. He described how he began to feel depressed at the age of 17, toward the end of his senior year in high school:

"I was triggered into a depression that lasted through the end of the summer. I had no energy, couldn't get out of bed, the usual depression stuff, suicidality. I didn't feel like doing anything." Subsequently he developed anxiety symptoms, associated with vague worries that someone would harm him. He began to have auditory hallucinations, hearing voices of "people shouting different voices inside my head." He felt he could tell what others were thinking: "I know people and can understand them and their thoughts and silly motives. It's like nothing profound, like basic bullshit." At the same time, "everything looked fake, like in a picture." These experiences persisted after the depression lifted. About 6 months later, he began staying up all night, missing classes, and had racing thoughts: "My mind wouldn't shut off, I kept thinking and thinking. Things were swirling around in my head." He began to experience what he called "panic attacks" accompanied by rapid heart rate, nausea, fear of going out, and worries about his food being poisoned.

It is not clear whether schizoaffective states represent a variant of schizophrenia or the coexistence of two separate disorders. The category of schizoaffective disorder has been a controversial one: *DSM-III* considered it to a diagnosis of exclusion, to be made only when either bipolar disorder or schizophrenia do not fit the clinical picture. *DSM-IV* defines it as a disorder with episodic mood disturbances similar to those seen in major depression or mania but also requires psychotic symptoms to have been present for at least 2 weeks outside of the episode of disturbed mood. Some consider schizoaffective disorder to be an atypical form of bipolar disorder; others, a subtype of schizophrenia. The results of a recent epidemiological study suggested that people with schizoaffective disorder have both schizophrenia and affective disorder (Kendler, McGuire, Gruenberg, & Walsh, 1995).

Deterioration in Psychosocial Functioning: A deterioration in level of functioning is always a feature of psychotic disorders. For adolescents, schoolwork and social activities are affected. A gradual but marked withdrawal from peers, school, and family resulting in almost total isolation often occurs. A distrust of others develops, and the adolescent becomes preoccupied by fantasy, as illustrated by the following case.

A 15-year-old boy lost interest in school team sports and turned to fishing by himself. He soon gave up this hobby and became absorbed in stamp collecting. He enmeshed himself in his solitary interests to the exclusion of all peer contact, becoming known as "the ghost" of his high school class. His only contact with his family was during his silent, short stay at the dinner table. He secluded himself for longer and longer periods in his bedroom, and his parents suspected that he was masturbating excessively. Within a short time more florid psychotic symptoms became evident and the diagnosis of schizophrenia was made.

These changes usually cause distress to both the adolescent and his family. Expressions of this distress from the teenager may take the form of complaints about feeling confused, being unable to concentrate, or feeling that his or her thoughts are out of control. Although in some cases parents are apparently oblivious to the problem, they may express a sense of anger and frustration, attributing their teenager's problems to lack of motivation or laziness.

Other Symptoms: Social inappropriateness is another common feature of psychotic disorders in adolescents. It may manifest itself in the carrying of current or recent fads to an extreme degree, for example, hair that is worn very long or short. The inappropriateness must be gauged in relation to the prevailing standards of the adolescent's peer community; peers will see such an adolescent as "out of it." A change toward sloppiness in personal appearance as well as a deterioration in personal hygiene also may have occurred. Although no one feature of the adolescent's clothing or personal grooming is grossly inappropriate, the combined effect of the whole creates a sense of oddness.

A variety of other clinical pictures may herald the onset of a psychotic disorder in adolescents. Unexplained physical symptoms are common, particularly pseudoneurological symptoms (Livingston, Taylor, & Crawford, 1988). Pseudocyesis has been described as the presenting symptom in an adolescent patient with an incipient thought disorder; this symptom was followed by a delusional miscarriage (Reichenbacher & Yates, 1987).

Etiology

The etiology of psychotic disorders is unknown. Both the schizophrenia-spectrum disorders and the bipolar disorders have been shown to be familial. Current evidence suggests that schizophrenia (or at least some forms of it) results from a neurodevelopmental vulnerability interacting with environmental stresses. There is evidence that a variety of physical conditions can increase risk, including genetic predisposition, birth trauma, and in utero infections.

BRAIN STRUCTURE AND FUNCTION

The search for specific lesions in the brains of schizophrenic or manic-depressive patients has pointed to abnormalities in processing pathways that affect higher brain centers. The limbic system, hippocampus, and amygdala carry projections that are involved in most higher cortical functions. In many histological and imaging studies, several of these regions have been implicated in the etiology of the two disorders.

Although routine psychometric testing often shows no abnormalities in cognitive functioning in schizophrenia, studies that used more refined neuropsychological testing have shown abnormalities that implicate the frontal and temporal lobes. A condition of "hypofrontality" has been found in neuroimaging studies, positron emission tomography (PET), and cerebral blood flow studies.

Computed tomography (CT scans), in which multiple X rays are taken and then analyzed to yield cross-sectional images of the brain, has yielded some important findings in patients with schizophrenia. These have included increased ventricular-to-brain ratios, cerebellar atrophy, and third ventricle enlargement. In patients with schizophrenia, enlarged ventricles have been found to be associated with medication response, negative symptoms, and cognitive impairment. Ventricular enlargement is the end result of loss of neuronal mass, as ventricles simply are the fluid-filled spaces within the brain. Enlarged ventricles are found in a variety of neurologic conditions that involve loss of brain tissue, such as alcoholism and dementia. Not all patients with schizophrenia have this finding; it has been found in adolescent patients (Schultz et al., 1983) as well as adults with histories of early onset and/or poor premorbid functioning (Morihisa, 1991), and could reflect birth or neonatal complications in these patients. The higher prevalence of schizophrenia among people who were born during the winter months suggests a viral infection is responsible in some cases. It is possible that insults to the brain that occur early in life manifest themselves later on, as the synaptic pruning that occurs during adolescent brain development exposes faulty architecture that was not previously apparent. For further discussion, see Chapter 5.

Premorbid Deficits: Other research has focused on identifying preexisting deficits in functioning as possible constituents of vulnerability. While there does not appear to be a specific preschizophrenic personality, some preexisting disturbance in psychological functioning is common. Prospective studies, using data gathered before the illness become overt, indicate varying kinds of psychopathology, ranging from a delinquent pattern of behavior to withdrawal. The preexistence of learning disabilities, attention deficit disorders, and mental retardation among children who later develop psychoses during adolescence has also been found (Chess, 1977; Watt, 1978). Specific deficits, called "process" features, also have been found. They include cognitive confusion and rigidity of thinking, which interfere with an individual's inability to cope with multiple aspects of the environment and result in overall low functioning. "Cognitive slippage," a mild type of thought disorder involving some looseness of association, has been found in children of schizophrenic parents (Arboleda & Holzman, 1985).

PSYCHOSOCIAL FACTORS

Although a variety of unfavorable childhood conditions have been implicated in the development of psychotic disorders, specifying precisely how these operate has been an elusive goal. In addition to the difficulties in measuring and defining stress, there is the added problem that what is stressful for a vulnerable individual may not be stressful for everyone. Although clinical case reports frequently cite stress factors as important precipitants of a psychotic episode, there are very few systematic studies of the impact of stress on the development of psychotic disorders in adolescence. One finding of a longitudinal study of children born to a schizophrenic parent showed that institutional rearing during early childhood increased the likelihood that the child would later develop schizophrenia (Parnas, Teasdale, & Schulsinger, 1985). Another group (Hellgren, Gillberg, & Enerskog, 1987) found that adolescents with psychotic disorders were twice as likely to have had a parent who died as were controls; they compared 40 adolescent inpatients with psychotic disorders to teenagers who were seen for school health problems and were free of psychiatric illness. The Israeli follow-up study of children of schizophrenic mothers showed an increased risk of developing schizophrenia in the kibbutz-raised children compared to the town-raised group (Mirsky et al., 1985); the difference was attributed to the possibility of increased stigmatization of a child who stands out as different in the kibbutz.

Family Studies: The notion that a negative intrafamilial environment could play a role in the pathogenesis of psychotic disorders, especially schizophrenia, began with the concept of "communication deviance" developed in the 1960s (Wynne & Singer, 1963). Although it generated much interest, this idea eventually was abandoned as unprovable, as it could not be demonstrated that these aberrant family interactions predated the onset of the illness. Subsequently "expressed emotion" (EE) was held to be an important factor in the etiology, course, and treatment of schizophrenia (Vaughn & Leff, 1976). The term refers to communications characterized by criticism, emotional overinvolvement, or intrusiveness expressed by relatives toward a psychiatrically ill family member. The work in this area has indicated that high levels of expressed emotion are associated with relapse in patients who are already ill as well as predictive of schizophrenic illness in adolescents with previous psychiatric disorders (Goldstein, 1985). This work remains controversial and has been criticized for not taking into account the effect that a patient's illness has on the family. As Goldstein has pointed out, it is possible that even though the schizophrenic disorder has not yet become fully manifest, it could still be having an effect on family interactions.

An additional factor that suggests that there is a dynamic interplay between the individual and the environment is the finding that both course and outcome are highly variable and even patients who appear to have a chronic deteriorating course may recover (M. Bleuler, 1974). While this fluidity is in and of itself not proof of an important role of the environment in pathogenesis, it is certainly consistent with such a hypothesis.

Development and Vulnerability: An intriguing hypothesis is that schizophrenia and other psychotic disorders may result from the impact of the developmental process itself on vulnerable individuals. The fact that the onset is so often in the late adolescent period, and this period is one of heightened psychosocial stressors, makes it plausible that growing up, and all the attendant demands that it places on the individual, may simply be too much for some vulnerable adolescents. The frequent clinical observation that the first psychotic episode so often follows upon a significant life change, such as going away to college, or rupture of an important relationship, lends credence to this view. Indeed, many of those who worked intensively with psychotic adolescents believed just this to be the case. Harry Stack Sullivan (1953) postulated that it was the adolescent's "essential experience of self" gone awry that led to a psychotic decompensation, as the self became repudiated and split off: "The personality is partly torn from its moorings and has moved from what was actually its developmental level into a state which we call the schizophrenic way of life" (quoted in Perry & Gawel, 1953, p. 327).

Others emphasized separation-individuation as the nemesis for adolescents vulnerable to psychosis (Ekstein, 1973).

SUBTYPING

Since the clinical manifestations of schizophrenia are so diverse, much research has been directed at identifying subtypes, in the belief that there actually may be several forms of this illness or, as Eugen Bleuler stated, a "group of schizophrenias" (1911/1950).

Two different patterns of onset of schizophrenia have been described, each having different prognostic implications. The acute onset, or reactive, type usually is associated with lack of serious prior personality impairment, often has a precipitating event, and is accompanied by confusion or emotionality. This type is particularly difficult to distinguish from other kinds of psychosis and has a good prognosis. The slow-onset type, often called process schizophrenia, is an insidious illness developing in a basically schizoid individual who often has a long history of maladjustment. This type tends to show progressive deterioration, hence a poorer prognosis.

POSITIVE AND NEGATIVE SYMPTOMS

A more recent distinction has been made on the basis on positive and negative symptoms. Positive symptoms include hallucinations, delusions, and disordered thinking. They tend to occur earlier in the course of the illness and may be more responsive to drug treatment. Although there is some disagreement about the definition of negative symptoms, these are generally considered to include withdrawal, blunting of affect, poverty of speech and content, asociality, anhedonia, and avolition. These are more enduring, often emerge later in the course of the illness, and have been associated with possible frontal lobe deficit (Weinberger, Aloia, Goldberg, & Berman, 1994). Negative symptoms have been termed a deficit syndrome, since they represent the absence of normal human characteristics. They have been shown to be preexistent in the process forms of schizophrenia and have been associated with physical brain abnormalities and with a more chronic course. They are more likely to be found in childhood-onset schizophrenia than later onset forms of this disorder. Negative symptoms are viewed as responsible for the poor psychosocial functioning associated with much of the morbidity in chronic schizophrenia. Compared to positive symptoms, they are less responsive to treatment with the traditional antipsychotic drugs, the neuroleptics.

Diagnosis

For a variety of reasons, psychotic disorders often are misdiagnosed when they occur during the adolescent period. The polymorphous nature of early forms of these disorders, and the fact that their presentation is colored by developmental features, makes them difficult to recognize. The lack of a history of past episodes complicates the task of making a diagnosis. Even when psychotic symptoms are clearly present in an adolescent patient, a correct diagnosis may not be made because of the clinician's reluctance to label the adolescent as having a serious and possibly long-term mental illness. Adolescents with psychotic symptoms are often reluctant to reveal them, fearing they are "crazy," and the suspiciousness and uncommunicativeness that are part of the illness challenge the psychiatrist's skill.

CLINICAL INTERVIEW

As with other disorders of adolescence, the cornerstones of diagnosis are the clinical interview with the adolescent and the gathering of information from parents and other sources. There are advantages to meeting with the youngster together with his or her parents for at least part of the initial session. Adolescents with psychotic symptoms not infrequently are so terrified of the encounter with a psychiatrist that they are virtually unable to communicate on their own. Additionally, because of the extreme suspiciousness that is common in such youngsters, meeting with the patient and parents separately can foster the adolescents' sense that the adults are conspiring about them. Finally, it is important for the parents to be made aware of the extent to which psychotic symptoms are present, and hearing about them directly from their child provides incontrovertible evidence of their existence.

HISTORY

A careful and thorough developmental history is a crucial part of the diagnostic assessment. Particular attention should be paid to gradual or sudden changes in adolescents' ability to function competently at home, at school, and in the community. As these adolescents often are not very communicative and are difficult to interview, this information may not be readily obtainable directly from patients, and parents should be asked about self-accusatory statements and comments about death or suicide. Finally, the importance of obtaining a family history of psychiatric disorder cannot be overemphasized. Often this is the only real clue as to the nature of the psychotic illness in adolescents, when prior history is unrevealing.

PHYSICAL FINDINGS

In functional psychosis, the general physical and neurological examinations usually will be normal. In acute-onset schizophrenia, disturbances in autonomic nervous system functioning, such as dilated pupils, cold extremities, and patchy areas of vasodilatation on the skin, are sometimes noted. Psychomotor disturbances are marked by a variety of symptoms, ranging from a marked decrease in activity (catatonia) to bizarre posturing, excited stereotypic movements, facial grimacing, and/or waxy flexibility. Dehydration may be present secondary to inadequate fluid intake in catatonic patients, and patients who have delusions involving food may be poorly nourished.

LABORATORY STUDIES

Unfortunately, no specific laboratory tests can be used to aid in the diagnosis of psychotic disorders in adolescents. PET, magnetic resonance imaging (MRI) and CT scans are done primarily to rule out the presence of space-occupying lesions. Although brain imaging studies are currently a very fruitful area of research, the abnormalities found in schizophrenic patients are not specific enough for them to be used as diagnostic tests. An electroencephalogram (EEG) remains a relatively simple and cost-effective procedure that can yield valuable results. In some cases EEG abnormalities are found. Usually they are inconclusive, but sometimes they are suggestive of temporal lobe epilepsy. Patients who have such a pattern often respond to anticonvulsant therapy.

Routine laboratory studies done before starting patients on the appropriate medication usually include complete blood counts and liver and thyroid function tests. Thyroid abnormalities are not uncommon, especially in affective disorders (Sokolov, Kutcher, & Joffe, 1994), and thyroid function studies (T3, T4, TSH) are now routinely done on new admissions in many psychiatric hospitals. Pregnancy testing also is usually done on adolescent girls admitted to psychiatric hospitals; it should always be done prior to starting psychotropic medication unless the clinician is certain that the patient is not pregnant.

Blood or urine drug screens are also fairly routine, because of the high prevalence of substance abuse in adolescents presenting with psychotic symptoms. Other than those tests needed for drug clearance, the use of laboratory tests should be informed by the history and physical examination. Since patients with psychotic illnesses often present with various physical complaints, it is important to do whatever is necessary at the outset to rule out any systemic disorder; however, multiple blind alleys to rule out physical illnesses should not be pursued to the point that appropriate treatment is delayed.

PSYCHOLOGICAL TESTING

Psychological testing, including tests of cognitive functioning such as the Wechsler Intelligence Scale for Children (WISC), Bender-Gestalt, and Draw-a-Person, as well as the projective tests such as the Rorschach and Thematic Apperception Test (TAT), can be helpful in revealing subtle disturbances in thought patterns as well as ruling out organic brain impairment. In adolescents with long-standing psychosocial impairment, patterns consistent with learning disabilities often are found. Neuropsychological testing frequently shows fronto-temporal lobe impairment. Although the Minnesota Multiphasic Personality Inventory (MMPI) contains a schizophrenia scale, and this test is often administered to adolescents to aid diagnosis, it is not a reliable method of diagnosing psychotic disorders (Davies, Lachar, & Gdowski, 1987). Clinicians should bear in mind that diagnosis should never be based on test findings alone.

DIFFERENTIAL DIAGNOSIS

Once the clinician is certain that a psychotic illness is present, the task is to rule out infectious, metabolic, neoplastic, and neurodegenerative diseases. Although the distinction between "organic" and "functional" psychotic disorders no longer seems valid, it is still important to identify disorders that have nonpsychiatric causes. Most of these can be ruled out by a careful history, physical examination, and routine laboratory studies. The presence of clouding or some alteration of consciousness, fever, or focal neurologic signs certainly points in the direction of a toxic, metabolic, or infectious etiology.

Head Injuries and Epilepsy: A schizophreniform illness has been described following head trauma that involved injury to the temporal lobe (Nasrallah, Fowler, & Judd, 1981). Temporal lobe

epilepsy has been shown to have an association with psychotic symptoms. These symptoms may occur transiently following a seizure or may be chronic; subclinical or subthreshold seizure activity has been implicated, and patients with an onset of epilepsy during adolescence and those with more refractory seizure disorders are at highest risk for psychoses (Umbricht, Degreff, Barr, Lieberman, Pollack, & Schaul, 1995).

Unusual Syndromes: Other conditions that have been found to be associated with psychotic symptoms in adolescents include lead intoxication (McCracken, 1987), Capgras syndrome (Jerome, 1986), and Kleine-Levin syndrome (Gillberg, 1987). The latter is an unusual periodic disorder characterized by somnolence, hyperphagia, and psychotic symptoms. The older literature contains several case reports of periodic psychosis of puberty; it has been suggested that this illness, which may be seen in adult women as well as adolescent girls, is related to hormonal changes during the menstrual cycle, but it has not been studied systematically (Severino & Yonkers, 1993).

Confusion with Other Psychiatric Disorders: When psychotic disorders present as more subtle forms of psychopathology, the differential diagnosis can be difficult and includes virtually every other psychiatric disorder. Various forms of anxiety and obsessive-compulsive symptoms may be present. Depression is very common. Psychotic disorders not infrequently present as conduct disorders; Lewis and colleagues have noted the high prevalence of previously unrecognized psychotic symptoms in youngsters who have been incarcerated for committing violent crimes (Lewis, Shanok, Pincus, & Glass, 1979). In some cases the youngster's delinquent behavior actually may be an attempt to mask the presence of more serious psychiatric symptoms, as illustrated by the following example.

A 15-year-old boy was transferred to a state hospital inpatient ward after a 2-week stay at a university hospital inpatient service, where he had been given a diagnosis of conduct disorder and sociopathy. He had been involved in vandalism and breaking and entering, which had earned him a police record. Inappropriate smiling was evident as he described his delinquent behavior, and he isolated himself from peers on the ward. Although initially he denied psychotic symptoms, subsequently he admitted hearing voices and acknowledged that he would prefer to be thought of as "bad" rather than "crazy."

Dissociative disorders can be accompanied by hallucinations. Careful inquiry can establish that the auditory or visual hallucinations are accompanied by "alterlike" presences whom are the patient perceives as attempting to influence his or her behavior. As these disorders are very often not diagnosed for many years after their onset, the presence of the hallucinations frequently is erroneously interpreted as evidence of a psychotic disorder.

Developmental Disorders: Occasionally adolescents with developmental disabilities of various types are misdiagnosed as having psychotic illnesses. This happens because they sometimes have inappropriate behavior and problems with social interactions that make them resemble patients with schizophrenia, particularly during adolescence, when gaps in their social skills become even more apparent than they were at an earlier age. As adolescents, these patients resemble those with the deficit forms of schizophrenia, but they do not have delusions and hallucinations. Although it is possible for autistic persons to develop schizophrenia and they not infrequently become seriously depressed, their risk for psychotic disorders does not appear increased over that of the general population (Volkmar & Cohen, 1991).

Because they are socially inappropriate, adolescents with Asperger's syndrome and certain kinds of learning disabilities may sometimes mistakenly be diagnosed as having psychotic disorders. Asperger's syndrome is a condition involving social impairments, oddities of verbal and nonverbal communication, and peculiar fantasies (Frith, 1991); it may be related to autism and is not thought to be part of the schizophrenia spectrum. An interesting type of learning disability, termed nonverbal learning disability, thought to be related to right hemisphere brain dysfunction, has been described. Individuals with this syndrome have higher verbal than nonverbal abilities and deficits in social nonverbal communication and visual perception. They have difficulty handling novel situations and as a result often appear strange and awkward, "autisticlike." They are often good readers but lack commensurate comprehension (Semrud-Clikeman & Hynd, 1990). A relationship between this syndrome and attention deficit hyperactivity disorder has been postulated. Its relationship to autism is not clear.

Feigned Psychosis: Rarely, adolescents feign psychotic symptoms as a way of coping with an overwhelmingly stressful situation. While akin to malingering, the degree to which conscious effort is involved is not easy to determine; this clinical entity may be what was formerly called hysterical psychosis. These patients are not without psychopathology, but they are not psychotic. Rather, they are using the feigned symptoms as an adaptive strategy to extricate themselves from an intolerable environment (Greenfeld, 1987). This situation probably happens much less than is believed; in the author's experience, it is much more common for adolescents to be accused of making up psychotic symptoms when they are actually present.

Cultural Influences on Symptoms: Finally, the clinician must remember that phenomena arising out of culturally defined and sanctioned experiences can be mistaken for psychotic symptoms. It is important, when dealing with an adolescent from a culture other than one's own, to understand the meaning of the experiences reported in the context of the culture, as illustrated by the following example:

A 16-year-old girl originally from Puerto Rico had been diagnosed as having schizophrenia after she reported seeing the devil. A Hispanic clinician who subsequently worked with the entire family learned that all three of the children had had a vision of the devil while they were playing alone in a field in their home country.

Once the just-discussed conditions have been ruled out, the psychiatrist is usually left with a differential diagnosis of schizophrenia or schizophreniform disorder, an affective disorder with psychotic symptoms, or the rather nonspecific categories of brief psychotic disorder and psychotic disorder not otherwise specified. Given the confusing clinical picture seen in many adolescent psychotic disorders, it is not surprising that the category psychotic disorder not otherwise specified is used fairly commonly. From a practical point of view, as we shall see in the following section, the major concern during the acute treatment phase is whether to use a mood-stabilizing drug or an antipsychotic, or both in combination.

Management

Early detection of psychotic disorders and prompt initiation of appropriate treatment is important in improving the prognosis and preventing chronicity in psychotic disorders. One hypothesis is that prompt initiation of drug therapy may halt neuronal changes that, if unchecked, become irreversible with time. Another rationale is that a major portion of the long-term functional impairment in these illnesses comes from a devastating impact of a prolonged period of disability on individuals' sense of their own competency as well as the erosion of skills required to work and function in society. This is particularly important in the case of adolescents; the advent of the psychotic disorder not only involves a deterioration from a prior level of functioning but results in derailment of normal development toward emotional and economic self-sufficiency.

GOALS OF MANAGEMENT

Management of these illnesses aims at maximizing the adolescent's capacity to function in as nearly a normal manner as possible. This is done by a two-pronged approach: the restoration of functions that have been lost and the prevention of further decompensation. Drug treatment along with psychosocial treatment form the cornerstones of management. Treatment can be conceptually divided into acute and ongoing phases.

THE ACUTE PHASE: ENGAGING THE PATIENT AND FAMILY IN TREATMENT

If at all possible, the cooperation of both the adolescent patient and family should be obtained as part of the process of initiating treatment. Adolescents who are undergoing psychotic decompensation often are lacking in the insight that would assist them in cooperating with a recommendation for appropriate treatment. In addition, they may be extremely suspicious of others, especially psychiatrists, whom they fear will find out about their "crazy" thoughts. Frequently confused and even terrified, they are struggling desperately to deny that there is anything wrong with them. If the physician suspects that a psychotic illness is developing in a patient who is still fairly functional in everyday life, but who is resistant to the idea of seeing a "shrink," the psychiatrist can try to maintain frequent contact with the patient, continue to attempt to develop a therapeutic alliance, and persuade the patient to become a willing participant in treatment. One way of doing this is to

focus on problems in the relationship between the adolescent and his or her parents, seeing them together. Another possibility is to work with the parents, keeping the option open for the adolescent to join the sessions at some point in the future. Still another approach is to suggest a follow-up visit in 3 to 4 weeks to "see how things are going" and reintroduce the idea of treatment. Obviously, if there is a danger of self-destructive behavior, or if it is apparent that the adolescent is rapidly decompensating, then the physician must insist very firmly to both the patient and family that inpatient psychiatric treatment be sought immediately. This can be done in a way that still respects the adolescent's fear of loss of autonomy. Saying something like "I know that you don't agree, but I am very concerned about what I see happening to you, and I feel that the only way this problem can be helped is by psychiatric hospitalization" may be sufficient to obtain at least the adolescent's acquiesence to this plan. When the adolescent patient is acutely psychotic and totally opposed to receiving any help, emergency commitment to a psychiatric hospital or a psychiatric unit in a general hospital may have to be accomplished. All states have provisions for such emergency involuntary admissions; the exact procedures that must be followed as well as how long the adolescent patient can be kept against his or her will vary considerably from state to state.

Hospitalization: Hospital treatment is indicated for the adolescent who is having an acute psychotic breakdown and/or who is in need of close supervision and vigorous therapeutic intervention. In addition to allowing a controlled administration of antipsychotic medications, the hospital environment provides a protective atmosphere in which external stimuli and demands are minimized, thus reducing the stress on the exquisitely vulnerable decompensating adolescent. With the reduction of external stresses, reconstitution sometimes will begin to occur in and of itself.

Addressing Developmental Deficits: Some adolescents with psychotic disorders are not necessarily undergoing acute decompensation but are so emotionally impaired that intensive rehabilitation or habilitation is needed. These youngsters are likely to have had long-standing impairment. They need more than medication and outpatient therapy. For the adolescent who has been dysfunctional since early childhood, the gains during inpatient or outpatient treatment may be limited, but there is still a possibility for emotional growth through the personality development and restructuring associated with adolescence. In a controlled, carefully structured environment, such an adolescent can slowly and gradually learn more appropriate ways of functioning socially and reach a higher level of personality integration. If the youngster is able to be maintained at home, partial hospitalization or a specialized school setting may be appropriate. Otherwise, residential treatment should be sought.

Outpatient Treatment: In adolescents whose impairment is not so severe, outpatient psychotherapy, antipsychotic medication, and supportive environmental manipulation may be sufficient. The adolescent who is capable of being maintained on an outpatient basis should have enough ego strength to be able to compensate for intermittently poor reality testing. Outpatient therapy for these youngsters frequently has to be continued on a long-term basis, often for several years, until patients have developed sufficient strength no longer to need the therapist to lend this kind of intensive help. As time goes on, the frequency of contact may be lessened, but it is worthwhile to have such patients "keep in touch" intermittently. The therapist who treats these kinds of adolescents needs to be prepared to become an ongoing and enduring part of their lives for many years.

PSYCHOPHARMACOLOGY

Adolescents are often resistant to taking prescribed medications because they perceive that doing so entails a threat to their sense of autonomy, and this is particularly true of the adolescent with a mental disorder. When the disorder itself interferes with insight and judgment and is accompanied by distrust and fear, the task of gaining the patient's cooperation is a Herculean one. A good patient-physician relationship is essential in trying to overcome this resistance. It is not uncommon for adolescents to experience improved functioning with successful drug therapy as their mind being "controlled" or taken over by the drug. Excessive sedation may reinforce a youngster's conviction that he or she is being "drugged."

For hospitalized adolescents, it is best to allow a period of close observation and evaluation to occur for at least 2 to 3 days during the initial phases in order to clarify the diagnosis before any drug therapy is begun. The use of benzodiazepines such as clonazepam can be helpful in calming anxiety and agitation while not obscuring the presence of psychotic symptoms.

Antipsychotic Drugs: The major tranquilizers and mood-stabilizing agents are indispensable adjuncts in the treatment of psychotic illnesses. The phenothiazines, of which the parent compound is chlorepromazine (Thorazine), the first drugs proven effective for schizophrenia, were later joined by the thiothixenes and butyrophenones. The so-called atypical antipsychotic drugs, of which risperidone and clozapine are the parent compounds, act by a different mechanism than causing dopaminergic system blockade and are becoming widely used for adolescent patients. All are effective in decreasing the agitation and psychotic thought processes; they differ in their tendency to cause sedation and involuntary motor movements.

The advent of so-called atypical or novel antipsychotics has been an exciting breakthrough in the treatment of schizophrenia and other psychotic disorders. These drugs have been found to be effective in treatment-resistant cases—that is, those that responded poorly to traditional antipsychotic drugs. They have been held to produce greater improvement in negative symptoms than traditional drugs (Kane & Freeman, 1994). There is some argument as to whether they actually target primary negative symptoms or produce their apparent advantage by simply failing to produce secondary negative symptoms (Carpenter, Conley, Buchanan, Breier, & Tamminga, 1995). What is indisputable is that they are effective and do have fewer of the parkinsonian side effects that make compliance with neuroleptics problematic for many patients. Clozapine is believed not to have the potential to produce tardive dyskinesia; it is, however, associated with a risk of seizures and agranulocytosis. It seems to be as effective in adolescents as with adults (Birmaher, Baker, Kapur, Quintana, & Ganguli, 1992). Because of the risks associated with clozapine, the Food and Drug Administration approved guidelines and the American Academy of Child and Adolescent Psychiatry Practice Parameters for the Treatment of Schizophrenia in Children and Adolescents stipulate that two neuroleptic drugs should be tried prior to clozapine (McClellan & Werry, 1994). This caveat does not apply to risperidone, which has rapidly gained popularity as a first-line drug for psychotic disorders. The potential of risperidone to produce tardive dyskinesia is unknown; it does produce extrapyramidal reactions, although less so than the high-potency neuroleptic drugs. There is a reasonable argument to be made for giving risperidone as a first-line drug for adolescents, given the importance of medication compliance in improving outcome and the potential for improved compliance because of reduced extrapyramidal side effects. An additional reason for using this drug is the possibility that reducing negative symptoms will improve outcome.

Dosing of Antipsychotic Drugs: Lower doses of antipsychotic medications than those commonly used in adults are often adequate for adolescents, who frequently have a higher degree of sensitivity to these agents. Additionally, because a young patient's first experience with psychotropic medication can have long-lasting effects on attitudes toward psychopharmacological treatment and affect future compliance, a great deal of caution is warranted in instituting medication and titrating it to effective doses. Extrapyramidal side effects, including muscular rigidity, tremor, or akathisia, can be extremely frightening to adolescents. The psychiatrist should take precautions so that they do not occur or at least that they do not progress to a severe state. Care must be taken to explain the possibility of side effects in advance and to reassure the patient that if side effects do occur, they are not serious and can be reduced or eliminated. The various antipsychotic drugs differ in their tendency to produce side effects as well as in their sedative properties. If more than a minimal dose of a high-potency neuroleptic such as haloperidol is prescribed, it is wise to administer an antiparkinsonian drug concomitantly. Although rarer, the gynecomastia and impotence that occasionally occur are particularly upsetting to adolescent males, and females may be equally disturbed by experiencing galactorrhea and/or amenorrhea.

Table 32.1 shows the dosage ranges for adults. A reasonable strategy is to begin at the lower end of the range when using these drugs for adolescent patients. Except for clozapine, blood levels are not useful in determining optimal doses of antipsychotic drugs. However, they can be helpful in differentiating neuroleptic toxicity from worsening illness. This may be a problem, for example, when increasing agitation develops in a patient on a phenothiazine.

Although some calming effect will be evident immediately after beginning treatment with antipsychotic drugs, the effect on the positive and negative psychotic symptoms can take up to 6 weeks or longer to occur; with clozapine, the response time may be several months. In a study of 70 first-episode schizophrenic patients, the mean and median times to remission were 36 weeks and 11 weeks, respectively (Lieberman et al., 1993). Therefore, it is erroneous to conclude that a drug is ineffective after only 2 to 3 weeks. Unfortunately, because of time pressures and the increasing emphasis on short-term approaches, adequate drug trials are not always done, and premature changes in medication are common.

Maintenance Drug Treatment: Once a favorable response occurs, the dose of antipsychotic medication should be reduced to the lowest dose necessary to maintain remission. Doing so will reduce or eliminate side effects as well as lessen the likelihood of tardive dyskinesia. While the role of maintenance drug treatment is well established in long-term psychotic disorders, it is less clear in patients who are recovering from their first episode. Prevention of relapse is paramount, not only because of the emotional and economic costs of psychotic episodes but also because responses to neuroleptic drugs are progressively poorer with each relapse (Wyatt, 1991). The usual dose of antipsychotic medication needed to maintain remission is 5 milligrams (mg) haloperidol or its equivalent per day. Current recommendations are that patients be kept on an antipsychotic drug for at least 1 year following a first episode and for at least 5 years following a recurrence. At the end of this time, gradual tapering of the drug may be begun, with careful monitoring of the patient for recurrence of prodromal signs and symptoms. It is important that the patient and family be educated as to what to look for, so as to be able to detect early signs of relapse and report them.

Tardive Dyskinesia: Tardive dyskinesia, a sometimes irreversible disorder characterized by a variety of abnormal movements and thought to be caused by damage to the striatal dopaminergic receptor sites, occurs in children and adolescents treated with phenothiazines, although it is more common in older patients who have been on high

TABLE 32.1

Available antipsychotic Drugs, Dosage, and Dosage Forms

	Dosage Range[a]	Parenteral Dosage	Galenic Forms
Phenothiazines			
Acetophenazine maleate (Tindal)	40–120	—	Oral
Chlorpromazine hydrochloride (Thorazine)	200–800	25–50	Oral, liquid injection, suppository
Fluphenazine hydrochloride fluphenazine decanoate (Prolixin-D) fluphenazine enanthate (Prolixin-E)	2–60	1.25–2.5 12.5–50 q 1–4 weeks	Oral, liquid, injection
Mesoridazine besylate (Serentil)	75–300	25	Oral, liquid, injection
Perphenazine (Trilafon)	8–32	5–10	Oral, liquid, injection
Thioridazine hydrochloride (Mellaril)	150–800		Oral, liquid, injection
Trifluoperazine hydrochloride (Stelazine)	5–20	1–2	Oral, liquid, injection
Triflupromazine hydrochloride (Vesprin)		20–60	Injection
Butyrophenone			
Haloperidol decanoate (Haldol)	5–30 40–100 25–100 q 1–4 weeks	5–10 haloperidol-D	Oral, injection
Dibenzodiazepine			
Clozapine (Clozaril)	100–900	—	Oral
Dibenzoxapine			
Loxapine succinate (Loxitane)	40–100	25	Oral, liquid, injection
Indole			
Molindone hydrochloride (Moban)	50–225		Oral, injection
Diphenylbutylpiperidine			
Pimozide (Orap)	2–6		Oral
Thioxanthenes			
Chlorprothixene (Taractan)	50–400	25–50	Oral, liquid, injection
Thiothixene hydrochloride (Navane)	5–30	2–4	Oral, liquid, injection
Benzisoxazole			
Risperidone (Risperdal)	4–8		Oral

Source: P. F. Buckley and H. Meltzer (1995), "Treatment of schizophrenia." In A. F. Schatzberg & C. B. Nemeroff (Eds.), *American psychiatric textbook of psychopharmacology* (2nd ed.). Washington, DC: American Psychiatric Press. Copyright 1995 by American Psychiatric Press. Reprinted with permission.
[a]The dosage ranges are representative of the effective doses that are generally used in clinical practice.

doses of these drugs for long periods of time. There is evidence that severe extrapyramidal reactions are predictive of later development of tardive dyskinesia (Chouinard, Annable, Ross-Chouinard, & Mercier, 1988).

Mood Stabilizers: Lithium is used for the treatment of acute manic episodes and as maintenance therapy to prevent or diminish the intensity of subsequent episodes in those manic-depressive patients with a history of mania. It is also used in combination with an antipsychotic drug to treat schizoaffective illness. On lithium the wide fluctuations of mood are reduced, manic behavior abates, and depressive episodes are fewer and less pronounced. Lithium alone is probably as effective as an antipsychotic in less severely excited manic patients. It is probably less effective than an antipsychotic in very hyperactive, disturbed, psychotic manic, or schizoaffective patients. Lithium also may be useful in patients with psychotic disorders where there is prominent mood lability, or impulsive or episodic violence or anger, or if overactivity, insomnia, pressured speech, irritability, or other common manic symptoms are part of a psychotic episode. The use of the phenothiazines along with lithium may be necessary during the

371

early days of treatment of acute episodes to calm the wild, manic behavior; clonazapam also may be helpful.

Lithium has been effective for treatment-resistant schizophrenia in adults, even when prominent affective symptoms are not present, and a trial of lithium would seem to be indicated in adolescents who do not respond to antipsychotic drugs alone.

Because of the neurotoxicity of neuroleptic drugs, an argument can be made for initiating treatment of a first psychotic episode with lithium alone, or lithium plus a minor tranquilizer such as clonazepam, to see if this will bring about resolution of the psychotic episode. If the patient improves, the benzodiazepine can be discontinued and maintenance doses of lithium used. This strategy is particularly attractive in cases where the diagnosis is unclear, as is so often the case in adolescents. Before deciding on such a course of action, the psychiatrist should have some indications that the disorder has a strong affective component.

Rapid establishment of a lithium level of 0.8 to 1.2 milliequivalent per liter (meq/L) is desired for acute psychosis, and an initial regimen of 300 mg 2 to 4 times a day is indicated in healthy adolescent patients. Serum levels should be obtained every 3 or 4 days in the beginning, with the dose adjusted as necessary to achieve a level of approximately 1.0 meq/L. In patients with possible renal impairment, the lower starting dose is indicated. Response in acutely manic states may require 5 to 14 days to occur, even with adequate blood levels. As blood levels stabilize, their frequency may be decreased to 2 times a week initially and eventually to once a week as long as the patient is stable.

Levels should be obtained about 12 hours after the last dose. For the treatment of acute manic states or psychotic excitement, 1.0 is the target level, but levels up to 1.5 meq/L are sometimes needed; acutely psychotic patients seem to tolerate higher levels without side effects. Cautious attempts to increase the level even higher have been recommended for patients whose mania is still uncontrolled despite a level of 1.5 meq/L for several days and who do not show side effects indicative of lithium toxicity, such as marked tremor, oversedation, vomiting, and ataxia (Schatzberg & Nemeroff, 1995).

Maintenance Therapy with Lithium: For maintenance therapy, lithium can be begun at 1 or 2 300 mg doses a day; weekly serum levels are often sufficient during dosage adjustment. A lithium level of 0.7 to 1.0 meq/L is generally considered appropriate, but levels as low as 0.4 to 0.6 meq/L have been reported to be effective in preventing relapses. Once a patient on maintenance lithium is stabilized adequately with weekly serum levels for a few weeks, monthly levels are sufficient, and after 6 months to a year of stability, levels every 3 months may suffice.

For either acute or more long-term conditions, trials of about 4 weeks with adequate or highest tolerated blood levels are usually sufficient to determine whether lithium will be clinically useful.

Side Effects of Lithium: Lithium side effects of weight gain, frequent urination, and tremors are especially troubling for many teenagers. This plus the necessity of frequent blood monitoring makes many adolescent patients refuse to even consider taking this drug. Valproate, which has been shown to be nearly as effective as lithium in acute mania (Freeman, Clothier, Pazzaglia, Lesem, & Swann, 1992), is being increasingly used as an alternative to lithium. Its efficacy in long-term treatment, however, has not yet been demonstrated, and it is occasionally associated with side effects of weight gain and temporary hair loss. Carbamazapine is another drug that is effective in some cases of bipolar illness. Both valproate and carbamazapine require blood monitoring, but not as frequently as lithium. For further discussion of treatment of bipolar disorders with lithium, see Chapter 30.

Antidepressants: Antidepressants are necessary for major depression with psychotic features; an antipsychotic drug may have to be given, as well. Antidepressants with or without mood stabilizers also are used in patients with schizoaffective disorders. As they recover from an acute psychotic episode, some patients with schizophrenia suffer from postpsychotic depression, and antidepressants are helpful in these patients. Serotonin reuptake inhibitors have replaced tricyclic antidepressants in popularity because of their relative safety and lack of side effects. However, there is still a place for the tricyclics, which have the benefit that monitoring of drug plasma levels can be helpful in determining whether to increase the dose. Usually a positive response to antidepressants will be seen within 2 to 3 weeks, but 4 to 6 weeks at adequate dosage levels should be allowed for a sufficient clinical trial. Bupropion has the potential to induce psychotic symptoms in patients who do not have them to begin with, and also can produce seizures so it is not a good choice for psychotic patients. (Antipsychotic drugs also lower the seizure threshold.) Experience with the newer antidepressants in psychotic patients is too limited to make any recommendations. For further discussion of drug treatment of affective disorders, please see Chapter 30.

It should be kept in mind that antidepressants can precipitate mania in vulnerable patients, that they have been linked to the initiation of rapid-cycling mood disorders, and that they can exacerbate psychotic symptoms. Of the antidepressants, bupropion has been felt to be less likely to precipitate mania, but evidence for this is equivocal.

PROBLEMS WITH POLYPHARMACY

It is not at all uncommon for the practicing psychiatrist to be faced with the necessity to initiate treatment rapidly despite considerable diagnostic uncertainty; this is perhaps true more often for the adolescent who presents with psychotic symptoms than in any other situation. Because these patients almost always have mood symptoms, as well, there is a strong temptation to initiate therapy with an antipsychotic drug plus an antidepressant or mood stabilizer at the same time. This approach has many problems. The possibility of adverse side effects is compounded, diminishing the prospects for compliance in the long term. If side effects emerge, it is often difficult to tell which medication is responsible for them, since many drugs have similar side effects. (Both selective serotonin reuptake inhibitors and neuroleptics can produce akathisia and galactorrhea, for example.) Once clinical improvement occurs, the clinician usually is reluctant to discontinue any drugs because it is not clear which one is responsible for the improvement. Patients usually are discharged as soon as they are stabilized enough for outpatient or partial hospital treatment. Once the patient is no longer in the hospital, changes in medication may be risky. The general guidelines for antipsychotic, antidepressants, and mood stabilizers are for them to be given for at least a year following remission of a first episode. Thus, the clinician really is committed to the continuation of multiple drugs for an extended period of time once they are started. The situation is far simpler

if therapy is initiated with a single drug and then continued to the point of maximal allowable dosage for an adequate period of time before changing to or adding other drugs.

PSYCHOSOCIAL TREATMENT

Studies of adults with schizophrenia have shown that a stable and ongoing therapeutic relationship is an important factor in outcome. General principles of psychotherapy with adolescents apply to working with those who are recovering from psychotic illnesses. In supportive psychotherapy, the modality most appropriate to these patients, the adolescent patient is encouraged to use his or her capacity for self-observation, judgment, and rational thinking in order to achieve a more realistic picture of self and others. Frequently, the therapist who works with an adolescent who has residual psychotic symptoms has to engage in an "ego-lending" process, supplying these rational thought processes through comments made during therapy sessions, as illustrated in the following examples.

An 18-year-old woman, who had chronic severe emotional impairment, needed to be told by her therapist that her mother's grossly inconsistent behavior and extreme emotional instability were due to an emotional disturbance within the mother, rather than solely to the patient's own "craziness," as she had so long believed.

A patient in therapy commented, "Yesterday I started to get the feeling of having a piece of glass in my throat. But I know I feel that way when I'm anxious." The therapist had previously made a link between her psychotic symptom and her feeling state.

Group therapy can be useful for adolescents who are recovering from a psychotic episode. The other members of an adolescent group are generally supportive of a youngster whose ego functioning is still very fragile, and the sense of connectedness to others in one's peer group is a salutary experience for the adolescent who feels isolated and alone. The presence of another youngster who has experienced psychotic symptoms but is now without them can be very reassuring. However, the adolescent whose thought processes are still very disorganized or who is experiencing frequent hallucinations is not a good candidate for group therapy as these symptoms are likely to be very anxiety provoking for the group and the group itself may create additional stress for the adolescent.

PSYCHOSOCIAL REHABILITATION

Treatment of adults has documented the effectiveness of psychosocial rehabilitation programs. These outpatient programs generally have a long-term focus and aim for producing maximal independent functioning, but gear their expectations toward realistic goals. A typical goal might be employment in a sheltered workshop, for example. Because of the general tendency to feel that adolescents should be "mainstreamed" in regular education programs, and the lack of emphasis on vocational training of most regular as well as special education programs, the concept of psychosocial rehabilitation has not been generally applied to younger patients. The extension of this model to adolescent treatment programs would appear to have much merit.

SCHOOL AND VOCATIONAL TRAINING

An important part of working with adolescent patients with long-term mental illness is guiding them toward appropriate school and vocational choices. Partly because intellectual functioning may not be obviously impaired, the patient and family may cling to inappropriately high expectations. The inevitable failure to realize these expectations will create additional stress and demoralization. A young person who has dropped out of college, for example, may delay making plans other than to resume an ambitious plan to return to a demanding academic curriculum and pursue graduate studies. Part-time enrollment at a community college may be a much more realistic choice, but one that may signify having given up on one's hopes and dreams. To guide the late adolescent toward activity that will be productive and have a high probability of success requires patience and tact on the part of the therapist. It is helpful to assist the patient and family to focus on the immediate future and think in terms of realistic short-term goals, which do not negate the possibility of loftier long-term ambitions. At the same time, the therapist does not want to damage further the patient's already battered self-esteem by suggesting that menial work is all that he or

she will ever be capable of. The truth is that it is not possible to predict ultimate functioning. Helping the patient achieve a compromise between his or her life's dream and what is possible is an important therapeutic goal, as illustrated by the following case.

Melissa, a formerly bright, vivacious young woman, had attended a prestigious college and majored in art history with dreams of becoming a professional artist. At the age of 19 she suffered her first psychotic episode and fairly quickly developed classical signs and symptoms of schizophrenia. Over the course of the next 2 years, she had a series of hospitalizations, and finally entered a day treatment program, much to her and her family's dismay, for it signaled chronicity and long-term nature of her illness. Eventually, with the support of the program, she was able to get a part-time job in a small art gallery and framing shop. She was elated at her success, which allowed her to maintain a view of herself as part of the world of art and artists.

Several approaches are applicable to the treatment of patients with psychotic disorders. Treatment must be tailored to the patient's individual needs and must address the enduring disability and incapacitation that so often accompanies these illnesses. In most cases, long-term treatment is necessary. Continuity of care is also important. Generally available treatment approaches, particularly for children and adolescents, are short term. In most systems, mental health services for children and adolescents have a cutoff age of eighteen, when patients become eligible to receive services designed for adults. This discontinuity occurs at a crucial transitional point in development for both normal and emotionally disturbed teenagers. As it also occurs during the peak age of onset of schizophrenia, it is a particularly unfortunate fact for adolescents with this illness. While an adolescent who is identified as in need of special educational help while he or she is still in school is legally entitled to the continuation of such support through age 21, those over 16 who drop out of school as a result of their illness are often ineligible for services.

WORK WITH FAMILIES

The majority of adolescents who are treated for psychotic illnesses will continue to live with their families at least until they reach adulthood. Work with families is essential in the treatment of all adolescents with severe psychiatric disorders, including psychotic illnesses. Although the exact methods and aims of such work may vary, one of the chief goals should always be to provide accurate information to families about the disorder and its prognosis. Doing so is often difficult when a family is reacting to the shock of finding out that a family member is severely ill. Parents and siblings need to be given as much information as they can handle. The psychiatrist can encourage them to learn as much as they can about these illnesses and tell them they will have the opportunity to become more knowledgeable as time goes on. They can be told that the course and outcome are very variable and much depends on the appropriateness of treatment. No useful purpose is served by providing misinformation or unrealistically optimistic statements about expectations for cure; neither are unremittingly gloomy predictions justified. Accurate information helps families to have realistic expectations. This in turn makes it easier for them to provide appropriate emotional support to their mentally ill adolescent so that they can foster a reasonable degree of autonomy and emotional emancipation.

Family Support and Outcome: Work with adults indicates that favorable outcomes are influenced by family support, education of patients and family members about the illness, psychosocial rehabilitation, and appropriate medication management. The work on expressed emotion suggests that family interactions should be an important focus of treatment with the goal of increasing support and reducing stressful interactions (Hogarty et al., 1991).

Difficulties in Obtaining Care: Families of adolescents with psychotic disorders face the very difficult task of trying to obtain appropriate treatment for their children in a time of increasing cost controls, when there continues to be a widespread lack of recognition that long-term mental illness in children and adolescents deserves treatment on an equal basis with other medical disorders. Some insurance policies specifically exclude coverage for any psychiatric treatment that is not defined as acute care. For the adolescent with a psychotic disorder, this means that anything other than a brief hospitalization or limited stay in a partial hospitalization program will not be covered. For some families, the best option is for them to be-

come involved with the public sector fairly early on. However, public sector options may be limited, as well, and families will need to become strong and effective advocates for their children's needs if they are to receive appropriate services.

Support Groups for Families: In recent years, largely owing to the advocacy efforts of families of people with long-term mental illnesses, the amount of support and information that is available to families has greatly increased. Groups such as the Alliance for the Mentally Ill have taken up the cause of children and adolescents with severe psychiatric disorders. These groups are generally listed in the yellow pages of the telephone book under mental health services; they also may be reached through various commercial computer on-line services. Psychiatrists can be helpful in suggesting to families that they involve themselves with such groups as a way of increasing their knowledge about their youngster's disorders, learning about treatment options, and receiving valuable emotional support as well as concrete help in obtaining necessary services.

SPECIAL CONSIDERATIONS WITH COMORBID SUBSTANCE ABUSE

The management of drug-induced psychotic states can be divided into two phases: acute and long term. Acute management is best carried out in a facility that can provide intensive, 24-hour medical supervision. The length of hospitalization required varies from a few days to several weeks. Major tranquilizers are helpful in controlling agitation and extreme anxiety. Haloperidol has been recommended as particularly helpful. Physical restraint should be avoided if possible.

In planning follow-up treatment for the adolescent with a drug-induced psychosis, or one who has comorbid substance abuse, many factors must be taken into account. These include the family, community, peers, and school; the extent and chronicity of previous drug use; and the presence of preexisting psychiatric illness or impairment. Seldom can the adolescent for whom drug use has become a way of life be treated successfully outside of a highly structured residential treatment program. In other cases, outpatient counseling or therapy can be attempted on a trial basis, with residential treatment remaining an option. Partial hospitalization offers an intermediate alternative. After-school programs serve as intensive outpatient treatment during the crucial after-school hours when most drug use occurs.

PROGNOSIS

There are few prospective follow-up studies of adolescents with psychotic disorders, and none of these is long term. Because of the heterogeneity of these disorders, predictions regarding outcome are almost impossible when they present as a first episode. It is generally considered that earlier age of onset is associated with a worse prognosis for both schizophrenia and affective disorders; this is presumed to be due to increased genetic loading resulting in earlier manifestation as well as greater severity of disorder. Other factors related to outcome are premorbid functioning, the presence of negative symptoms, and gender. (Females have better outcome as well as later onset.) The presence of mood symptoms is a good prognostic sign, as is acute onset. There is evidence that duration of symptoms before treatment is related to outcome, independent of age of onset (Loebel et al., 1992).

Although many adolescents who are the victims of a single drug-induced psychotic episode will recover completely, others, even though treated appropriately, will remain persistently psychotic and eventually become indistinguishable from chronic schizophrenic patients. One study of patients hospitalized for a drug abuse–related psychotic episode showed that among those who remained persistently psychotic, a positive family history of schizophrenia was likely (Tsuang, Simpson, & Kronfol, 1982). A comparison of patients with drug-induced psychoses with and without positive family histories showed that those with relatives with schizophrenia were on average 2 years younger than those without this presumed genetic loading. Thus, it appears that drug use can hasten the onset of schizophrenia in genetically vulnerable individuals.

Special note must be made of the risk of suicide in psychotic patients. The risk of suicide, already increased in adolescence and young adulthood, is magnified in the presence of a psychotic disorder. Over the course of their illness, one-fourth of patients with schizophrenia attempt suicide, and 8 to 10% actually kill themselves. The rate of suicide for bipolar disorder is even higher: almost 20% (Goodwin & Jamison, 1990). There is always a risk that an acutely psychotic patient will respond to delusional ideas or command hallucinations by harming him- or herself. There is also the danger that the patient who is recovering from a psychotic episode will feel overwhelmed by depression and hopelessness, and view suicide as preferable to a life of despair.

Many studies point to the importance of treatment in outcome. Patients who are maintained on appropriate medication clearly do much better than those who are not. There is evidence that multiple recurrences cause progressive deterioration, perhaps through producing some irreversible changes in the brain. Compliance with medication is therefore very important, and anything that enhances compliance will improve outcome. The therapeutic alliance, that all-important part of work with adolescents, has been shown to be crucial to the treatment of schizophrenia, and it is likely that it is similarly important in the treatment of other psychotic disorders, as well.

Conclusion

In summary, when a psychotic disorder presents during adolescence, the diagnosis is often unclear and becomes manifest only after continued observation and evaluation of the patient over time. In spite of the fact that psychotic disorders remain enigmas in many ways, much has been learned about medical and psychosocial treatment approaches that has important implications for treatment of adolescents with these illnesses. The advent of newer antipsychotic drugs holds the promise of exciting breakthroughs in treatment. The importance of prolonged periods of disability and recurrent relapses for long-term outcome has particular implications for the adolescent period and argues for aggressive, continuous, and comprehensive treatment. The knowledge that the course of schizophrenia is extremely variable and that good outcomes, including apparently complete recovery, can occur even after years of incapacitating illness, is cause for optimism. The study of premorbid personality, as well as the manifestations of psychotic disorders in adolescents, is important in and of itself but also can offer the hope of achieving a better understanding of some of the leading causes of adult psychiatric morbidity.

REFERENCES

American Psychiatric Association. (1994). *Diagnostic and statistical manual of mental disorders* (4th ed.). Washington, DC: Author.

Andreason, N. C., & Powers, P. S. (1976). Psychosis, thought disorder and regression. *American Journal of Psychiatry, 133*, 522–526.

Arboleda, C., & Holzman, P. S. (1985). Thought disorder in children at risk for psychosis. *Archives of General Psychiatry, 42*, 1004–1013.

Birmaher, B., Baker, B., Kapur, S., Quintana, H., & Ganguli, R., (1992). Clozapine for the treatment of adolescents with schizophrenia. *Journal of the American Academy of Child and Adolescent Psychiatry, 31*, 160–164.

Bleuler, E. (1950). *Dementia praecox or the group of schizophrenias.* Translated by J. Zinkin. New York: International Press. Originally published 1911.

Bleuler, M. (1974). The long term course of the schizophrenic psychoses. *Psychological Medicine, 4*, 244–254.

Caplan, R. (1994). Thought disorder in childhood. *Journal of the American Academy of Child and Adolescent Psychiatry, 33*, 605–615.

Carlson, G. A., Fennig, S., & Bromet, E. J. (1994). The confusion between bipolar disorder and schizophrenia in youth: Where does it stand in the 1990s? *Journal of the American Academy of Child and Adolescent Psychiatry, 33*, 453–460.

Carpenter, W. T., Conley, R. R., Buchanan, R. W., Breier, A., & Tamminga, C. A. (1995). Patient response and resource management: Another view of clozapine treatment of schizophrenia. *American Journal of Psychiatry, 152*, 827–832.

Chess, S. (1977). Evolution of behavior disorder in a group of mentally retarded children. *Journal of the American Academy of Child and Adolescent Psychiatry, 16*, 1–18.

Chouinard, G., Annable, L., Ross-Chouinard, A., & Mercier, P. (1988). A five-year prospective longitudinal study of tardive dyskinesia: Factors predicting appearance of new cases. *Journal of Clinical Psychopharmacology, 8*, 21s–26s.

Davies, A., Lachar, D., & Gdowski, C. (1987). Assessment of PIC and MMPI scales in adolescent psychosis: A caution. *Adolescence, 22*, 571–578.

Ekstein, R. (1973). The schizophrenic adolescent's struggle toward and against separation and individuation. *Adolescent Psychiatry, 2*, 5–24.

Flaherty, L., & Sarles, R. M. (1981). Psychoses during adolescence: A review. *Journal of Adolescent Health Care, 1*, 301–307.

Freeman, T. W., Clothier, J. L., Pazzaglia, P., Lesem, M. D., & Swann, A. C. (1992). A double-blind comparison of valproate and lithium in the treatment of acute mania. *American Journal of Psychiatry, 149*, 108–111.

Frith, U. (Ed.). (1991). *Autism and Asperger syndrome.* New York: Cambridge University Press.

Ghadirian, A. M., & Roux, N. (1995). Prevalence and symptoms at onset of bipolar illness among adolescents. *Psychiatric Services, 46*, 402–404.

Gillberg, C. (1987). Kleine-Levin syndrome: Unrecognized diagnosis in adolescent psychiatry. *Journal of the American Academy of Child and Adolescent Psychiatry, 26*, 793–794.

Goldstein, M. (1985). Family factors that antedate the onset of schizophrenia and related disorders: The results of a fifteen year prospective longitudinal study. *Acta Psychiatrica Scandinavia, 71*, 7–18.

Goodwin, K., & Jamison, R. (1990). *Manic-depressive illness.* New York: Oxford University Press.

Gossett, J., Lewis, S., & Barnhart, D. (1983). *To find a way.* New York: Brunner/Mazel.

Greenfeld, D. (1987). Feigned psychosis in a 14-year-old girl. *Hospital and Community Psychiatry, 38*, 73–75.

Hellgren, L., Gillberg, C., & Enerskog, I. (1987). Antecedents of adolescent psychoses: A population-based study of school health problems in children who develop psychoses in adolescence. *Journal of the American Academy of Child and Adolescent Psychiatry, 26*, 351–355.

Hogarty, G. E., Anderson, C. M., Reiss, D. J., Kornblith, S., Greenwald, D. P., Ulrich, R. F., & Carter, M. (1991). Family psychoeducation, social skills training, and maintenance chemotherapy in the aftercare treatment of schizophrenia, II: Two-year effects of a controlled study on relapse and expressed emotion. *Archives of General Psychiatry, 43*, 633–642.

Jerome, L. (1986). Capgras syndrome. *British Journal of Psychiatry, 148*, 750–751.

Kane, J. M., & Freeman, H. L. (1994). Towards more effective antipsychotic treatment. *British Journal of Psychiatry, 165* (Suppl. 25), 22–31.

Kendler, K. S., McGuire, M. B., Gruenberg, A. M., & Walsh, D. (1995). Examining the validity of DSM-III-R schizoaffective disorder and its putative subtypes in the Roscommon family study. *American Journal of Psychiatry, 152*, 755–764.

Kraeplin, E. (1971). *Dementia praecox and paraphrenia.* New York: Kreiger. (Originally published 1919.)

Lewis, D. O., Shanok, S. S., Pincus, J. H., & Glass, G. H. (1979). Violent juvenile delinquents: Psychiatric, neurological, psychological and abuse factors. *Journal of the American Academy of Child and Adolescent Psychiatry, 18*, 307–319.

Lieberman, J. A., Jody, D., Geisler, S., Alvir, J., Loebel, A., Szymanski, S., Woerner, M., & Borenstein, M. (1993). Time course and biological predictors of treatment response in first episode schizophrenia. *Archives of General Psychiatry, 50*, 369–376.

Livingston, R., Taylor, J. L., & Crawford, S. L. (1988). A study of somatic complaints and psychiatric diagnosis in children. *Journal of the American Academy of Child and Adolescent Psychiatry, 27*, 185–187.

Loebel, A. D., Lieberman, J. A., Alvir, J. M. J., Mayerhoff, D. I., Geisler, S. H., & Szymanski, S. R. (1992). Duration of psychosis and outcome in first-episode schizophrenia. *American Journal of Psychiatry, 149*, 1183–1188.

Marengo, J., & Harrow, M. (1985). Thought disorder: A function of schizophrenia, mania, or psychosis? *Journal of Nervous and Mental Diseases, 173*, 35–41.

Mattanah, J. F. J., Becker, D. F., Levy, K. N., Edell, W. S., & McGlashan, T. H. (1995). Diagnostic stability in adolescents followed up 2 years after hospitalization. *American Journal of Psychiatry, 152*, 889–894.

McClellan, J., & Werry, J. (1994). Practice parameters for assessment and treatment of children and adolescents with schizophrenia. *Journal of the American Academy of Child and Adolescent Psychiatry, 33*, 616–635.

McCracken, J. T. (1987). Lead intoxication psychosis in an adolescent. *Journal of the American Academy of Child and Adolescent Psychiatry, 26*, 274–276.

Meijer, M., & Treffers, P. (1991). Borderline and schizotypal disorders in children and adolescents. *British Journal of Psychiatry, 158*, 205–212.

Mirsky, A. F., Silberman, E. K., Latz, A., & Nagler, S. (1985). Adult outcomes of high-risk children: Differential effects of town and kibbutz rearing. *Schizophrenia Bulletin, 11*, 150–154.

Morihisa, J. M. (1991). Advances in neuroimaging technologies. In A. Stoudemire, & B. S. Fogel (Eds.), *Medical psychiatric practice* (pp. 3–28). Washington, DC: American Psychiatric Press.

Parnas, J., Teasdale, T. W., & Schulsinger, H. (1985). Institutional rearing and diagnostic outcome in children of schizophrenic mothers. *Archives of General psychiatry, 42*, 762–769.

Patterson, W. M., Logan, W. E., & Vandewalle, M. B. (1982). PCP psychosis in a general hospital. *Military Medicine, 147*, 311–312.

Pearson, G. T. (1987). Long-term treatment needs of hospitalized adolescents. *Adolescent Psychiatry, 14*, 342–357.

Perry, H. S., & Gawel, M. L. (Eds.). (1953). *The interpersonal theory of psychiatry*. New York: W. W. Norton.

Reichenbacher, T., & Yates, A. (1987) Pseudocyesis as the presenting symptom in an adolescent patient with an incipient thought disorder. *Journal of Adolescent Health Care, 8*, 456–459.

Schatzberg, A. F., & Nemeroff, C. (1995). Mood stabilizers. In A. F. Schatzberg & C. Nemeroff (Eds.), *American Psychiatric textbook of psychopharmacology*, Washington, DC: American Psychiatric Press.

Schulsinger, H. (1976). A ten year follow-up of children of schizophrenic mothers: A clinical assessment. *Acta Psychiatrica Scandinavia, 53*, 371–386.

Schultz, S. C., Koller, M. M., Kishore, P. R., Hamer, R. M., Gehl, J. J., & Friedel, R. O. (1983). Ventricular enlargement in teenage patients with schizophrenia spectrum disorder. *American Journal of Psychiatry, 140*, 1592–1595.

Semrud-Clikeman, M., & Hynd, G. (1990). Right hemisphere dysfunction in nonverbal learning disabilities: Social, academic and adaptive functioning in adults and children. *Psychological Bulletin, 107*, 196–209.

Severino, S. K., & Yonkers, K. A. (1993). A literature review of psychotic symptoms associated with the premenstruum. *Psychosomatics, 34*, 299–306.

Sokolov, S. T. H., Kutcher, S. P., & Joffe, R. T. (1994). Basal thyroid indices in adolescent depression and thyroid disorder. *Journal of the American Academy of Child and Adolescent Psychiatry, 33*, 469–475.

Tsuang, M. T., Simpson, J. C., & Kronfol, Z. (1982). Subtypes of drug abuse with psychosis: Demographic characteristics, clinical features, and family history. *Archives of General Psychiatry, 39*, 141–147.

Umbricht, D., Degreef, G., Barr, W. B., Lieberman, J. A., Pollack, S., Schaul, N. (1995). Postictal and chronic psychoses in patients with temporal lobe epilepsy. *American Journal of Psychiatry, 152*, 224–231.

Vaughn, C., & Leff, J. (1976). The influence of family and social factors on the course of psychiatric illness: A comparison of schizophrenic and depressed neurotic patients. *British Journal of Psychiatry, 129*, 125–137.

Volkmar, F. R., Cohen, D. J. (1991). Comorbid association of autism and schizophrenia. *American Journal of Psychiatry, 148*, 1705–1707.

Watt, N. F. (1978). Patterns of childhood social development in adult schizophrenics. *Archives of General Psychiatry, 36*, 160–165.

Weinberger, D. R., Aloia, M. S., Goldberg, T. E., & Berman, K. F. (1994). The frontal lobes and schizophrenia. *Journal of Neuropsychiatry and Clinical Neurosciences, 6*, 419–427.

Wolff, S., & Chick, J. (1980). Schizoid personality in childhood: A controlled follow-up study. *Psychological Medicine, 10*, 85–100.

Wyatt, R. J. (1991). Early intervention with neuroleptics may decrease the long-term morbidity of schizophrenia. *Schizophrenia Research, 5*, 201–202.

Wynne, L. C. & Singer, M. T. (1963). Thought disorder and family relations of schizophrenics, I: A research strategy. *Archives of General Psychiatry, 9*, 191–198.

Young, T. J. (1987). PCP use among adolescents. *Child Study Journal, 17*, 55–66.

SECTION III
Special Aspects of Psychiatric Treatment
of Adolescents

33 / Psychotherapy of the Adolescent

John E. Meeks

Psychotherapy is a valuable element in the treatment of any psychiatrically impaired adolescent. The extent to which other treatment modalities are utilized varies widely according to the patient's diagnosis and current adaptive state. Many adolescents can be treated with psychotherapy alone, particularly if the therapist has a wide range of techniques including dynamic understanding, capacity for cognitive interventions, and a basic mastery of behavioral techniques. Other adolescents require additional interventions, which may even be the primary treatment approach. These may include medication, remedial education, specialized intervention in response to chemical dependency, skill training, and other specialized techniques. However, even in these cases the clinician needs basic psychotherapeutic skills in order to elicit a treatment alliance with the patient and a cooperative and understanding involvement in the treatment undertaking, regardless of its elements.

The Therapeutic Alliance

The first and most important part of developing a psychotherapeutic relationship with an adolescent patient is the evolution of a therapeutic alliance (Meeks & Bernet, 1990). The difficulties encountered in establishing this alliance vary with many factors in the patient's situation. The age of the patient, the degree and nature of nurturing experiences in the past, the patient's cognitive sophistication, the circumstances of the referral, and countless other factors can influence the patient's willingness to understand and accept the therapist's desire to be helpful within the limitations of the psychotherapeutic contract. These limitations are important factors in the therapeutic alliance because the patient often has wishes and sometimes real needs for help that would be more appropriate for a parent or other adults to provide. The psychotherapist offers a kind of help that may

be difficult for the frightened, angry, betrayed, and sometimes defeated adolescent to value. In addition to the disappointments adolescents may feel regarding the limits of the psychotherapist's offers to them, they are equally frightened by dangers that the clinician may represent to their already troubled efforts to gain the degree of self-assurance and self-sufficiency that they wish.

One of the major obstacles to developing a therapeutic alliance with an adolescent is his or her fear of dependency. This fear is often most marked in the early adolescent, who has only a precarious hold on newfound independence from parents. This tenuous perch is frequently troubled by intense dependency yearnings occasioned by the anxieties created when the young adolescent attempts to move out of the family confines and more into the peer group and the wider community. Since young adolescents have relatively limited adaptive capacities, they often find it extremely difficult to manage conflicts with peers, society's demands, and their own increased sexual and aggressive drives. The young adolescents' strong efforts to gain support from the peer group makes it difficult for them to turn comfortably to adults for help of any kind, especially help that would suggest that they are inept, unable to manage stress, or unable to relate comfortably to peers.

Similar problems are encountered in youngsters of almost any age who have major doubts regarding their basic adaptive skills. This includes teenagers with a history of attention deficit hyperactivity disorder, learning disability, or other developmental defects that have cast a shadow on their experience of successful mastery of self and the environment. Characteristically, young adolescents fear dependent relationships and tend to utilize primitive defenses, such as denial, displacement, and omnipotent fantasy. The offer of a psychotherapeutic relationship is felt as a threat and frequently rejected. (See Chapter 15 for further discussion of this point.)

Even in these youngsters, however, persistence is often repaid with the development of a workable therapeutic alliance. In youngsters who are more self-confident and who have had more fortunate relationships with previous caregivers, the alliance is developed somewhat more easily. In all cases, however, the process of psychotherapy itself as well as the developmental stresses of adolescence ensure that the alliance never runs smoothly. The psychotherapist can anticipate the need to re-create the alliance periodically in the course of contact with any adolescent. Indeed, it is this continual process of reexamination of the therapeutic relationship between the adolescent and the therapist that provides the powerful emotional learning experience essential to successful treatment.

The Early Process of Alliance Development

The key element in developing a therapeutic alliance is the capacity to respond empathically to the adolescent's resistances to the very process of therapy and to recognize and respond to elements of negative transference as they begin to appear in the interaction with the therapist. Most of the responsibility of this work falls on the therapist, since adolescent patients are rarely able to discuss their doubts and hesitations about the relationship directly. At times, it would appear that the adolescent is not aware of some of the troubling thoughts that are hovering just outside of consciousness and yet markedly affecting the interaction. Very often the initial efforts to describe difficulties in the therapy are attributed to other people in the adolescent's life. It is a useful rule of thumb to assume that all of the adolescent's complaints about adults are disguised complaints about the therapist or statements of fears that the adolescent has regarding the therapeutic process. Consider the following case example.

Mike, a 14-year-old youngster referred to psychotherapy because of poor school performance, social withdrawal, and depressive symptoms, was cooperative in therapy sessions but volunteered little and seemed very remote.

In his third session he began to talk with more affect about a teacher at school. He said he really hated the teacher's class because the teacher "had a thousand stupid rules" so that "you're afraid to even breathe because it might break some stupid rule." The therapist commented that it was obvious that this teacher really rubbed Mike the wrong way and had created a situation where Mike did not feel free to learn as much as he would like or to enjoy himself as he might wish. The therapist went on to comment that some youngsters found the rules in therapy somewhat annoying. Mike initially stated that he did not have any complaints about the therapist's rules but casually commented that he sometimes wished that he could come for his session when he really had something to talk about rather than at a set time each week. The therapist accepted this complaint and commented that it must be frustrating not to be able to come right away when something important is on your mind. The patient then gained a little more courage and complained that the therapist did not always answer questions or offer advice when Mike felt that he needed "some answers." The therapist responded to Mike's comments with appreciation of his frankness and promised to take those complaints into consideration. The therapist explained that he would feel more comfortable in offering advice as he came to know Mike better and explained that Mike's honesty with him about the interaction in the room was very helpful in moving the therapist to that position.

The adolescent patient often shows some fairly typical misunderstandings of the therapy relationship; these are related both to the developmental phase and to the experiences with adults that most adolescents have had. Often the youngsters expect the therapist to be moralistic or to try to control their behavior; sometimes they expect the therapist to behave like a teacher asking for performance and judging the quality of that output. Frequently they expect the therapist to try to act superior to them and to demonstrate the greater power that is associated with adulthood. When the adolescent makes these accusations directly, it is probably most useful just to agree that if therapy worked in that way, it would indeed be unacceptable. If it is possible to question the perception without appearing overly defensive or argumentative, that is usually wise also. For example, when the adolescent is reasonably calm, the therapist can ask: "Could you help me with that? Explain what I said or did that led you to believe that I am trying to tell you what to do."

It is also a good idea to ask the adolescent what others, especially parents, may have told him or her about treatment. If adolescents have been told in essence that they are coming to therapy to straighten our their behavior or to get their act together, the youngsters' fear that the therapist has a control agenda in mind is not unreasonable.

The second aspect of importance in developing a therapeutic alliance with the adolescent is to accept without question positive attributions that he or she may make to the psychotherapeutic process. Even if the therapist knows that these may be frustrated in the future, it is appropriate to accept them as an early basis for connection with the troubled patient. It is probably true that most people who go for psychotherapy harbor unrealistic wishes and expectations of magical help; certainly this is true of the adolescent patient with his or her age-appropriate expectations of adult support and direction. This acceptance of positive transference should not lead the therapist to exceed the therapeutic role by encouraging unrealistic expectations or promising help that cannot be delivered in the psychotherapeutic role. In other words, the adolescent may need to idealize the therapist, but the therapist does not need to encourage the idealization.

The third important element in developing the early alliance is the recognition and empathic response to the adolescent's pain. This is particularly important with younger adolescents, but adolescents in general are somewhat cautious regarding exposing pain and unhappiness. For many of them the opening up of such wounds is not only somewhat overwhelming to their coping abilities, it is also an embarrassing admission of weakness and dependency that flies in the face of their efforts to mature and emancipate. For these reasons, the therapist needs to be very alert to even hints of pain and suffering revealed by the adolescent. These should not be ignored and need to be recognized and responded to.

Unfortunately, simply responding may not be sufficiently supportive to many adolescent patients. They will be carefully assessing the therapist's response for both its adequacy and its sensitivity to their need for dignity and independent stature. Usually it is best for therapists to err on the side of understatement in response and to hope that at the same time appropriate recognition of the intensity of the pain is conveyed. The adolescent's ability to accept therapeutic concern is quickly destroyed if the therapist is perceived as "mushy" or infantilizing. Adolescents may accept best brief, idiomatic reactions, such as: "Phew! Not so easy to bounce back after something like

that, eh?" or "That sounds like a tough one." Later in the therapeutic process, when the adolescent has come to understand that the therapist can be trusted with intense emotion without misunderstanding vulnerability as total surrender or incompetence on the patient's part, these difficult areas can be explored with the therapist offering clearer expressions of the depth of his or her understanding.

The final general area of technique that assists in the development of the therapeutic alliance is the process of teaching the patient role to the adolescent. Earlier I mentioned the need to correct any misapprehension adolescents may have regarding what is expected of them in the therapeutic relationship. In the fairly early phases of treatment, however, opportunities usually arrive to recognize and praise those behaviors that are the positive elements of the patient's role in the alliance. The earliest opportunity for this kind of intervention often occurs when the patient is able to open up for the first time regarding family issues, problems with friends, or other significant troubled interactions. Such occurrences offer the therapist the opportunity to respond within the framework of the therapeutic alliance, commenting perhaps, "That's very interesting," "I can see that you have given that a lot of thought," or "That's very helpful to me in understanding some of the difficulties that you told me about." Comments like these let the patient know that this kind of interaction will be most useful in this specific relationship. The youngster gradually learns that the expression of strong feelings and affects is acceptable and welcome, and that his or her statements will be utilized to understand and help the patient and not to make judgmental comments or statements about how he or she "should" feel.

A second event that frequently occurs in early phases of therapy is for the patient to challenge the therapist to explain some event, symptom, or response. The therapist often feels in a difficult spot since failure to offer some constructive evaluation might be seen as excessive passivity, therapeutic ineptitude, or simply withholding of help. On the other hand, too-active early interpretation or even clarification may frighten patients, lead them to fear that the therapist has the capacity to read their mind, or simply encourage inappropriate dependency. It is sometimes useful to say "I have some ideas about that but I think the work will go better if you tell me how you've got it figured first. After all, I've noticed that you're pretty good at figuring out things and that you're a good observer."

Patients often can accept this challenge and are then willing to provide their own assessment. If this assessment is at all accurate, it opens the opportunity to the therapist to support a patient's further work by saying "You must be really smart because that's pretty much what I was thinking" (assuming, of course, that the patient has a sense of humor). Sometimes the therapist then can add one further thought to demonstrate availability and readiness to "think with the patient" as he or her attempts to understand and unravel feelings and reactions.

Finally, there is usually an opportunity in therapy to respond to the patient's report of having handled a problem situation with greater skill than in the past. This report of success should be viewed as a very complex communication. First of all, the patient is checking to see if the therapist agrees that the new response is indeed more healthy. In addition, however, the adolescent is checking out the possibility that the therapist may take too much credit for the improvement, may be trying to direct the patient's behavior, or may respond to the new behavior in a primarily moralistic way. Consequently, it is important to first ask how the patient feels about the new behavior. Sometimes one gets a bit of a surprise, as in the following example.

Paul, a 15-year-old adolescent referred for a variety of acting-out behaviors, included among his symptoms fierce verbal battles with his volatile father that at times came very close to fisticuffs. Paul responded positively to the opportunity for psychotherapy and showed an aptitude for psychological exploration and the expression of feelings. He clearly enjoyed his sessions and rapidly showed a calming that influenced his behaviors at school and with his friends. In his fifth session Paul reported that he and his father had gotten into a disagreement but that he had not exploded and indeed had even suggested to his father that they discuss the disagreement later when both of them were calm.

The therapist asked, "How did you feel about handling it this way? I realize in the past you would have lost your temper."

Paul stared levelly at the therapist for a few moments and then said, "Like a wimp."

Of course, the therapist recognized that Paul's behavior was more adaptive, but the awareness that Paul could not escape the feeling that he had capitulated to his father was an important issue to address in therapy and to be alert for in the transference with the therapist. Once what Paul had actually experienced in this interaction with his father was understood, it became possible to explore the boy's attitude toward masculinity and his enormous ambivalence toward his father, whom he both idealized and feared.

Parental Involvement and the Early Development of the Therapeutic Alliance

It is important to recognize that the therapeutic alliance with the adolescent occurs because of permission granted by the parents for the adolescent to become emotionally involved with an adult outside the family. The parents' attitudes toward the therapeutic relationship may include varying degrees of anxiety, jealousy, and distrust depending on their relationship with the adolescent and on their own emotional makeup. However, the therapist can do a great deal to encourage parental support of the therapeutic alliance. Of course, it is sometimes necessary for the parents to have active treatment themselves, either as participants in family therapy or in marital or individual psychotherapy of their own. Recognizing the situations where therapy is essential if there is to be any chance for the adolescent to progress in treatment is a function of the diagnostic process, discussed elsewhere. It is obvious that adolescents are unlikely to be treated successfully when their parents are involved in direct child abuse, heavy drug use, or active and direct scapegoating. However, there are also more subtle family situations involving enmeshment, loss of generational boundaries, or other patterns that so imprison adolescents that successful moves toward individuation are unlikely without parental change.

Even nonabusive parents may require help in understanding the therapeutic process and developing a cooperative pro-therapy bond with the adolescent's therapist. First of all, it seems important to have a direct contact with the parents in a face-to-face setting. The adolescent can be invited to attend the session, particularly if the patient is at all anxious about parental involvement in the therapy process. However, it is unwise for the therapist to agree to exclude the parents from contact. Adolescents who insist that the therapist never talk to their parents are creating an unrealistic situation. In such cases, adolescents are working on the premise that they can deal with their lives without any parental involvement, which is patently a fantasy, particularly for young adolescents. For the therapist to accept such a premise at the start of therapy causes the work to begin in an extremely unrealistic way. Adolescents who initially deny the therapist contact with parents should be counseled at length as to the unfeasibility of this approach. In fact, adolescents should be encouraged to permit the therapist to have easy and regular contact with the parents. Adolescents should be told that the therapist will not discuss matters with the parents without informing the adolescent ahead of time that these discussions will occur and that the therapist will use reasonable judgment in maintaining sensitive communications.

The parents, particularly if they are not in conjoint therapy, should be encouraged to call the therapist with any questions, information, or concerns. Doing so eases their anxiety and provides the therapist with valuable information. Calls from parents that involve comments or questions that are clearly intrusive, manipulative, or excessively demanding indicate a need for a more intensive intervention with them. However, most parents are quite cooperative and do not abuse the telephone privilege in any way.

Parents should be given to understand that they retain all parental authority, prerogatives, and responsibilities. Some parents are concerned that they should check with the therapist before taking any position with their youngster around rules, expectations, and the like. Obviously, the therapist will assure the parents that that is not the goal of therapy. The therapist does not compete with the parents, dictate to them how to run their family,

or otherwise intrude on the parent-child relationship. Any suggestions to the parents should be confined to remarks about what might be helpful to the therapy rather than directions for improving parenting. This approach helps to clarify the distinction between the therapist, who is interested in understanding and assisting in the growth process, as compared to the parents, whose role is to direct, limit, and control the adolescent. It is vital that the therapist communicate to the parents his or her wish to have them as allies; they must be greatest source of strength, support, nurturance, and direction for their son or daughter. Therapy should be seen as a process dedicated to improving the parent-child relationship, not replacing it.

At times it is necessary for the therapist to suggest to the parents different behaviors that might be more effective in promoting growth in an adolescent. However, even at these times it is important to recognize both the positive quality of the parents' motivations and their good intentions.

Intense concern, the impulse to be helpful, and pain and frustration when their child is having difficulties are almost universal among parents of adolescent patients. These feelings need to be recognized and accepted even when the therapist is suggesting more effective parenting techniques.

The therapist must explain to the parents that he or she must feel free to discuss any contacts with them with the patient. In fact, it is appropriate to tell parents to talk with the youngster about calls that they intend to make to the therapist. The goal of all these approaches is to decrease any distrust or suspicion of collusion between the parents and the therapist that the adolescent might be concerned about.

The Interdisciplinary Team

As mentioned earlier, some adolescents require multiple interventions that include psychotherapy. Often it falls upon the adolescent's psychotherapist to ensure the cooperation of various specialists who may be involved in the treatment process. Building an interdisciplinary team that can survive efforts at splitting is a complex process that cannot be treated entirely in the framework of a discussion of psychotherapy. However, the basic elements include general agreement on treatment goals, clear assignment of specific responsibilities to various team members, and the establishment of a mechanism whereby the team can respond quickly and in the very early stages to any efforts to split (Gunderson, 1978).

The Alliance in Other Psychotherapeutic Modalities

In some cases psychotherapy may best be approached by utilizing conjoint family therapy or group psychotherapy rather than the individual format. Although the therapeutic alliance in these treatment settings shares many common elements with the therapeutic alliance in individual work, there are some differences.

The process of forming an alliance in family therapy has been referred to as "joining" the family (Minuchin, 1974). This joining refers to a process through which the therapist is granted a special temporary membership in the family setting with a special role. That role is to comment on family interactions and to alter those that seem dysfunctional or destructive to family members. The special techniques of the various schools of family psychotherapy are beyond the scope of this chapter. However, the family therapist requires the same empathic objectivity and nonjudgmental stance that is necessary to gain acceptance in individual psychotherapy (Scharff & Scharff, 1987). In maintaining the alliance in the family therapy of an adolescent, it is even more crucial than in individual therapy for the therapist to avoid any semblance of taking on a parenting role.

Adolescent group psychotherapy often is a powerful and effective intervention. Some of the work of developing an alliance needs to occur in individual sessions prior to placing the patient in the group setting. These individual sessions are directed toward determining treatment goals that the adolescent could present in group therapy, providing an opportunity for discussion of apprehensions that the adolescent may have regarding joining a group, and the early explanation of the role and function of the other members of the group. The therapist must emphasize the mutual interdependence of group members, the value that each member brings to the group, and the need for open discussion of all interactions among group members. Within the framework of group functioning and the objectives of the group, it is then possible to explain the need for group rules and expectations, requirements that the adolescent might otherwise resent as another example of adult interference. It is also important to explain that the therapist's role is one of focusing and clarifying group interactions rather than a teacher or instructor, at least in groups that are directed particularly toward dynamic psychotherapy (Meeks, 1973).

Many other effective groups are not exploratory but are aimed toward shaping behavior in a more constructive direction, for example, helping a youngster deal with chemical dependency or to find alternatives to delinquent behavior (Berkovitz, 1972). As a rule, the alliance in these groups is more narcissistic with a somewhat charismatic leader who may well have overcome the very habit patterns that the group is attempting to master.

The Middle Phases of Treatment—Utilizing the Therapeutic Alliance

Early in the midphases of psychotherapy the therapist attempts to establish primary themes that both he or she and the patient agree are worthy of careful scrutiny and repeated evaluation. These themes are of infinite variety in terms of their individual presentation; however, they tend to focus on several basic human concerns. The degree to which each concern is important to an individual patient gradually becomes clear in the early phases of treatment.

One general basic theme in psychotherapy of many adolescent patients is that of fear. This subject includes fears of aloneness, of physical damage, and of rejection, plus a whole variety of anxieties that are so shadowy that adolescents cannot even give them a name. With the support of the therapeutic alliance, patients become increasingly able to address fears and to relinquish symptoms of avoidance and varieties of disorganization and defeat. The second basic theme that tends to occur in the psychotherapy of adolescents is their problem in balancing their need for relationships, intimacy, and support with their equally felt need for independence and self-direction. In its extreme form, this is a battle between isolation and merger. Adolescents are able to use the therapeutic alliance to come to understand that dependency can be mature and permissible when it is helpful to overall adaptation. They can understand that it is possible to meet the needs of others because one chooses to do so rather than out of a fear of rejection (with the answering resentment and sense of suffocation).

The third most common theme is anxiety around the expression of impulses. Fears of being shamed, guilty reactions to sexual or aggressive urges, and even conflicts between incompatible impulsive drives within adolescents themselves are all familiar areas in the psychotherapeutic journey.

In the course of the therapeutic process, these themes are given names and titles drawn from a patient's own words and experiences as these are shared with the therapist. In other words, a common language gradually develops that bonds the therapist and the patient ever more tightly in their mutual effort to gain greater comfort, freedom, and maturity for the adolescent patient.

Much of the middle part of psychotherapy requires addressing these themes as they express themselves in day-to-day interactions with others. The patient is involved in "working through," a process that requires repetition and the opportunity to encounter the same problem in other guises. When this occurs often enough, the capacity to generalize the experience to most encounters gradually can be achieved.

As this working-through process continues, the patient also grows through the interactions with the therapist. In successful psychotherapy, the patient tends to internalize both the therapist and the process of therapy itself (Williams, 1986). Adolescents frequently express this quite directly as a shyly confessed desire someday to become a therapist. The therapist should accept and validate this statement; if the alliance is actually in place, the adolescent is already acting as a psychotherapist to one patient—him- or herself. It is also true

that therapists frequently observe in therapy a gradual shift in the feeling tone of self-observation. Early in therapy if patients look at areas of themselves that are regarded as difficulties, their attitude is frequently harsh and critical. As therapy continues, they often identify with the empathic and yet objective attitude of the therapist who is able to confront problems and shortcomings without criticism or anger.

Unfortunately for us as therapists, not all of the constructive events in psychotherapy are so pleasant and congruent with our identity as helpers. Patients also grow from our deficiencies, and they gradually become comfortable in letting us know about some of these negative experiences in treatment.

Patients face a crisis when their therapist has an empathic failure (Kohut, 1971). Given the patient's complexity, the therapist's humanness, and the variety of external factors that may affect the treatment process, this is an inevitable event in psychotherapy. There will be times when we simply do not understand what the patient is actually trying to tell us, as the following case example shows.

Marshall, a 17-year-old youngster with significant impairment of his self-development and identity, was able to use psychotherapy effectively largely because of a strong idealizing and mirroring transference with the therapist. As the therapy continued, Marshall became somewhat uncomfortable with the threat of merger and demonstrated this by beginning to come late to therapy sessions. He was sure that the therapist would be angry about this and was abjectly apologetic about not coming on time. The therapist, in a misguided effort to help Marshall with his conflict said, "I mainly feel bad because you're losing part of your time."

This "harmless" remark infuriated Marshall, who said, "I never thought of it as just my time. I thought we were working together."

Empathic failures occur in many other ways, as in situations where the therapist is tired or where countertransference disrupts the clear understanding of the patient's needs. In any event, it is important to recognize that these occurrences permit the patient the minor frustrations that are necessary to growth, assuming that these frustrations occur within a framework in which the therapist is usually empathically in tune.

In a similar way, transference disappointments allow the patient to grow. Again, these are inevitable since the patient will bring to therapy hopes and wishes that are beyond the scope of the therapist to provide—often beyond the scope of what any human being could provide to another. It is interesting, however, that therapists sometimes feel apologetic and deficient when they are unable to provide completely for their patients' needs. Complaints of this kind, namely that therapy has not completely removed all difficulties or that the therapist's treatment has not resulted in the patient's being able to find a suitable girlfriend or boyfriend, need simply to be accepted calmly. Indeed, the patient's unhappiness should be granted and he or she should be allowed to be unhappy. At times it is necessary to point out directly to patients that their expectations are beyond the scope of what the therapist can provide and to suggest alternative ways that their needs might be met. With some chronically complaining adolescents, there may even be a time where the therapist needs to suggest that a decision should be made. Would they like to continue to work on improving their lives and their circumstances, or would they prefer an engraved plaque from the therapist stating that they have justifiable reasons for continued unhappiness?

One therapeutic disappointment that occurs regularly and provides the opportunity for psychotherapeutic work and the patient's growth occurs when the therapist is absent and unable to meet with the patient. Absences for illness, vacations, professional meetings, and other reasons are not planned around the patient's desires or needs. Sometimes an absence occurs at the very time when the patient feels the greatest need of support, help, or assistance. At those times the absence is obviously resented, and the patient feels considerable anger, disappointment, and disillusionment. Adolescent patients rarely are able to complain directly about their therapist's absence but tend to show their response indirectly by missed sessions, increased symptoms, increased complaints against the therapist, and other evidence that the smooth progress of the therapeutic alliance has been disrupted.

As a rule, direct and stereotyped comments regarding the patient's response to absences are not effective in helping adolescents make the connection between their sense of disappointment and the occurrence of the feelings and behaviors that they are now experiencing. It is important to stay with the time-honored technique of dealing with defenses first and finding shared language around the event before attempting to deal with the absence. For example, the therapist can comment on difficulties that the patient reports in a session by saying "Well, I sure picked a rotten time to be out of town." Such a comment gives the patient a chance to say "You sure did" and express anger within the framework of normal communication rather than in jargon.

The Closing Phases of Psychotherapy

As psychotherapy continues, the adolescent begins to show certain behavior patterns that suggest he or she has accomplished much of the process that therapy was intended to achieve. Several indicators may appear that suggest that the therapist should consider moving toward a termination phase of the treatment process.

If the patient is consistently using problem-solving techniques that include a capacity for friendly but honest self-observation and moderately competent expression of needs and feelings to others, this suggests that the tools of psychotherapy have now become the patient's own possession.

A similar comment can be made regarding the patient's capacity to mother him- or herself rather than to deny the need for nurture, care, limits, and direction and manipulate others to take that role. As the patient makes some reasonably sensible decisions around self-care, this indicates an internalization of a positive nurturing figure that shows caring is now part of the adolescent's developing ego skills.

Improved relationships with peers and adults outside the therapy situation are very positive indications that the gains in therapy are real and can be generalized to other situations. It is especially positive if these improved relationships are occurring even in situations where some conflict exists and where considerable efforts and flexibility have been needed on the adolescent's part to achieve a successful situation.

It is also important to observe the accuracy with

which the adolescent views others. Increased insight into the motivations of other people and hidden reasons for behavior (without using these insights in a competitive or manipulative way) are a real indication that the adolescent has reached a new level of maturity.

Finally, the patient's ability to reach some kind of closure on the plan to become a psychotherapist is an interesting guide to readiness for discharge. Many patients simply "outgrow" the wish to be a psychotherapist because, in the course of therapy, their own aptitudes and interests have become much more central than their identification and attachment to the therapist. Indeed, it is interesting to observe how often patients in this terminal phase of therapy will begin to think of other people who need the therapist's services. It is as if they know that they soon will be leaving and they want to be sure that the therapist does not feel abandoned.

Discussing Termination

Often the therapist must be the one to mention the possibility of termination. This is an interesting reversal of the prevailing tone of the early phases of therapy with an adolescent, which often are replete with threats to quit therapy, angry statements that therapy is useless, and assertions that the therapist is at best inept if not downright dangerous. However, once a positive alliance is developed and the patient has constructively utilized the therapist over a period of time, the adolescent may be reluctant to give up this trusted adult friend, even when he or she no longer needs the special expertise and formal arrangements of psychotherapy.

Even if patients bring up termination themselves, they often experience discussion of the possibility as a rejection. It is crucial to pick up clues that patients are feeling that the therapist is tired of them, has better things to do, is disappointed with them, or for one of a million reasons no longer wishes to remain close to them. The therapist must clarify that termination is being discussed because of a patient's progress and that the therapist enjoys and is totally supportive of this newfound strength. If a patient responds to the danger of rejection

by prematurely fleeing therapy or proposing to do so, it is important for the therapist to try to circumvent actively this less than constructive end to the treatment process.

Many approaches may be useful, depending on the patient. In some cases the therapist can utilize the shared language and experience to comment on the patient's difficulty with saying good-bye or attempt to avoid sad feelings even when they are mixed with satisfaction and a sense of accomplishment. With some patients to bring up appropriate procedural comments, such as the need to tie up some loose ends or the need to sum up treatment. Some patients respond well to the suggestion that there are appropriate processes in saying good-bye that are important to follow both for the patients' own benefit and because the therapist would appreciate them.

It is also important to recognize that countertransference can interfere with termination in a variety of ways. Obviously, some patients are terminated prematurely because the therapist actually does have negative feelings toward them. Self-observation and peer or other supervision should help to prevent occurrences of that kind. On the other hand, positive countertransference feelings toward an adolescent may lead the therapist to prolong treatment beyond the point that is appropriate. It is always possible to find a few more problems that need resolution, particularly in young adolescents; however, they should not be expected to achieve an emotional balance beyond their developmental level even with the best of psychotherapeutic intervention.

The therapist should feel comfortable with an adolescent's need to maintain some contact with the "real object" (that is, the adult friend) that the therapist has become. It is entirely appropriate and desirable for adolescents who have terminated psychotherapy to keep their therapist informed of their progress, and they often do exactly that. Contacts regarding important milestones such as graduations, successful athletic accomplishments, and the like are quite common and should be accepted and responded to with a brief encouraging note.

Therapists also should be alert to adolescents who are feeling guilty about abandoning them. Particularly those adolescents who have had enmeshed family relationships with hidden messages of need for inappropriate support may feel that their newfound capacity to be on their own and their desire to leave therapy are hurtful and show lack of gratitude toward the therapist. With these youngsters, it is important to support independent functioning. The therapist may respond to some of their anxious concerns by saying "I know you're really looking forward to college and you're going to be tremendously busy, but if you have a moment I'll always be glad to hear how things are going for you." Such a comment both states that you do not have expectations of major involvement and yet indicates that the patient's more independent functioning is a source of pleasure rather than a threat.

Finally, in the process of termination, it is important not to forget the parents. They need to be kept informed regarding plans in this direction. Often they will respond with anxiety since they have come to see the therapist as a major source of support and stability to the adolescent and to family relationships. To some extent they, too, feel that their relationship is being terminated and suffer a sense of loss that may need to be discussed to varying degrees.

Problems in Psychotherapy

ABSENCES AND LATENESS

Many adolescents have difficulty adjusting to the regular schedule of psychotherapy. Some of them are already overly scheduled with school and extracurricular activities and experience the formality of regular therapy sessions as yet another burden that they may resist. Other adolescents are not well organized and have difficulty in getting to school on time or even arriving at activities that they enjoy, such as meetings with friends or athletic games.

If lateness persists, it is useful to raise questions about difficulties of arriving places on time and to inquire whether this is typical of many activities of the adolescent or specific to therapy. It is also important to note that considerable allowance should be made for adolescents who get themselves to their sessions on public transportation, which may not be entirely dependable. With patients who are brought by their parents, the lateness may represent parental acting out rather than

the adolescents' problem. In any case, the important goal is to determine what feelings and attitudes are actually encoded in the behavior of tardiness rather than to reverse that behavior rapidly. It is important to continue ending sessions on time even if the patient is late and does not get the full allotted session. Doing so is necessary to maintain the structure of the treatment process and to enable the therapist to avoid feelings of resentment or of being manipulated.

Persistent absences from therapy are, of course, a much more serious problem. It is obvious that no therapy can proceed if the patient does not arrive for sessions. Early in therapy missed sessions usually represent open and passive resistance to the treatment process. Some patients are unwilling for a variety of reasons to state directly to their parents and to the therapist that they do not want to engage in psychotherapy, but their behavior says that that is the case. They vote with their feet! It is important not to accept excuses for these misses and to reevaluate quickly the entire treatment contract, utilizing parental support when available to encourage attendance. If this brings anger more directly into the treatment process, so much the better.

Later in the treatment process, when transference is a real issue, the patient may miss sessions to avoid dealing with important therapeutic material. Sometimes this is only temporary and the patient is able to return having better prepared his or her defenses or having become better able to deal with the issues in treatment. Since these are genuine pieces of acting out, usually unconscious, it is important to proceed carefully in exploring their meaning or in suggesting connections with the treatment material. An approach of sympathetic understanding about the difficulty of coming to sessions when feelings are intense may permit patients at least to consider the possibility that their mind protected them from this discomfort by allowing them to forget that the session was scheduled. The practical question of charging for missed sessions is one that each therapist must resolve. It is not as clear cut as in charging for the missed sessions of adults. With adolescents, often the parents must pay for their children's acting out, since, from a practical point of view, even if the patients were held directly responsible, they usually would not have the financial means to cover the cost. It is my practice to point out to the parents the financial hardship it creates for me if patients do not attend and to ask their involvement in deciding the most effective way to deal with an absentee problem in their youngster. A practical approach that sometimes is effective is to hold the patient responsible for some portion of the cost of missed sessions, for example, the amount of one week's allowance.

SILENCE

Many adolescents get themselves to treatment, even on time, but then are silent. Sometimes this takes the form of appearing to have little to say although they seem cooperative and respond to questions with brief answers. However, the session stretches on with many quiet times. In other cases it is obvious that the patient is withholding speech and means this as an angry attack on the process of psychotherapy. Other times it is clear that the patient would like to speak but is too anxious, tense, or confused to be able to enter in to a meaningful discussion.

It is obvious that the therapist's first job when faced with a silent patient is to make a differential diagnosis of the type of silence and the probable dynamics behind it. Some adolescents grow up in families where there is little discussion and silence is a normal mode of life. These adolescents often have poorly developed verbal skills and find no comfort in easy conversation. These patients respond best to sympathy, patience, and modeling of comfortable conversation. Often they need to be taught that there are many subtle things to be said about situations or about their feelings that have simply never occurred to them before. If this is done with warmth and eager acceptance of a growing ability to communicate, these patients often show considerable progress over a few months of therapeutic effort. Many times their symptoms, often varieties of depression and withdrawal, improve as their capacity to talk to another human being is slowly strengthened.

Other patients are blocked from speaking easily because of fears of appearing overly dependent, needy, or vulnerable. This is often true of adolescent boys, who are very frightened of reaching out to others for fear of losing their image of masculine strength. These patients must be approached first in areas that are comfortable for them, such as athletics, and may respond best to

therapists who have some genuine interest and knowledge in these areas. Sometimes it is possible for the therapist to bridge from these areas by talking about sports stars who have gotten into difficulty because of psychiatric or drug problems and by modeling a willingness to be less than invincible him- or herself.

Other patients are silent because they are overwhelmed with anxiety and become too upset when they begin to talk about their concerns. This vulnerability needs to be understood; indeed, the patient should be supported in a gradual approach to the exploration of psychic pain. Many patients of this kind, often from families where intrusiveness is common, feel comforted and supported by the therapist's willingness to permit a comfortable silence and to share a companionable, supportive, undemanding approach to life's difficulties.

The angry adolescent who uses silence as a weapon needs help in turning this anger into a verbal pattern that can be understood and perhaps constructively approached. Since the adolescent knows that the psychiatrist requires speech and shared thought in order to do his or her job, the angry adolescent is tempted to render the therapist helpless and inept by withholding the tools that he or she requires. Unfortunately, at the same time the patient is injuring him- or herself and removing the possibility of progress. If the therapist continually presents this observation without rancor or personal retaliation for the adolescent's anger, sometimes the youngster can be helped to begin to put the anger into words.

EXTERNAL TRAUMATIC EVENTS

At times in the course of the psychotherapy of an adolescent, a major traumatic life event arises: the death of a parent or some other person close to the adolescent, the loss of an important relationship as in the geographic move of a best friend, or a personal trauma such as being physically attacked or raped. Such major traumas change the entire texture of the psychotherapeutic relationship for some time. In effect, the previous therapeutic contract is no longer valid. At this point the adolescent patient needs help in dealing with so massive a threat to ego functioning. The therapist mainly becomes important as another adult who is kindly disposed toward the adolescent, understands the stress that he or she is experiencing, and is willing to support the adolescent through the inevitable emotional unrest. At the same time, unlike other adults in the adolescent's life, the therapist needs to protect the therapeutic alliance that will be necessary to the patient when psychotherapy can be resumed once again. In other words, the therapist needs to evaluate supportive behaviors at the time of stress to be sure that they do not remove him or her from the professional status that would be required to conduct exploratory psychotherapy, if that is the patient's long-term need. For example, the adolescent therapist might think twice about actually attending the funeral of a patient's parent or best friend unless it can be assured that the patient will not turn to the therapist as a real object with appropriate expectations of physical comforting or other interactions that would later be inappropriate to the therapeutic relationship. At the same time, it is important that the therapist not appear to be so caught up in the formalities of the therapeutic relationship that he or she cannot show simple human support and caring. For example, if the patient becomes ill and has to be hospitalized or undergo surgery, it is entirely appropriate for the therapist to visit to show concern and a wish to maintain a positive interaction with the patient. There are no definite guidelines for the therapist in these circumstances, and each case must be judged according to the patient's need. Doing so sometimes requires the therapist to carefully evaluate his or her own motivations and the potential for countertransference traps in these highly charged emotional circumstances.

PARENTAL INTERFERENCE

In spite of the fact that the treatment relationship has been clarified in the development of therapeutic contract and the parents seem basically allied with the therapist, problems still can arise due to parental interference. Often this occurs because the parents feel unable effectively to manage some aspect of the adolescent's life that they feel to be important. Unfortunately, often these are areas that are normal parts of adolescent behavior, such as arguing with the parents, sexual experimentation, refusal to accept parental goals, and the like. In view of the therapist's excellent relationship with the adolescent, parents often be-

lieve that he or she could influence these things in the appropriate direction. Parents sometimes begin this kind of interference with the phrase "I feel that if you would speak to Betty about . . ." They then present the area of their concern. It is important, of course, not to become involved in this position of *in loco parentis,* especially when a parent actually is demonstrating a difficulty in accepting the adolescent's individuation. At the same time, the therapist must retain the parents' cooperation and support for the overall therapeutic effort.

Often both goals can be accomplished by explaining again the limitations of the therapeutic relationship and the ways in which it differs from the appropriate authority position of the parent. The therapist also can point out that the effectiveness of his or her role would be lost if it is expanded to include elements of parental function. Sometimes it is helpful to offer sessions to the parents so that they can be supported and even assisted in their parenting effort. At the same time, it is important in these interactions continually to remind the parents of the adolescent's need to emancipate and the likelihood that, even if they are challenged during adolescent development, parental values will not be forgotten in the long term.

If the parents' discomfort with the adolescent's growth is extreme, of course, they should be referred for separate counseling and psychotherapy. Excessive involvement too close to the adolescent's treatment may be incompatible with successful treatment (Diamond, Serrano, Dickey, & Sonis, 1996).

SPECIAL TREATMENT PARAMETERS

In many situations, psychotherapy must include other interactions with the patient not typically considered a part of exploratory treatment. The most common is the use of medication during psychotherapy. The concomitant use of appropriate psychoactive medication can be a positive element in psychotherapy so long as its possible role as an irrational factor in the transference and countertransference is understood and dealt with in the treatment process. For example, the patient may experience medication from the therapist as an unwarranted parental control mechanism or as a magic gift from an omnipotent ally. Minor side effects may lead the patient to doubt the therapist's benign intentions, and the need to explore a variety of medications as therapeutic trials may be mistaken by the adolescent as indecision or failure on the part of the therapist.

In some cases of severe illness, medication needs to begin on an inpatient basis so that appropriate supervision and support can be present until the desired pharmacological effect is achieved. In other cases, it is wise to delay the onset of even indicated medication until there is a therapeutic alliance so that the patient can accept treatment with a pharmacological agent as a positive partial approach that is melded into a larger treatment plan under the supervision of a knowledgeable and caring therapist. Schowalter (1989) has reviewed this subject in a most useful way.

Another parameter of treatment concerns youngsters who are physically ill or who have eating disorders or other problems that require careful monitoring of their physical state at the same time that they are engaged in the psychotherapeutic relationship. Often it is wise to have this function carried out by a colleague; it is so directly connected in adolescent minds to parental monitoring and concern for their well-being that they have difficulty seeing it as an objective part of the treatment process. When this kind of arrangement cannot be made, the therapist simply has to point out continually the objective reality of the relationship and attempt to avoid misinterpretations.

UNSUCCESSFUL THERAPY

At times therapists face situations in which ongoing psychotherapeutic efforts with an adolescent patient seem ineffective. It is important to assess such a situation carefully before reaching this kind of conclusion. Therapeutic ambition can be thwarted by very slow progress, particularly if it is accompanied by a good deal of negative verbalization from the patient. In a fit of injured pride, a therapist can decide to disrupt therapy that is in fact quite important and positive for the involved youngster. This kind of misinterpretation of the therapist's importance and positive role in the patient's life is quite common in work with severely disturbed adolescents. Consider the next case example.

Sheila, a social worker in a school program for severely emotionally disturbed youngsters, was required to leave the program due to her husband's unavoidable move to another city. She predicted to the staff that when she announced her departure it would cause applause from Roger, a very angry and constantly disruptive and complaining member of her therapy group. In fact, when she announced that she was leaving, Roger broke into inconsolable tears.

In other cases, the perception that treatment is moving too slowly or not at all is correct. Sometimes this is because the original prescription of outpatient psychotherapy was incorrect and the patient in fact is in need of inpatient treatment, residential care, or some other more structured approach. Other times it means that other elements should be added to the treatment, such as group psychotherapy, remedial education, or other aids to the patient's development of ego skills. Ideally, these decisions should be assessed with the patient and the family before concerns are expressed about the productivity of treatment. As a rule, it is better to inquire as to the views of all involved before having to face embarrassing and uncomfortable questions from the family. It goes without saying, on the other hand, that if the family does raise questions, the therapist should address them immediately rather than assuring everyone that things are fine (Offord & Bennett, 1994).

A wise early response to questions on anyone's part regarding the effectiveness of therapy is to ask for a consultation with a colleague. Consultations can bring a fresh point of view to the treatment situation, which may not only provide insights into transference or countertransference blocks that are present but also serve as a reassessment of the treatment plan and an opportunity for the patient and family to review treatment progress. Interestingly, consultations often are followed by an improvement in the course of treatment, even if continuation with the same therapist and same treatment plan are recommended.

If treatment is going poorly without clear explanation, it is also important to consider the possibility that the patient is secretly involved in drug use or has problems that did not surface in the original evaluation, such as learning disabilities or minor neurological problems. A reevaluation of the entire situation is indicated, including a careful evaluation of countertransference. Unfortunately, therapists are not able to treat every patient who comes to them for help. For a variety of reasons, individual therapists find particular difficulty in being useful to certain kinds of patients or to certain kinds of families. When these problems are recognized, if they cannot be ameliorated through the therapist's personal therapy or supervision, the patient should be transferred to a different therapist with as much speed as possible.

Occasionally a therapist attempts to treat a patient who may be treatable at another time and place but is simply unavailable for treatment in the present. Sometimes it is useful to accept the patient's wish to deal with things without treatment for a while and suggest that the need for treatment should be reviewed at some future date. This circumstance can occur even at certain points in very successful treatment. Consider the case of Howard.

Howard, a 17-year-old high school senior, suffered an acute depressive psychosis, probably triggered by his anticipation of leaving home and going to college. He was treated in a hospital for 3 weeks, then in day hospital for an additional 2 months. In the course of this treatment, he was seen individually in psychotherapy, initially 3 times a week, tapering down gradually to once a week. The treatment was extremely successful. Not only did Howard's psychosis clear, but he gained valuable insight into the family background and personality characteristics that had made him so vulnerable to separation trauma. However, as he began to function in a relatively normal way, he became increasingly uncomfortable in psychotherapy since he saw it as a reminder of his severe breakdown and because he found that the exploration of some issues still brought back the fear that he would once again lose control and lose his sanity.

He indicated that he needed a hiatus in therapy in order to stabilize himself and gain confidence in his ability to manage his day-to-day affairs. This request was granted and he remained out of therapy, successfully returning to college and to an appropriate social life. After 6 months he returned to psychotherapy, where he was once again comfortable in working on some of his long-standing problems.

Conclusion

Psychotherapy of the adolescent is a complex process that can utilize a variety of modalities as well as a range of interventions. These approaches extend from those that are primarily cognitive, behavioral, or supportive to those that are exploratory and utilize information derived from the exploration of transference. These strategies work only if they are tailored individually to fit the needs of the patient and if they recognize that both the patient and the patient's family need to understand and support the aims and methods of the therapeutic approach. Considered in this flexible way, psychotherapy remains central to all psychiatric treatment of the disturbed adolescent.

REFERENCES

Berkowitz, I. H. (1972). *Adolescents grow in groups.* New York: Brunner/Mazel.

Diamond, G. S., Serrano, A. C., Dickey, M., & Sonis, W. A. (1996). Current status of family-based outcome and process research. *Journal of the American Academy of Child and Adolescent Psychiatry, 35,* 6–16.

Gunderson, J. (1978). Defining the therapeutic process in psychiatric milieus. *Psychiatry, 41,* 327–335.

Kohut, H. (1971). *The analysis of the self.* New York: International Universities Press.

Meeks, J. E. (1973). Structuring the early phase of group psychotherapy with adolescents. *International Journal of Child Psychotherapy, 2,* 391–405.

Meeks, J. E., & Bernet, W. (1990). *The fragile alliance* (4th ed.). Malabor, FL: E. Krieger Publishing.

Minuchin, S. (1974). *Families and family therapy.* Cambridge, MA: Harvard University Press.

Offord, D. R., & Bennett, K. J. (1994). Conduct disorder: Long-term outcomes and intervention effectiveness. *Journal of the American Academy of Child and Adolescent Psychiatry, 33,* 1069–1078.

Scharff, D. E., & Scharff, J. S. (1987). *Object relations family therapy.* Northvale, NJ: Jason Aronson.

Schowalter, J. (1989). Psychodynamics and medication. *Journal of American Academy of Child and Adolescent Psychiatry, 28,* 681–684.

Williams, F. S. (1986). The psychoanalyst as both parent and interpreter for adolescent patients. *Adolescent Psychiatry, 13,* 164–177.

34 / Special Considerations in Psychopharmacological Treatment of Adolescents

Lois T. Flaherty and Debra M. Katz

Dramatic developments in the past decade have moved psychopharmacological treatment into an increasingly prominent position within the field of adolescent psychiatry. There has been an explosion in research and development of new drugs. The advent of managed care has meant increasing emphasis on short-term treatment, which often involves drug therapy. However, most published research on psychopharmacology deals with adults and, to a lesser extent, prepubertal children. Nonetheless, in spite of the continuing relative paucity of studies demonstrating efficacy of this kind of treatment in adolescents, psychiatrists who treat adolescents are increasingly relying on pharmacotherapy, drawing on published research on adults and children as well as their own clinical experience. However, because of the unique psychological and physiological features of adolescence, psychopharmacologic management in the adolescent patient is a complex and challenging task. The informed use of psychotropic medication in adolescent patients must take into account the effects of pubertal development on medication efficacy and the influence of psychosocial developmental tasks of adolescence on medication compliance. This chapter highlights general principles of drug treatment of adolescent patients but does not address specific dosages or treatment regimens, which are covered elsewhere.

Variables Affecting Adolescents' Drug Responses

While it is generally taken for granted that children differ from adults in their physical responses to psychotropic medications, it is not always appreciated that adolescents differ not only from children but from adults as well in their responses to these agents. The growing body of knowledge about anatomical and neurotransmitter maturation provides evidence that brain development continues into the late adolescent period. Therefore, there is a scientific explanation for why drugs that affect the brain show variability in efficacy during this phase.

How a drug works is also dependent on its interactions with various receptors in the brain. These interactions are in turn determined by the number of receptors, how they are distributed, and their sensitivity and mechanism of action. We do know that receptors are subject to modification by many naturally occurring brain chemicals as well as by drugs. We are beginning to understand something about how normal growth and development affect them. But comparatively little is known about the influence of growth and development on drug-receptor interactions. Nor is the impact of drugs on the developing brain well understood; the possibility that long-term effects could occur must be weighed in the clinical decision-making process (Vitiello & Jensen, 1995).

Burke and Puig-Antich (1990) reported poor clinical efficacy of tricyclic antidepressants in the adolescent population. They hypothesized that sex hormones, which increase during puberty, have an antagonist role on the antidepressant effect of imipramine. This antagonism may be related to competition at the receptor level or diminished receptor affinity. In addition, competition for the liver's metabolizing enzymes with gonadal hormones may explain the lower doses of these drugs needed during adolescence and their decreased efficacy.

It has been suggested that high gonadal steroid levels associated with adolesecence may significantly inhibit monoamine transmitter function (Kye & Ryan, 1995); while animal studies provide some supportive evidence of this, data based on research in this area are extremely sparse. Another hypothesis is that gonadal hormones may compete with drugs for the liver's metabolizing enzymes; this would account for the fact that adolescents are sometimes very sensitive to psychotropic drugs and need lower doses even than children. However, this is a poorly understood area.

The size of the liver relative to body weight is much greater in children than in adults. For example, the liver of a toddler is 40 to 50% greater and that of a 6-year-old is 30% greater than the liver of an adult. This means that for children, the dose of drugs metabolized by the liver needs to be larger per kilogram of body weight (Briant, 1978). However, as adolescents approach adults with regard to liver metabolic activity, the dose of some drugs actually may have to be *lowered* as the patient goes from childhood to adolescence. This is often true of stimulants, for example.

Another reason why results may be less than optimal is that diagnosis of disorders is often uncertain in the adolescent period. In an effort to establish a comprehensive approach to medicating an adolescent patient, a careful clinician considers both target symptomatology and diagnostic accuracy (Green, 1991). But the reality is that definitive diagnosis is often difficult to attain in an adolescent, either because the clinical presentation is colored by developmental changes or because the illness is not yet in its fully developed form. For example, in adolescence, affective illnesses, especially bipolar illness, may present with a wide spectrum of symptomatology, making diagnosis difficult. The clinician does not have the knowledge afforded by psychiatric history of past episodes. Nor does he or she have the luxury of a "crystal ball" to see what the natural course of illness will be over time.

COMORBIDITY

The increased prevalence of comorbidity and the relatively high probability that depression in adolescence is actually an early manifestation of bipolar disorder ("occult bipolarity") may account for relatively modest effects of antidepressants in this age group. Conditions that are commonly comorbid with depression include conduct disorder and borderline personality disorder; the presence of conduct disorder has been shown to decrease antidepressant response in depressed children and the borderline personality disorder is associated with a poorer response to antidepressants in adults (Kye & Ryan, 1995).

It has been suggested that high gonadal steroid levels associated with adolescence may significantly inhibit monamine transmitter function (Kye & Ryan, 1995); there is some supportive evidence of this from animal studies, but data based on research in this area are extremely sparse. Another hypothesis is that gonadal hormones may compete with drugs for the liver's metabolizing enzymes; this would account for the fact that adolescents are sometimes very sensitive to psychotropic drugs and need lower doses even than children. However, this is a poorly understood area.

Medication Choices

The choice of medications frequently is based on specfic target symptoms rather than on a complete diagnostic formulation. In the absence of a firm diagnosis, it behooves the clinician to identify measurable target symptoms that can be monitored quantitatively and qualitatively over time. For example, it may be appropriate to consider the use of lithium or carbamazapine in a 16-year-old with impulsivity, poor school performance, irritability, mood lability, and a family history of bipolar disorder even when classic symptoms of depression and/or mania are not apparent.

In most cases, the psychiatrist searching for information about a particular drug will not find published reports of carefully controlled clinical trials in adolescents. In fact, what may be found is evidence suggesting that psychopharmacologic treatment is ineffective in teenagers. For example, much of the literature on antidepressants in adolescents does not show clear-cut efficacy in this population. However, many of the studies involve small groups of patients, heterogeneous samples, may not have used washout periods, or have other problems that may have made efficacy difficult to detect. Knowing that a drug has been well studied in adults and aware that there is a great deal of continuity between adolescence and adulthood for many illnesses, such as depression, the psychiatrist can feel confident in prescribing a drug that has proven efficacy and a reasonable risk/benefit ratio. In general, substantial clinical experience with a drug in adults should be sufficient to allow the clinician a measure of comfort in using the drug in adolescents.

The *Physician's Desk Reference* (PDR), which publishes U.S. Food and Drug Administration (FDA) guidelines, generally gives age 12 as the cutoff for drugs approved for use in adults, so that the issue of "unapproved" use of medications is less of a consideration when treating adolescents than it is for children. Nonetheless, a physician is likely to be faced with the necessity of prescribing a drug for an indication not mentioned in the prescribing information, as for example, carbamazapine for impulse control disorders. The FDA restricts the claims that may be made by drug companies for their products; these restrictions are not meant to limit prescribing of drugs by physicians (Laughren, 1996). Since many drugs simply have not been subjected to FDA-approved testing in children and adolescents, product information must include the caveat "safety and effectiveness in children have not been established."

New FDA regulations have allowed possible approval of medications in children and adolescents based on extrapolation of research on drug efficacy with adults. The FDA has asked that drug manufacturers reexamine data already obtained from studies on adults and consider this as well as any supporting data from studies on children, and where appropriate, apply for approval for changes in labeling. The agency also has incorporated a rule that studies in pediatric populations will be required for approval of new drugs if it is likely these agents will be used in these populations. These new regulations represent substantial changes and are likely to stimulate much more research in child and adolescent psychopharmacology (Laughren, 1996). In the meantime, the best approach for the clinician, and one that is legally defensible, is to be familiar with the studies published in the scientific literature, be able to evaluate them critically, and use them as a basis for practice.

Issues of Compliance

Few studies specifically address medication compliance in adolescent psychiatric patients. Bastiaens (1995) assessed medication compliance in 30 adolescents 20 months postpsychiatric hospitalization. The adolescents and their parents had been assessed during the hospitalization regarding their knowledge and attitudes toward medications for psychiatric disorders. The adolescents received an intensive education about their medications while they were in the hospital. These authors found that the best predictor of posthospital medication compliance was prior attitude toward taking psychiatric medications. Neither being well informed about the medication nor having parents' favorably disposed toward its use was sufficient to ensure compliance. The authors suggest that the best approach is to work with the adolescent patient to modify negative feelings about taking medication.

Clinical experience suggests that noncompliance with medication is widespread in adolescent psychiatric patients, and our understanding of adolescent development informs us as to why this is so. Even if adolescent patients overtly agree to take medication, they are often less than fully compliant. The developmental tasks of separation and individuation in adolescence directly influence the formation of a trusting relationship with the prescribing psychiatrist. As adolescents gain an autonomous identity and begin to separate from their parents, they often engage in distancing and devaluation with all adult figures of authority. They may devalue the social/political norms as the "establishment" and find alternative ways to manage themselves in their environment. This includes idealizing "counterculture" leaders and rejecting authoritarian figures in the mainstream of society. These predictable and normative adolescent behaviors are exaggerated in many psychiatrically ill teenagers. The result may be an adolescent patient's refusal even to consider taking medication or various other forms of noncompliance.

Noncompliance may take the form of skipping pills, taking doses other than those prescribed, combining prescribed medication with unprescribed drugs, or initiating unannounced drug holidays. The adolescent patient will rarely reveal this information spontaneously and may deny it when asked. The dynamics of noncompliance in many adolescent patients are similar to those that have been described in borderline adult patients. These dynamics include fears of being controlled by the therapist and the symbolic equation of medication with good or bad nurturance (Havens, 1968). The psychiatrist must work actively with these transference issues. For adolescents for whom self-destructiveness is an ingrained pattern, noncompliance with medication is part of an established pattern of behavior.

Frequently, for adult patients, a trusting, at times even parental transference relationship with the psychiatrist helps to motivate them to comply with medication while tolerating untoward effects. If the psychiatrist treating an adolescent patient takes on this kind of transference role, the patient, in an attempt to maintain some semblance of autonomy, may rebel against treatment and be noncompliant with taking medication.

With adolescent patients, as with children, parents' attitudes toward psychiatric medications are very important. The motivation and ability of the responsible adults to support the adolescent's taking medication should always be taken into account. Unlike the case with children, parents' support of the treatment and their agreement with the prescribing of medication, while necessary, is not sufficient to ensure compliance.

Parents who have themselves had substance abuse problems often are very reluctant to allow their adolescents to take prescribed medications. Parents not infrequently get tangled in their adolescent's resistance toward treatment, including the taking of medication, by attempting to control the behavior of their child. Some parents have been known to reward regular attendance at psychiatric appointments and be punitive if directions are not followed to the letter. This attempt to enforce compliance with treatment directly opposes the developmental task of adolescence to take responsibility for oneself. A struggle for control ensues, which becomes a standoff with irate, frustrated parents on the one side opposed by an adolescent whose level of functioning is impaired secondary to being without needed medication. The patient sees the psychiatrist as allied with the parents; the parents see him or her as ineffective; and a negative treatment alliance with the patient and his or her family develops. To prevent this kind of impasse, the psychiatrist must set up a reliable and predictable framework within which effective work can take place. The adolescent needs to feel autonomous in this relationship without parental intrusion. The parents need to develop their own trusting alliance with the psychiatrist; they can then feel informed about the treatment while allowing a separate and confidential relationship to develop between their adolescent and the psychiatrist.

Establishing a solid therapeutic alliance with an adolescent patient is essential for good medication compliance. The work on forming an effective alliance begins with the initial sessions, which usually takes place after the psychiatrist has accepted the referral and has had telephone contact with the parents. It is the authors' practice to begin the initial session with a 15-minute meeting with the adolescent and the parents together to discuss the evaluation process. The reasons for the consultation are reviewed. The rules of confidentiality are explained. Parents are assured that the psychiatrist will never compromise the safety of the adolescent and that confidentiality will be breached if the adolescent is suicidal or homicidal or at risk of any harm. Parents are also told in very clear terms that issues regarding sexual activity, drug use and abuse, and confidential discussions will not be shared with them unless necessary to ensure safety or the adolescent gives permission.

The Pharmacotherapeutic Alliance

Once these ground rules are established, the parents are excused and the adolescent is interviewed alone. The goal of the initial session is to begin to create an alliance based on trust and honesty. Even when the psychiatrist is seeing the adolescent only for evaluation and medication monitoring, it is important that rapport be established. This rapport has been referred to as the pharmacotherapeutic alliance (Gutheil, 1982). In this relationship the psychiatrist actively enlists the adolescent in mutually shared treatment goals. The goal is for the doctor and patient to work in harmony as observers and evaluators of the treatment process. If the adolescent can take an active role in the treatment, he or she will gain a sense of control and independence, which in turn fosters achievement of age-appropriate developmental milestones. The utilization of self-reporting scales to monitor treatment response is one way to foster active participation. First, it enhances the capacity for reflection and self-observation. Second, this allows the adolescent to understand that the problem be addressed—for example, depression—has multiple components. Further, by objectifying the disorder, the treatment process itself may become less threatening and intrusive.

The necessity of ruling out pregnancy prior to beginning treatment with psychotropic medications and the need to discuss with the adolescent the potential for drug interactions with street drugs and alcohol creates an opportunity to discuss drug use and sexual activity in depth. The clinician should review safe sex practices (i.e., condom use and ways to protect oneself from contracting sexually transmitted disease and AIDS). In addition, frank discussions about alcohol and drug use should be encouraged while assuring the teenager of protecting his or her confidentiality. A teenager may be using alcohol or cocaine as a way to self-medicate depressive or manic episodes of a bipolar mood disorder. However, he or she may have been afraid to discuss this with anyone for fear of being labeled an addict and condemned by family members. It is essential that in the working relationship between the psychiatrist and the teenager, a nonjudgmental approach be taken.

The psychiatrist must make a determination about whether substance abuse or dependency is present and then make sure appropriate treatment is undertaken before embarking on a psychopharmacological treatment program. Of course, when an adolescent patient is engaged in potentially dangerous activities, parents must be informed. This is sometimes best done in carefully planned family sessions in which the therapist coaches and supports the adolescent in sharing information.

Once a decision is made that medication is indicated, it is necessary to present this recommendation to the adolescent and parents in ways that make sense to them. The psychiatrist may wish to bring this up first with the adolescent before talking with the parents. A subsequent discussion may be with the parents alone or with the parents and adolescent together. If, following an initial one-to-one discussion, the adolescent is included in the meeting with the parents, he or she will have the opportunity to hear again about the role of medication in the treatment, reinforcing and enhancing understanding. The psychiatrist should discuss the risks of not treating the disorder with medication as well as the risks involved in using medication.

Many publications and printed materials are available to help adolescents and parents understand the role of medications in their treatment (Dulcan, 1992). These can be helpful both at the time treatment is initiated and in cases where

parents or adolescents are reluctant to consider medications, so that they have an opportunity to become more fully informed prior to making a final decision. There is evidence from general pediatric practice that educational efforts and improved communication with the parent can improve compliance. For further discussion of this, see Chapter 35.

At times it is advisable to postpone using medication for an adolescent patient. A patient who is very much opposed to considering it initially can be told that the issue can be reconsidered at a later time, after a trial period of therapy alone. The same is true when parents are unwilling to allow psychopharmacologic treatment. An adolescent who is involved in substance abuse should be given the opportunity to become drug-free and committed to abstinence prior to beginning a psychotropic medication.

Classes of Medications

For each class of medications used in the treatment of adolescent psychiatric patients, specific compliance and psychological issues prevail.

STIMULANTS

Stimulants are used most commonly in the treatment of attention deficit hyperactivity disorder (ADHD) and narcolepsy (Green, 1991). Stimulants and effective in adolescents with symptoms of ADHD, although response rate is lower than for children (Evans & Pelham, 1991; Klorman, Brumaghim, Fitzpatrick, & Borgstedt, 1990). Often those who are treatment resistant are referred to child and adolescent psychiatrists for further evaluation. The psychiatrist who treats adolescents often sees patients who were diagnosed as children with ADHD and started on methylphenidate, the most commonly prescribed stimulant. The parents of such teenagers complain that, over time, the beneficial effects of the stimulants have worn off, and their adolescent child is again displaying the behaviors that occasioned the original referral for psychiatric help. The psychiatrist must not assume either that the original diagnosis was correct or that medication was used appropriately. In addition, the great majority of children with

ADHD receive inadequate treatment. ADHD has many symptoms, including hyperactivity, poor school performance, irritability, and impulsivity, symptoms that also may characterize overanxious disorder and depression. It is therefore essential that a detailed history of symptomatology and medication efficacy be obtained even in the adolescent who has a long history of being treated with stimulants. Often a careful clinician will identify a different diagnostic possibility to explain the treatment nonresponsiveness. Alternatively, the fact that prior clinical trials were inadequate may come to light.

Despite evidence to the contrary, many parents have held to the common belief that most children grow out of their ADHD symptomatology when they reach adolescence. In reality, many adolescents with ADHD will display the same clinical picture they did as children; others will develop more serious difficulties. With the introduction of pubertal hormonal changes and age-dependent psychosocial stressors, there may be an exaggeration of impulsivity, inattentiveness, and acting-out behavior resembling conduct disorder. These individuals embrace rebelliousness as they strive for autonomy. In other cases, oppositional defiant disorder or conduct disorder has been superimposed on the ADHD. Stimulants are effective for symptoms of these disruptive behavior disorders when they are comorbid conditions with ADHD.

Dependency and Abuse of Stimulants: Chemical dependency on prescribed psychotropic agents is an area of continuing exploration. Although there have been a few cases in which adolescents were either addicted or dependent on these agents (Jaffe, 1991), these cases are the exception.

A new sociocultural phenomenon has occurred that affects the attitudes of adolescents toward all drugs, especially those with a potential for misuse. Many adolescents are worried about the possibility of addiction. Teenagers in the 1980s and early 1990s have been inundated with the "Just say no" campaign of the Reagan era and the prevailing antidrug sentiment of our society. The notion of being healthy by staying "substance free" has created resistance on the part of these adolescents to taking potentially beneficial medications. These teenagers need reassurance that their medication will not cause addiction or dependence. It is worthwhile to help the adolescent focus on his or her ability to control the taking of the medication as prescribed.

The authors of a recent comprehensive review of drug treatment of attention deficit hyperactivity disorder assert that there are "no scientific data confirming the abuse of prescribed stimulants by ADHD children who are receiving appropriate diagnosis and careful follow-up" (Spencer et al., 1996, p. 425). They also point out that previous work by their group has shown that the most commonly abused substance among adolescents and adults with ADHD is marijuana, not stimulants (Biederman et al., 1995). Nonetheless, myths persist about widespread abuse of stimulants by teens for whom these drugs are prescribed for treatment of ADHD.

There have been reports of adolescents selling their methylphenidate to classmates and friends; the authors' patients have reported being approached by other students at school who have offered to buy their medications, and they report such abuse is widespread, although there are no reliable data. One adolescent patient of one author "snorted" his methylphenidate in order to induce weight loss so that he could qualify for his school's wrestling team; one adolescent patient of the other author sold his medication to other students so that they could lose weight. These are serious problems; however, they do not entail abuse of stimulant medication in the usual sense. The paucity of published reports and virtual absence of abusers of prescribed stimulants in drug treatment programs argues that such abuse is indeed rare. Nonetheless, the potential for stimulants to get into the wrong hands is reason for caution; recently the manufacturer of Ritalin has incorporated warnings to parents about the need to monitor closely their children's medication.

Medication Compliance: Compliance is likely to be compromised when an adolescent has had negative experiences with taking medications for ADHD as a child. Either the medication is seen as ineffective, or side effects were problematic. Often, in such cases, a clinician who takes a careful history finds that prior treatment was sporadic and inconsistent, and a good trial of medication with accurate monitoring of response never occurred. It is challenging to win the trust of a teenager to attempt a new trial of an agent rejected in the past. Time and patience are necessary to educate the patient and the family about what probably happened and how it can be avoided in the future.

Medication compliance is influenced by the side effect profile of the medication as experienced by the adolescent (Green, 1991). Irritability, insomnia, anorexia, and dysphoria may not be well tolerated by individuals on stimulants. Black male adolescents may be at higher risk for elevated blood pressure on stimulants (Brown & Sexson, 1989). Many adolescent girls welcome the appetite suppressant features of stimulants as an aid to controlling unwanted weight gain. However, adolescents with a proclivity to thinness may find the inability to maintain a desired heavier weight a reason not to take the stimulants as prescribed, as illustrated in the following example:

Susie: Susie, a 5 foot 10 inch, 16-year-old who weighed 115 pounds, revealed to her psychiatrist that she has been "cheeking" her stimulant medication for the past 8 years, concealing this from her family while continuing to have poor school performance and impulsive behavior. She had been switched from methylphenidate to dextroamphetamine and then to pemoline because of what was felt to be poor clinical responses. She reported that with the onset of puberty, she had minimal breast development and felt she was "skin and bones." She feels embarrassed in the gym when she needs to shower and has been called "stringbean" by her peers. She reported that when she took the medication, she could never eat enough to maintain her ideal body weight or feel comfortable with her lack of feminity.

In many cases, side effects to stimulants as well as other drugs can be avoided by beginning the medication at a low dose, even one that is likely to be subtherapeutic, and explaining that the dose likely will have to be increased. For many drugs, tolerance to side effects develops, and once this occurs, the dose can be increased gradually, waiting at each increased dose until the side effects disappear or decrease, until therapeutic levels are attained. Patients also can be told that if side effects do not go away and are intolerable, it is almost always possible to switch to another drug that will not have them. For Susie, for example, a tricyclic antidepressant, clonidine, or bupropion may have been an effective alternative.

ANTIDEPRESSANTS AND LITHIUM

The medication management of affective disorders in adolescence is complicated and challenging. Depressed or manic adolescents must first accept the fact that an affective state beyond their control is affecting their daily functioning. The symptoms of hopelessness and worthlessness that are core features of depression strike at the heart of adolescents' strivings for autonomy and self-worth. They commonly feel weak and inadequate when they are unable to manage these affects and when their level of functioning is adversely affected. Depressed adolescents, in a desperate attempt to maintain a sense of competency, may not reveal these symptoms to their family and peer group. In addition, parents, teachers, and friends may minimize an adolescent's distress by rationalizing serious dysfunction and attributing it to "typical teenage behavior." Focus on deterioration in academic performance and isolation and decreased socialization with peers as signs of a psychiatric disorder can help to objectify the illness as well as emphasize its impact in ways that are difficult for the parents or teenager to deny. By labeling these phenomena part of an illness rather than a weakness or failing, the clinician can help restore a measure of self-esteem.

Depression Interferes with Acceptance and Compliance: Depressed adolescents often have difficulty accepting medication; they view it as another sign that they are incompetent and cannot handle their problems on their own. They are likely to say, if they begin to improve, that it is the medication working and not they themselves. They need help in recognizing that medication can do nothing by itself without their working on their problems, and their improvement is very much a consequence of their hard work.

For a depressed and anxious adolescent whose passivity and inactivity have become a comforting modus operandi, the increased activation that results from antidepressants may exacerbate anxiety. This in turn may lead to noncompliance in taking medication.

Issues Associated with Specific Agents

In addition to these general problems adolescents have accepting drug treatment for an affective illness, the clinician needs to keep in mind that certain compliance and treatment issues are associated with specific agents.

TRICYCLIC ANTIDEPRESSANTS

Until the advent of serotonin reuptake inhibitors, tricyclic antidepressants were the most commonly used antidepressants for adolescents. Side effects of sedation and weight gain, as well as the dry mouth and constipation so commonly seen in these medications, make them as problematic for adolescents as they are for adults. However, it is well to remember that these side effects are not universal, and for a given patient one of these drugs may be well tolerated and effective. Although there have been no reports of sudden death in adolescents taking tricyclic antidepressants, the reports of cardiotoxicity in children, although rare, have given psychiatrists pause in using these drugs in adolescents. Electrocardiogram monitoring is recommended in patients under 16 and in any patients who have known cardiac problems.

MONOAMINE OXIDASE INHIBITORS

Monoamine oxidase inhibitors, while indicated for the use in major depression and panic disorder in adults, have limited usefulness in adolescents. They may be indicated in adolescents who are nonresponders to other antidepressants who can assure dietary compliance. In a retrospective chart review of 23 adolescent patients treated with either tranylcypromine sulfate or phenelzine administered alone or in conjunction with a tricyclic antidepressant, Ryan and colleagues (1988) reported that of the total group studied, 74% had a good or fair response, but about 30% were noncompliant with the dietary restrictions. Even though only 2 patients had significant symptoms after ingesting tyramine-containing foods, the authors urged caution and careful monitoring of patients for whom these drugs are prescribed and advised against their use in impulsive adolescents or those who may abuse drugs. It has been suggested that adherence to a difficult restrictive diet in developmentally appropriate rebellious adolescents is unattainable and quite risky.

LITHIUM

It is well established that lithium is a drug whose compliance is tenuous in all age groups of patients. Adults with bipolar illness to not like the loss of hypomanic creativity and success while tolerating a host of adverse effects. Adolescents do not well tolerate the untoward effects of lithium, such as weight gain and an exacerbation of facial acne. In the adolescent population, one's appearance is central to peer acceptance. While enjoying self-expression through outrageous clothing and hairstyles, teenagers do not want to be noticed for imperfections in appearance. A teenage girl being treated with lithium as an adjunct to an antidepressant for impulsivity, mood lability, and episodes of rage became noncompliant when a 10-pound weight gain made her feel unattractive and further ostracized her from her peers. Emphasis on a trusting relationship with the psychiatrist where the teenager is an empowered participant in treatment may contribute to better compliance with lithium. Recent indications that valproate may be as effective as lithium for bipolar disorders, and also have fewer troublesome side effects, offer the possibility of this drug as an alternative that may be better tolerated by adolescent patients.

SEROTONIN REUPTAKE INHIBITORS

The serotonin reuptake inhibitors offer the important advantages of having relatively few side effects, virtual absence of lethality of overdoses, and no known cardiotoxicity, and for these reasons they have become increasingly prescribed for depression in adolescents. They also have some efficacy in anxiety disorders. It is good to remember that these drugs are not without side effects, some of which can be difficult to distinguish from depressive symptoms, a fact that can make dosing difficult. They all can cause anorexia, restlessness and agitation, insomnia, daytime fatigue, and sexual dysfunction, all of which might be signs of worsening depression as well as side effects. Thus, increasing the dose in response to the appearance of these manifestations might only serve to worsen them. Additionally, blood levels are not useful in determining dose as they are with tricyclic antidepressants. The best advice is to make sure the recommended therapeutic dose is maintained for sufficient length of time, usually 4 weeks, before increasing it. In adolescents, the therapeutic dose is frequently less than that for adults.

BUPROPION

Bupropion is also relatively free of side effects, although it has a slight risk of seizures. In addition to its efficacy in depression, it has been found to be effective in some conduct disorders with aggressive behavior as well as with ADHD.

The newer antidepressants, velafaxine and nefazadone, have not been studied systematically in children and adolescents. In case reports, venlafaxine has been reported to have some efficacy in ADHD; if this impression is confirmed, the drug may have particular utility because of its antianxiety and antiobsessional effects (Pleak & Gormly, 1995).

ANTIPSYCHOTICS

Since the advent of better diagnostic tools and alternative psychotropic agents, neuroleptics are used to a lesser degree in the adolescent population than was formerly the case. The traditional antipsychotics are still the first-choice agents in the treatment of childhood schizophrenia and autism (Green, 1991; McClellan & Werry, 1994). They are also used in the treatment of severely aggressive conduct-disordered children. Two neuroleptics, haloperidol and pimozide, are used for Tourette's disorder. The most common use of neuroleptics in adolescents with no previous psychiatric history is for psychotic symptoms, which may represent the onset of schizophrenia. An adolescent may begin to express paranoid ideation, delusional thought, or exhibit disorganized thinking and withdrawn behavior. It is essential to take a slow methodical approach when medicating an adolescent who may be frightened of his or her deterioration or suspicious of authorities. The psychiatrist is challenged to create a trusting relationship where the serious potential adverse effects of neuroleptic malignant syndrome and tardive dyskinesia can be discussed without fostering noncompliance. Attaining informed consent with utilization of available supports may allow for a trial during which the patient is able to appreciate more fully to potential benefit of the medication and negative attitudes will decrease, as the following case example illustrates.

John: John had his first psychotic break at age 17 and was hospitalized and treated with haloperidol. Within 24 hours he had a severe dystonic reaction and was treated with intramuscular injections of dimenhydri-

nate. Since that time he has been reluctant to take any antipsychotic medication, with the result that his thought disorder greatly impaired his level of functioning. By the age of 24 he had been hospitalized on a chronic care unit of a state hospital for 2 years. He consistently refused any trial of antipsychotic medication, stating a fear of being poisoned and becoming a robot. Documentation in his hospital record noted a 4-month period during which he was compliant with medication and living in a community residence free from psychotic symptoms. His case was considered for involuntary medication. Upon approval, he was given a trial with haloperidol and benztropine. In 3 weeks his delusional thinking diminished and auditory hallucinations disappeared. When his thoughts became more organized, he was able to report his fear of the medication dating back to his bad experience as an adolescent.

In general, it is best to begin neuroleptics at low doses and gradually increase the dose. Acutely agitated psychotic patients should be treated in the hospital, and agitation often can be managed effectively with benzodiazapines, such as lorazepam, until the neuroleptic has taken effect. There is no advantage to so-called rapid neuroleptization; this practice carries the risk of producing an extreme dyskinesia that may have the long-term result of medication refusal, in addition to the risk of neuroleptic malignant syndrome. Although haloperidol is the most widely prescribed of the traditional antipsychotics, other, lower-potency neuroleptics that have more sedating properties and less propensity for extrapyramidal side effects should be considered in initiating treatment, particularly when agitation and anxiety are prominent.

ATYPICAL ANTIPSYCHOTIC DRUGS

The advent of newer, so-called atypical antipsychotic medications, such as clozapine and risperidone, has given the clinician important alternatives for treatment of schizophrenia and other psychoses. Studies of these drugs in adolescents, although limited, show comparable efficacy to that found in adults (Campbell & Cueva, 1995). Although clozapine is not considered a first-line drug because of the risk of agranulocytosis, some have argued that in children and adolescents it may be preferable to neuroleptics because of the decreased potential for tardive dyskinesia and its putative greater efficacy (Frazier et al., 1994). Risperidone has rapidly moved to the forefront in popularity of antipsychotic drugs prescribed because of its efficacy and low incidence of extrapyramidal side effects, but its potential to cause tardive dyskinesia is unknown. Newer drugs, such as olanzapine and sertindole, offer promise but await studies in the adolescent age group.

BENZODIAZEPINES

Adolescents frequently complain of anxiety and sleep disturbances, and may request medications for these. Here the problem is not a potential for noncompliance but a danger of abuse or dependence if benzodiazepines are used. In general, it is best to try to identify the underlying cause and treat it. If in fact a primary anxiety disorder is present, then the treatment should be geared toward the primary diagnosis, such as panic disorder. The psychiatrist should keep in mind that sleep disturbances usually are symptoms of other disorders, such as depression, and will improve as the disorder improves. There is some evidence that clonazepam may be useful in the treatment of panic disorder and neuroleptic-induced akathisia in adolescents (Kutcher Reiter, Gardner, & Klein, 1992). Data are very limited on the safety and efficacy of anxiolytics and sedative-hypnotics in adolescents. These drugs can cause paradoxical excitation and disinhibition, leading to worsening of aggressive and explosive behavior in patients for whom dyscontrol is a problem.

Multidrug Therapy

The use of more than one drug at a time is sometimes necessary. The dictum that polypharmacy generally should be avoided has been replaced by the precept that rational use of more than one selective agent is sometimes necessary (Wilens et al., O'Connor, 1995). Combined pharmacotherapy is indicated in the treatment of depressive episodes in which a bipolar disorder is suspected, when a mood-stabilizing agent such as lithium may be combined with an antidepressant, or postpsychotic depression in schizophrenia, when an antidepressant and an antipsychotic may be coadministered, or when the coexistence of two pharmacologically responsive disorders is suspected, such as ADHD and mania. For conditions that are known to respond to monodrug and treatment, the clinician should determine that an adequate dose of the primary drug has been given for an adequate period of time before adding another drug. An alternative strategy to augmentation with a second drug is to change to another drug. In almost all conditions for which psychotropic drugs are prescribed, there are cases in which one of a class of drugs is more effective than another for a given patient. This is true for stimulants, antidepressants, and neuroleptics. In cases where an additional medication is needed—for example, to control extreme anxiety or insominia—the use of a relatively short-acting drug, such as a benzodiazepine, for limited periods of time, until the clinician is certain of having achieved maximal benefit from the primary drug, is preferable to adding another drug whose effects are cumulative.

Conclusion

Many special considerations apply to the psychopharmacological treatment of adolescents. Diagnosis is difficult, and adolescent patients sometimes refuse drug treatment. Even if they agree to it, they often have great difficulty correctly taking medication as prescribed. Accurate titration of medication to a dose that maximizes efficacy and minimizes untoward effects is challenging in this population. In prescribing psychotropic medication to adolescents, as with other age groups, forming a therapeutic alliance is essential. This chapter has highlighted some of the general issues involved in psychopharmacologic treatment of adolescents. The reader is referred to the chapters on specific disorders for a more complete discussion of treatment.

REFERENCES

Bastiaens, L. (1995). Compliance with pharmacotherapy in adolescents: Effects of patients' and parents' knowledge and attitudes toward treatment. *Journal of Child and Adolescent Psychopharmacology, 5*, 39–48.

Biederman, J., Wilens, T., Mick, E., Milberger, S., Faraone, S., & Spencer, T. (1995). Psychoactive substance abuse disorder in adults with attention deficit hyperactivity disorder. *American Journal of Psychiatry, 152*, 1652–1658.

Briant, R. H. (1978). An introduction to clinical pharmacology. In J. S. Werry (Ed.), *Pediatrc psychopharmacology: The use of behavior-modifying drugs in children* (pp. 203–229). New York: Brunner/Mazel.

Brown, R. T., & Sexson, S. B. (1989). Effects of methylphenidate on cardiovascular responses in attention deficit hyperactivity disordered adolescents. *Journal of Adolescent Health Care, 10*, 179–183.

Burke, P., & Puig-Antich, J. (1990). Psychobiology childhood depression. In M. Lewis & S. M. Miller (Eds.), *Handbook of developmental psychopathology* (pp. 327–339). New York: Plenum Press.

Campbell, M., & Cueva, J. (1995). Psychopharmacology in child and adolescent psychiatry: A review of the past seven years. Part II. *Journal of the American Academy of Child and Adolescent Psychiatry, 34*, 1262–1272.

Dulcan, M. K. (1992). Information for parents and youth on psychotropic medications. *Journal of Child and Adolescent Psychopharmacology, 2*, 81–101.

Evans, S. W. & Pelham, W. E. (1991). Psychostimulant effects on academic and behavioral measures for ADHD junior high school students in a lecture format classroom. *Journal of Abnormal Child Psychology, 19*, 537–552.

Frazier, J. A., Gordon, C. T., McKenna, K., Lenane, M. C., Jih, D., & Rapoport, J. L. (1994). An open trial of clozapine in 11 adolescents with childhood onset schizophrenia. *Journal of the American Academy of Child and Adolescent Psychiatry, 33*, 658–663.

Green, W. H. (1991). *Child and adolescent clinical psychopharmacology*. Baltimore: Williams & Wilkins.

Gutheil, T. G. (1982). The psychology of psychopharmacology. *Bulletin of the Menninger Clinic, 46* (4), 321–330.

Havens, L. L. (1968). Some difficulties in giving schizophrenic and borderline patients medication. *Psychiatry, 31*, 44–50.

Jaffe, S. L. (1991). Intranasal abuse of prescribed methylphenidate by an alcohol and drug abusing adolescent with ADHD. *Journal of American Academy of Child and Adolescent Psychiatry, 30* (5), 773–775.

Klorman, R., Brumaghim, J. T., Fitzpatrick, P. A., & Borgstedt, A. D. (1990). Clinical effects of a controlled trial of methylphenidate on adolescents with attention deficit disorder. *Journal of the American Academy of Child and Adolescent Psychiatry, 29*, 702–709.

Kutcher, S. P., Reiter, S., Gardner, D. M., & Klein, R. G. (1992). The pharmacotherapy of anxiety disorders in children and adolescents. *Psychiatric Clinics of North America, 15*, 41–67.

Kye, C., & Ryan, N. (1995). Pharmacologic treatment of child and adolescent depression. In M. A. Riddle (Ed.), Pediatric Psychopharmacology II. *Child and Adolescent Psychiatric Clinics of North America, 4*, 261–281.

Laughren, T. P. (1996). Regulatory issues in pediatric psychopharmacology. *Journal of the American Academy of Child and Adolescent Psychiatry, 35*, 1276–1282.

McClellan, J., & Werry, J. (1994). Practice parameters for the assessment and treatment of children and adolescents with schizophrenia. *Journal of the American Academy of Child and Adolescent Psychiatry, 33*, 616–635.

Pleak, R. R., & Gormly, L. J. (1995). Effects of venlafaxine treatment for ADHD in a child [letter]. *American Journal of Psychiatry, 152*, 1099.

Ryan, N. D., Puig-Antich, J., Rabinovich, H., Fried, J., Ambrosini, P., Meyer, V., Torres, D., Dachille, S., & Mazzie, D. (1988). MAOIs in adolescent major depression unresponsive to tricyclic antidepressants. *Journal of the American Academy of Child and Adolescent Psychiatry, 27*, 755–758.

Spencer, T., Biederman, J., Wilens, T., Harding, M., O'Donnell, D., & Griffen, S. (1996). Pharmacotherapy of attention deficit hyperactivity disorder across the life cycle. *Journal of the American Academy of Child and Adolescent Psychiatry, 35*, 409–432.

Vitiello, B., & Jensen, P. S. (1995). Developmental perspectives in pediatrc psychopharmacology. *Psychopharmacology Bulletin, 31*, 75–81.

Wilens, T., Spencer, T., Biederman, J., Wozniak, J., & O'Connor, D. (1995). Combined pharmacotherapy: An emerging trend in pediatric psychopharmacology. *Journal of the American Academy of Child and Adolescent Psychiatry, 34*, 110–112.

35 / Compliance with Medical Regimens

Sheridan Phillips

Compliance with treatment is generally considered a crucial factor in the outcome of any treatment. However, the frequency with which patients in general fail to comply with treatment recommendations has been well documented (Haynes, Taylor, & Sachett, 1979). Adolescent patients pose particular difficulties with regard to compliance, since they are generally expected to take at least partial responsibility for following treatment regimens but at the same time are often struggling with conflicts over autonomy and authority. Compliance issues are particularly challenging for psychiatrically ill adolescents, whose autonomy and authority struggles are likely to be intensified or even to constitute the core of the treatment.

Successful treatment for a variety of disorders is now available, thanks to the effort of generations of medical researchers. Patients' refusal to follow these treatment regimens, or to follow them appropriately, is therefore a frequent source of frustration for health care providers. Failure to comply with treatment clearly can have adverse consequences for patients and their families. It can also have broader social consequences. For example, if only half of the 200,000 teenagers treated annually for gonorrhea comply with the full course of antibiotics, this contributes substantially to the reservoir of communicable disease (Cromer & Tarnowski, 1989).

Most of the research on compliance has focused on general medical care and not specifically on adolescent psychiatric care. However, psychiatric treatment of adolescents can be considered a special case of medical treatment, and it is likely that the same principles apply. In light of the increasing use of psychopharmacological approaches to treat adolescents, it behooves psychiatrists to be aware of measures that can enhance their patients' compliance with drug treatment. Also, psychiatrists who consult in primary care settings are often asked to assist other physicians in working with adolescents who are noncompliant with medical treatment.

Compliance with medical treatment can include following through with referrals for specialized services, keeping appointments with the primary care provider/facility, following a medication and/or behavioral regimen, and prevention (e.g., contraception). This chapter addresses the first three issues, focusing on recommendations for increasing compliance. Reproductive health issues are discussed in chapter 20.

Compliance with Referrals

In general, patients are less likely to comply with mental health or behavioral referrals than they are with referrals for medical or surgical intervention. Compliance is more likely when the referral recommendation comes from the primary care provider, in contrast to referrals made in an emergency room or as the result of a health screening program. Patients with acute illnesses are less likely to comply with referrals than are those with a chronic disease. However, symptomatic status does influence compliance, with symptomatic patients being substantially more likely than asymptomatic patients to follow through with a referral recommendation.

In the case of mental health consultation or referral, this author (Phillips, 1992) has suggested that acceptance of the referral recommendation will be enhanced by "normalizing" the problem and the recommendation. This includes drawing the analogy to use of other specialized services (e.g., accountants, plumbers) and conveying that this is a routine component of comprehensive health care. Toward that end, I recommend that mental health specialists be included as members of group practices or general health clinics where all providers share charts, personnel, and facilities. Similarly, referral is easier in organized systems of care where a range of services is provided and steps are taken to minimize bureaucratic barriers in going from one level of service to another, as, for example, from inpatient to outpatient treatment. Parent and patient support groups within a general clinic can also destigmatize mental health treatment by focusing on enhancing problem-solving and coping with issues related to the child's disease or disorder.

Many referrals fail during transition to a different provider and site. Transitions can be facilitated by including a mental health specialist on site. The presence of this specialist conveys the message that such referrals are common, not "abnormal," and clearly signals the referring physician's confidence in the specialist. It is also easy and natural to arrange a personal introduction. If an off-site referral is necessary, I have suggested (1992) that personal contact is the key to successful transition. Optimally, the specialist should come to the primary care site to meet the patient and family and, if possible, conduct the first session there.

Compliance with Appointments

Reported rates of failed appointments range from 15 to 75%, with substantial variation between populations, sites, and nature of treatment. It is often unclear how many failed appointments represent cancellations vs. "no shows." It is also difficult to estimate a true dropout rate. For example, Deyo and Inui (1980) studied a general medical clinic for adults and found that 40% of patients who missed two consecutive appointments subsequently returned to the clinic in the next 15 months.

Surveys of patients who failed to keep appointments indicate that approximately one-quarter never intended to return and one-quarter encountered family-related problems that hindered compliance, such as the lack of a baby-sitter, transportation, or money. The remainder of patients report that they forgot or were confused about when the appointment was scheduled. These outcomes appear to be a function of four variables: the patient (and family), the environment, the provider, and the process.

Multiple studies of patient characteristics have found statistically significant but relatively small effects of demographic variables: Noncompliance rates are higher for patients who are lower in age, socioeconomic status, and education. However, these findings are of limited clinical utility because they are not sufficiently powerful to assist prediction of individual patients' compliance. They do serve, however, to heighten concern about noncompliance in facilities that serve such populations.

The lack of good demographic predictors has prompted investigation of patient beliefs and values. The Health Beliefs Model hypothesizes that a patient's compliance is a function of his or her perception of the disease, including its perceived severity, his or her susceptibility to disease, belief in the efficacy of treatment, and the cost/benefit ratio of intervention. While some studies have found modest relationships between health beliefs and appointment keeping, this area of research has not progressed sufficiently to enable prediction of individual patient compliance.

Thus currently it is not possible to predict a patient's compliance with appointments on the basis of demographic or belief factors. Physicians are also unable to predict patient compliance; several studies have found their predictions to be no better than chance. A more useful approach may be to target efforts to increase compliance with patients who have a history of broken appointments because this appears to be a better predictor than the other variables described above. Possibly the best strategy may be simply to ask the patient if he or she plans to return. Haynes, Taylor, and Sackett (1979) report that the patient's estimate of compliance explained an astounding 52% of the variance, in contrast to the 5 to 25% typically accounted for by demographics or beliefs.

Environmental factors also contribute to appointment keeping. While whether is related to failed appointments, it is of less significance than access to the health facility. Distance from home to the facility appears not to be important, but transportation is. Family stability and size, and the presence of small children at home, is also a major factor. It thus seems clear that compliance with appointments will be enhanced if patients have appropriate transportation and if brief child care can be provided at the health facility.

Provider characteristics also seem related to compliance, although methodological constraints have hampered documenting specific details of these characteristics. Some key deterrents to good provider-patient interactions are impersonality, brevity of encounter, and lack of communication, particularly of emotional issues. In general, patients who have had satisfactory interactions with the physician and facility, and who are confident of their ability to provide successful treatment, are more likely to comply with future appointments. Continuity of provider also enhances compliance; when patients are treated by one to four providers, they are more likely to keep appointments than are patients who encounter more than four different providers.

Finally, the process of scheduling appointments and characteristics of the facility also impact on compliance. Approximately half of patients with failed appointments report that they did not know an appointment was scheduled, thought it was for a different day or time, or simply forgot. Thus, communicating the specifics regarding the next appointment needs to be crystal clear, preferably with the patient receiving a card noting the date, day, and time. It may be useful for this card to be of an unusual color and shape. Telephone and mail reminders (one to five days before) have been used in a variety of sites. While results are mixed, most studies report a substantial improvement (20 to 75%) in appointment keeping. Mailed reminders have been found to be more cost effective than phone calls. They are also more useful for populations in which many patients do not have telephones.

Relevant facility variables include location (neighborhood clinics typically report greater compliance) and timing. The average waiting time to see the physician is a key variable, as is the lag time between a request for an appointment and when it is scheduled. Time between appointments is also relevant, with greater compliance found for more frequent appointments. Frankel and Hovell (1978) report that reducing the scheduled lag time from 1 to 2 weeks to 1 to 2 days reduced a no-show rate of 50% to 5%. They also reported a comparison of individual appointments vs. a block time with either an assigned or unassigned physician, and found that either type of appointment with an assigned physician improved both the show rate and the percentage of patients who arrived on time. (Physicians were more prompt, too.) The worst combination was block-time ap-

pointment with an unassigned physician. Other investigators have employed financial incentives, such as a $5 coupon for keeping an appointment on time. Although results have been mixed, most studies report improved compliance that was cost effective when personnel costs were included.

While children's compliance with appointments is largely a function of parental motivation, many additional factors affect adolescents' compliance. As patients enter adolescence, their desire for confidentiality can hinder access to health care. Even when payment for services is not an issue, teenagers who seek care without parental knowledge still must be able to pay for transportation. Privacy issues may also hinder the use of either mailed or phoned reminders of appointments. Finally, teenagers may be reluctant to continue to see a "child" psychiatrist, or a pediatrician, especially in an office where the waiting area is filled with small children and decorated with pictures of bunnies. This fact has prompted some pediatricians to use a more neutral office decor and to schedule their adolescent patients at blocks of times identified as "teen" hours.

Compliance with a Treatment Regimen

There is now substantial evidence that at least one-third of patients do not comply with a recommended course of treatment. When this relates to prevention or necessitates sustained action, as with chronic illness, the compliance rate is only about 50%. Even with a 10-day antibiotic regimen for otitis media, between 40 to 80% of children do not receive the entire course. Studies of compliance with both medication and behavioral regimens (see Cromer & Tarnowski, 1989) indicate that adolescents are more likely to exhibit noncompliance than are younger children. However, noncompliance does not appear to be a simple linear function of age; investigations of college students have found them to be significantly more compliant than their younger peers. These findings have important implications for psychopharmacologic treatment of adolescents, since most regimens are unlikely to produce immediate perceptible benefit and many involve unpleasant side effects.

Compliance with a treatment regimen is in part related to the same factors as is compliance with appointments, although these are not perfectly correlated. Thus, intervention efforts have focused on clear communication and education, altering health-related beliefs, improving provider-patient interaction, and increasing environmental support. In addition, various aspects of the treatment regimen have been modified, or tailored to the individual patient, in attempts to improve compliance.

The most fundamental issue is to ensure that patients understand the purpose and details of the treatment regimen. Most important, patients must be able to recall what is expected of them after the visit. Ley (1972) has shown that approximately 50% of information given to patients is forgotten 15 minutes after leaving the physician. This suggests that, at a minimum, the provider should have a written set of instructions for the patient, which is reviewed and discussed with the patient during the visit, highlighting the key details.

Patient instructions should be assessed carefully for clarity and reading level. The U.S. Department of Health and Human Services (1989) has published a pamphlet providing guidelines for developing and pretesting patient materials. Providers who are unable to devote extensive time to devising patient materials should at least ask for an honest review by several different individuals. Even terms such as "evening" and "with meals" are open to varying interpretation. Other instructions are even more obscure. For example, the author's husband recently underwent cataract surgery in a world-renowned facility and received instructions that included the admonition "No sex involving straining." While providing entertainment during the recuperative process, such instructions are not likely to engender the desired behavior.

While a good start, ensuring that patients understand the regimen will not generally produce adequate compliance. This is particularly true when treatment is complex, inconvenient, expensive, chronic, or requires an altered lifestyle. In general, simplifying the regimen and/or tailoring it to the individual patient will improve compliance. When possible, treatment should be streamlined

by reducing the number of medications prescribed and the number of doses per day, and by administering different medications simultaneously. Similarly, the regimen should be as short as possible. Matching the regimen to the patient's daily activities will also minimize forgetfulness and enhance compliance. This is especially important when the regimen continues beyond symptomatic relief and there are no longer symptoms present to act as a reminder. Lima, Nazarian, Charney, and Lahti (1976) have reported improved compliance as a function of reminder stickers and a picture of a clock indicating when pills should be taken.

In long-term treatment, the expense can be reduced by prescribing generic drugs and/or encouraging shopping for the cheapest prescription rates. Following the introduction of a regimen, Maiman and Rodewald (1992) recommend scheduling follow-up visits in quick succession and telephoning patients after three or four days to assess progress with treatment. If the regimen requires major lifestyle changes, these should be introduced one at a time, reinforcing appropriate behavior and allowing it to stabilize before adding the next change.

With complex and extensive regimens, tailoring them to the individual patient and providing ongoing monitoring and support is time consuming. Physicians can enlist the efforts of other health care providers, such as nurses, physician assistants, psychologists, and pharmacists to provide additional assessment, clarification, and reinforcement. Short-term, focused groups can also assist patients and their families to solve problems and develop adaptive strategies. Peer counselors have been very useful in nonpsychiatric settings, because they provide a "coping" model of a peer with the same illness or disorder who struggled initially with the same fears and difficulties but was eventually able to manage the illness appropriately. Research on observational learning has shown that the greatest amount of fear reduction and adaptive behavior will result from the use of a coping model who is slightly older but of the same sex as the patient. This approach has not been used extensively in psychiatric settings but has potential benefit.

Greater physician knowledge of strategies to increase compliance can significantly improve patient outcome. Maiman, Becker, Liptak, and Nazarian (1988) provided pediatricians with written materials describing compliance-enhancing techniques; another group also participated in a five-hour tutorial for further discussion of these approaches. Mothers of children treated for otitis media by both groups of pediatricians were significantly more likely to administer the antibiotic regimen correctly and consistently than were mothers of children treated by control-group pediatricians.

The physician-patient relationship is clearly a key factor in compliance. Patient dissatisfaction and noncompliance is generally focused on lack of information, inability to understand the physician's responses to questions, impersonality, and lack of discussion regarding prevention. Improving communication, meeting expectations of the medical visit, and enhancing affective interaction (e.g., the patient feeling that the physician is friendly and understands the complaint) has improved compliance with treatment of otitis media and asthma. For long-term regimens, such as for juvenile diabetes or dialysis, physicians may find it useful to develop a written therapeutic contract that describes the treatment goal, the obligations of both physician and patient, and a time frame for assessing progress and evaluating the efficacy of treatment to that point. Such contracts formalize mutual expectations and clarify both short-term and long-term goals.

Attention to developmental issues is also a key element in compliance, particularly with a long-term regimen or one that impacts significantly on lifestyle. Children and many young adolescents are functioning cognitively at the level of concrete operations, limiting their ability to understand abstract concepts and the long-term consequences of health behavior. Young adolescents with chronic illnesses may enter adolescence with psychological or social delays if they have a history of poor school performance, parental overprotection, and difficulties with peers.

The onset of adolescence can substantially alter a child's attitudes and compliance with medical treatment. As teenagers work on the developmental task of individuation and separation from the family, they may resist the demands of a treatment regimen perceived to be imposed by parents and physicians. With the increased importance of the peer group, teenagers will be reluctant to appear different from their peers. This is most clearly a problem when the treatment regimen affects physical appearance (e.g., a Milwaukee brace), activities, or diet. However, just the idea of having to take medication, particularly during the day, can present challenges for the teenager who, for example, may be seen "taking drugs" or self-administering insulin injections.

Teenagers' compliance will be enhanced by encouraging them to assume progressively more responsibility for their health care as they proceed through adolescence. The teenager should be actively included in discussions of diagnosis and treatment and should participate in management decisions. Although family support is still important, the teenager in reality increasingly becomes the key player in management, which should be acknowledged explicitly. Rather than presenting treatment as physician or parental wishes, aspects of the treatment regimen can be presented as a series of "if-then" statements (e.g., if you want to be able to control your mood swings, then you will need to . . .).

Adolescents with chronic medical illnesses, such as diabetes, asthma, or kyphoscolios, present challenges for their primary care physicians as well as for mental health professionals who may be asked to work with them to improve their compliance with medical treatment. Particularly when the regimen is extensive and multifaceted, the provider should work with the patient to determine how treatment might be modified to maximize compliance and outcome. This entails examining each aspect of the regimen and clarifying which components are crucial and which are merely advisable. A series of "trade-offs" may enable a teenager to comply fully with vital elements of care while compromising on others that are not essential to good care but have important personal ramifications for the adolescent. For example, it may be socially or emotionally important for a diabetic teenager to frequent fast-food restaurants with her friends. Rather than insisting on rigid dietary adherence and inviting rejection of the entire nutritional regimen, it is advisable to assist her in identifying items she can order there that will not seriously violate her dietary requirements. In general, compliance is fostered by addressing teenagers' needs and concerns and allowing them as much control as possible.

Treating the adolescent patient is inevitably a time-consuming process. These are patients "in training," and they are thus not readily able to describe symptoms and concerns, raise questions, and solve problems. The physician who cares for teenagers must therefore routinely allow more time for their visits and be particularly alert to subtle expression of concerns or difficulties. It is helpful to normalize issues (e.g., "A lot of teenagers have been worried about . . . Have you had any thoughts about that?"), particularly when treatment may impact on body image, sexual development, or peer interaction.

Management of the adolescent is also complicated by the need to relate both to the teenager and to the parents. Whether the physician works primarily with the teenager or typically sees patient and parents together, it is important to define the ground rules to all concerned and to allow some opportunity to see the adolescent alone and the parents alone. The teenager's confidentiality should be protected, but it is also important to inform parents of their child's progress. In most states, adolescents have the right to obtain at least some forms of medical treatment without parental consent or knowledge. Nonetheless, generally

teenagers, especially young adolescents, are best served if their families are involved at some point in treatment. In any case, physicians should be clear about the limits of confidentiality. It may be useful to inform teenagers that there are also limits of confidentiality for adult patients. Management of complex, long-term regimens will be enhanced by enlisting appropriate family support. If family interactions are inadequate or destructive, family therapy would be indicated as part of comprehensive health care.

In summary, noncompliance with medical treatment is a multifaceted problem, representing an interaction of patient characteristics and beliefs, provider characteristics, aspects of the health facility, environmental obstacles, and aspects of the treatment regimen. Recommendations for improving compliance have addressed education, provider-patient interaction, facilitating access, modifying the treatment regimen, enlisting family support, and using other health care providers. Successful intervention is likely to require a multifactoral approach, combining several different strategies to promote compliance.

REFERENCES

Cromer, B. A., & Tarnowski, K. J. (1989). Noncompliance in adolescents: A review. *Journal of Developmental and Behavioral Pediatrics, 10,* 207–215.

Deyo, R. A., & Inui, T. S. (1980). Dropouts and broken appointments: A literature review and agenda for future research. *Medical Care, 18,* 1146–1157.

DuRant, R. H., Seymore, C., & Jay, M. S. (1991). Adolescents' compliance with therapeutic regimens. In W. R. Hendee (Ed.), *The health of adolescents* (pp. 468–494). San Francisco: Jossey-Bass.

Frankel, B. S., & Hovell, M. F. (1978). Health service appointment keeping: A behavioral view and critical review. *Behavioral Modification, 2,* 435–464.

Friedman, I. M., & Litt, I. F. (1987) Adolescents' compliance with therapeutic regimens. *Journal of Adolescent Health Care, 8,* 52–67.

Friedman, S. B., Fisher, M., & Schonberg, S. K. (Eds.). (In press). *Comprehensive adolescent health care* (2nd ed.). St. Louis: Mosby-Year Book.

Haynes, R. B., Taylor, D. W., & Sackett, D. L. (Eds.) (1979). *Compliance in health care.* Baltimore: Johns Hopkins University Press.

Ley, P. (1972). Primacy, rate importance, and the recall of medical statements. *Journal of Health and Social Behavior, 13,* 311–316.

Lima, J., Hazarian, L., Charney, E., & Lahti, C. (1976).

Compliance with short-term antimicrobial therapy: Some techniques that help. *Pediatrics, 57,* 383–386.

Maiman, L. A., Becker, M. H., Liptak, G. S., & Nazarian, L. F. (1988). Improving pediatricians' compliance-enhancing practices: A randomized trial. *American Journal of Diseases of Children, 142,* 773–779.

Maiman, L. A., & Rodewald, L. E. (1992). Compliance with pediatric health care recommendations. In R. A. Hoekelman, S. B. Friedman, N. M. Nelson, & H. M. Siedel (Eds.), *Primary pediatric care* (2nd ed., pp. 146–150). St. Louis; C. V. Mosby.

Phillips, S. (1992). Psychosocial intervention with adolescents. In S. B. Friedman, M. Fisher, S. K. Schonberg (Eds.), *Comprehensive adolescent health care.* St. Louis: Quality Medical Publishing.

Phillips, S., Sarles, R. M., Friedman, S. B., & Boggs, J. E. (In press). Consultation and referral for behavioral and developmental problems. In. R. A. Hoekelman, S. B. Friedman, N. Nelson, & H. M. Seidel (Eds.), *Primary pediatric care* (3rd ed.). St. Louis: Mosby-Year Book.

U.S. Department of Health and Human Services, Public Health Service. (1989). *Making health communication programs work: A planner's guide* (NIH Publication No. 89-1493). Bethesda, MD: National Institute of Health.

36 / Legal Issues: Legal Status of Adolescents

Richard A. Ratner

The legal status of what we now call adolescence has changed gradually but dramatically as society and its notions of childhood have changed. In the earliest civilizations, including the Hebrews and the Romans and extending through the 16th century in Europe, children as a class had little status. For the most part, parents were free to treat their children as they chose, with what laws that existed in this area forbidding children to harm their parents. Children were thought of as little adults with many of the responsibilities but none of the rights of adults.

As civilization developed, childhood was "discovered." Legal systems began to deal with the ways children differed from adults, including the degree to which they were responsible for their behavior and the degree to which both their parents and the state were responsible for them.

With the further evolution of society, it has become clear that children do not turn into adults overnight. We have discovered adolescence, a lengthy period of transition during which time the individual can be said to be neither a child nor an adult in every legal respect. A youth may be old enough to choose a parent in a custody dispute but not old enough to drive, drink, or bear full adult responsibility for a criminal act. Nor is age alone a guarantee that a youth has the capacity for reason; there is wide variation in the degree of maturity present in any given sample of 15-year-olds.

This fact has created problems for the law, which operates categorically: One is competent or not, guilty or not, of adult years or not. To cope with these matters, most modern societies have developed a juvenile court system separate from the adult courts. The history of the juvenile justice system reflects the tension between those who view adolescents more like children and those who would treat them more like adults.

Adolescents and their parents or guardians may become involved with the courts under at least three distinct circumstances. The first is when the juvenile is the perpetrator of a criminal act, such as rape, robbery, or murder. The second is when the juvenile becomes involved in behaviors that, while not criminal if committed by an adult, are grounds for the courts to assume supervision of the youngster. Examples of these "status offenses" include defiance of parents' rules, running way, or truancy. The third is when the teenager is suspected of being a victim of the behavior of his or her caregivers, as in cases of child abuse, neglect, and abandonment.

Although some of these examples involve youths as victims rather than perpetrators, all of these situations are handled by a juvenile court system that is separate and distinct from the adult courts. Since the end of the 1940s, every state has had in place such a separate court for dealing with young people. There is considerable variation from state to state with respect to the operation of these courts, including even their names. In Michigan, for example, juvenile matters are handled by the Probate Court, while in other states the courts may be named family courts or juvenile courts.

The Juvenile Court System

The appearance of a separate juvenile court system in this country is a relatively recent phenomenon, with the first court specifically for juveniles having been created by statute in Illinois in 1899. However, it represented the culmination of a movement that had its roots in the early years of the 19th century, when a wave of reform resulted in the creation, in 1825, of the New York House of Refuge, specifically to house youthful vagrants and offenders (Sacks & Reader, 1992).

The reformers were motivated by a belief that children were punished too cruelly and that the practice of housing young lawbreakers with older criminals would have a corrupting effect on the youths. The guiding philosophy was that education, religion, and hard work would rehabilitate these children, who often were seen as having been led astray by unfit parents.

The juvenile court system grew out of the efforts of the Child-Savers, a loosely termed group made up largely of middle-class women who recognized that the Houses of Refuge had degenerated into virtual prisons. The advent of juvenile courts was a triumph of the approach to juvenile crime they originated, which came to be known as the rehabilitative ideal. Historically it has been opposed by those who emphasize discipline and punishment (Margolis, 1988).

Implicit in the notion of rehabilitation was treatment, and the court clinic as an adjunct to the juvenile court was developed for this purpose. William Healy, M.D., established the nation's first such clinic in 1909. Healy's career brought him into contact with Sigmund Freud and into analysis with Franz Alexander. He collaborated with Alexander in the application of analytic techniques to delinquents.

The Child Guidance movement fostered the further development of treatment as an alternative to punishment. It was instrumental in applying an interdisciplinary model to the treatment of delinquents and their families. The first inpatient psychiatric units also were created as a result of this "marriage" of psychiatry and juvenile justice (Levine, Ewing, & Hager, 1987).

The traditional goal of the adult courts had always been deterrence through isolation and punishment. Because of the primacy of the rehabilitative ideal, however, juvenile courts operated in a very different way. For example, unlike adult courts, the proceedings of juvenile courts were confidential in order to protect the offender from the stigma of being labeled a criminal.

At the same time, the usual constitutional safeguards that protected adult defendants from the state in adult court did not exist in juvenile court. These included such "due process" safeguards (guaranteed by the 14th Amendment to the Constitution) as the rights to counsel, to confrontation and cross-examination of the accuser, and even to a transcript of the proceedings for purposes of appeal.

The rationale for a system that did not guarantee these rights was that the juvenile court did not exist to punish offenders; rather, its mission was to protect the child whose crime was viewed as evidence of his or her problems (Guyer, 1985). In this sense, the court existed as a manifestation not of the state's police powers but of its *parens patriae* function. The notion of *parens patriae*, derived from English common law, describes the state's (once the monarch's) prerogative to act as the guardian of those who are "disabled." One such "disability" is the lack of a mature understanding of one's criminal acts, which can be found in, among others, "infants, idiots and lunatics" (quoted in Quen, 1989).

By the 1960s there was widespread dissatisfaction with the system of juvenile justice. Juvenile delinquency was perceived to be on the rise as problems of drug abuse and juvenile gangs were ever more frequently reported. Adherents of a retributionist approach to juvenile justice pointed to judicial leniency as one cause.

Proponents of rehabilitation were also unhappy with the court system but for different reasons. They came to feel that the courts had too often abused their discretion in sentencing young people, resulting in excessive sentences to state schools. Worse yet, in a classic example of history repeating itself, the schools themselves had become virtual caricatures of the therapeutic institutions originally envisioned by reformers. Underfunding led to overcrowding and inadequate or absent treatment programs. Soon instances of abuse and cruelty on the part of untrained and indifferent caregivers began to surface. (Margolis, 1988; Silberman, 1978). Rather than oases for troubled youth, these schools became "finishing schools" that prepared them to embark on a life of crime.

In 1966, the case of Gerald Gault, which typified the kinds of abuses that had become too typical of the juvenile justice system, reached the Supreme court (*In re Gault,* 1967). Gault was a 15-year-old Arizona youth who was arrested and charged with making lewd telephone calls, convicted on the flimsiest of evidence, and sentenced to confinement in a state school for a maximum of 6 years. As an adult, the same crime would have resulted in a fine of $5 to $50 or imprisonment for not more than 2 months.

The Court concluded from its review in the *Gault* case and in a series of related seminal decisions that the juvenile courts as they then functioned, routinely, and often profoundly, violated the constitutional rights of young people in their charge. As the Court stated in *Kent v. U.S.* (1966), ". . . there must be grounds for concern that the child receives the worst of both worlds: that he gets neither the protection accorded to adults nor the solicitious care and rejuvenative treatment postulated for children" (p. 556).

As a result, the Court ushered in a new era in juvenile justice by granting an entire series of due process safeguards to youths in the juvenile court system. These provisions included, among others, the right to counsel, to notice of the charges, to a transcript of the proceedings, to confrontation and cross-examination, and to the right against self-incrimination. Other landmark cases granted juveniles the right to proof beyond reasonable doubt in order to be found guilty (*In re Winship*, 1970) and clarified the circumstances under which older juveniles could be "transferred" to the jurisdiction of an adult court (*Kent v. U.S.*, 1966). The Court stopped short, however, of extending the right of trial by jury to juveniles (*McKeiver v. Pennsylvania*, 1971).

In the 20 years following *Kent* and *Gault*, the trend to further due process protection in juvenile court has been joined by the movement toward deinstitutionalization, which was already in vogue with respect to adult mental hospitals. The Juvenile Justice and Delinquency Prevention Act of 1974 established the Office of Juvenile Justice and Delinquency Prevention, which granted funds to states to encourage deinstitutionalization and preventive approaches.

Mental health professionals applauded many of these changes but were troubled by others. Because state schools and other public institutions had been largely ineffective in the rehabilitation of youthful offenders, many advocates for youth came to believe that rehabilitation itself "did not work." This became a rationale for those who valued punishment over rehabilitation to advocate a get-tough approach that coincided with the ascendancy of a politically conservative presidency.

Over the past 5 years, advocates of society's more punitive impulses have gained ground on supporters of the rehabilitative model in the arena of public policy, and nowhere is this better illustrated than in recent changes in the states' approach to transferring minors to adult court. While the *Kent* case made it clear that a juvenile could not be transferred without a hearing that would consider the pros and cons of such a decision (with amenability to treatment constituting a very significant reason to keep the minor in juvenile court), states began to circumvent such hearings by legislating different methods of transfer. Chief among these are "automatic" transfers based on the seriousness of the crime and the age of the juvenile and transfers made at prosecutorial discretion—where it is up to the prosecutor rather than the courts to decide in which court, juvenile or adult, the accused should be tried.

The effect of these changes will be to send more juveniles accused of committing the most serious crimes to adult court, where the adversarial system holds complete sway and where the range of penalties may include (in certain states) death. In these cases the offender's rehabilitative potential will have a limited effect on the court's decisions, and the opportunities for treatment that still exist in the juvenile court will be unavailable.

Sensational crimes in which younger and younger juveniles commit ever more vicious acts have done their part to sour the public on the value of the juvenile court. Many prosecutors view treatment as simply a means of escaping incarceration and of doubtful efficacy. Defense counsel for their part have long been soured on the ability of the juvenile court system to deliver on its promises of treatment and rehabilitation. As a result, they often concentrate their efforts on extricating their clients from any form of structure and supervision. This leaves the juvenile court judge, charged with final responsibility for the disposition of his or her cases, as potentially the only person who approaches each case with a mind open to the recommendations of mental health workers.

The psychiatrist appearing as an expert witness will discover that the climate of juvenile court today is more adversarial and more cynical than in years past (Ratner & Nye, 1992). These changes result from the cumulative effects on the courts over the past 30 years of the trends noted earlier. However, it can be argued that precisely for these reasons, psychiatric input in juvenile court is more important than ever before.

The Juvenile Court: Structure and Function

While there is a certain similarity of juvenile court procedure to the processes of adult court, the unique nature of this court makes each stage different in important respects. The process can be divided into three general stages: intake, adjudication, and disposition; these correspond roughly to pretrial procedures, trial, and sentencing in adult court.

The intake phase of a delinquency hearing is handled by specially trained probation officers or social workers. Factfinding occurs during intake, and a decision is made either to dismiss the case (if probable cause that the crime was committed by the youth cannot be demonstrated) or to move it forward.

If a juvenile is willing to admit responsibility for the act with which he or she is charged, he or she may be a candidate for diversion, a process by which the case is shunted away from the court if the youth agrees to such provisions as making restitution, seeking counseling, or donating time to community service.

If the young person denies the crime or if it is a serious crime involving violence for which diversion is not available, the court proceeds formally toward adjudication.

Once formal proceedings before a judge are begun, the suspected perpetrator must be represented by counsel. The courts are obligated to provide an attorney if the youth is indigent and cannot afford one. Should the youth admit to the crime, a lengthy hearing aimed toward ascertaining guilt or innocence is unnecessary, and the case proceeds to the phase of disposition. However, if the youth denies responsibility, a date for the adjudicatory hearing, analogous to a trial in adult court, is set.

Unlike adult court, guilt or innocence is determined by a judge rather than a jury. To protect the confidentiality of the juvenile, the juvenile court is closed to spectators, and the records are not public. On the other hand, the hearing unfolds similarly to an adult trial in the sense that both prosecution and defense present their cases via examination and cross-examination of witnesses and closing statements. For a finding of delin-

quency, the judge must use the same standard of proof, beyond a reasonable doubt, as in adult court.

The terminology of the juvenile court differs from that of adult court and continues to reflect its rehabilitative mission. Thus, the term "adjudicated delinquent" is used rather than a finding of "guilty," and rather than the term "sentencing," which implies punishment, the term "disposition" is used.

The juvenile court's mission is to rehabilitate youths rather than simply punish them. Disposition is the core of this function. Often the attorneys involved pay more attention to this phase of the case than to others, because it may be crucial to the future of the adjudicated delinquent.

Disposition, like adjudication, is a judicial decision. Possible dispositions run the gamut from probation, to confinement in a youth correctional institution, to placement in a residential treatment center or group home.

Should a youth be felt to be suffering from a mental disorder or defect, the court may place him or her in a psychiatric hospital for further evaluation and treatment. In some states, the juvenile court judge has the authority to require that parents as well as their children enter into family treatment programs if it is felt that these will alleviate the underlying difficulties.

Under certain circumstances, adolescents, typically age 15 or older, who are believed to have committed crimes may be turned over to the adult court for trial. This process, variously known as "waiver," "transfer," or "bindover," results in the youth's becoming an adult defendant. By so doing he or she loses the protection of the juvenile court, including confidentiality and sealed records and, if convicted, is exposed to the full gamut of adult sentencing.

Age at the time of the offense and the seriousness of the crime together establish "eligibility" for waiver. Typically, a hearing must then be held to determine whether probable cause exists to believe the youth is guilty. Should such a finding be made, a further hearing, known as a transfer hearing, is scheduled. At this time the judge considers a variety of factors in making a decision. Most of these relate to the overall issue of the youth's amenability to treatment and rehabilitation.

Ironically, juveniles are sometimes treated

more leniently in adult court, where they are first offenders, than in juvenile court, where they are often recidivists. On the other hand, when the crime is vicious and outrageous enough, transfer to adult court may open up the potential for capital punishment in states that have a death penalty.

Capital Punishment

At this writing, the Supreme Court has refused to rule the death penalty unconstitutional for offenders who are at least 16 years old at the time of their crimes (*Wilkins v. Missouri, Stanford v. Kentucky*), although in an earlier decision (*Thompson v. Oklahoma*) it prevented the execution of a teenager who was 15 at the time of his crime. To be sure, youthful offenders in adult court are entitled to the same procedural guarantees as adults when capital punishment is being considered. However, most advocates for youth are opposed to capital punishment for teenagers, on the grounds that they are still developing emotionally and are always candidates for rehabilitation. The American Society for Adolescent Psychiatry has taken this position on numerous occasions since 1987, when its amicus curiae brief was entered in the Supreme Court case of *Thompson v. Oklahoma*.

Varieties of Involvement of Adolescents with the Juvenile Court

JUVENILE DELINQUENCY

A delinquent act is an ordinary criminal act that is committed by a minor. Traditionally, society has treated such youth differently from adult felons, who, if found guilty, are punished for their acts. The basis for the difference is that adults are considered to be responsible for their actions, while young perpetrators are as a class viewed as disabled, and as such they are considered to require the protection of the state via its *parens patriae* function (Quen, 1989) rather than punishment. The "disability" lies in the young person's theoreti-

cal lack of the capacity to think and behave in a mature fashion.

Legally, to be adjudicated delinquent is not to be found guilty. Rather, it is an alternative to a finding of guilt, which can take place only if the defendant is felt to be fully responsible for the crimes. Juvenile status means as a matter of law that the offender is not held to be fully responsible for his or her actions.

The age of majority for these purposes is set by the states. Typically it is 18, but the juvenile court often can maintain jurisdiction until the offender reaches the age of 21.

Once arrested, a youth may be detained for a variable period of time until trial. In most jurisdictions, a detention hearing must be held within a certain time period to determine if detention should be continued. At this hearing, the court must be convinced of the following (singly or together) if it wishes to continue holding the detainee: first, that a crime has been committed; second, that there is probable cause to believe that the detainee committed it; and third, that if not held the youth will either be in imminent danger or will pose a danger to others or will flee the jurisdiction.

Preventive detention is the practice of detaining an individual before trial because it is anticipated that he or she will commit further crimes in the interim. The constitutionality of preventive detention for juveniles was upheld in the 1984 Supreme Court decision *Schall v. Martin*.

Fundamental to our legal system is the notion that an individual must be competent for trial before the trial can occur. Competency means that an individual possesses the requisite mental state to make sensible decisions on his or her own behalf with the assistance of an attorney. To try an incompetent individual would be no different under the law from trying a comatose or an absent person.

Juvenile courts generally follow the criteria for competency used in adult courts as set out in the Supreme Court decision in *Dusky v. United States* (1960): that the individual possesses a rational and factual grasp of the charges and proceedings against him or her and that he or she is able to cooperate with counsel with a reasonable degree of rational understanding. While a serious mental illness or a significant degree of mental retardation is the usual basis for a finding of incompetence, the mere existence of mental illness is not sufficient for such a finding.

When the issue of mental competency is raised, the court often requires the testimony of psychiatrists. In many jurisdictions, a finding of incompetency by the court leads to dismissal of the charges; in others, it results in referral for treatment and return to court when competency is restored.

In adult court, a defendant may be acquitted of guilt by reason of insanity if he or she suffered from a mental disease or defect at the time of the crime that impaired his or her capacity to act purposefully (criminal intent). If the defendant lacked criminal intent—that is, he or she did not knowingly and deliberately act criminally, then he or she cannot be held responsible for the crime.

In the relatively rare circumstances that an insanity defense is mounted in juvenile court (Harrington & Keary, 1980), psychiatric expertise may be called on to determine the individual's mental state at the time of the crime.

STATUS OFFENDERS

Many youths come to the attention of the juvenile courts because of such acts as running away, truancy, or simply being unmanageable by their parents. Because these behaviors would not be crimes if committed by adults and because it is their state of "being" that brings them before the court, such youths are referred to as status offenders. In different states these young people are variously known as persons in need of supervision (PINS), children in need of supervision (CHINS), and juveniles in need of supervision (JINS) as well as "wayward" children or "incorrigibles."

Many jurisdictions attempt to separate the handling of such offenders from that of delinquents, who are considered to be more seriously impaired. Under the influence of the proponents of deinstitutionalization, some states have removed status offenders from the jurisdiction of the juvenile court altogether (Sacks & Sacks, 1980). In these cases, placement in a secure (locked) setting is not an option, and participation in any form of treatment is often voluntary. The inability of the legal system to do anything about the youngster's out-of-control behavior is a frequent source of therapeutic frustration for parents and the professionals they consult.

Other states fall along a spectrum in their handling of these cases, with the extreme being a primarily "deterrence" model in which status offenders are handled very similarly to delinquents: detention and secure settings are important dispositions.

THE ABUSED AND NEGLECTED ADOLESCENT

A distinction is usually made between "abuse" on the one hand and "neglect" or "maltreatment" on the other. Abuse usually is defined as harm inflicted on the young person by a caregiver. Physical injury and sexual intercourse or molestation are nearly always specified, and in many states psychological abuse is considered, as well.

Neglect refers not to actions but to the inactions of caregivers that may jeopardize the health or safety of their children. Examples include not providing for such basic needs as food, clothing, shelter, and medical care and abandonment of the child for periods of time. In some states, parental behavior that is "immoral," such as substance abuse or criminal behavior, may qualify as "neglect."

Professionals such as physicians and teachers are required by law to report suspected abuse or neglect. Once such a report is made—to Child Protective Services or the police—an investigation is initiated. As in the intake phase of delinquency adjudication, the investigating agency must make a choice either to handle the situation informally by referring the parents or the family as a whole for training, education, or treatment or to petition the court for a hearing. In the latter case, a hearing to determine whether the child is abused or neglected will be scheduled at which both the youth and the parents or other caregivers are typically represented by attorneys.

If such a finding is made, depending on the severity of the situation, the child may be removed temporarily from parental custody and made a ward of the court or of the commissioner of Social Services, while the parents may be required to engage in education and treatment. In extreme cases, the court may preside over a hearing that results in the termination of parental rights.

Termination refers to the permanent dissolution of the parent-child relationship; the parents are no longer considered legally related to the child, and accordingly no longer have any responsibility for him or her. Typically it is a "voluntary" procedure in which parents surrender the young person to a state agency that oversees placement in a foster home or adoption. It results from compelling evidence of unfitness, neglect, harm to the child, or abandonment by the parents.

THE EMANCIPATED ADOLESCENT

Emancipation is defined as a situation in which a minor, usually under the age of 18, is

released from some or all of the disabilities of childhood and receive[s] the rights and duties of adulthood. Emancipation also may release parents from their rights and duties, including the right to the custody and control of their child; the right to receive the child's earnings; and the duty to support, maintain, protect, and educate their child. (Guggenheim & Sussman, 1985, p. 190)

Emancipation differs from termination of parental rights in that it does not result in a legal dissolution of the parental relationship. And, unlike termination, it is typically initiated by the parents themselves in order to redefine the pattern of their obligations toward their child. Marriage or service in the armed forces usually results in an "automatic" emancipation, as does the mere fact of attaining one's majority. "Partial" emancipations may occur with respect to certain rules and regulations ordinarily imposed by the parents for various time periods during a child's minority. Most emancipation takes place informally without the involvement of a court.

Emancipation by court order can take place, as can termination of parental rights, based on outrageous treatment by parents of their children. Typically, however, children must be older adolescents, 16 or older, for emancipation to be an option. A younger teenager, unable to function on his or her own, is more likely to be a candidate for termination, assuming that the parents cannot provide the minimum necessary safety and protection to which every child is entitled.

CONSENT TO TREATMENT AND CONFIDENTIALITY

One important issue for clinicians concerns whether a minor has the right to consent to his or her own medical care. In the case of emancipated minors, the answer is usually yes, although in the case of other young people, the consent of the parents traditionally has been required. There are many exceptions to this rule, however, that depend on such factors as the nature and severity of the medical condition and, in some states, whether a child may qualify as a mature minor.

If a condition is a medical emergency, a young person generally may be treated without parental consent. Such a finding does not require the threat of imminent death, but only that a delay in treatment will endanger a child's health or that treatment is necessary to ameliorate pain. In the case of psychiatric treatment, it is possible to interpret this requirement fairly broadly; however, in practice it is rare that treatment is continued beyond an initial few sessions without involving parents, for clinical reasons as well as the fact that parents usually are responsible for paying for treatment. This kind of situation is most likely to arise in clinics, especially in school-based settings, where teenagers are encouraged to seek help on their own.

Many states allow treatment of mature minors without parental consent. This status may be defined by age or by mental capacity to understand and appreciate the nature of the intervention and its possible consequences. Physicians are not required to treat mature minors without parental consent unless a medical emergency exists, but one who does would be well advised to document carefully both the basis for his or her medical judgement and the process by which consent is gained.

The decade of the 1980s saw a gradual shift toward allowing minors to be treated without parental consent for a variety of conditions. For example, drug and alcohol treatment, prenatal care, and treatment for venereal disease may all be provided without parental consent.

With respect to birth control, nonprescription contraceptives are available to anyone who can pay for them, regardless of age. Prescription birth control products may be provided without parental consent under circumstances that differ in different states. Whether minors have the right to obtain prescription birth control devices without parental consent remains in litigation in various jurisdictions.

Abortion is generally permitted without parental consent, although details differ by jurisdiction, and recent years have seen a trend toward requiring at least parental notification, if not consent. Parents, on the other hand, do not have the right to force a pregnant daughter to have an abortion, and the law allows a pregnant minor female access to prenatal care regardless of whether the parents approve of continuing the pregnancy.

Confidentiality of medical treatment for minors remains a medical standard but is subject to both the same limitations placed on confidentiality of treatment for adults and to certain limiting factors unique to the patient's status as a minor. In the former category, the presence of venereal disease must be reported, as must (more pertinently for

psychiatrists) allegations of physical or sexual abuse.

In the latter category, states differ in terms of what circumstances, if any, require a treating physician to give notice to parents or guardians regarding the treatment. Some states leave it to the discretion of the physician but only if he or she feels that notice is important to protect the health of the young person. Some states require notice to the parents of an immature and unemancipated minor who has chosen to undergo an abortion, but in general the principle of confidentiality outweighs any obligation to report to parents.

REFERENCES

Dusky v. United States. 362 U.S. 402 (1960).

Guggenheim, M., & Sussman, A. (1985). *The rights of young people.* New York: Bantam Books.

Guyer, M. J. (1985). Commentary: The juvenile justice system. In D. Schetky & E. Benedek (Eds.), *Emerging issues in child psychiatry and the law* (pp. 159–179). New York: Brunner/Mazel.

Harrington, M. M., & Keary, A. (1980). The insanity defense in juvenile delinquency proceedings. *Bulletin of the American Academy of Psychiatry and the Law, 8* (3), 272–279.

In re Gault. 387 U.S. 1 (1967).

In re Winship. 397 U.S. 358 (1970).

Kent v. United States. 383 U.S. 541 (1966).

Levine, M., Ewing, C. P., & Hager, R. (1987). Juvenile and family mental health law in sociohistorical context. *International Journal of Law & Psychiatry, 10,* 91–111.

Margolis, R. J. (1988). *Out of harm's way: The emancipation of juvenile justice.* New York: The Edna McConnell Clark Foundation.

McKeiver v. Pennsylvania. 403 U.S. 528 (1971).

Quen, J. (1989). The historical challenge of juvenile criminality. In R. Rosner & H. Schwartz (Eds.), *Juvenile psychiatry and the law* (pp. 3–13). New York: Plenum Press.

Ratner, R., & Nye, S. (1992). Court testimony: The psychiatrist as witness. In M. Kalogerakis (Ed.), *Handbook of psychiatric practice in the juvenile justice system.* Washington, DC: American Psychiatric Press.

Sacks, H., & Reader, W. D. (1992). *History of the juvenile court.* In M. Kalogerakis (Ed.), *Handbook of psychiatric practice in the juvenile justice system.* Washington, DC: American psychiatric Press.

Sacks, H. S., & Sacks, H. L. (1980). Status offenders: Emerging issues and new approaches. In D. Schetky & E. Benedek (Eds.), *Child psychiatry and the law* (pp. 156–194). New York: Brunner/Mazel.

Schall v. Martin. 467 U.S. 253 (1984).

Silberman, C. E. (1978). *Criminal violence, criminal justice.* New York: Random House.

Stanford v. Kentucky. 109 S. Ct. 2969 (1989).

Thompson v. Oklahoma. 108 S. Ct. 2687 (1988).

Wilkins v. Missouri. 109 S. Ct. 2969 (1989).

37 / Psychiatric Hospitalization of Adolescents

Marc Amaya and W. V. Burlingame

The Historical Context and Legal Landmarks

The creation of inpatient psychiatric units specifically designed for children and adolescents was a natural outgrowth of the child welfare movement that characterized the United States during the first half of the 20th century. The mental health professionals who staffed these pioneering units recognized the sometimes deleterious effects of housing child or adolescent patients with adults and therefore separated their youthful psychiatric patients from them. They also brought a developmental perspective to their understanding of child and adolescent psychopathology. When these first child and adolescent psychiatric units were established in the 1940s and 1950s, little consideration was given to who might legally consent for the treatment provided. In those years minors had few rights as "persons" under the law; parents or guardians were solely responsible for making critical decisions such as those related to hospitalization. In addition, little distinction was made in the law between hospitalization for medical reasons (such as surgery) and hospitalization for psychiatric treatment.

Two U.S. Supreme Court decisions changed the legal landscape dramatically. In the first of these (*In re Gault*, 1967), the Court reversed decades of casual attention to the procedural and due process rights of minors. This indifference had resulted from the presumption that the then-current editions of juvenile justice, with their unrestrained judicial discretion and procedural laxity, did in fact operate "in the best interests of the child." Gerald Gault was a 15-year-old Arizona boy who was charged and found guilty of having

made obscene telephone calls to a neighbor. He was sentenced to a state correctional facility for the remainder of his minority (6 years). The same crime would have netted no more than 60 days in jail or a fine of $50 if committed by an adult in that state. The Supreme Court ultimately held that Gault's constitutional rights (and those of all other minors who were similarly incarcerated) had been violated. The Court ruled that Arizona had failed to provide Gault with proper notice of charges against him, had neglected his right to counsel, had not given him the right to examine witnesses, and had failed to provide him with an avenue for appellate review. Justice Abe Fortas, writing for the majority, observed that for minors facing incarceration, "It would be extraordinary if our Constitution did not require the procedural regularity and the exercise of care implied in the phrase 'due process.'" He added that "The condition of being a boy does not justify a kangaroo court" (*In re Gault*, 1967, pp. 27–28). Although the constitutional issue had arisen in a different domain (juvenile justice), the *Gault* decision subsequently was cited in several cases in which the authority of parents and guardians to consent to the admission and treatment of their minor children in psychiatric facilities was challenged. The contention advanced was that a minor child's loss of liberty when placed in an institution such as a psychiatric hospital was effectively the same as the loss of liberty that occurred in the juvenile correctional system; therefore, minor children faced with possible admission to a psychiatric facility should be provided with the due process protections afforded by *Gault*.

During the 1970s two cases—one from Georgia and the other from Pennsylvania—ascended through the federal judiciary and culminated in *Parham v. J.R.* (1979). The alleged abuses cited in *Parham* were familiar; the plaintiffs argued that (1) parents did not always act in the best interests of their children; (2) the term of institutional placement could be and often was indefinite when a state agency acted as a child's guardian (due to

The authors wish to acknowledge the kind and informed assistance provided in the preparation of this manuscript by their colleague Paul M. Brinich, Ph.D., director of Psychological Services at Children's Psychiatric Institute of John Umstead Hospital, Butner, North Carolina.

the lack of a family placement); (3) decisions made by institutional admissions personnel could be biased or otherwise in error; and (4) the event of psychiatric hospitalization was itself traumatic and created social stigmata. The remedy proposed by the plaintiffs in *Parham* was to mandate judicial review of all psychiatric admissions of minor children. However, in a stunning and controversial decision, the Burger Court reversed previous lower court decisions and held that, while states were *free* to require the protections afforded by due process, there was no constitutional basis for *requiring* judicial review of decisions by parents or guardians who seek psychiatric hospitalization of their minor children. Chief Justice Warren Burger wrote, "Although we acknowledge the fallibility of medical and psychiatric diagnosis, we do not accept the notion that shortcomings of specialists can always be avoided by shifting the decision . . . to an untrained judge" (*Parham v. J.R.*, 1979, p. 2508). The Court then proceeded to require, as a constitutional floor, the involvement of a "neutral factfinder" in determining psychiatric admission of minors: "We conclude that the risk of error inherent in the parental decision to have a child institutionalized for mental health care is sufficiently great that some kind of inquiry should be made by a 'neutral factfinder' to determine whether the statutory requirements for admission are satisfied" (*Parham v. J.R.*, 1979, p. 2506). In practice, this "neutral factfinder" is, in most instances, the admissions officer or attending psychiatrist.

Although various observers have accused the Court of ambivalence and inconsistency regarding the rights of children, in the 15 years since the *Parham* decision there have been few serious challenges to parental authority in this matter when it is supported by professional judgment. The exceptions have occurred in those states where additional due process protections were already in place prior to *Parham* or where some basis of right was found under the particular state's constitution (as in California). At present it seems likely that the conservative shift in the Court, reflected in the different relative weights assigned to child and parental rights in *Gault* and in *Parham*, will be maintained during the 1990s. Lower courts appear unlikely to take up the cause of the "reluctant volunteer" (i.e., minor children admitted "voluntarily" by parents over the children's objections).

In some ways this particular issue has been muted by the fact that pressures of health care funding and "managed care" have dramatically reduced lengths of stay in many child and adolescent inpatient psychiatric facilities, thus creating a formidable series of obstacles to the use of this form of treatment. Meanwhile, attention has shifted to a variety of other issues related to the hospitalization of children and adolescents.

Issues of Consent

TYPES OF VOLUNTARY ADMISSION OF MINOR CHILDREN

Given that the constitutional standard for psychiatric admission requires only the concurrence of a "neutral fact finder" and that matters are otherwise left entirely to the states, four distinct types or models for voluntary admission of minors are now visible, as well as numerous hybrids and variants of these entities. They include the traditional model, shared authority, judicial review, and administrative or clinical review.

The Traditional Model: The traditional model for the voluntary admission of a minor child to a psychiatric facility is one in which a parent or guardian unilaterally consents for such treatment. This model is prevalent in roughly one-third to one-half of the states; the main variations that appear involve age specifications. For example, in Idaho parents may consent for the admission of their children until the age of 18 years. In contrast, South Carolina allows 16- and 17-year-olds to consent to their own admissions and discharges. The traditional model, with its inherent paternalism (insofar as it vests all authority in parents and mental health professionals), is most likely to trigger the resentment and oppositionalism of authority-sensitive adolescents. On the other hand, it is also the model that affords most protection to the treatment process. This protection is a significant feature when attempting to treat conduct-disordered and other oppositional youth, particularly when the admission can be enforced by the courts and law enforcement personnel.

Shared Authority: The shared authority model of voluntary admission is one in which the authority to consent to psychiatric hospitalization is shared between parents and their adolescent children. The virtue of this approach is that minors and their parents must agree regarding the decision to seek psychiatric hospitalization; under the best of circumstances, they enter that treatment with an initial alliance that may not be present in the traditional model. The model is attractive to those who are sensitive to the developmental issues of adolescence and who see the sharing of authority as a way of building an alliance between a minor child and his or her parents. The disadvantage of this model lies in the fact that one party can refuse consent and thus block critically necessary inpatient psychiatric treatment. In New Mexico, for example, children younger than 12 years must cosign admissions documents while older youths admit themselves. In approximately a dozen other states some form of dual consent is required. It remains to be seen how this model affects the *efficacy* of treatment, although some researchers have undertaken a systematic examination of the competency of youths to make informed decisions regarding their own treatment (Weithorn & Campbell, 1982). It also remains to be seen whether the United Nations Convention on the Rights of the Child (1991), which has stressed self-determination and the participation of youths in decisions affecting their welfare, will have implications for American children who have been referred for psychiatric hospitalization. Investigations of the courses of those youths who refuse to consent to treatment would be of great interest and relevance.

Judicial Review: The third model of voluntary admission of minor children is one in which courts are assigned statutory responsibility to review such admissions. This was the method sought by the plaintiffs in *Parham*; it was to be left to judges to determine whether statutory criteria for hospitalization had been met in individual cases. Judicial review currently exists in its purest form in North Carolina. There a district court must review every psychiatric admission of a minor within 10 days of the date of admission. While parents (or guardians), together with appropriate mental health professionals, can authorize a minor child's initial admission, the district court must concur with this decision. The court reviews the relevant evidence and considers statutory criteria in a hearing in which the minor, represented by counsel, may contest his or her admission. If the court ratifies

the admission, the minor patient may then contest his or her hospitalization at specified intervals. Other states have less exacting procedures; judicial review may be required, for example, only if the minor child objects to the admission. Judicial review has two principal advantages: It may protect the child and the hospital from an unjustified admission, and it purports to convey a sense of justice through its process. Unfortunately, it also may create considerable turmoil, uncertainty, and even trauma for a variety of parties, as Amaya and Burlingame (1981) have described.

Administrative or Clinical Review: Administrative or clinical review attempts to impose checks and balances on parental and professional authority by requiring that independent mental health administrators and professionals review the psychiatric hospitalizations of minor children. A number of states have experimented with these methods, hoping to substitute independent clinical judgment for those of judges who, as cited in *Parham*, usually are untrained in matters of mental health and illness. Another sometimes explicit goal of administrative review is the considered allocation of access to scarce resources. This model may require extensive collaboration between local community mental health personnel and the staff of youth services units within regional psychiatric hospitals. A "single portal of entry" may be defined, and it becomes the responsibility of the portal-of-entry reviewer to decide how to use available resources. Such a process has little or nothing to do with a parent's or minor's right to consent or to withhold consent; it is, however, a very real aspect of the model, an aspect that may facilitate a continuum of care and may operate to enhance the most efficient use of existing resources.

These four models are obviously not mutually exclusive. Enormous diversity exists and no force operates to bring about national uniformity. At present there is also no consensus regarding the balance that should be struck among these various models of voluntary psychiatric admission of minors and between the potentially conflicting interests of parents and children. Statutory provisions continue to evolve in response to local pressures and needs. While several states created due process protections following *Gault*, the *Parham* decision brought most efforts to expand judicial review to a halt. Readers who wish for a more detailed discussion of these issues and the various ways in which states have dealt with this problem are referred to Weithorn (1988), to Burlingame and Amaya (1985), and to a practitioner-oriented discussion of issues regarding the psychiatric hospitalization of minors (Burlingame & Amaya, 1992).

Before concluding this section on the voluntary admission of minors, it must be acknowledged that the decision to seek psychiatric hospitalization for a child is no longer confined to the child, his or her parents, mental health professionals, judges, and agency administrators. Third-party payers (whether a health insurance company, a managed care entity, a health maintenance organization, Medicaid, or other source of reimbursement) are taking a very active part in the admission procedure. While these payers have little *legal* standing (in that they cannot prevent a child from entering or force a child to leave a hospital), they are able and willing to veto reimbursement for hospital services. In all probability, this will remain as the most difficult issue in child and adolescent inpatient psychiatric practice during the 1990s. Legislation and case law that define the responsibility and accountability of a third-party payer when that payer prohibits reimbursement for psychiatric services is only beginning to emerge. Worth mentioning, however, is that there have been a number of enormous settlements and judgments against attending physicians and hospitals when harm befell a patient who was discharged prematurely because insurance benefits had expired. At this writing, even if services have been requested by a minor child and his or her parents, even if they have been deemed appropriate by a licensed mental health professional, and even if they have survived judicial and administrative review, a third-party payer may still refuse to reimburse for them.

OTHER FORMS OF COMMITMENT

In addition to the voluntary admission of minors, all states provide for involuntary hospitalization by civil commitment. This procedure, which in most states applies to children and adolescents as well as to adults, permits physicians and psychologists to commit persons to psychiatric facilities, subject to judicial review. The criteria for involuntary commitment are set out in statute and

have been the subject of several Supreme Court decisions. The overarching standard is dangerousness to self or others. Beyond that, state statutes vary in their specificity regarding criterion behaviors, recency of the behaviors, and dangerousness of the behaviors (to self, others, or property). In practice, the statutory criteria for voluntary admissions (e.g., the presence of a psychiatric condition warranting inpatient treatment) are always less stringent than the dangerousness standard. As a result, child advocates who seek to enlarge the liberty interests of adolescents first propose a single standard of dangerousness for the involuntary commitment of both minors and adults; they further propose that *all* other admissions require the consent of the patient; whether child or adult. Were these proposals to be enacted nationally, the result would be a very significant reduction in the number of psychiatric beds occupied by minors. On the one hand, many psychiatrically troubled minors would fail to meet dangerousness criteria; on the other hand, these same minors often would refuse to consent to their hospitalization.

Aside from the issues of voluntary and involuntary *inpatient* admissions, a number of states have also experimented with *outpatient* commitments. Outpatient commitment provides a mechanism by which mental health professionals may use the police power of the state to secure and to impose treatment that is less intrusive and less expensive than inpatient hospitalization. It also provides a means of enforcing treatment compliance, particularly with medication, in order to prevent decompensation and readmission. This procedure has been employed with adults and minors alike; if and when a patient fails to comply with outpatient procedures, the outpatient commitment facilitates the patient's return to the hospital as an inpatient.

OTHER ISSUES RELATED TO CONSENT

Historically, a single "blanket" consent for treatment was considered sufficient for "voluntary" admission; in the case of minors, this was executed by the parent or guardian. For the involuntarily committed patient, child or adult, such a consent was considered redundant inasmuch as the court had essentially removed that person's right to consent. Certain other classes of patients were considered "incompetent" and had guardians appointed or had the institution assume the role of de facto guardian. However, in an increasingly consumer-oriented society in which litigious remedies are pursued by patients who may have been harmed by clinicians, the blanket consent has given way to the doctrine of informed consent. Informed consent requires that permission be secured for specific interventions or activities that are thought to incur risk. Informed consent, which often entails a detailed explanation of the benefits and risks of specific interventions or activities, may now be sought for the following: the administration of neuroleptic medication or any psychoactive medication; the provision of sex education and condoms to hospitalized minors; screening for HIV; seclusion and restraint; deprivation of patients' rights, which are identified in statute or by policy; any release of otherwise confidential information; audio and videotaping; surgical interventions; electroshock; certain recreational or therapeutic activities (e.g., use of tools or bicycles, hiking, or weight-lifting, particularly when the patients involved are medicated, suffer from seizure disorders, or have a history of self-injury); visits by outside parties; attendance at external Alcoholics or Narcotics Anonymous meetings; and participation in any research that involves activity beyond the retrospective analysis of chart data. (This list is only partial and illustrative and does not encompass all the possibilities and actualities.)

Aside from the risk/benefit discussion, informed consent is oftentimes limited and is typically documented on a facility form in which a staff member witnesses the giving of consent and indicates that the required information was transmitted. Although such documentation demonstrates that consent has been secured and that information has been provided, it does not, of course, mitigate negligence or the provision of a less than acceptable standard of care. States and treatment facilities vary considerably in the extent to which they secure informed consent for the matters just listed. For example, decisions to seclude or restrain a patient, or to deprive him or her of specific rights (such as visitation), are not typically matters of parental consent; parents often are asked, however, if they wish to be notified should such actions be taken.

Traditionally, the person holding the right to consent to admission is the one who would also consent to the use of any procedures that put a patient at risk. However, as shared authority has blurred the issue of consent, many clinicians and facilities now attempt to secure consent from both the parent or guardian and the minor patient. Even when the legal authority to consent is clearly and exclusively invested in parents, some clinicians and facilities also seek "assent" (often signed assent) from minor patients and provide them with a great deal of information about the risks and benefits associated with a particular procedure or activity. Clinicians and facilities that do so are mindful that minors, upon achieving majority, may sue for perceived wrongful treatment. When there is a disagreement about appropriate treatment between a facility's professional staff and the patient or parent, the facility may use these informed consent procedures to highlight the areas of disagreement and to document why alternative measures will be inadequate. When a facility is empowered or chooses to implement treatment without further patient or parent permission, and the parent comes to object to that treatment, the recourse of the parent is to remove the child from the hospital. This may in turn leave the parent vulnerable to charges of medical neglect and then to interventions by social services personnel. Most treatment facilities, as well as most state departments of mental health that operate public sector hospitals, have developed elaborate protocols for the utilization of treatment modalities that put patients at risk, for securing consent to or giving notice of their administration, and for the administration of treatment against a minor patient's wishes. Practitioners will want to be aware of these protocols and should adhere to them scrupulously.

CONFIDENTIALITY

Mental health professionals have a responsibility, usually embodied in statute, to maintain the privacy of their patients. This means that mental health professionals may not disclose information obtained in the course of rendering professional services. The only exceptions occur when there is clear danger to the patient or others; when the patient or, in the case of minors, in many states, the parent consents to the release of information, or when other mandates specified in state statute (e.g., the reporting of neglect and abuse) supersede the right to privacy.

As the authority to consent has become blurred, matters of confidentiality have become correspondingly more complex. In general, the person empowered to consent for treatment also controls confidentiality. Strictly speaking, when parents are the gatekeepers of consent, children and adolescents are not permitted to have secrets from them, and professionals are not allowed to maintain privacy except to the degree to which parents permit. For this reason, it is critical that professionals and institutions clarify from the outset what sort of information will remain confidential and from whom. Psychotherapists need to clarify with their patients what information will remain confidential from parents and the remainder of the treatment team, and what information will be included in the patients' records or chart. Group and family therapists need to consider the same issues. All parties need to be mindful that in many states, the child or adolescent, upon achieving majority, may gain access to his or her medical records. Finally, the records of parent and family treatment may need to be maintained separately from the records of the child's treatment; the purpose for such separation is that, when records of the identified patient are released at subsequent points, the privacy of other parties is not inadvertently compromised. Koocher and Keith-Spiegel (1990) provide a more extended discussion of this complex and vexing issue.

Contemporary Issues

CRITERIA FOR VOLUNTARY ADMISSION AND CONTINUED HOSPITALIZATION

Of late, pressures have emanated from advocates of the liberty interests of youth, as well as from cost-conscious managed care contractors, for psychiatric hospitals to adopt a strict and highly exclusive criterion of dangerousness for both the psychiatric admission and the continued inpatient treatment of minors. Many thoughtful clinicians, however, argue that the psychiatric hospitalization of a minor may be justified by patient need even in the absence of symptom acuity, particularly when regression, deterioration, decompensation, or a resumption of dangerousness would occur if the structures and interventions of inpatient

treatment were removed by a premature discharge. Attempts to tie length of stay to diagnosis have been notoriously unsuccessful in psychiatry, thus leaving admission criteria as well as appropriate length of stay in much controversy. The following baseline conditions for justifying psychiatric admission and continuing hospitalization are often embedded in statutes, in peer review criteria, and in the acuity criteria developed by third-party carriers.

Demonstrated Need: There must be a demonstrated need for the inpatient evaluation or treatment of a psychiatric disorder as defined in a standard nosology. Admissions should occur only for the evaluation and treatment of acute and severe psychiatric conditions that place the adolescent at risk or render him or her severely dysfunctional. A psychiatric admission that is arranged exclusively to provide respite to a child's caregivers, that substitutes for a more appropriate juvenile detention or correctional placement, or that simply fills a gap following the failure of a foster placement constitutes a violation of the child's rights and a misuse of the psychiatric unit. In like manner, hospitalization should not be continued merely because a postdischarge placement is not available.

Appropriateness of Placement: Psychiatric hospitalization must be the *least restrictive, least intensive, appropriate,* and *available* intervention for evaluation and treatment. Inpatient hospitalization necessarily compromises many of the normal developmental needs of adolescence: the need to exercise autonomy, the need to progress educationally and vocationally in concert with peers, the need to participate in family life, and the need to explore the wider context of community life. Less costly, less intensive, and less restrictive modalities—such as outpatient psychotherapy, case management, residential treatment, therapeutic foster placement, and partial hospitalization—must be considered and become the objects of advocacy if not available.

Appropriate Treatment Program: The inpatient treatment facility must provide a comprehensive, individualized, and appropriate treatment program. This principle is violated when, for example, a state psychiatric facility is besieged by involuntary commitments that exceed its bed capacity, the resources of its staff, and its ability to ensure the health and safety of its patients. It is also violated when a thinly staffed private psychiatric facility fails to provide adequate educational and vocational programming or recreational opportunities to its patients, or when such a facility, due to distance or lack of staff resources, cannot offer necessary and regular family therapy and parent counseling. In recent years, there has been increasing interest paid to "intensity-of-service" criteria (K. W. Stevenson, personal communication, 1991). This approach specifies, in addition to the clinical criteria for admission and continued stay, the forms and levels of treatment programming for children and adolescents that must be in place. It emphasizes the participation of practitioners with additional training in child and adolescent specialties. Criteria such as these may become additional requirements for reimbursement; if so, they would amplify the present, overly general prescriptions of the traditional accrediting bodies.

In recent years, the criteria for admission and continued stay in hospital psychiatric units have become increasingly mired in controversy; the advent of a national health care plan may provide the only escape from these conflicts. Administrative costs of third-party carriers reach unconscionable levels, while managed care contractors implement more and more restrictive criteria for admission and impose arbitrary caps on lengths of stay. The ultimate dilemma occurs when the 5th day, the 30th day, or some other arbitrarily determined cutoff point has been reached but the patient has not been stabilized and cannot safely be discharged. The family's insurance carrier then refuses to pay for continued inpatient treatment; and neither the hospital nor the child's family can absorb the ongoing costs of inpatient treatment. In times past, Medicaid funding served as a partial backstop, as did the adolescent units in publicly funded state psychiatric facilities. However, many states have been faced with fiscal crises that have forced them to close or to limit their public programs and to severely restrict Medicaid funds (which are contingent upon a state's ability to match federal dollars). At the same time, other highly visible groups of youthful patients are competing for these newly restricted Medicaid resources (e.g., juvenile AIDS patients). All of this occurs while both research and clinical experience continue to demonstrate the need for and efficacy

of long-term inpatient treatment for particular psychiatric conditions in childhood and adolescence (Bleiberg, 1990).

CRITICS AND CRITICISM

No coverage of issues related to psychiatric hospitalization of adolescents would be complete without some mention of the scathing and articulate indictments that have been voiced by several contemporary critics. Particularly notable among these is Weithorn (1988), who provided a compelling analysis of the diverse trends that she believes have led to a "skyrocketing" in the rate of psychiatric admission of "troublesome" youth. The *Parham* decision clearly established a legal basis for parents and practitioners to hospitalize children and adolescents without administrative, clinical, or judicial checks or oversight; the massive upsurge in admission rates (fourfold in private facilities) occurred in the 5 years immediately following *Parham*. Many for-profit corporate hospital chains found psychiatric hospitalization comparatively inexpensive to provide and therefore profitable. The legal underpinning provided by *Parham* set the stage for the aggressive marketing of inpatient psychiatric services in the private sector. These events were contemporaneous with a deinstitutionalization in juvenile corrections; the federal government greatly reduced the youthful populations of training, industrial, and reform schools by requiring the removal of "status" offenders (i.e., runaways, truants, and the "undisciplined") from these settings, in exchange for federal funds. Weithorn argues that these youth were simply "transinstitutionalized" (due in part to the lack of community resources) from old juvenile correctional facilities to new for-profit psychiatric units. Other facilitating factors included the advent of Medicaid funding for psychiatric hospitalization of minors, the existence of imprecise and unverified conceptualizations in current psychopathology (especially the diagnosis of conduct disorder), and the presence of insurance plans that reimbursed handsomely for inpatient treatment but not for less expensive outpatient and day treatment programs. The coexistence of ostensibly defensible diagnoses and of financial incentives to hospitalize led to the rapid growth of adolescent psychiatric facilities. Weithorn concludes her critique by urging that inpatient psychiatric units be reserved for psychotic, suicidal, and other profoundly disturbed youth, while community programs be given the responsibility for maintaining adolescents with conduct disorders (whom she believes are less disturbed and many only be manifesting normal developmental processes). Although Weithorn overstates her case at times and seems naive in her understanding of the adolescent conduct disorder and Axis II psychopathology in general, her arguments are compelling and should be reviewed and considered by thoughtful practitioners. As a footnote, to the extent that Weithorn is correct in asserting that attending psychiatrists in the for-profit chains have enormous financial incentives to hospitalize, those psychiatrists can scarcely fill the role of the "neutral factfinder." Were this trend to continue, one wonders if it might not set the stage for an eventual revisitation of *Parham* in the federal courts.

In the years since the original Weithorn (1988) publication, circumstances have continued to evolve at a rapid rate. A number of states that utilized Medicaid dollars for psychiatric hospitalization of minors have felt increasingly burdened by the need for the state to match the funds and have severely limited length of stay, either arbitrarily (5 or 10 days of hospitalization) or through highly restrictive acuity criteria (continuing manifest dangerousness). In a number of states, reversals of the trends cited by Weithorn are occurring: Only those youths with the most acute and risky of psychiatric conditions are admitted; significant numbers of adolescent units are closing or reintegrating their patients in general psychiatric units; and, in a few instances, acting-out adolescents are being "transinstitutionalized" back to juvenile justice facilities where they are crowding detention centers and training schools.

Of note also is the increased interest in alternatives to expensive psychiatric hospitalization, as permitted by Medicaid waivers that authorize the use of Medicaid funds for residential treatment, day treatment, therapeutic foster care, and other outpatient services. Several for-profit hospital chains have been quick to develop residential treatment units that supplanted their closed adolescent psychiatric beds when their states adopted Medicaid waivers and began to discourage psychiatric hospitalization. These residential programs were financially advantageous in that they substan-

tially reduced costly medical, psychiatric, and nursing services, as well as various quality control and oversight mechanisms, and were thus quite competitive for Medicaid dollars. Residential treatment was also in keeping with the trend toward privatization of services that led many public entities to contract with private providers in ways that were unanticipated in earlier years. In this regard, probably the grandest experiment to attempt to implement a continuum of care and to diminish reliance on psychiatric hospitalization was the Fort Bragg Demonstration Project. This was an $80 million undertaking of the Department of Defense to test whether implementing a continuum of mental health and substance abuse services for children and adolescents was more cost effective and clinically advantageous than reliance on traditional outpatient and inpatient services. The findings of this carefully controlled study were somewhat discouraging, however: The number and length of inpatient hospitalizations was reduced, but the ultimate costs were higher and the clinical outcomes were no better than those of the comparison sites (Bickman, 1996).

And amid the welter of currents and countercurrents, there remain several equally articulate professionals who continue to speak for the merits of extended, intensive psychiatric hospitalization (Bleiberg, 1990; Rinsley, 1990). What is cited are the increasing numbers of youths with enormously complex and resistant psychopathology in which borderline features or conditions intermingle with posttraumatic stress disorder, attention deficit hyperactivity disorder, mood disorder, substance abuse, severe behavioral acting out, risk-laden and self-injurious activity, debilitated or abusive family systems, and diminished or absent community support networks. Due to their behavioral excesses, these youths are simply not manageable in less secure residential placements and witness multiple short-term hospitalizations that serve only to manage crises while briefly providing the illusion of "treatment"; these youths may then come to be seen as treatment failures or as untreatable and suitable only for correctional placement. From this point of view, what is required is definitive inpatient treatment lasting for a year or longer in which the critical bonding and trust issues are addressed as well as deficits in impulse management and the lack of family provision. Unfortunately, when left untreated, these disorders ultimately are expressed in antisocial activity or are masked by severe substance abuse. Further, brief hospitalizations may only add to the litany of ruptured relationships and unrequited trust, while the piecemeal or "wraparound" community services fail to achieve the necessary integration and fail to constitute the crucible in which bonding deficits are addressed and lasting character change can be accomplished. These critics of the contemporary scene find it disheartening that our society cannot provide secure, extended inpatient treatment to that group of severely disturbed children and adolescents who will respond to nothing less. Bleiberg (1990) and Rinsley (1990), in particular, have provided thoughtful accounts of the rationales and details of this form of treatment.

REFERENCES

Amaya, M., & Burlingame, W. (1981). Judicial review of psychiatric admissions. *Journal of the American Academy of Child Psychiatry, 20,* 761–776.

Bickman, L. (1996). A continuum of care. *American Psychologist, 51,* 689–701.

Bleiberg, E. (1990). The clinical challenge of children and adolescents with severe personality disorders. *Bulletin of the Menninger Clinic, 54,* 107–120.

Burlingame, W., & Amaya, M. (1985). Psychiatric commitment of children and adolescents: Issues, current practices, and clinical impact. In D. H. Schetky & E. P. Benedek (Eds.), *Emerging issues in child psychiatry and the law* (pp. 229–249). New York: Brunner/Mazel.

Burlingame, W., & Amaya, M. (1992). Psychiatric commitment of children and adolescents. In D. H. Schetky & E. P. Benedek (Eds.), *Clinical handbook of child psychiatry and the law* (pp. 292–307). Balti-more: Williams & Wilkins.

In re Gault. 387 U.S. 1 (1967).

Koocher, G., & Keith-Spiegel, P. D. (1990). *Children, ethics, and the law.* Lincoln: University of Nebraska Press.

Parham v. J.R. 442 U.S. 584 (1979).

Rinsley, D. (1990). The severely disturbed adolescent: Indications for hospital and residential treatment. *Bulletin of the Menninger Clinic, 54,* 3–12.

U.N. convention on the rights of the child: Unofficial summary of articles. (1991). *American Psychologist, 46,* 50–52.

Weithorn, L. A. (1988). Mental hospitalization of troublesome youth: An analysis of skyrocketing admission rates. *Stanford Law Review, 40,* 773–838.

Weithorn, L. A., & Campbell, S. B. (1982). The competency of children and adolescents to make informed treatment decisions. *Child Development, 53,* 1589–1598.

38 / The College Years: A Final Phase of Adolescent Development

Ghislaine D. Godenne

This chapter addresses the developmental issues confronting today's college student and their resolution through the process of maturation with or without the help of psychotherapy.

Developmental Issues

Although a few intellectually precocious students enter college while they are still in the midst of adolescence, most students enter college in the last phase of their adolescent period. It is during this phase that the finishing touch is put on the developmental tasks of adolescence, tasks that various authors have delineated in their writings and that I briefly cover later in this chapter. In a monograph the Group for the Advancement of Psychiatry published in 1968, a number of tasks to be accomplished during adolescence were mentioned. These included acquiring independence from their parents toward whom in later years they will return in a relationship of equality; forming an identity, knowing and accepting their sexuality, establishing moral values by which to live and committing themselves to their professional choice; and being ready to establish an intimate, loving, and lasting relationship.

In order to accomplish these tasks, the adolescent will have to acquire independence, self-esteem, and an identity of his or her own.

INDEPENDENCE

Moving from a dependent to an independent status takes place gradually during the adolescent period. If there has been continuity in the child's socialization, the transition will be smooth (Benedict, 1938). Family relations play an important role in attaining independence, as it is through the family that one normally acquires basic trust, a sense of competence, and a sense of continuity that, together with achieving one's identity, are necessary conditions to reach independence.

It is in college that adolescents test their newly acquired "relative" independence (relative, as most students are still dependent financially on their parents). Some students experience their sudden freedom with anxiety and a tendency to regress to a dependent status. Indeed, even high school students who loudly professed their rights to independence suddenly become silent for fear that they will be granted the full independence they so noisily demanded in the recent past. In regressing to a more dependent phase of life, students often experience acute anxiety that stems from a strong ambivalence between loving the parents who gratify their dependent needs while hating them for doing so.

Other students entering college look frantically for new experiences. They abuse drugs or alcohol or become promiscuous in order to prove to themselves that they are now independent. Egan and Cowan (1980) describe this behavior as "counter-dependent." Others see it as "pseudoindependence," which gives the youth a false sense of autonomy; indeed, for the first time he or she is solely responsible for his or her actions. To be truly autonomous, however, it is necessary to obtain not only complete independence but also individuation from parents and form a separate identity (Cobb, 1992). Once students have gone through the stages of dependence and counterdependence and have reached independence, Egan and Cowan suggest a final stage, that of "interdependence," in which the young person accepts the fact that there is no shame in needing others nor fault in being needed. Male students have more difficulty than female students taking this last step as masculinity in their eyes implies being completely self-sufficient.

SELF-ESTEEM

The self-image of college students is still strongly influenced by their body image, which in turn influences their self-esteem. An adolescent who felt unpopular in high school and blamed it on physical characteristics may enter college looking for a new start and thus anxiously awaits peers' reactions. Female students are known to go on diets the summer before entering college in order to make themselves more attractive to their peers. In a course on adolescence and youth I taught at the Johns Hopkins University, students were offered extra credit if they wrote their own autobiographies. In the autobiographies, over 60% of the students were still concerned about their appearance. In group therapy sessions, female and male students alike on a hot summer day might be seen wearing jackets; females admit they want to hide their breasts, while males attempt to cover up their lack of muscle development. Although it is generally held that boys have a more positive body image than girls, my experience with college students does not confirm this belief. Indeed, many male students spend inordinate amounts of time in the athletic center building up their muscles, with some even using anabolic steroids to look more masculine. The present-day concern about body image has led to the increasing prevalence of anorexia and bulimia among the college population. Although eating disorders were once a prerogative of female students, now males are showing up with similar disorders. Occasionally both female and male students unhappy with their looks seek cosmetic surgery.

Toward the end of their college or sometimes graduate school years, most students learn to value themselves and others with a measuring rod that has less to do with looks and more with achievement. Their self-esteem now relies heavily on the reassurance given by others that they are worthwhile. Consequently, they are often crushed by the disparaging comments of those who, in order to aggrandize themselves, degrade their peers. Succeeding academically, socially, and athletically has become the basis of how the students feel about themselves at this stage of development. Only when youths know and accept who they are, regardless of looks and/or successes, will they reach an inner sense of worth that is no longer dependent on how they appear to others. To ac-

cept who one is, one has to reconstruct in more realistic terms the ego ideal one has formed in adolescence. In some way one has to reshape it by taking into accounts one's own strengths and weaknesses.

Narcissistic wounds are frequent among college students: a poor grade, a broken date, a sports mistake, or a loss in the student council election can throw students into deep despair, sometimes to the point of suicide. A student's suicide attempt not uncommonly follows a confrontation with the police; despite how minor the infraction has been, the student cannot face the shame of an arrest. Indeed, shame engenders maladaptive responses to anger such as other or self-directed hostility. On the other hand, guilt engenders constructive reactions (Tangney, Wagner, Hill-Barlow, Marschall, & Gramzow, 1996).

IDENTITY

It is essential for college youths to achieve a "true identity" (Marcia, 1966) as one's future is highly influenced by one's identity. In high school identity is based mainly on the here and now. Body image, peer acceptance, and one's role in the community are what forms one's identity. In college, however, it has to be redefined by taking into consideration concerns about the future such as career and role in the society (Cobb, 1992). Once he or she has decided on a field of interest, the college student must choose a major that will open the door to various career possibilities from which he or she will then make a career choice. Female students also have to choose between having a full-time professional career or being a full-time wife and mother. Some accept placing their career on a back burner until their children are grown, a choice that will lead to some discontinuity in their lives. Others decide to attempt to become "supermoms."

Family structures are changing, and so are the roles of males and females and the identity inherent to those roles. Although more has been written on the female revolution, male students also face changing roles. While most college women still want to fill the conventional role of wife and mother, they also aspire to careers. They will, however, be able to realize their newfound identity only if the men of tomorrow are comfortable with sharing the roles of provider and housewife that were conventionally assigned to men and women respectively.

For Marcia (1966), to form a "true identity," one has to experience a "crisis" and make a "commitment." In the crisis, one experiences confusion and anxiety as one faces a variety of choices, such as career, values, and religious beliefs. Once the choice is made and one makes a commitment to it, a pattern of life is established and inner peace is achieved. Some students enter college without having had an identity crisis. Instead they were handed an identity by their families, teachers, and/or peers, who thought they knew what "was best for their future." They accepted without even questioning the role assigned to them. Once in college, however, away from earlier influences, they finally have to confront the haunting question: "Who am I really?" Thus, what was blindly accepted in high school is questioned anew. Family values are challenged or even discarded, albeit temporarily. Prejudices are reexamined, reshaped, reduced, or even eliminated. For the first time students come to realize that although they are unique, separate from others, and entitled to their own ideas, they have to respect those who express opinions at variance with their own. Career choices are no longer as clear cut as they once seemed. College opens new vistas and new interests, and the major chosen upon entering college might no longer fit the dreams. The identity with which the young person entered college was not a "true identity"; rather, as Marcia terms it, it was a "foreclosed identity." These awarenesses propel students into existential crises that will lead to the formation of true identities without which they would never quite feel content with their lives. Such crises prompt some students to take a leave of absence, a period of moratorium, in order to reflect on what is going on within themselves, discover their true identities, and make a commitment to the needs and aspirations of their newly discovered selves.

The kind of relationships students have with their families will facilitate or exaggerate their identity crises. Most parents want the best for their children, but some do not realize that what they see as the best will not necessarily provide their children with a lifelong sense of contentment. Some parents are so convinced of their wisdom that they oppose any career change by threatening to withhold financial support should

their child deviate from the lifelong goal they have established for him or her.

Erikson (1982) describes each stage of life as a crisis from which a successful resolution involves a "higher-order concept that acts to synthesize the competing alternatives" (Sprinthall & Collins, 1988, p. 151). Prior to adolescence, one has to have reached hope (the resolution of basic trust versus mistrust), will (the resolution of autonomy versus shame and doubt), purpose (stemming from initiative versus guilt), and competence (the successful outcome of mastery versus inferiority). In the next two stages of life—adolescence and young adulthood—one has to be capable not only of fidelity, the resolution of the antithesis of identity versus identity diffusion, but also of love, the synthesis of intimacy versus isolation. Both fidelity and love require the ability to trust one's self in order to be able to trust others; however, to trust one's self, one has to know who one is. Knowing who one is evolves from a sense of sameness, one's identification with the group to which one belongs—a college student, a member of a fraternity or sorority—and a sense of differentiation, seeing oneself as an individual separate from the group. Indeed, we all have a need to belong. Students who do not feel a sense of sameness or belongingness experience loneliness. In addition, they feel unrelated, ignored, and misunderstood by their peer group. For Erikson (1959), "The sense of ego identity . . . is the accrued confidence that the inner sameness and continuity are matched by the sameness and continuity of one's meaning for others, as evidenced in the tangible promise of a "career" (p. 228). In order to achieve ego identity, one's early identifications have to be integrated gradually by one's ego. Blos (1979) belives that late adolescence is primarily a phase of ego identity consolidation and as such is a decisive turning point in one's life. For Perry (1968), the formation of an identity is the final step in the intellectual and psychological development of college students. He mentions that in college, students progress from a stage of dualism (in which ideas are good or bad), to a stage of relativism (where they accept the possibility that more than one view of the world can be correct), to the stage of commitment (in which they finally adopt a particular set of values).

To love, the synthesis of Erikson stage of intimacy versus isolation, one has to experience a

433

sense of mutuality in which one's needs, thoughts, and feelings are shared with the loved one without fearing a loss of identity. While intimacy is achieved only when one is able to make deep mutual disclosures and share vulnerability, friendship implies loyalty, mutual respect, and a sharing of thoughts. Insofar as students are at different stages in their capacity for intimacy, painful feelings of abandonment due to broken romances occur when one partner fails to commit.

Finally, moral values, religious affiliations, and all other beliefs inherited from the past have to be, at this stage of life, reevaluated in order to fit one's true identity. Reevaluating does not imply rejecting the past but reshaping it.

An important component of one's identity is one's sexual identity. In college, students learn to differentiate among infatuation, friendship, intimacy, and sexual attraction. Although college is no longer the place where most students have their first sexual experience, it is there that they gradually learn to make love with, and not to, another person. While "making love" they become less preoccupied with their body performance and more attentive to their partner's well-being. In this postadolescent phase, sexual experimentation is common: Blos (1962) writes, "In the realm of sexual drive, experimentation is evident in the relations with potential love objects which represent all possible combinations of degraded and idealized, of sexual and tender love" (p. 151). Through their sexual activities some students look for physical closeness, some for dominance, or some even to express hostility.

Some freshmen who have come from a milieu in which sex was never mentioned become very distressed at the amount of sexual talk and/or activity in the dorms. This atmosphere where sexual activity is common and openly discussed makes for another of those elements of discontinuity that Benedict mentions as being responsible for difficulty during adolescence.

Knowing one's sexual preference is an integral part of one's identity. In the last decade, as society has accepted, if not condoned, homosexual lifestyles, students are freer to examine their sexual preferences. Although today's college students accept a homosexual orientation with less fear, they do have to face challenges spared the heterosexual students. They often go through an agonizing time before reaching a definite conclusion about their sexual orientation; during this time some students experiment with both homosexual and heterosexual relations. For most homosexual students, coming out of the closet, and especially breaking the news to their parents, creates a great deal of anxiety.

"Date rape" recently has become a major concern on college campuses. While it undoubtedly has existed for many years, now that women are demanding equality and any kind of sexual harassment has been officially condemned, women find it easier to report date rape. Finkelston and Oswalt (1995) found through a study of 140 female students that 5% had been date-raped but had not reported it due to shame and/or guilt regarding the event. College administrators have created judicial courts to handle the increasing number of cases brought to their attention.

Pregnancy among students is no longer rare. During a psychiatric evaluation, it is no longer exceptional to hear that a female student has had or is planning to have an abortion and suffers pangs of guilt and pain about it.

While sexual activity is common, the fear of AIDS has put somewhat of a damper on sexual activities in colleges; many college students practice "safe sex" and have become more discriminating about their sexual partners.

Special Issues Facing Minority Groups

AFRICAN AMERICAN AND ASIAN STUDENTS

Colleges, today more than in the past, are a melting pot of ethnic backgrounds in which minority students are challenged to consolidate their own ethnic identities. Cross (1987) outlines four steps in the formation of such an identity, steps that start as soon as the child enters school but usually are not completed before college. They are (1) the preencounter, when the individual identifies with the dominant culture; (2) the encounter, when through experiencing flagrant discrimination the individual becomes aware of his or her ethnicity; (3) the immersion, the phase in which the minority adolescent highly values the ways of his or her ethnic group and devalues those

434

of the dominant culture; and (4) the internalization, when the student values him- or herself and others for what he or she really is and not according to the ethnic group he or she belongs to.

In a mainly white college, African American and Asian students are constantly aware that they belong to a minority and have to fend for themselves, as the administration usually provides them with little tangible support. Programs for minority students, although well intentioned, tend to isolate them from the mainstream; by remaining with their own ethnic group, minority students fail to enlarge their horizons and never identify with the population of their alma mater. Those who choose to move away from their own ethnic group and join the majority are considered traitors by students of their own race. African American students who felt accepted by their peers in mainly white preparatory schools often experience, once in college, a very different situation. African American students accuse them of being "black on the outside but white on the inside," and white students do not necessarily accept them among their own. African American students who turn for help to a college counseling service are often seen by white therapists who have little firsthand experience of the oppression, discrimination, and prejudice they have experienced. The therapists have trouble understanding the black students' distrust of a mainly white faculty and administration and may tend to resent the black students' anger toward the society in which they live.

The situation is somewhat different for Asian students but it is by no means less difficult. Unlike African American students, Asian students do not form a homogeneous group: They are as different as the culture of the countries they originally came from. For all of them, however, the Western world challenges most of their beliefs. Their religions, which at home play a major role in their lives, are almost nonexistent in the West. Family values by which they live and die are given little importance in the Western culture, where instead material possessions dominate the scene. They are misunderstood by their teachers, administrators, peers, and even counselors when they show little emotion, do not participate in the classroom, and are so afraid to fail or not live up to expectations that they become sleepless and even paralyzed when faced with completing a term paper.

Parents of minority students often have very high expectations for their children. They sacrifice a great deal to send them to college; as a reward, they expect their children to make the top of their class. Asian students frequently become suicidal after failing an exam; their failure makes them feel worthless, and they are ready to pay with their lives for the shame they caused their parents.

Ideally, college counseling and/or psychotherapy centers should have on staff counselors of different ethnic backgrounds. White therapists who treat African American students should keep in mind the African American cultural taboo against psychiatry; the therapists may have to accept, in the early phases of treatment, the devaluation of their profession by the black student patient. For black patients to feel comfortable enough to share their concerns, therapists may have to use innovative techniques and deviate from their usual modus operandi. White therapists sometimes question their ability to work with African American students, as it is often not clear to them where they come from and also where they want to go.

White therapists working with Asian students and even first-generation Asian students should take time to study the mores, customs, and values of the cultures the students come from. They should refrain from applying North American standards in evaluating their patients. According to Pedersen (1995), "All learning occurs in a cultural context. Successful counseling can be achieved by training healthcare providers to interpret behaviors in their cultural context."

Regardless of the student's country of origin, traveling to a foreign country requires some adjustment, which only those who have experienced it can fully understand. All foreign students get some comfort in talking to a counselor who has lived or visited their country. Although a visit does not do much more than skim the surface of a country's culture, at least it is better than complete ignorance of the nation. A diversified and well-traveled counseling staff is undoubtedly a plus for a counseling center, especially now, when more and more foreign students are studying in North American universities.

TRANSFER AND COMMUTING STUDENTS

At least at the beginning of the academic year, some transfer students have trouble adjusting to a new college. The college administrat··· ·ds to ignore this group of students; rarely are they included in the freshmen orientation week or "adopted" by alumni families who would orient them to the city. They feel left out (and they often are!) by their peers who have already formed a steady circle of friends and are disinclined to include them. In addition to their lack of welcome, they are still dealing with feelings, pleasant or unpleasant, about the college they left. Other transfer students, however, blossom from the very beginning in their new college, especially if it is the one they had aspired to enter earlier.

Commuting students in a mainly residential college usually do not feel part of the college life. Usually they do not participate in campus events, as they do not live on campus, and due to their small numbers, they do not receive special attention from the administration. For commuters college often seems to be merely a sophisticated version of high school, but whereas in high school they shared the same predicament with all their peers, in college they face their college experience alone.

Psychotherapy on College Campuses

Important psychological tasks face the college student. Some mature without the need for outside help. Others just need a helping hand to walk through these last stages of adolescence. A few experience severe difficulties and turn to our profession to help them navigate toward adulthood. Despite a national tendency to believe that all psychological problems during college are developmental problems, reports from psychiatric services on campuses show, without exception, an increase in severe mental illness in this population. The reason for such an increase is unknown; however, I believe that the dissolution of families plays a large role in this distressing finding. In addition, the apparent futility of obtaining a degree in higher education (students hear about Ph.D. graduates working as hotel doormen), the unsettling world situation, and the frightening escalation of violence at home and abroad all add stress to a difficult phase of life in which major tasks have to be accomplished. A few years ago the students

who came for help at the Counseling and Psychiatric Services of Johns Hopkins University were given, in order of frequency, the following psychiatric diagnoses: adjustment disorder with depressed mood, personality disorders, substance abuse, affective psychoses, bulimia, general anxiety and panic disorders, identity disorders, brief reactive psychoses, and schizophrenia.

Lately college counseling services have paid a lot of attention to attention deficit disorder (ADD) with or without hyperactivity (ADHD). Among 42 upper Midwest university students diagnosed by the treating psychiatrist with ADHD, the "presenting problems included ADHD symptoms, mood symptoms, nonspecific learning disabilities, and academic underachievement"; to this list the authors added a series of associated problems, including drug and/or alcohol abuse, dependency, legal problems, and eating disorders (Heiligenstein & Keeling, 1995, p. 226).

Today many college psychiatric services that earlier were staffed by psychiatrists are being phased out and replaced by counseling and student developmental centers. Where in the past students were offered unlimited psychotherapy or even psychoanalysis, now unfortunately they are entitled only to limited services and are referred elsewhere in the community if their condition warrants more intensive help. Adolescent psychiatrists are the most qualified to treat the college youth, as this age shares many characteristics with adolescence. Indeed, college students are often immature, self-conscious, unsure of their true identity, and conflicted by their dependence on their parents. Their heterosexual relationships are often transitory and, as such, a source of major upheaval in their lives. They are eager to challenge adults, including their therapists. However, unlike their younger peers, for them school often takes a significant precedence over their therapy, and when quick results are not forthcoming they are prone to drop out of treatment without further notice. Long vacations and/or the short life span of their status as students interferes in their forming strong transference relationships with their therapists. The majority of them are bright, sophisticated, verbal, and well motivated, and often they are the ones who initiate their therapy.

Most counseling and/or psychiatric services on campuses offer an array of different forms of therapy: individual, group, couple, long term or short term, and with or without the adjunct of pharmacotherapy. The kind of therapy students are referred to is based on the seriousness, extent, and duration of their problem; their motivation (are they seeking help under duress from their professors, dean of students, or on their own volition?), the status of their finances (if they are referred to the community), the time they have available for therapy, their past experiences, and the professional orientation of an available therapist.

Although group therapy is often the treatment of choice for many college students, students on a college campus are often reluctant at first to try this modality. They see their problems as unique and believe no one would understand them or care enough to try to understand them. They are afraid of a possible lack of confidentiality and fear that if their peers know they are in group therapy, they will look down on them. Therapists themselves are sometimes reluctant to refer a patient to a group in the narcissistic belief that no one could be of as much help to the student as the therapist. However, once involved in a group, students welcome the support they get from other members. They also feel reassured that they are not the only ones who have problems, and they enjoy not being under as much pressure to talk as in individual therapy. From an administrative point of view, group therapies serve a useful purpose: they free individual therapy hours and reduce waiting lists.

Along with group therapy, short-term therapy and time-limited therapy have become the main forms of treatment on campuses. In short-term therapy, the number of sessions is set from the onset and is strictly enforced. In time-limited therapy, although the patient is told that the number of sessions is limited, this rule is not adhered to rigidly. If the student requires more help at the end of the planned number of sessions, additional sessions are added. Contrary to common belief, short-term therapy is not for the novice therapist; it should be carried out only by an experienced therapist when there is a focused problem; the student exhibits a capacity for insight and a high degree of relatedness to the therapist; there is a clear psychodynamic formulation of the problem; and the student is eager to work in treatment.

Treating students on campus is not without drawbacks. For some students, it generates feelings akin to sibling rivalry; others are concerned about being seen by peers or teachers or afraid that confidentiality will not be respected or that their being in psychotherapy will be part of their student records. Some students try to use their being seen in the college mental health clinic as an excuse not to turn in assignments, to drop a course after the cut-off date, or even not to take a quiz or final exam. On-campus therapists occasionally find themselves in the difficult predicament of working with the best friend or worst enemy of a student they are seeing in therapy. As they cannot use in treatment what they have learned confidentially through other sources, they might become so burdened by the information they are privy to that they become less effective in their work. Nevertheless, advantages for students seen on campus outweigh the disadvantages: they will not have to lose time traveling to their therapist's office, they probably will not have to pay for the visits or will be charged on a sliding scale, and they are seeing therapists who are familiar with their college or university.

From 1973 to 1992 students at Johns Hopkins University were offered unlimited psychiatric sessions. (The first 10 sessions were free to the student; after that they were charged on a sliding scale.) One out of five undergraduates used the services offered by the clinic at some time during their college years. In the 1989–1990 academic year, the median number of visits was 4.5 per student while the average number of visits was 15 per student. (Some students were in psychoanalysis.) A study done in 1975–1976 on the Johns Hopkins University campus showed that freshmen were mainly seen suffering from physical symptoms, sophomores from depression, and seniors from relationship problems. It is of interest to note that twice during any academic year, the number of referrals to a campus clinic peaks. Although the peaks occur in the fall and early spring, which correspond to test time, one should not overlook the anxiety associated with going home for Thanksgiving or making plans for the summer vacation. For some freshmen, preparing to go home for their first vacation since entering college is stressful; they wonder not only if they will still have their own bedroom but also if they will still fit in their family's way of life. Will they be allowed the independence they enjoy in college, or will they once again fall under family rules such as those concerning curfews? Occasionally students report being afraid that once home, they will not be allowed to return to campus because of family problems, financial problems, or even their own or their parents' separation anxiety. Looking ahead to summer vacation involves making plans on how to spend it. Some students are conflicted by the choices open to them: going home and getting a job in their community or staying near their college and getting a job locally. Those students who are involved in a serious relationship wonder what a separation will do to it; students who have not

done well academically are concerned about facing the anger or disappointment of their parents. Seniors face identical problems but on a larger scale; they have to adjust to leaving the college environment they have called home for four years.

It is hoped that when students leave the university holding well-deserved, diplomas, they also will walk out confident of having achieved the developmental tasks required to embark successfully in the adult world.

REFERENCES

Benedict, R. (1938). Continuities and discontinuities in cultural conditioning. *Psychiatry*, 1, 161–167.

Blos, P. (1962). *On adolescence. A psychoanalytic interpretation.* New York: Free Press.

Blos, P. (1979). *The adolescent passage: Developmental issues.* New York: International Universities Press.

Cobb, N. J. (1992). *Adolescence—continuity, change and diversity.* Palo Alto, CA: Mayfield Publishing.

Cross, W. E., Jr. (1987). A two-factor theory of black identity: Implications for the study of identity development in minority children. In J. S. Phinney & M. J. Rotheram (Eds.), *Children's ethic socialization* (pp. 113–133). Beverly Hills, CA: Sage Publications.

Egan, G., & Cowan, M. A. (1980). *Moving into adulthood. Themes and variations in self-directed development for effective living.* Belmont, CA: Brooks/Cole.

Erikson, E. H. (1950). *Childhood and society.* New York: W. W. Norton.

Erikson, E. H. (1959). *Identity and the life cycle. Psychological Issues*, 1.

Erikson, E. H. (1982). *The life cycle completed.* New York: W. W. Norton.

Finkelston, L., & Oswalt, R. (1995). College date rape: Incidence and reporting. *Psychological Reports*, 77 (2), 526.

Glasscole, R., & Fishman, M. E. (1973). *Mental health on the campus: A field study.* Washington, DC: American Psychiatric Association.

Godenne, G. D. (1977, January). Is being a college student a hazardous occupation? *The Johns Hopkins Magazine*, 36–41.

Godenne, G. D. (1984). College students. *Clinical Update in Adolescent Psychiatry*, 1, (16) pp. 1–12.

Group for the Advancement of Psychiatry (1968). *Normal adolescence: Its dynamics and impact.* Group for

the Advancement of Psychiatry (Vol. 6, Report no. 68). New York: Author.

Group for the Advancement of Psychiatry. (1983). *Friends and lovers in college years.* New York: Mental Health Materials Center.

Heiligenstein, E., & Keeling, R. P. (1995). Presentation of unrecognized attention deficit hyperactivity disorder in college students. *Journal of American College Health*, 43 (5), 226–228.

Marcia, J. E. (1966). Development and validation of ego-identity status. *Journal of Personality and Social Psychology*, 3, 551–559.

Nikelly, A. G. (1966). *A guide for adjusting to college . . . mental health for students.* Springfield, IL: Charles C Thomas.

Pedersen, P. B. (1995). Culture-centered counseling skills as a preventive strategy for college health services. *Journal of American College Health*, 44 (1), 20–26.

Perry, W. G. (1968). *Forms of intellectual and ethical development in college years.* New York: Holt, Rinehart and Winston.

Sprinthall, N. A., & Collins, W. A. (1988). *Adolescent psychology. A developmental view* (2nd ed.). New York: Random House.

Sue, D. W., & Sue, D. (1990). *Counseling the culturally different: Theory and practice* (2nd ed.). New York: John Wiley & Sons.

Tangney, J. P., Wagner, P. E., Hill-Barlow, D., Marschall, D. E., & Gramzow, R. (1996). Relationship of shame and guilt to constructive versus destructive responses to anger across the lifespan. *Journal of Personality and Social Psychology*, 70 (4), 797–809.

Whitaker, L. C., & Slimak, R. E. (Eds.) (1990). *College student suicide.* New York: Haworth Press.

SUBJECT INDEX

NAME INDEX

460

Printed in the United States
146455LV00002B/28/A

9 780471 550761